# MAD®
## about the
# MOVIES

**Special Warner Bros. Edition**

# MAD

## *about the*

# MOVIES

**Special Warner Bros. Edition**

**By "The Usual Gang of Idiots"**

**Edited by Nick Meglin & John Ficarra**

**Introduction by Gene Siskel & Roger Ebert**

**MAD**

New York York

**BOOKS**™

# MAD BOOKS

## William Gaines Founder

**Jenette Kahn** President & Editor-in-Chief

**Paul Levitz** Executive Vice President & Publisher

**Nick Meglin & John Ficarra** Editors (*MAD*)

**Charlie Kadau** Senior Editor

**David Shayne** Associate Editor

**Nadina Simon** Art Director

**Charles Kochman** Editor (Licensed Publishing)

**Elisabeth Vincentelli** Assistant Editor

**Trent Duffy** Managing Editor

**Dan Brown** Director•Business Development & Mass Market Sales

**Patrick Caldon** VP•Finance & Operations

**Dorothy Crouch** VP•Licensed Publishing

**Lillian Laserson** VP•Legal Affairs

**Bob Rozakis** Executive Director•Production

*Though Alfred E. Neuman wasn't the first to say "A fool and his money are soon parted," here's your chance to prove the old adage right—subscribe to MAD! Simply call 1-800-4-MADMAG and mention code 9BMA1. Operators are standing by (the water cooler).*

# CONTENTS

**LEARNED TO BE A MOVIE CRITIC BY READING MAD MAGAZINE.** I learned a lot of other things from the magazine too, including a whole new slant on society. *MAD* supplied the first ironic humor to appear in my life. One day I was a trusting, credulous youth who approached the Princess Theater with pennies and nickels grasped in my sweaty palm, eager to see the latest matinee adventures of my heroes Lash La Rue and Whip Wilson. The next day I was a *MAD* reader, and could look down with scorn upon my classmates who sat goggle-eyed through clichés and stereotypes.

*MAD*'s parodies made me aware of the machine inside the skin—of the way a movie might look original on the outside, while inside it was just recycling the same dumb old formulas. I did not read the magazine, I plundered it for clues to the universe. Studying each issue carefully, I learned about standard dialogue and obligatory scenes, cardboard characters and giant gaps in plausibility, and "Scenes We'd Like to See." Pauline Kael lost it at the movies; I lost it at *MAD* Magazine.

Today's moviegoers are surrounded by a sea of cynical media. It was more innocent in the far-off days of my youth in downstate Illinois. It was in *MAD* Magazine, for example, that I was first exposed to the very notion of a foreign-language film. I thought all movies were in English. After all, everyone I knew spoke English, didn't they? And had I ever seen a subtitled film? Certainly not. I knew theoretically that in places like France they spoke another language—but even there I figured they had to understand at least enough English to go to the movies.

*MAD* ended my illusions with an article satirizing inaccurately translated subtitles. A hooker under a street lamp made proposals that looked steamy in the drawings but were completely innocent in the subtitles. Come to think of it, that might also have been the first place where I learned about hookers. In my bucolic hometown, surrounded by waving fields of soybeans, the only people who stood under street lamps were waiting for the bus.

I am particularly pleased that this first collection of *MAD* movie parodies focuses on the contributions of Warner Bros. (I know that the studio and the magazine are owned by the same giant conglomerate, but, hey, coincidences happen.) Every studio had its style, and Warner Bros. always had the best hard-boiled crime melodramas—a tradition extending right up to modern times in movies like *Dirty Harry* and *Lethal Weapon*. The studio's tone was set early on, when founding brother Jack L. Warner called a meeting of his producers and writers and told them, "Don't give me any more pictures where they write with feathers!"

The greatest of all Warner Bros. movies is without a doubt *Casablanca*, which *MAD* manhandles in a parody that begins with the observation that, at Rick's Place—excuse me, Reek's Place—no one could look at the owner's brooding face and ask if there was a happy hour. When the Marx Brothers announced plans to make *A Night in Casablanca*, Warners threatened to sue them, charging that the title ripped off their classic. Groucho fired back: "You probably have the right to use the name Warner, but what about Brothers? Professionally, we were brothers long before you were."

*MAD*'s parodies not only destroyed my innocence, they also helped to demythologize the Hollywood movie star. When *MAD* was born, people still took stars seriously. They were treated like gods, or royalty. People actually asked them to sign scraps of paper! Within a few years *MAD* had so completely warped the national value system that matinee idols were laughingstocks, and the only actors who could get work looked like extras from a Dickens novel. Tab Hunter was out, Anthony Perkins was in, and *MAD* gets the credit.

My only regret is that more moviegoers don't learn from *MAD*'s movie parodies. Study this book and never again be taken in by *Mars Attacks!* *MAD* and its influence have simply made some kinds of movies impossible. *Scream* and *Scream 2*, for example, are a tribute to *MAD*: horror movies have started making fun of themselves as a preventive measure.

The proof that *MAD* has good taste in movies is that, generally speaking, the magazine hasn't satirized bad ones. This volume targets such films as *Who's Afraid of Virginia Woolf?*, *Bonnie and Clyde*, and *The Right Stuff*. Pretty good choices. I love the whole *fershlugginer* thing. Congratulations to the Usual Gang of Idiots.

—**Roger Ebert**

I AM KNOWN FOR DISAGREEING WITH ROGER EBERT, BUT I CERTAINLY DON'T THIS TIME. His essay is wise and perhaps definitive. I just wish *MAD*'s "Usual Gang of Idiots" (the UGOI) hadn't taken out the parts where Roger said he owes me fifty bucks, that he confesses I'm his idol, and that he was wrong to give a positive review to the Burt Reynolds film *Cop and a Half*.

But Roger is right on target to acknowledge that for our generation *MAD*, through features such as "Scenes We'd Like to See," was our first exposure to film criticism. Indeed, Roger has even compiled a little book (*Ebert's Little Movie Glossary*, Andrews and McMeel, $12.95—not cheap!) full of such similar movie clichés—including at least one I supplied: "The Talking Killer," who suddenly contracts logorrhea (look it up!) once he has his intended victim in his sights and can't stop talking until the man has time to escape, setting up a chase scene. Once, just once, in a scene *I'd* like to see, the killer is at a loss for words and simply blows away the quavering, *fershlugginer* (try to look it up!) sucker. Only then does the gunman start talking, and at that point I couldn't care if he recited, say, a list of the twenty-three auxiliary verbs: "Am, is, are, was, were, be, been; do, does, did; have, has, had; shall, should; will, would; can, could; may, might, must, ought."

In retrospect, what I also admire about the *MAD* movie satires is that the writers and artists took on the finest, most acclaimed films of the times and didn't settle for puncturing easy targets. It's one thing to skewer a supposed blockbuster that fails to succeed; it's quite another to tackle a Stanley Kubrick masterpiece like "201 Minutes of a Space Idiocy" (available in *MAD About the Sixties*, Little, Brown, $19.95—certainly not cheap!). Says one space traveler: "I'll swear someone just threw a bone at our spaceship!" And the monolith is referred to as both a "prehistoric transistor radio" and a "handball court that plays music." And the phone call home from space? In the *MAD* satire, an operator says, "Deposit $17,500 for the first three minutes, plus 10¢ for the overtime!"

One could also argue that the *MAD* movie satires inspired not only a generation of critics but filmmakers as well. Weren't the hilarious parodies by the Zucker-Abrahams-Zucker team (the *Airplane!* and *Naked Gun* movies) made in the same spirit? You bet your *potrzebie* (pointless to look up)! The closest the UGOI have come was *MAD*'s *Up the Academy* (1980), but all that was truly *MAD* was the licensed title. For some reason no one thought to ask any of the Usual Gang to write the screenplay, and the film suffered because of that.

A challenge: It's about time someone asked *MAD*'s UGOI to write an original screenplay better than those they've parodied. Roger and I will bring our thumbs to the premiere (I'm addicted to Twizzlers, by the way; Roger would like his usual case of Raisinets).

Hoohah!

—**Gene Siskel**

# AN ILLUSTRATED HISTORY OF WARNER BROS.

BY ARNIE KOGEN, ILLUSTRATED BY MORT DRUCKER

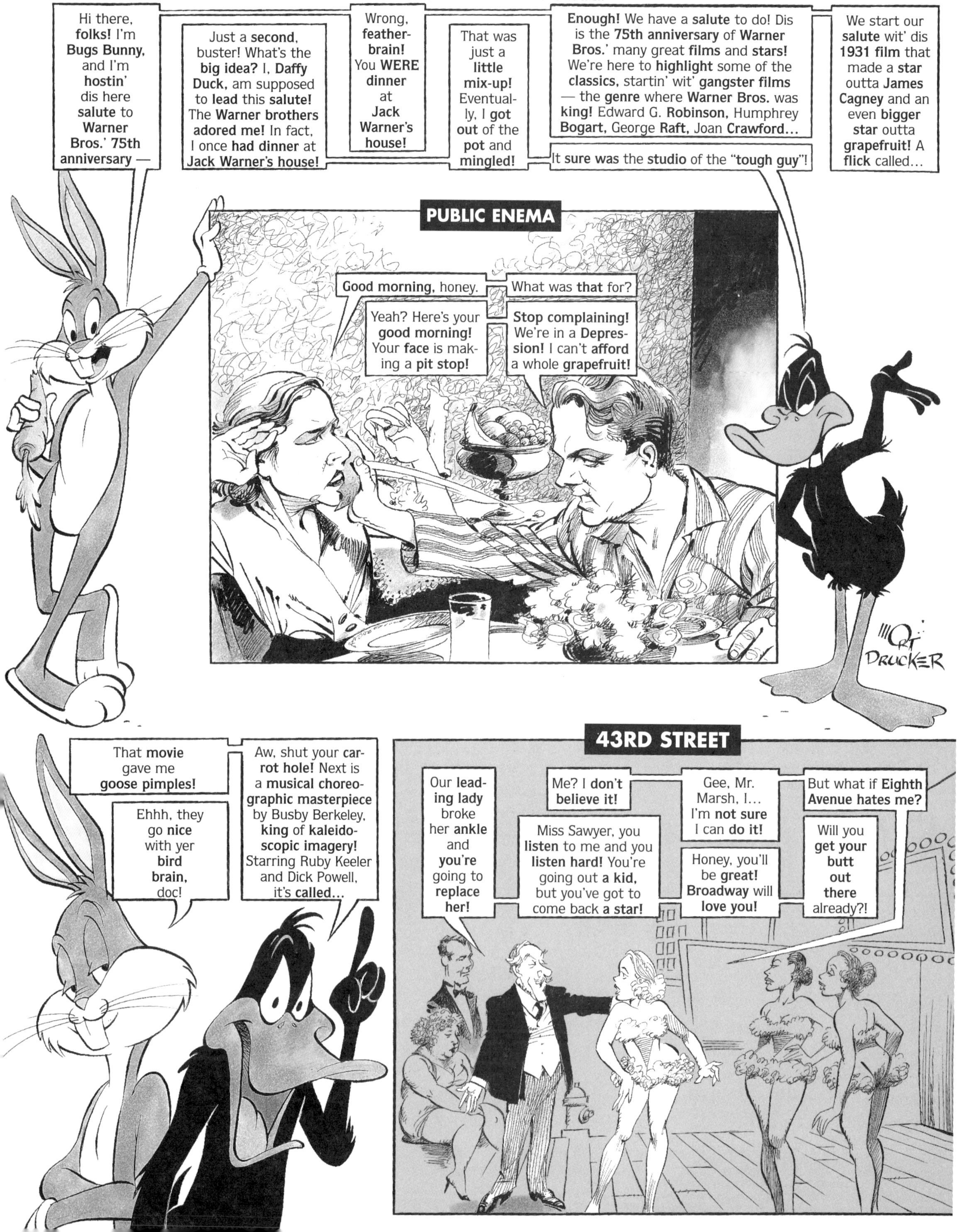

Hi there, folks! I'm Bugs Bunny, and I'm hostin' dis here salute to Warner Bros.' 75th anniversary —
Just a second, buster! What's the big idea? I, Daffy Duck, am supposed to lead this salute! The Warner brothers adored me! In fact, I once had dinner at Jack Warner's house!
Wrong, feather-brain! You WERE dinner at Jack Warner's house!
That was just a little mix-up! Eventually, I got out of the pot and mingled!
Enough! We have a salute to do! Dis is the 75th anniversary of Warner Bros.' many great films and stars! We're here to highlight some of the classics, startin' wit' gangster films — the genre where Warner Bros. was king! Edward G. Robinson, Humphrey Bogart, George Raft, Joan Crawford...
It sure was the studio of the "tough guy"!
We start our salute wit' dis 1931 film that made a star outta James Cagney and an even bigger star outta grapefruit! A flick called...
PUBLIC ENEMA
Good morning, honey.
What was that for?
Yeah? Here's your good morning! Your face is making a pit stop!
Stop complaining! We're in a Depression! I can't afford a whole grapefruit!
MORT DRUCKER
That movie gave me goose pimples!
Ehhh, they go nice with yer bird brain, doc!
Aw, shut your carrot hole! Next is a musical choreographic masterpiece by Busby Berkeley, king of kaleidoscopic imagery! Starring Ruby Keeler and Dick Powell, it's called...
43RD STREET
Our leading lady broke her ankle and you're going to replace her!
Me? I don't believe it!
Miss Sawyer, you listen to me and you listen hard! You're going out a kid, but you've got to come back a star!
Gee, Mr. Marsh, I... I'm not sure I can do it!
Honey, you'll be great! Broadway will love you!
But what if Eighth Avenue hates me?
Will you get your butt out there already?!

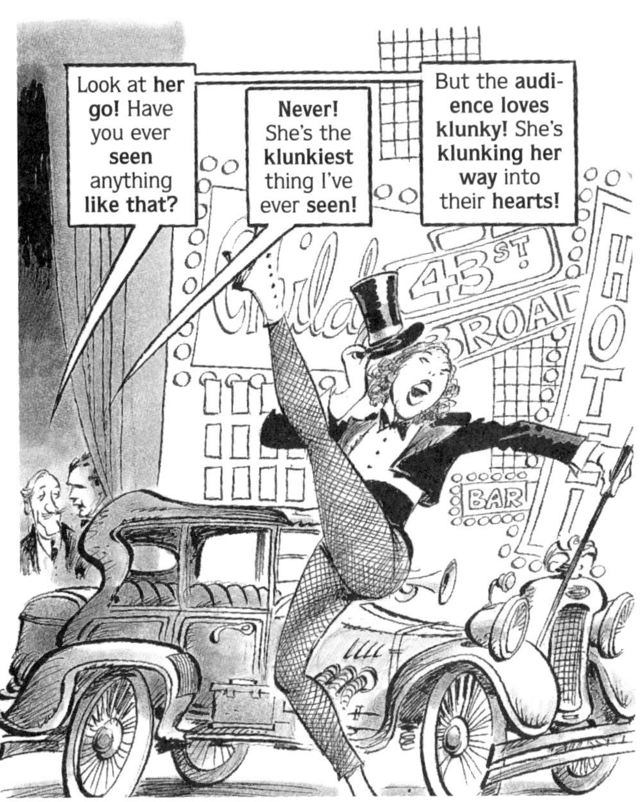
Look at her go! Have you ever seen anything like that?
Never! She's the klunkiest thing I've ever seen!
But the audience loves klunky! She's klunking her way into their hearts!
43RD
BROADWAY
HOTEL
BAR

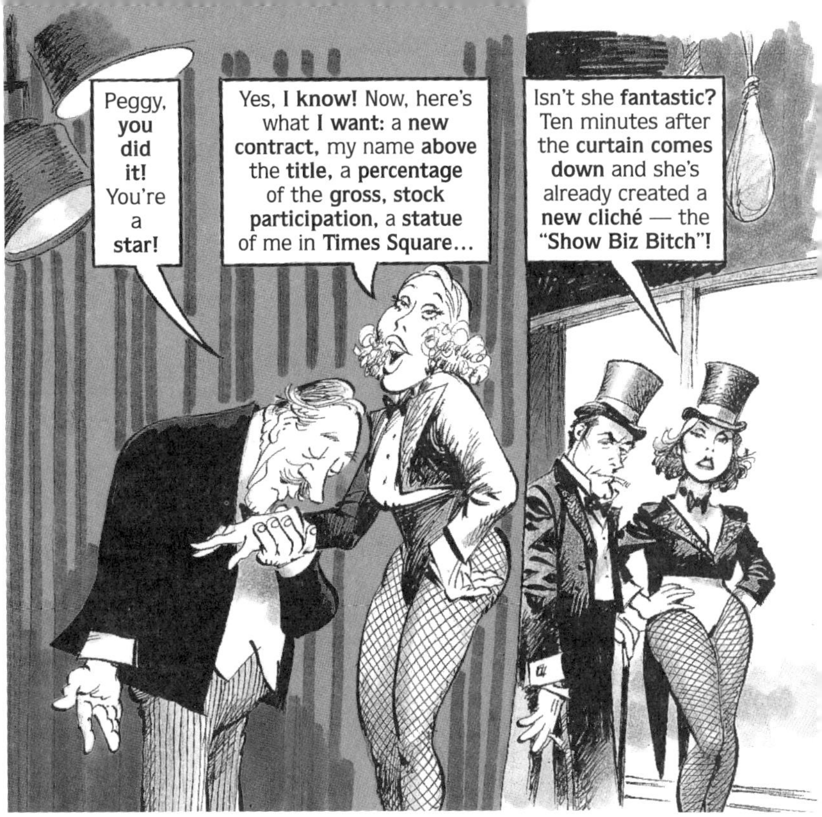
Peggy, you did it! You're a star!
Yes, I know! Now, here's what I want: a new contract, my name above the title, a percentage of the gross, stock participation, a statue of me in Times Square...
Isn't she fantastic? Ten minutes after the curtain comes down and she's already created a new cliché — the "Show Biz Bitch"!

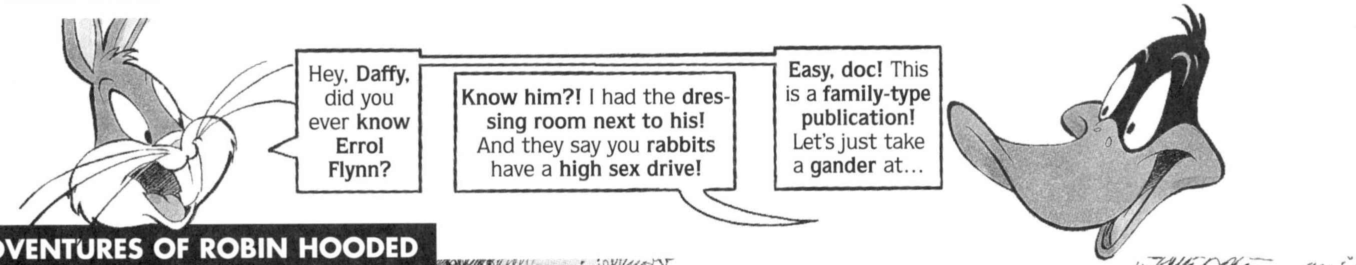
Hey, Daffy, did you ever know Errol Flynn?
Know him?! I had the dressing room next to his! And they say you rabbits have a high sex drive!
Easy, doc! This is a family-type publication! Let's just take a gander at...

## THE ADVENTURES OF ROBIN HOODED

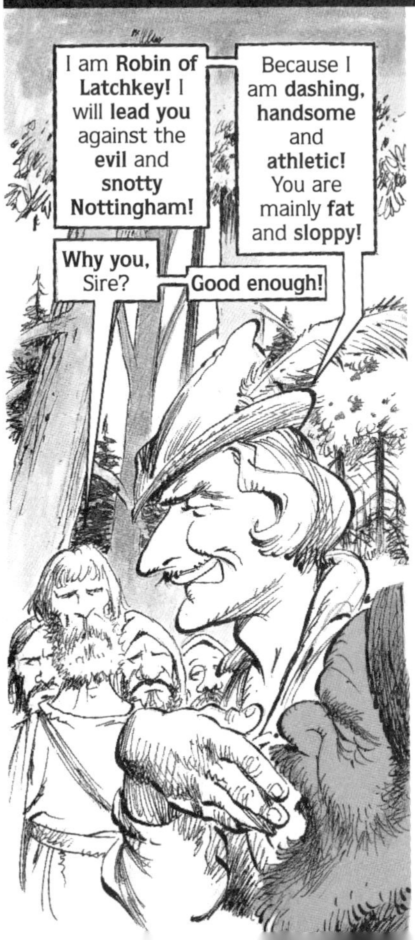
I am Robin of Latchkey! I will lead you against the evil and snotty Nottingham!
Why you, Sire?
Because I am dashing, handsome and athletic! You are mainly fat and sloppy!
Good enough!

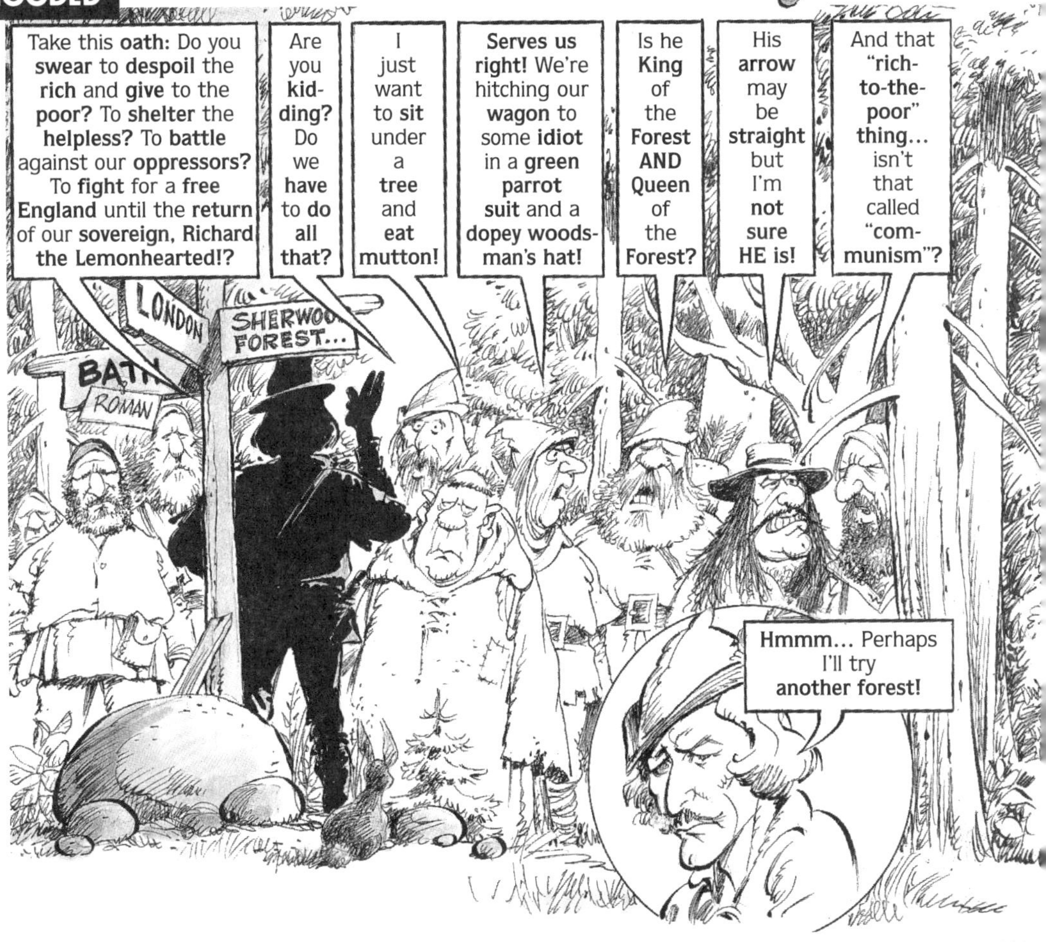
Take this oath: Do you swear to despoil the rich and give to the poor? To shelter the helpless? To battle against our oppressors? To fight for a free England until the return of our sovereign, Richard the Lemonhearted!?
Are you kidding? Do we have to do all that?
I just want to sit under a tree and eat mutton!
Serves us right! We're hitching our wagon to some idiot in a green parrot suit and a dopey woodsman's hat!
Is he King of the Forest AND Queen of the Forest?
His arrow may be straight but I'm not sure HE is!
And that "rich-to-the-poor" thing... isn't that called "communism"?
LONDON
SHERWOOD FOREST...
BATH
ROMAN
Hmmm... Perhaps I'll try another forest!

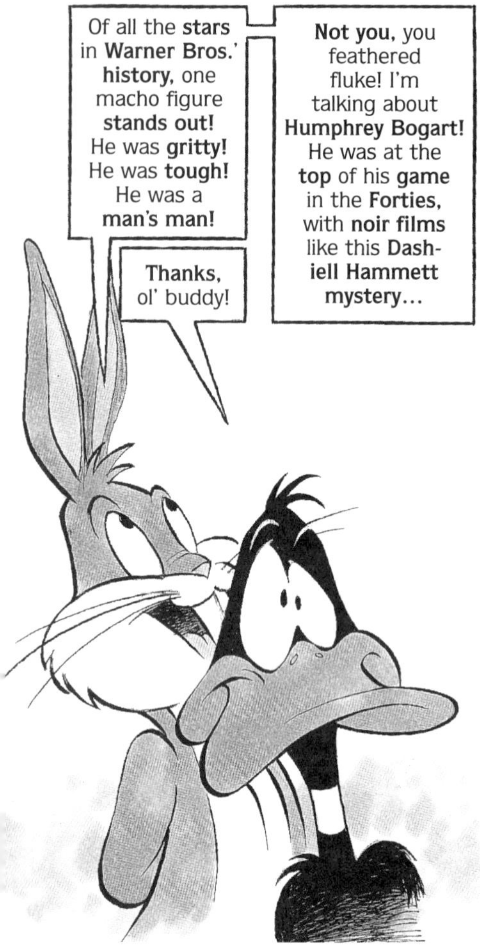
Of all the stars in Warner Bros.' history, one macho figure stands out! He was gritty! He was tough! He was a man's man!
Not you, you feathered fluke! I'm talking about Humphrey Bogart! He was at the top of his game in the Forties, with noir films like this Dashiell Hammett mystery…
Thanks, ol' buddy!

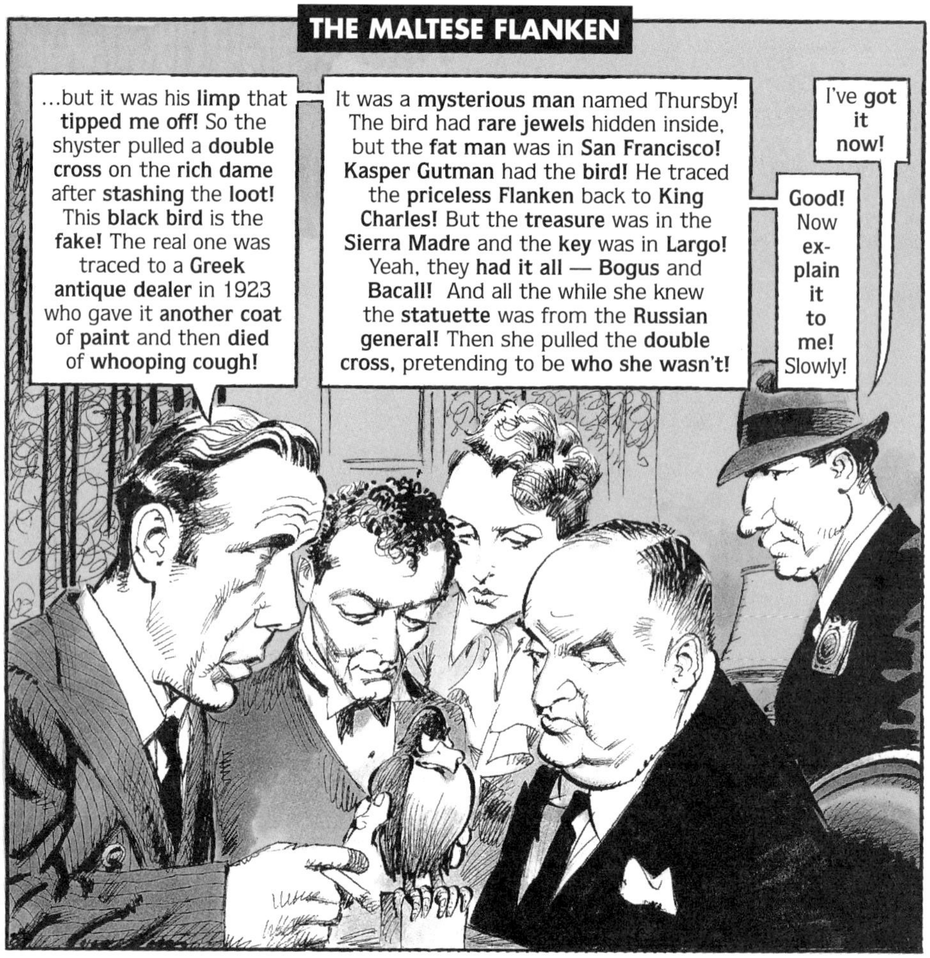
THE MALTESE FLANKEN
…but it was his limp that tipped me off! So the shyster pulled a double cross on the rich dame after stashing the loot! This black bird is the fake! The real one was traced to a Greek antique dealer in 1923 who gave it another coat of paint and then died of whooping cough!
It was a mysterious man named Thursby! The bird had rare jewels hidden inside, but the fat man was in San Francisco! Kasper Gutman had the bird! He traced the priceless Flanken back to King Charles! But the treasure was in the Sierra Madre and the key was in Largo! Yeah, they had it all — Bogus and Bacall! And all the while she knew the statuette was from the Russian general! Then she pulled the double cross, pretending to be who she wasn't!
I've got it now!
Good! Now explain it to me! Slowly!

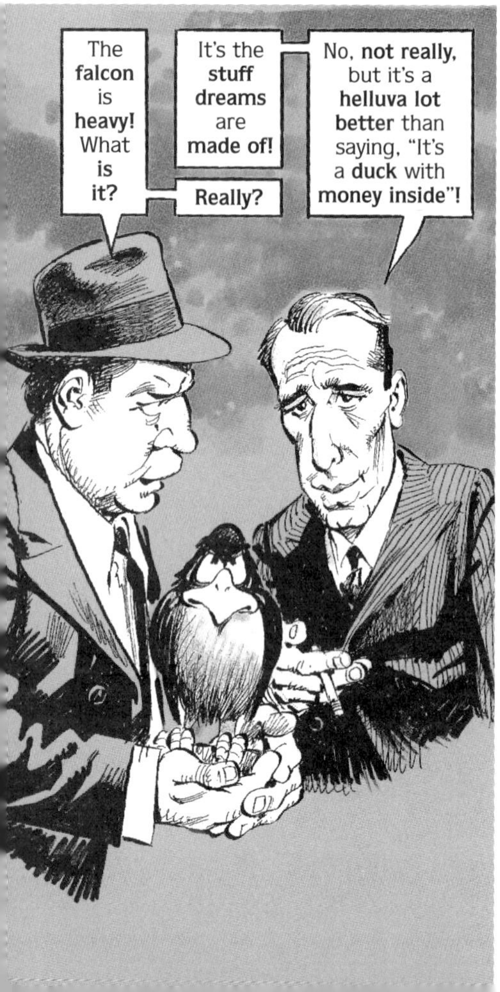
The falcon is heavy! What is it?
It's the stuff dreams are made of!
Really?
No, not really, but it's a helluva lot better than saying, "It's a duck with money inside"!

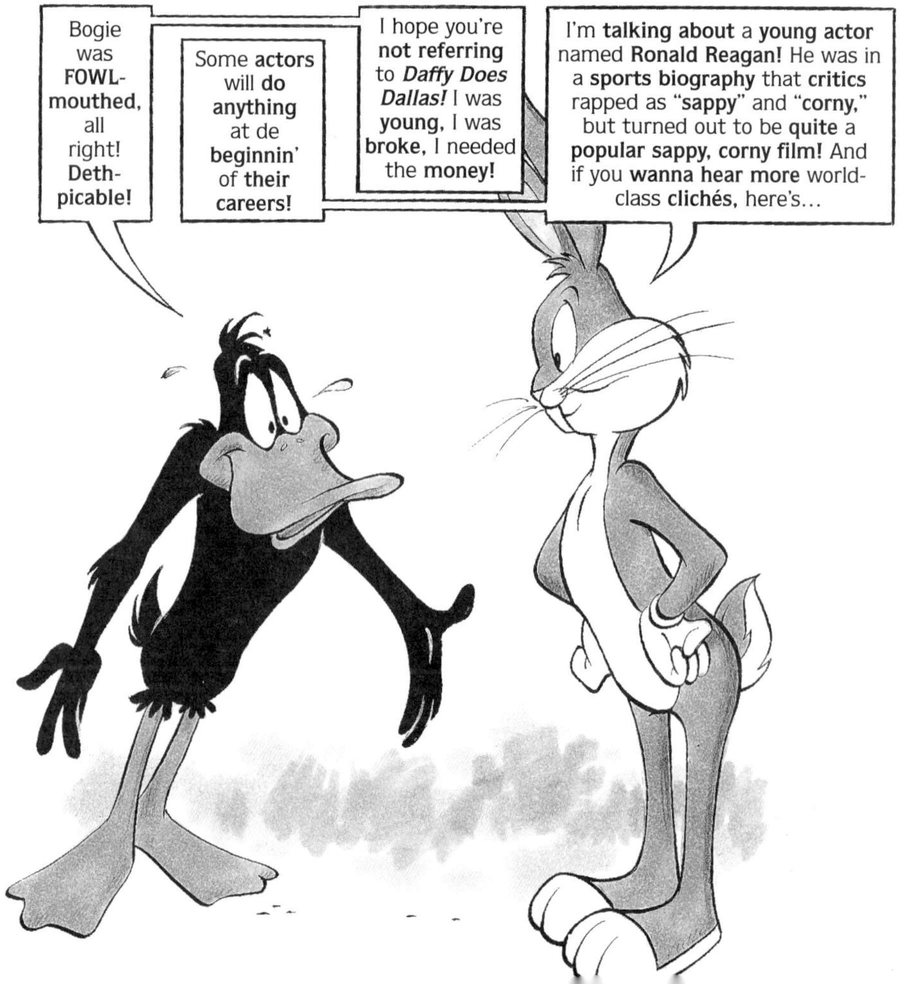
Bogie was FOWL-mouthed, all right! Dethpicable!
Some actors will do anything at de beginnin' of their careers!
I hope you're not referring to Daffy Does Dallas! I was young, I was broke, I needed the money!
I'm talking about a young actor named Ronald Reagan! He was in a sports biography that critics rapped as "sappy" and "corny," but turned out to be quite a popular sappy, corny film! And if you wanna hear more world-class clichés, here's…

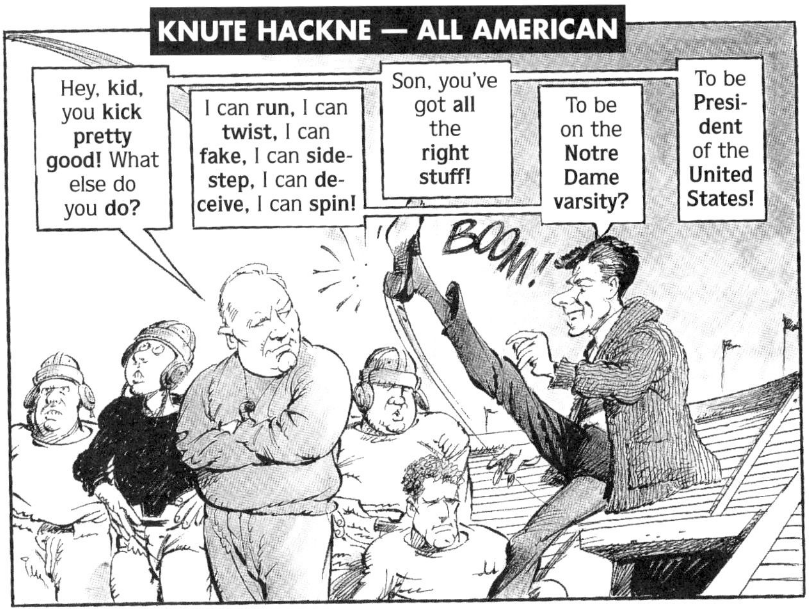
KNUTE HACKNE — ALL AMERICAN
Hey, kid, you kick pretty good! What else do you do?
I can run, I can twist, I can fake, I can side-step, I can de-ceive, I can spin!
Son, you've got all the right stuff!
To be on the Notre Dame varsity?
To be President of the United States!
BOOM!

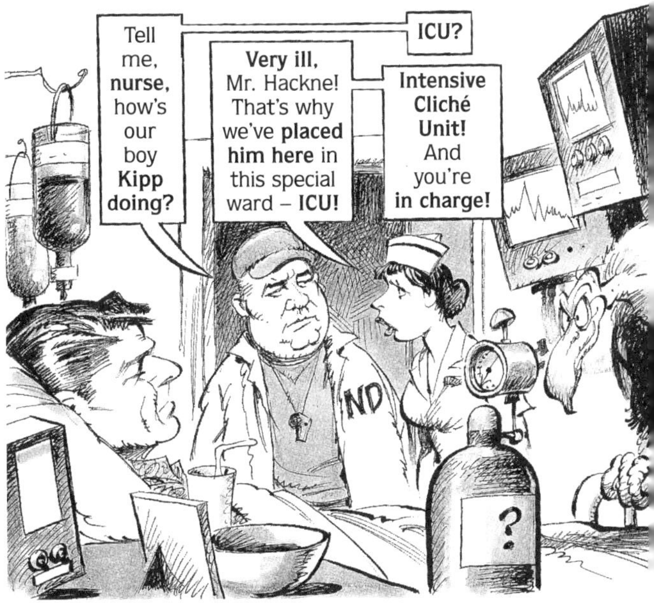
Tell me, nurse, how's our boy Kipp doing?
Very ill, Mr. Hackne! That's why we've placed him here in this special ward – ICU!
ICU?
Intensive Cliché Unit! And you're in charge!
ND
?

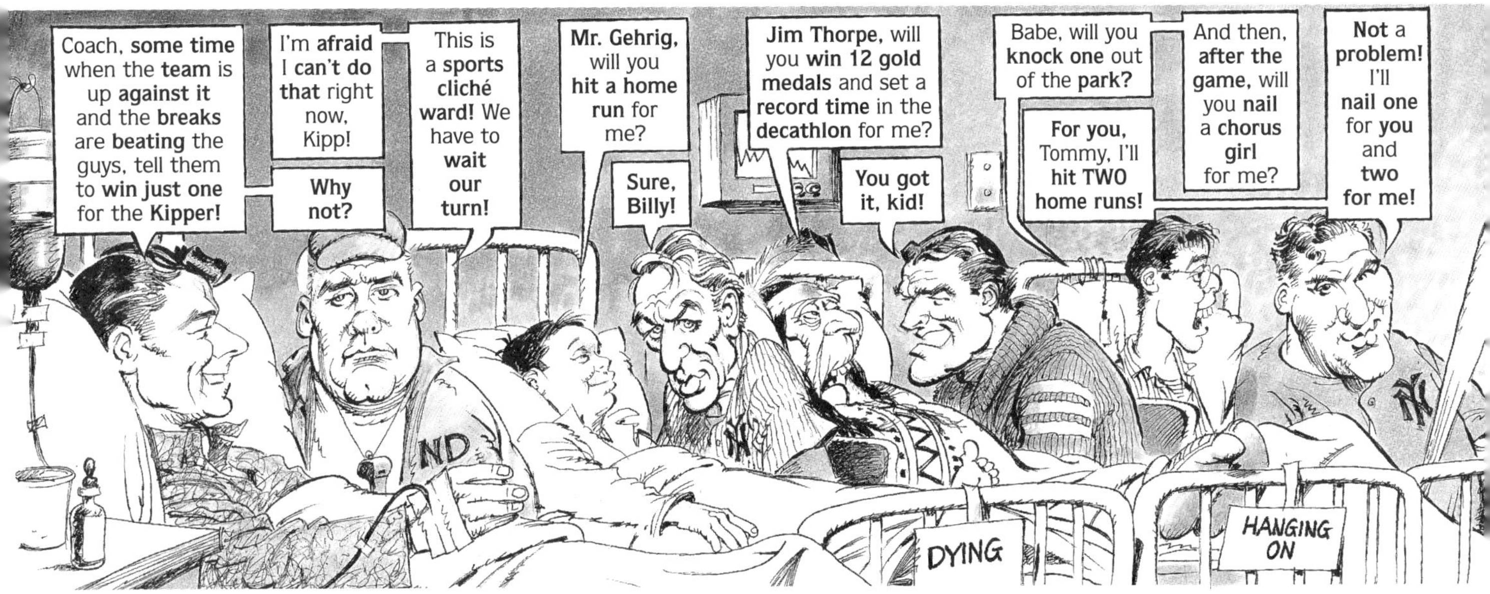
Coach, some time when the team is up against it and the breaks are beating the guys, tell them to win just one for the Kipper!
I'm afraid I can't do that right now, Kipp!
Why not?
This is a sports cliché ward! We have to wait our turn!
Mr. Gehrig, will you hit a home run for me?
Sure, Billy!
Jim Thorpe, will you win 12 gold medals and set a record time in the decathlon for me?
You got it, kid!
Babe, will you knock one out of the park?
For you, Tommy, I'll hit TWO home runs!
And then, after the game, will you nail a chorus girl for me?
Not a problem! I'll nail one for you and two for me!
ND
DYING
HANGING ON

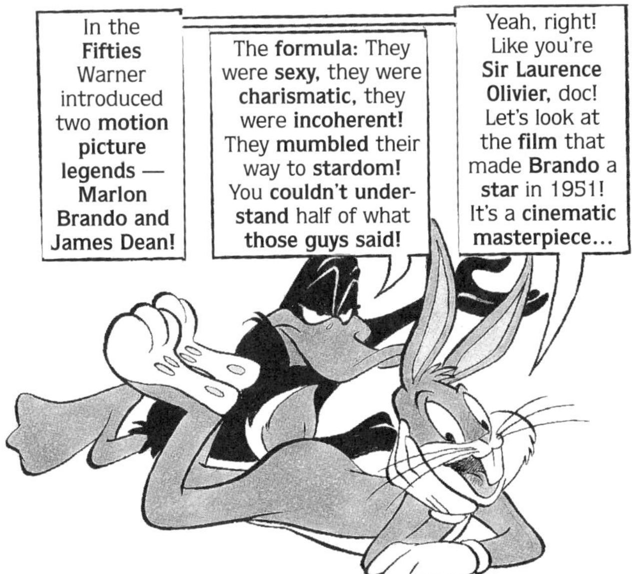
In the Fifties Warner introduced two motion picture legends — Marlon Brando and James Dean!
The formula: They were sexy, they were charismatic, they were incoherent! They mumbled their way to stardom! You couldn't under-stand half of what those guys said!
Yeah, right! Like you're Sir Laurence Olivier, doc! Let's look at the film that made Brando a star in 1951! It's a cinematic masterpiece...

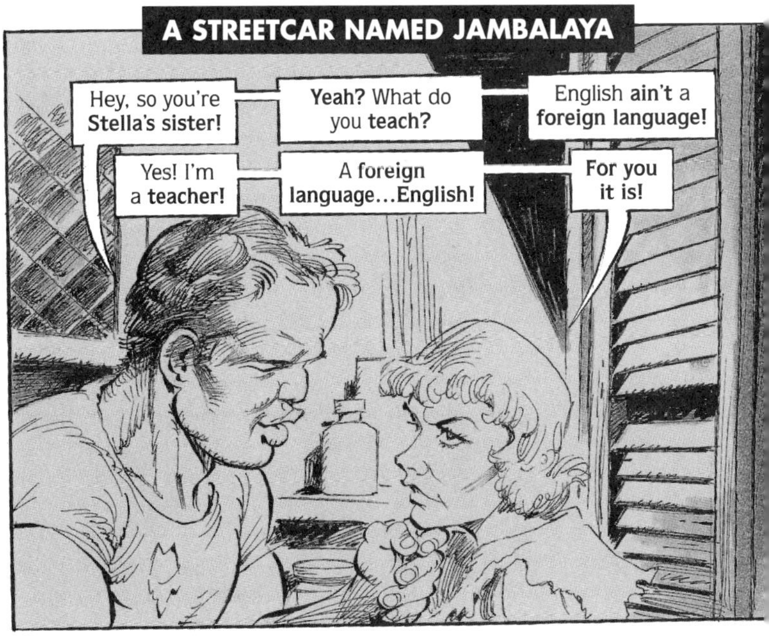
A STREETCAR NAMED JAMBALAYA
Hey, so you're Stella's sister!
Yes! I'm a teacher!
Yeah? What do you teach?
A foreign language...English!
English ain't a foreign language!
For you it is!

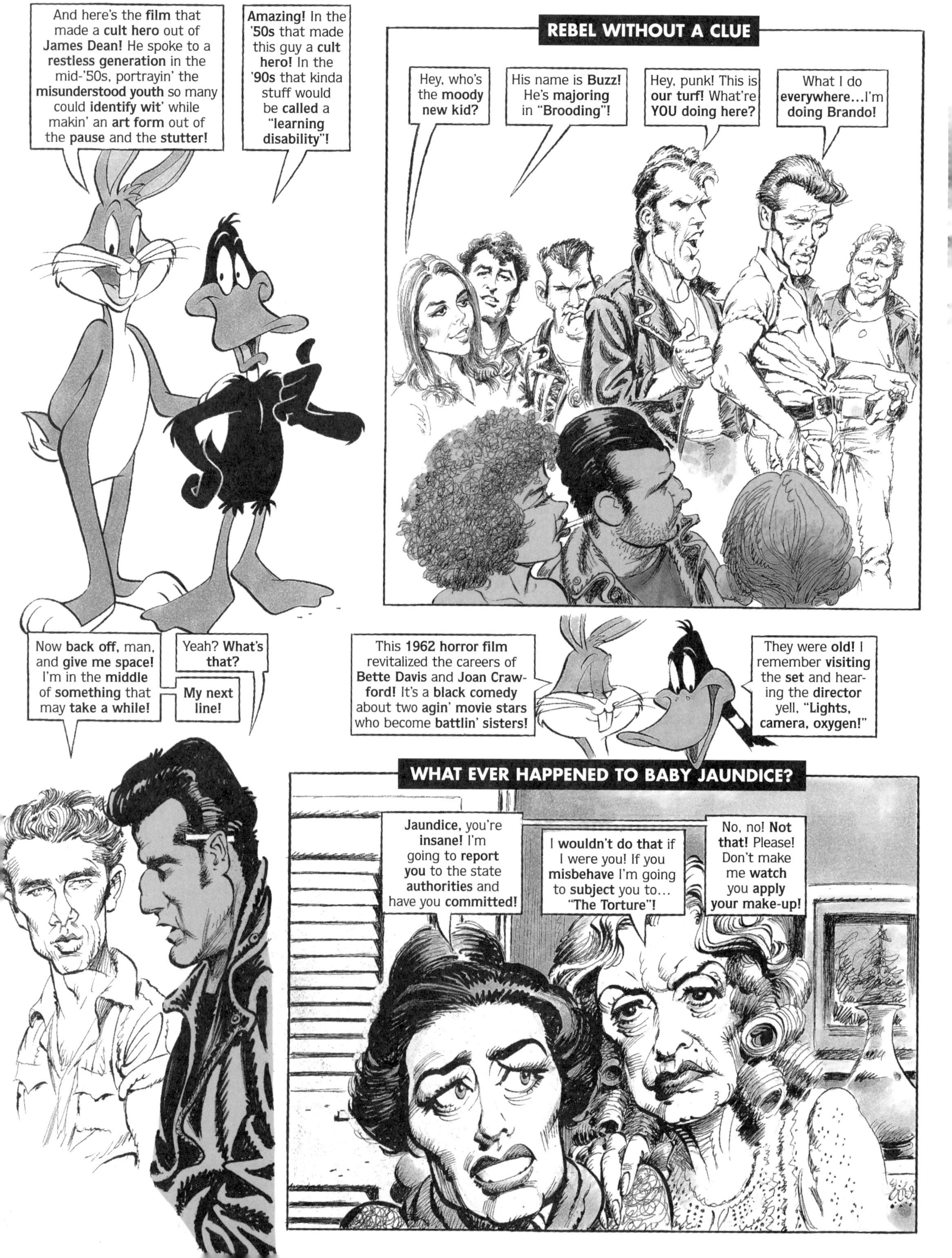

And here's the film that made a cult hero out of James Dean! He spoke to a restless generation in the mid-'50s, portrayin' the misunderstood youth so many could identify wit' while makin' an art form out of the pause and the stutter!
Amazing! In the '50s that made this guy a cult hero! In the '90s that kinda stuff would be called a "learning disability"!
REBEL WITHOUT A CLUE
Hey, who's the moody new kid?
His name is Buzz! He's majoring in "Brooding"!
Hey, punk! This is our turf! What're YOU doing here?
What I do everywhere…I'm doing Brando!
Now back off, man, and give me space! I'm in the middle of something that may take a while!
Yeah? What's that?
My next line!
This 1962 horror film revitalized the careers of Bette Davis and Joan Crawford! It's a black comedy about two agin' movie stars who become battlin' sisters!
They were old! I remember visiting the set and hearing the director yell, "Lights, camera, oxygen!"
WHAT EVER HAPPENED TO BABY JAUNDICE?
Jaundice, you're insane! I'm going to report you to the state authorities and have you committed!
I wouldn't do that if I were you! If you misbehave I'm going to subject you to… "The Torture"!
No, no! Not that! Please! Don't make me watch you apply your make-up!

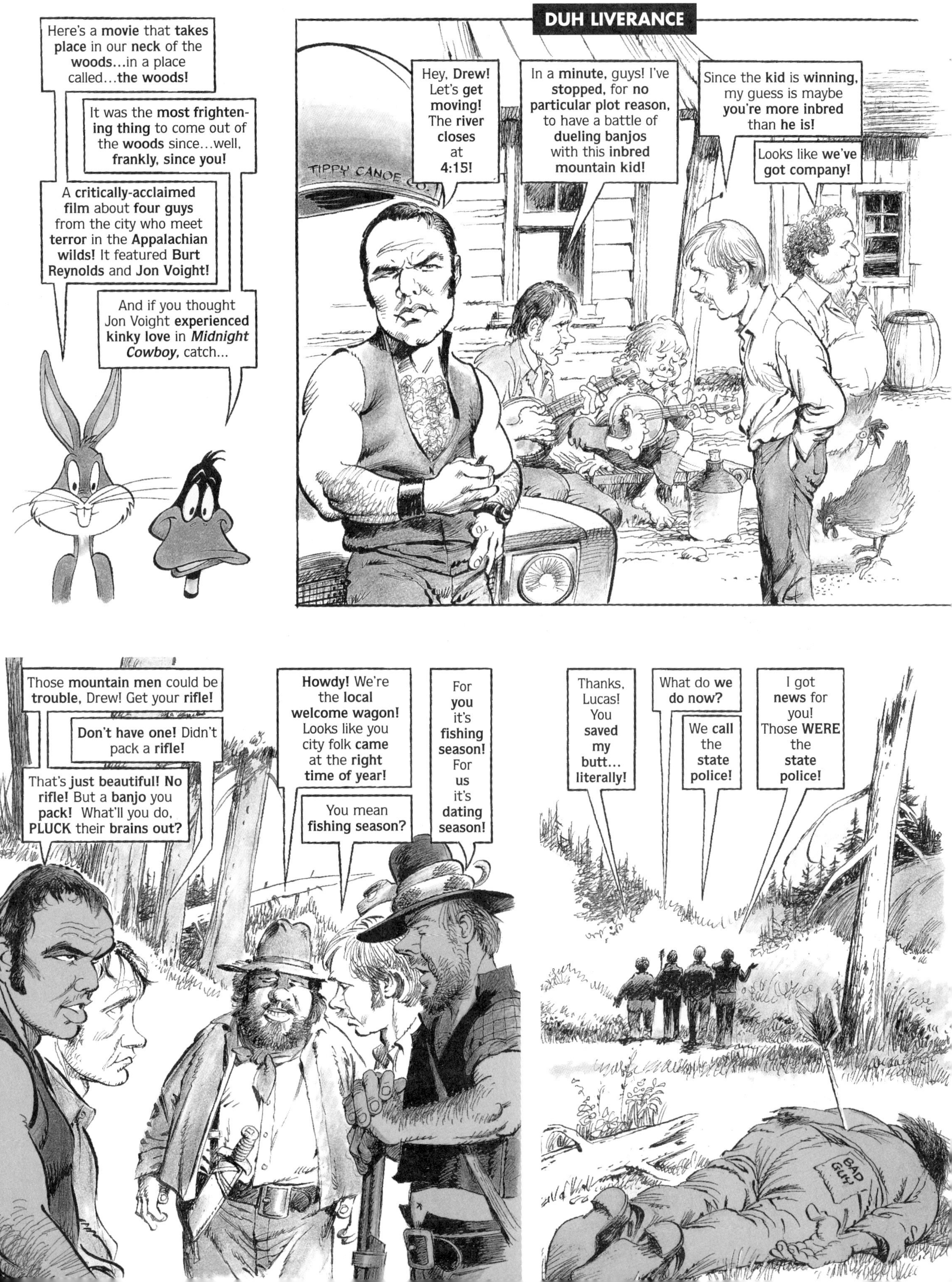
DUH LIVERANCE
Here's a movie that takes place in our neck of the woods...in a place called...the woods!
It was the most frightening thing to come out of the woods since...well, frankly, since you!
A critically-acclaimed film about four guys from the city who meet terror in the Appalachian wilds! It featured Burt Reynolds and Jon Voight!
And if you thought Jon Voight experienced kinky love in Midnight Cowboy, catch...
Hey, Drew! Let's get moving! The river closes at 4:15!
TIPPY CANOE CO.
In a minute, guys! I've stopped, for no particular plot reason, to have a battle of dueling banjos with this inbred mountain kid!
Since the kid is winning, my guess is maybe you're more inbred than he is!
Looks like we've got company!
Those mountain men could be trouble, Drew! Get your rifle!
Don't have one! Didn't pack a rifle!
That's just beautiful! No rifle! But a banjo you pack! What'll you do, PLUCK their brains out?
Howdy! We're the local welcome wagon! Looks like you city folk came at the right time of year!
You mean fishing season?
For you it's fishing season! For us it's dating season!
Thanks, Lucas! You saved my butt... literally!
What do we do now?
We call the state police!
I got news for you! Those WERE the state police!
BAD GUY

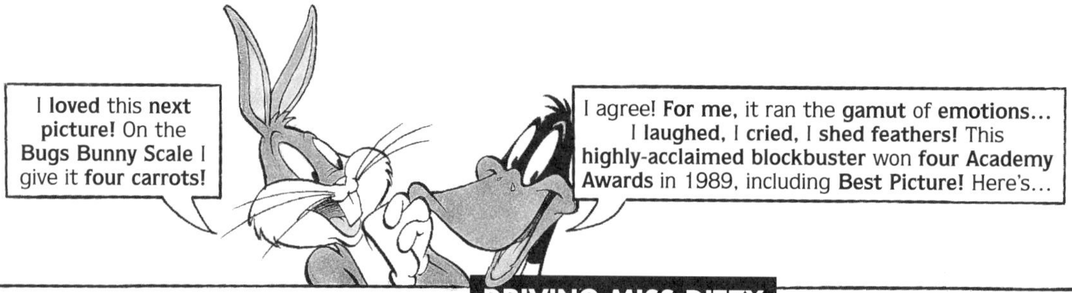
I loved this next picture! On the Bugs Bunny Scale I give it four carrots!
I agree! For me, it ran the gamut of emotions… I laughed, I cried, I shed feathers! This highly-acclaimed blockbuster won four Academy Awards in 1989, including Best Picture! Here's…

## DRIVING MISS DITZY

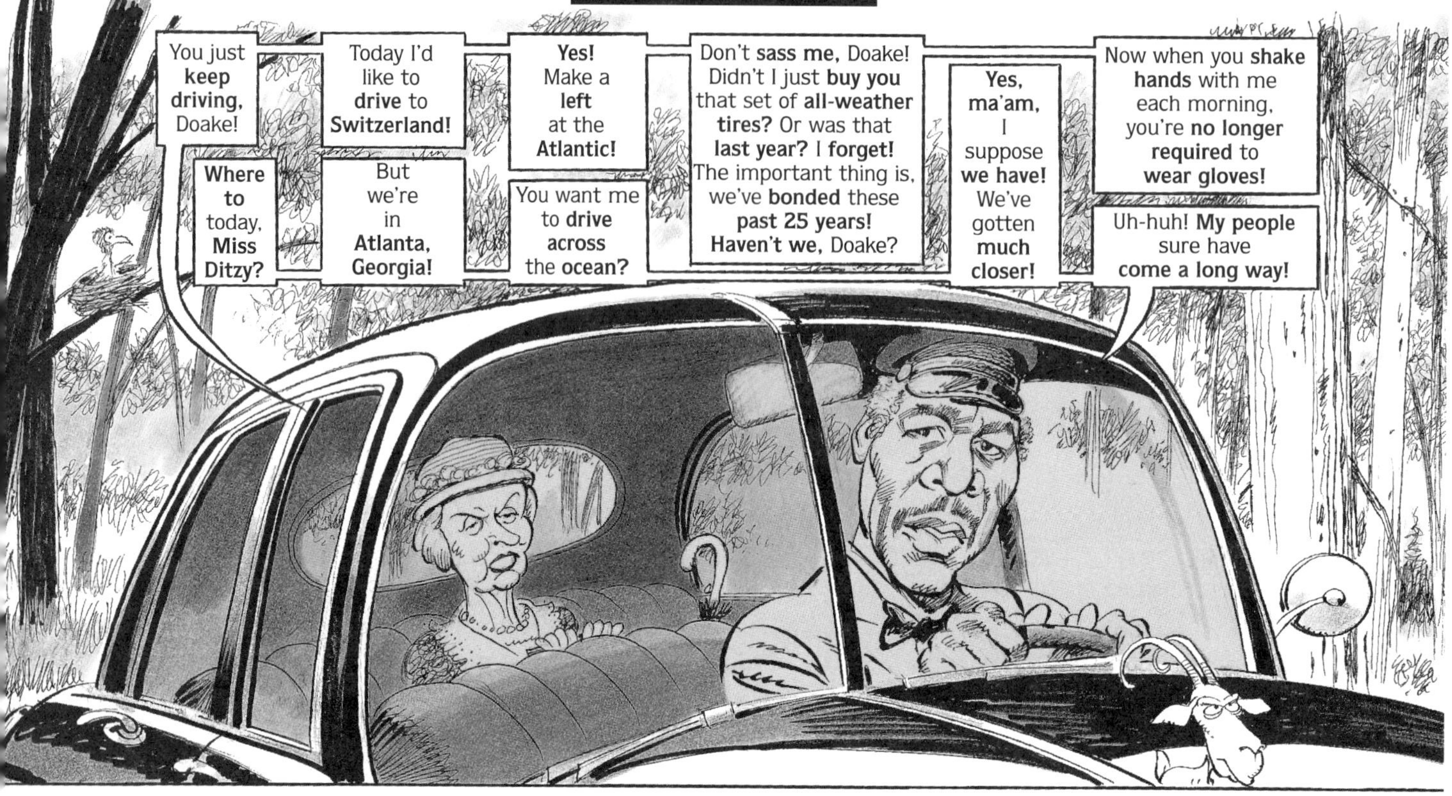
You just keep driving, Doake!
Where to today, Miss Ditzy?
Today I'd like to drive to Switzerland!
But we're in Atlanta, Georgia!
Yes! Make a left at the Atlantic!
You want me to drive across the ocean?
Don't sass me, Doake! Didn't I just buy you that set of all-weather tires? Or was that last year? I forget! The important thing is, we've bonded these past 25 years! Haven't we, Doake?
Yes, ma'am, I suppose we have! We've gotten much closer!
Now when you shake hands with me each morning, you're no longer required to wear gloves!
Uh-huh! My people sure have come a long way!

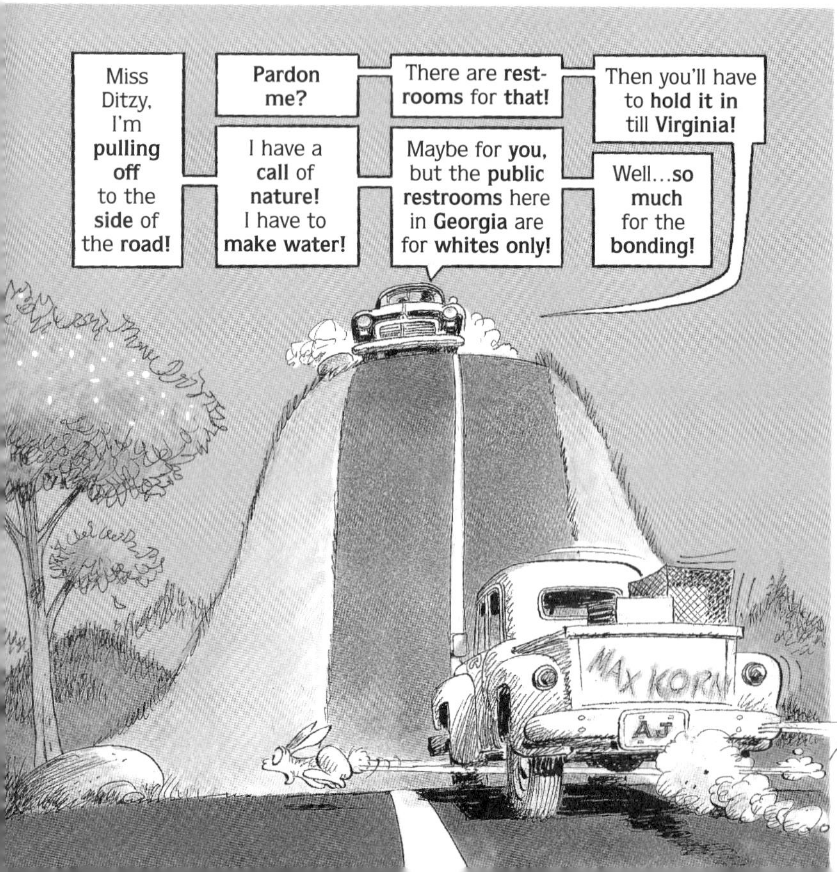
Miss Ditzy, I'm pulling off to the side of the road!
Pardon me?
I have a call of nature! I have to make water!
There are rest-rooms for that!
Maybe for you, but the public restrooms here in Georgia are for whites only!
Then you'll have to hold it in till Virginia!
Well…so much for the bonding!
MAX KORN
AJ

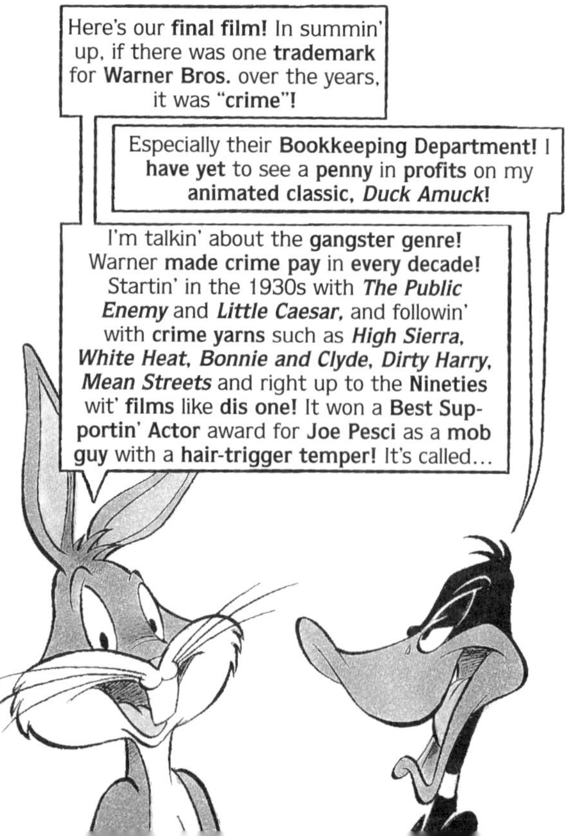
Here's our final film! In summin' up, if there was one trademark for Warner Bros. over the years, it was "crime"!
Especially their Bookkeeping Department! I have yet to see a penny in profits on my animated classic, *Duck Amuck*!
I'm talkin' about the gangster genre! Warner made crime pay in every decade! Startin' in the 1930s with *The Public Enemy* and *Little Caesar*, and followin' with crime yarns such as *High Sierra, White Heat, Bonnie and Clyde, Dirty Harry, Mean Streets* and right up to the Nineties wit' films like dis one! It won a Best Sup-portin' Actor award for Joe Pesci as a mob guy with a hair-trigger temper! It's called…

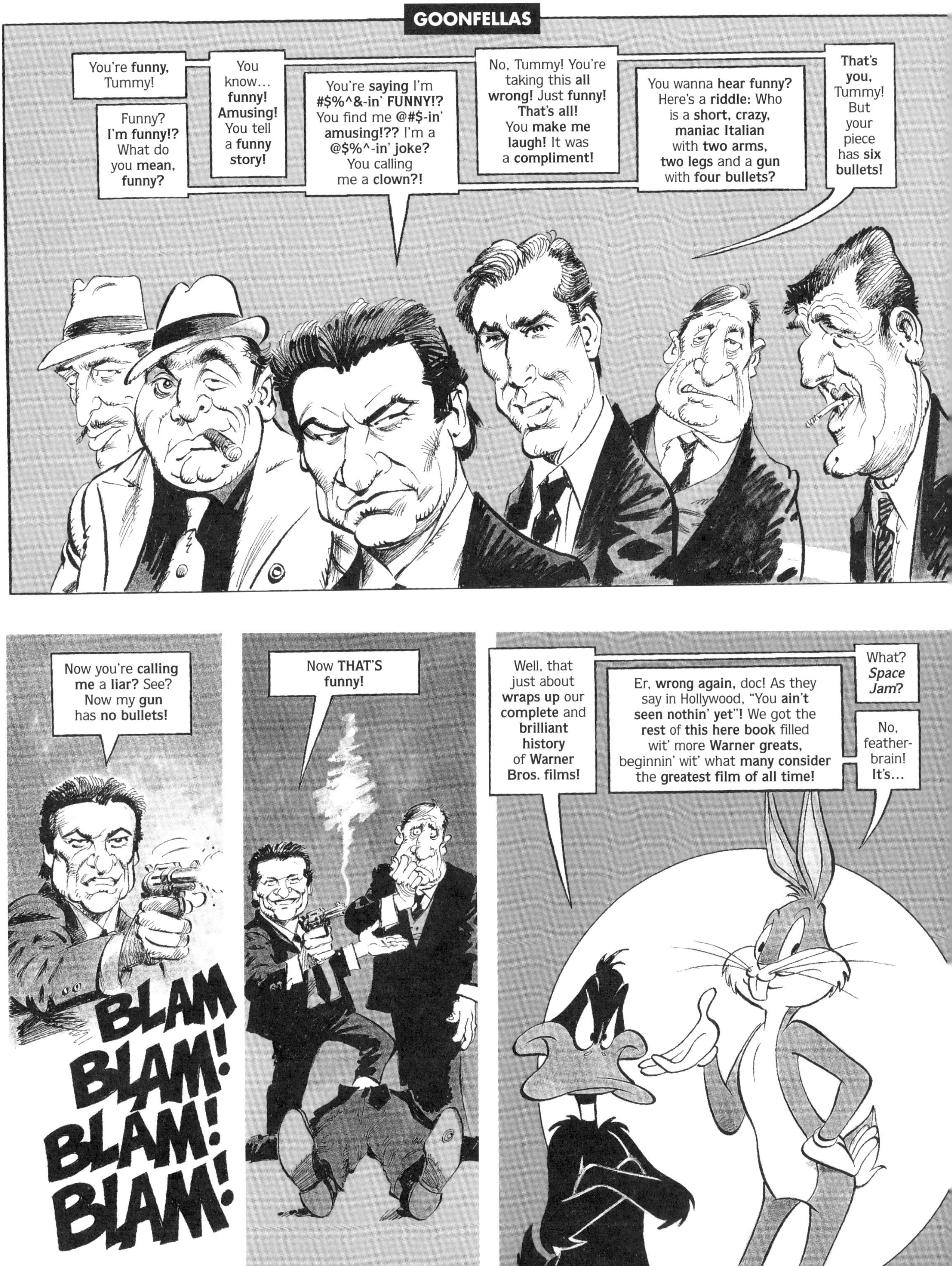
GOONFELLAS
You're funny, Tummy!
Funny? I'm funny!? What do you mean, funny?
You know… funny! Amusing! You tell a funny story!
You're saying I'm #$%^&-in' FUNNY!? You find me @#$-in' amusing!?? I'm a @$%^-in' joke? You calling me a clown?!
No, Tummy! You're taking this all wrong! Just funny! That's all! You make me laugh! It was a compliment!
You wanna hear funny? Here's a riddle: Who is a short, crazy, maniac Italian with two arms, two legs and a gun with four bullets?
That's you, Tummy! But your piece has six bullets!
Now you're calling me a liar? See? Now my gun has no bullets!
BLAM
BLAM!
BLAM!
BLAM!
Now THAT'S funny!
Well, that just about wraps up our complete and brilliant history of Warner Bros. films!
What? Space Jam?
Er, wrong again, doc! As they say in Hollywood, "You ain't seen nothin' yet"! We got the rest of this here book filled wit' more Warner greats, beginnin' wit' what many consider the greatest film of all time!
No, feather-brain! It's…

SLAY IT AGAIN, SAM DEPT.

Of all the satires of all the movies in all the humor magazines in the world, this one ended up in ours!

# CA

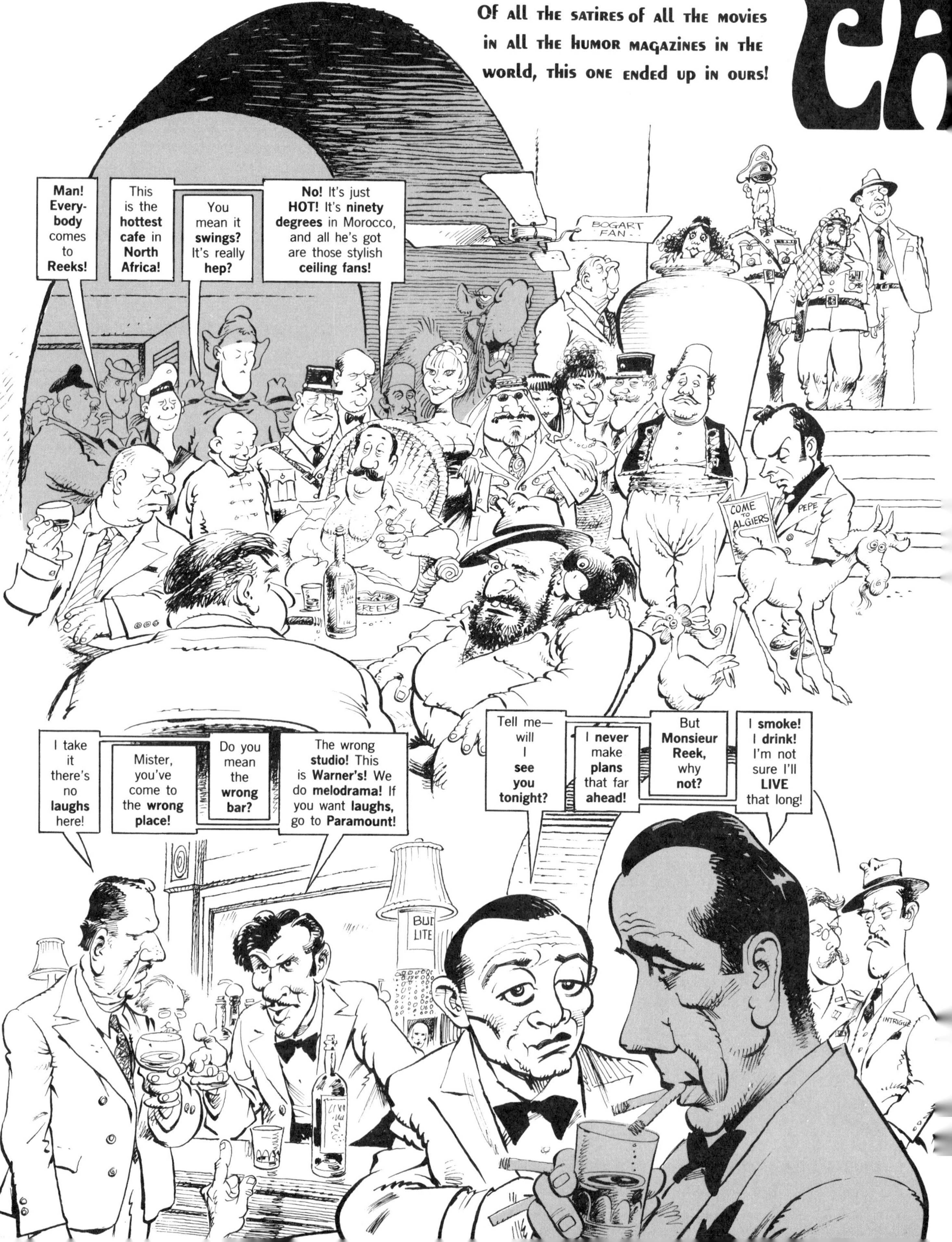

Man! Everybody comes to Reeks!
This is the hottest cafe in North Africa!
You mean it swings? It's really hep?
No! It's just HOT! It's ninety degrees in Morocco, and all he's got are those stylish ceiling fans!
BOGART FAN
REEKS
COME TO ALGIERS
PEPE
I take it there's no laughs here!
Mister, you've come to the wrong place!
Do you mean the wrong bar?
The wrong studio! This is Warner's! We do melodrama! If you want laughs, go to Paramount!
Tell me—will I see you tonight?
I never make plans that far ahead!
But Monsieur Reek, why not?
I smoke! I drink! I'm not sure I'll LIVE that long!
BUD LITE
INTRIGUE

# SABONKERS

ARTIST: MORT DRUCKER WRITER: ARNIE KOGEN

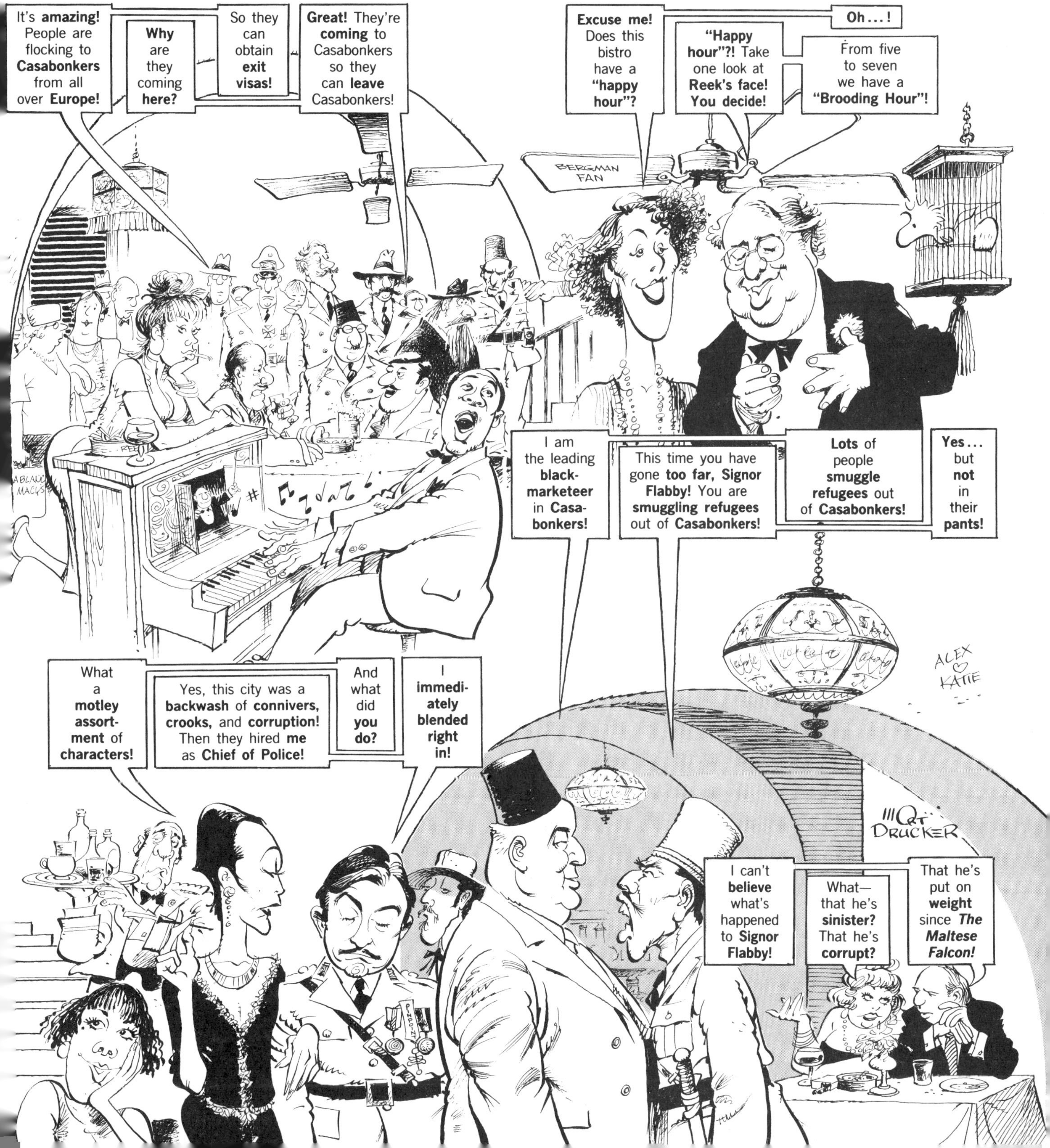

It's **amazing!** People are flocking to **Casabonkers** from all over **Europe!**
**Why** are they coming **here?**
So they can obtain **exit visas!**
**Great!** They're **coming** to Casabonkers so they can **leave** Casabonkers!
**Excuse me!** Does this bistro have a **"happy hour"?**
**Oh . . . !**
From five to seven we have a **"Brooding Hour"!**
**"Happy hour"?!** Take one look at **Reek's face! You decide!**
BERGMAN FAN
I am the leading **black-marketeer** in **Casa-bonkers!**
This time you have gone **too far, Signor Flabby!** You are **smuggling refugees** out of **Casabonkers!**
**Lots** of people **smuggle refugees** out of **Casabonkers!**
**Yes . . .** but **not** in their **pants!**
What a **motley assort-ment** of **characters!**
Yes, this city was a **backwash** of **connivers, crooks,** and **corruption!** Then they hired **me** as **Chief of Police!**
And what did **you do?**
I **immedi-ately blended right in!**
I can't **believe** what's happened to **Signor Flabby!**
What— that he's **sinister?** That he's **corrupt?**
That he's put on **weight** since ***The Maltese Falcon!***

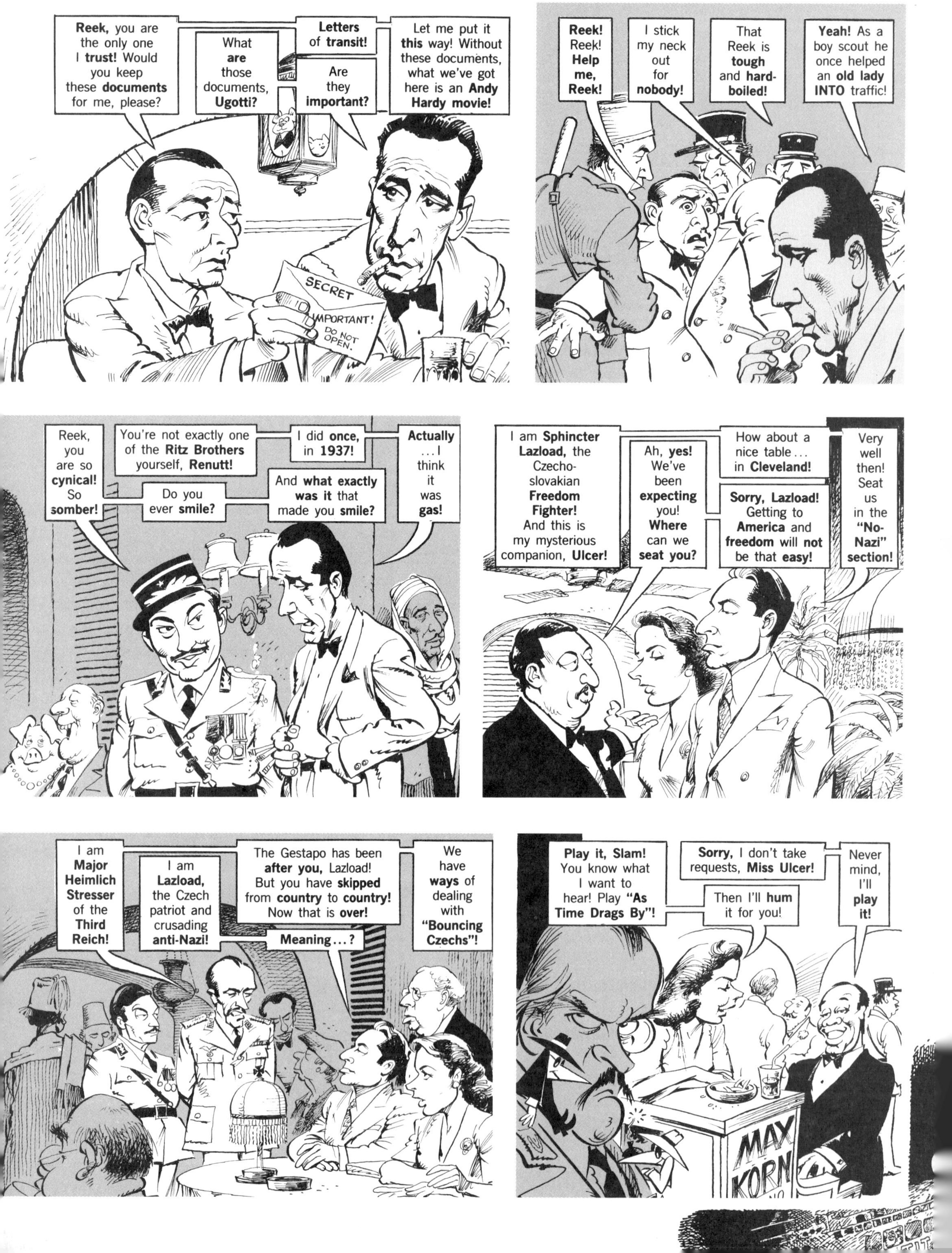
Reek, you are the only one I trust! Would you keep these documents for me, please?
What are those documents, Ugotti?
Letters of transit!
Are they important?
Let me put it this way! Without these documents, what we've got here is an Andy Hardy movie!
SECRET
IMPORTANT!
DO NOT OPEN.
Reek! Reek! Help me, Reek!
I stick my neck out for nobody!
That Reek is tough and hard-boiled!
Yeah! As a boy scout he once helped an old lady INTO traffic!
Reek, you are so cynical! So somber!
You're not exactly one of the Ritz Brothers yourself, Renutt!
Do you ever smile?
I did once, in 1937!
And what exactly was it that made you smile?
Actually . . . I think it was gas!
I am Sphincter Lazload, the Czecho-slovakian Freedom Fighter! And this is my mysterious companion, Ulcer!
Ah, yes! We've been expecting you! Where can we seat you?
How about a nice table . . . in Cleveland!
Sorry, Lazload! Getting to America and freedom will not be that easy!
Very well then! Seat us in the "No-Nazi" section!
I am Major Heimlich Stresser of the Third Reich!
I am Lazload, the Czech patriot and crusading anti-Nazi!
The Gestapo has been after you, Lazload! But you have skipped from country to country! Now that is over!
Meaning . . . ?
We have ways of dealing with "Bouncing Czechs"!
Play it, Slam! You know what I want to hear! Play "As Time Drags By"!
Sorry, I don't take requests, Miss Ulcer!
Then I'll hum it for you!
Never mind, I'll play it!
MAX KORN

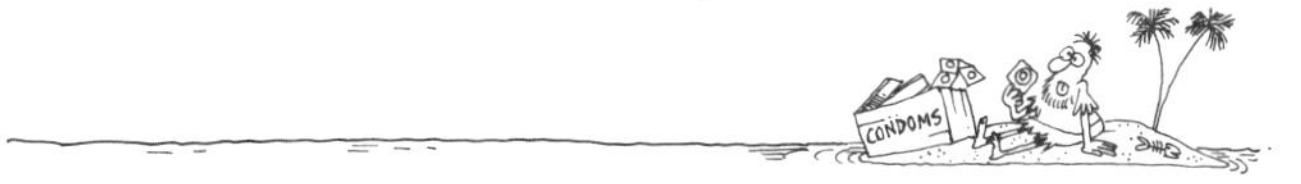
CONDOMS

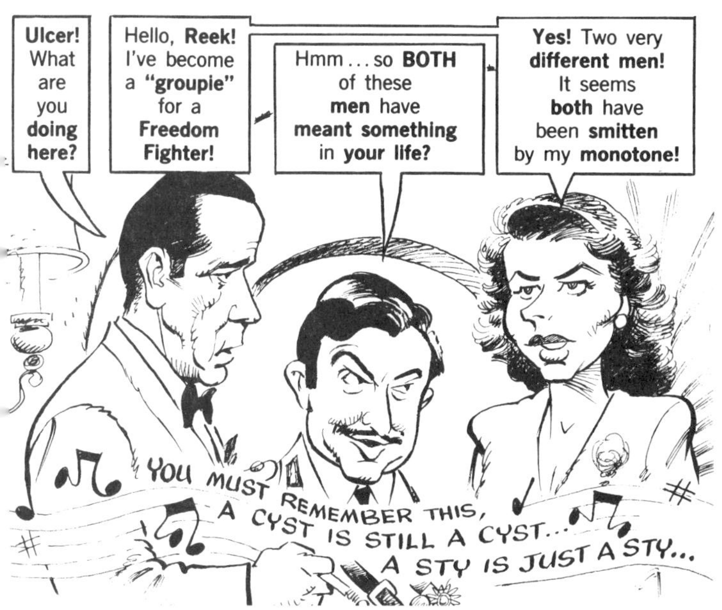
Ulcer! What are you doing here?
Hello, Reek! I've become a "groupie" for a Freedom Fighter!
Hmm ... so BOTH of these men have meant something in your life?
Yes! Two very different men! It seems both have been smitten by my monotone!
YOU MUST REMEMBER THIS, A CYST IS STILL A CYST... A STY IS JUST A STY...

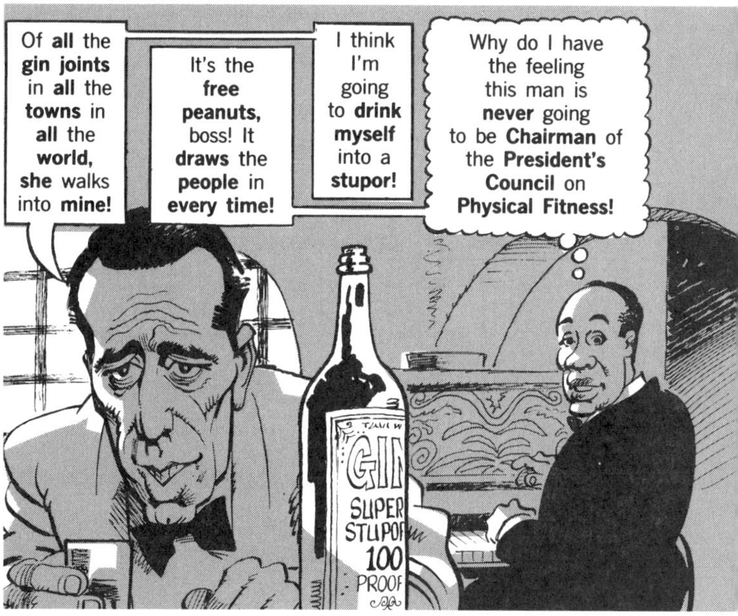
Of all the gin joints in all the towns in all the world, she walks into mine!
It's the free peanuts, boss! It draws the people in every time!
I think I'm going to drink myself into a stupor!
Why do I have the feeling this man is never going to be Chairman of the President's Council on Physical Fitness!
GIN
SUPER
100
PROOF

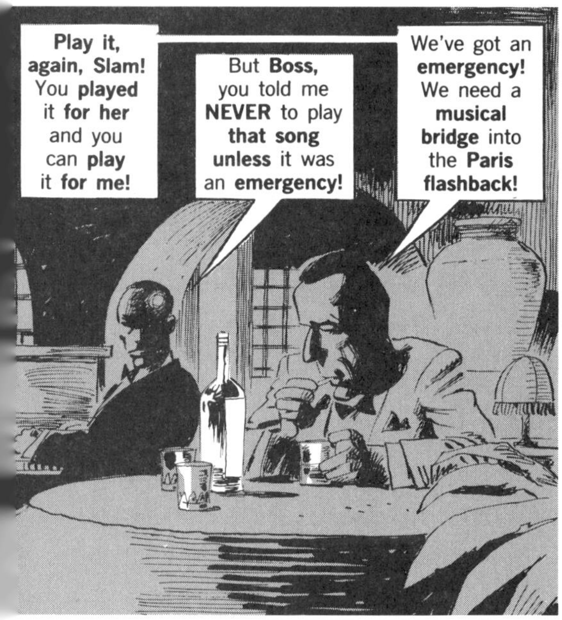
Play it, again, Slam! You played it for her and you can play it for me!
But Boss, you told me NEVER to play that song unless it was an emergency!
We've got an emergency! We need a musical bridge into the Paris flashback!

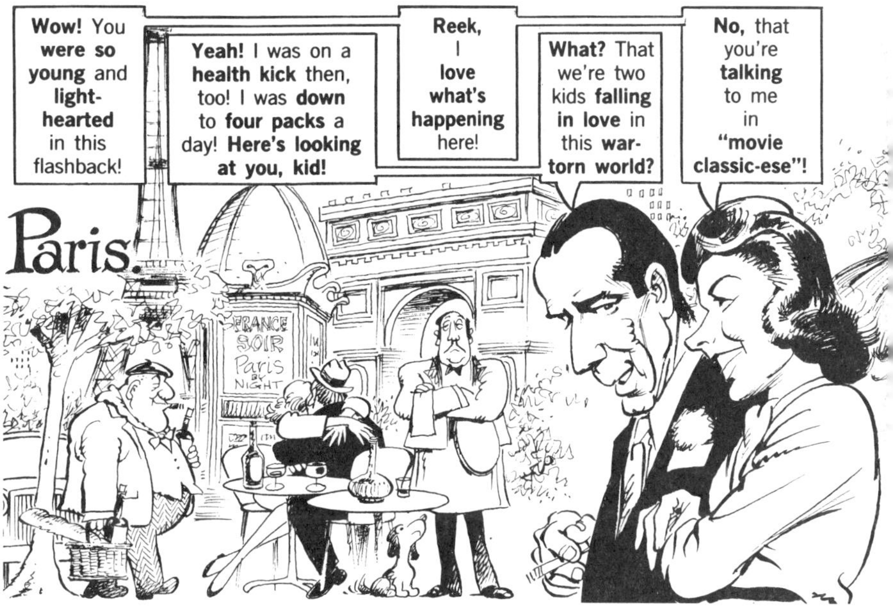
Wow! You were so young and light-hearted in this flashback!
Yeah! I was on a health kick then, too! I was down to four packs a day! Here's looking at you, kid!
Reek, I love what's happening here!
What? That we're two kids falling in love in this war-torn world?
No, that you're talking to me in "movie classic-ese"!
Paris
FRANCE SOIR
Paris BY NIGHT

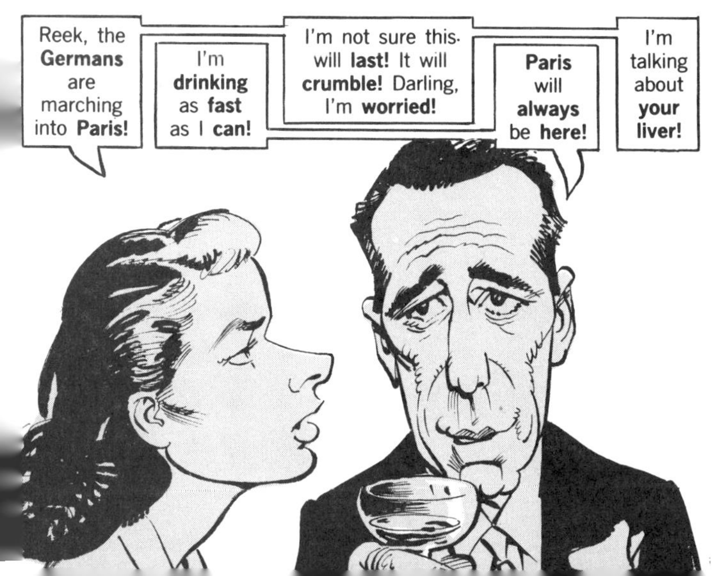
Reek, the Germans are marching into Paris!
I'm drinking as fast as I can!
I'm not sure this will last! It will crumble! Darling, I'm worried!
Paris will always be here!
I'm talking about your liver!

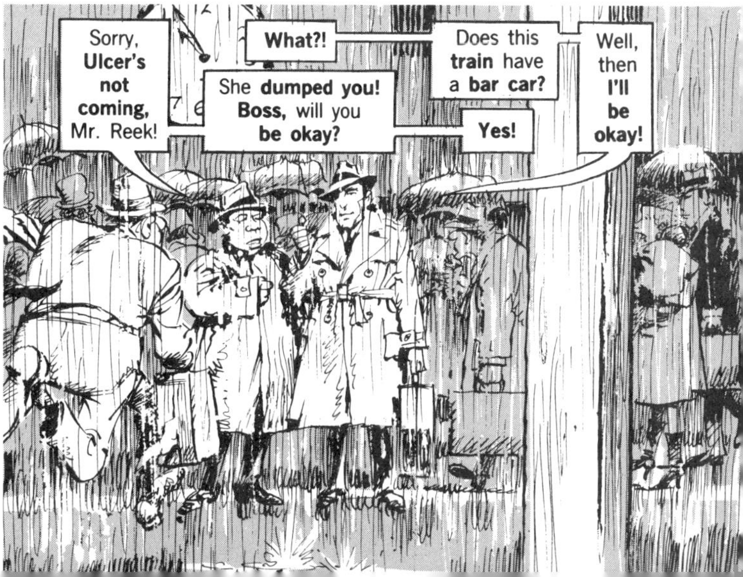
Sorry, Ulcer's not coming, Mr. Reek!
What?!
She dumped you! Boss, will you be okay?
Does this train have a bar car?
Yes!
Well, then I'll be okay!

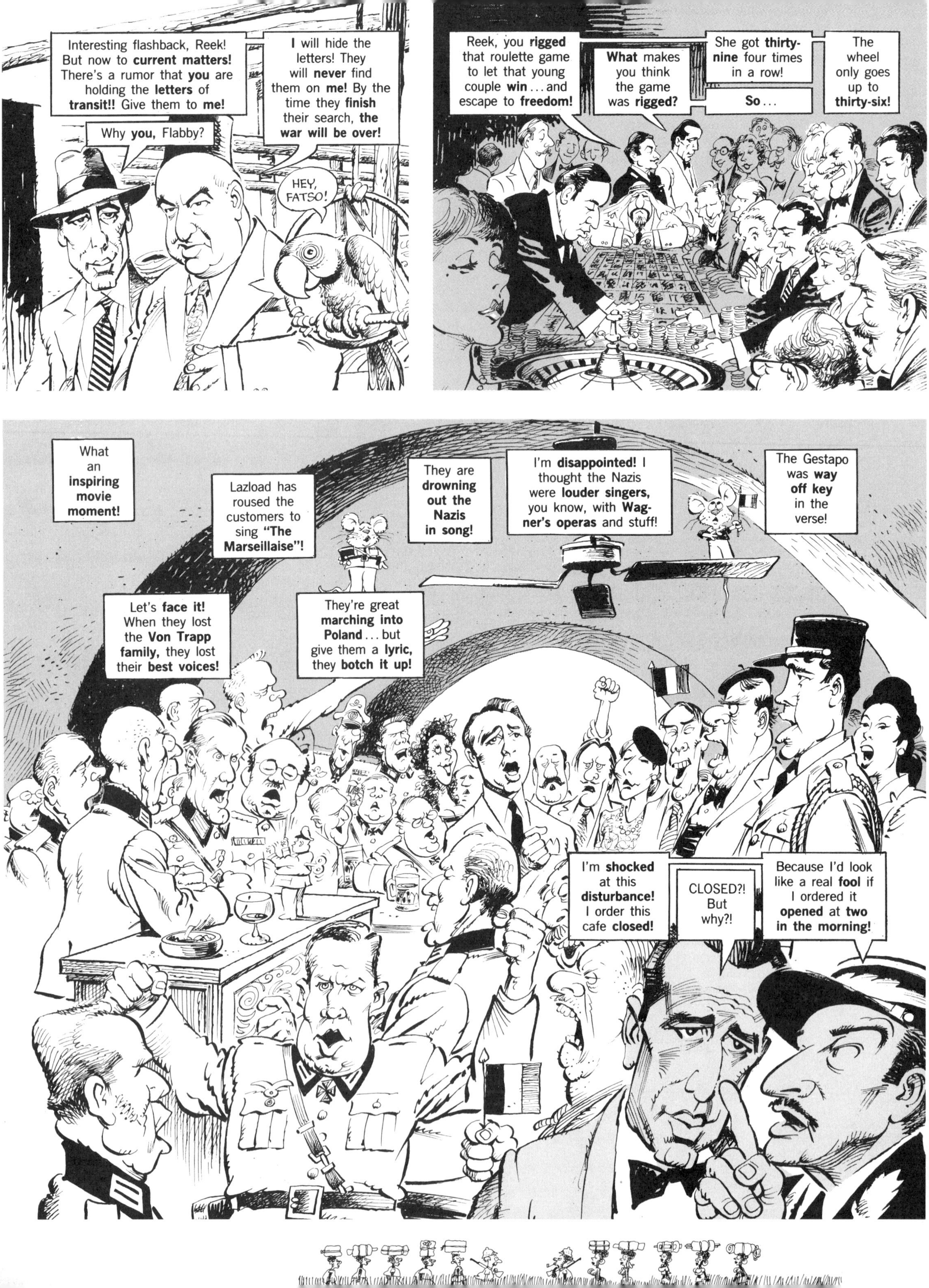
Interesting flashback, Reek! But now to current matters! There's a rumor that you are holding the letters of transit!! Give them to me!
Why you, Flabby?
I will hide the letters! They will never find them on me! By the time they finish their search, the war will be over!
HEY, FATSO!
Reek, you rigged that roulette game to let that young couple win . . . and escape to freedom!
What makes you think the game was rigged?
She got thirty-nine four times in a row!
So . . .
The wheel only goes up to thirty-six!
What an inspiring movie moment!
Lazload has roused the customers to sing "The Marseillaise"!
They are drowning out the Nazis in song!
I'm disappointed! I thought the Nazis were louder singers, you know, with Wagner's operas and stuff!
The Gestapo was way off key in the verse!
Let's face it! When they lost the Von Trapp family, they lost their best voices!
They're great marching into Poland . . . but give them a lyric, they botch it up!
I'm shocked at this disturbance! I order this cafe closed!
CLOSED?! But why?!
Because I'd look like a real fool if I ordered it opened at two in the morning!

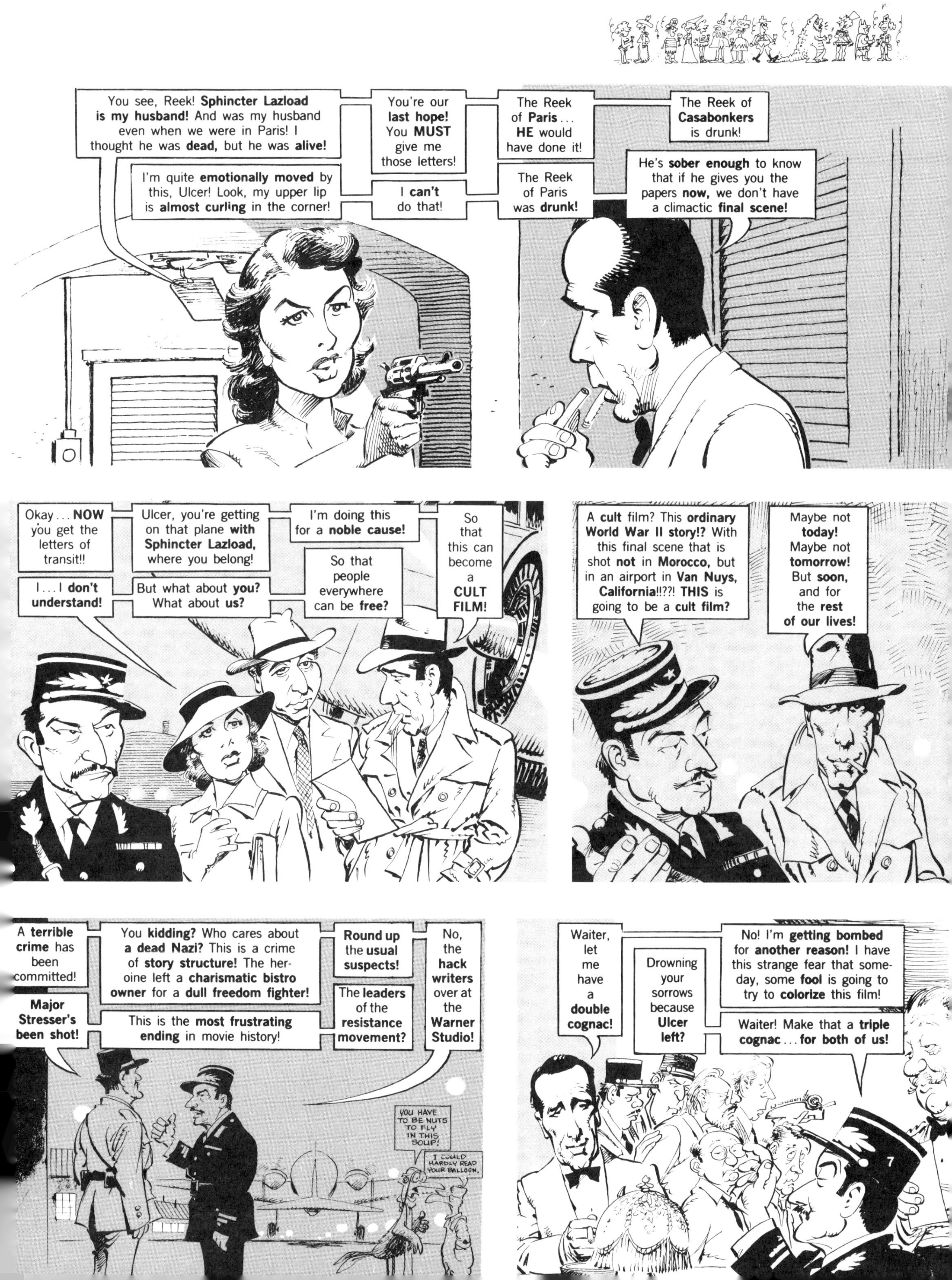
You see, Reek! Sphincter Lazload is my husband! And was my husband even when we were in Paris! I thought he was dead, but he was alive!
You're our last hope! You MUST give me those letters!
I'm quite emotionally moved by this, Ulcer! Look, my upper lip is almost curling in the corner!
I can't do that!
The Reek of Paris... HE would have done it!
The Reek of Casabonkers is drunk!
The Reek of Paris was drunk!
He's sober enough to know that if he gives you the papers now, we don't have a climactic final scene!
Okay... NOW you get the letters of transit!!
Ulcer, you're getting on that plane with Sphincter Lazload, where you belong!
I'm doing this for a noble cause!
So that this can become a CULT FILM!
I... I don't understand!
But what about you? What about us?
So that people everywhere can be free?
A cult film? This ordinary World War II story!? With this final scene that is shot not in Morocco, but in an airport in Van Nuys, California!!??! THIS is going to be a cult film?
Maybe not today! Maybe not tomorrow! But soon, and for the rest of our lives!
A terrible crime has been committed!
You kidding? Who cares about a dead Nazi? This is a crime of story structure! The heroine left a charismatic bistro owner for a dull freedom fighter!
Round up the usual suspects!
No, the hack writers over at the Warner Studio!
Major Stresser's been shot!
This is the most frustrating ending in movie history!
The leaders of the resistance movement?
YOU HAVE TO BE NUTS TO FLY IN THIS SOUP!
I COULD HARDLY READ YOUR BALLOON.
Waiter, let me have a double cognac!
Drowning your sorrows because Ulcer left?
No! I'm getting bombed for another reason! I have this strange fear that someday, some fool is going to try to colorize this film!
Waiter! Make that a triple cognac... for both of us!

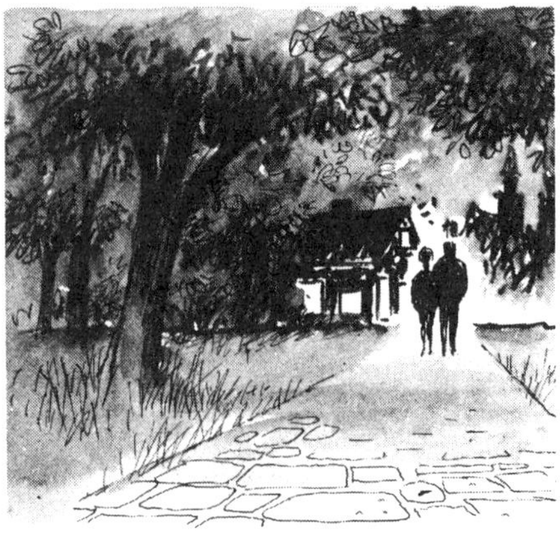

When they first set out to make a film of this successful Broadway play, they decided that they'd need two middle-aged ugly people to play the hero and heroine. Then they decided that they'd also like to make *money* with this film!

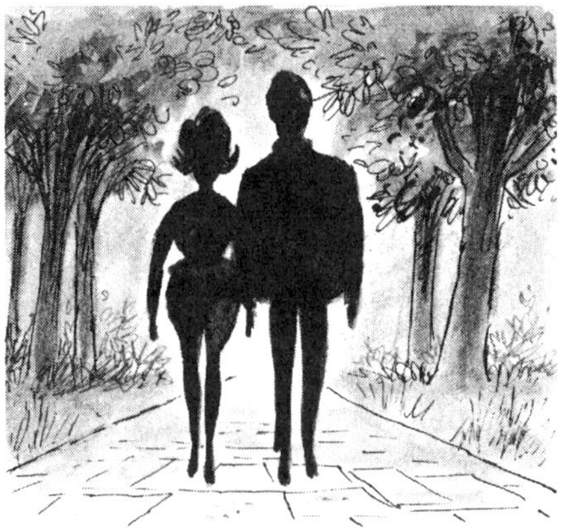

So they hired Liz and Dick! You won't *believe* how the make-up man has camouflaged Liz's beauty and sex appeal—turning her into an ugly, middle-aged bag! Brace yourself! Here comes that hideous, overblown, sexless blob now!

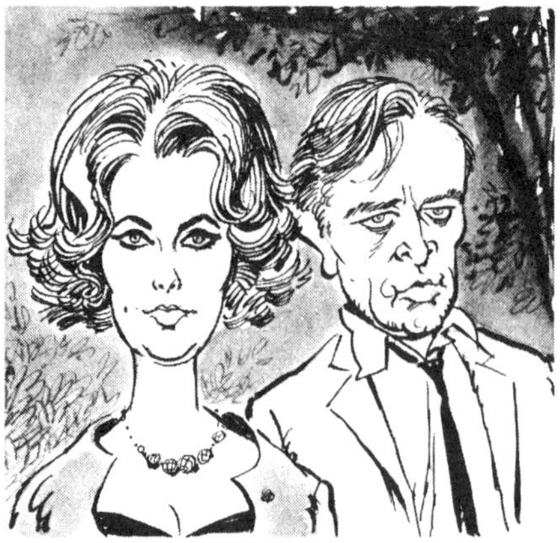

See those three lines around her eyes! And see those four grey hairs! And see how ugly she looks all over! Yeccchhh! All we know is: We certainly wouldn't want our mother to look like her! Our *girl friend,* yeah! But not our mother!

**Now get ready for a movie excursion into the world of sex, profanity, screaming, drinking and blood-curdling parlor games that never quite answers the question the whole world is asking . . . mainly:**

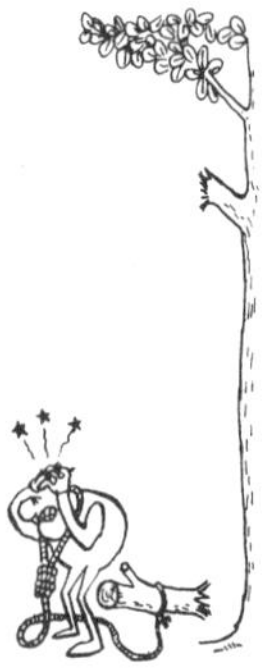

# WHO IN HECK IS VIRGINIA WOOLFE?

ARTIST: MORT DRUCKER WRITER: LARRY SIEGEL

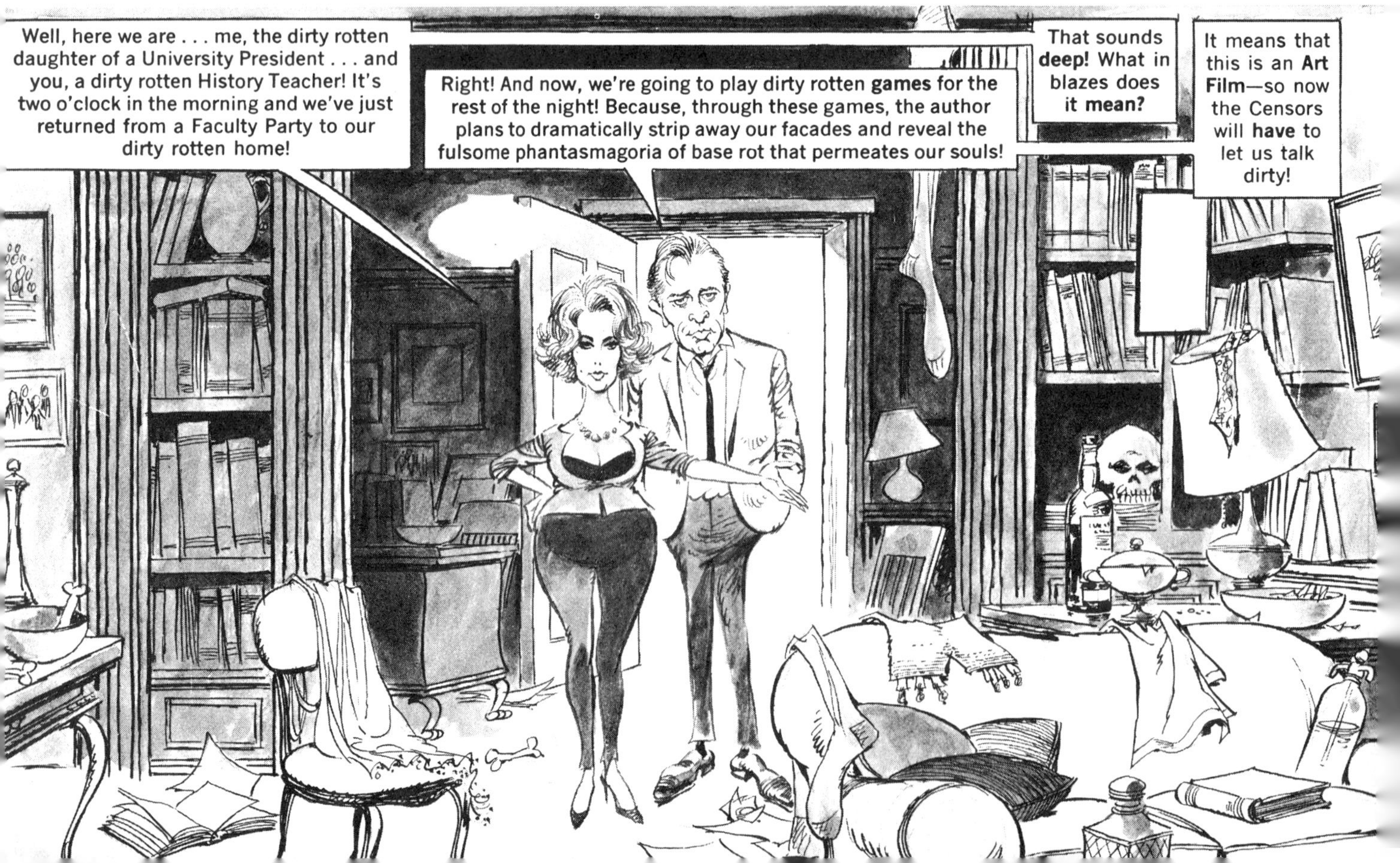
Well, here we are . . . me, the dirty rotten daughter of a University President . . . and you, a dirty rotten History Teacher! It's two o'clock in the morning and we've just returned from a Faculty Party to our dirty rotten home!
Right! And now, we're going to play dirty rotten **games** for the rest of the night! Because, through these games, the author plans to dramatically strip away our facades and reveal the fulsome phantasmagoria of base rot that permeates our souls!
That sounds **deep!** What in blazes does **it mean?**
It means that this is an **Art Film**—so now the Censors will **have** to let us talk dirty!

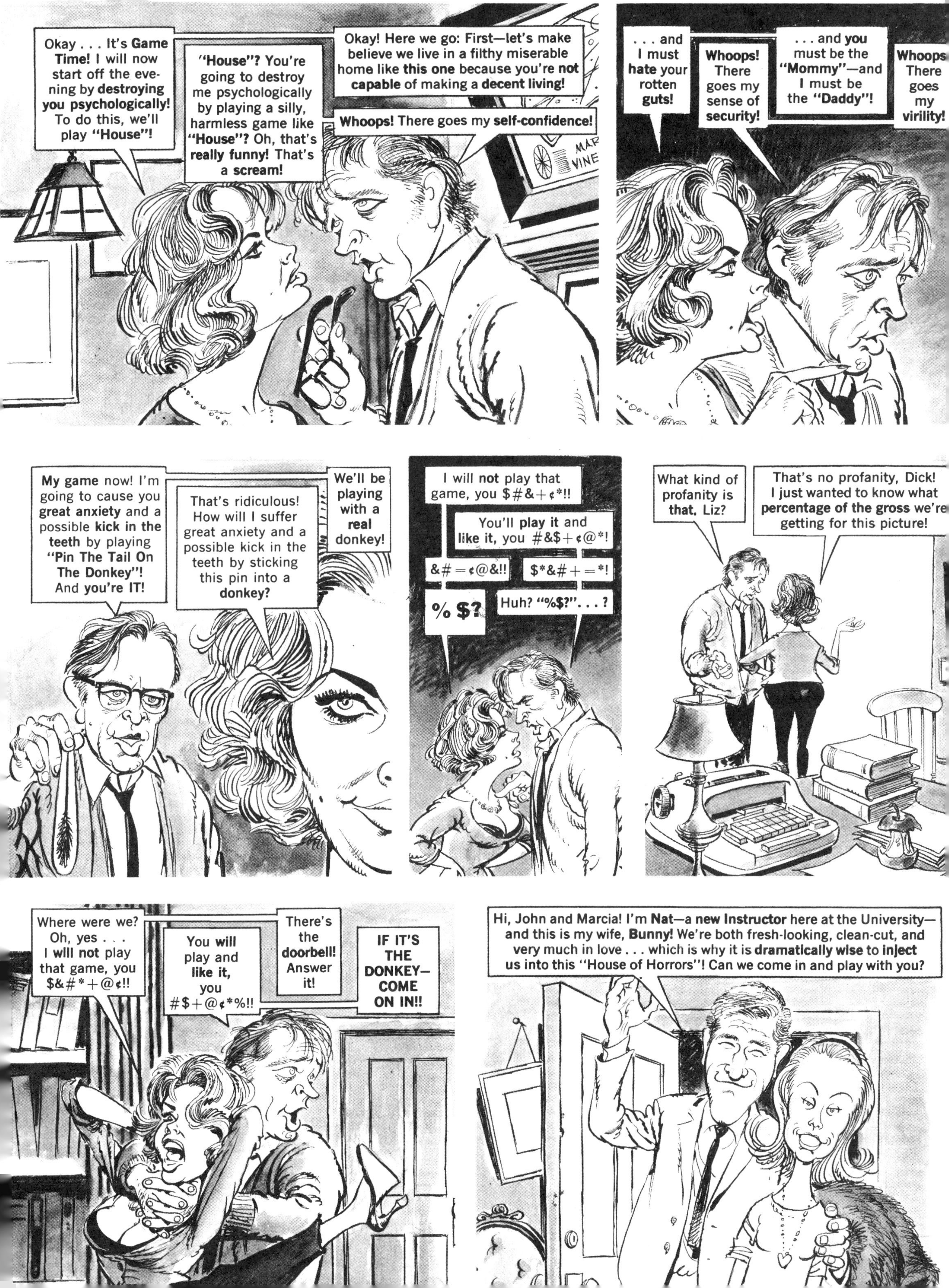
Okay . . . It's Game Time! I will now start off the evening by destroying you psychologically! To do this, we'll play "House"!
"House"? You're going to destroy me psychologically by playing a silly, harmless game like "House"? Oh, that's really funny! That's a scream!
Okay! Here we go: First—let's make believe we live in a filthy miserable home like this one because you're not capable of making a decent living!
Whoops! There goes my self-confidence!
. . . and I must hate your rotten guts!
Whoops! There goes my sense of security!
. . . and you must be the "Mommy"—and I must be the "Daddy"!
Whoops There goes my virility!
My game now! I'm going to cause you great anxiety and a possible kick in the teeth by playing "Pin The Tail On The Donkey"! And you're IT!
That's ridiculous! How will I suffer great anxiety and a possible kick in the teeth by sticking this pin into a donkey?
We'll be playing with a real donkey!
I will not play that game, you $#&+¢*!!
You'll play it and like it, you #&$+¢@*!
&#=¢@&!!
$*&#+=*!
% $?
Huh? "%$?". . . ?
What kind of profanity is that, Liz?
That's no profanity, Dick! I just wanted to know what percentage of the gross we're getting for this picture!
Where were we? Oh, yes . . . I will not play that game, you $&#*+@¢!!
You will play and like it, you #$+@¢*%!!
There's the doorbell! Answer it!
IF IT'S THE DONKEY—COME ON IN!!
Hi, John and Marcia! I'm Nat—a new Instructor here at the University—and this is my wife, Bunny! We're both fresh-looking, clean-cut, and very much in love . . . which is why it is dramatically wise to inject us into this "House of Horrors"! Can we come in and play with you?

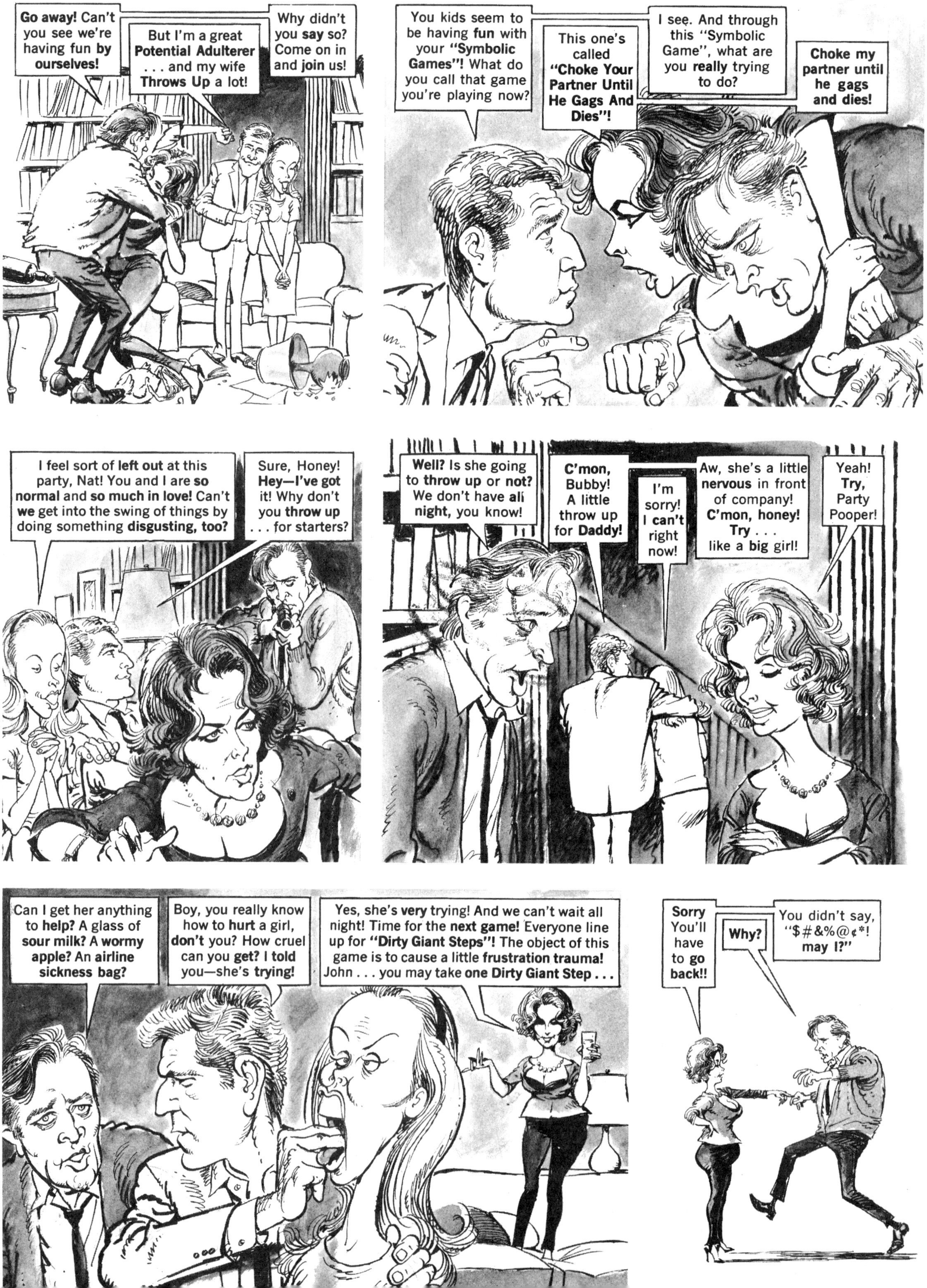

Go away! Can't you see we're having fun by ourselves!
But I'm a great Potential Adulterer . . . and my wife Throws Up a lot!
Why didn't you say so? Come on in and join us!
You kids seem to be having fun with your "Symbolic Games"! What do you call that game you're playing now?
This one's called "Choke Your Partner Until He Gags And Dies"!
I see. And through this "Symbolic Game", what are you really trying to do?
Choke my partner until he gags and dies!
I feel sort of left out at this party, Nat! You and I are so normal and so much in love! Can't we get into the swing of things by doing something disgusting, too?
Sure, Honey! Hey—I've got it! Why don't you throw up . . . for starters?
Well? Is she going to throw up or not? We don't have all night, you know!
C'mon, Bubby! A little throw up for Daddy!
I'm sorry! I can't right now!
Aw, she's a little nervous in front of company! C'mon, honey! Try . . . like a big girl!
Yeah! Try, Party Pooper!
Can I get her anything to help? A glass of sour milk? A wormy apple? An airline sickness bag?
Boy, you really know how to hurt a girl, don't you? How cruel can you get? I told you—she's trying!
Yes, she's very trying! And we can't wait all night! Time for the next game! Everyone line up for "Dirty Giant Steps"! The object of this game is to cause a little frustration trauma! John . . . you may take one Dirty Giant Step . . .
Sorry You'll have to go back!!
Why?
You didn't say, "$#&%@¢*! may I?"

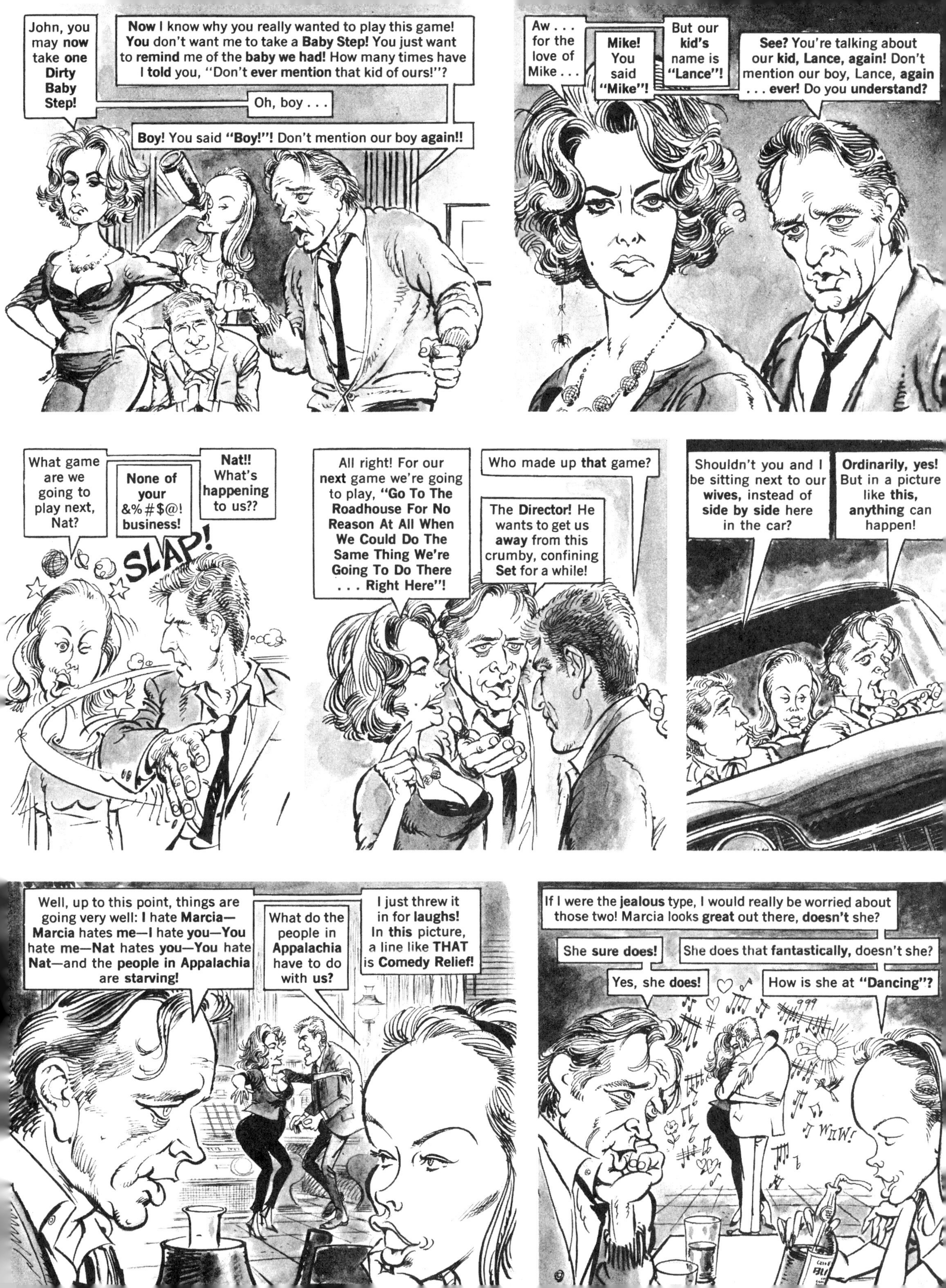
John, you may now take one Dirty Baby Step!
Now I know why you really wanted to play this game! You don't want me to take a Baby Step! You just want to remind me of the baby we had! How many times have I told you, "Don't ever mention that kid of ours!"?
Oh, boy . . .
Boy! You said "Boy!"! Don't mention our boy again!!
Aw . . . for the love of Mike . . .
Mike! You said "Mike"!
But our kid's name is "Lance"!
See? You're talking about our kid, Lance, again! Don't mention our boy, Lance, again . . . ever! Do you understand?
What game are we going to play next, Nat?
None of your &%#$@! business!
Nat!! What's happening to us??
SLAP!
All right! For our next game we're going to play, "Go To The Roadhouse For No Reason At All When We Could Do The Same Thing We're Going To Do There . . . Right Here"!
Who made up that game?
The Director! He wants to get us away from this crumby, confining Set for a while!
Shouldn't you and I be sitting next to our wives, instead of side by side here in the car?
Ordinarily, yes! But in a picture like this, anything can happen!
Well, up to this point, things are going very well: I hate Marcia—Marcia hates me—I hate you—You hate me—Nat hates you—You hate Nat—and the people in Appalachia are starving!
What do the people in Appalachia have to do with us?
I just threw it in for laughs! In this picture, a line like THAT is Comedy Relief!
If I were the jealous type, I would really be worried about those two! Marcia looks great out there, doesn't she?
She sure does!
She does that fantastically, doesn't she?
Yes, she does!
How is she at "Dancing"?
WHW!

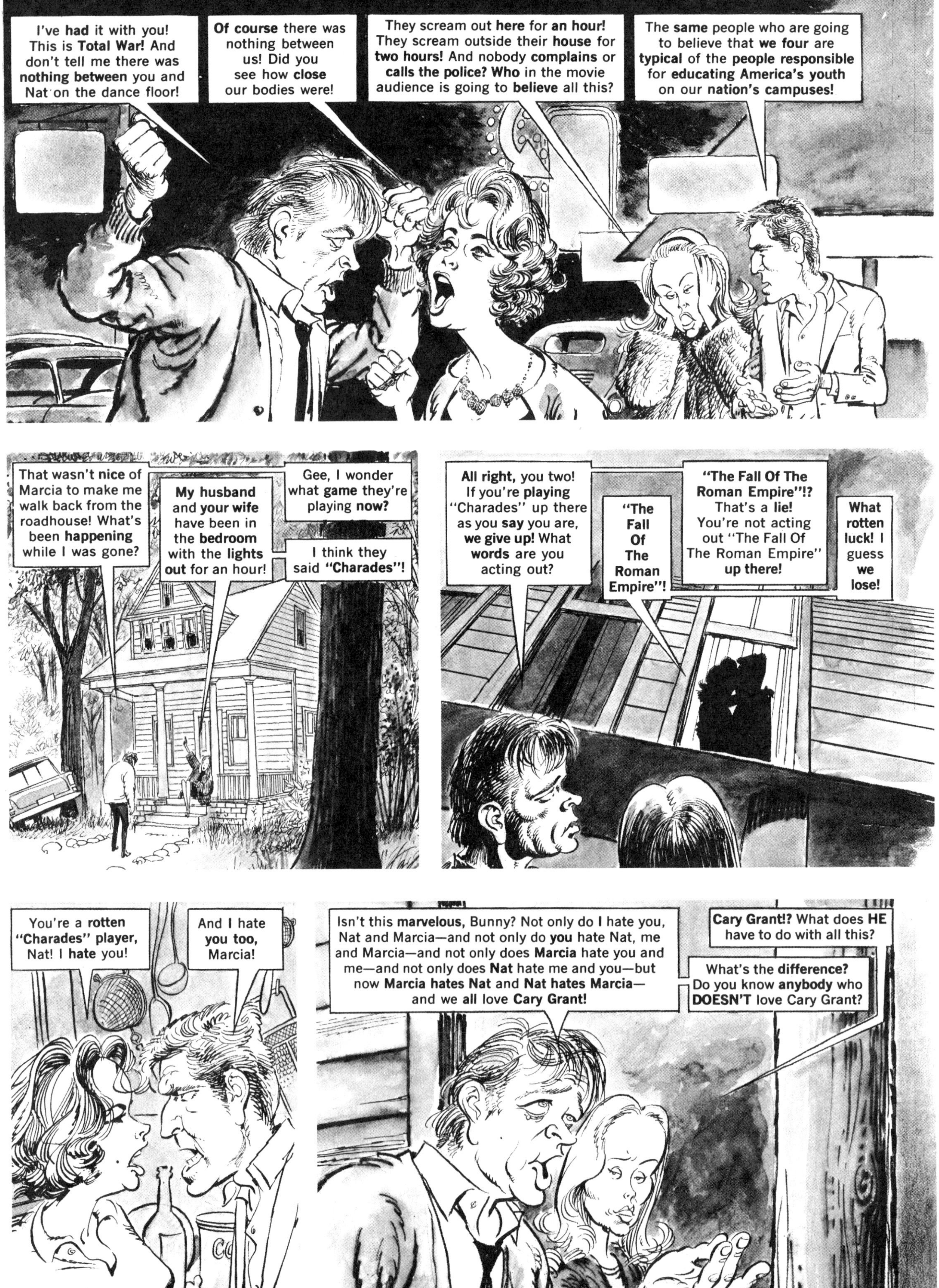
I've had it with you! This is Total War! And don't tell me there was nothing between you and Nat on the dance floor!
Of course there was nothing between us! Did you see how close our bodies were!
They scream out here for an hour! They scream outside their house for two hours! And nobody complains or calls the police? Who in the movie audience is going to believe all this?
The same people who are going to believe that we four are typical of the people responsible for educating America's youth on our nation's campuses!
That wasn't nice of Marcia to make me walk back from the roadhouse! What's been happening while I was gone?
My husband and your wife have been in the bedroom with the lights out for an hour!
Gee, I wonder what game they're playing now?
I think they said "Charades"!
All right, you two! If you're playing "Charades" up there as you say you are, we give up! What words are you acting out?
"The Fall Of The Roman Empire"!
"The Fall Of The Roman Empire"!? That's a lie! You're not acting out "The Fall Of The Roman Empire" up there!
What rotten luck! I guess we lose!
You're a rotten "Charades" player, Nat! I hate you!
And I hate you too, Marcia!
Isn't this marvelous, Bunny? Not only do I hate you, Nat and Marcia—and not only do you hate Nat, me and Marcia—and not only does Marcia hate you and me—and not only does Nat hate me and you—but now Marcia hates Nat and Nat hates Marcia—and we all love Cary Grant!
Cary Grant!? What does HE have to do with all this?
What's the difference? Do you know anybody who DOESN'T love Cary Grant?

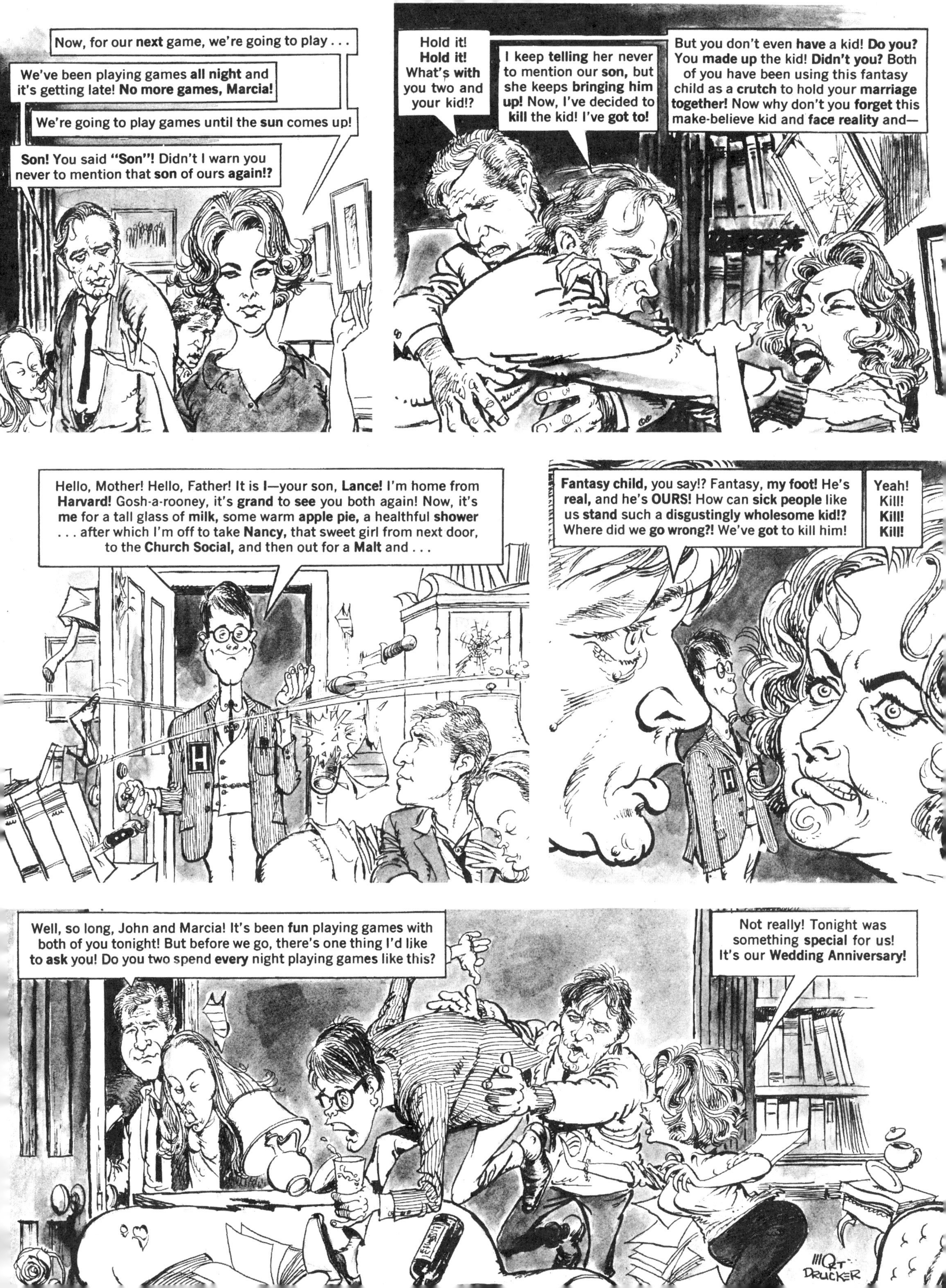
Now, for our next game, we're going to play . . .
We've been playing games all night and it's getting late! No more games, Marcia!
We're going to play games until the sun comes up!
Son! You said "Son"! Didn't I warn you never to mention that son of ours again!?
Hold it! Hold it! What's with you two and your kid!?
I keep telling her never to mention our son, but she keeps bringing him up! Now, I've decided to kill the kid! I've got to!
But you don't even have a kid! Do you? You made up the kid! Didn't you? Both of you have been using this fantasy child as a crutch to hold your marriage together! Now why don't you forget this make-believe kid and face reality and—
Hello, Mother! Hello, Father! It is I—your son, Lance! I'm home from Harvard! Gosh-a-rooney, it's grand to see you both again! Now, it's me for a tall glass of milk, some warm apple pie, a healthful shower . . . after which I'm off to take Nancy, that sweet girl from next door, to the Church Social, and then out for a Malt and . . .
Fantasy child, you say!? Fantasy, my foot! He's real, and he's OURS! How can sick people like us stand such a disgustingly wholesome kid!? Where did we go wrong?! We've got to kill him!
Yeah! Kill! Kill! Kill!
Well, so long, John and Marcia! It's been fun playing games with both of you tonight! But before we go, there's one thing I'd like to ask you! Do you two spend every night playing games like this?
Not really! Tonight was something special for us! It's our Wedding Anniversary!
MORT DRUCKER

If you're a "TV Late Show" film buff, you're probably aware of the important roles certain "props" played in old movies. In fact, some of these "props"

# A MAD GUID
# SHOW" CLICH

## MONSTER MOVIE TORCH

Always used by hunchback-assistant to antagonize monster . . . and always used again later on by villagers to track down monster-murderer of hunchback-assistant and other assorted victims.

## CATHEDRAL RADIO

Device used to interrupt love scenes . . . and engagements . . . with announcement that the Japanese have attacked Pearl Harbor. Hero and heroine defer marriage plans until the world can be made a better place to live. At film's end, they are reunited in Guadalcanal —he's a Navy pilot and she's a nurse.

## NOBLE PILOT WRENCH

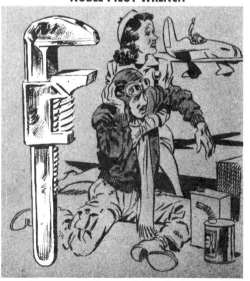

Test pilots Tom and Jim both love Sue. One of them has to test the dangerous X-14. Jim, convinced that Sue loves Tom, pretends to let him take up the X-14. But when Tom looks up to check the weather, Jim hits him on the head with the prop wrench, takes the X-14 up himself, and is never seen again.

## BROKEN AMULET NECKLACE

Handsome Arab beggar boy defies death by scaling wall of Caliph's palace in wild attempt to reach Princess who he loves. Evading guards, he finally gets to her, only to discover . . . by fitting together their broken amulet necklaces . . . that they are brother and sister! Love affair is over before it begins.

## TRAGEDY-IDENTIFYING LIFE PRESERVER

Used several ways for dramatic effec For example, we see a wreckage-strew oily sea. Prop life-preserver floa by. It says . . . "Lusitania"! Or we s a young honeymoon couple smooching o deck. They move off, revealing ship name on prop life-preserver. The po kids! They're sailing on the "Titanic

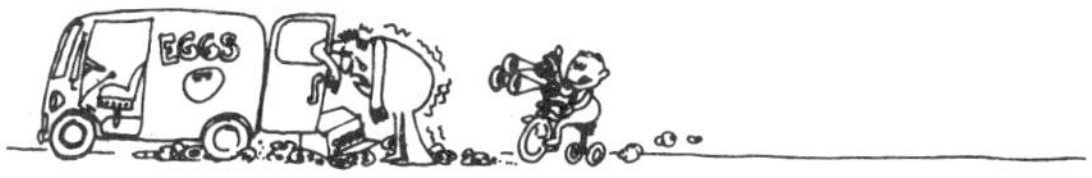
EGGS

were used so often, they actually achieved "cliché" status. For those of you who don't know what in heck we're talking about, we now present this article:

# E TO "TV LATE
# É MOVIE PROPS

ARTIST:
ANGELO TORRES
WRITER:
PAUL PETER PORGES

### SUSPENSION MICROPHONE

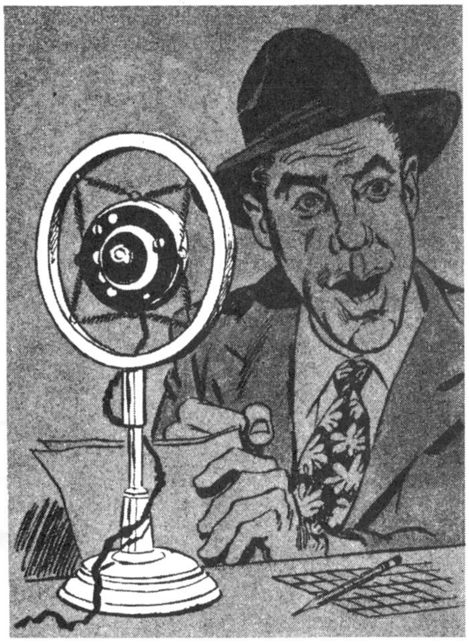

Used effectively by the Announcer at the ballpark to tell the little boy with the fatal illness who's lying in the hospital, holding the autographed baseball, that the Slugger has hit one over the fence just for him—bringing on a sudden miracle cure for the boy.

### THIS-WILL-MAKE-YOU-TALK HYPODERMIC NEEDLE

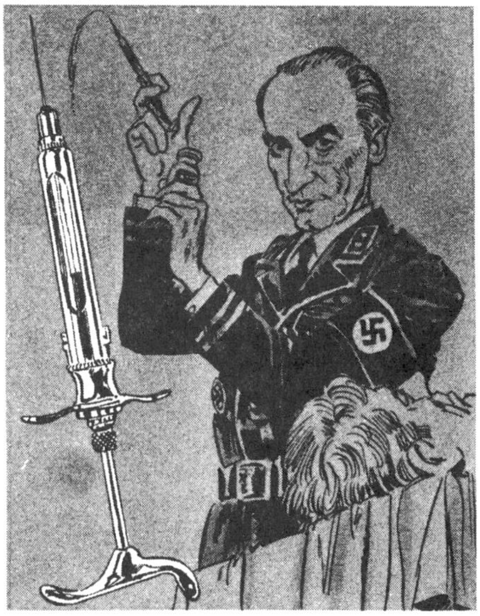

After brutal torture has failed, the sadistic Nazi officer has one method left to make Allied undercover agent reveal location of Gen. Eisenhower's headquarters and the time, place and size of upcoming invasion of Europe: the injection of — gasp — truth serum!

### TIN CUPS, TIN PLATES AND UTENSILS

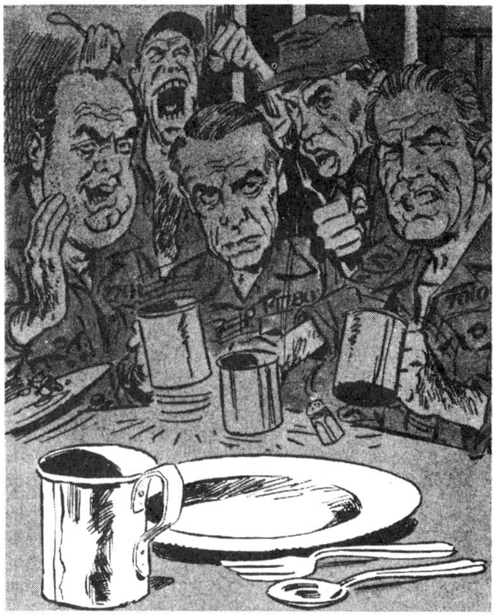

Invariably used by inmates in Prison pictures to bang on mess hall tables and clang across cell bars to register their dissatisfaction with the lousy food, the indifferent Warden, the cruel guards, the intolerable working conditions, and the impossible script.

### BAIL OF NEWSPAPERS

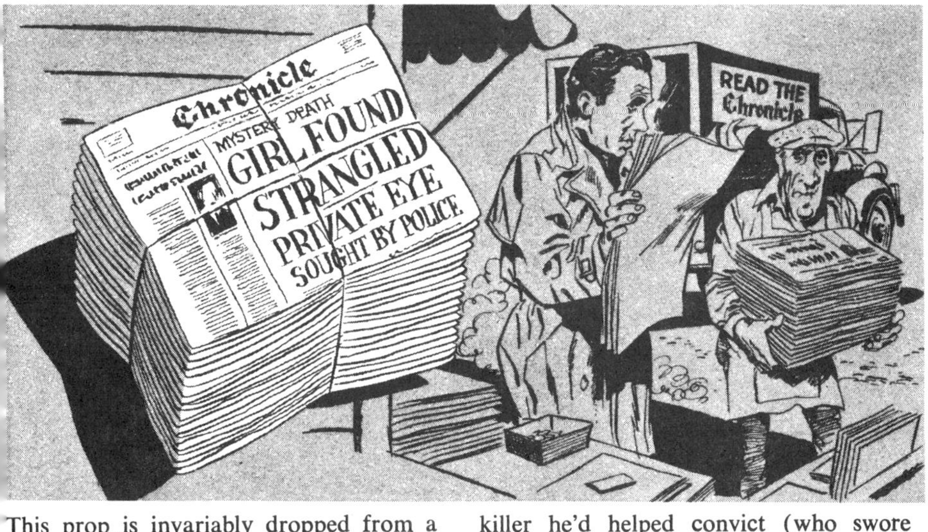
Chronicle
MYSTERY DEATH
GIRL FOUND
STRANGLED
PRIVATE EYE
SOUGHT BY POLICE
READ THE
Chronicle

This prop is invariably dropped from a truck at the feet of our hero who, as the newsstand dealer cuts the string, learns by the headlines that (1) the killer he'd helped convict (who swore revenge) has escaped from prison, or (2) the girl he was with last night is dead, and he's wanted for her murder!

### SMALL TOWN TRAFFIC CONTROLLER

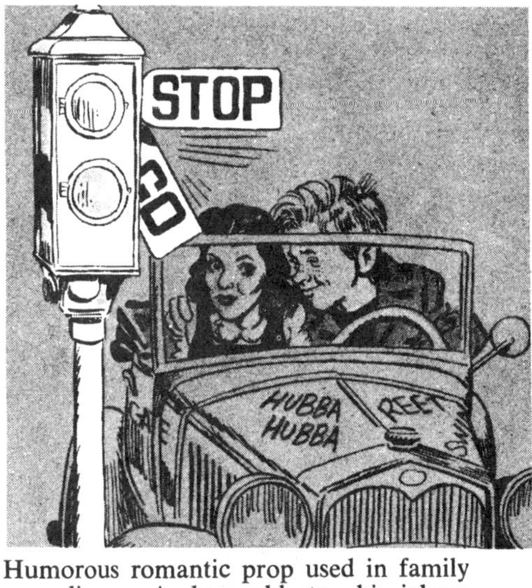
STOP
GO
HUBBA
HUBBA
REET

Humorous romantic prop used in family comedies so Andy could stop his jalopy and kiss Polly while sign changed from stop to go to stop to go to stop to—

## RE-BREATHING BAG

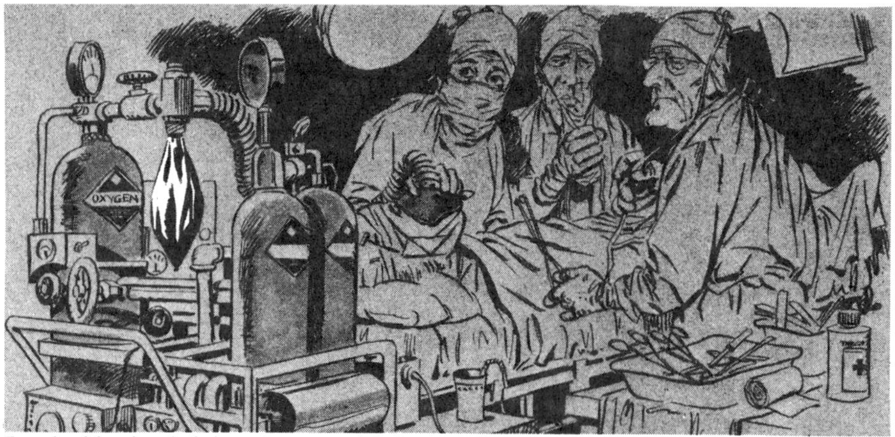
OXYGEN

Invaluable in helping lay movie fans follow the progress of an operation. Everything is going along fine while bag expands and contracts regularly. Any faltering or collapse is signal for Surgeon to whisper, "Quick, Nurse — the adrenalin!" If injection works, bag will resume expansion and contraction. If bag remains deflated, Surgeon will snap off rubber gloves and throw them to the floor in disgust while the Nurse solemnly pulls a sheet over body.

## EXTENSION TELEPHONE

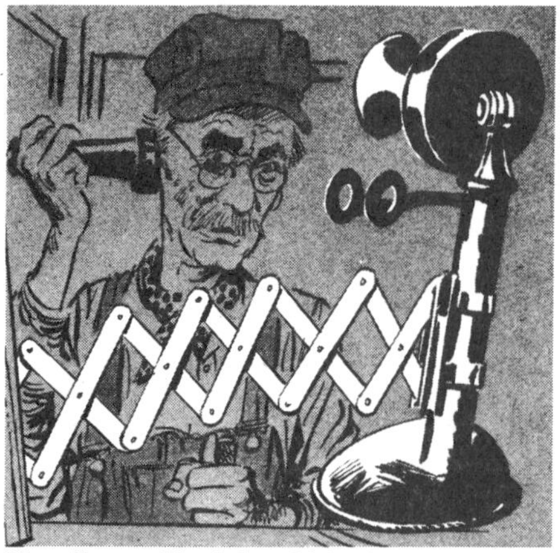

Usually grabbed by Old Timer in green eyeshade who calls ahead and stops the "Cannonball Express" from crossing the dynamited trestle. Sometimes grabbed by hotshot City Editor who yells, "Stop the press! We're re-making Page One!"

## EASILY-SMASHED MIRROR

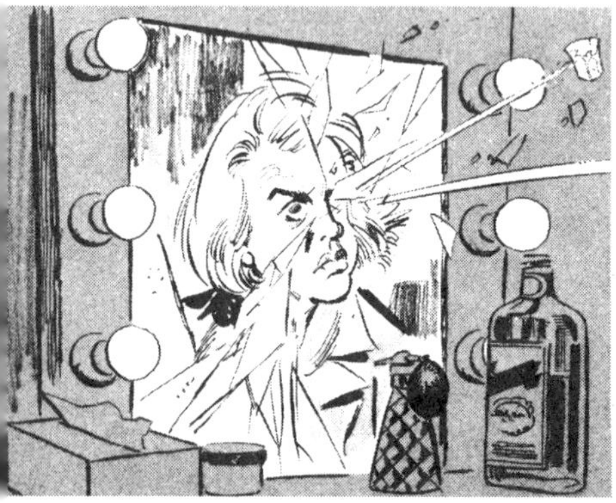

It's a sure bet that at some point in the big Broadway Star's career, she'll reach that low point when she'll look at herself in the mirror, filled with self-contempt and loathing, and fling her whisky glass at her reflection . . . smashing the mirror into smithereens. However, like mirror, her life will be almost impossible to put back together.

## SLIDING BEER GLASS

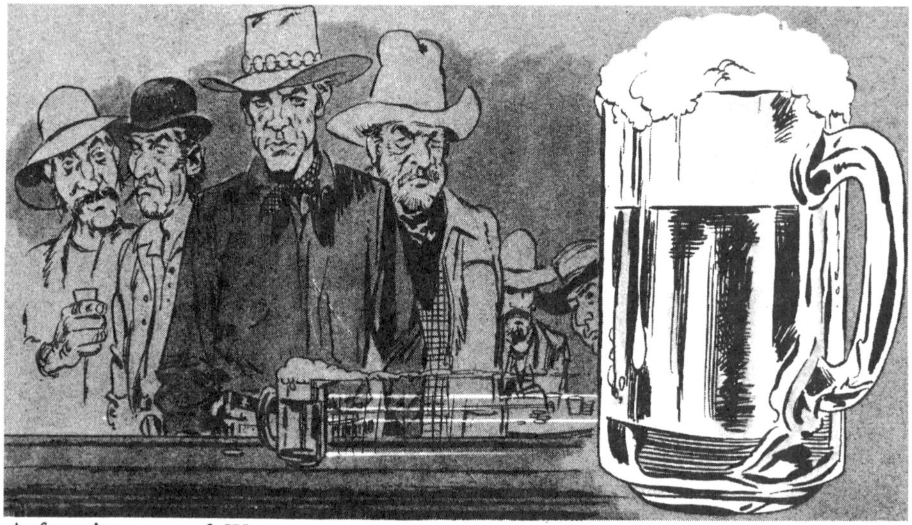

A favorite prop of Western movies for bringing the noisy festivities in the saloon to a dead stop, the beer glass always slides 30 feet down bar and comes to rest right in front of tall lonesome stranger who just walked in.

## PAINTING WITH EYEHOLES

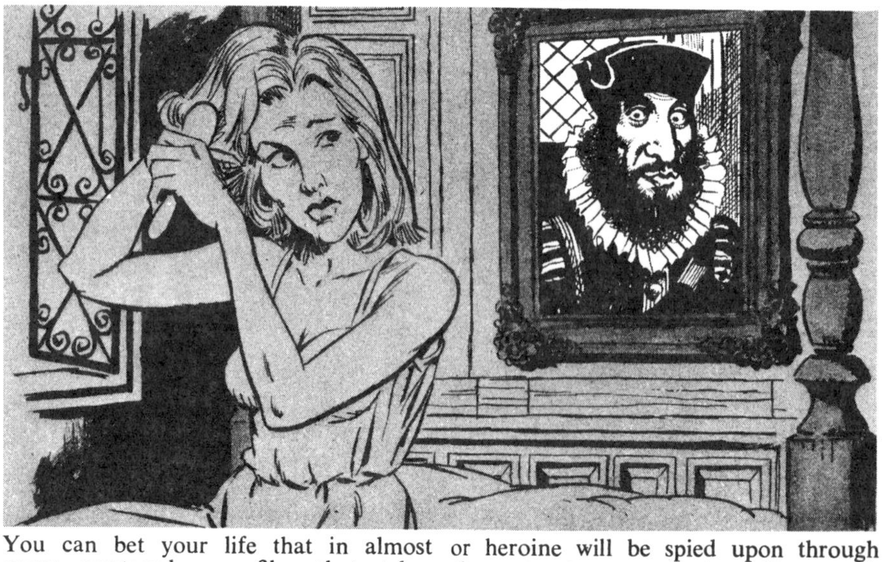

You can bet your life that in almost every mystery-horror film that takes place in a creepy old house, our hero or heroine will be spied upon through the cut-out eyes of the old portrait hanging over the fireplace . . . or bed.

## BROADWAY-BOUND DANCING SHOES

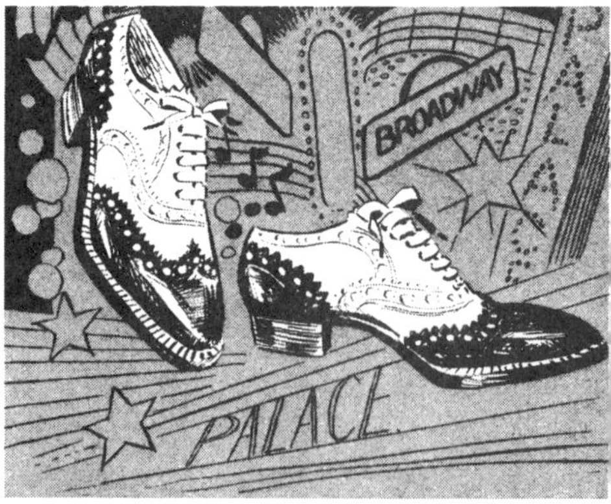
BROADWAY
PALACE

Some eager youngsters have put a show together in a barn. Our hero, wearing two-tone prop shoes, knocks everybody dead with his dance routine including famous talent scout who just happened to be out front. Shoes are then shown dancing across country in a series of montage shots, bound for Broadway and that big break at the Palace Theater.

## "AMERIKANISCHER SCHWEINHUND" PERISCOPE

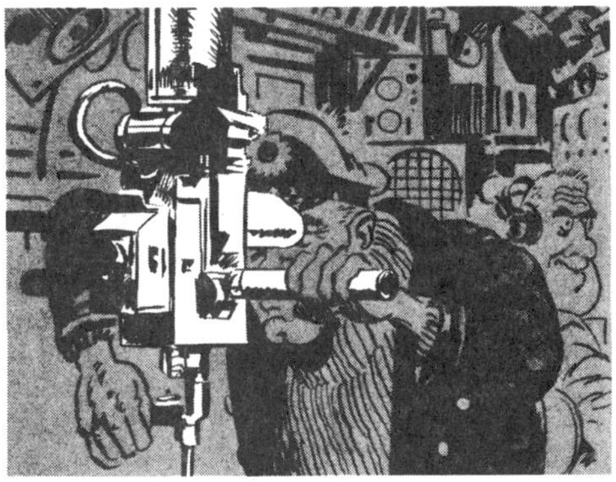

After several touching scenes aboard the troop transport in which the boys have exchanged memories, jokes, bits of homespun philosophy and photos of loved ones, film always cuts suddenly to this prop. Look for the evil Nazi Sub Commander, followed by a torpedo.

## HOT TOWEL BROILER

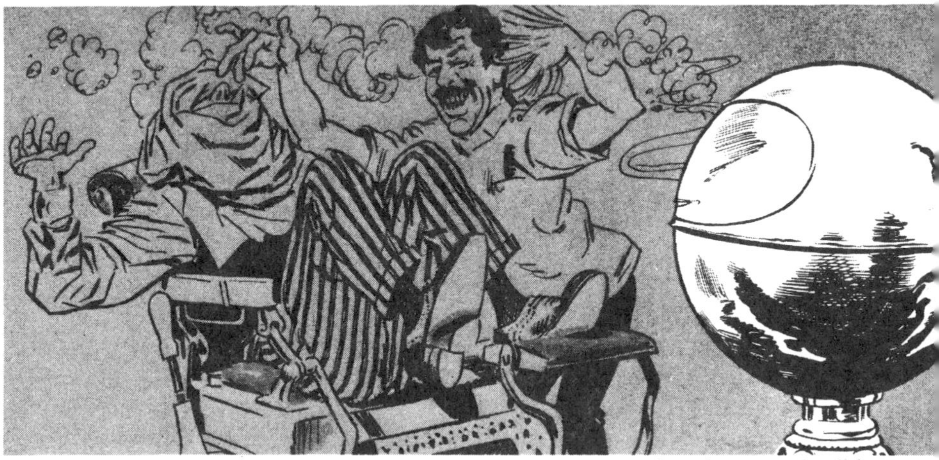

Back in days when men's "hairstylists" were known as "barbers," they not only cut hair, but they also shaved people. In comedy films, the fun started when the barber turned to the broiler prop, took out a steaming hot towel, did a little painful dance, and dropped it on the face of a prone and helpless villain – like a crusty bank president, a skinflint landlord or a city slicker.

## TELL-TALE CIGARETTE BUTT

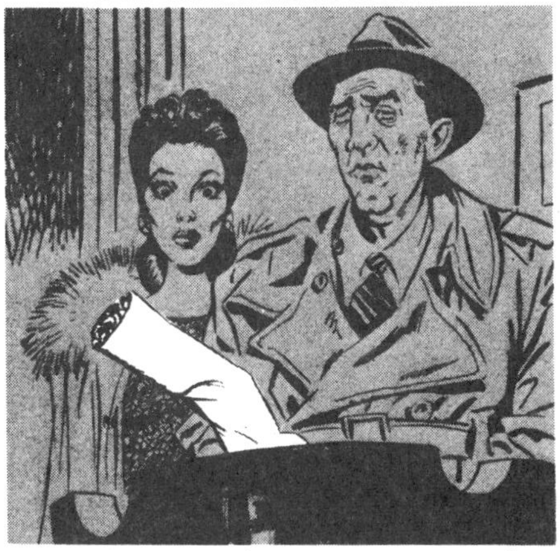

Main character always spots prop when dropping in unexpectedly. If the main character is a detective, it means he surprised the girl and the murderer. If the main character is a woman, the butt is usually lipstick-smeared, and it means her lover is cheating on her.

## WEATHER-BEATEN INN SIGN

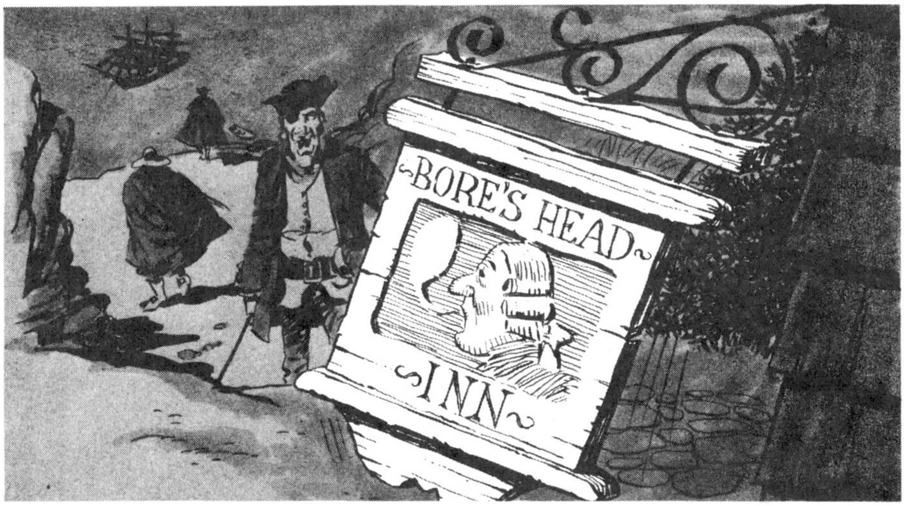
BORE'S HEAD
INN

Creaky old gimmick that's always used to establish the scene (usually on the English coast) where the smugglers or the ship-wreckers are meeting to make plans or split the swag. You can bet that the sign will be swinging wildly in a torrential downpour and suddenly illuminated by a flash of lightning.

## SLOWLY ROTATING CEILING FAN

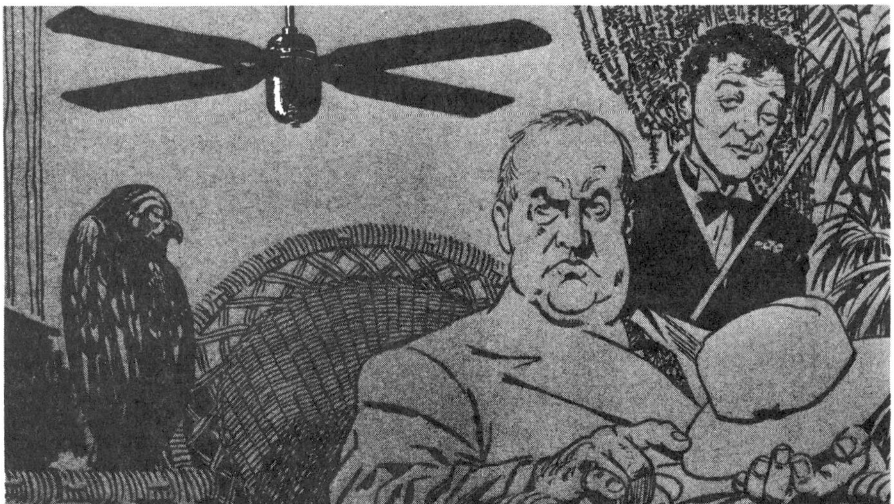

Always used for setting the scene in either a steaming tropic jungle or the Casbah. The slower the fan turns, the more oppressive the heat (and the plot) becomes. Look for intrigue, treachery, spies, murder – and Sidney Greenstreet.

## TUMBREL CART

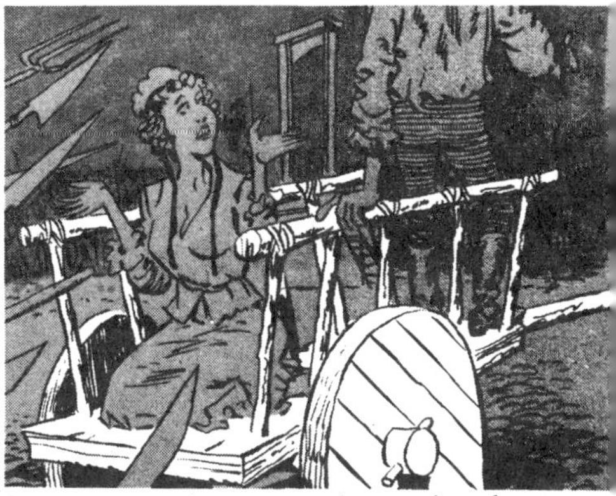

Prop wagon always seen in movies about French Revolution. It was used to carry condemned to Guillotine and was geared to move painfully slow to give inhuman jeering crowd an opportunity to hurl insults at prisoner, and also to give prisoner time to do a final voice-over – like maybe, "'Tis a far, far better thing I do than I have ever done . . ."

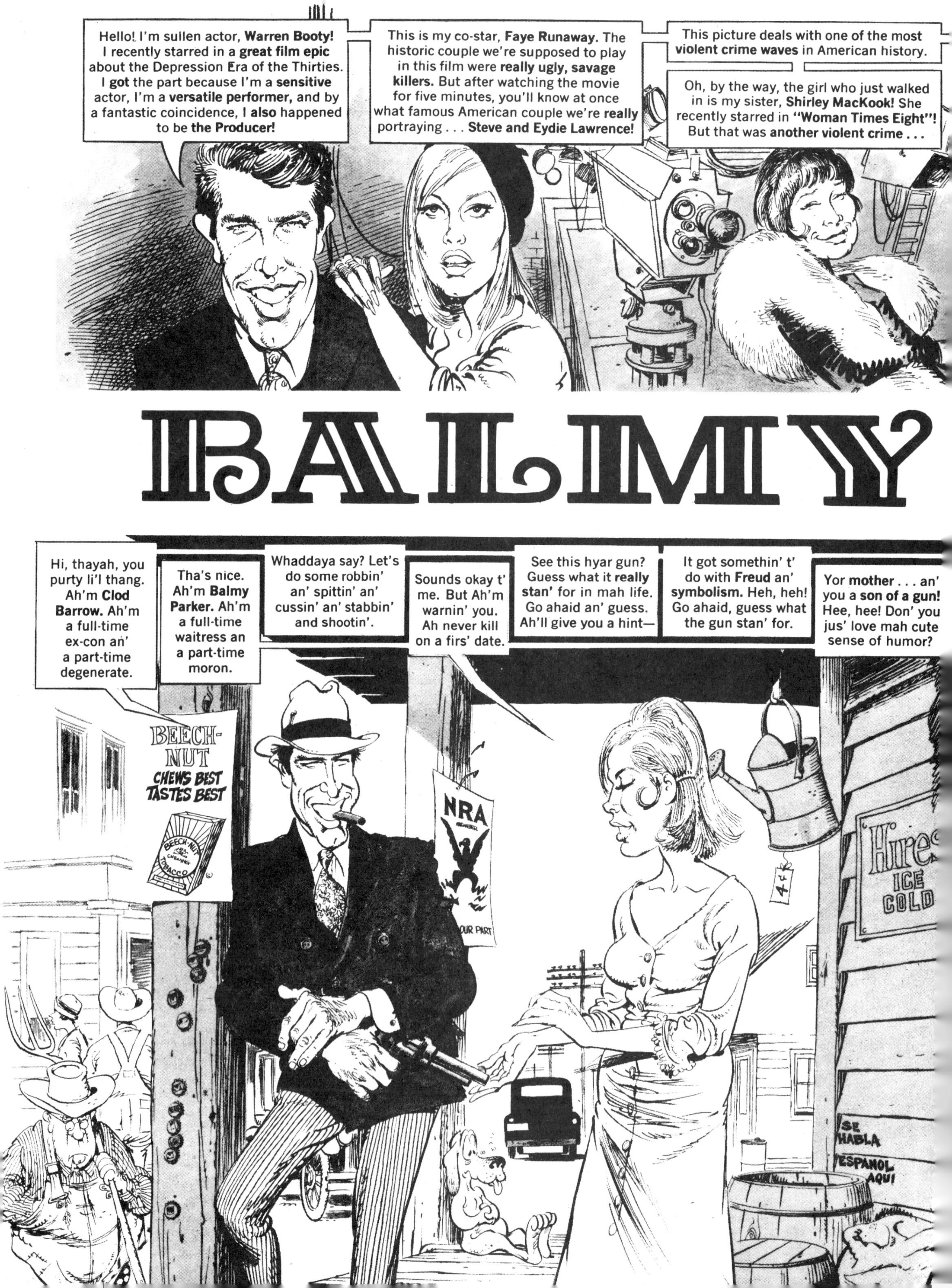

Hello! I'm sullen actor, Warren Booty! I recently starred in a great film epic about the Depression Era of the Thirties. I got the part because I'm a sensitive actor, I'm a versatile performer, and by a fantastic coincidence, I also happened to be the Producer!
This is my co-star, Faye Runaway. The historic couple we're supposed to play in this film were really ugly, savage killers. But after watching the movie for five minutes, you'll know at once what famous American couple we're really portraying . . . Steve and Eydie Lawrence!
This picture deals with one of the most violent crime waves in American history.
Oh, by the way, the girl who just walked in is my sister, Shirley MacKook! She recently starred in "Woman Times Eight"! But that was another violent crime . . .
BALMY
Hi, thayah, you purty li'l thang. Ah'm Clod Barrow. Ah'm a full-time ex-con an' a part-time degenerate.
Tha's nice. Ah'm Balmy Parker. Ah'm a full-time waitress an a part-time moron.
Whaddaya say? Let's do some robbin' an' spittin' an' cussin' an' stabbin' and shootin'.
Sounds okay t' me. But Ah'm warnin' you. Ah never kill on a firs' date.
See this hyar gun? Guess what it really stan' for in mah life. Go ahaid an' guess. Ah'll give you a hint—
It got somethin' t' do with Freud an' symbolism. Heh, heh! Go ahaid, guess what the gun stan' for.
Yor mother . . . an' you a son of a gun! Hee, hee! Don' you jus' love mah cute sense of humor?
BEECH-NUT
CHEWS BEST TASTES BEST
NRA
Hires ICE COLD
SE HABLA ESPANOL AQUI

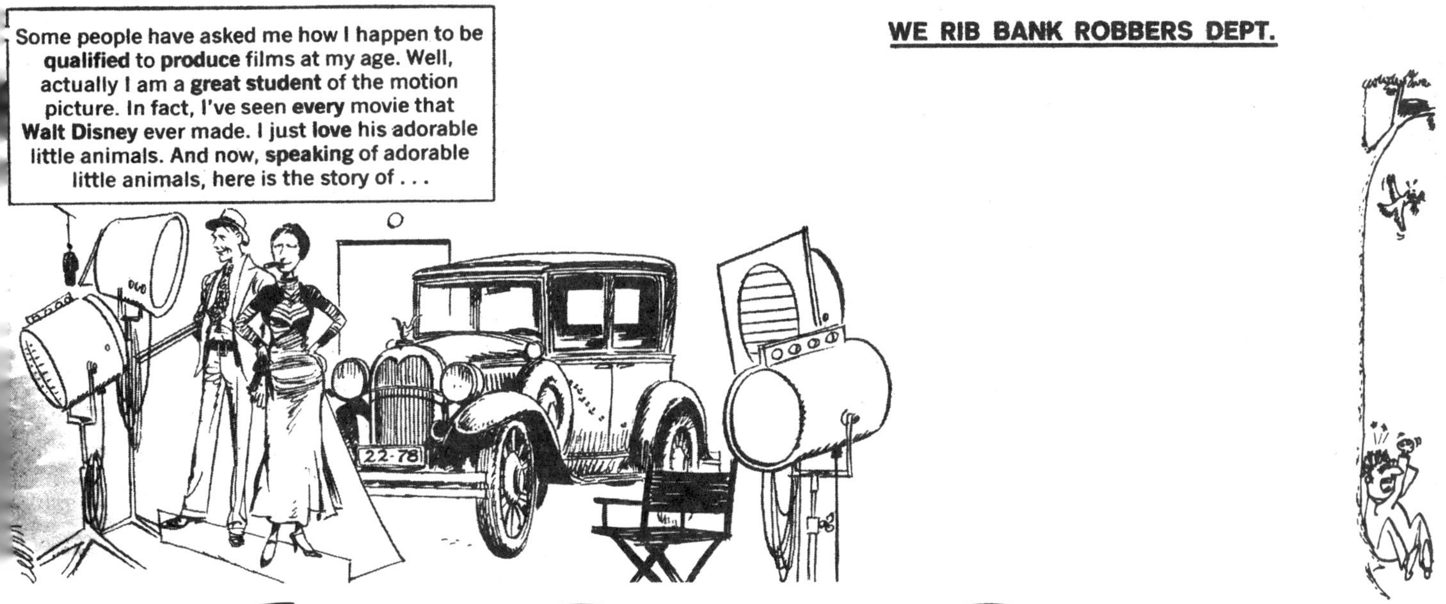
Some people have asked me how I happen to be **qualified** to **produce** films at my age. Well, actually I am a **great student** of the motion picture. In fact, I've seen **every** movie that **Walt Disney** ever made. I just **love** his adorable little animals. And now, **speaking** of adorable little animals, here is the story of . . .
22-78

# AND CLOD

ARTIST: MORT DRUCKER WRITER: LARRY SIEGEL

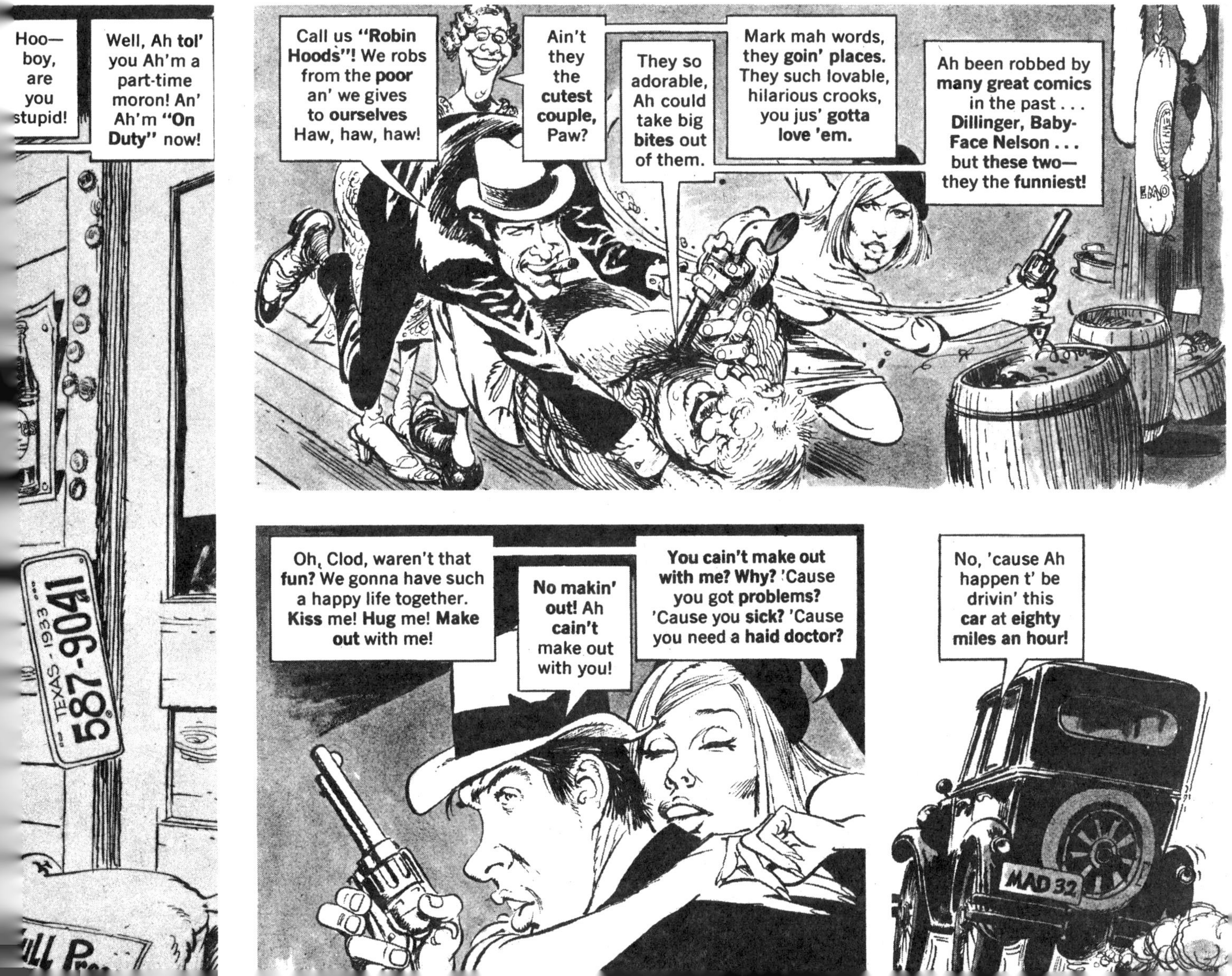
Hoo—boy, are you stupid!
Well, Ah **tol'** you Ah'm a part-time moron! An' Ah'm **"On Duty"** now!
TEXAS - 1933
587-9041
Call us **"Robin Hoods"!** We robs from the **poor** an' we gives to **ourselves** Haw, haw, haw!
Ain't they the **cutest couple,** Paw?
They so adorable, Ah could take big **bites** out of them.
Mark mah words, they **goin' places.** They such lovable, hilarious crooks, you jus' **gotta love 'em.**
Ah been robbed by **many great comics** in the past . . . **Dillinger, Baby-Face Nelson . . .** but **these two—** they the **funniest!**
Oh, Clod, waren't that **fun?** We gonna have such a happy life together. **Kiss** me! **Hug** me! **Make out** with me!
**No makin' out!** Ah **cain't** make out with you!
**You cain't make out with me? Why?** 'Cause you got **problems?** 'Cause you **sick?** 'Cause you need a **haid doctor?**
No, 'cause Ah happen t' be drivin' this **car at eighty** miles an hour!
MAD 32

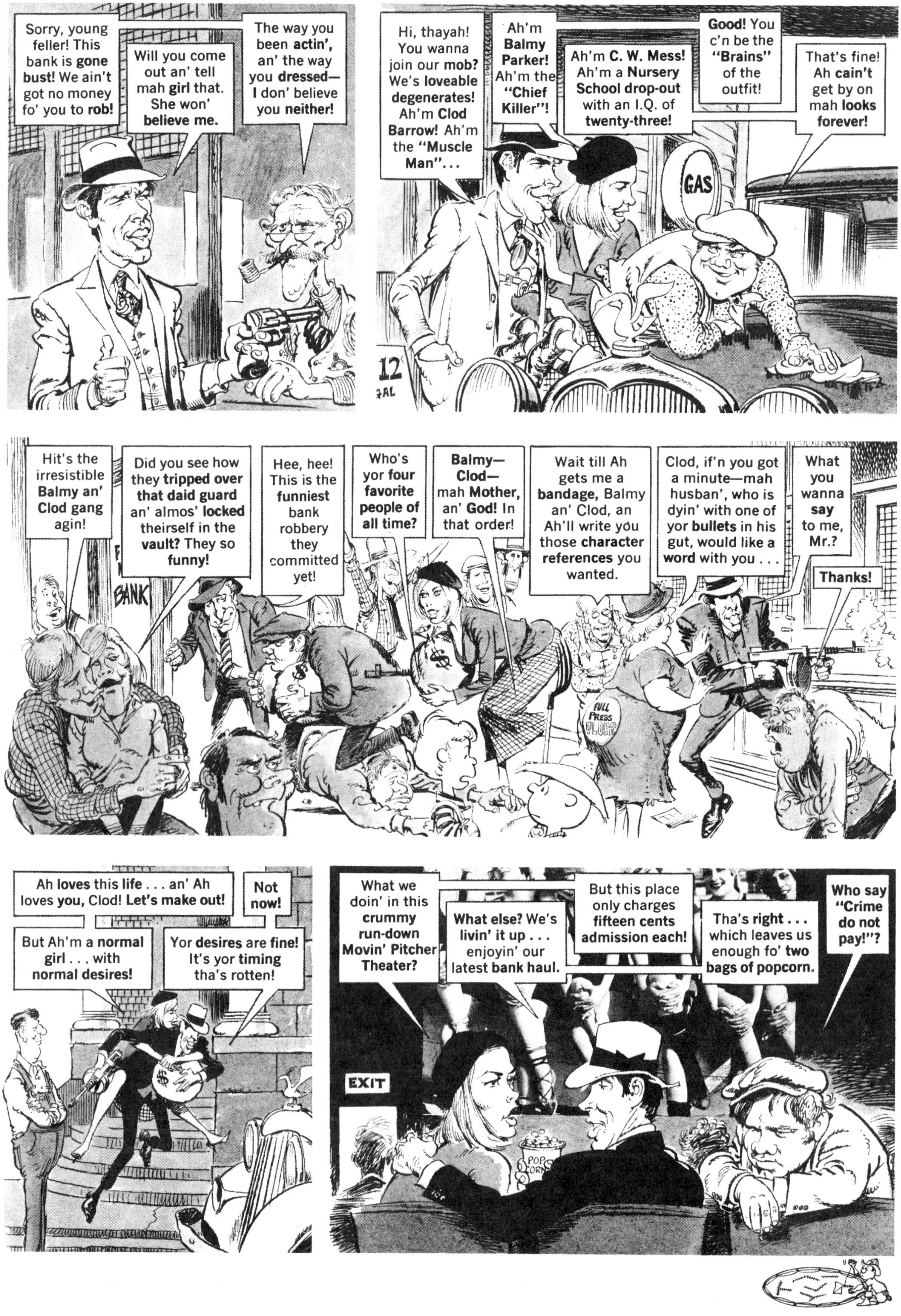

Sorry, young feller! This bank is gone bust! We ain't got no money fo' you to rob!
Will you come out an' tell mah girl that. She won' believe me.
The way you been actin', an' the way you dressed— I don' believe you neither!
Hi, thayah! You wanna join our mob? We's loveable degenerates! Ah'm Clod Barrow! Ah'm the "Muscle Man"...
Ah'm Balmy Parker! Ah'm the "Chief Killer"!
Ah'm C. W. Mess! Ah'm a Nursery School drop-out with an I.Q. of twenty-three!
Good! You c'n be the "Brains" of the outfit!
That's fine! Ah cain't get by on mah looks forever!
GAS
Hit's the irresistible Balmy an' Clod gang agin!
Did you see how they tripped over that daid guard an' almos' locked theirself in the vault? They so funny!
Hee, hee! This is the funniest bank robbery they committed yet!
Who's yor four favorite people of all time?
Balmy— Clod— mah Mother, an' God! In that order!
Wait till Ah gets me a bandage, Balmy an' Clod, an Ah'll write you those character references you wanted.
Clod, if'n you got a minute—mah husban', who is dyin' with one of yor bullets in his gut, would like a word with you . . .
What you wanna say to me, Mr.?
Thanks!
BANK
FULL PRESS FLOUR
Ah loves this life . . . an' Ah loves you, Clod! Let's make out!
Not now!
But Ah'm a normal girl . . . with normal desires!
Yor desires are fine! It's yor timing tha's rotten!
What we doin' in this crummy run-down Movin' Pitcher Theater?
What else? We's livin' it up . . . enjoyin' our latest bank haul.
But this place only charges fifteen cents admission each!
Tha's right . . . which leaves us enough fo' two bags of popcorn.
Who say "Crime do not pay!"?
EXIT
POP CORN

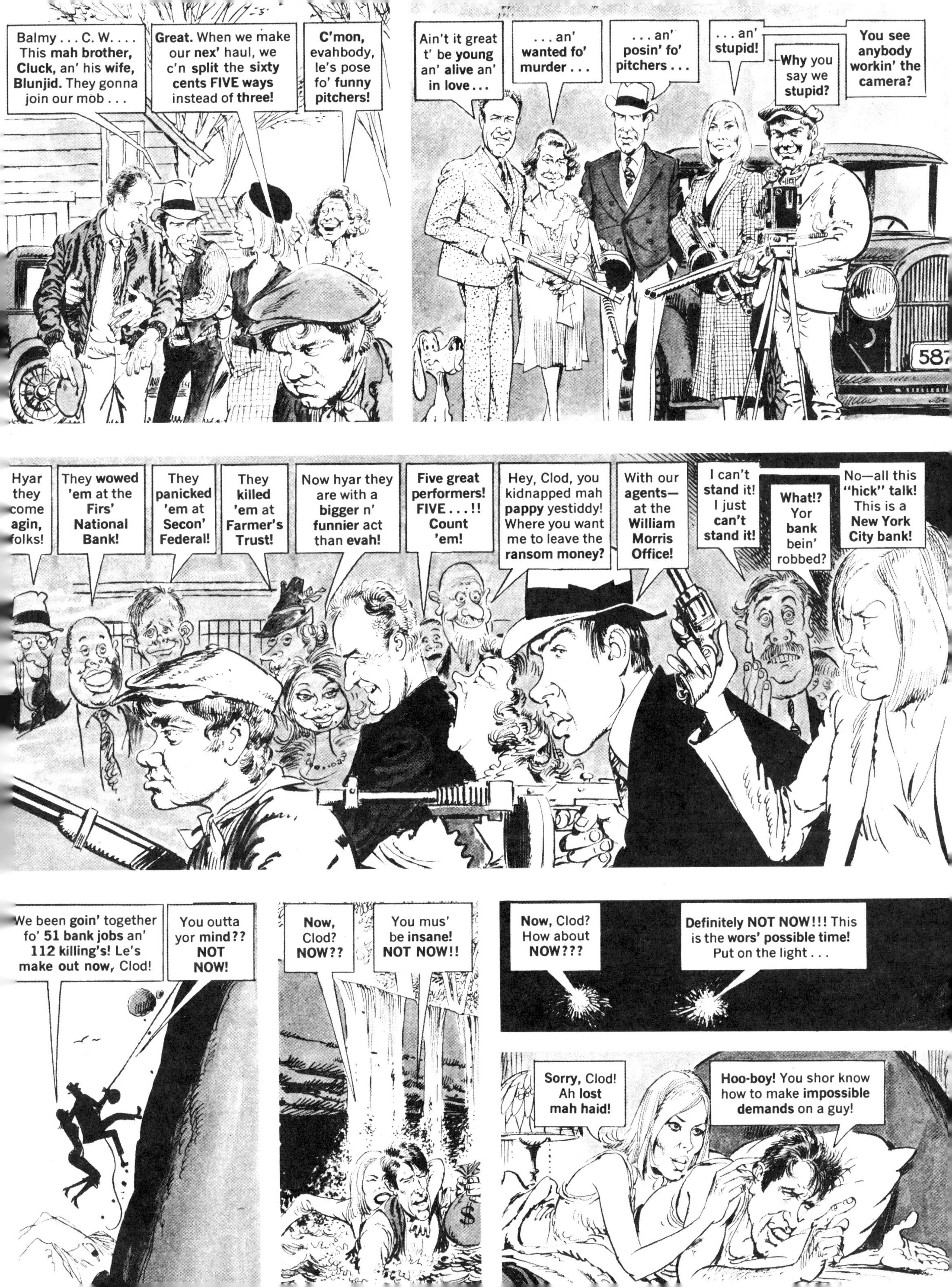

Balmy . . . C. W. . . . This mah brother, Cluck, an' his wife, Blunjid. They gonna join our mob . . .
Great. When we make our nex' haul, we c'n split the sixty cents FIVE ways instead of three!
C'mon, evahbody, le's pose fo' funny pitchers!
Ain't it great t' be young an' alive an' in love . . .
. . . an' wanted fo' murder . . .
. . . an' posin' fo' pitchers . . .
. . . an' stupid!
Why you say we stupid?
You see anybody workin' the camera?
587
Hyar they come agin, folks!
They wowed 'em at the Firs' National Bank!
They panicked 'em at Secon' Federal!
They killed 'em at Farmer's Trust!
Now hyar they are with a bigger n' funnier act than evah!
Five great performers! FIVE . . . !! Count 'em!
Hey, Clod, you kidnapped mah pappy yestiddy! Where you want me to leave the ransom money?
With our agents— at the William Morris Office!
I can't stand it! I just can't stand it!
What!? Yor bank bein' robbed?
No—all this "hick" talk! This is a New York City bank!
We been goin' together fo' 51 bank jobs an' 112 killing's! Le's make out now, Clod!
You outta yor mind?? NOT NOW!
Now, Clod? NOW??
You mus' be insane! NOT NOW!!
Now, Clod? How about NOW???
Definitely NOT NOW!!! This is the wors' possible time! Put on the light . . .
Sorry, Clod! Ah lost mah haid!
Hoo-boy! You shor know how to make impossible demands on a guy!

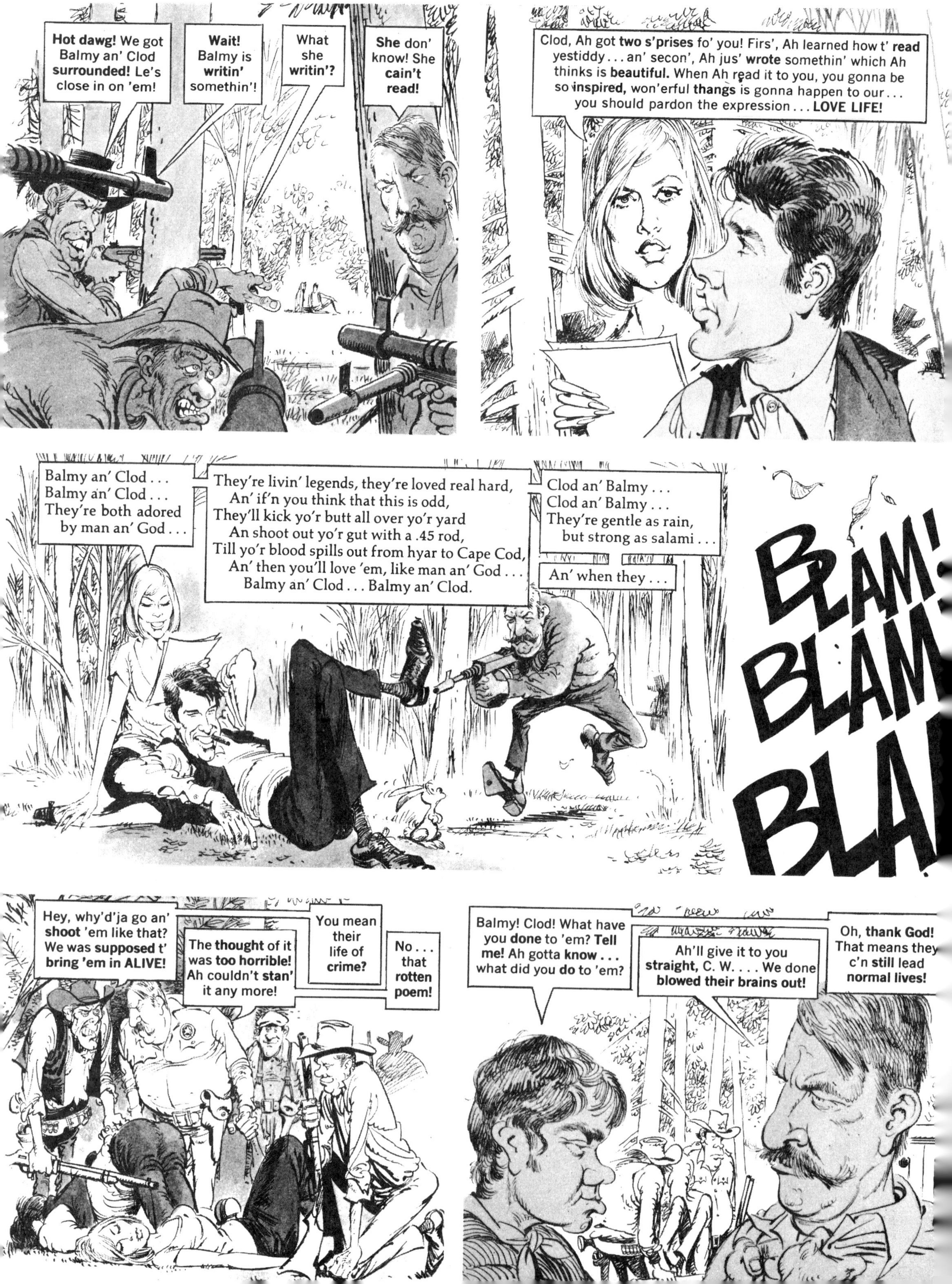
Hot dawg! We got Balmy an' Clod surrounded! Le's close in on 'em!
Wait! Balmy is writin' somethin'!
What she writin'?
She don' know! She cain't read!
Clod, Ah got two s'prises fo' you! Firs', Ah learned how t' read yestiddy . . . an' secon', Ah jus' wrote somethin' which Ah thinks is beautiful. When Ah read it to you, you gonna be so inspired, won'erful thangs is gonna happen to our . . . you should pardon the expression . . . LOVE LIFE!
Balmy an' Clod . . . Balmy an' Clod . . . They're both adored by man an' God . . .
They're livin' legends, they're loved real hard, An' if'n you think that this is odd, They'll kick yo'r butt all over yo'r yard An shoot out yo'r gut with a .45 rod, Till yo'r blood spills out from hyar to Cape Cod, An' then you'll love 'em, like man an' God . . . Balmy an' Clod . . . Balmy an' Clod.
Clod an' Balmy . . . Clod an' Balmy . . . They're gentle as rain, but strong as salami . . .
An' when they . . .
BLAM! BLAM! BLA
Hey, why'd'ja go an' shoot 'em like that? We was supposed t' bring 'em in ALIVE!
The thought of it was too horrible! Ah couldn't stan' it any more!
You mean their life of crime?
No . . . that rotten poem!
Balmy! Clod! What have you done to 'em? Tell me! Ah gotta know . . . what did you do to 'em?
Ah'll give it to you straight, C. W. . . . We done blowed their brains out!
Oh, thank God! That means they c'n still lead normal lives!

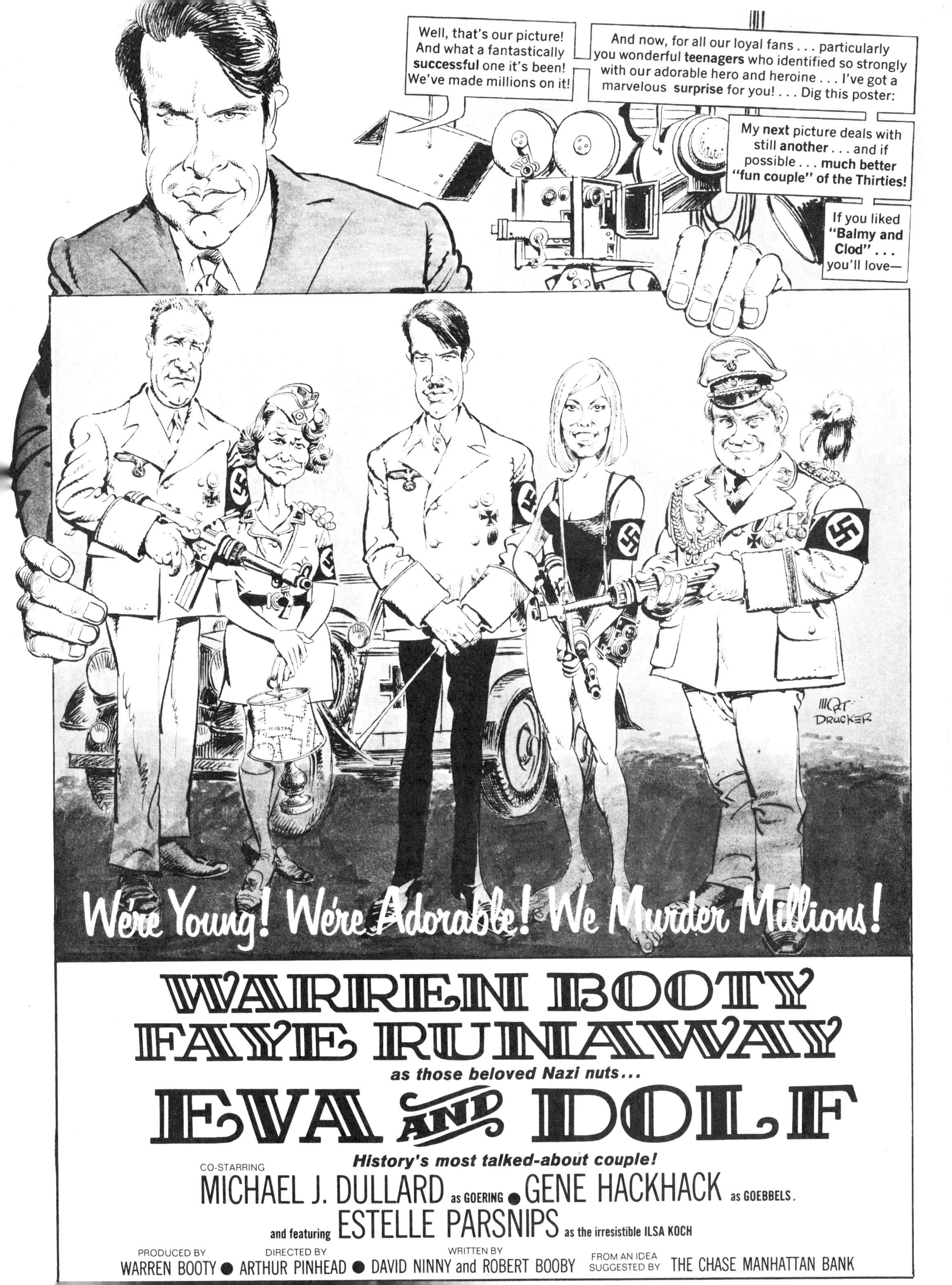
Well, that's our picture! And what a fantastically successful one it's been! We've made millions on it!
And now, for all our loyal fans . . . particularly you wonderful teenagers who identified so strongly with our adorable hero and heroine . . . I've got a marvelous surprise for you! . . . Dig this poster:
My next picture deals with still another . . . and if possible . . . much better "fun couple" of the Thirties!
If you liked "Balmy and Clod" . . . you'll love—
MORT DRUCKER
We're Young! We're Adorable! We Murder Millions!
WARREN BOOTY
FAYE RUNAWAY
as those beloved Nazi nuts...
EVA AND DOLF
History's most talked-about couple!
CO-STARRING
MICHAEL J. DULLARD as GOERING • GENE HACKHACK as GOEBBELS,
and featuring ESTELLE PARSNIPS as the irresistible ILSA KOCH
PRODUCED BY WARREN BOOTY • DIRECTED BY ARTHUR PINHEAD • WRITTEN BY DAVID NINNY and ROBERT BOOBY
FROM AN IDEA SUGGESTED BY THE CHASE MANHATTAN BANK

**ESCAPE-GOAT DEPT.**

Years ago, when they made a prison picture, you knew exactly what was going on. The guards were all sadistic and the prisoners were all regular guys under their tough exteriors. But today, things are different. Today,

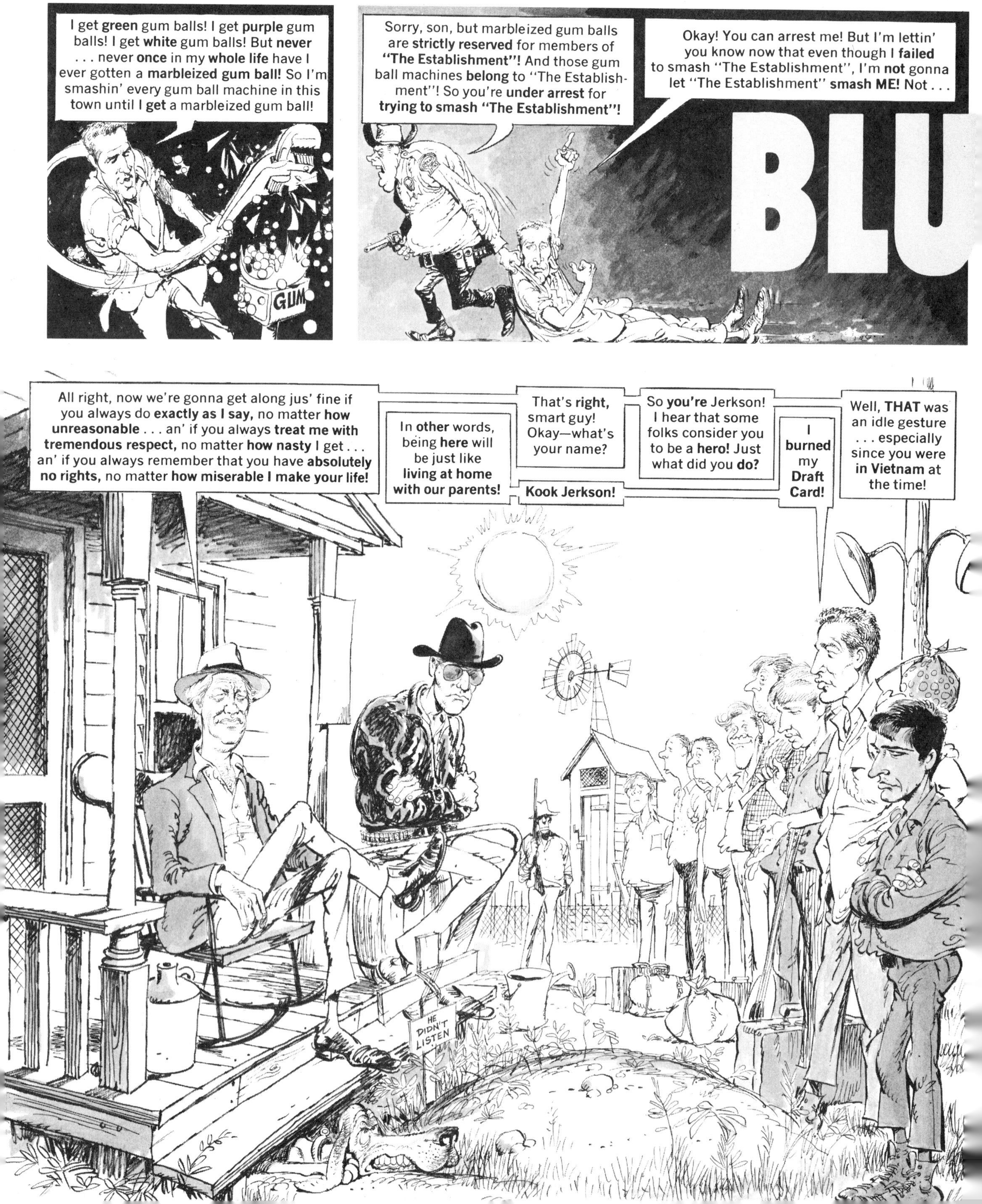
I get green gum balls! I get purple gum balls! I get white gum balls! But never . . . never once in my whole life have I ever gotten a marbleized gum ball! So I'm smashin' every gum ball machine in this town until I get a marbleized gum ball!
GUM
Sorry, son, but marbleized gum balls are strictly reserved for members of "The Establishment"! And those gum ball machines belong to "The Establishment"! So you're under arrest for trying to smash "The Establishment"!
Okay! You can arrest me! But I'm lettin' you know now that even though I failed to smash "The Establishment", I'm not gonna let "The Establishment" smash ME! Not . . .
BLU
All right, now we're gonna get along jus' fine if you always do exactly as I say, no matter how unreasonable . . . an' if you always treat me with tremendous respect, no matter how nasty I get . . . an' if you always remember that you have absolutely no rights, no matter how miserable I make your life!
In other words, being here will be just like living at home with our parents!
That's right, smart guy! Okay—what's your name?
Kook Jerkson!
So you're Jerkson! I hear that some folks consider you to be a hero! Just what did you do?
I burned my Draft Card!
Well, THAT was an idle gesture . . . especially since you were in Vietnam at the time!
HE DIDN'T LISTEN

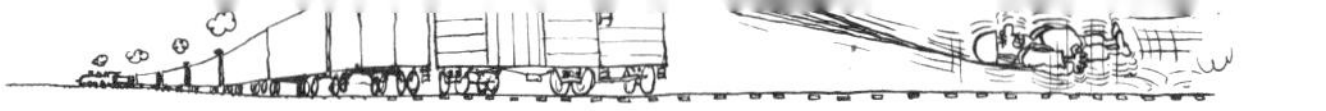

a prison picture isn't really about prison and prisoners. Today, it's all symbolism, and you have to figure out what's going on. Like f'rinstance in this MAD version of a recent prison picture that begins like this:

# E-EYED KOOK

ARTIST: MORT DRUCKER WRITER: STAN HART

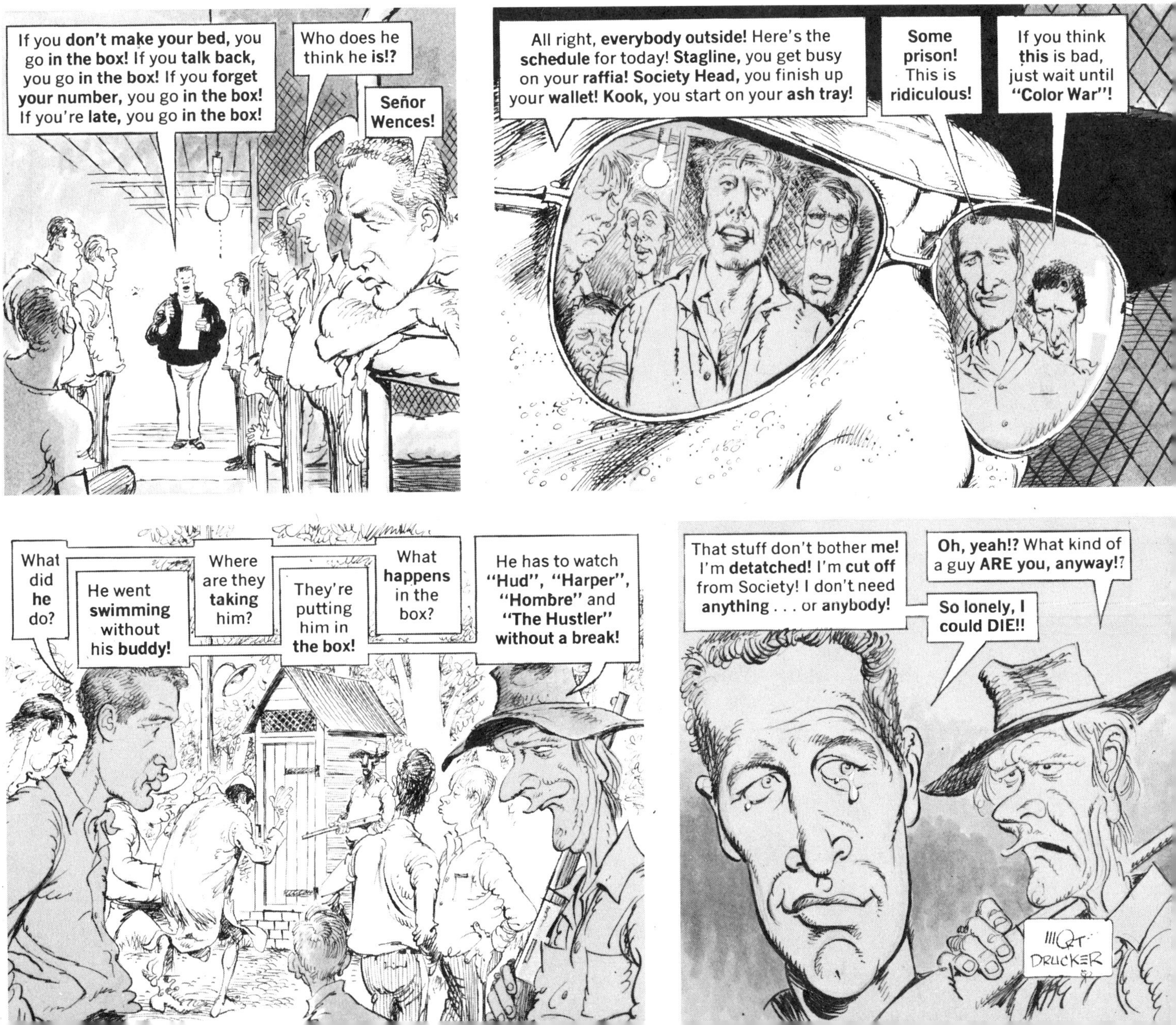

If you **don't make your bed,** you go **in the box!** If you **talk back,** you go **in the box!** If you **forget your number,** you go **in the box!** If you're **late,** you go **in the box!**
Who does he think he **is!?**
**Señor Wences!**
All right, **everybody outside!** Here's the **schedule** for today! **Stagline,** you get busy on your **raffia! Society Head,** you finish up your **wallet! Kook,** you start on your **ash tray!**
**Some prison!** This is **ridiculous!**
If you think **this** is bad, just wait until **"Color War"!**
What did **he** do?
He went **swimming** without his **buddy!**
Where are they **taking** him?
They're putting him in **the box!**
What **happens** in the box?
He has to watch **"Hud", "Harper", "Hombre"** and **"The Hustler" without a break!**
That stuff don't bother **me!** I'm **detatched!** I'm **cut off** from Society! I don't need **anything** . . . or **anybody!**
**Oh, yeah!?** What kind of a guy **ARE you, anyway!?**
**So lonely, I could DIE!!**
MORT DRUCKER

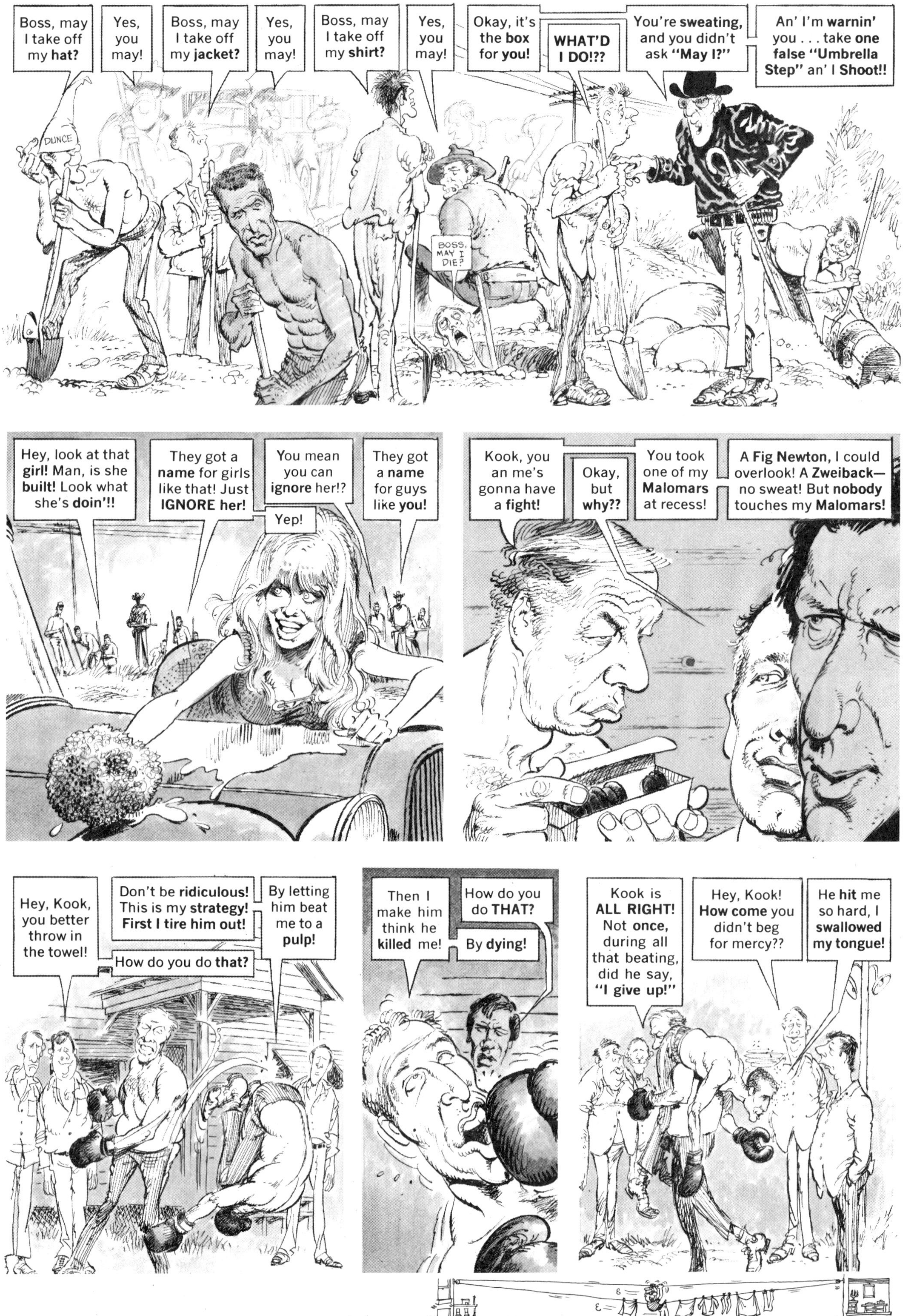
Boss, may I take off my **hat?**
Yes, you may!
Boss, may I take off my **jacket?**
Yes, you may!
Boss, may I take off my **shirt?**
Yes, you may!
Okay, it's the **box** for **you!**
**WHAT'D I DO!??**
You're **sweating,** and you didn't ask **"May I?"**
An' I'm **warnin'** you . . . take **one false "Umbrella Step"** an' I **Shoot!!**
DUNCE
BOSS, MAY I DIE?
Hey, look at that **girl!** Man, is she **built!** Look what she's **doin'!!**
They got a **name** for girls like that! Just **IGNORE her!**
You mean you can **ignore** her!?
Yep!
They got a **name** for guys like **you!**
Kook, you an me's gonna have a **fight!**
Okay, but **why??**
You took one of my **Malomars** at recess!
A **Fig Newton,** I could overlook! A **Zweiback**— no sweat! But **nobody** touches my **Malomars!**
Hey, Kook, you better throw in the towel!
Don't be **ridiculous!** This is my **strategy! First I tire him out!**
How do you do **that?**
By letting him beat me to a **pulp!**
Then I make him think he **killed** me!
How do you do **THAT?**
By **dying!**
Kook is **ALL RIGHT!** Not **once,** during all that beating, did he say, **"I give up!"**
Hey, Kook! **How come** you didn't beg for mercy??
He **hit** me so hard, I **swallowed my tongue!**

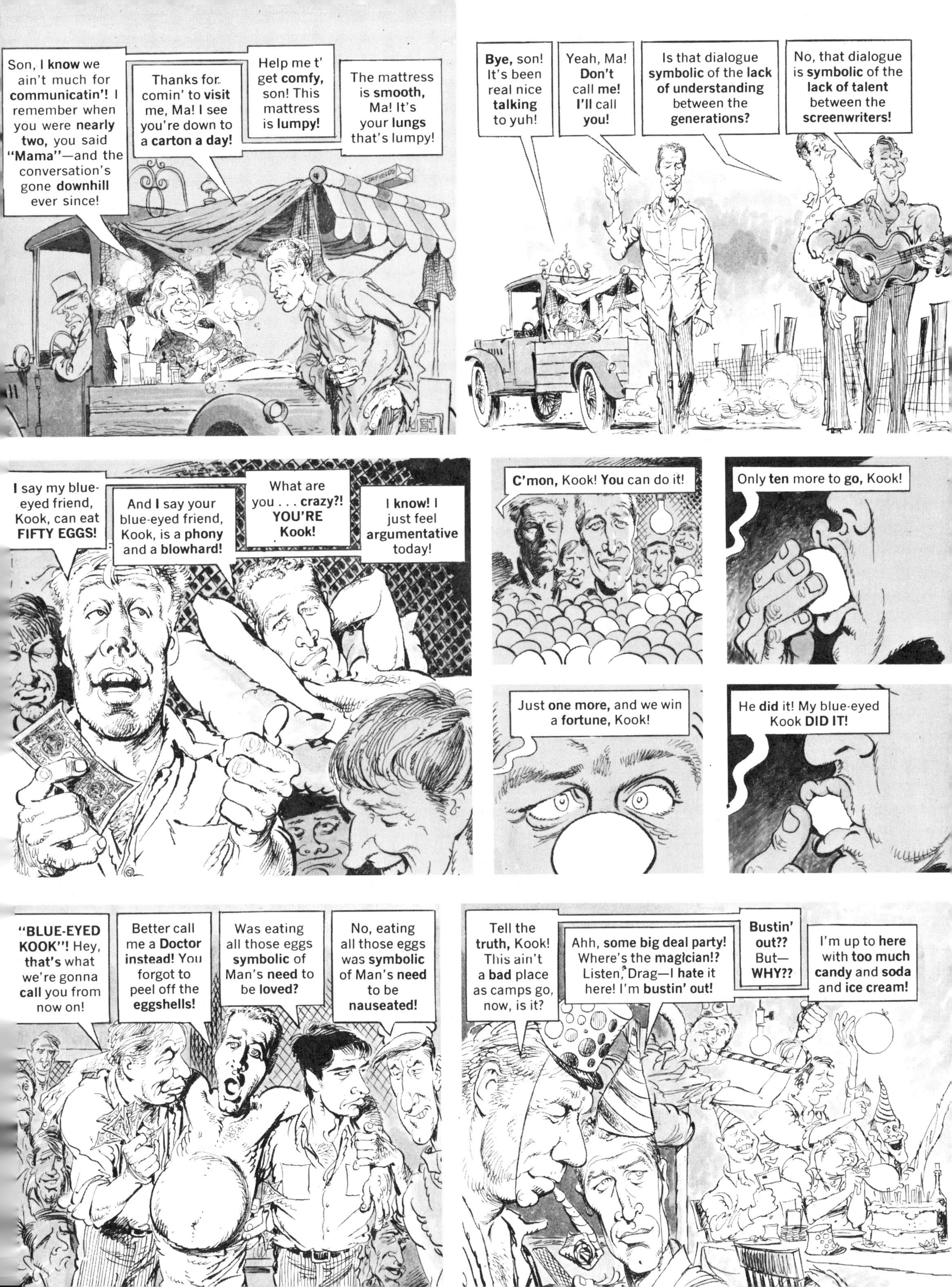
Son, I know we ain't much for communicatin'! I remember when you were nearly two, you said "Mama"—and the conversation's gone downhill ever since!
Thanks for comin' to visit me, Ma! I see you're down to a carton a day!
Help me t' get comfy, son! This mattress is lumpy!
The mattress is smooth, Ma! It's your lungs that's lumpy!
Bye, son! It's been real nice talking to yuh!
Yeah, Ma! Don't call me! I'll call you!
Is that dialogue symbolic of the lack of understanding between the generations?
No, that dialogue is symbolic of the lack of talent between the screenwriters!
I say my blue-eyed friend, Kook, can eat FIFTY EGGS!
And I say your blue-eyed friend, Kook, is a phony and a blowhard!
What are you . . . crazy?! YOU'RE Kook!
I know! I just feel argumentative today!
C'mon, Kook! You can do it!
Only ten more to go, Kook!
Just one more, and we win a fortune, Kook!
He did it! My blue-eyed Kook DID IT!
"BLUE-EYED KOOK"! Hey, that's what we're gonna call you from now on!
Better call me a Doctor instead! You forgot to peel off the eggshells!
Was eating all those eggs symbolic of Man's need to be loved?
No, eating all those eggs was symbolic of Man's need to be nauseated!
Tell the truth, Kook! This ain't a bad place as camps go, now, is it?
Ahh, some big deal party! Where's the magician!? Listen, Drag—I hate it here! I'm bustin' out!
Bustin' out?? But— WHY??
I'm up to here with too much candy and soda and ice cream!

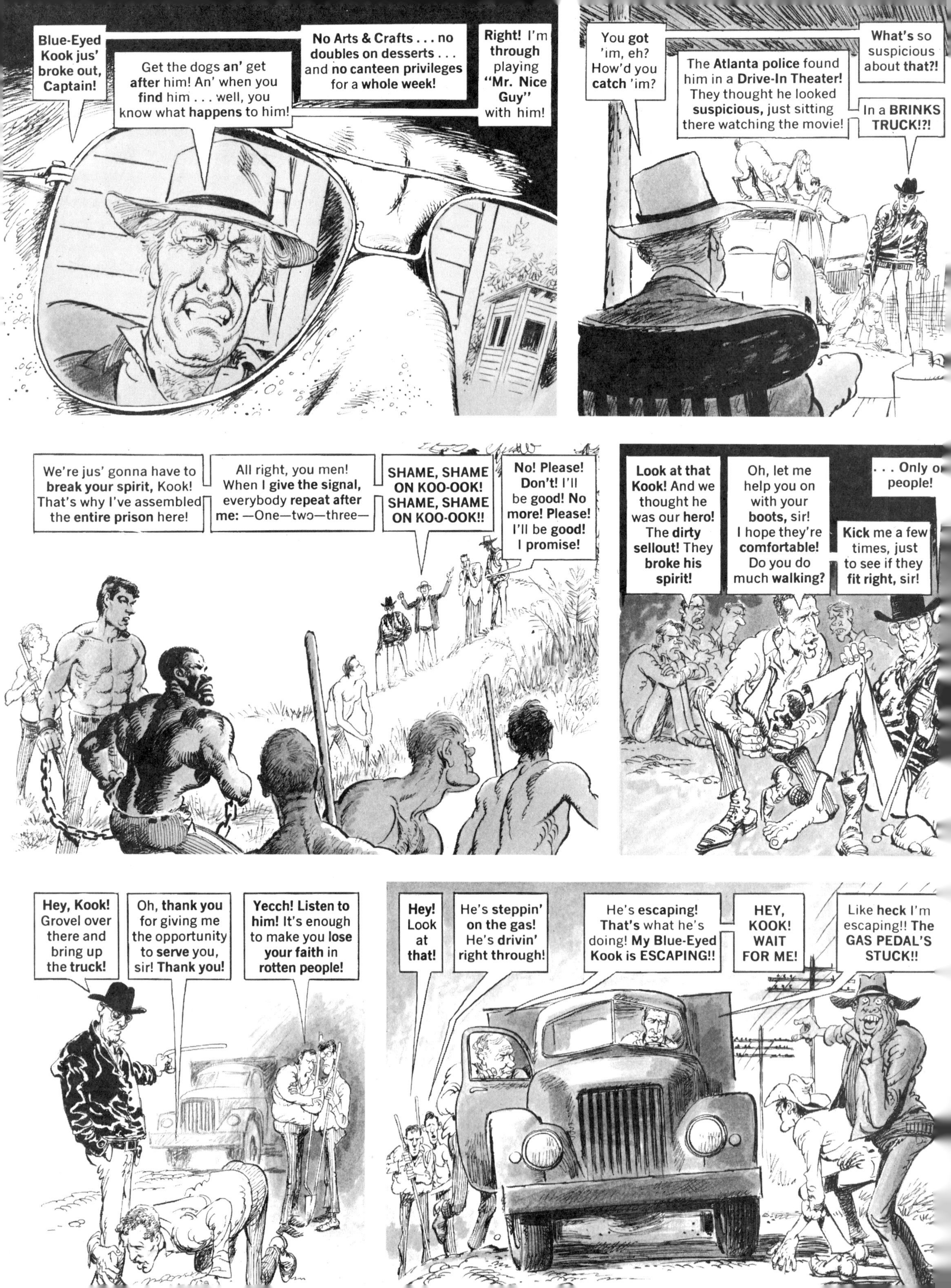

Blue-Eyed Kook jus' broke out, Captain!
Get the dogs an' get after him! An' when you find him . . . well, you know what happens to him!
No Arts & Crafts . . . no doubles on desserts . . . and no canteen privileges for a whole week!
Right! I'm through playing "Mr. Nice Guy" with him!
You got 'im, eh? How'd you catch 'im?
The Atlanta police found him in a Drive-In Theater! They thought he looked suspicious, just sitting there watching the movie!
What's so suspicious about that?!
In a BRINKS TRUCK!?!
We're jus' gonna have to break your spirit, Kook! That's why I've assembled the entire prison here!
All right, you men! When I give the signal, everybody repeat after me: —One—two—three—
SHAME, SHAME ON KOO-OOK! SHAME, SHAME ON KOO-OOK!!
No! Please! Don't! I'll be good! No more! Please! I'll be good! I promise!
Look at that Kook! And we thought he was our hero! The dirty sellout! They broke his spirit!
Oh, let me help you on with your boots, sir! I hope they're comfortable! Do you do much walking?
. . . Only
people!
Kick me a few times, just to see if they fit right, sir!
Hey, Kook! Grovel over there and bring up the truck!
Oh, thank you for giving me the opportunity to serve you, sir! Thank you!
Yecch! Listen to him! It's enough to make you lose your faith in rotten people!
Hey! Look at that!
He's steppin' on the gas! He's drivin' right through!
He's escaping! That's what he's doing! My Blue-Eyed Kook is ESCAPING!!
HEY, KOOK! WAIT FOR ME!
Like heck I'm escaping!! The GAS PEDAL'S STUCK!!

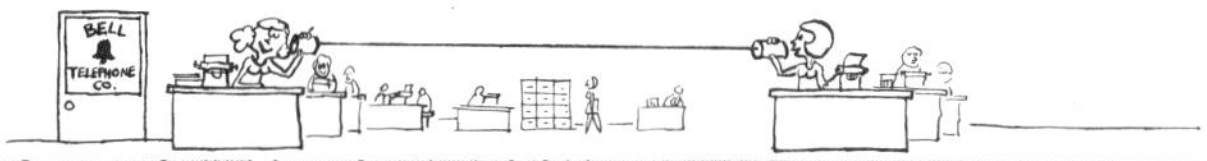
BELL
TELEPHONE CO.

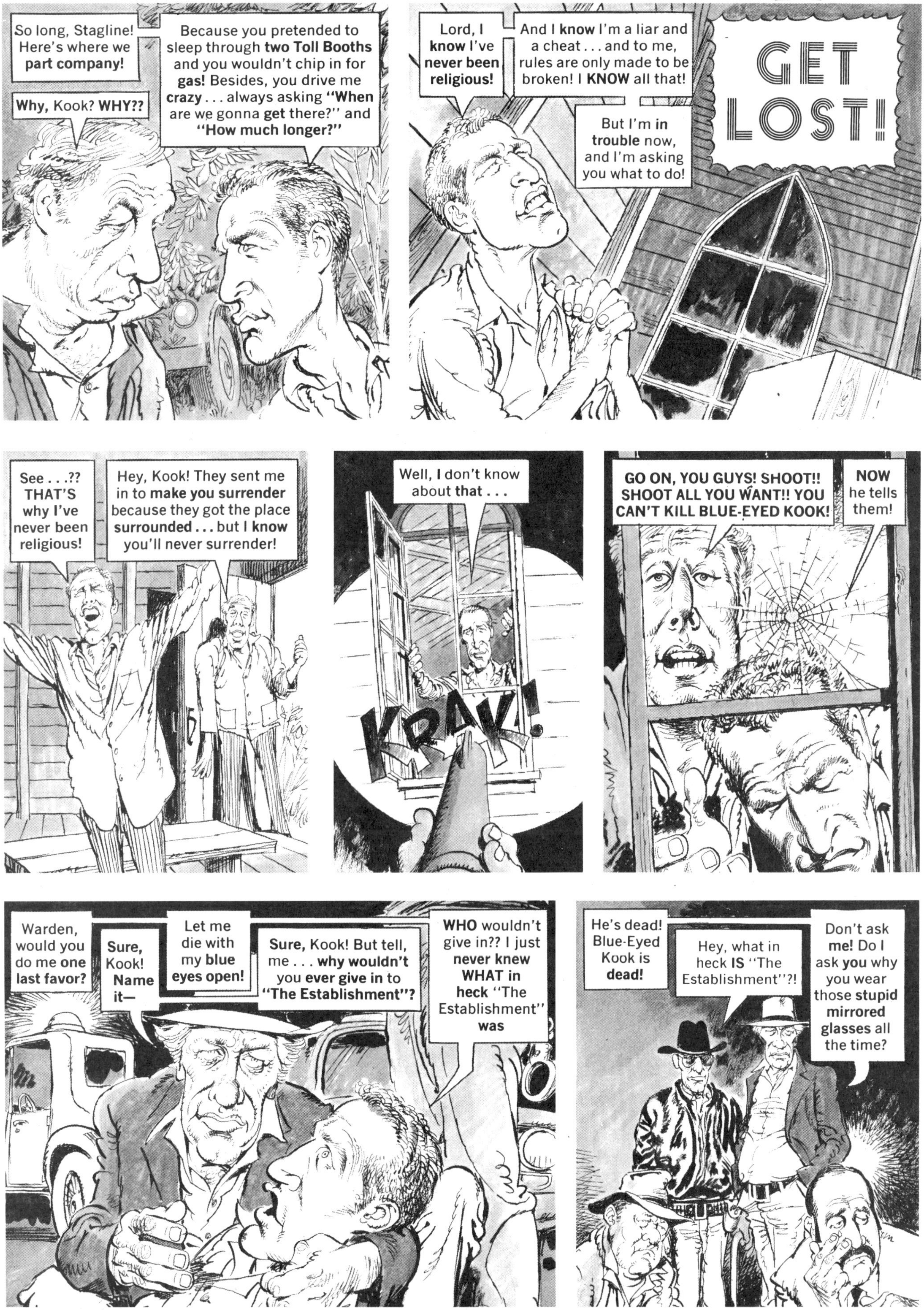
So long, Stagline! Here's where we part company!
Why, Kook? WHY??
Because you pretended to sleep through two Toll Booths and you wouldn't chip in for gas! Besides, you drive me crazy . . . always asking "When are we gonna get there?" and "How much longer?"
Lord, I know I've never been religious!
And I know I'm a liar and a cheat . . . and to me, rules are only made to be broken! I KNOW all that!
But I'm in trouble now, and I'm asking you what to do!
GET LOST!
See . . .?? THAT'S why I've never been religious!
Hey, Kook! They sent me in to make you surrender because they got the place surrounded . . . but I know you'll never surrender!
Well, I don't know about that . . .
KRAK!
GO ON, YOU GUYS! SHOOT!! SHOOT ALL YOU WANT!! YOU CAN'T KILL BLUE-EYED KOOK!
NOW he tells them!
Warden, would you do me one last favor?
Sure, Kook! Name it—
Let me die with my blue eyes open!
Sure, Kook! But tell, me . . . why wouldn't you ever give in to "The Establishment"?
WHO wouldn't give in?? I just never knew WHAT in heck "The Establishment" was
He's dead! Blue-Eyed Kook is dead!
Hey, what in heck IS "The Establishment"?!
Don't ask me! Do I ask you why you wear those stupid mirrored glasses all the time?

GOD SAVE McQUEEN DEPT.

No matter what kind of role he plays, Steve McQueen is always Steve McQueen! He was Steve McQueen when he did his *sailor bit* in "The Sand Pebbles"! He was Steve McQueen when he did his *illegitimate father bit* in "Love With A Proper Stranger"! He was Steve McQueen when he did his *sophisticated crook bit* in "The Thomas Crown Affair"! And if you've seen his latest . . . in which he plays a detective, then you'll have to agree that he's still Steve McQueen, even when he does his . . .

# "BULLBIT"

ARTIST: MORT DRUCKER WRITER: AL JAFFEE

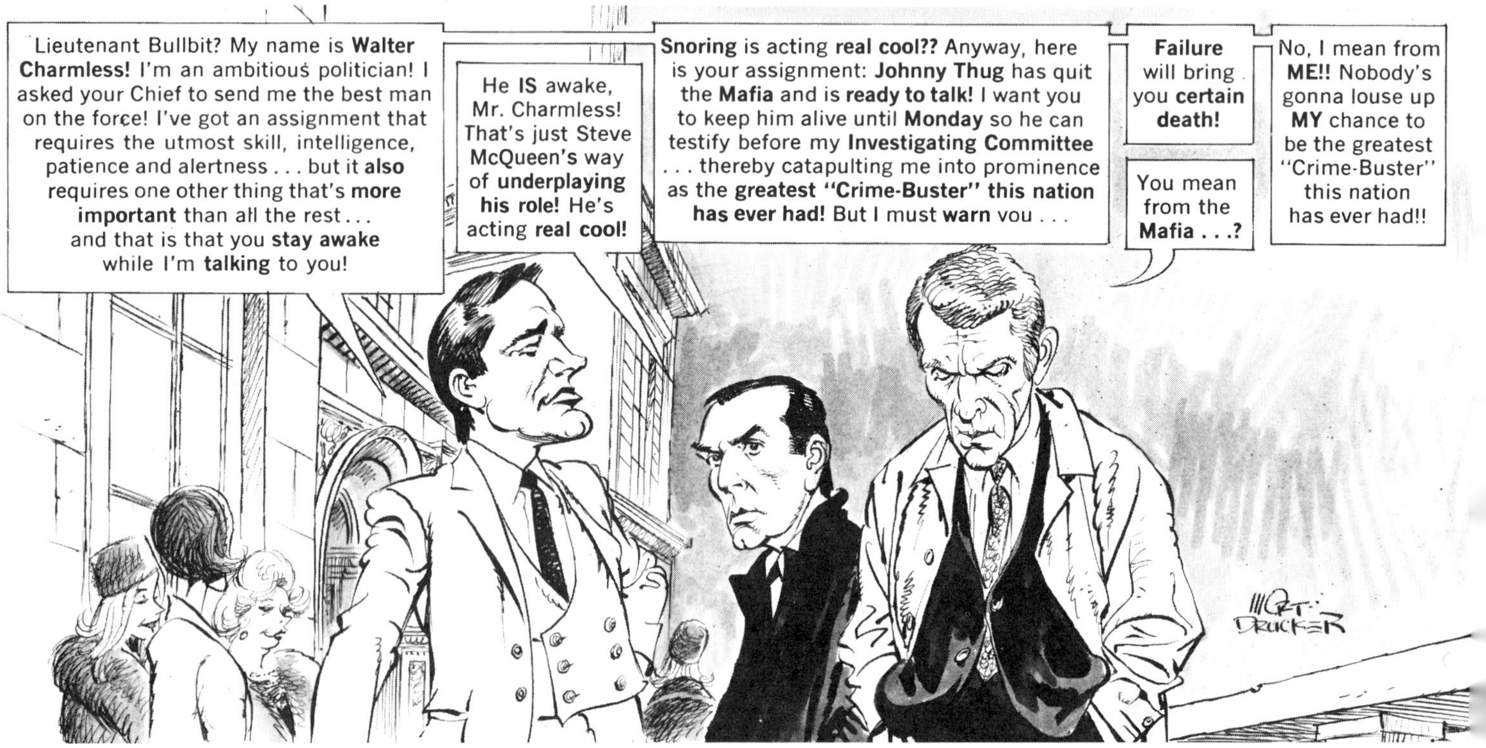
Lieutenant Bullbit? My name is **Walter Charmless!** I'm an ambitious politician! I asked your Chief to send me the best man on the force! I've got an assignment that requires the utmost skill, intelligence, patience and alertness . . . but it **also** requires one other thing that's **more important** than all the rest . . . and that is that you **stay awake** while I'm **talking** to you!
He **IS** awake, Mr. Charmless! That's just Steve McQueen's way of **underplaying his role!** He's acting **real cool!**
**Snoring** is acting **real cool??** Anyway, here is your assignment: **Johnny Thug** has quit the **Mafia** and is **ready to talk!** I want you to keep him alive until **Monday** so he can testify before my **Investigating Committee** . . . thereby catapulting me into prominence as the **greatest "Crime-Buster" this nation has ever had!** But I must **warn** you . . .
**Failure** will bring you **certain death!**
You mean from the **Mafia . . .?**
No, I mean from **ME!!** Nobody's gonna louse up **MY** chance to be the greatest "Crime-Buster" this nation has ever had!!
MORT DRUCKER

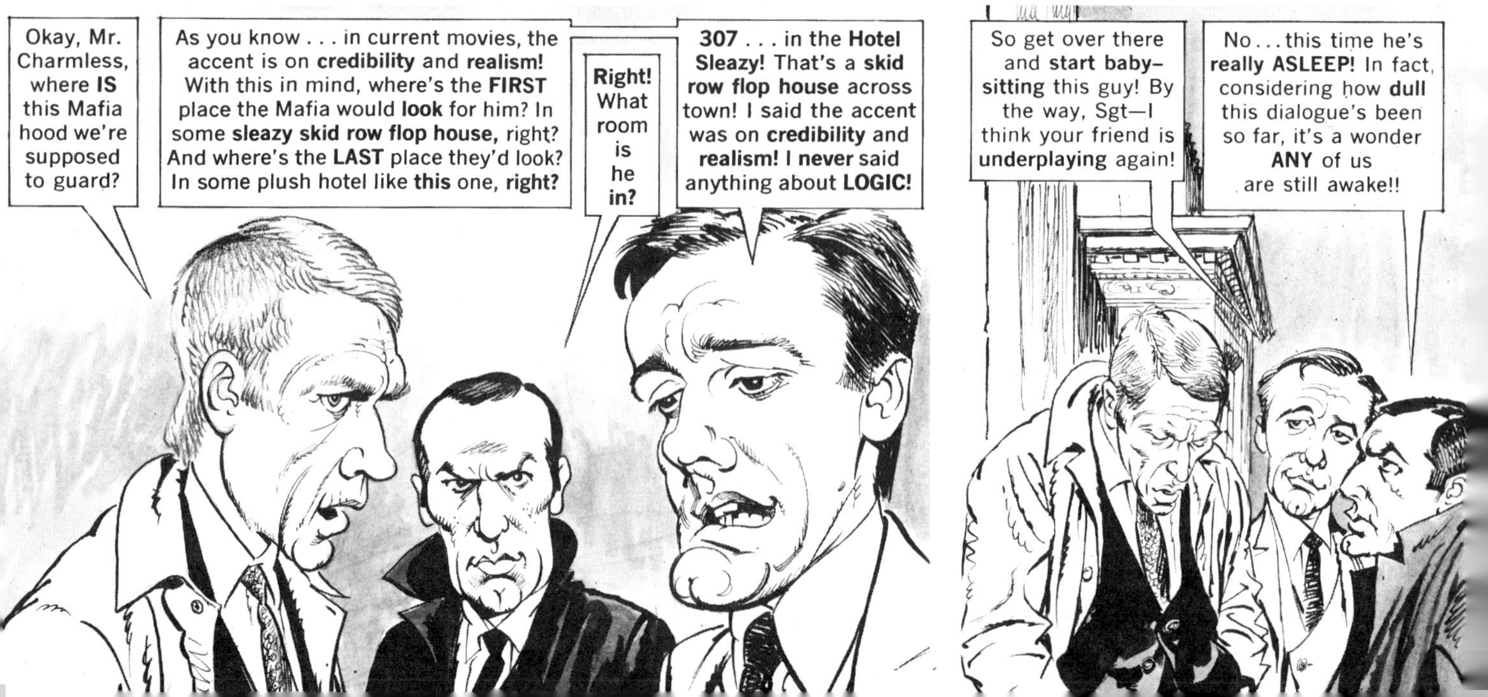
Okay, Mr. Charmless, where **IS** this Mafia hood we're supposed to guard?
As you know . . . in current movies, the accent is on **credibility** and **realism!** With this in mind, where's the **FIRST** place the Mafia would **look** for him? In some **sleazy skid row flop house,** right? And where's the **LAST** place they'd look? In some plush hotel like **this** one, **right?**
**Right!** What room is he **in?**
**307** . . . in the **Hotel Sleazy!** That's a **skid row flop house** across town! I said the accent was on **credibility** and **realism! I never** said anything about **LOGIC!**
So get over there and **start baby-sitting** this guy! By the way, Sgt—I think your friend is **underplaying** again!
No . . . this time he's **really ASLEEP!** In fact, considering how **dull** this dialogue's been so far, it's a wonder **ANY** of us are still awake!!

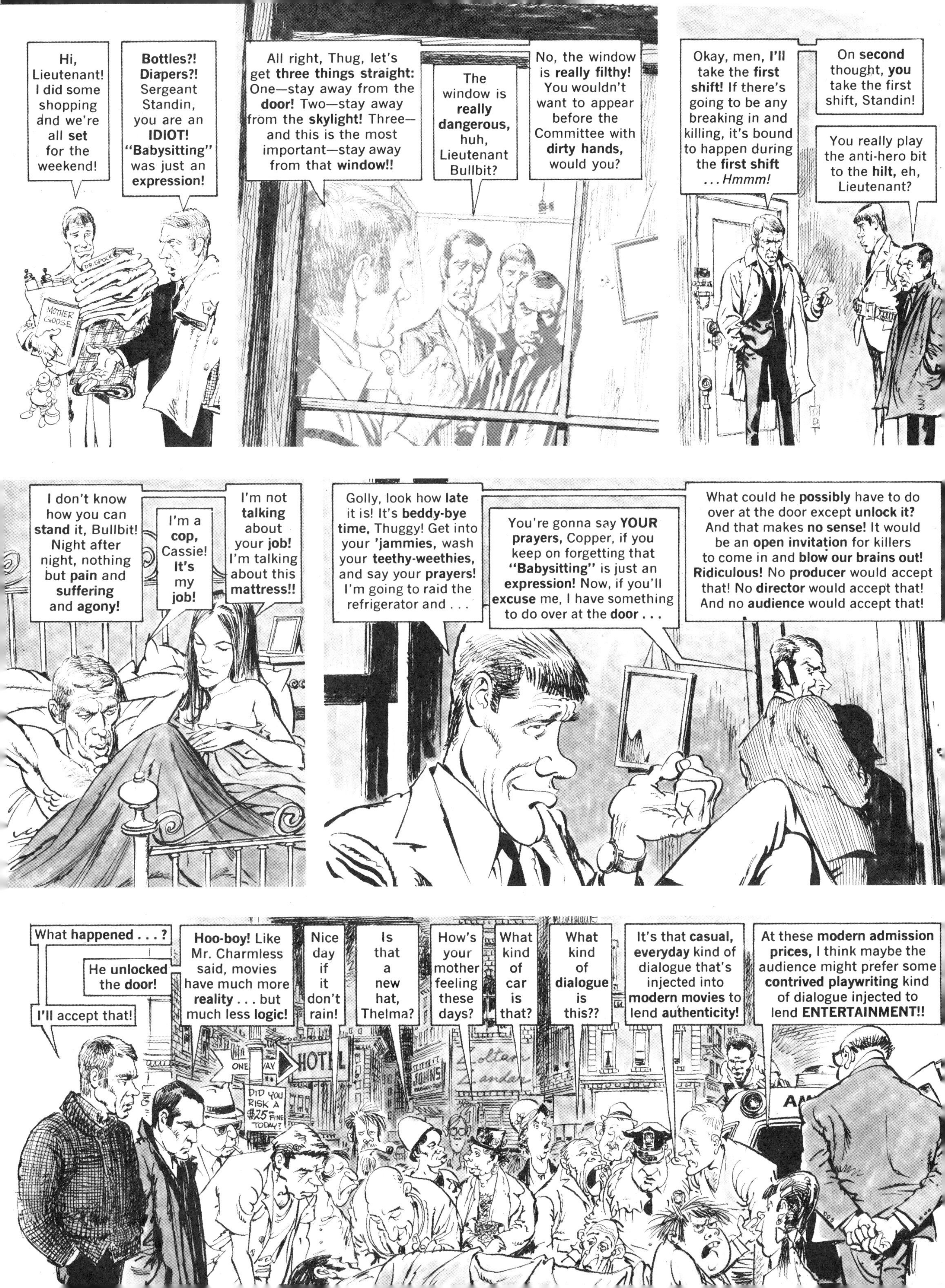
Hi, Lieutenant! I did some shopping and we're all **set** for the weekend!
**Bottles?! Diapers?!** Sergeant Standin, you are an **IDIOT! "Babysitting"** was just an **expression!**
DR. SPOCK
MOTHER GOOSE
All right, Thug, let's get **three things straight:** One—stay away from the **door!** Two—stay away from the **skylight!** Three—and this is the most important—stay away from that **window!!**
The window is **really dangerous,** huh, Lieutenant Bullbit?
No, the window is **really filthy!** You wouldn't want to appear before the Committee with **dirty hands,** would you?
Okay, men, **I'll** take the **first shift!** If there's going to be any breaking in and killing, it's bound to happen during the **first shift** *. . . Hmmm!*
On **second** thought, **you** take the first shift, Standin!
You really play the anti-hero bit to the **hilt,** eh, Lieutenant?
I don't know how you can **stand** it, Bullbit! Night after night, nothing but **pain** and **suffering** and **agony!**
I'm a **cop,** Cassie! **It's** my **job!**
I'm not **talking** about your **job!** I'm talking about this **mattress!!**
Golly, look how **late** it is! It's **beddy-bye time,** Thuggy! Get into your **'jammies,** wash your **teethy-weethies,** and say your **prayers!** I'm going to raid the refrigerator and . . .
You're gonna say **YOUR prayers,** Copper, if you keep on forgetting that **"Babysitting"** is just an **expression!** Now, if you'll **excuse** me, I have something to do over at the **door . . .**
What could he **possibly** have to do over at the door except **unlock it?** And that makes **no sense!** It would be an **open invitation** for killers to come in and **blow our brains out! Ridiculous!** No **producer** would accept that! No **director** would accept that! And no **audience** would accept that!
What **happened . . . ?**
He **unlocked** the **door!**
**I'll** accept that!
**Hoo-boy!** Like Mr. Charmless said, movies have much more **reality** . . . but much less **logic!**
ONE WAY
HOTEL
DID YOU RISK A $25 FINE TODAY?
JOHNS
Nice day if it don't rain!
Is that a new hat, Thelma?
How's your mother feeling these days?
What kind of car is that?
What kind of **dialogue** is this??
It's that **casual, everyday** kind of dialogue that's injected into **modern movies** to lend **authenticity!**
At these **modern admission prices,** I think maybe the audience might prefer some **contrived playwriting** kind of dialogue injected to lend **ENTERTAINMENT!!**

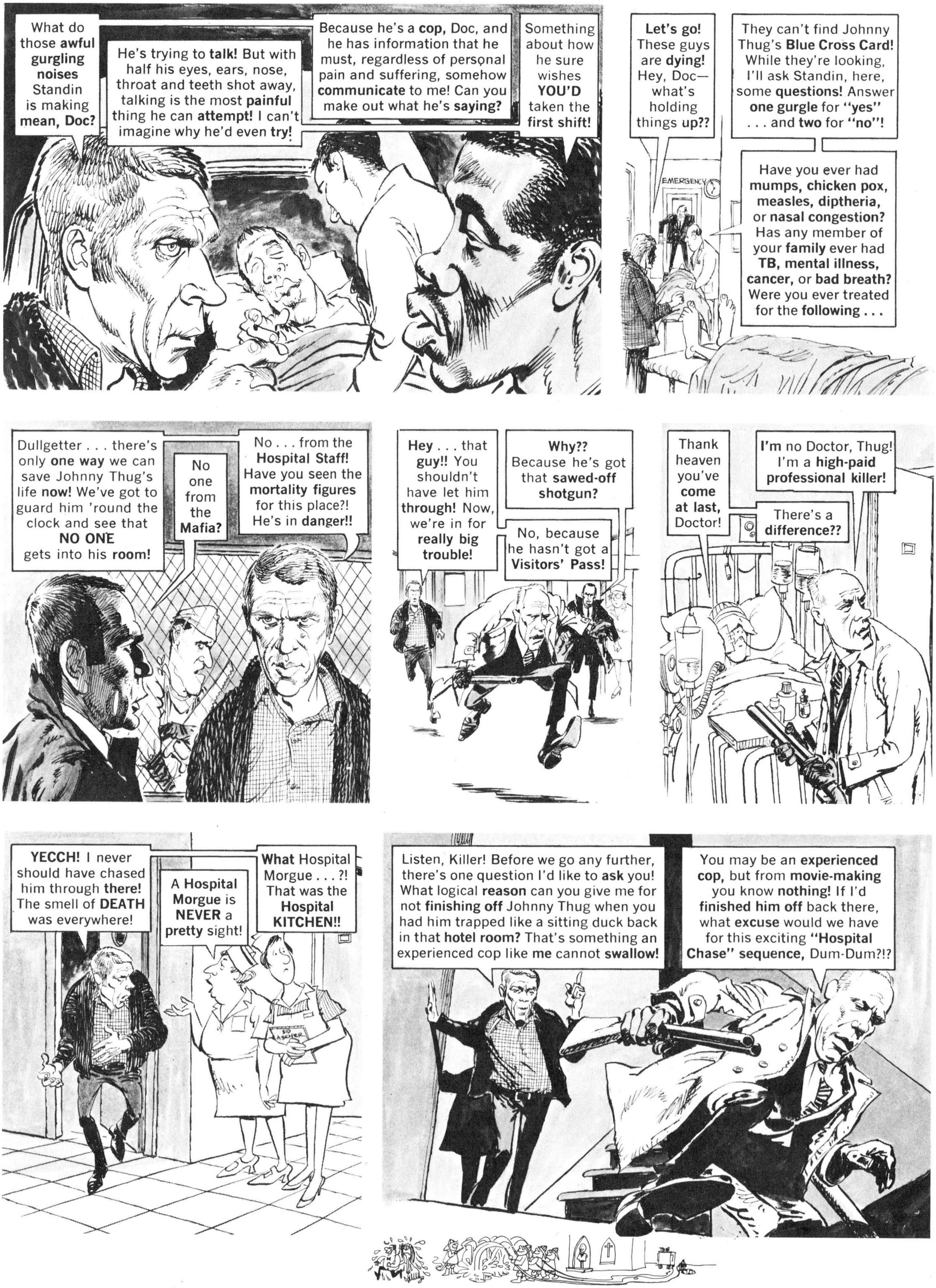
What do those awful gurgling noises Standin is making mean, Doc?
He's trying to talk! But with half his eyes, ears, nose, throat and teeth shot away, talking is the most painful thing he can attempt! I can't imagine why he'd even try!
Because he's a cop, Doc, and he has information that he must, regardless of personal pain and suffering, somehow communicate to me! Can you make out what he's saying?
Something about how he sure wishes YOU'D taken the first shift!
Let's go! These guys are dying! Hey, Doc— what's holding things up??
They can't find Johnny Thug's Blue Cross Card! While they're looking, I'll ask Standin, here, some questions! Answer one gurgle for "yes" . . . and two for "no"!
EMERGENCY
Have you ever had mumps, chicken pox, measles, diptheria, or nasal congestion? Has any member of your family ever had TB, mental illness, cancer, or bad breath? Were you ever treated for the following . . .
Dullgetter . . . there's only one way we can save Johnny Thug's life now! We've got to guard him 'round the clock and see that NO ONE gets into his room!
No one from the Mafia?
No . . . from the Hospital Staff! Have you seen the mortality figures for this place?! He's in danger!!
Hey . . . that guy!! You shouldn't have let him through! Now, we're in for really big trouble!
Why?? Because he's got that sawed-off shotgun?
No, because he hasn't got a Visitors' Pass!
Thank heaven you've come at last, Doctor!
I'm no Doctor, Thug! I'm a high-paid professional killer!
There's a difference??
YECCH! I never should have chased him through there! The smell of DEATH was everywhere!
A Hospital Morgue is NEVER a pretty sight!
What Hospital Morgue . . . ?! That was the Hospital KITCHEN!!
SID ASCHER
Listen, Killer! Before we go any further, there's one question I'd like to ask you! What logical reason can you give me for not finishing off Johnny Thug when you had him trapped like a sitting duck back in that hotel room? That's something an experienced cop like me cannot swallow!
You may be an experienced cop, but from movie-making you know nothing! If I'd finished him off back there, what excuse would we have for this exciting "Hospital Chase" sequence, Dum-Dum?!?

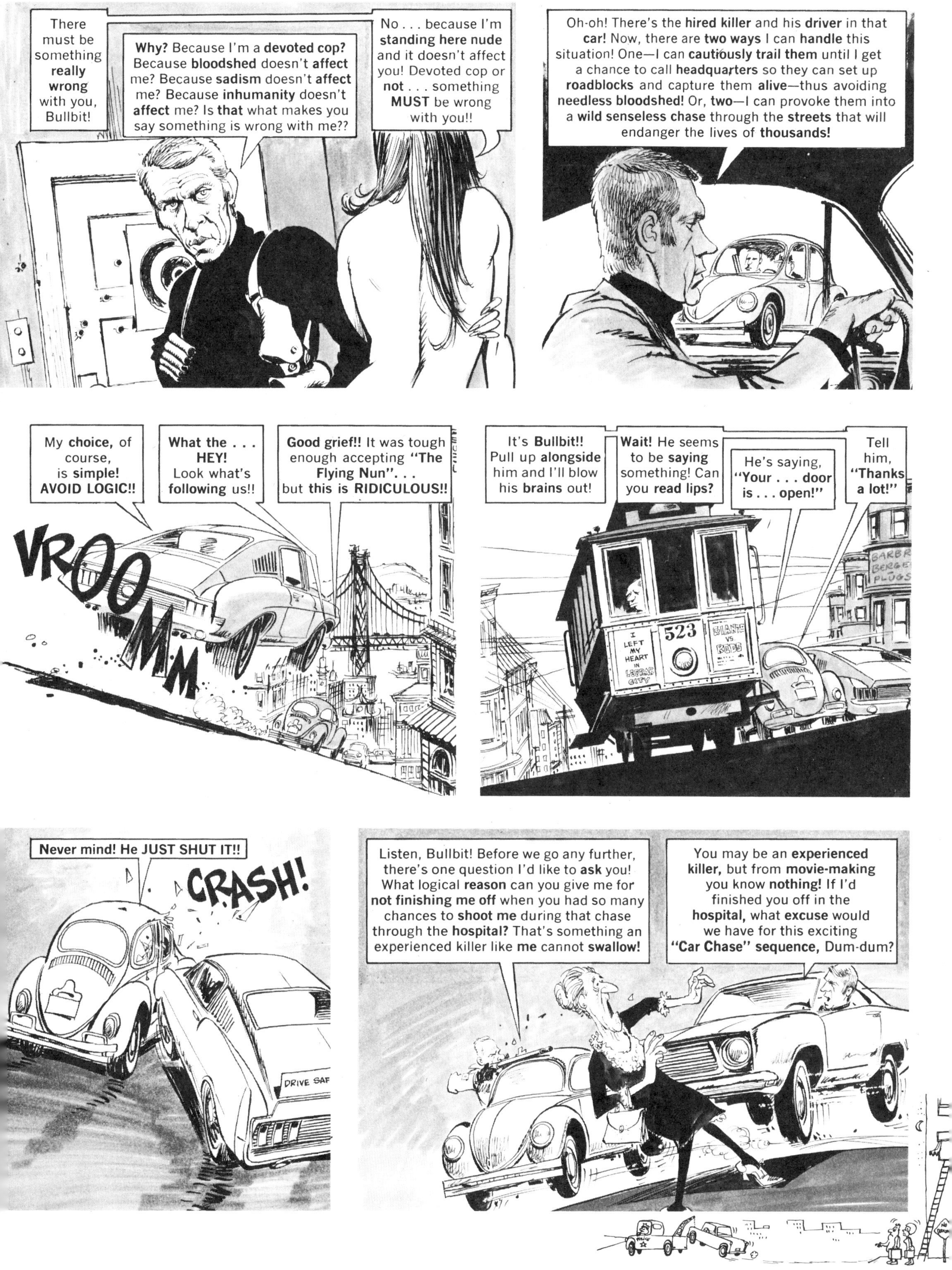
There must be something **really wrong** with you, Bullbit!
**Why?** Because I'm a **devoted cop?** Because **bloodshed** doesn't **affect** me? Because **sadism** doesn't **affect** me? Because **inhumanity** doesn't **affect** me? Is **that** what makes you say something is wrong with me??
No . . . because I'm **standing here nude** and it doesn't affect you! Devoted cop or **not** . . . something **MUST** be wrong with you!!
Oh-oh! There's the **hired killer** and his **driver** in that **car!** Now, there are **two ways** I can **handle** this situation! One—I can **cautiously trail them** until I get a chance to call **headquarters** so they can set up **roadblocks** and capture them **alive**—thus avoiding **needless bloodshed!** Or, **two**—I can provoke them into a **wild senseless chase** through the **streets** that will endanger the lives of **thousands!**
My **choice,** of course, is **simple! AVOID LOGIC!!**
**What the . . . HEY!** Look what's **following** us!!
**Good grief!!** It was tough enough accepting **"The Flying Nun"**. . . but **this is RIDICULOUS!!**
VROOOMMM
It's **Bullbit!!** Pull up **alongside** him and I'll blow his **brains** out!
**Wait!** He seems to be **saying** something! Can you **read lips?**
He's saying, **"Your . . . door is . . . open!"**
Tell him, **"Thanks a lot!"**
523
I LEFT MY HEART IN LEFRAK CITY
**Never mind! He JUST SHUT IT!!**
CRASH!
Listen, Bullbit! Before we go any further, there's one question I'd like to **ask** you! What logical **reason** can you give me for **not finishing me off** when you had so many chances to **shoot me** during that chase through the **hospital?** That's something an experienced killer like **me** cannot **swallow!**
You may be an **experienced killer,** but from **movie-making** you know **nothing!** If I'd finished you off in the **hospital,** what **excuse** would we have for this exciting **"Car Chase" sequence,** Dum-dum?

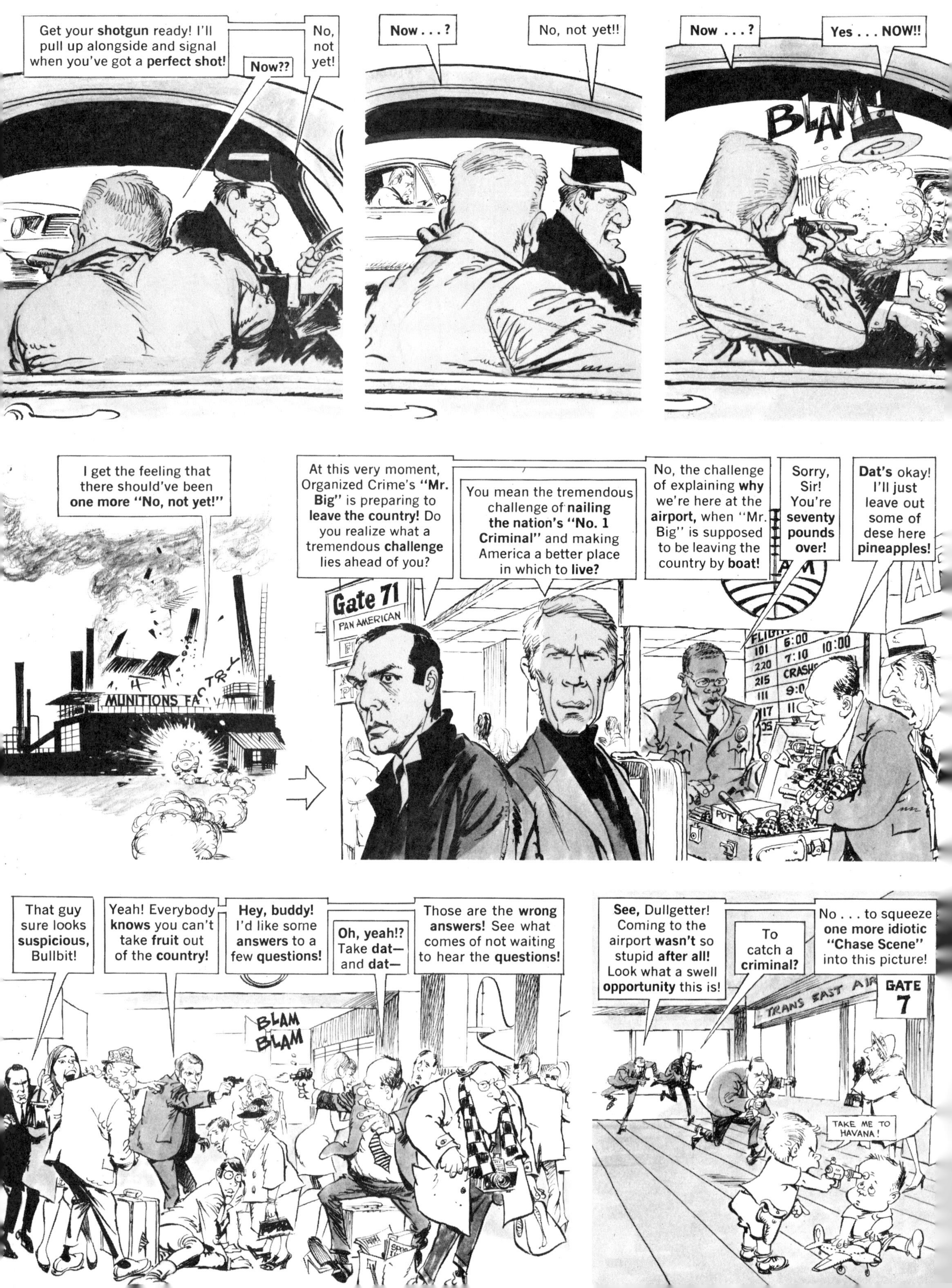

Get your shotgun ready! I'll pull up alongside and signal when you've got a perfect shot!
Now??
No, not yet!
Now . . . ?
No, not yet!!
Now . . . ?
Yes . . . NOW!!
BLAM!
I get the feeling that there should've been one more "No, not yet!"
MUNITIONS FA
FACTORY
At this very moment, Organized Crime's "Mr. Big" is preparing to leave the country! Do you realize what a tremendous challenge lies ahead of you?
You mean the tremendous challenge of nailing the nation's "No. 1 Criminal" and making America a better place in which to live?
No, the challenge of explaining why we're here at the airport, when "Mr. Big" is supposed to be leaving the country by boat!
Sorry, Sir! You're seventy pounds over!
Dat's okay! I'll just leave out some of dese here pineapples!
Gate 71
PAN AMERICAN
POT
That guy sure looks suspicious, Bullbit!
Yeah! Everybody knows you can't take fruit out of the country!
Hey, buddy! I'd like some answers to a few questions!
Oh, yeah!? Take dat— and dat—
Those are the wrong answers! See what comes of not waiting to hear the questions!
BLAM BLAM
See, Dullgetter! Coming to the airport wasn't so stupid after all! Look what a swell opportunity this is!
To catch a criminal?
No . . . to squeeze one more idiotic "Chase Scene" into this picture!
TRANS EAST AIR
GATE 7
TAKE ME TO HAVANA!

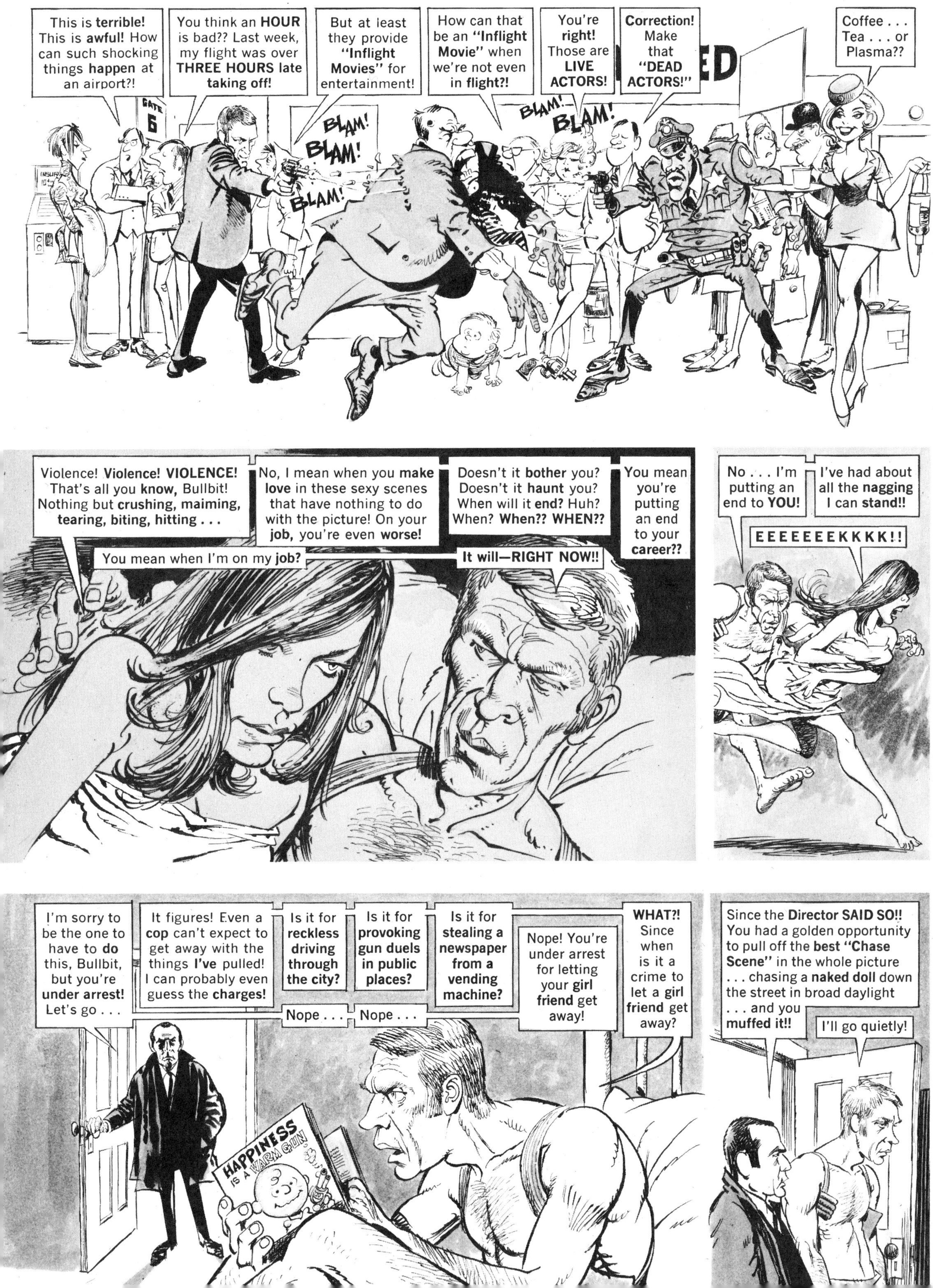

This is terrible! This is awful! How can such shocking things happen at an airport?!
You think an HOUR is bad?? Last week, my flight was over THREE HOURS late taking off!
But at least they provide "Inflight Movies" for entertainment!
How can that be an "Inflight Movie" when we're not even in flight?!
You're right! Those are LIVE ACTORS!
Correction! Make that "DEAD ACTORS!"
Coffee . . . Tea . . . or Plasma??
GATE 6
BLAM! BLAM! BLAM!
BLAM! BLAM!
Violence! Violence! VIOLENCE! That's all you know, Bullbit! Nothing but crushing, maiming, tearing, biting, hitting . . .
You mean when I'm on my job?
No, I mean when you make love in these sexy scenes that have nothing to do with the picture! On your job, you're even worse!
Doesn't it bother you? Doesn't it haunt you? When will it end? Huh? When? When?? WHEN??
You mean you're putting an end to your career??
It will—RIGHT NOW!!
No . . . I'm putting an end to YOU!
I've had about all the nagging I can stand!!
EEEEEEEKKKKK!!
I'm sorry to be the one to have to do this, Bullbit, but you're under arrest! Let's go . . .
It figures! Even a cop can't expect to get away with the things I've pulled! I can probably even guess the charges!
Is it for reckless driving through the city?
Nope . . .
Is it for provoking gun duels in public places?
Nope . . .
Is it for stealing a newspaper from a vending machine?
Nope! You're under arrest for letting your girl friend get away!
WHAT?! Since when is it a crime to let a girl friend get away?
HAPPINESS IS A WARM GUN
Since the Director SAID SO!! You had a golden opportunity to pull off the best "Chase Scene" in the whole picture . . . chasing a naked doll down the street in broad daylight . . . and you muffed it!!
I'll go quietly!

**THE WRONG ARM OF THE LAW DEPT.**

Say! What ever happened to those "nice" movie detectives of years ago? Remember? They were all pleasant, good-natured guys with no hang-ups. *Charlie Chan,* the *Thin Man* . . . even the *Shadow* enjoyed a healthy laugh once in a while. But look what's happening today. Every new movie detective that comes along appears to have a problem. You know who we're talking about. Detectives like moody, semi-bewildered Steve McQueen in "Bullet" . . . bigoted, neurotic Gene Hackman in "The French Connection" . . . and now **this** guy: a taciturn, trigger-happy, morose, sadistic, psychotic farblungit known as—what else?—

# DIRT

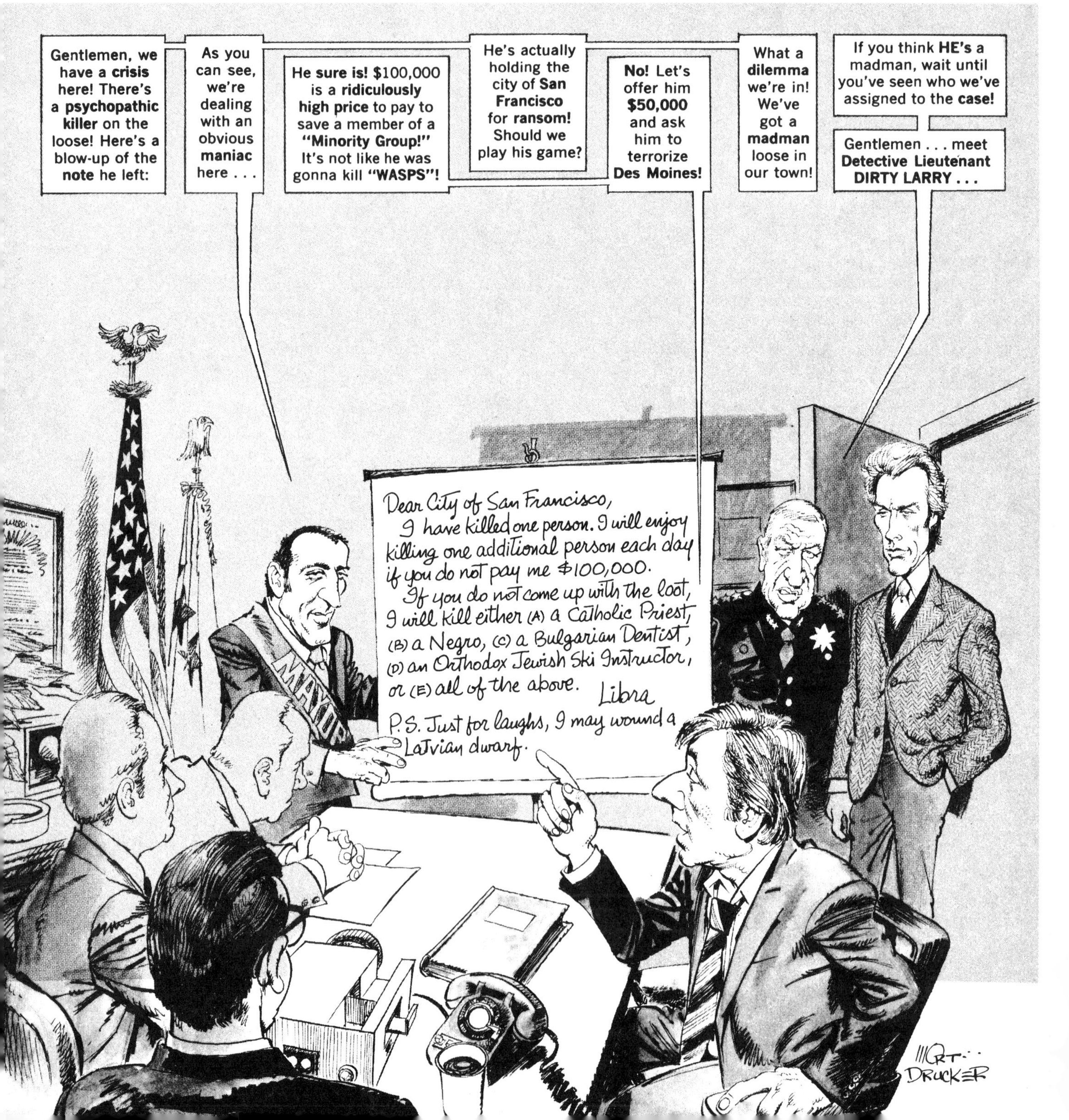

Gentlemen, we have a crisis here! There's a psychopathic killer on the loose! Here's a blow-up of the note he left:
As you can see, we're dealing with an obvious maniac here . . .
He sure is! $100,000 is a ridiculously high price to pay to save a member of a "Minority Group!" It's not like he was gonna kill "WASPS"!
He's actually holding the city of San Francisco for ransom! Should we play his game?
No! Let's offer him $50,000 and ask him to terrorize Des Moines!
What a dilemma we're in! We've got a madman loose in our town!
If you think HE's a madman, wait until you've seen who we've assigned to the case!
Gentlemen . . . meet Detective Lieutenant DIRTY LARRY . . .
Dear City of San Francisco,
I have killed one person. I will enjoy killing one additional person each day if you do not pay me $100,000.
If you do not come up with the loot, I will kill either (A) a Catholic Priest, (B) a Negro, (C) a Bulgarian Dentist, (D) an Orthodox Jewish Ski Instructor, or (E) all of the above.
Libra
P.S. Just for laughs, I may wound a Latvian dwarf.
MAYOR
MORT DRUCKER

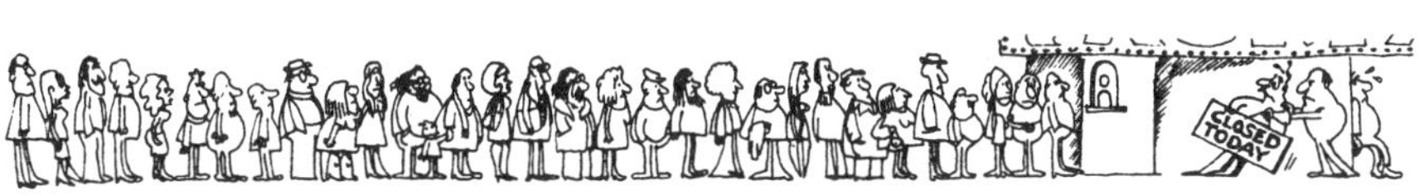
CLOSED TODAY

# Y LARRY

ARTIST:
MORT DRUCKER

WRITER:
ARNIE KOGEN

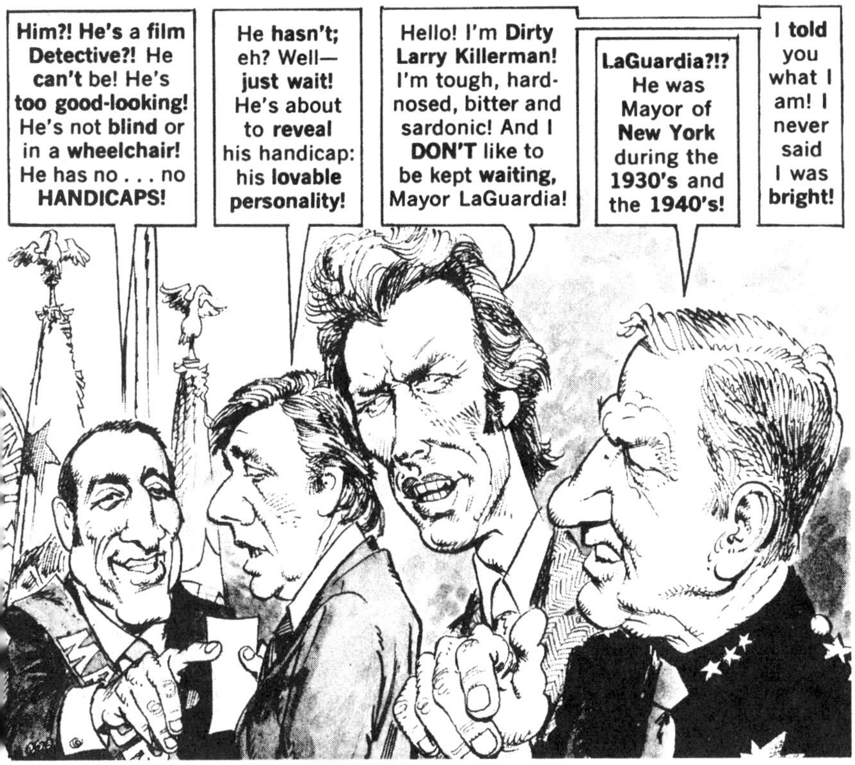
Him?! He's a film Detective?! He can't be! He's too good-looking! He's not blind or in a wheelchair! He has no . . . no HANDICAPS!
He hasn't; eh? Well— just wait! He's about to reveal his handicap: his lovable personality!
Hello! I'm Dirty Larry Killerman! I'm tough, hard-nosed, bitter and sardonic! And I DON'T like to be kept waiting, Mayor LaGuardia!
LaGuardia?!? He was Mayor of New York during the 1930's and the 1940's!
I told you what I am! I never said I was bright!

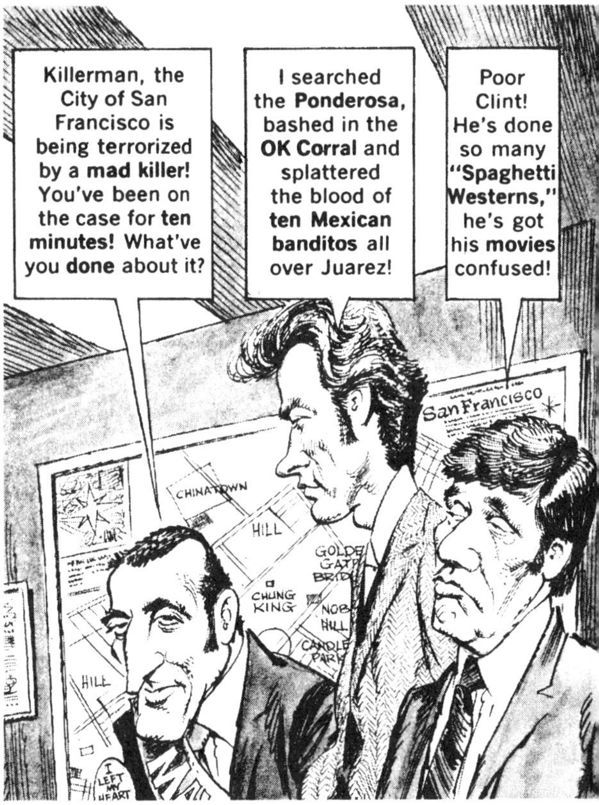
Killerman, the City of San Francisco is being terrorized by a mad killer! You've been on the case for ten minutes! What've you done about it?
I searched the Ponderosa, bashed in the OK Corral and splattered the blood of ten Mexican banditos all over Juarez!
Poor Clint! He's done so many "Spaghetti Westerns," he's got his movies confused!
San Francisco
CHINATOWN
HILL
CHUNG KING

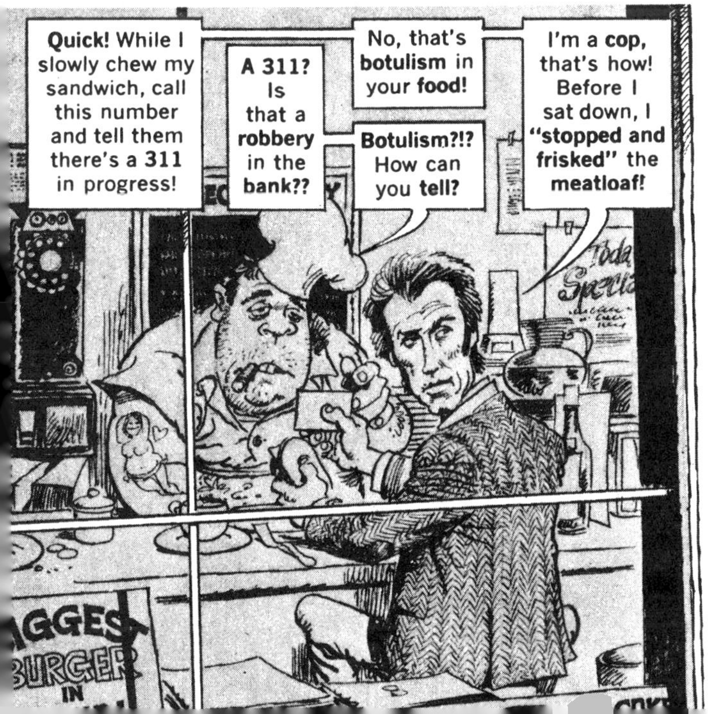
Quick! While I slowly chew my sandwich, call this number and tell them there's a 311 in progress!
A 311? Is that a robbery in the bank??
No, that's botulism in your food!
Botulism?!? How can you tell?
I'm a cop, that's how! Before I sat down, I "stopped and frisked" the meatloaf!

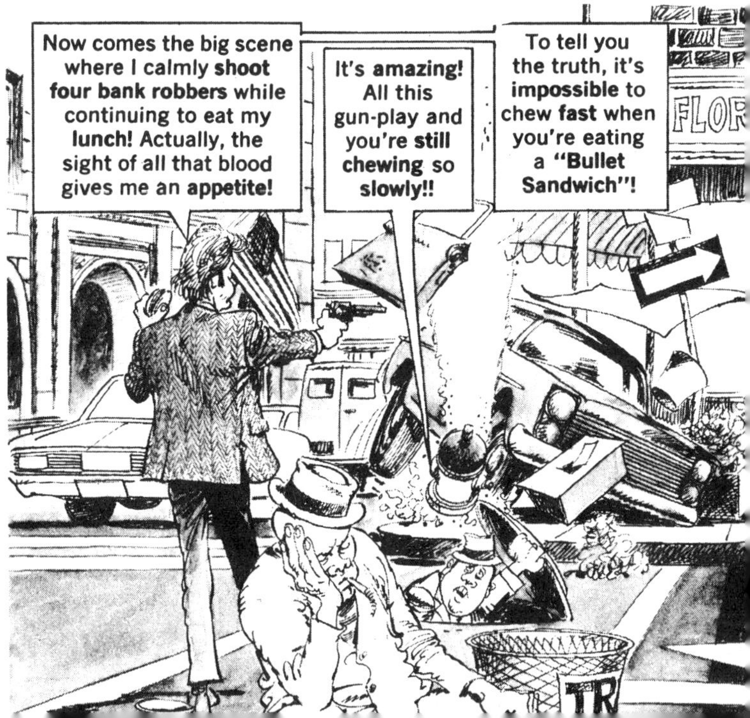
Now comes the big scene where I calmly shoot four bank robbers while continuing to eat my lunch! Actually, the sight of all that blood gives me an appetite!
It's amazing! All this gun-play and you're still chewing so slowly!!
To tell you the truth, it's impossible to chew fast when you're eating a "Bullet Sandwich"!

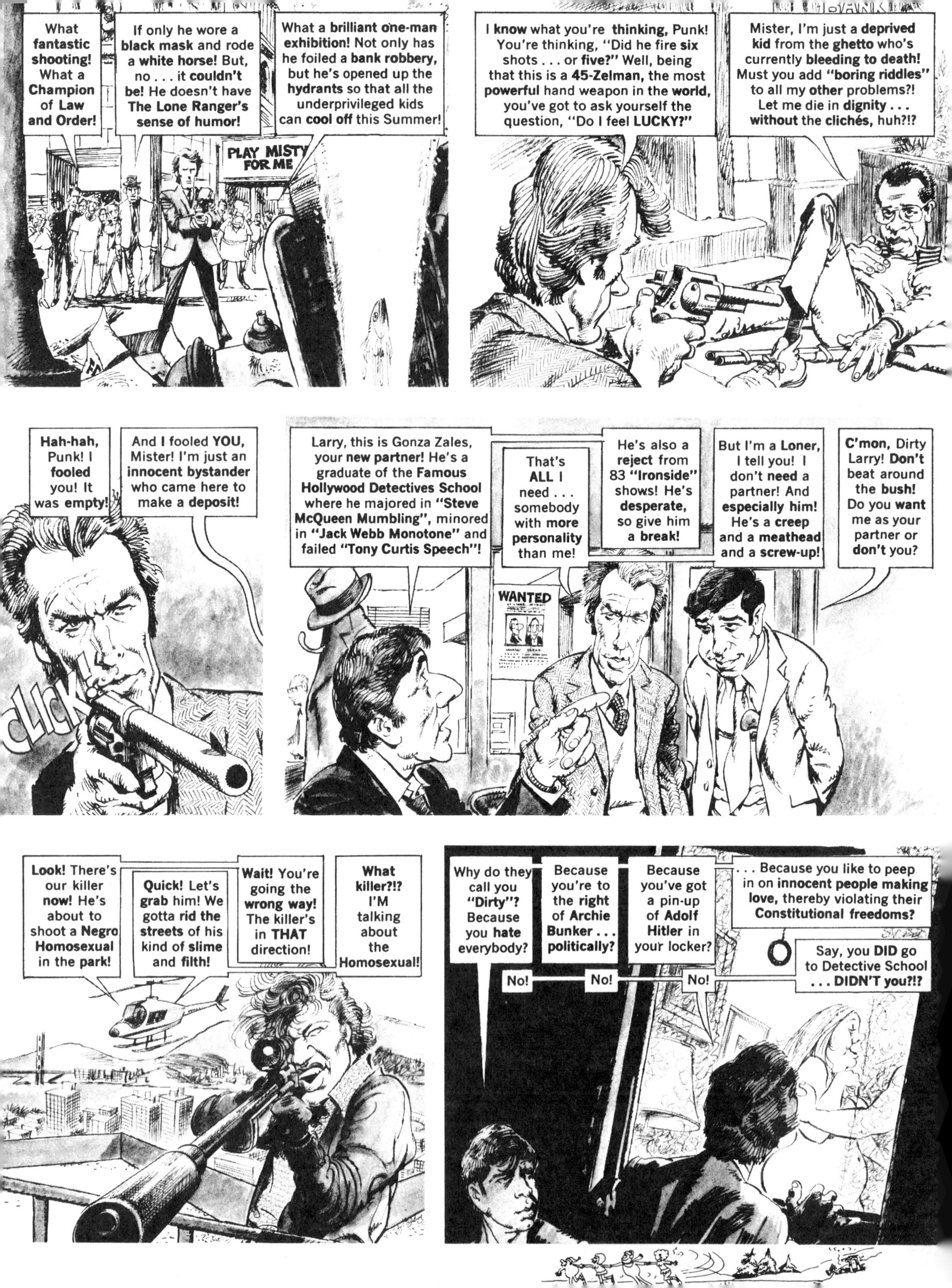

What fantastic shooting! What a Champion of Law and Order!
If only he wore a black mask and rode a white horse! But, no . . . it couldn't be! He doesn't have The Lone Ranger's sense of humor!
What a brilliant one-man exhibition! Not only has he foiled a bank robbery, but he's opened up the hydrants so that all the underprivileged kids can cool off this Summer!
PLAY MISTY FOR ME
I know what you're thinking, Punk! You're thinking, "Did he fire six shots . . . or five?" Well, being that this is a 45-Zelman, the most powerful hand weapon in the world, you've got to ask yourself the question, "Do I feel LUCKY?"
Mister, I'm just a deprived kid from the ghetto who's currently bleeding to death! Must you add "boring riddles" to all my other problems?! Let me die in dignity . . . without the clichés, huh?!?
Hah-hah, Punk! I fooled you! It was empty!
And I fooled YOU, Mister! I'm just an innocent bystander who came here to make a deposit!
CLICK!
Larry, this is Gonza Zales, your new partner! He's a graduate of the Famous Hollywood Detectives School where he majored in "Steve McQueen Mumbling", minored in "Jack Webb Monotone" and failed "Tony Curtis Speech"!
That's ALL I need . . . somebody with more personality than me!
He's also a reject from 83 "Ironside" shows! He's desperate, so give him a break!
But I'm a Loner, I tell you! I don't need a partner! And especially him! He's a creep and a meathead and a screw-up!
C'mon, Dirty Larry! Don't beat around the bush! Do you want me as your partner or don't you?
WANTED
Look! There's our killer now! He's about to shoot a Negro Homosexual in the park!
Quick! Let's grab him! We gotta rid the streets of his kind of slime and filth!
Wait! You're going the wrong way! The killer's in THAT direction!
What killer?!? I'M talking about the Homosexual!
Why do they call you "Dirty"? Because you hate everybody?
No!
Because you're to the right of Archie Bunker . . . politically?
No!
Because you've got a pin-up of Adolf Hitler in your locker?
No!
. . . Because you like to peep in on innocent people making love, thereby violating their Constitutional freedoms?
Say, you DID go to Detective School . . . DIDN'T you?!?

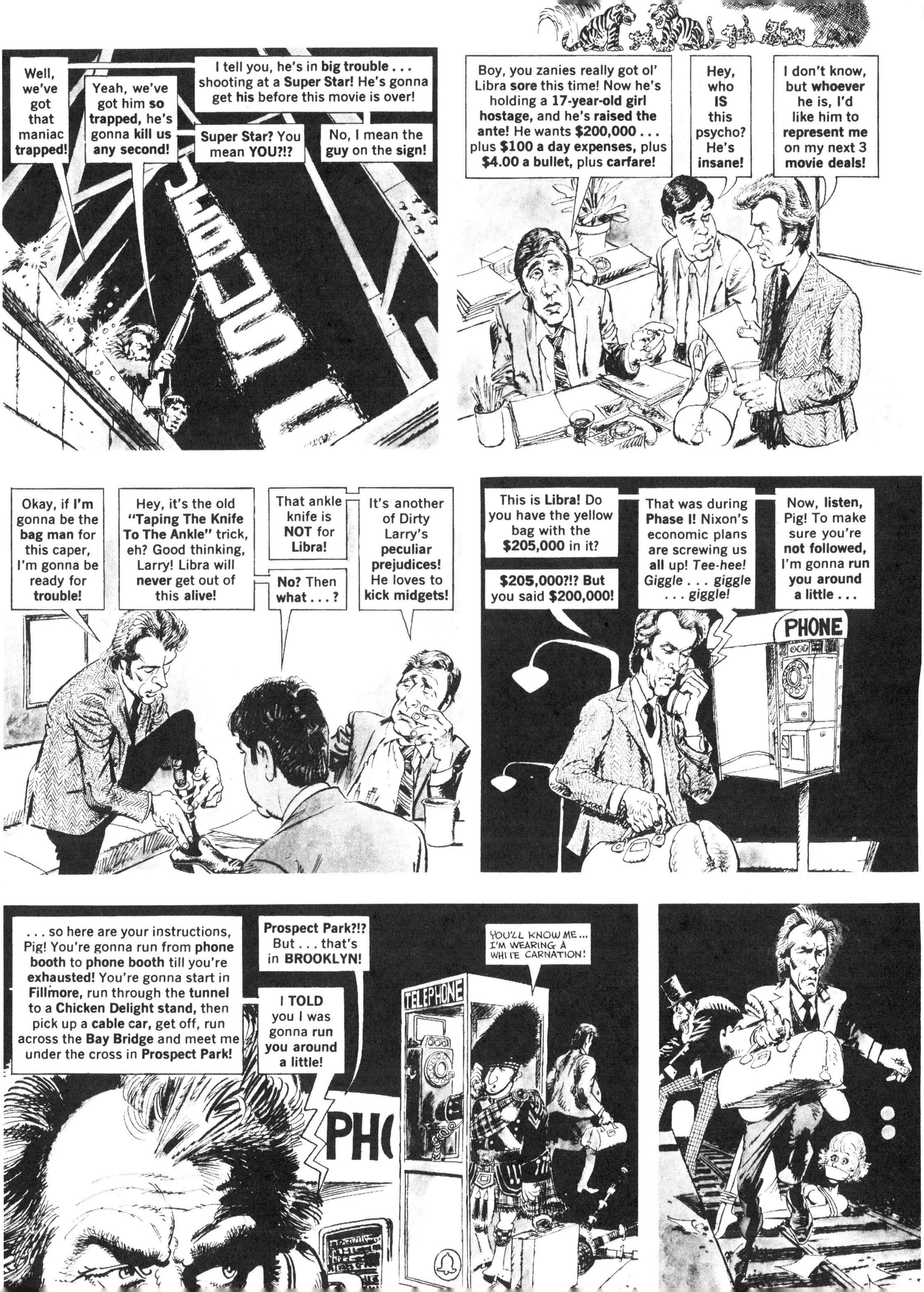

Well, we've got that maniac trapped!
Yeah, we've got him so trapped, he's gonna kill us any second!
I tell you, he's in big trouble . . . shooting at a Super Star! He's gonna get his before this movie is over!
Super Star? You mean YOU?!?
No, I mean the guy on the sign!
Boy, you zanies really got ol' Libra sore this time! Now he's holding a 17-year-old girl hostage, and he's raised the ante! He wants $200,000 . . . plus $100 a day expenses, plus $4.00 a bullet, plus carfare!
Hey, who IS this psycho? He's insane!
I don't know, but whoever he is, I'd like him to represent me on my next 3 movie deals!
Okay, if I'm gonna be the bag man for this caper, I'm gonna be ready for trouble!
Hey, it's the old "Taping The Knife To The Ankle" trick, eh? Good thinking, Larry! Libra will never get out of this alive!
That ankle knife is NOT for Libra!
No? Then what . . . ?
It's another of Dirty Larry's peculiar prejudices! He loves to kick midgets!
This is Libra! Do you have the yellow bag with the $205,000 in it?
$205,000?!? But you said $200,000!
That was during Phase I! Nixon's economic plans are screwing us all up! Tee-hee! Giggle . . . giggle . . . giggle!
Now, listen, Pig! To make sure you're not followed, I'm gonna run you around a little . . .
PHONE
. . . so here are your instructions, Pig! You're gonna run from phone booth to phone booth till you're exhausted! You're gonna start in Fillmore, run through the tunnel to a Chicken Delight stand, then pick up a cable car, get off, run across the Bay Bridge and meet me under the cross in Prospect Park!
Prospect Park?!? But . . . that's in BROOKLYN!
I TOLD you I was gonna run you around a little!
PHO
TELEPHONE
YOU'LL KNOW ME... I'M WEARING A WHITE CARNATION!

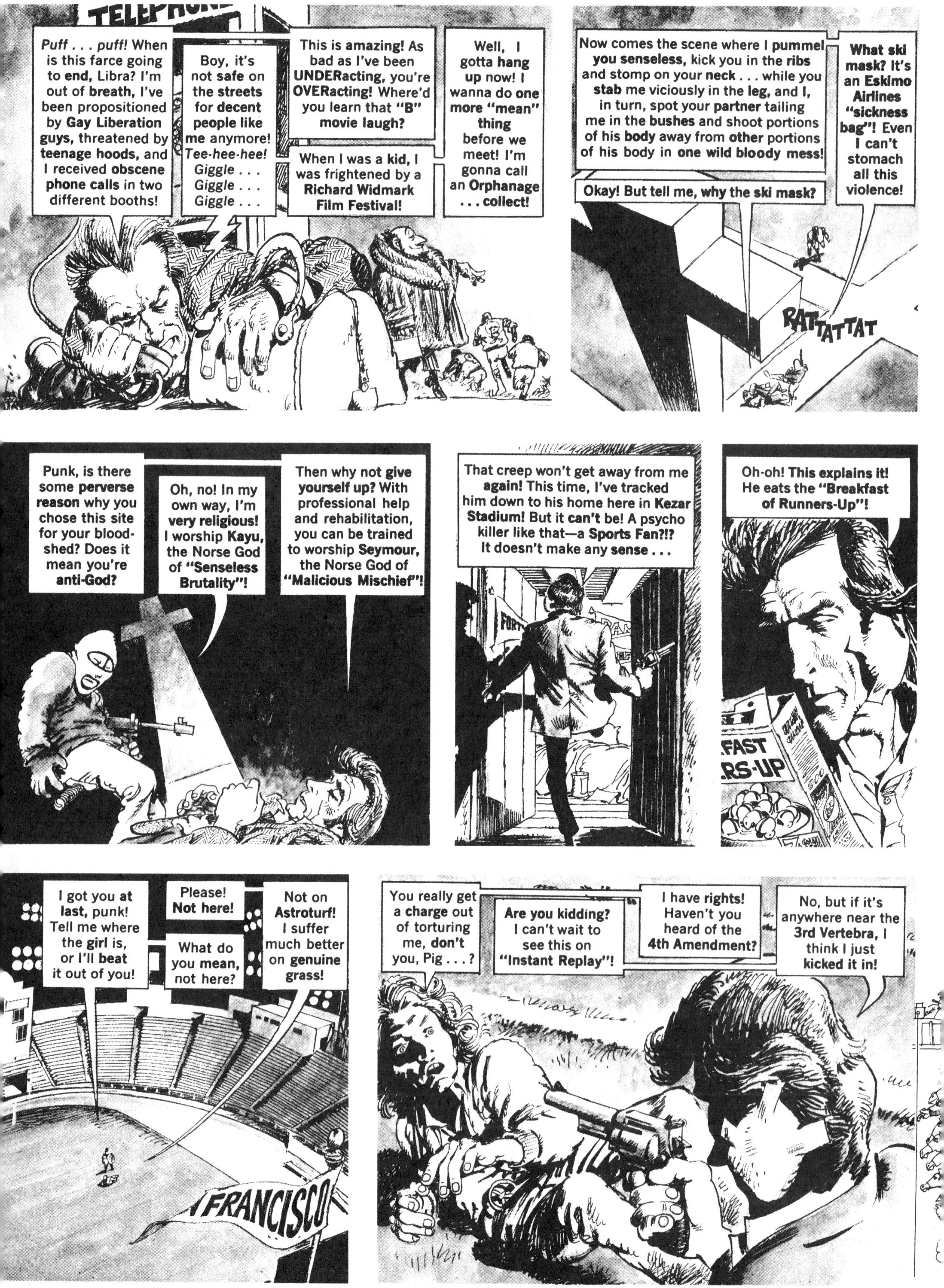

TELEPHONE
*Puff . . . puff!* When is this farce going to **end,** Libra? I'm out of **breath,** I've been propositioned by **Gay Liberation guys,** threatened by **teenage hoods,** and I received **obscene phone calls** in two different booths!
Boy, it's not **safe** on the **streets** for **decent people like me** anymore! *Tee-hee-hee!* Giggle . . . Giggle . . . Giggle . . .
This is **amazing!** As bad as I've been **UNDERacting,** you're **OVERacting!** Where'd you learn that **"B" movie laugh?**
When I was a **kid,** I was frightened by a **Richard Widmark Film Festival!**
Well, I gotta **hang up** now! I wanna do **one more "mean" thing** before we meet! I'm gonna call an **Orphanage . . . collect!**
Now comes the scene where I **pummel you senseless,** kick you in the **ribs** and stomp on your **neck** . . . while you **stab** me viciously in the **leg,** and I, in turn, spot your **partner** tailing me in the **bushes** and shoot portions of his **body** away from **other** portions of his body in **one wild bloody mess!**
**Okay! But tell me, why the ski mask?**
**What ski mask? It's an Eskimo Airlines "sickness bag"!** Even I can't stomach all this violence!
RATTATTAT
Punk, is there some **perverse reason** why you chose this site for your blood-shed? Does it mean you're **anti-God?**
Oh, no! In my own way, I'm **very religious!** I worship **Kayu,** the Norse God of **"Senseless Brutality"!**
Then why not **give yourself up?** With professional help and rehabilitation, you can be trained to worship **Seymour,** the Norse God of **"Malicious Mischief"!**
That creep won't get away from me **again!** This time, I've tracked him down to his home here in **Kezar Stadium!** But it **can't** be! A psycho killer like that—a **Sports Fan?!?** It doesn't make any **sense . . .**
Oh-oh! **This explains it!** He eats the **"Breakfast of Runners-Up"!**
FAST
RS-UP
I got you **at last,** punk! Tell me where the **girl** is, or I'll **beat** it out of you!
Please! **Not here!**
What do you **mean,** not here?
Not on **Astroturf!** I suffer much better on **genuine grass!**
FRANCISCO
You really get a **charge** out of torturing me, **don't** you, Pig . . . ?
**Are you kidding?** I can't wait to see this on **"Instant Replay"!**
I have **rights!** Haven't you heard of the **4th Amendment?**
No, but if it's anywhere near the **3rd Vertebra,** I think I just **kicked it in!**

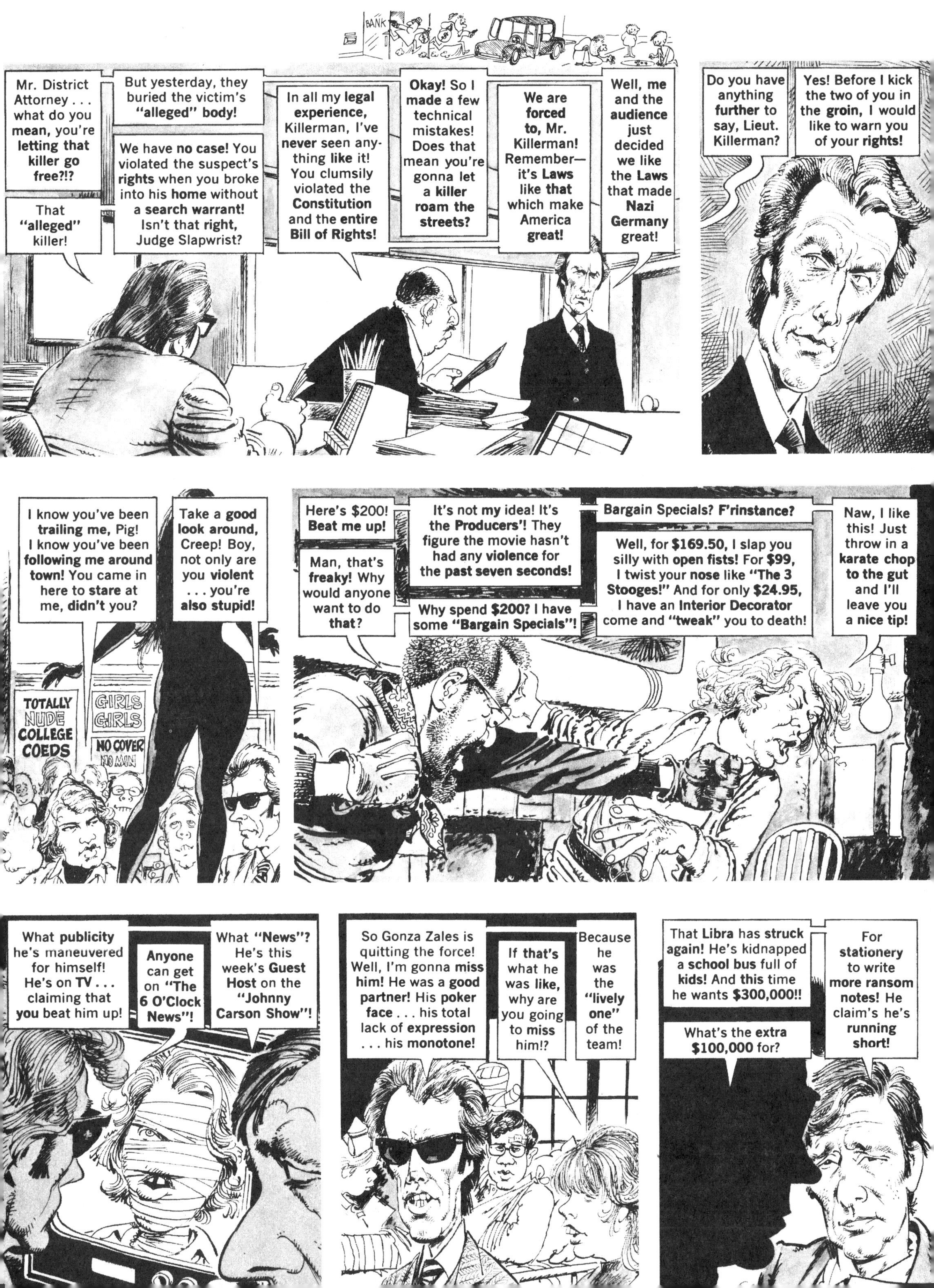
BANK
Mr. District Attorney . . . what do you mean, you're letting that killer go free?!?
But yesterday, they buried the victim's "alleged" body!
That "alleged" killer!
We have no case! You violated the suspect's rights when you broke into his home without a search warrant! Isn't that right, Judge Slapwrist?
In all my legal experience, Killerman, I've never seen anything like it! You clumsily violated the Constitution and the entire Bill of Rights!
Okay! So I made a few technical mistakes! Does that mean you're gonna let a killer roam the streets?
We are forced to, Mr. Killerman! Remember—it's Laws like that which make America great!
Well, me and the audience just decided we like the Laws that made Nazi Germany great!
Do you have anything further to say, Lieut. Killerman?
Yes! Before I kick the two of you in the groin, I would like to warn you of your rights!
I know you've been trailing me, Pig! I know you've been following me around town! You came in here to stare at me, didn't you?
Take a good look around, Creep! Boy, not only are you violent . . . you're also stupid!
TOTALLY NUDE COLLEGE COEDS
GIRLS GIRLS
NO COVER NO MIN
Here's $200! Beat me up!
Man, that's freaky! Why would anyone want to do that?
It's not my idea! It's the Producers'! They figure the movie hasn't had any violence for the past seven seconds!
Why spend $200? I have some "Bargain Specials"!
Bargain Specials? F'rinstance?
Well, for $169.50, I slap you silly with open fists! For $99, I twist your nose like "The 3 Stooges!" And for only $24.95, I have an Interior Decorator come and "tweak" you to death!
Naw, I like this! Just throw in a karate chop to the gut and I'll leave you a nice tip!
What publicity he's maneuvered for himself! He's on TV . . . claiming that you beat him up!
Anyone can get on "The 6 O'Clock News"!
What "News"? He's this week's Guest Host on the "Johnny Carson Show"!
So Gonza Zales is quitting the force! Well, I'm gonna miss him! He was a good partner! His poker face . . . his total lack of expression . . . his monotone!
If that's what he was like, why are you going to miss him!?
Because he was the "lively one" of the team!
That Libra has struck again! He's kidnapped a school bus full of kids! And this time he wants $300,000!!
What's the extra $100,000 for?
For stationery to write more ransom notes! He claim's he's running short!

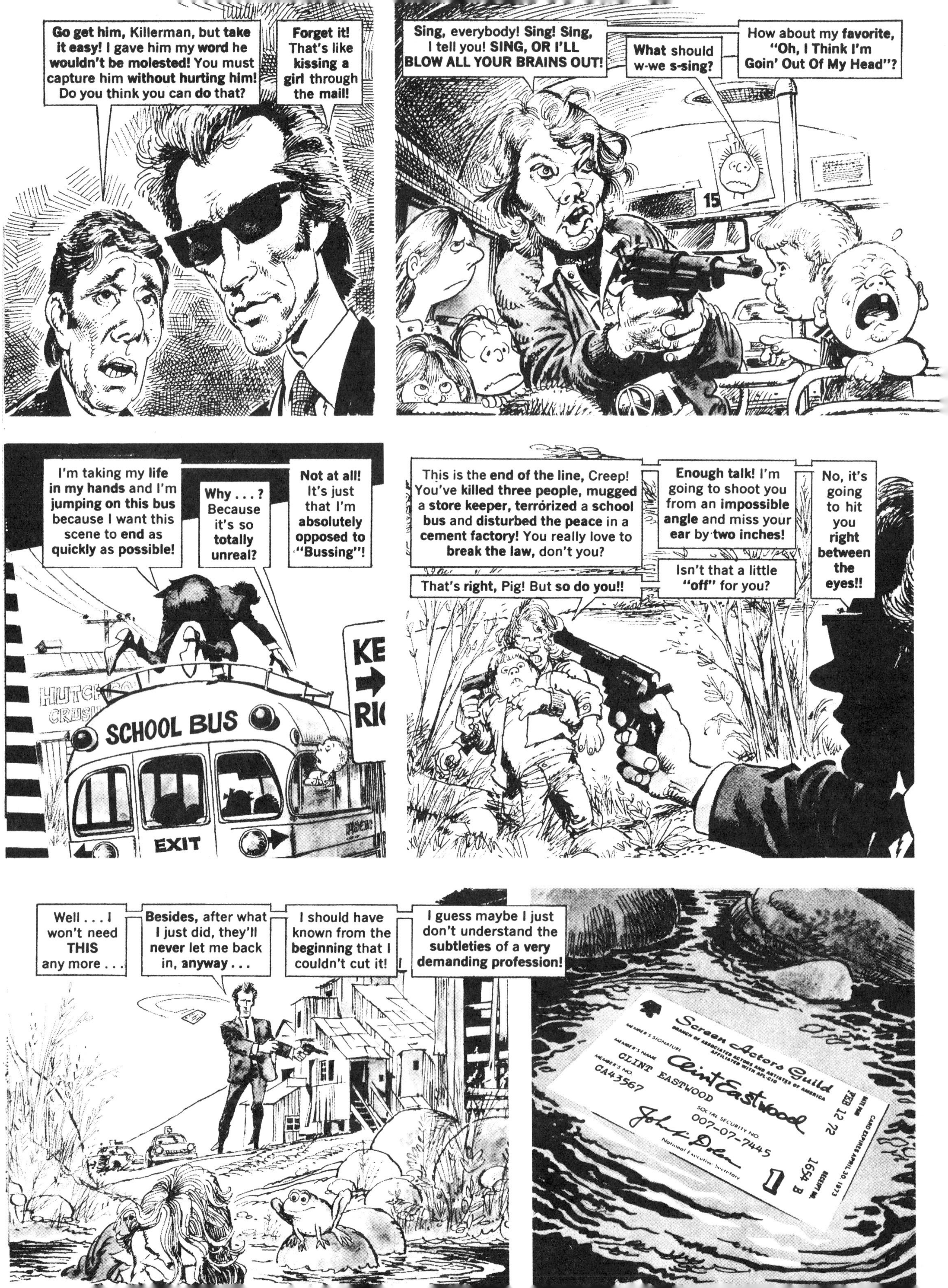

Go get him, Killerman, but take it easy! I gave him my word he wouldn't be molested! You must capture him without hurting him! Do you think you can do that?
Forget it! That's like kissing a girl through the mail!
Sing, everybody! Sing! Sing, I tell you! SING, OR I'LL BLOW ALL YOUR BRAINS OUT!
What should w-we s-sing?
How about my favorite, "Oh, I Think I'm Goin' Out Of My Head"?
15
I'm taking my life in my hands and I'm jumping on this bus because I want this scene to end as quickly as possible!
Why . . . ? Because it's so totally unreal?
Not at all! It's just that I'm absolutely opposed to "Bussing"!
SCHOOL BUS
EXIT
This is the end of the line, Creep! You've killed three people, mugged a store keeper, terrorized a school bus and disturbed the peace in a cement factory! You really love to break the law, don't you?
That's right, Pig! But so do you!!
Enough talk! I'm going to shoot you from an impossible angle and miss your ear by two inches!
Isn't that a little "off" for you?
No, it's going to hit you right between the eyes!!
Well . . . I won't need THIS any more . . .
Besides, after what I just did, they'll never let me back in, anyway . . .
I should have known from the beginning that I couldn't cut it!
I guess maybe I just don't understand the subtleties of a very demanding profession!
Screen Actors Guild
CLINT EASTWOOD
CA43567
SOCIAL SECURITY NO.
007-07-7445
National Executive Secretary
FEB 12 72

# Scenes We'd Like to See

**The Cops Close In**

ART—MORT DRUCKER

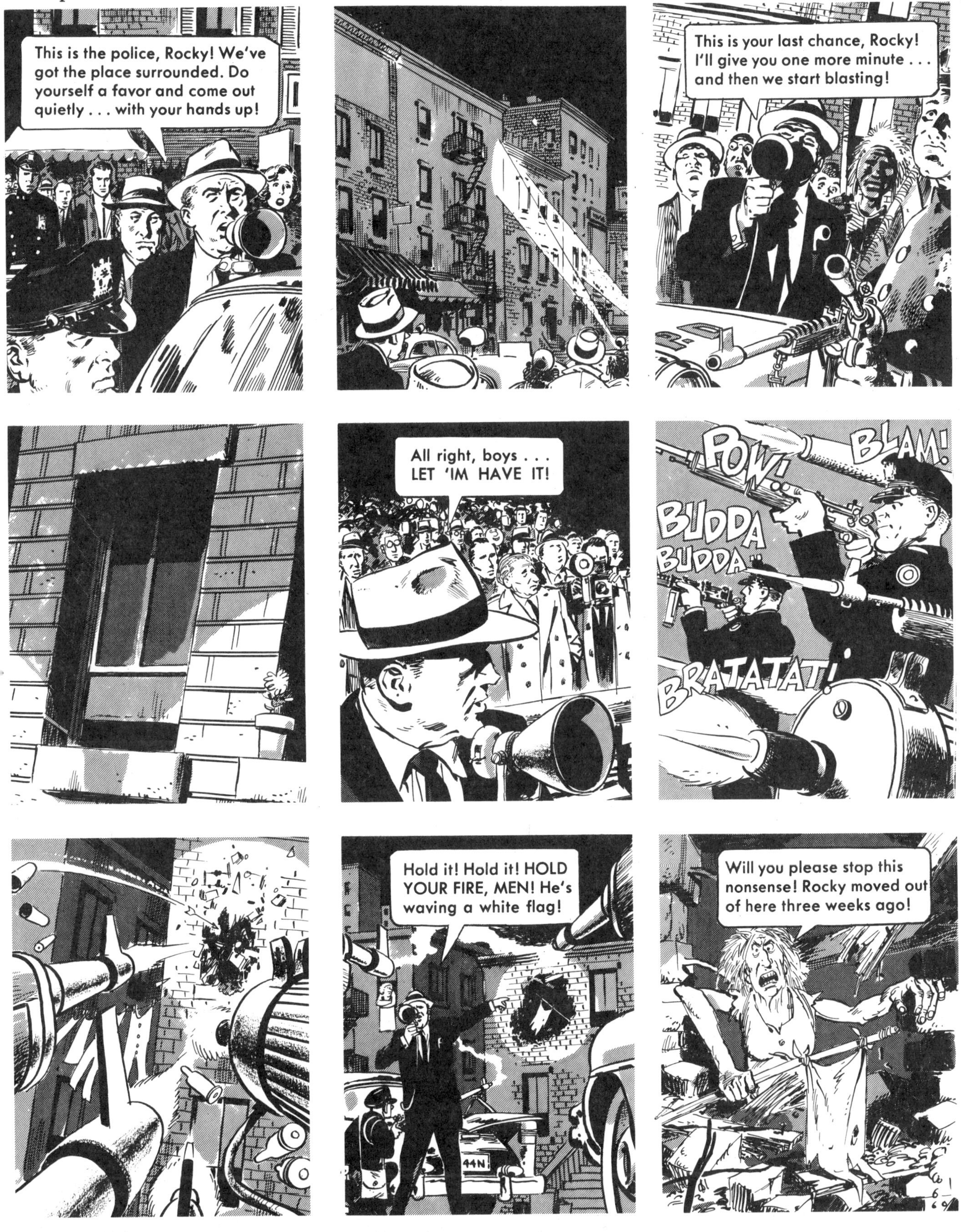

This is the police, Rocky! We've got the place surrounded. Do yourself a favor and come out quietly . . . with your hands up!
This is your last chance, Rocky! I'll give you one more minute . . . and then we start blasting!
All right, boys . . . LET 'IM HAVE IT!
POW!
BLAM!
BUDDA BUDDA
BRATATAT!
Hold it! Hold it! HOLD YOUR FIRE, MEN! He's waving a white flag!
44N
Will you please stop this nonsense! Rocky moved out of here three weeks ago!

**DE SADEST STORY EVER TOLD DEPT.**

Us moral people all hate violence, right? Let's hear it for "Anti-Violence"! *Yayyy!* Stanley Kubrick also hates violence, right? Let's hear it for Stanley Kubrick! *Yayyy!* And let's hear it for his new movie, which shows how horrible violence is! *Yay*— Uh— Hey, wait a minute! If Mr. Kubrick's new movie is so "Anti-Violence," how come it's jam-packed with the worst, sickening, most disgusting violence imaginable? Let's face it, Stanley, baby! Your movie is really . . .

# ACR

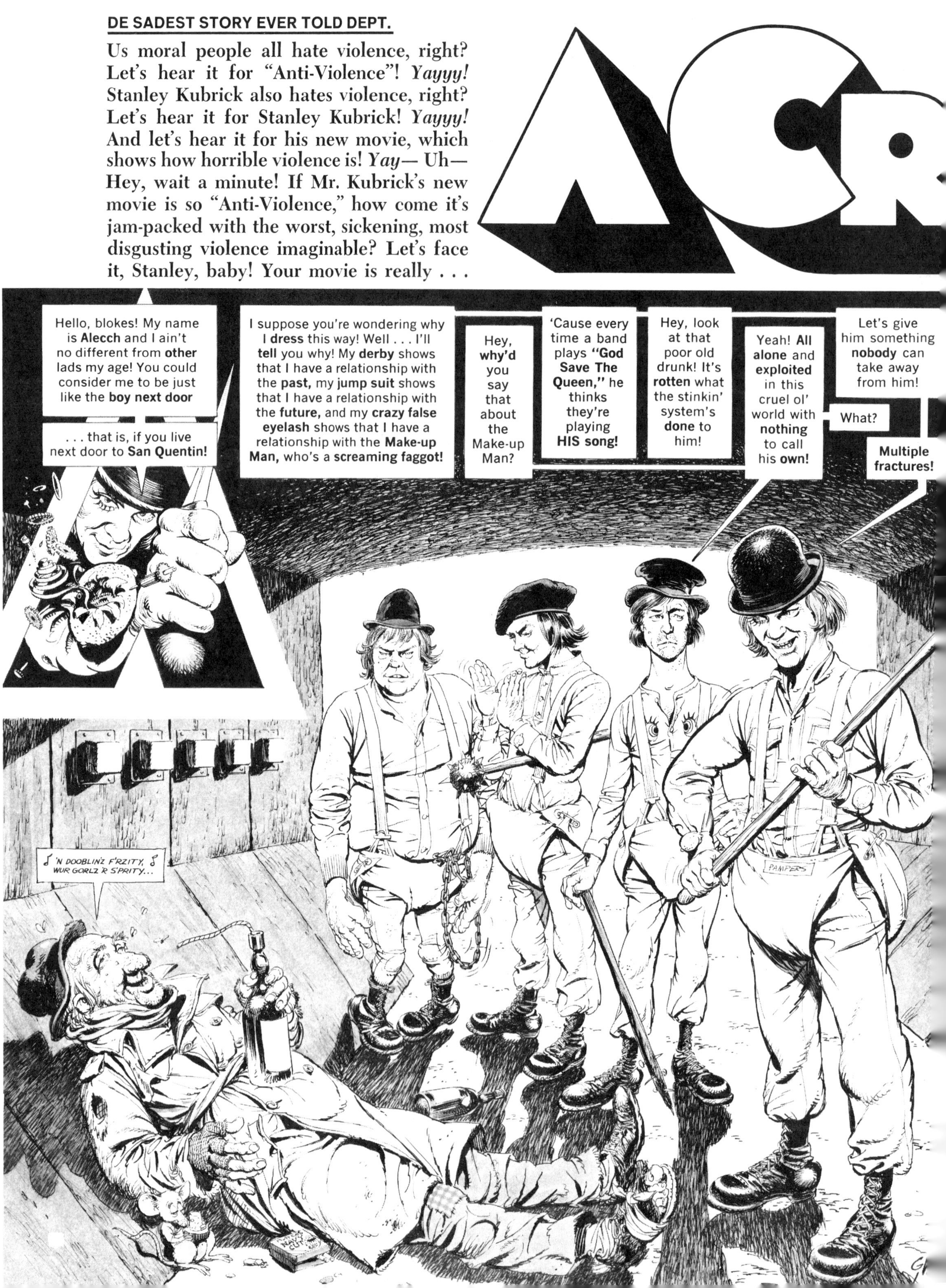

Hello, blokes! My name is **Alecch** and I ain't no different from **other** lads my age! You could consider me to be just like the **boy next door**
. . . that is, if you live next door to **San Quentin!**
I suppose you're wondering why I **dress** this way! Well . . . I'll **tell** you why! My **derby** shows that I have a relationship with the **past,** my **jump suit** shows that I have a relationship with the **future,** and my **crazy false eyelash** shows that I have a relationship with the **Make-up Man,** who's a **screaming faggot!**
Hey, **why'd** you say that about the Make-up Man?
'Cause every time a band plays **"God Save The Queen,"** he thinks they're playing **HIS song!**
Hey, look at that poor old drunk! It's **rotten** what the stinkin' system's **done** to him!
Yeah! **All alone** and **exploited** in this cruel ol' world with **nothing** to call his **own!**
Let's give him something **nobody** can take away from him!
What?
**Multiple fractures!**
'N DOOBLIN'Z F'RZITY, WUR GORLZ 'R S'PRITY...
PAMPERS

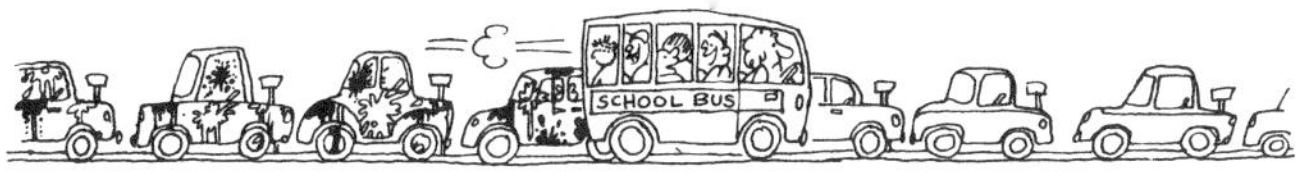

SCHOOL BUS


# OCKWORK LEMON

ARTIST: GEORGE WOODBRIDGE WRITER: STAN HART

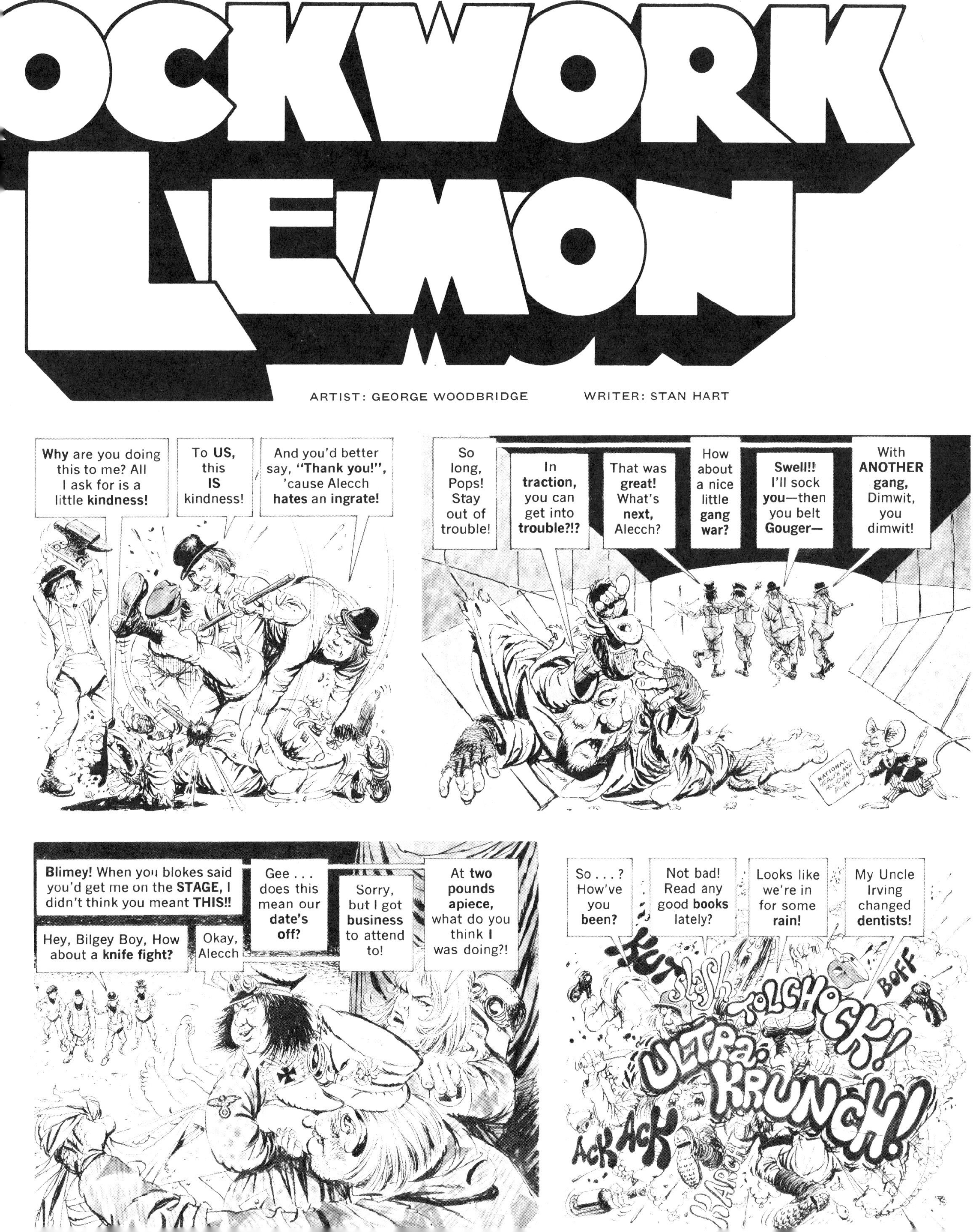

Why are you doing this to me? All I ask for is a little kindness!
To US, this IS kindness!
And you'd better say, "Thank you!", 'cause Alecch hates an ingrate!
So long, Pops! Stay out of trouble!
In traction, you can get into trouble?!?
That was great! What's next, Alecch?
How about a nice little gang war?
Swell!! I'll sock you—then you belt Gouger—
With ANOTHER gang, Dimwit, you dimwit!
NATIONAL HEALTH AND ACCIDENT PLAN
Blimey! When you blokes said you'd get me on the STAGE, I didn't think you meant THIS!!
Hey, Bilgey Boy, How about a knife fight?
Okay, Alecch
Gee . . . does this mean our date's off?
Sorry, but I got business to attend to!
At two pounds apiece, what do you think I was doing?!
So . . . ? How've you been?
Not bad! Read any good books lately?
Looks like we're in for some rain!
My Uncle Irving changed dentists!
TOLCHOCK!
BOFF
ULTRA-
KRUNCH!
ACK ACK

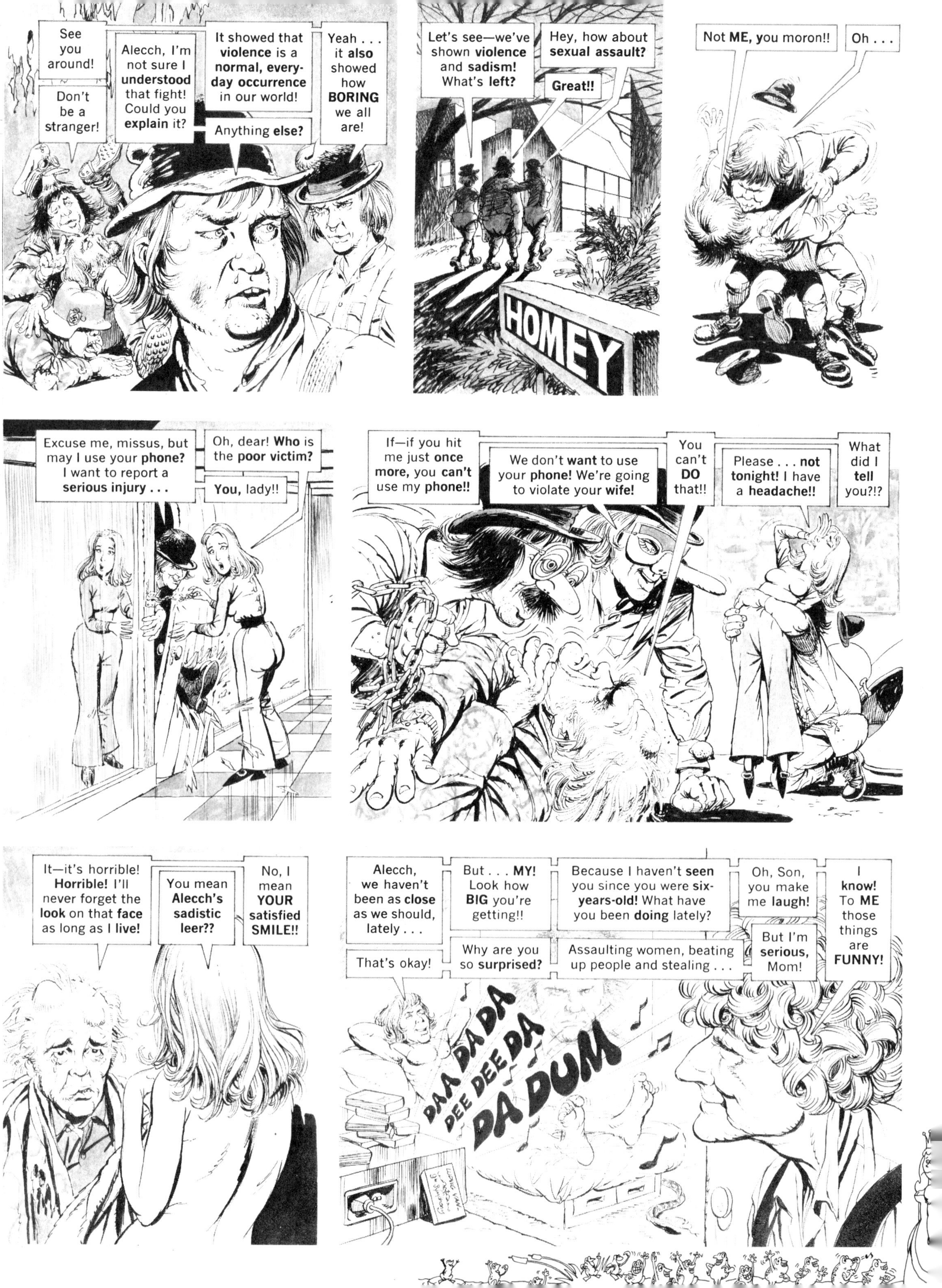
See you around!
Alecch, I'm not sure I understood that fight! Could you explain it?
It showed that violence is a normal, every-day occurrence in our world!
Yeah . . . it also showed how BORING we all are!
Don't be a stranger!
Anything else?
Let's see—we've shown violence and sadism! What's left?
Hey, how about sexual assault?
Great!!
HOMEY
Not ME, you moron!!
Oh . . .
Excuse me, missus, but may I use your phone? I want to report a serious injury . . .
Oh, dear! Who is the poor victim?
You, lady!!
If—if you hit me just once more, you can't use my phone!!
We don't want to use your phone! We're going to violate your wife!
You can't DO that!!
Please . . . not tonight! I have a headache!!
What did I tell you?!?
It—it's horrible! Horrible! I'll never forget the look on that face as long as I live!
You mean Alecch's sadistic leer??
No, I mean YOUR satisfied SMILE!!
Alecch, we haven't been as close as we should, lately . . .
That's okay!
But . . . MY! Look how BIG you're getting!!
Why are you so surprised?
Because I haven't seen you since you were six-years-old! What have you been doing lately?
Assaulting women, beating up people and stealing . . .
Oh, Son, you make me laugh!
But I'm serious, Mom!
I know! To ME those things are FUNNY!
DA DA DA DEE DEE DA DA DUM

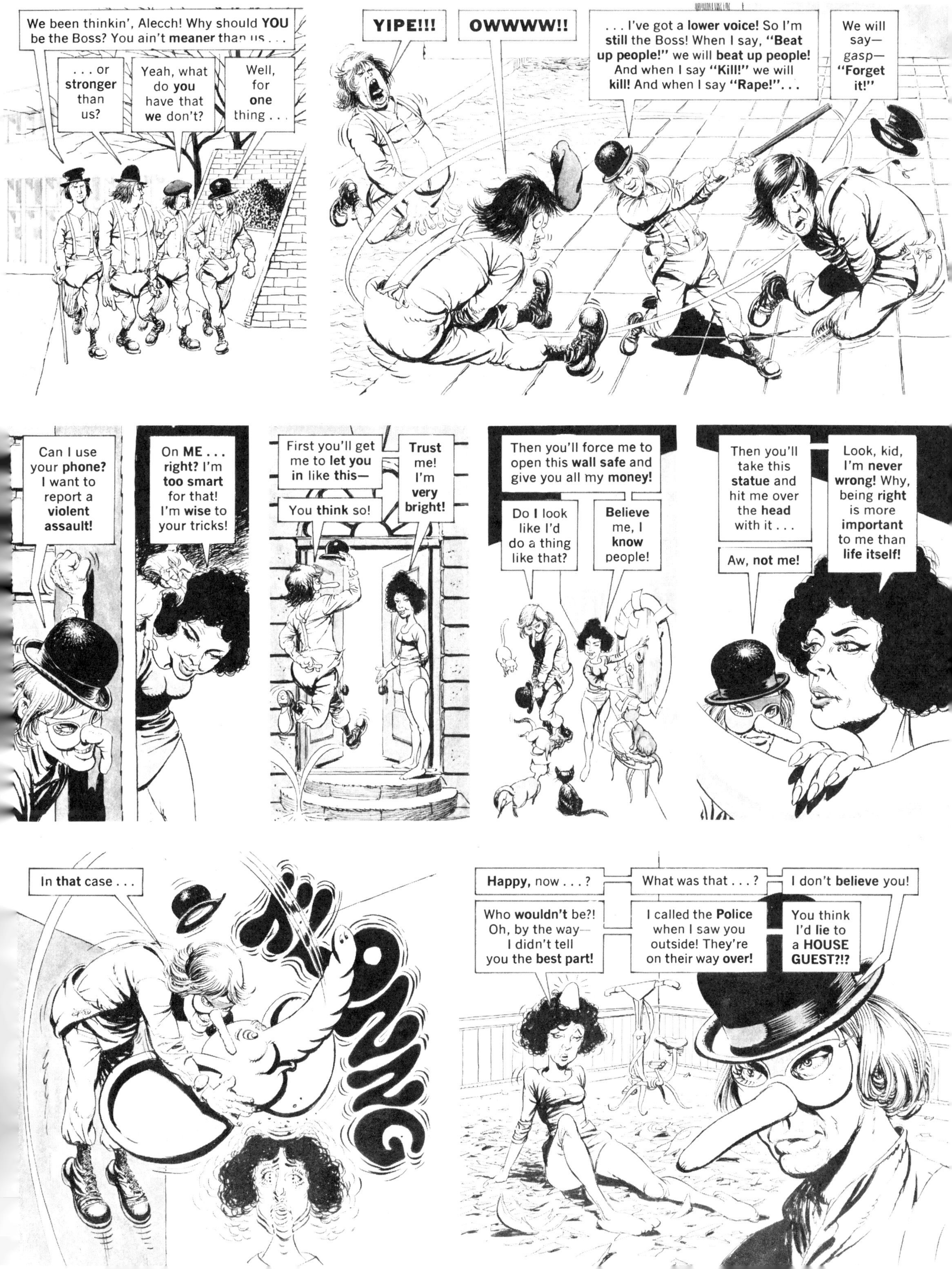
We been thinkin', Alecch! Why should YOU be the Boss? You ain't meaner than us . . .
. . . or stronger than us?
Yeah, what do you have that we don't?
Well, for one thing . . .
YIPE!!!
OWWWW!!
. . . I've got a lower voice! So I'm still the Boss! When I say, "Beat up people!" we will beat up people! And when I say "Kill!" we will kill! And when I say "Rape!". . .
We will say—gasp—"Forget it!"
Can I use your phone? I want to report a violent assault!
On ME . . . right? I'm too smart for that! I'm wise to your tricks!
First you'll get me to let you in like this—
You think so!
Trust me! I'm very bright!
Then you'll force me to open this wall safe and give you all my money!
Do I look like I'd do a thing like that?
Believe me, I know people!
Then you'll take this statue and hit me over the head with it . . .
Aw, not me!
Look, kid, I'm never wrong! Why, being right is more important to me than life itself!
In that case . . .
Happy, now . . . ?
Who wouldn't be?! Oh, by the way—I didn't tell you the best part!
What was that . . . ?
I called the Police when I saw you outside! They're on their way over!
I don't believe you!
You think I'd lie to a HOUSE GUEST?!?

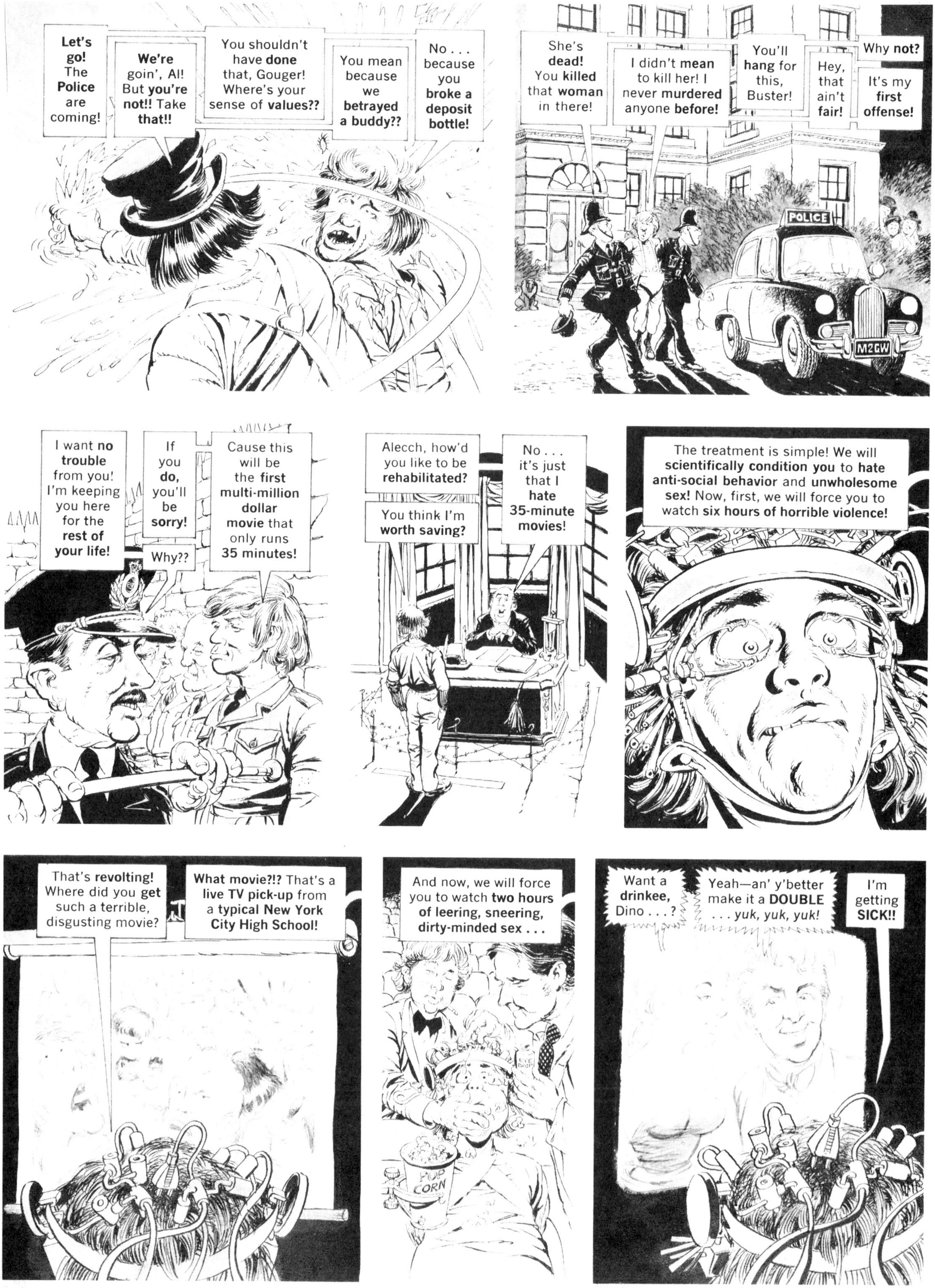
Let's go! The Police are coming!
We're goin', Al! But you're not!! Take that!!
You shouldn't have done that, Gouger! Where's your sense of values??
You mean because we betrayed a buddy??
No . . . because you broke a deposit bottle!
She's dead! You killed that woman in there!
I didn't mean to kill her! I never murdered anyone before!
You'll hang for this, Buster!
Hey, that ain't fair!
Why not?
It's my first offense!
POLICE
M2GW
I want no trouble from you! I'm keeping you here for the rest of your life!
If you do, you'll be sorry!
Why??
Cause this will be the first multi-million dollar movie that only runs 35 minutes!
Alecch, how'd you like to be rehabilitated?
You think I'm worth saving?
No . . . it's just that I hate 35-minute movies!
The treatment is simple! We will scientifically condition you to hate anti-social behavior and unwholesome sex! Now, first, we will force you to watch six hours of horrible violence!
That's revolting! Where did you get such a terrible, disgusting movie?
What movie?!? That's a live TV pick-up from a typical New York City High School!
And now, we will force you to watch two hours of leering, sneering, dirty-minded sex . . .
POP CORN
Want a drinkee, Dino . . . ?
Yeah—an' y'better make it a DOUBLE . . . yuk, yuk, yuk!
I'm getting SICK!!

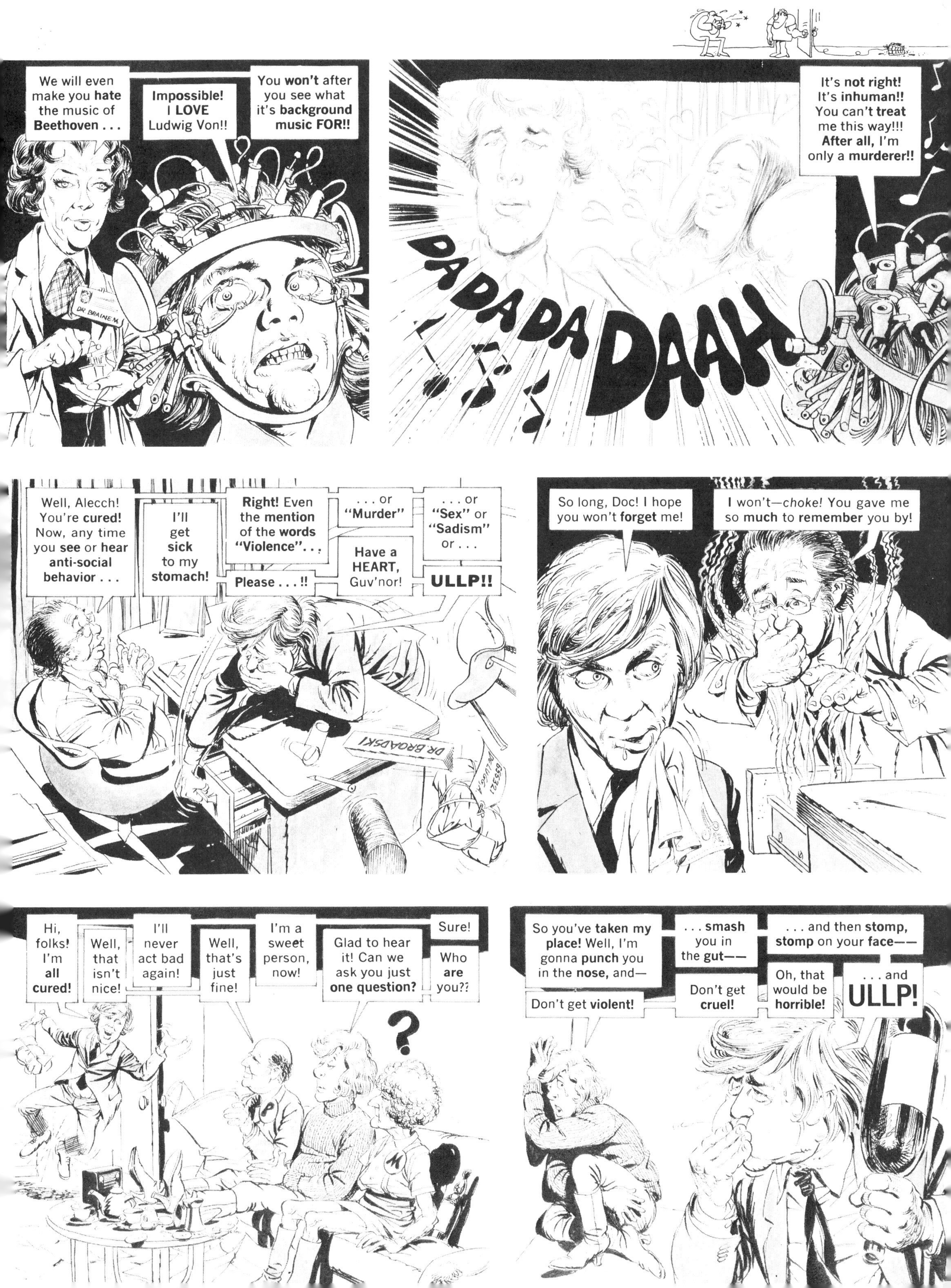

We will even make you **hate** the music of **Beethoven . . .**
**Impossible! I LOVE** Ludwig Von!!
You **won't** after you see what it's **background music FOR!!**
DR. BRAINE'M
It's **not right!** It's **inhuman!!** You can'**t treat** me this way!!! **After all,** I'm only a **murderer!!**
DA DA DA DAAH
Well, Alecch! You're **cured!** Now, any time you **see** or **hear anti-social behavior . . .**
I'll get **sick** to my **stomach!**
**Right!** Even the **mention** of the **words "Violence". . .**
Please . . . !!
. . . or **"Murder"**
Have a **HEART,** Guv'nor!
. . . or **"Sex"** or **"Sadism"** or . . .
**ULLP!!**
DR. BROADSKI
So long, Doc! I hope you won't **forget** me!
I won't—*choke!* You gave me so **much** to **remember** you by!
Hi, folks! I'm **all cured!**
Well, that isn't nice!
I'll never act bad again!
Well, that's just fine!
I'm a sweet person, now!
Glad to hear it! Can we ask you just **one question?**
Sure!
Who **are** you??
?
So you've **taken my place!** Well, I'm gonna **punch** you in the **nose,** and—
Don't get **violent!**
**. . . smash** you in the **gut——**
Don't get **cruel!**
. . . and then **stomp, stomp** on your **face——**
Oh, that would be **horrible!**
. . . and **ULLP!**

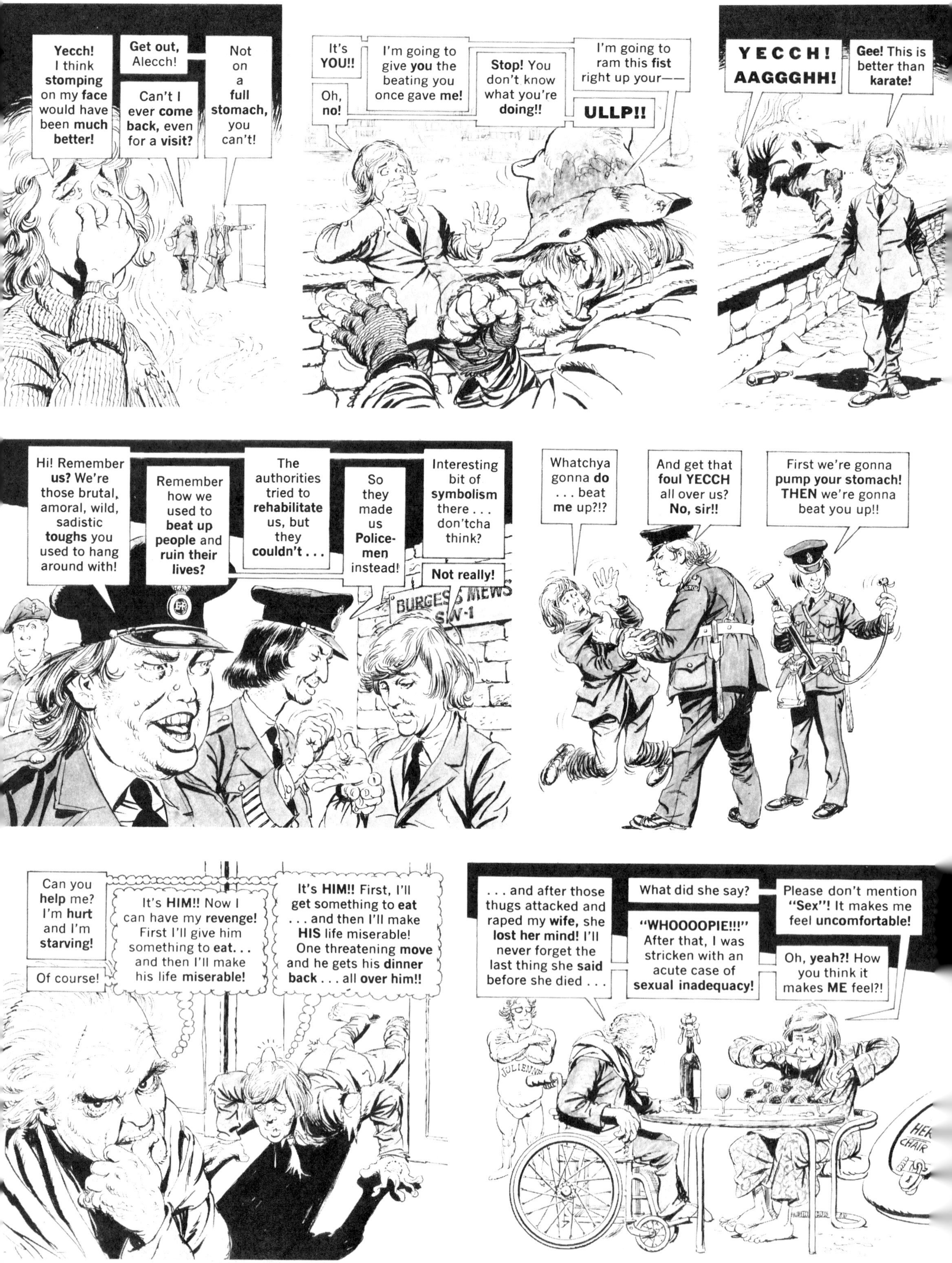

Yecch! I think stomping on my face would have been much better!
Get out, Alecch!
Can't I ever come back, even for a visit?
Not on a full stomach, you can't!
It's YOU!!
Oh, no!
I'm going to give you the beating you once gave me!
Stop! You don't know what you're doing!!
I'm going to ram this fist right up your——
ULLP!!
YECCH! AAGGGHH!
Gee! This is better than karate!
Hi! Remember us? We're those brutal, amoral, wild, sadistic toughs you used to hang around with!
Remember how we used to beat up people and ruin their lives?
The authorities tried to rehabilitate us, but they couldn't . . .
So they made us Policemen instead!
Interesting bit of symbolism there . . . don'tcha think?
Not really!
Whatchya gonna do . . . beat me up?!?
And get that foul YECCH all over us? No, sir!!
First we're gonna pump your stomach! THEN we're gonna beat you up!!
Can you help me? I'm hurt and I'm starving!
Of course!
It's HIM!! Now I can have my revenge! First I'll give him something to eat. . . and then I'll make his life miserable!
It's HIM!! First, I'll get something to eat . . . and then I'll make HIS life miserable! One threatening move and he gets his dinner back . . . all over him!!
. . . and after those thugs attacked and raped my wife, she lost her mind! I'll never forget the last thing she said before she died . . .
What did she say?
"WHOOOOPIE!!!" After that, I was stricken with an acute case of sexual inadequacy!
Please don't mention "Sex"! It makes me feel uncomfortable!
Oh, yeah?! How you think it makes ME feel?!

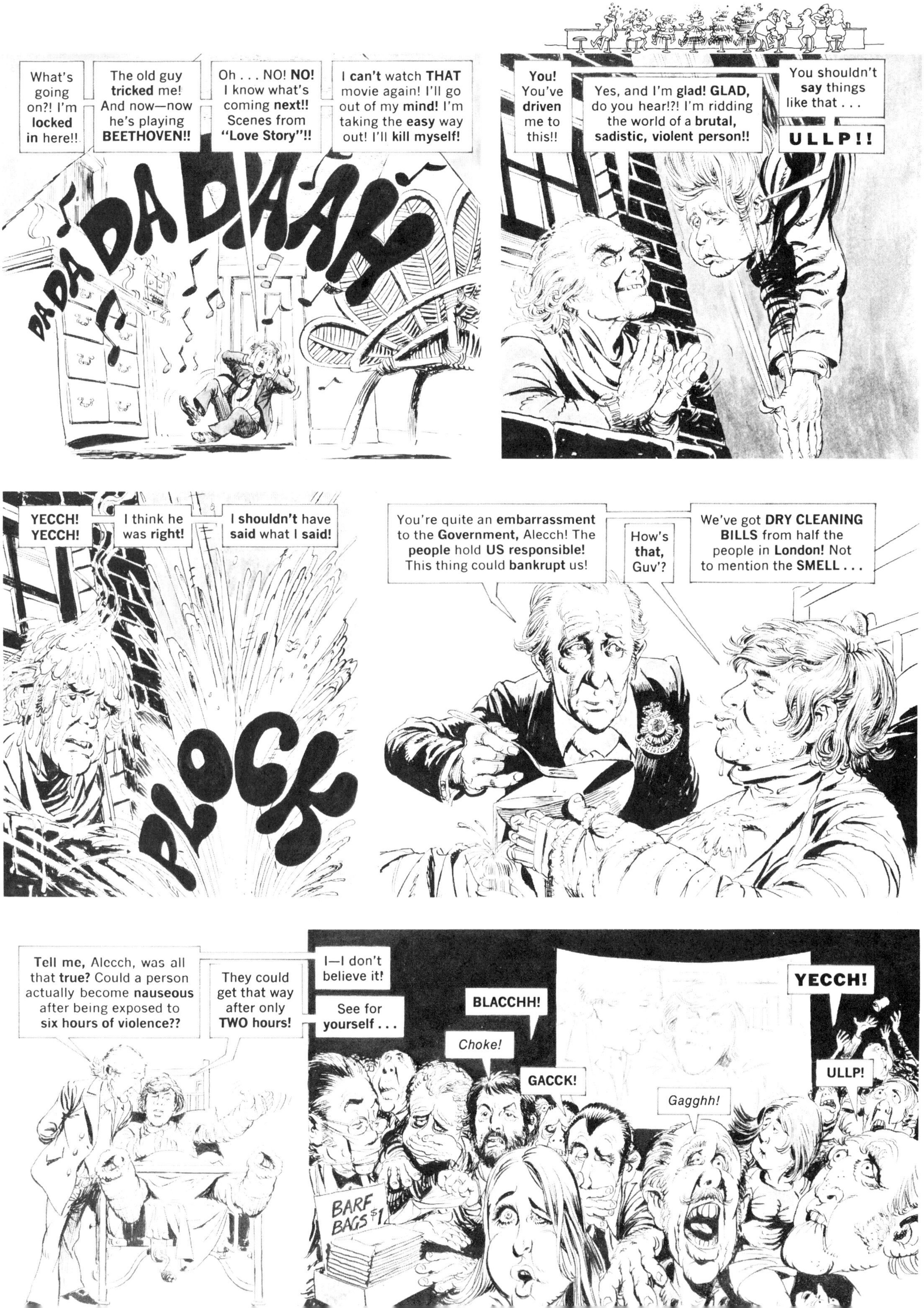
What's going on?! I'm **locked** in here!!
The old guy **tricked** me! And now—now he's playing **BEETHOVEN!!**
Oh . . . NO! **NO!** I know what's coming **next!!** Scenes from **"Love Story"!!**
I **can't** watch **THAT** movie again! I'll go out of my **mind!** I'm taking the **easy** way out! I'll **kill myself!**
DA DA DA DAAAH
**You!** You've **driven** me to this!!
Yes, and I'm **glad! GLAD,** do you hear!?! I'm ridding the world of a **brutal, sadistic, violent person!!**
You shouldn't **say** things like that . . .
**ULLP!!**
**YECCH! YECCH!**
I think he was **right!**
I **shouldn't** have **said** what I **said!**
PLOCK
You're quite an **embarrassment** to the **Government,** Alecch! The **people** hold **US responsible!** This thing could **bankrupt** us!
How's **that,** Guv'?
We've got **DRY CLEANING BILLS** from half the people in **London!** Not to mention the **SMELL . . .**
**Tell me,** Alecch, was all that **true?** Could a person actually become **nauseous** after being exposed to **six hours of violence??**
They could get that way after only **TWO hours!**
I—I don't believe it!
See for **yourself . . .**
**BLACCHH!**
*Choke!*
**GACCK!**
*Gagghh!*
**YECCH!**
**ULLP!**
BARF BAGS $1

**HOLLYWOOD DEPT.**

# Scenes We'd Like to See

## Driving The Golden Spike

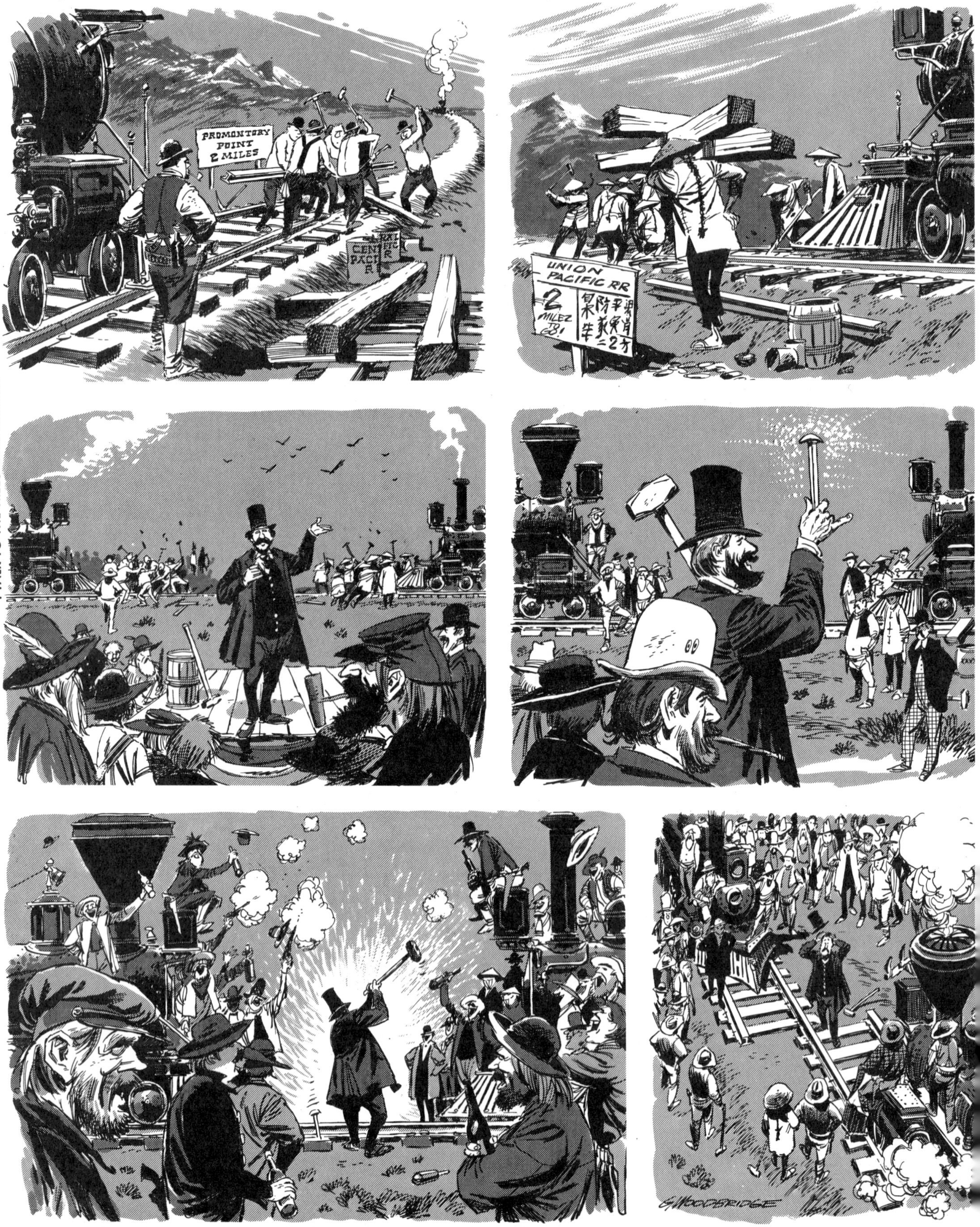

PROMONTORY POINT 2 MILES
UNION PACIFIC RR
2 MILEZ TO GO!
G. WOODBRIDGE


**I TALK TO THE TREES—Paul Winchell

ART—GEORGE WOODBRIDGE STORY BY EUGENE ST. JEAN

DIATRIBAL LEGEND DEPT.

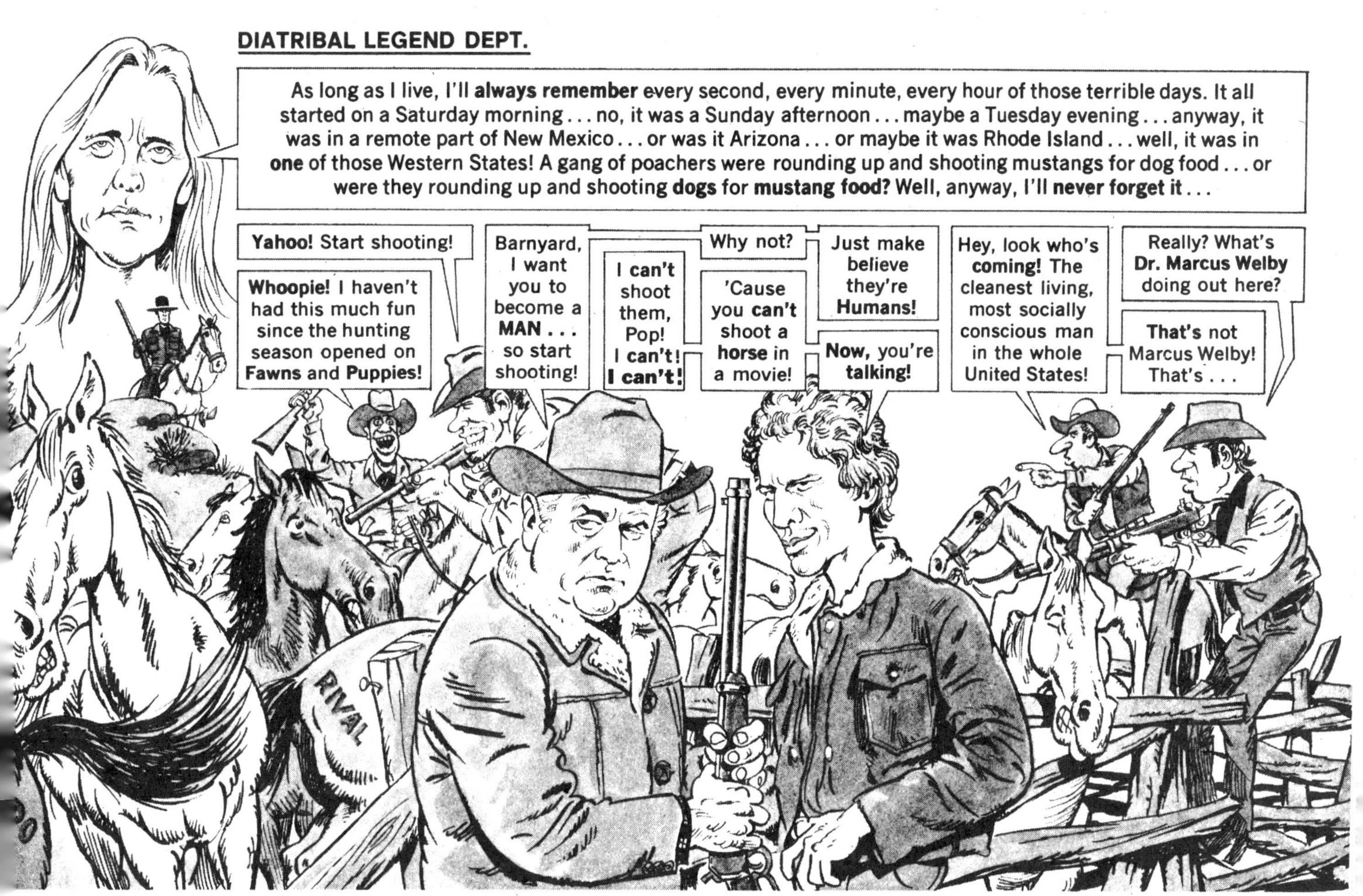
As long as I live, I'll **always remember** every second, every minute, every hour of those terrible days. It all started on a Saturday morning . . . no, it was a Sunday afternoon . . . maybe a Tuesday evening . . . anyway, it was in a remote part of New Mexico . . . or was it Arizona . . . or maybe it was Rhode Island . . . well, it was in **one** of those Western States! A gang of poachers were rounding up and shooting mustangs for dog food . . . or were they rounding up and shooting **dogs** for **mustang food?** Well, anyway, I'll **never forget it** . . .
**Yahoo!** Start shooting!
**Whoopie!** I haven't had this much fun since the hunting season opened on **Fawns** and **Puppies!**
Barnyard, I want you to become a **MAN . . .** so start shooting!
I **can't** shoot them, Pop! I **can't!** **I can't!**
Why not?
'Cause you **can't** shoot a **horse** in a movie!
Just make believe they're **Humans!**
**Now,** you're **talking!**
Hey, look who's **coming!** The cleanest living, most socially conscious man in the whole United States!
Really? What's **Dr. Marcus Welby** doing out here?
**That's** not Marcus Welby! That's . . .
RIVAL

# BILLY JOCK

ARTIST: ANGELO TORRES    WRITER: STAN HART

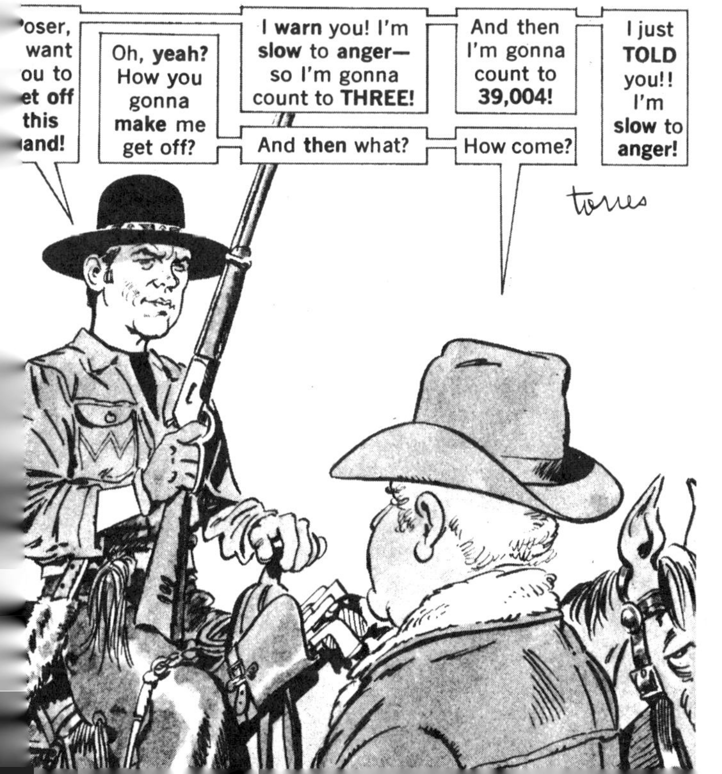
oser, want ou to et off this and!
Oh, **yeah?** How you gonna **make** me get off?
I **warn** you! I'm **slow** to **anger—** so I'm gonna count to **THREE!**
And **then** what?
And then I'm gonna count to **39,004!**
How come?
I just **TOLD** you!! I'm **slow** to **anger!**
torres

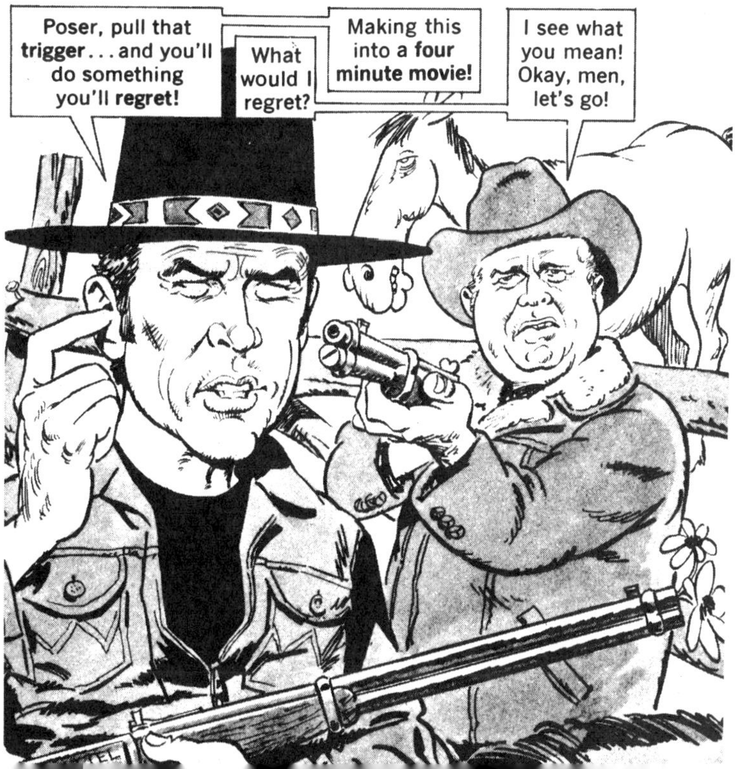
Poser, pull that **trigger** . . . and you'll do something you'll **regret!**
What would I regret?
Making this into a **four minute movie!**
I see what you mean! Okay, men, let's go!

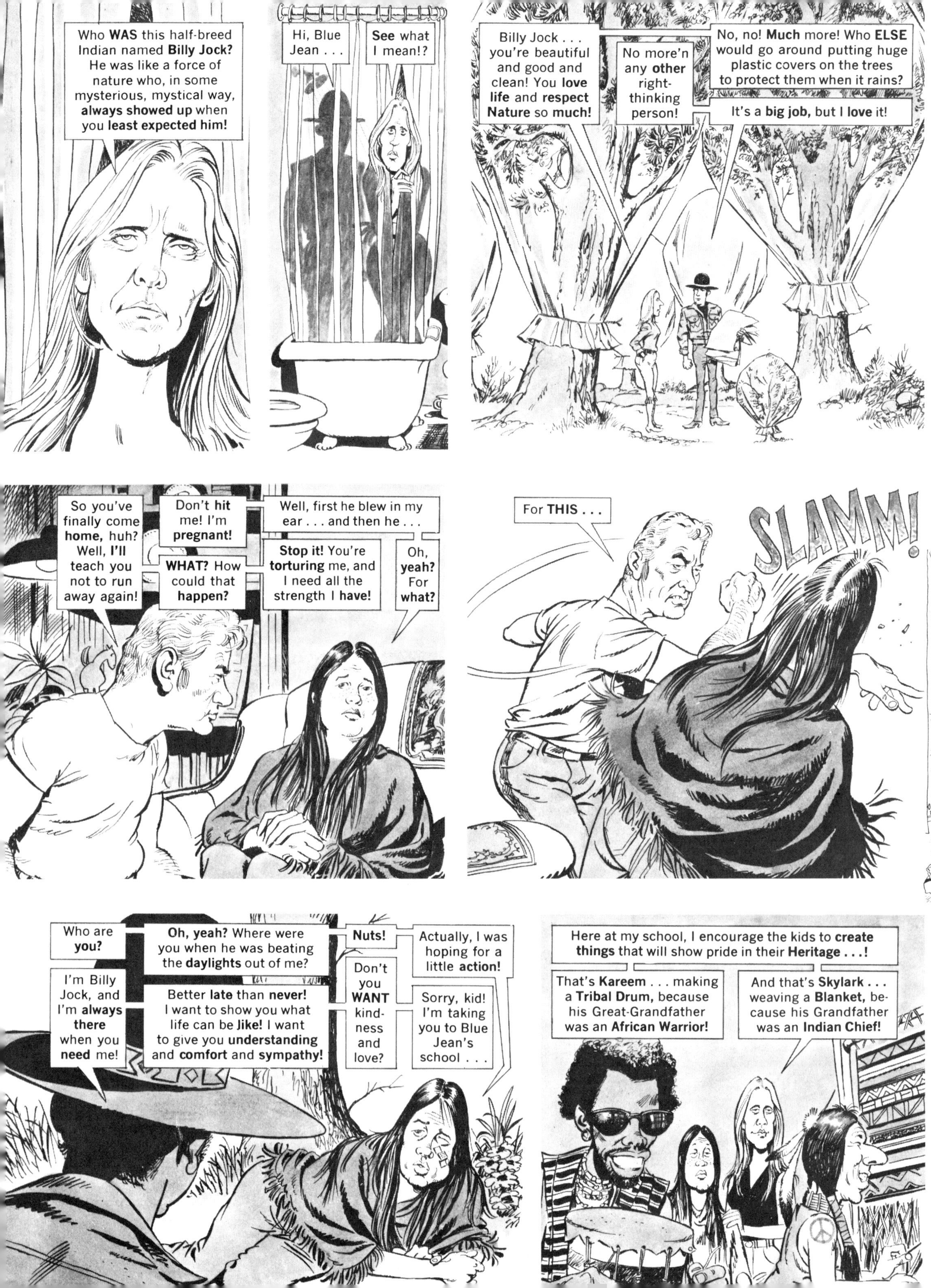

Who WAS this half-breed Indian named Billy Jock? He was like a force of nature who, in some mysterious, mystical way, always showed up when you least expected him!
Hi, Blue Jean . . .
See what I mean!?
Billy Jock . . . you're beautiful and good and clean! You love life and respect Nature so much!
No more'n any other right-thinking person!
No, no! Much more! Who ELSE would go around putting huge plastic covers on the trees to protect them when it rains?
It's a big job, but I love it!
So you've finally come home, huh? Well, I'll teach you not to run away again!
Don't hit me! I'm pregnant!
WHAT? How could that happen?
Well, first he blew in my ear . . . and then he . . .
Stop it! You're torturing me, and I need all the strength I have!
Oh, yeah? For what?
For THIS . . .
SLAMM!
Who are you?
I'm Billy Jock, and I'm always there when you need me!
Oh, yeah? Where were you when he was beating the daylights out of me?
Better late than never! I want to show you what life can be like! I want to give you understanding and comfort and sympathy!
Nuts!
Don't you WANT kindness and love?
Actually, I was hoping for a little action!
Sorry, kid! I'm taking you to Blue Jean's school . . .
Here at my school, I encourage the kids to create things that will show pride in their Heritage . . .!
That's Kareem . . . making a Tribal Drum, because his Great-Grandfather was an African Warrior!
And that's Skylark . . . weaving a Blanket, because his Grandfather was an Indian Chief!

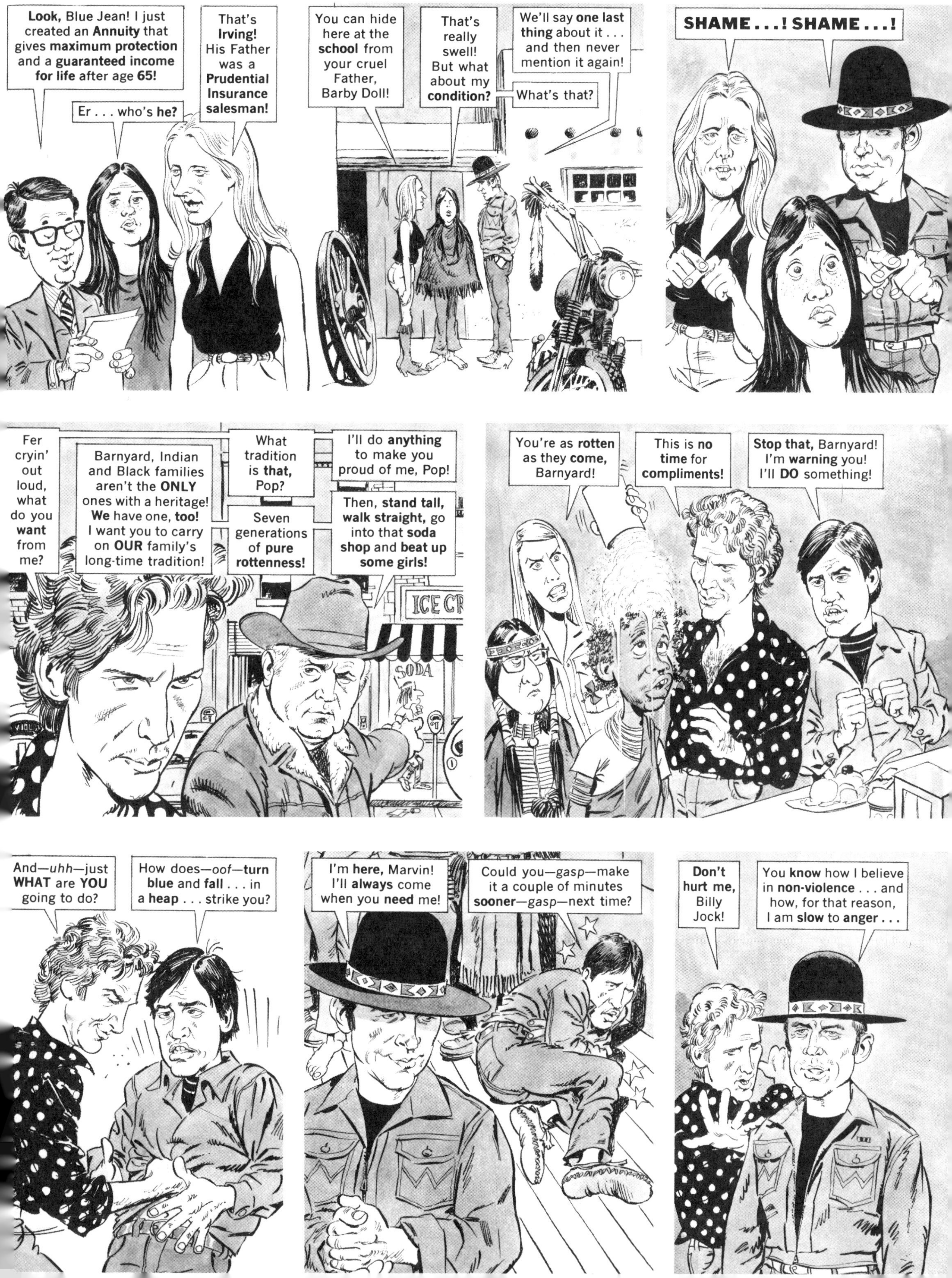
Look, Blue Jean! I just created an Annuity that gives maximum protection and a guaranteed income for life after age 65!
Er . . . who's he?
That's Irving! His Father was a Prudential Insurance salesman!
You can hide here at the school from your cruel Father, Barby Doll!
That's really swell! But what about my condition?
What's that?
We'll say one last thing about it . . . and then never mention it again!
SHAME . . . ! SHAME . . . !
Fer cryin' out loud, what do you want from me?
Barnyard, Indian and Black families aren't the ONLY ones with a heritage! We have one, too! I want you to carry on OUR family's long-time tradition!
What tradition is that, Pop?
Seven generations of pure rottenness!
I'll do anything to make you proud of me, Pop!
Then, stand tall, walk straight, go into that soda shop and beat up some girls!
ICE CR
SODA
You're as rotten as they come, Barnyard!
This is no time for compliments!
Stop that, Barnyard! I'm warning you! I'll DO something!
And—uhh—just WHAT are YOU going to do?
How does—oof—turn blue and fall . . . in a heap . . . strike you?
I'm here, Marvin! I'll always come when you need me!
Could you—gasp—make it a couple of minutes sooner—gasp—next time?
Don't hurt me, Billy Jock!
You know how I believe in non-violence . . . and how, for that reason, I am slow to anger . . .

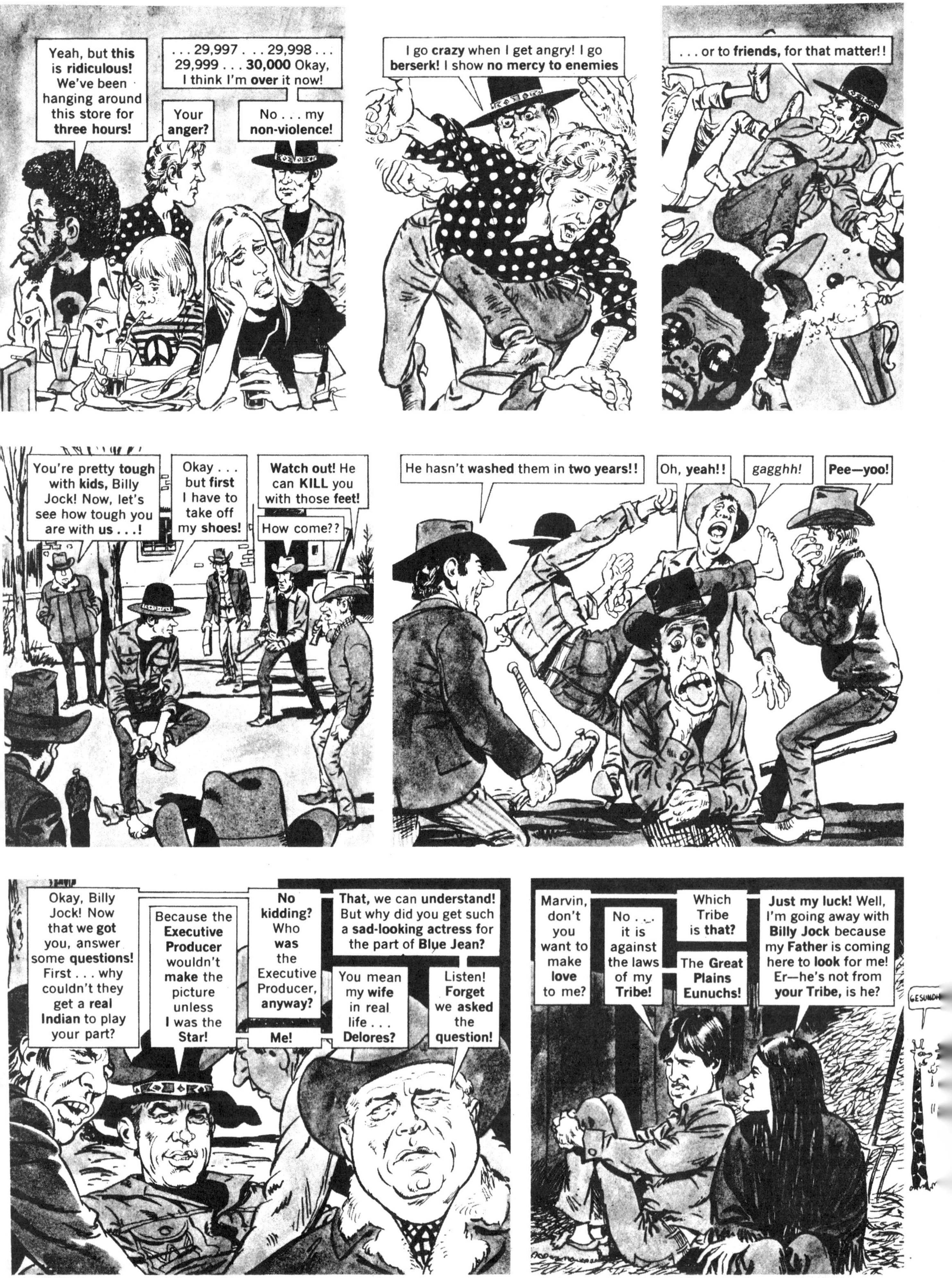

Yeah, but this is ridiculous! We've been hanging around this store for three hours!
. . . 29,997 . . . 29,998 . . . 29,999 . . . 30,000 Okay, I think I'm over it now!
Your anger?
No . . . my non-violence!
I go crazy when I get angry! I go berserk! I show no mercy to enemies
. . . or to friends, for that matter!!
You're pretty tough with kids, Billy Jock! Now, let's see how tough you are with us . . .!
Okay . . . but first I have to take off my shoes!
Watch out! He can KILL you with those feet!
How come??
He hasn't washed them in two years!!
Oh, yeah!!
gagghh!
Pee—yoo!
Okay, Billy Jock! Now that we got you, answer some questions! First . . . why couldn't they get a real Indian to play your part?
Because the Executive Producer wouldn't make the picture unless I was the Star!
No kidding? Who was the Executive Producer, anyway?
Me!
That, we can understand! But why did you get such a sad-looking actress for the part of Blue Jean?
You mean my wife in real life . . . Delores?
Listen! Forget we asked the question!
Marvin, don't you want to make love to me?
No . . . it is against the laws of my Tribe!
Which Tribe is that?
The Great Plains Eunuchs!
Just my luck! Well, I'm going away with Billy Jock because my Father is coming here to look for me! Er—he's not from your Tribe, is he?

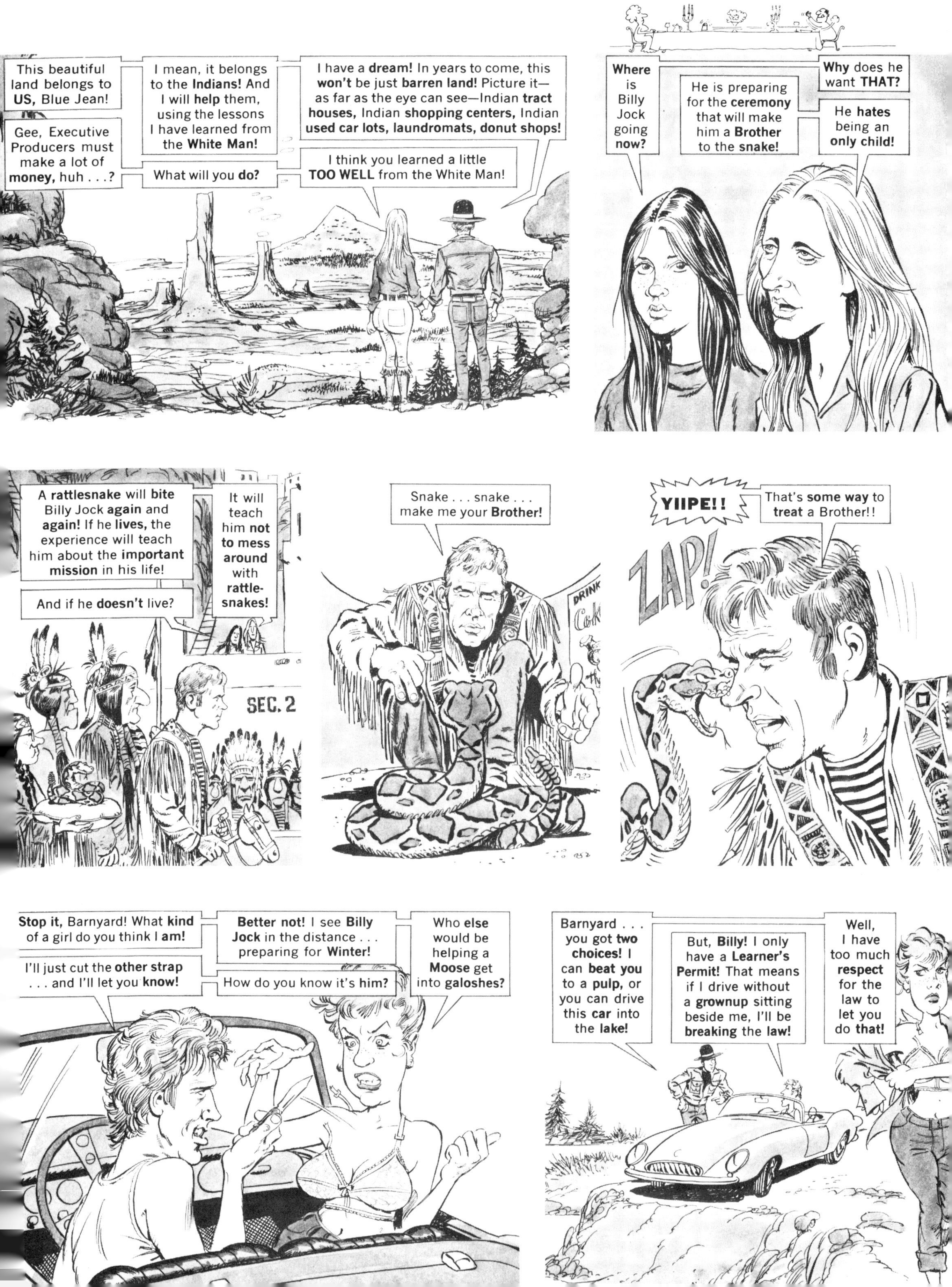

This beautiful land belongs to **US,** Blue Jean!
Gee, Executive Producers must make a lot of **money,** huh . . .?
I mean, it belongs to the **Indians!** And I will **help** them, using the lessons I have learned from the **White Man!**
What will you **do?**
I have a **dream!** In years to come, this **won't** be just **barren land!** Picture it—as far as the eye can see—Indian **tract houses,** Indian **shopping centers,** Indian **used car lots, laundromats, donut shops!**
I think you learned a little **TOO WELL** from the White Man!
**Where** is Billy Jock going **now?**
He is preparing for the **ceremony** that will make him a **Brother** to the **snake!**
**Why** does he want **THAT?**
He **hates** being an **only child!**
A **rattlesnake** will **bite** Billy Jock **again** and **again!** If he **lives,** the experience will teach him about the **important mission** in his life!
And if he **doesn't** live?
It will teach him **not to mess around** with **rattle-snakes!**
SEC. 2
Snake . . . snake . . . make me your **Brother!**
YIIPE!!
ZAP!
That's **some way** to **treat** a Brother!!
**Stop it,** Barnyard! What **kind** of a girl do you think I **am!**
I'll just cut the **other strap** . . . and I'll let you **know!**
**Better not!** I see **Billy Jock** in the distance . . . preparing for **Winter!**
How do you know it's **him?**
Who **else** would be helping a **Moose** get into **galoshes?**
Barnyard . . . you got **two choices!** I can **beat you** to a **pulp,** or you can drive this **car** into the **lake!**
But, **Billy!** I only have a **Learner's Permit!** That means if I drive without a **grownup** sitting beside me, I'll be **breaking** the **law!**
Well, I have too much **respect** for the law to let you do **that!**

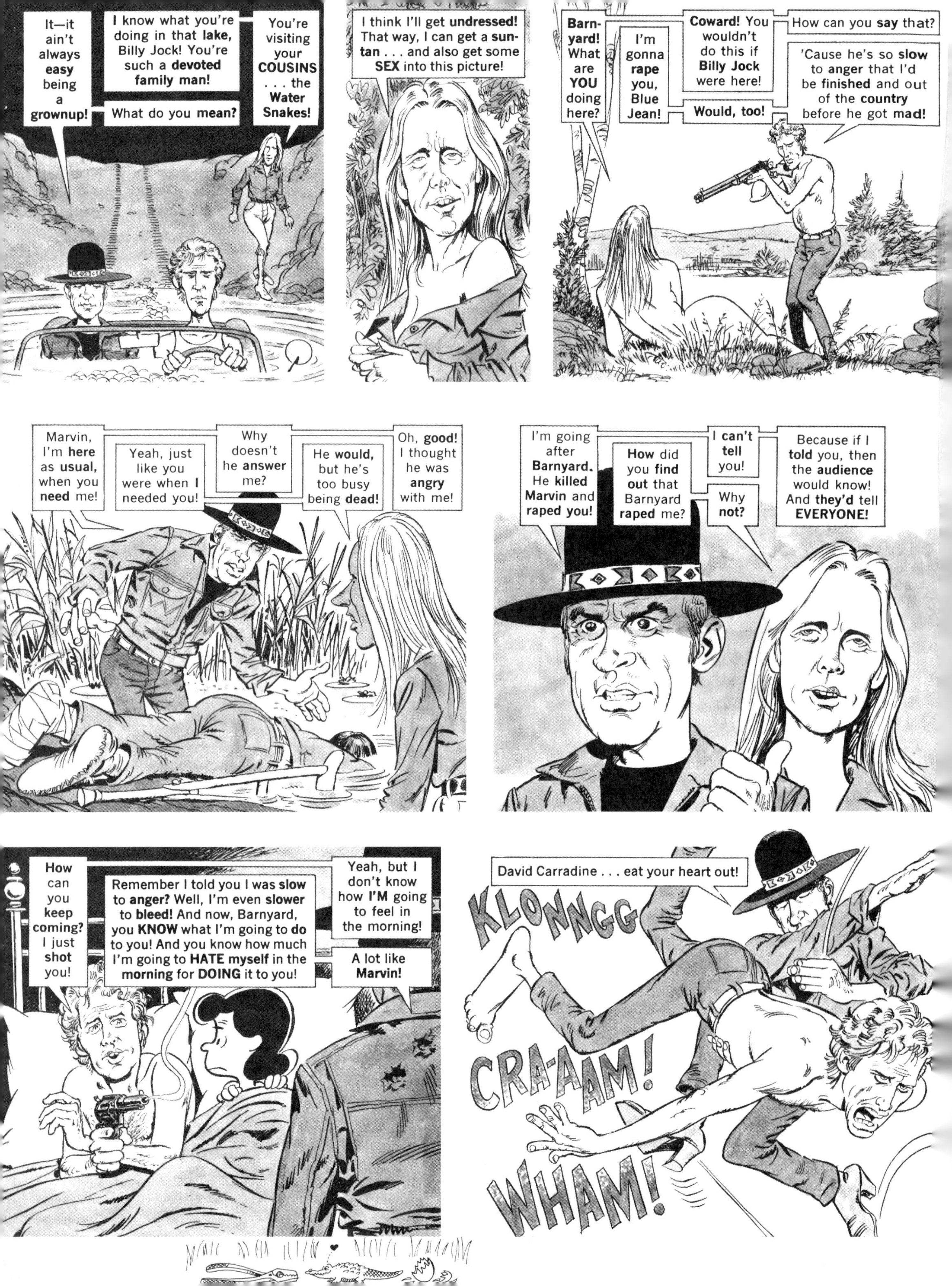

I know what you're doing in that lake, Billy Jock! You're such a devoted family man!
What do you mean?
You're visiting your COUSINS . . . the Water Snakes!
It—it ain't always easy being a grownup!
I think I'll get undressed! That way, I can get a suntan . . . and also get some SEX into this picture!
Barnyard! What are YOU doing here?
I'm gonna rape you, Blue Jean!
Coward! You wouldn't do this if Billy Jock were here!
Would, too!
How can you say that?
'Cause he's so slow to anger that I'd be finished and out of the country before he got mad!
Marvin, I'm here as usual, when you need me!
Yeah, just like you were when I needed you!
Why doesn't he answer me?
He would, but he's too busy being dead!
Oh, good! I thought he was angry with me!
I'm going after Barnyard. He killed Marvin and raped you!
How did you find out that Barnyard raped me?
I can't tell you!
Why not?
Because if I told you, then the audience would know! And they'd tell EVERYONE!
How can you keep coming? I just shot you!
Remember I told you I was slow to anger? Well, I'm even slower to bleed! And now, Barnyard, you KNOW what I'm going to do to you! And you know how much I'm going to HATE myself in the morning for DOING it to you!
Yeah, but I don't know how I'M going to feel in the morning!
A lot like Marvin!
David Carradine . . . eat your heart out!
KLONNGG
CRA-AAM!
WHAM!

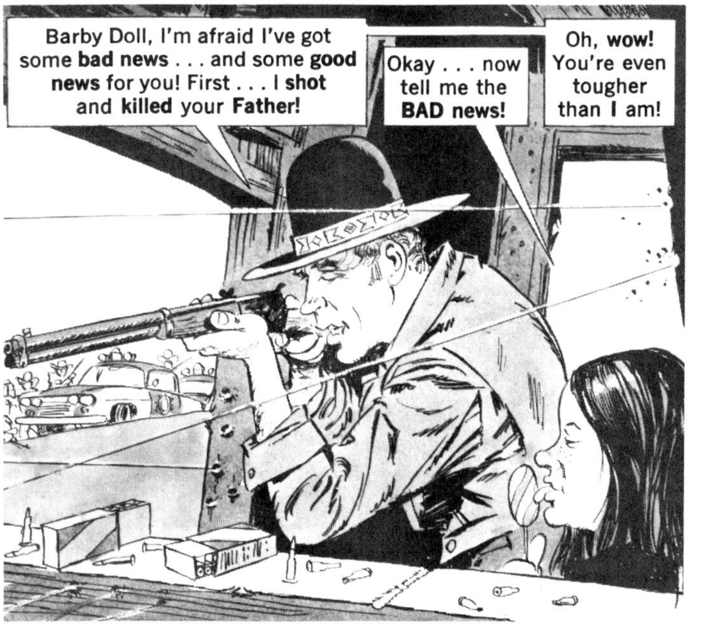
Barby Doll, I'm afraid I've got some bad news . . . and some good news for you! First . . . I shot and killed your Father!
Okay . . . now tell me the BAD news!
Oh, wow! You're even tougher than I am!

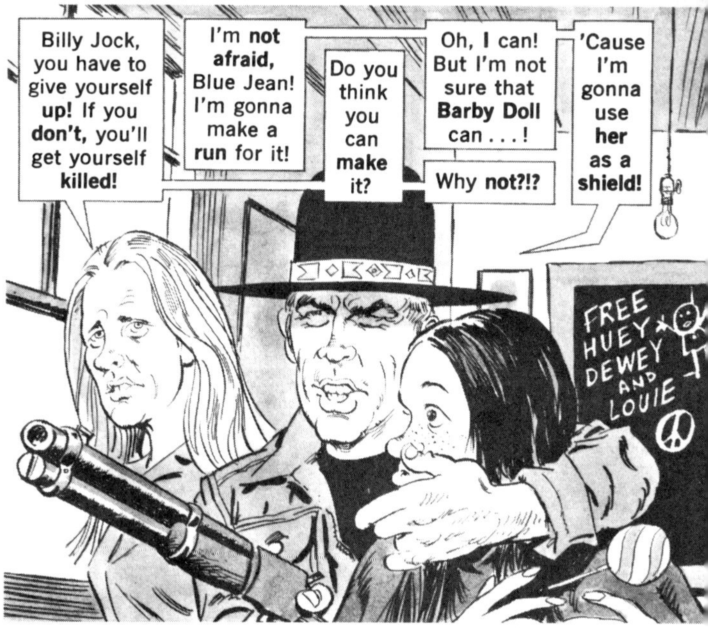
Billy Jock, you have to give yourself up! If you don't, you'll get yourself killed!
I'm not afraid, Blue Jean! I'm gonna make a run for it!
Do you think you can make it?
Oh, I can! But I'm not sure that Barby Doll can . . . !
Why not?!?
'Cause I'm gonna use her as a shield!
FREE HUEY DEWEY AND LOUIE

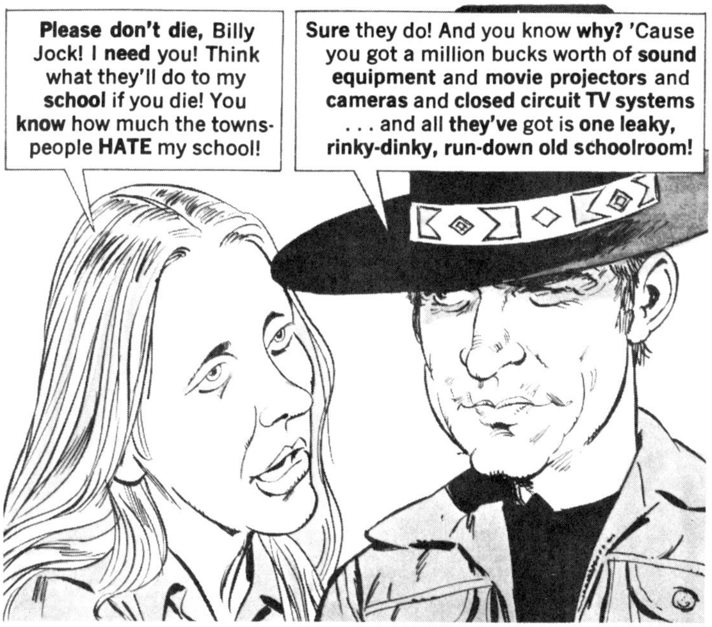
Please don't die, Billy Jock! I need you! Think what they'll do to my school if you die! You know how much the towns-people HATE my school!
Sure they do! And you know why? 'Cause you got a million bucks worth of sound equipment and movie projectors and cameras and closed circuit TV systems . . . and all they've got is one leaky, rinky-dinky, run-down old schoolroom!

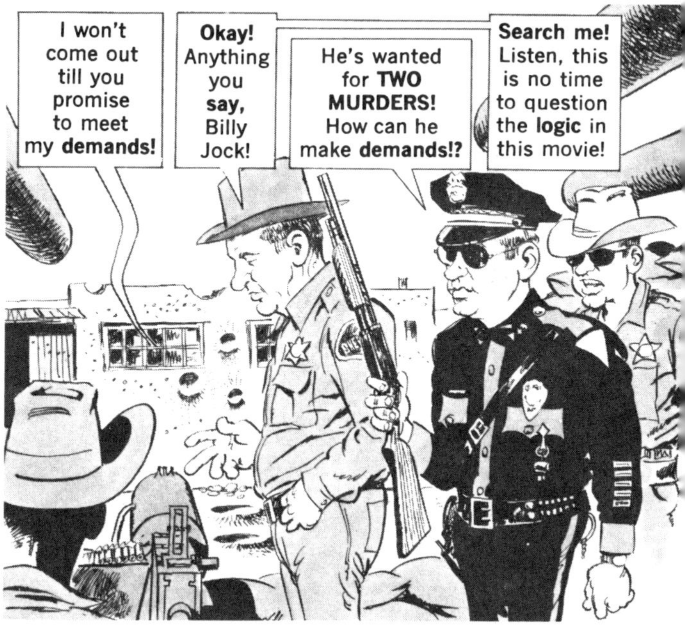
I won't come out till you promise to meet my demands!
Okay! Anything you say, Billy Jock!
He's wanted for TWO MURDERS! How can he make demands!?
Search me! Listen, this is no time to question the logic in this movie!

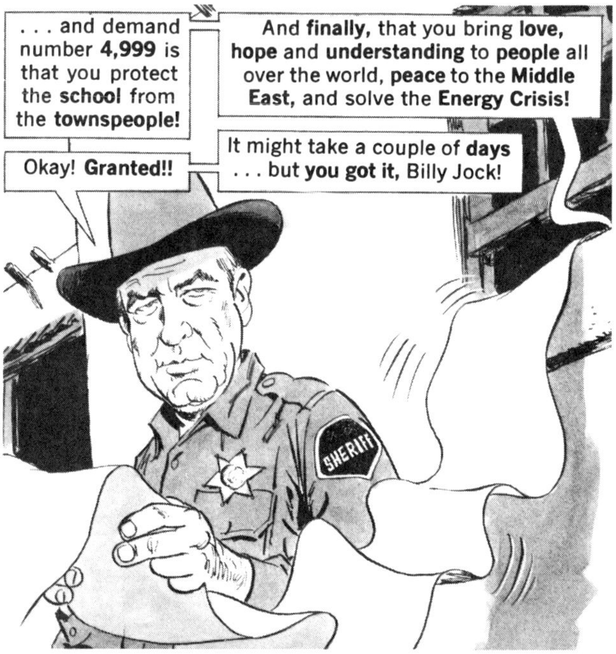
. . . and demand number 4,999 is that you protect the school from the townspeople!
And finally, that you bring love, hope and understanding to people all over the world, peace to the Middle East, and solve the Energy Crisis!
Okay! Granted!!
It might take a couple of days . . . but you got it, Billy Jock!
SHERIFF

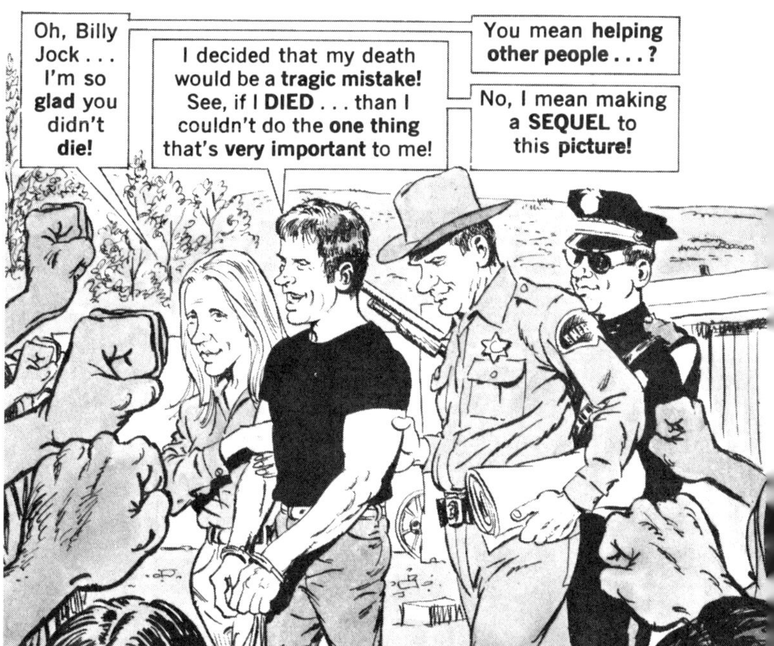
Oh, Billy Jock . . . I'm so glad you didn't die!
I decided that my death would be a tragic mistake! See, if I DIED . . . than I couldn't do the one thing that's very important to me!
You mean helping other people . . . ?
No, I mean making a SEQUEL to this picture!

**BETWEEN THE DEVIL AND THE HOLY SEE DEPT.**

Remember the good old days when Hollywood used to make horror movies about vampires, werewolves, zombies, seventy foot apes and other assorted monsters? Let's face it, they were all disgusting creatures, but there was still something kinda harmless and loveable about them. Well, those days are gone forever. Today's film makers have come up with something *really* disgusting. Yessiree, you screamed at "Frankenstein," you shrieked at "Dracula" and you shuddered at "King Kong," but take it from us . . . those guys were all a bunch of pussycats when compared to . . .

# THE E

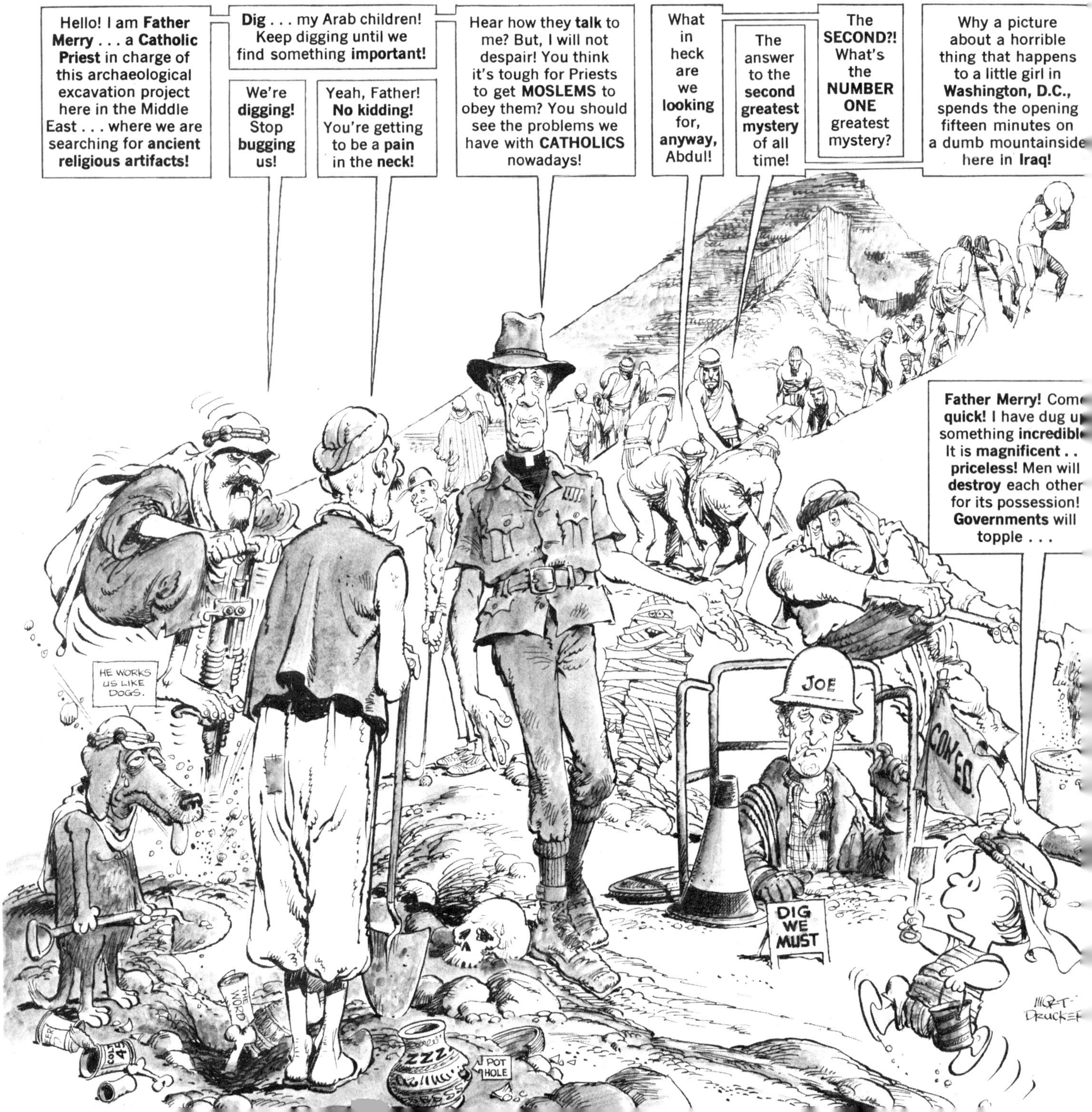

Hello! I am **Father Merry** . . . a **Catholic Priest** in charge of this archaeological excavation project here in the Middle East . . . where we are searching for **ancient religious artifacts!**
**Dig** . . . my Arab children! Keep digging until we find something **important!**
We're **digging!** Stop **bugging** us!
Yeah, Father! **No kidding!** You're getting to be a **pain** in the **neck!**
Hear how they **talk** to me? But, I will not despair! You think it's tough for Priests to get **MOSLEMS** to obey them? You should see the problems we have with **CATHOLICS** nowadays!
What in heck are we **looking** for, **anyway,** Abdul!
The answer to the **second greatest mystery** of all time!
The **SECOND?!** What's the **NUMBER ONE** greatest mystery?
Why a picture about a horrible thing that happens to a little girl in **Washington, D.C.,** spends the opening fifteen minutes on a dumb mountainside here in **Iraq!**
**Father Merry!** Com **quick!** I have dug u something **incredibl** It is **magnificent . . priceless!** Men will **destroy** each other for its possession! **Governments** will topple . . .
HE WORKS US LIKE DOGS.
JOE
DIG WE MUST
CON ED.
POT HOLE
THE WORD
MORT DRUCKER

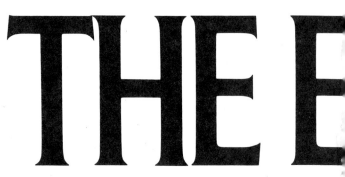

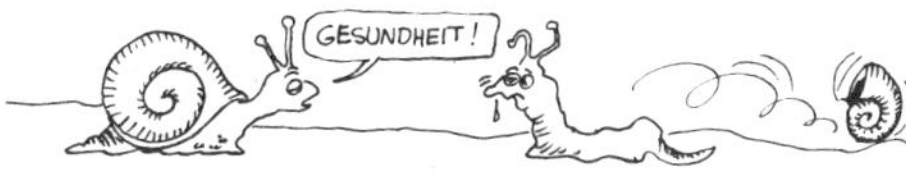

GESUNDHEIT!


# CCHORCIST

ARTIST: MORT DRUCKER WRITER: LARRY SIEGEL

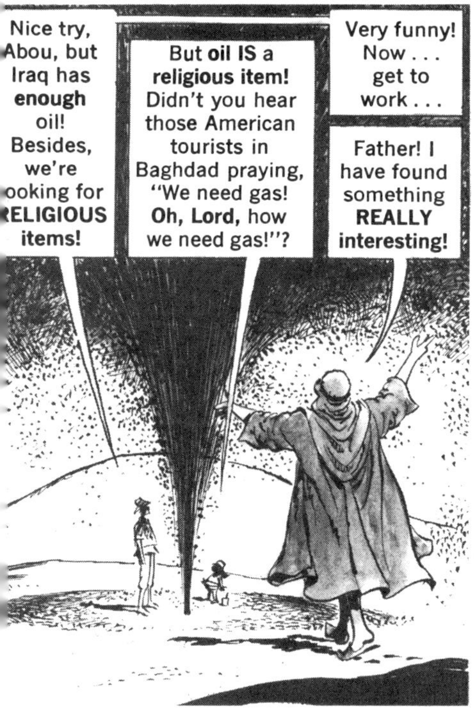

Nice try, Abou, but Iraq has enough oil! Besides, we're ooking for ELIGIOUS items!
But oil IS a religious item! Didn't you hear those American tourists in Baghdad praying, "We need gas! Oh, Lord, how we need gas!"?
Very funny! Now . . . get to work . . .
Father! I have found something REALLY interesting!


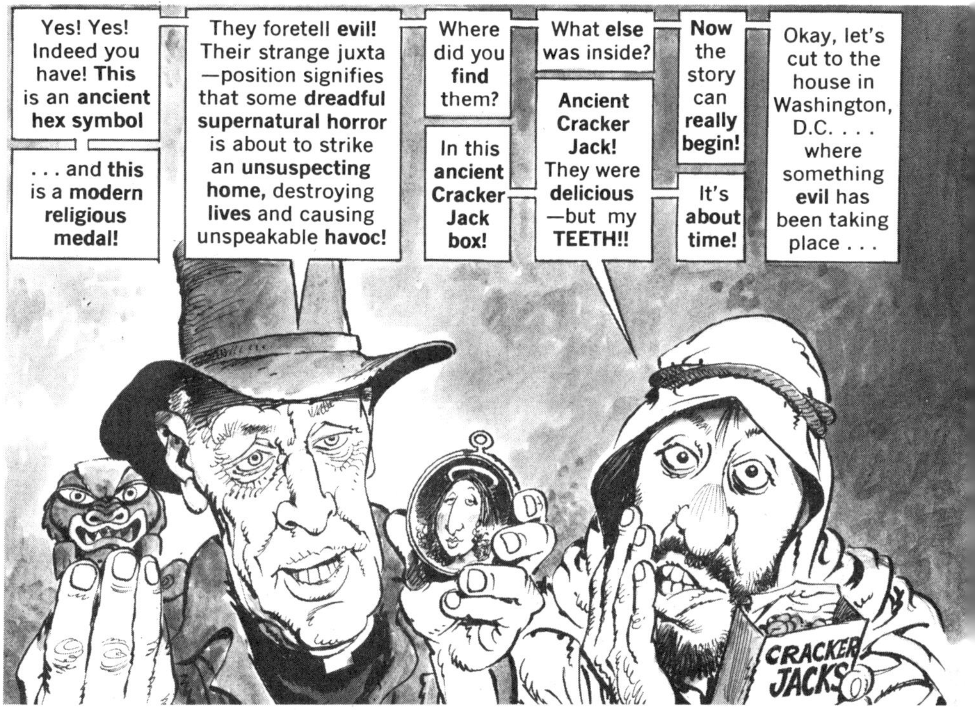

Yes! Yes! Indeed you have! This is an ancient hex symbol
. . . and this is a modern religious medal!
They foretell evil! Their strange juxta—position signifies that some dreadful supernatural horror is about to strike an unsuspecting home, destroying lives and causing unspeakable havoc!
Where did you find them?
In this ancient Cracker Jack box!
What else was inside?
Ancient Cracker Jack! They were delicious—but my TEETH!!
Now the story can really begin!
It's about time!
Okay, let's cut to the house in Washington, D.C. . . . where something evil has been taking place . . .
CRACKER JACKS


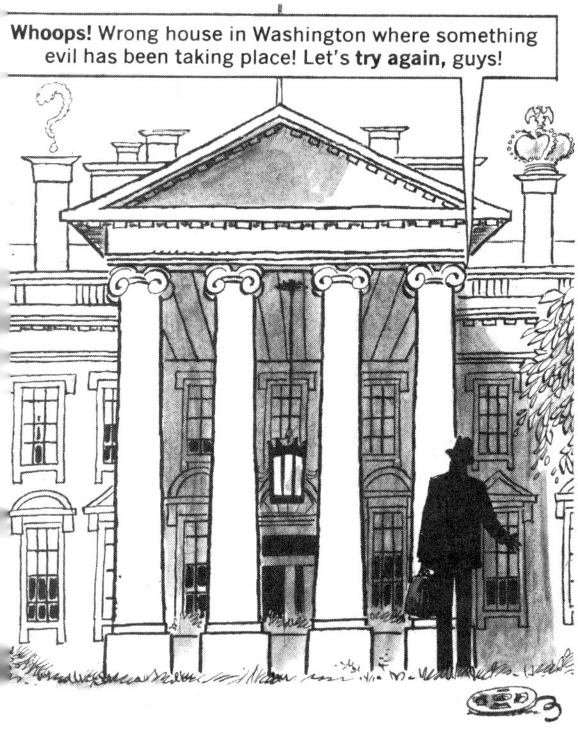

Whoops! Wrong house in Washington where something evil has been taking place! Let's try again, guys!


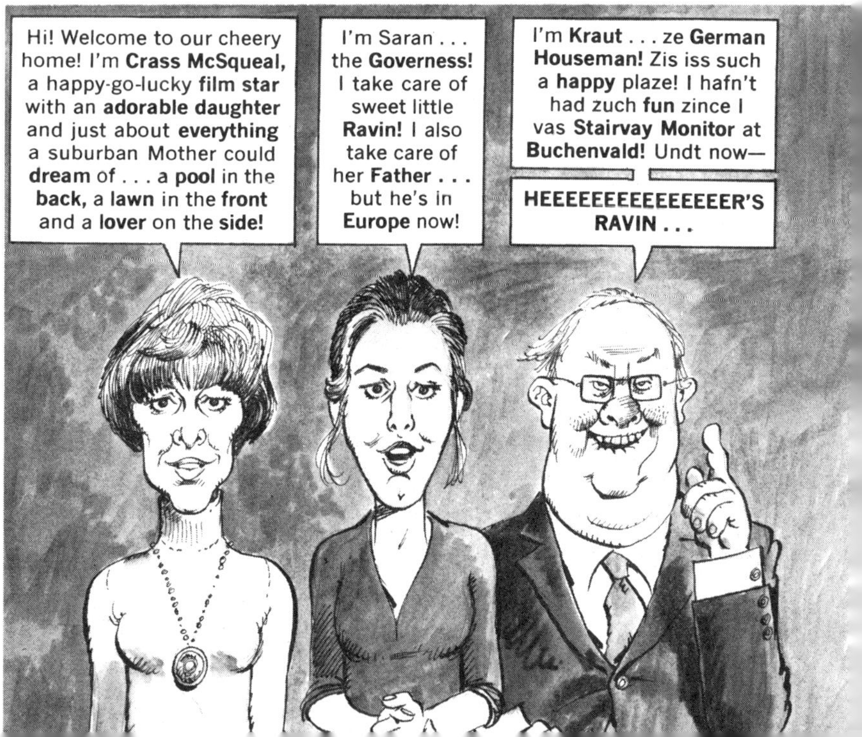

Hi! Welcome to our cheery home! I'm Crass McSqueal, a happy-go-lucky film star with an adorable daughter and just about everything a suburban Mother could dream of . . . a pool in the back, a lawn in the front and a lover on the side!
I'm Saran . . . the Governess! I take care of sweet little Ravin! I also take care of her Father . . . but he's in Europe now!
I'm Kraut . . . ze German Houseman! Zis iss such a happy plaze! I hafn't had zuch fun zince I vas Stairvay Monitor at Buchenvald! Undt now—
HEEEEEEEEEEEEEEER'S RAVIN . . .

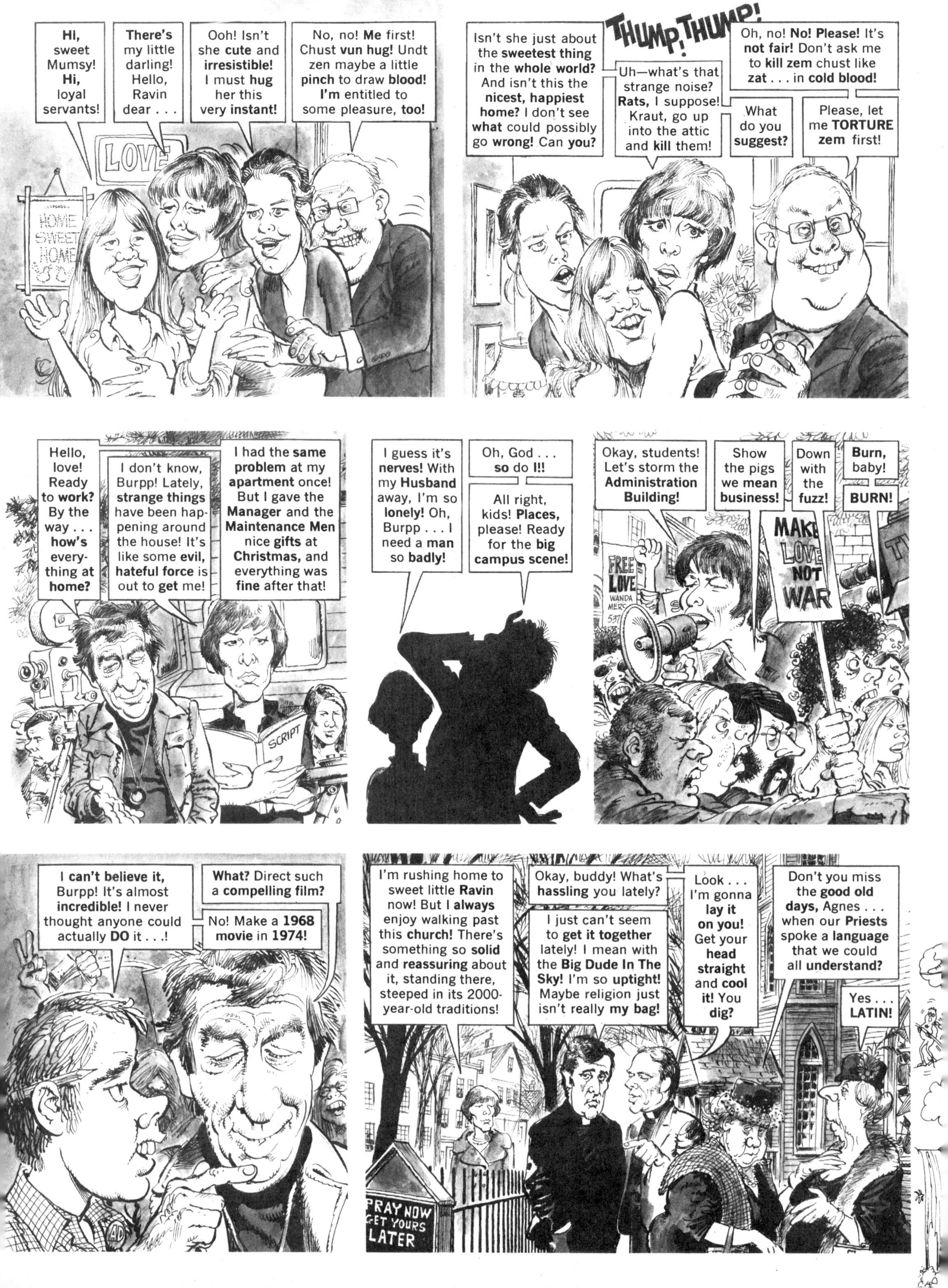

Hi, sweet Mumsy! Hi, loyal servants!
There's my little darling! Hello, Ravin dear . . .
Ooh! Isn't she cute and irresistible! I must hug her this very instant!
No, no! Me first! Chust vun hug! Undt zen maybe a little pinch to draw blood! I'm entitled to some pleasure, too!
LOVE
HOME SWEET HOME
THUMP! THUMP!
Isn't she just about the sweetest thing in the whole world? And isn't this the nicest, happiest home? I don't see what could possibly go wrong! Can you?
Uh—what's that strange noise? Rats, I suppose! Kraut, go up into the attic and kill them!
Oh, no! No! Please! It's not fair! Don't ask me to kill zem chust like zat . . . in cold blood!
What do you suggest?
Please, let me TORTURE zem first!
Hello, love! Ready to work? By the way . . . how's every-thing at home?
I don't know, Burpp! Lately, strange things have been hap-pening around the house! It's like some evil, hateful force is out to get me!
I had the same problem at my apartment once! But I gave the Manager and the Maintenance Men nice gifts at Christmas, and everything was fine after that!
SCRIPT
I guess it's nerves! With my Husband away, I'm so lonely! Oh, Burpp . . . I need a man so badly!
Oh, God . . . so do I!!
All right, kids! Places, please! Ready for the big campus scene!
Okay, students! Let's storm the Administration Building!
Show the pigs we mean business!
Down with the fuzz!
Burn, baby!
BURN!
FREE LOVE
MAKE LOVE NOT WAR
I can't believe it, Burpp! It's almost incredible! I never thought anyone could actually DO it . . .!
What? Direct such a compelling film?
No! Make a 1968 movie in 1974!
I'm rushing home to sweet little Ravin now! But I always enjoy walking past this church! There's something so solid and reassuring about it, standing there, steeped in its 2000-year-old traditions!
Okay, buddy! What's hassling you lately?
I just can't seem to get it together lately! I mean with the Big Dude In The Sky! I'm so uptight! Maybe religion just isn't really my bag!
Look . . . I'm gonna lay it on you! Get your head straight and cool it! You dig?
Don't you miss the good old days, Agnes . . . when our Priests spoke a language that we could all understand?
Yes . . . LATIN!
PRAY NOW GET YOURS LATER

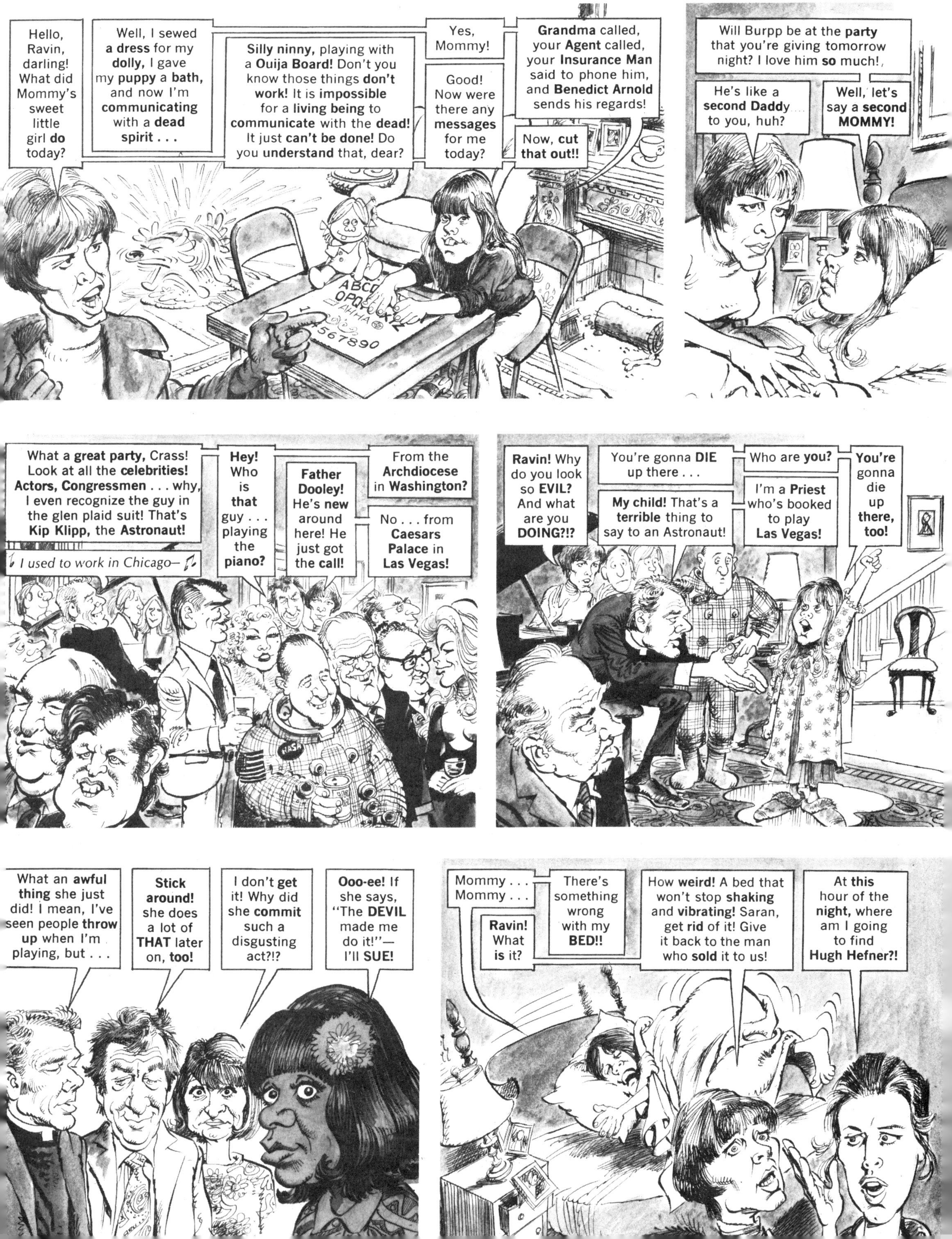

Hello, Ravin, darling! What did Mommy's sweet little girl **do** today?
Well, I sewed **a dress** for my **dolly,** I gave my **puppy** a **bath,** and now I'm **communicating** with a **dead spirit** . . .
**Silly ninny,** playing with a **Ouija Board!** Don't you know those things **don't work!** It is **impossible** for a **living being** to **communicate** with the **dead!** It just **can't be done!** Do you **understand** that, dear?
Yes, Mommy!
Good! Now were there any **messages** for me today?
**Grandma** called, your **Agent** called, your **Insurance Man** said to phone him, and **Benedict Arnold** sends his regards!
Now, **cut that out!!**
ABCD
OPQ
1234567890
Will Burpp be at the **party** that you're giving tomorrow night? I love him **so** much!
He's like a **second Daddy**.... to you, huh?
Well, let's say a **second MOMMY!**
What a **great party,** Crass! Look at all the **celebrities! Actors, Congressmen** . . . why, I even recognize the guy in the glen plaid suit! That's **Kip Klipp,** the **Astronaut!**
*I used to work in Chicago—*
**Hey!** Who is **that** guy . . . playing the **piano?**
**Father Dooley!** He's **new** around here! He just got **the call!**
From the **Archdiocese** in **Washington?**
No . . . from **Caesars Palace** in **Las Vegas!**
NASA
**Ravin!** Why do you look so **EVIL?** And what are you **DOING?!?**
You're gonna **DIE** up there . . .
**My child!** That's a **terrible** thing to say to an Astronaut!
Who are **you?**
I'm a **Priest** who's booked to play **Las Vegas!**
**You're** gonna die up **there, too!**
What an **awful thing** she just did! I mean, I've seen people **throw up** when I'm playing, but . . .
**Stick around!** she does a lot of **THAT** later on, **too!**
I don't **get** it! Why did she **commit** such a disgusting act?!?
**Ooo-ee!** If she says, "The **DEVIL** made me do it!"— I'll **SUE!**
Mommy . . . Mommy . . .
**Ravin!** What **is** it?
There's something wrong with my **BED!!**
How **weird!** A bed that won't stop **shaking** and **vibrating!** Saran, get **rid** of it! Give it back to the man who **sold** it to us!
At **this** hour of the **night,** where am I going to find **Hugh Hefner?!**

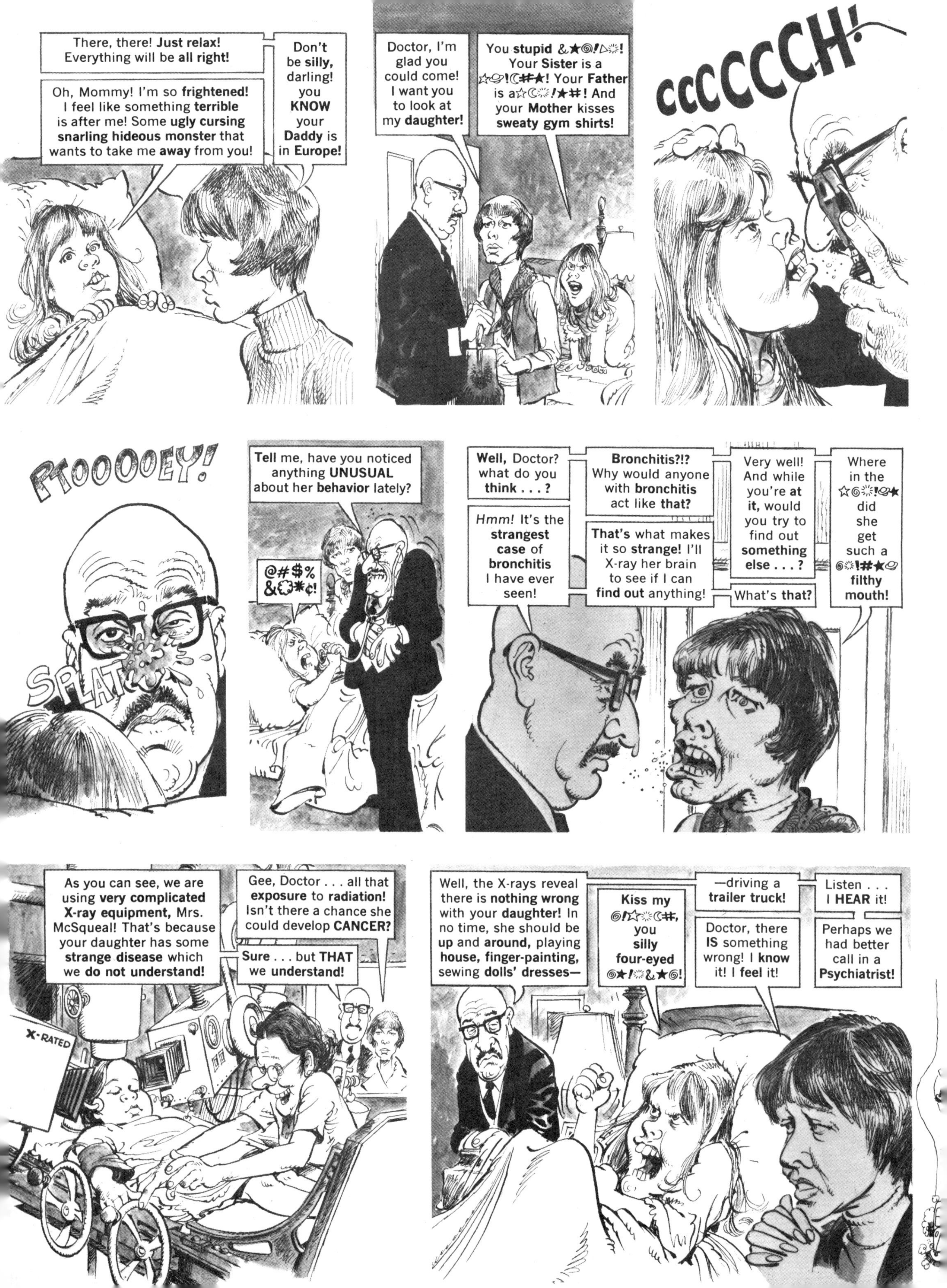
There, there! Just relax! Everything will be all right!
Oh, Mommy! I'm so frightened! I feel like something terrible is after me! Some ugly cursing snarling hideous monster that wants to take me away from you!
Don't be silly, darling! you KNOW your Daddy is in Europe!
Doctor, I'm glad you could come! I want you to look at my daughter!
You stupid &★@!△☼! Your Sister is a ☆@!☾#★! Your Father is a☆☾☼!★#! And your Mother kisses sweaty gym shirts!
CCCCCCH!
PTOOOOEY!
SPLAT
Tell me, have you noticed anything UNUSUAL about her behavior lately?
@#$% &✪*¢!
Well, Doctor? what do you think . . . ?
Hmm! It's the strangest case of bronchitis I have ever seen!
Bronchitis?!? Why would anyone with bronchitis act like that?
That's what makes it so strange! I'll X-ray her brain to see if I can find out anything!
Very well! And while you're at it, would you try to find out something else . . . ?
What's that?
Where in the ☆@☼!@★ did she get such a @☼!#★@ filthy mouth!
As you can see, we are using very complicated X-ray equipment, Mrs. McSqueal! That's because your daughter has some strange disease which we do not understand!
Gee, Doctor . . . all that exposure to radiation! Isn't there a chance she could develop CANCER?
Sure . . . but THAT we understand!
X-RATED
Well, the X-rays reveal there is nothing wrong with your daughter! In no time, she should be up and around, playing house, finger-painting, sewing dolls' dresses—
Kiss my @!☆☼☾#, you silly four-eyed @★!☼&★@!
—driving a trailer truck!
Doctor, there IS something wrong! I know it! I feel it!
Listen . . . I HEAR it!
Perhaps we had better call in a Psychiatrist!

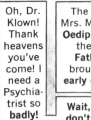

Oh, Dr. Klown! Thank heavens you've come! I need a Psychiatrist so **badly!**

The way I see it, Mrs. McSqueal, your **Oedipus Complex** is the result of a **Father fixation** brought on by an **early enema,** and—

**Wait,** Doctor! You **don't** understand!

All right! How's **this?** You have a **pathological fear** of **sex** as a result of a **deep-rooted psychosis** arising from a **traumatic pre-natal hernia!**

**No,** Doctor! **No!!**

My, my! Aren't we **picky** today! All right, you have **dementia praecox,** and **THAT'S IT!** I'm a very **busy man!**

Doctor, it's **not ME!** It's my **little girl!**

**Look** at her, Doctor! Look at this **room!** The bed is shaking, and she's covered with **blood,** and she's violating a **cross,** and that weird evil **voice** is coming out of her mouth!

What am I going to **do??**

I **assure** you, Mrs. McSqueal, you have **nothing** to **worry** about!

I **don't?!?**

Nope! But your **little** girl—now **SHE's** got a **problem!**

Yiccchhh! Le'me **out** of here!!

**What's** going on, Saran? There's a **big crowd** outside!

**Bad news,** Mrs. McSqueal! **Burpp** was mincing around in **Ravin's room,** and now the **window's** smashed and he's lying **dead** in the **alley** outside the **house!**

Oh . . . **no! Poor Burpp!** If I told him **once,** I told him a **million** times: **Don't** try to fly home in a **FOG!**

Uh . . . I'm **Lt. Kindergarten!** Can you tell me where I can find a Priest named **Father Tsouris?**

:Yes! I'm Father Tsouris!

**YOU?!?** Excuse me for being **personal,** Father, but what's a **Priest** doing running around a **track** on a Sunday morning?

Listen . . . the way **Church attendance** is nowadays, what **ELSE** is there to do! Did you ever try **SURFING** in this weather?

TRACK

Father, we just found a Director named **Burpp Denims** with his **head** turned **completely around!**

I **met** him once! It **HAS** to be an **improvement!**

No, you **don't** understand! He's **dead** . . . and we suspect an **evil force** is at work!

Oh, well, there's a **LOT** of that **going around** here in Washington!

Well, if you get any **ideas** about the murder, **call** me! Meanwhile— if you're not **doing** anything some evening, how would you like to go to a **movie** with me?

**Love to!** How about **Christmas Eve?**

**You're** not **doing** any- thing on **Christmas Eve?!?**

Oh! How **idiotic** of me! Why, I forgot all about the **Roller Derby!** Let's make it **Easter Sunday!**

It's **MY** ☀☆◎★ **room,** so get your ☆#!★⦰ **out** of it!

Listen to that **language!** And look what she's **doing** to her **Mother!**

Isn't zat **cute?** Our little girl iss **growing up!** She's getting more like a **normal teenager** every day!

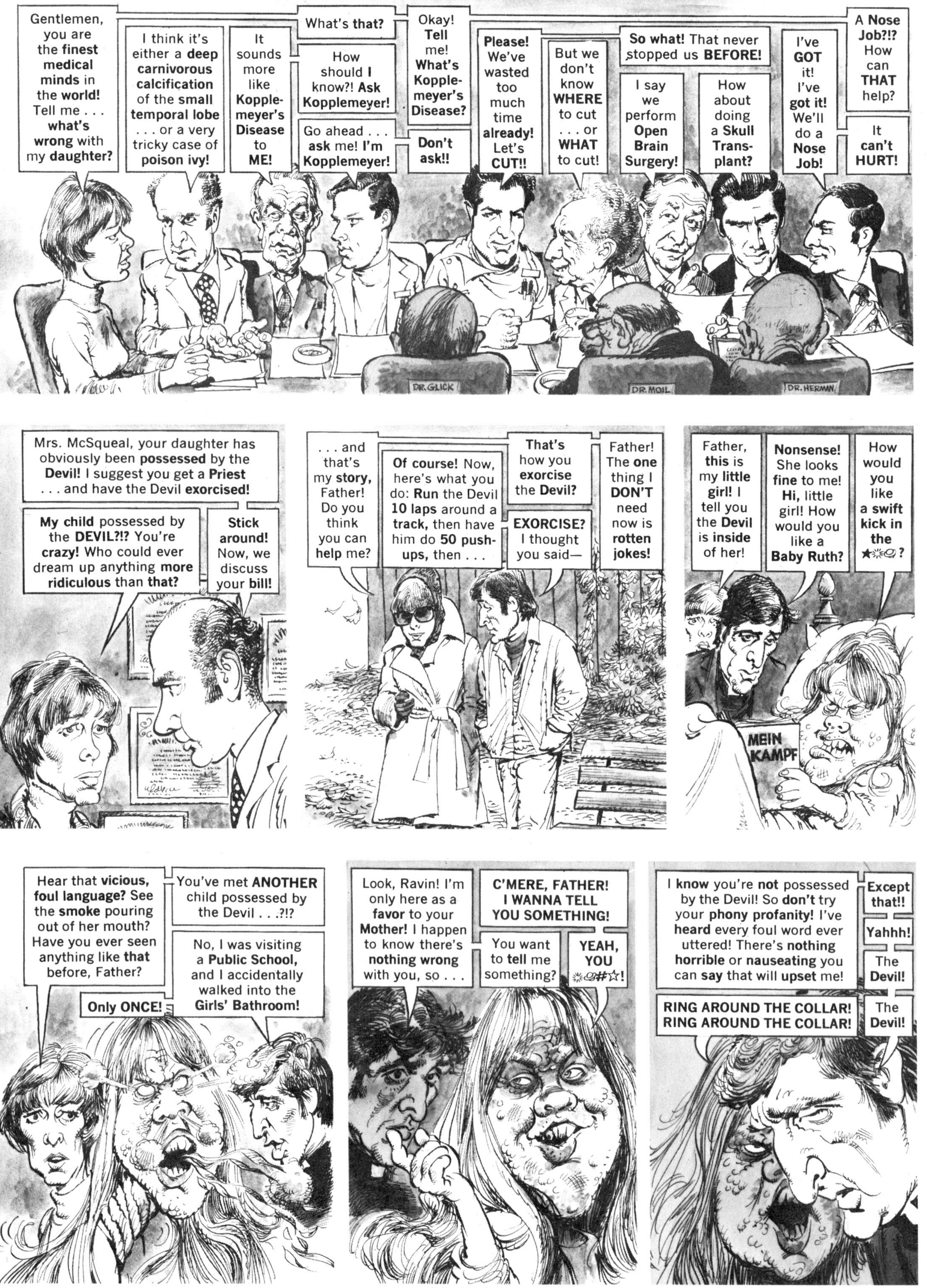

Gentlemen, you are the **finest medical minds** in the **world!** Tell me . . . **what's wrong** with my **daughter?**
I think it's either a **deep carnivorous calcification** of the **small temporal lobe** . . . or a very tricky case of **poison ivy!**
It sounds more like **Kopplemeyer's Disease** to **ME!**
What's **that?**
How should **I** know?! **Ask Kopplemeyer!**
Go ahead . . . **ask** me! **I'm Kopplemeyer!**
Okay! **Tell** me! **What's Kopplemeyer's** Disease?
**Don't ask!!**
**Please!** We've wasted too much time **already!** Let's **CUT!!**
But we don't know **WHERE** to cut . . . or **WHAT** to cut!
**So what!** That never stopped us **BEFORE!**
I say we perform **Open Brain Surgery!**
How about doing a **Skull Transplant?**
I've **GOT** it! I've **got it!** We'll do a **Nose Job!**
A **Nose Job?!?** How can **THAT** help?
It **can't HURT!**
DR. GLICK
DR. MOIL
DR. HERMAN
Mrs. McSqueal, your daughter has obviously been **possessed** by the **Devil!** I suggest you get a **Priest** . . . and have the Devil **exorcised!**
**My child** possessed by the **DEVIL?!?** You're **crazy!** Who could ever dream up anything **more ridiculous** than **that?**
**Stick around!** Now, we discuss your **bill!**
. . . and that's my **story,** Father! Do you think you can **help** me?
**Of course!** Now, here's what you do: **Run** the Devil **10 laps** around a **track,** then have him do **50 push-ups,** then . . .
**That's** how you **exorcise** the **Devil?**
**EXORCISE?** I thought you said—
Father! The **one** thing I **DON'T** need now is **rotten jokes!**
Father, **this** is my **little girl!** I tell you **the Devil** is **inside** of her!
**Nonsense!** She looks **fine** to me! **Hi,** little girl! How would you like a **Baby Ruth?**
How would you like **a swift kick in the** ★☼@?
MEIN KAMPF
Hear that **vicious, foul language?** See the **smoke** pouring out of her mouth? Have you ever seen anything like **that** before, Father?
**Only ONCE!**
You've met **ANOTHER** child possessed by the Devil . . .?!?
No, I was visiting a **Public School,** and I accidentally walked into the **Girls' Bathroom!**
Look, Ravin! I'm only here as a **favor** to your **Mother!** I happen to know there's **nothing wrong** with you, so . . .
**C'MERE, FATHER! I WANNA TELL YOU SOMETHING!**
You want to **tell** me something?
**YEAH, YOU** ☼@#☆!
I **know** you're **not** possessed by the Devil! So **don't** try your **phony profanity!** I've **heard** every foul word ever uttered! There's **nothing horrible** or **nauseating** you can **say** that will **upset** me!
**RING AROUND THE COLLAR! RING AROUND THE COLLAR!**
**Except that!!**
**Yahhh!**
**The Devil!**
**The Devil!**

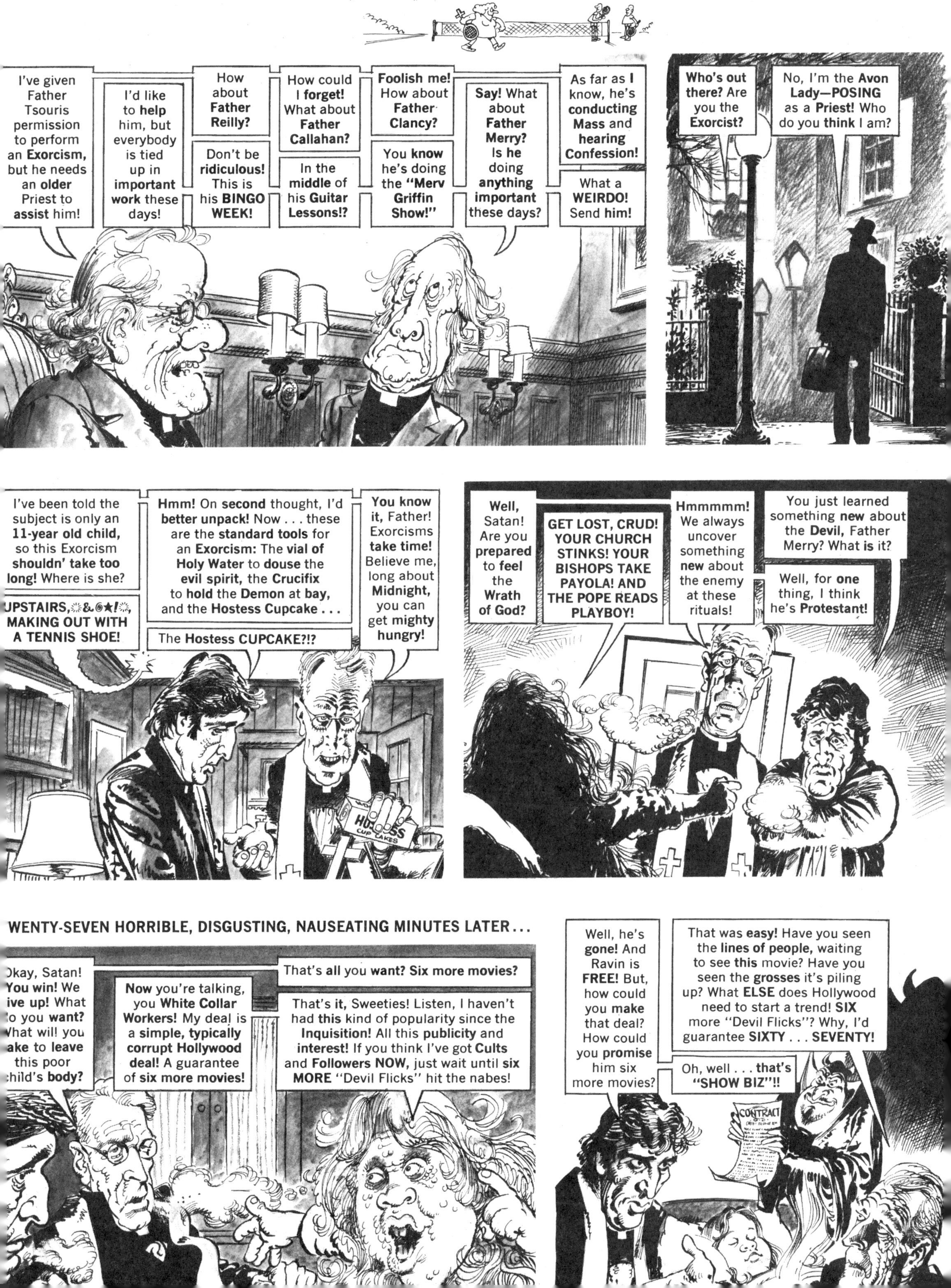

I've given Father Tsouris permission to perform an Exorcism, but he needs an older Priest to assist him!
I'd like to help him, but everybody is tied up in important work these days!
How about Father Reilly?
Don't be ridiculous! This is his BINGO WEEK!
How could I forget! What about Father Callahan?
In the middle of his Guitar Lessons!?
Foolish me! How about Father Clancy?
You know he's doing the "Merv Griffin Show!"
Say! What about Father Merry? Is he doing anything important these days?
As far as I know, he's conducting Mass and hearing Confession!
What a WEIRDO! Send him!
Who's out there? Are you the Exorcist?
No, I'm the Avon Lady—POSING as a Priest! Who do you think I am?
I've been told the subject is only an 11-year old child, so this Exorcism shouldn' take too long! Where is she?
UPSTAIRS, ☼&@★!☼, MAKING OUT WITH A TENNIS SHOE!
Hmm! On second thought, I'd better unpack! Now . . . these are the standard tools for an Exorcism: The vial of Holy Water to douse the evil spirit, the Crucifix to hold the Demon at bay, and the Hostess Cupcake . . .
The Hostess CUPCAKE?!?
You know it, Father! Exorcisms take time! Believe me, long about Midnight, you can get mighty hungry!
HOSTESS CUP CAKES
Well, Satan! Are you prepared to feel the Wrath of God?
GET LOST, CRUD! YOUR CHURCH STINKS! YOUR BISHOPS TAKE PAYOLA! AND THE POPE READS PLAYBOY!
Hmmmmm! We always uncover something new about the enemy at these rituals!
You just learned something new about the Devil, Father Merry? What is it?
Well, for one thing, I think he's Protestant!
WENTY-SEVEN HORRIBLE, DISGUSTING, NAUSEATING MINUTES LATER . . .
Okay, Satan! You win! We ive up! What o you want? What wil! you ake to leave this poor hild's body?
Now you're talking, you White Collar Workers! My deal is a simple, typically corrupt Hollywood deal! A guarantee of six more movies!
That's all you want? Six more movies?
That's it, Sweeties! Listen, I haven't had this kind of popularity since the Inquisition! All this publicity and interest! If you think I've got Cults and Followers NOW, just wait until six MORE "Devil Flicks" hit the nabes!
Well, he's gone! And Ravin is FREE! But, how could you make that deal? How could you promise him six more movies?
That was easy! Have you seen the lines of people, waiting to see this movie? Have you seen the grosses it's piling up? What ELSE does Hollywood need to start a trend! SIX more "Devil Flicks"? Why, I'd guarantee SIXTY . . . SEVENTY!
Oh, well . . . that's "SHOW BIZ"!!
CONTRACT

PLOT-BOILER DEPT.

**When you have problems and you don't want to think about them, what do you do? You go to the movies to take your mind off things, right? Wrong! Today, they're making movies that only *add* to your worries! Like—if you enjoy taking cruises, you can worry about dying in a "Poseidon Adventure"! Or if you live in the Los Angeles area, you can worry about dying in an "Earthquake"! Or, as is the case in this latest disaster epic, if you live or work in a modern, glass-walled skyscraper, you can worry about dying in—**

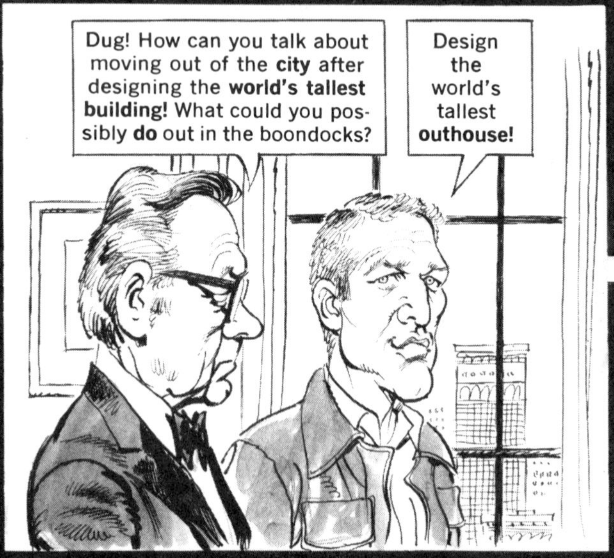
Dug! How can you talk about moving out of the **city** after designing the **world's tallest building!** What could you possibly **do** out in the boondocks?
Design the world's tallest **outhouse!**

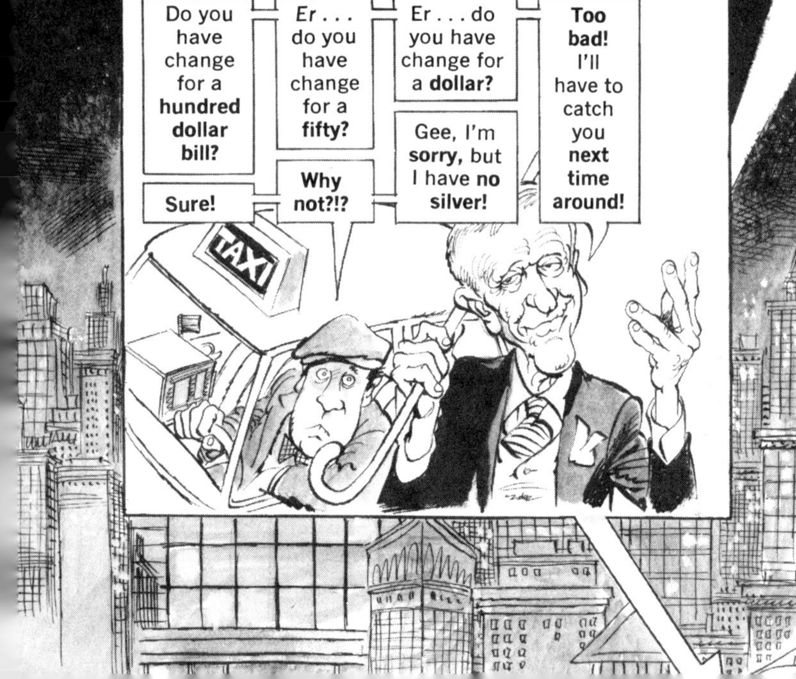
Do you have change for a **hundred dollar bill?**
Sure!
*Er . . .* do you have change for a **fifty?**
**Why not?!?**
Er . . . do you have change for a **dollar?**
Gee, I'm **sorry,** but I have **no silver!**
**Too bad!** I'll have to catch you **next time around!**
TAXI

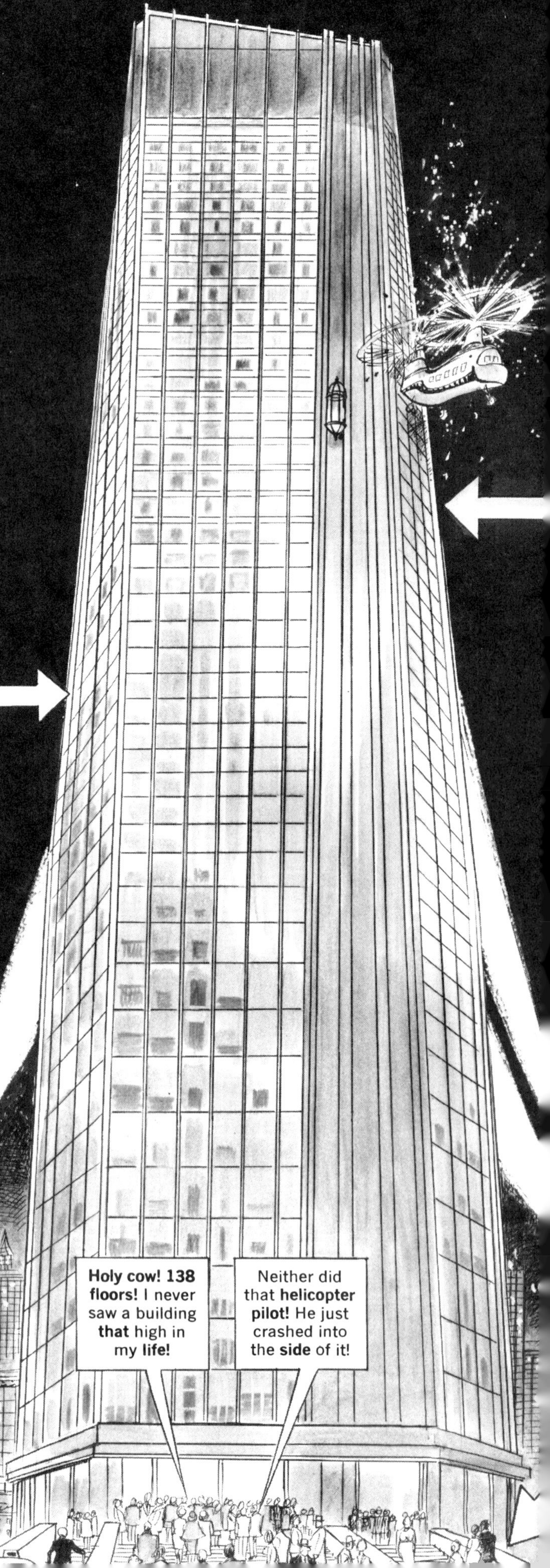
**Holy cow! 138 floors!** I never saw a building **that** high in my **life!**
Neither did that **helicopter pilot!** He just crashed into the **side** of it!

# THE TOWERING STERNO

ARTIST: MORT DRUCKER WRITER: DICK DE BARTOLO

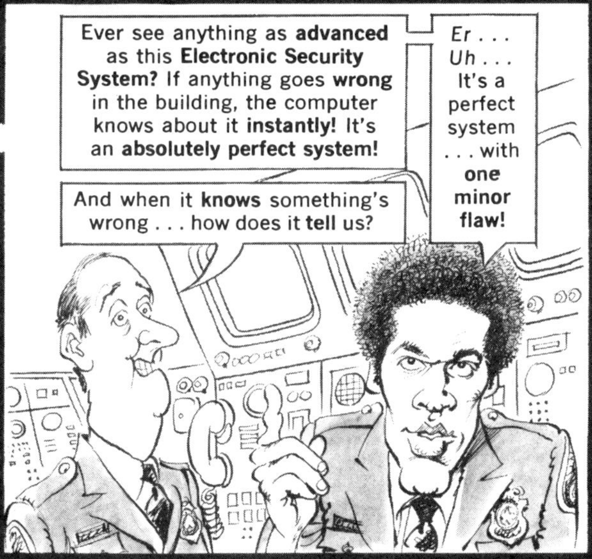
Ever see anything as advanced as this Electronic Security System? If anything goes wrong in the building, the computer knows about it instantly! It's an absolutely perfect system!
And when it knows something's wrong . . . how does it tell us?
Er . . . Uh . . . It's a perfect system . . . with one minor flaw!

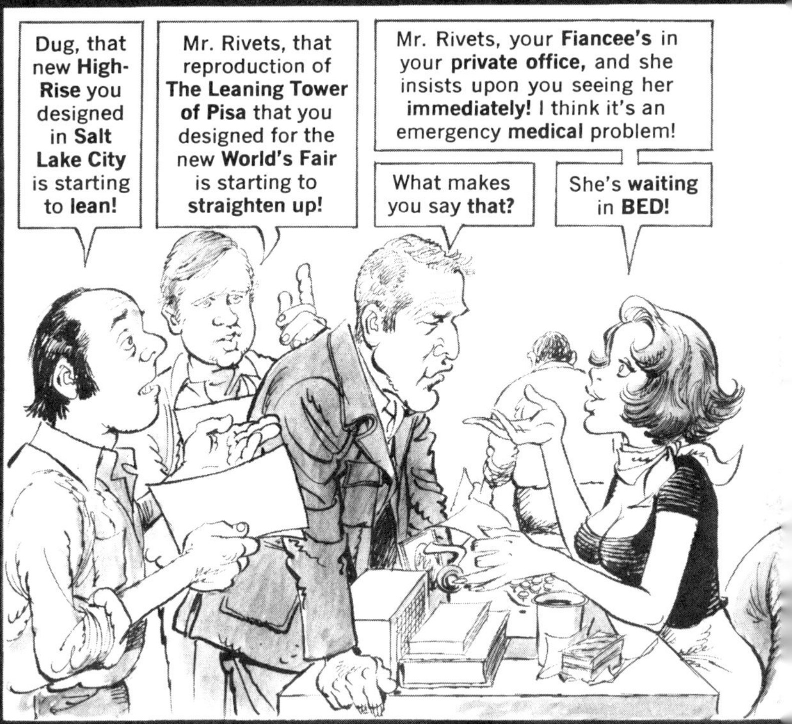
Dug, that new High-Rise you designed in Salt Lake City is starting to lean!
Mr. Rivets, that reproduction of The Leaning Tower of Pisa that you designed for the new World's Fair is starting to straighten up!
Mr. Rivets, your Fiancee's in your private office, and she insists upon you seeing her immediately! I think it's an emergency medical problem!
What makes you say that?
She's waiting in BED!

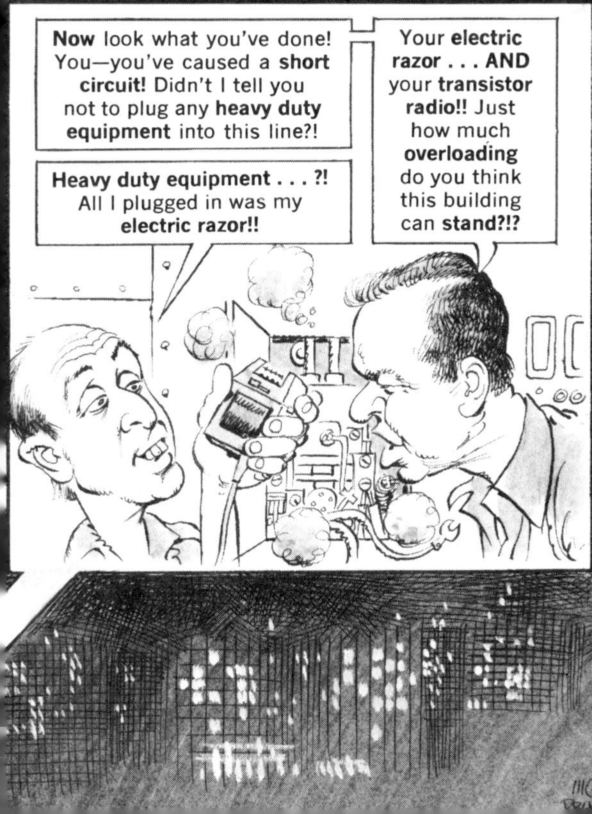
Now look what you've done! You—you've caused a short circuit! Didn't I tell you not to plug any heavy duty equipment into this line?!
Heavy duty equipment . . . ?! All I plugged in was my electric razor!!
Your electric razor . . . AND your transistor radio!! Just how much overloading do you think this building can stand?!?

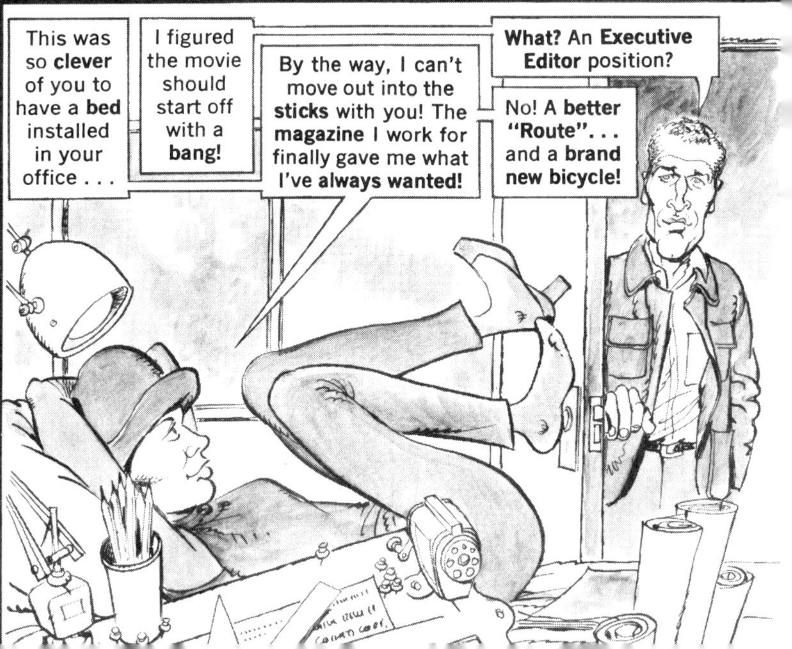
This was so clever of you to have a bed installed in your office . . .
I figured the movie should start off with a bang!
By the way, I can't move out into the sticks with you! The magazine I work for finally gave me what I've always wanted!
What? An Executive Editor position?
No! A better "Route". . . and a brand new bicycle!

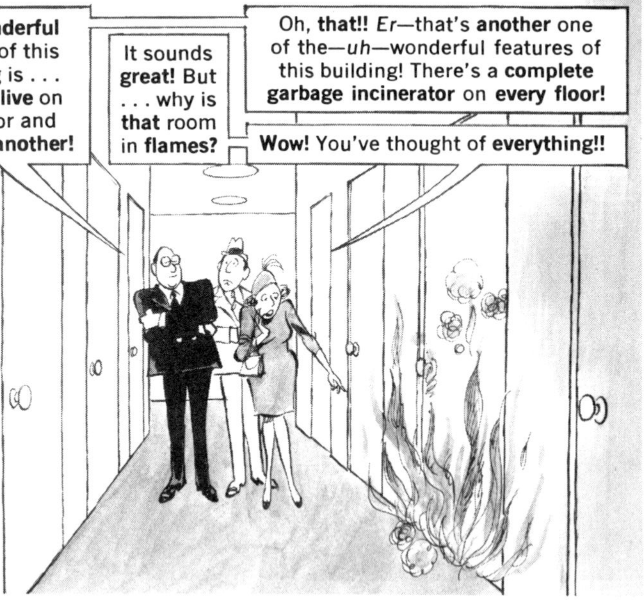
The wonderful feature of this building is . . . you can live on one floor and work on another!
It sounds great! But . . . why is that room in flames?
Oh, that!! Er—that's another one of the—uh—wonderful features of this building! There's a complete garbage incinerator on every floor!
Wow! You've thought of everything!!

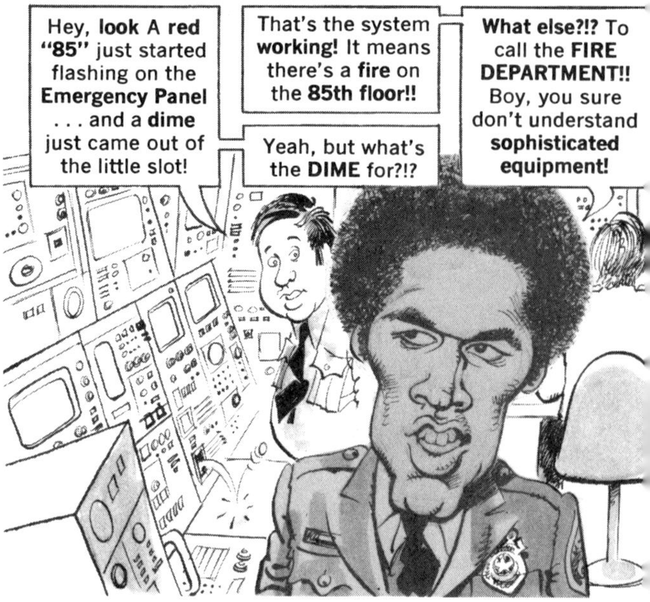
Hey, look A red "85" just started flashing on the Emergency Panel . . . and a dime just came out of the little slot!
That's the system working! It means there's a fire on the 85th floor!!
Yeah, but what's the DIME for?!?
What else?!? To call the FIRE DEPARTMENT!! Boy, you sure don't understand sophisticated equipment!

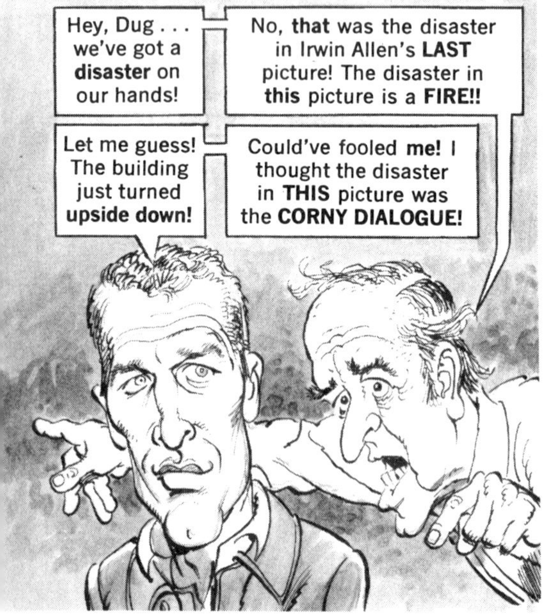
Hey, Dug . . . we've got a disaster on our hands!
No, that was the disaster in Irwin Allen's LAST picture! The disaster in this picture is a FIRE!!
Let me guess! The building just turned upside down!
Could've fooled me! I thought the disaster in THIS picture was the CORNY DIALOGUE!

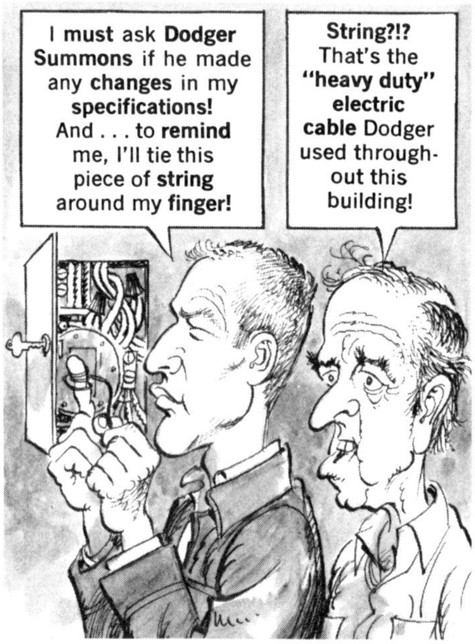
I must ask Dodger Summons if he made any changes in my specifications! And . . . to remind me, I'll tie this piece of string around my finger!
String?!? That's the "heavy duty" electric cable Dodger used throughout this building!

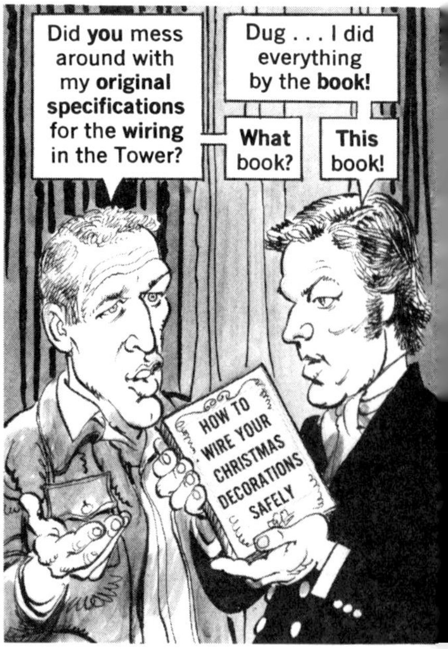
Did you mess around with my original specifications for the wiring in the Tower?
Dug . . . I did everything by the book!
What book?
This book!
HOW TO WIRE YOUR CHRISTMAS DECORATIONS SAFELY

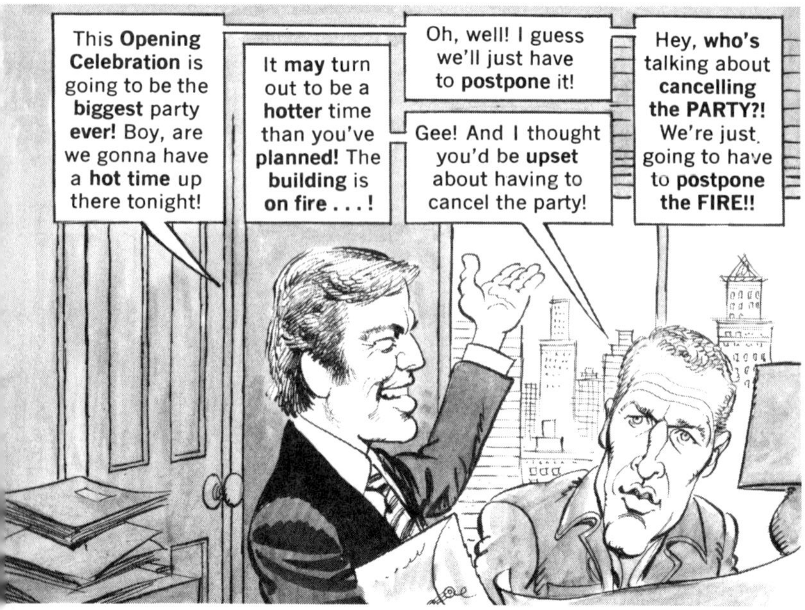
This Opening Celebration is going to be the biggest party ever! Boy, are we gonna have a hot time up there tonight!
It may turn out to be a hotter time than you've planned! The building is on fire . . . !
Oh, well! I guess we'll just have to postpone it!
Gee! And I thought you'd be upset about having to cancel the party!
Hey, who's talking about cancelling the PARTY?! We're just going to have to postpone the FIRE!!

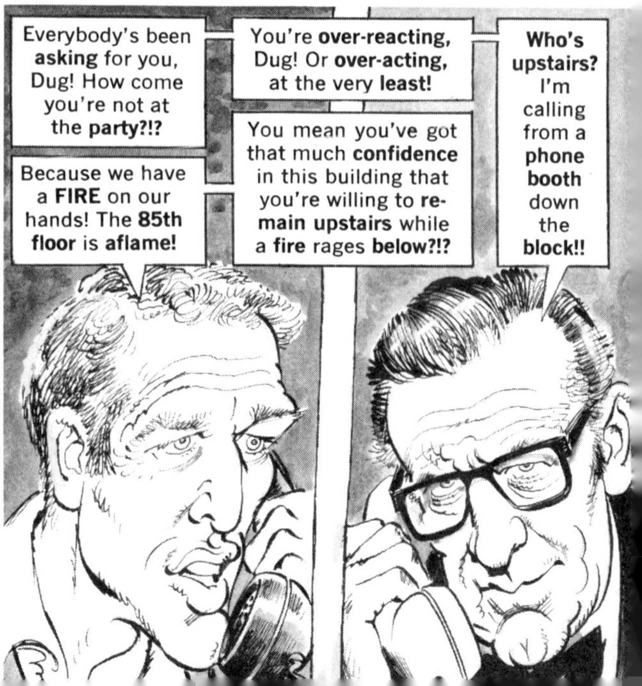
Everybody's been asking for you, Dug! How come you're not at the party?!?
Because we have a FIRE on our hands! The 85th floor is aflame!
You're over-reacting, Dug! Or over-acting, at the very least!
You mean you've got that much confidence in this building that you're willing to remain upstairs while a fire rages below?!?
Who's upstairs? I'm calling from a phone booth down the block!!

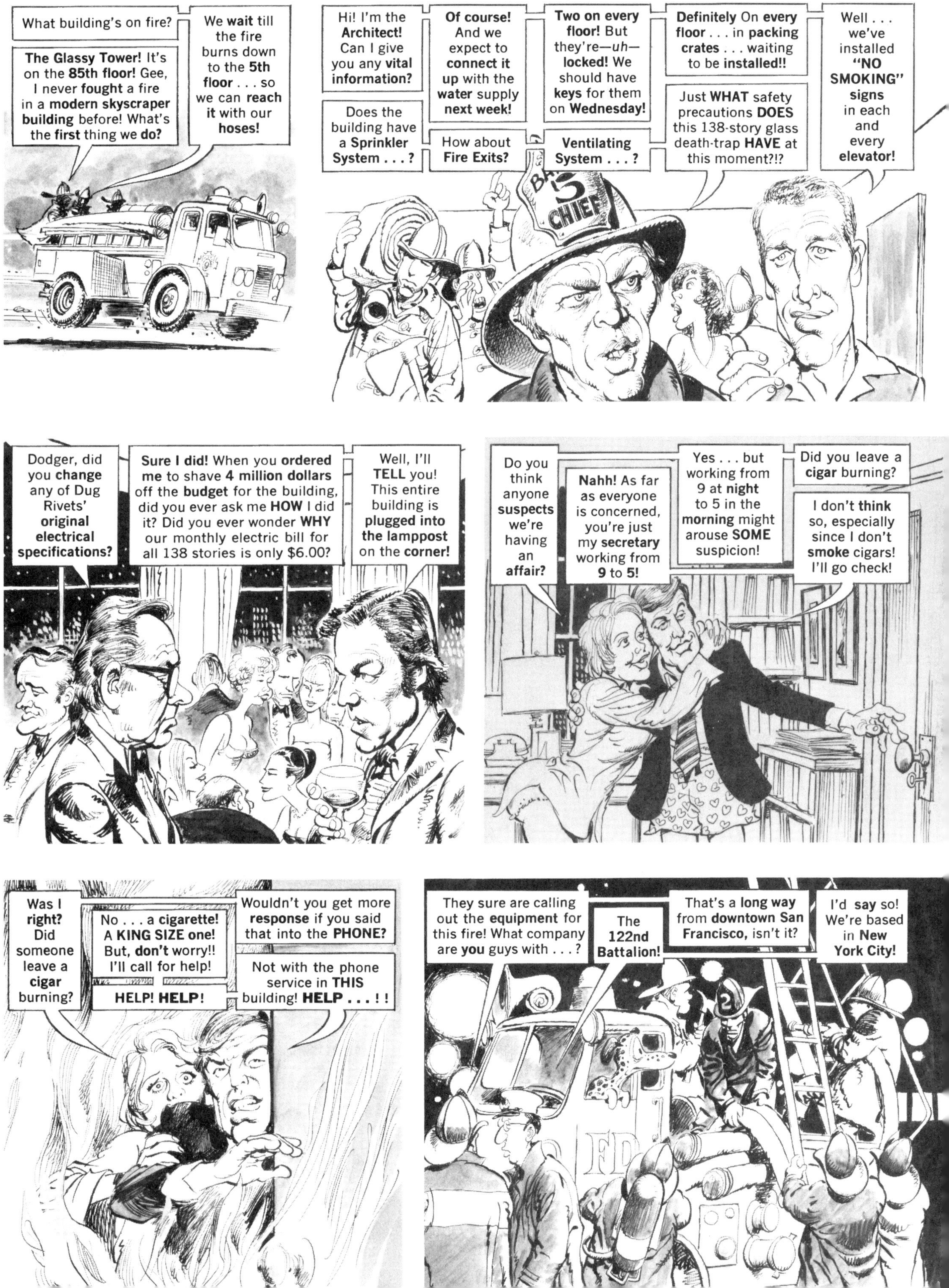
What building's on fire?
The Glassy Tower! It's on the 85th floor! Gee, I never fought a fire in a modern skyscraper building before! What's the first thing we do?
We wait till the fire burns down to the 5th floor . . . so we can reach it with our hoses!
Hi! I'm the Architect! Can I give you any vital information?
Does the building have a Sprinkler System . . . ?
Of course! And we expect to connect it up with the water supply next week!
How about Fire Exits?
Two on every floor! But they're—uh—locked! We should have keys for them on Wednesday!
Ventilating System . . . ?
Definitely On every floor . . . in packing crates . . . waiting to be installed!!
Just WHAT safety precautions DOES this 138-story glass death-trap HAVE at this moment?!?
Well . . . we've installed "NO SMOKING" signs in each and every elevator!
BAT 5 CHIEF
Dodger, did you change any of Dug Rivets' original electrical specifications?
Sure I did! When you ordered me to shave 4 million dollars off the budget for the building, did you ever ask me HOW I did it? Did you ever wonder WHY our monthly electric bill for all 138 stories is only $6.00?
Well, I'll TELL you! This entire building is plugged into the lamppost on the corner!
Do you think anyone suspects we're having an affair?
Nahh! As far as everyone is concerned, you're just my secretary working from 9 to 5!
Yes . . . but working from 9 at night to 5 in the morning might arouse SOME suspicion!
Did you leave a cigar burning?
I don't think so, especially since I don't smoke cigars! I'll go check!
Was I right? Did someone leave a cigar burning?
No . . . a cigarette! A KING SIZE one! But, don't worry!! I'll call for help!
HELP! HELP!
Wouldn't you get more response if you said that into the PHONE?
Not with the phone service in THIS building! HELP . . . ! !
They sure are calling out the equipment for this fire! What company are you guys with . . . ?
The 122nd Battalion!
That's a long way from downtown San Francisco, isn't it?
I'd say so! We're based in New York City!
FD

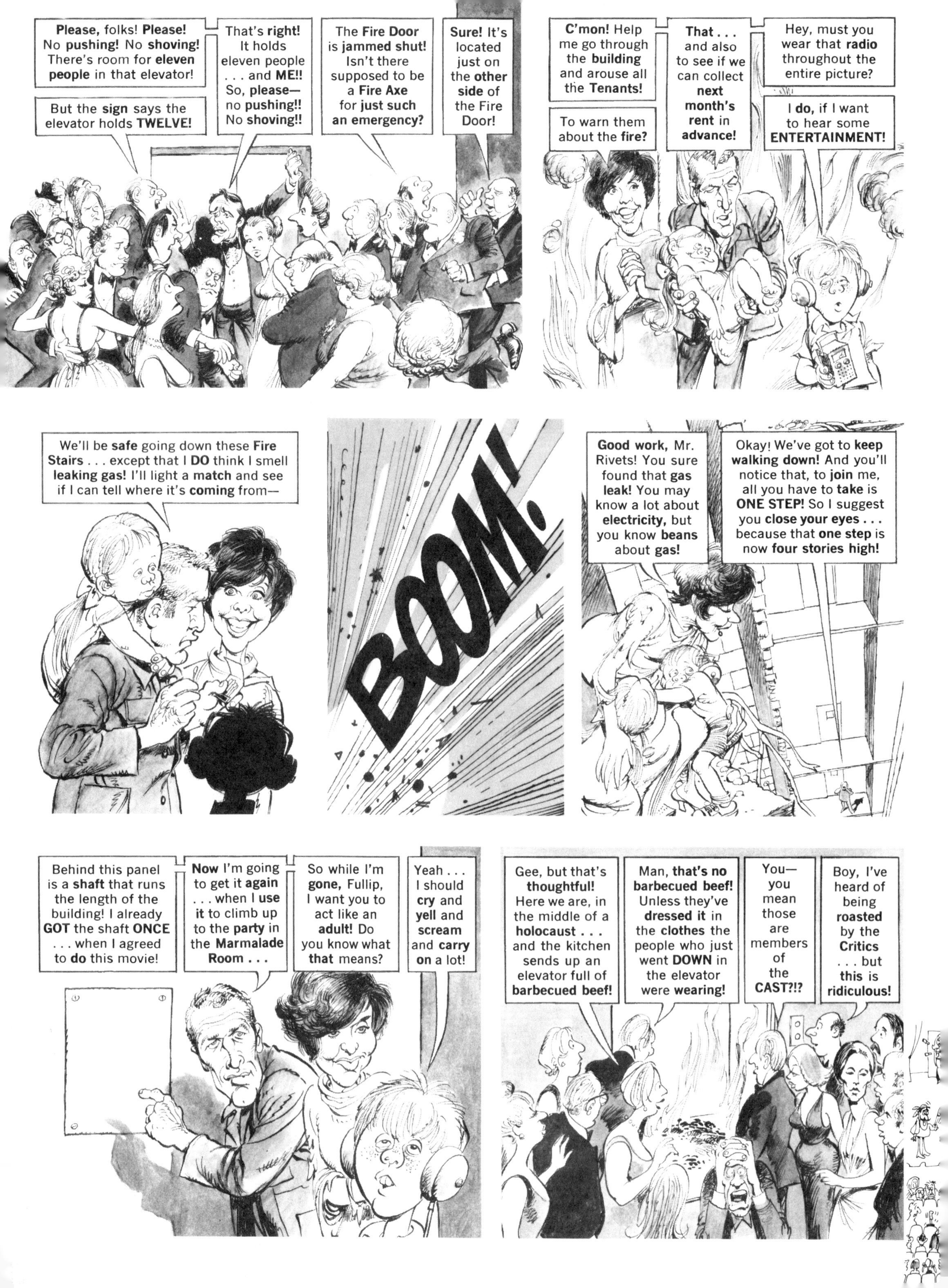

Please, folks! Please! No pushing! No shoving! There's room for eleven people in that elevator!
But the sign says the elevator holds TWELVE!
That's right! It holds eleven people . . . and ME!! So, please— no pushing!! No shoving!!
The Fire Door is jammed shut! Isn't there supposed to be a Fire Axe for just such an emergency?
Sure! It's located just on the other side of the Fire Door!
C'mon! Help me go through the building and arouse all the Tenants!
To warn them about the fire?
That . . . and also to see if we can collect next month's rent in advance!
Hey, must you wear that radio throughout the entire picture?
I do, if I want to hear some ENTERTAINMENT!
We'll be safe going down these Fire Stairs . . . except that I DO think I smell leaking gas! I'll light a match and see if I can tell where it's coming from—
BOOM!
Good work, Mr. Rivets! You sure found that gas leak! You may know a lot about electricity, but you know beans about gas!
Okay! We've got to keep walking down! And you'll notice that, to join me, all you have to take is ONE STEP! So I suggest you close your eyes . . . because that one step is now four stories high!
Behind this panel is a shaft that runs the length of the building! I already GOT the shaft ONCE . . . when I agreed to do this movie!
Now I'm going to get it again . . . when I use it to climb up to the party in the Marmalade Room . . .
So while I'm gone, Fullip, I want you to act like an adult! Do you know what that means?
Yeah . . . I should cry and yell and scream and carry on a lot!
Gee, but that's thoughtful! Here we are, in the middle of a holocaust . . . and the kitchen sends up an elevator full of barbecued beef!
Man, that's no barbecued beef! Unless they've dressed it in the clothes the people who just went DOWN in the elevator were wearing!
You— you mean those are members of the CAST?!?
Boy, I've heard of being roasted by the Critics . . . but this is ridiculous!

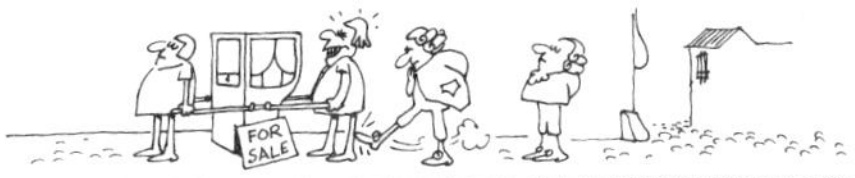
FOR SALE

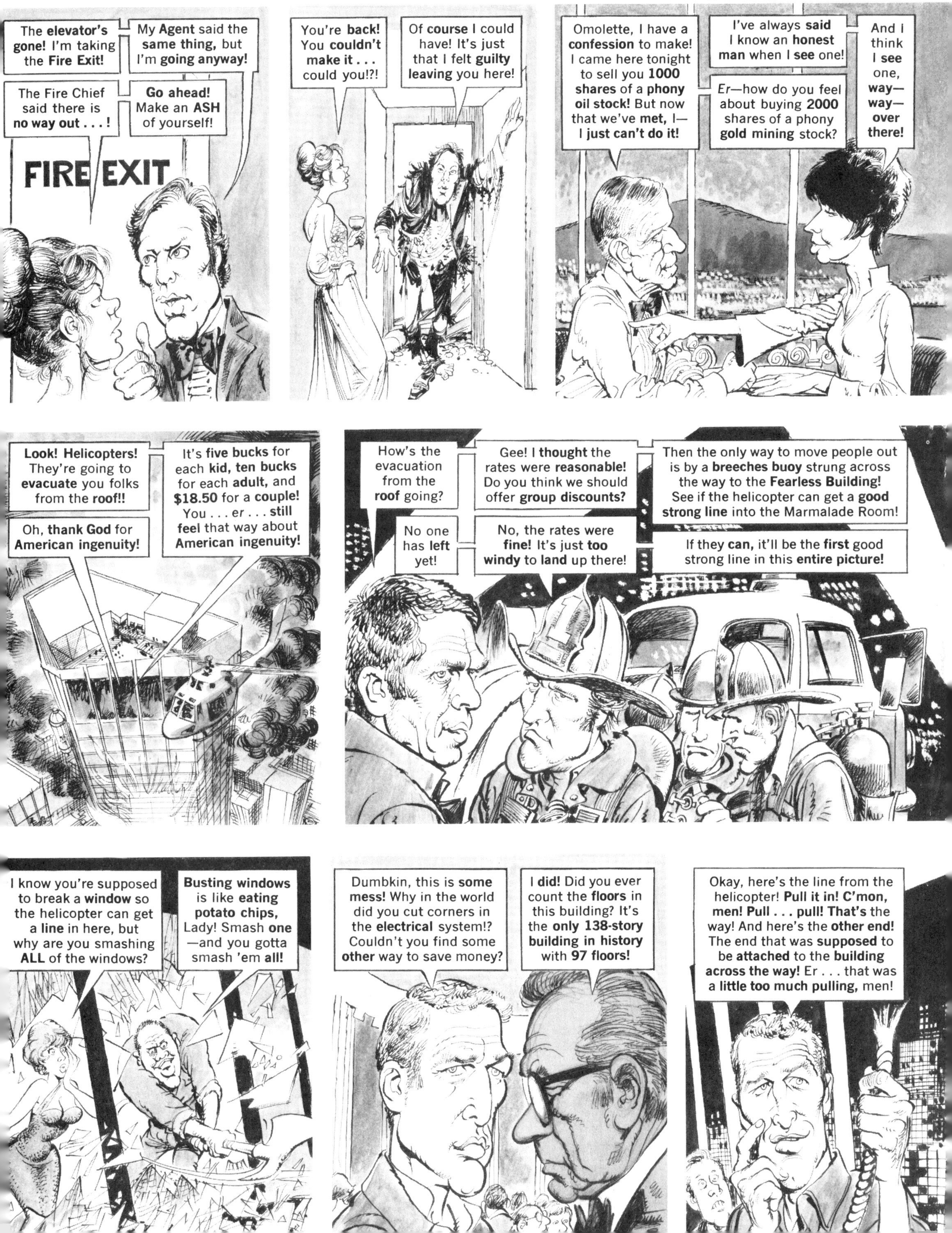
The elevator's gone! I'm taking the Fire Exit!
My Agent said the same thing, but I'm going anyway!
The Fire Chief said there is no way out . . . !
Go ahead! Make an ASH of yourself!
FIRE EXIT
You're back! You couldn't make it . . . could you!?!
Of course I could have! It's just that I felt guilty leaving you here!
Omolette, I have a confession to make! I came here tonight to sell you 1000 shares of a phony oil stock! But now that we've met, I— I just can't do it!
I've always said I know an honest man when I see one!
Er—how do you feel about buying 2000 shares of a phony gold mining stock?
And I think I see one, way—way—over there!
Look! Helicopters! They're going to evacuate you folks from the roof!!
Oh, thank God for American ingenuity!
It's five bucks for each kid, ten bucks for each adult, and $18.50 for a couple! You . . . er . . . still feel that way about American ingenuity!
How's the evacuation from the roof going?
No one has left yet!
Gee! I thought the rates were reasonable! Do you think we should offer group discounts?
No, the rates were fine! It's just too windy to land up there!
Then the only way to move people out is by a breeches buoy strung across the way to the Fearless Building! See if the helicopter can get a good strong line into the Marmalade Room!
If they can, it'll be the first good strong line in this entire picture!
I know you're supposed to break a window so the helicopter can get a line in here, but why are you smashing ALL of the windows?
Busting windows is like eating potato chips, Lady! Smash one—and you gotta smash 'em all!
Dumbkin, this is some mess! Why in the world did you cut corners in the electrical system!? Couldn't you find some other way to save money?
I did! Did you ever count the floors in this building? It's the only 138-story building in history with 97 floors!
Okay, here's the line from the helicopter! Pull it in! C'mon, men! Pull . . . pull! That's the way! And here's the other end! The end that was supposed to be attached to the building across the way! Er . . . that was a little too much pulling, men!

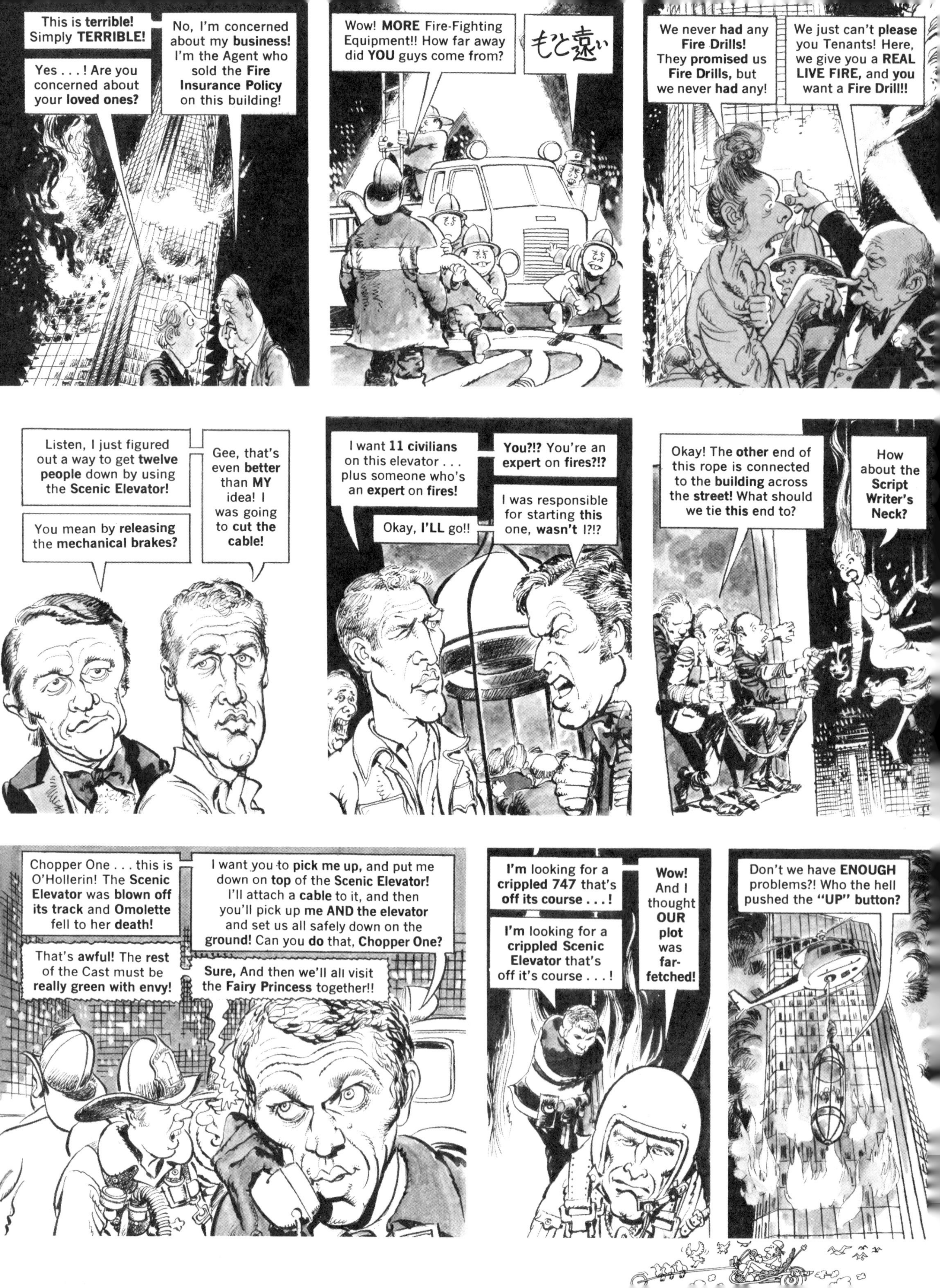

This is terrible! Simply TERRIBLE!
Yes . . . ! Are you concerned about your loved ones?
No, I'm concerned about my business! I'm the Agent who sold the Fire Insurance Policy on this building!
Wow! MORE Fire-Fighting Equipment!! How far away did YOU guys come from?
もっと遠い
We never had any Fire Drills! They promised us Fire Drills, but we never had any!
We just can't please you Tenants! Here, we give you a REAL LIVE FIRE, and you want a Fire Drill!!
Listen, I just figured out a way to get twelve people down by using the Scenic Elevator!
You mean by releasing the mechanical brakes?
Gee, that's even better than MY idea! I was going to cut the cable!
I want 11 civilians on this elevator . . . plus someone who's an expert on fires!
Okay, I'LL go!!
You?!? You're an expert on fires?!?
I was responsible for starting this one, wasn't I?!?
Okay! The other end of this rope is connected to the building across the street! What should we tie this end to?
How about the Script Writer's Neck?
Chopper One . . . this is O'Hollerin! The Scenic Elevator was blown off its track and Omolette fell to her death!
That's awful! The rest of the Cast must be really green with envy!
I want you to pick me up, and put me down on top of the Scenic Elevator! I'll attach a cable to it, and then you'll pick up me AND the elevator and set us all safely down on the ground! Can you do that, Chopper One?
Sure, And then we'll all visit the Fairy Princess together!!
I'm looking for a crippled 747 that's off its course . . . !
I'm looking for a crippled Scenic Elevator that's off it's course . . . !
Wow! And I thought OUR plot was far-fetched!
Don't we have ENOUGH problems?! Who the hell pushed the "UP" button?

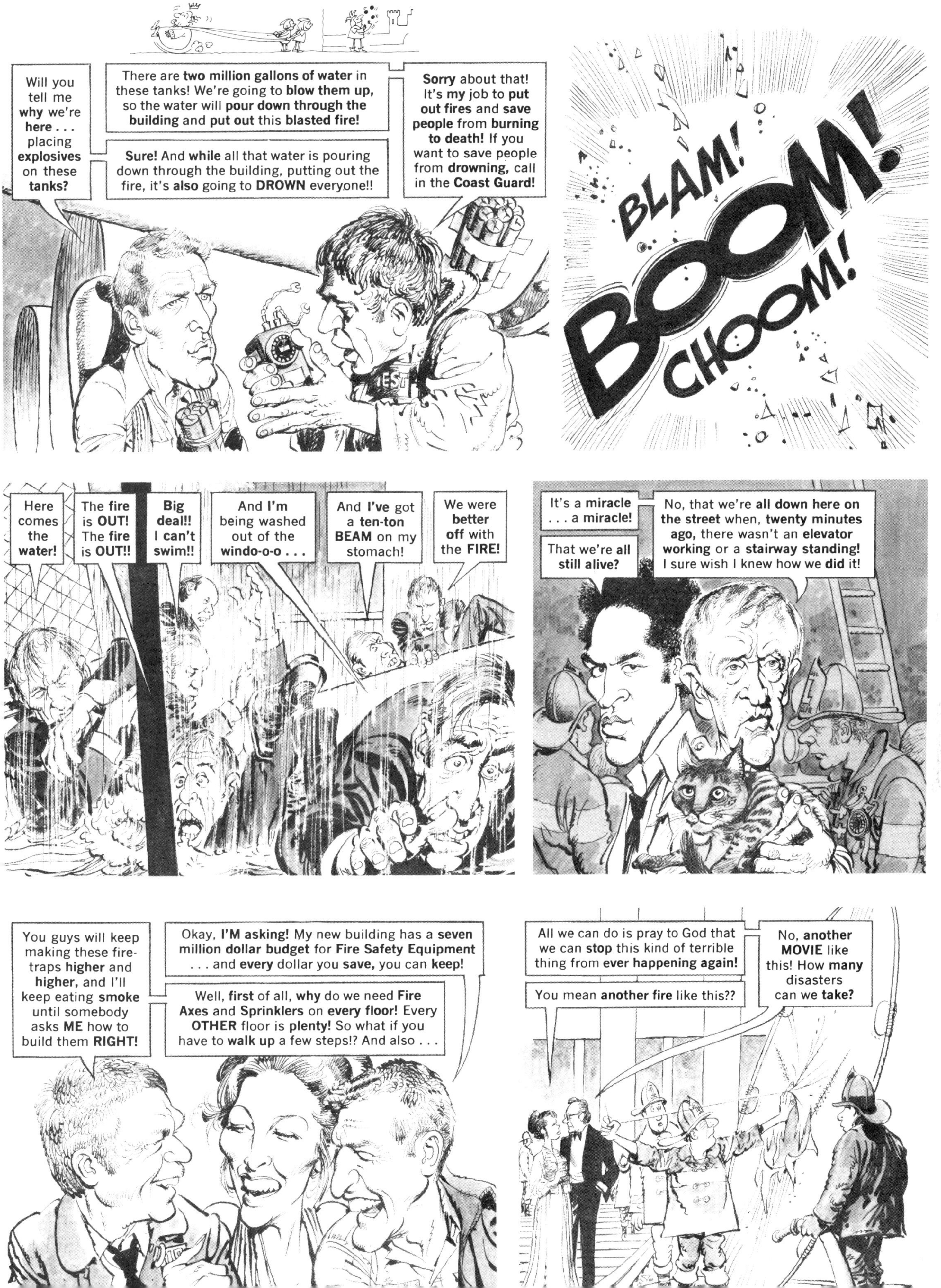

Will you tell me why we're here . . . placing explosives on these tanks?
There are two million gallons of water in these tanks! We're going to blow them up, so the water will pour down through the building and put out this blasted fire!
Sure! And while all that water is pouring down through the building, putting out the fire, it's also going to DROWN everyone!!
Sorry about that! It's my job to put out fires and save people from burning to death! If you want to save people from drowning, call in the Coast Guard!
BLAM! BOOM! CHOOM!
Here comes the water!
The fire is OUT! The fire is OUT!!
Big deal!! I can't swim!!
And I'm being washed out of the windo-o-o . . .
And I've got a ten-ton BEAM on my stomach!
We were better off with the FIRE!
It's a miracle . . . a miracle!
That we're all still alive?
No, that we're all down here on the street when, twenty minutes ago, there wasn't an elevator working or a stairway standing! I sure wish I knew how we did it!
You guys will keep making these fire-traps higher and higher, and I'll keep eating smoke until somebody asks ME how to build them RIGHT!
Okay, I'M asking! My new building has a seven million dollar budget for Fire Safety Equipment . . . and every dollar you save, you can keep!
Well, first of all, why do we need Fire Axes and Sprinklers on every floor! Every OTHER floor is plenty! So what if you have to walk up a few steps!? And also . . .
All we can do is pray to God that we can stop this kind of terrible thing from ever happening again!
You mean another fire like this??
No, another MOVIE like this! How many disasters can we take?

WITHDRAWAL SIMPLETONS DEPT.

For a while there, we were being treated to a rash of bank robbery films in which the criminals were clever, their plans ingenious and the execution brilliant. However, we are now threatened with a new, sickening trend in bank robbery films . . . inspired by the success of this latest farce . . . in which the criminals are IDIOTS who get themselves all loused up one hot

# DUM-DU

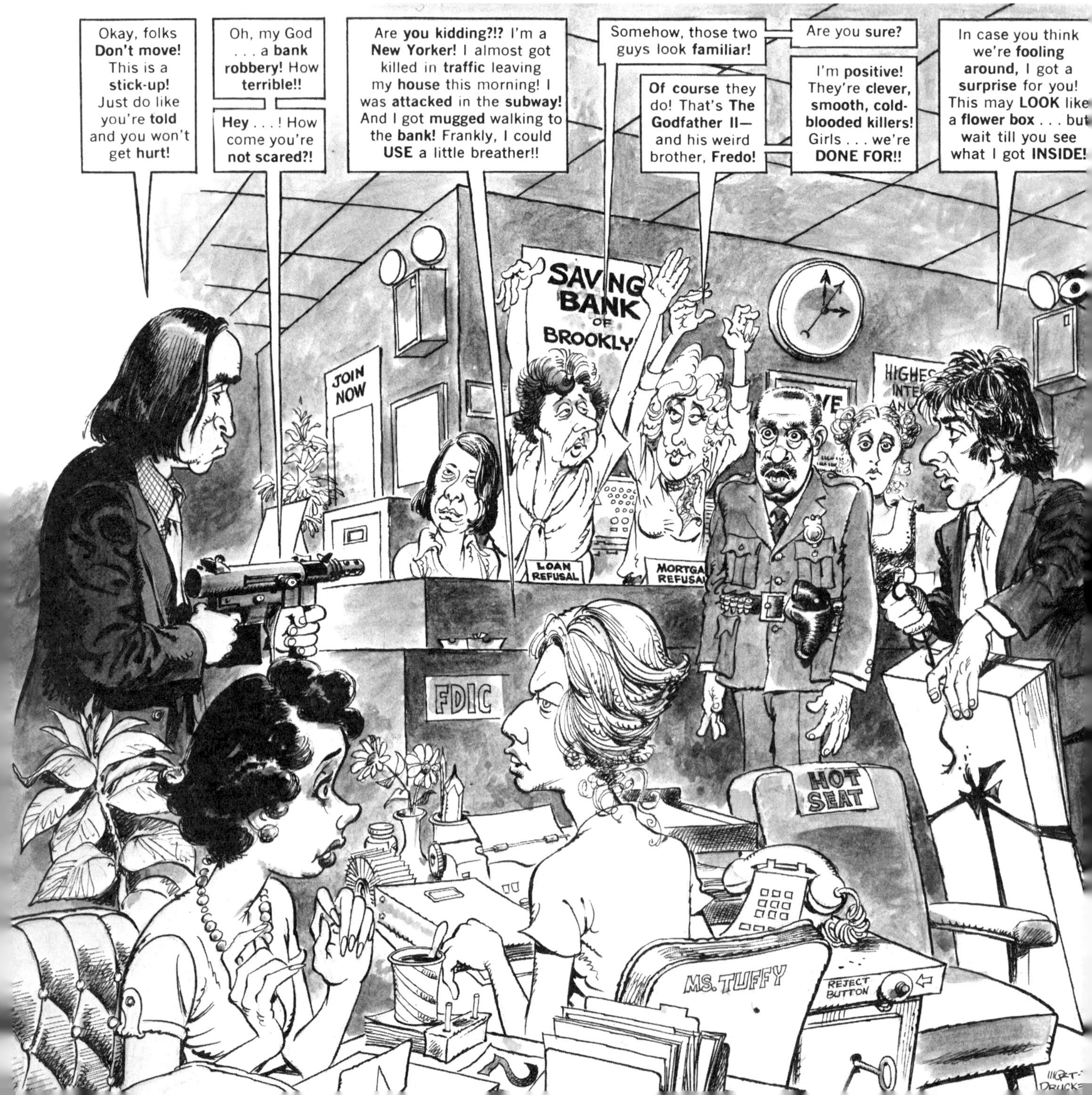

Okay, folks Don't move! This is a stick-up! Just do like you're told and you won't get hurt!
Oh, my God . . . a bank robbery! How terrible!!
Hey . . . ! How come you're not scared?!
Are you kidding?!? I'm a New Yorker! I almost got killed in traffic leaving my house this morning! I was attacked in the subway! And I got mugged walking to the bank! Frankly, I could USE a little breather!!
Somehow, those two guys look familiar!
Of course they do! That's The Godfather II— and his weird brother, Fredo!
Are you sure?
I'm positive! They're clever, smooth, cold-blooded killers! Girls . . . we're DONE FOR!!
In case you think we're fooling around, I got a surprise for you! This may LOOK like a flower box . . . but wait till you see what I got INSIDE!
SAVING BANK OF BROOKLY
JOIN NOW
LOAN REFUSAL
MORTGA REFUSA
FDIC
HOT SEAT
MS. TUFFY
REJECT BUTTON

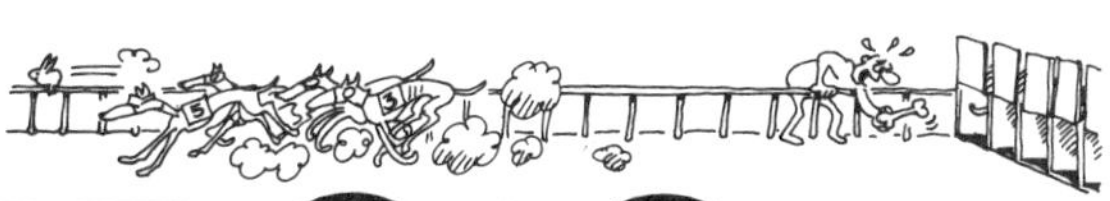

# M AFTERNOON

ARTIST: MORT DRUCKER WRITER: LARRY SIEGEL

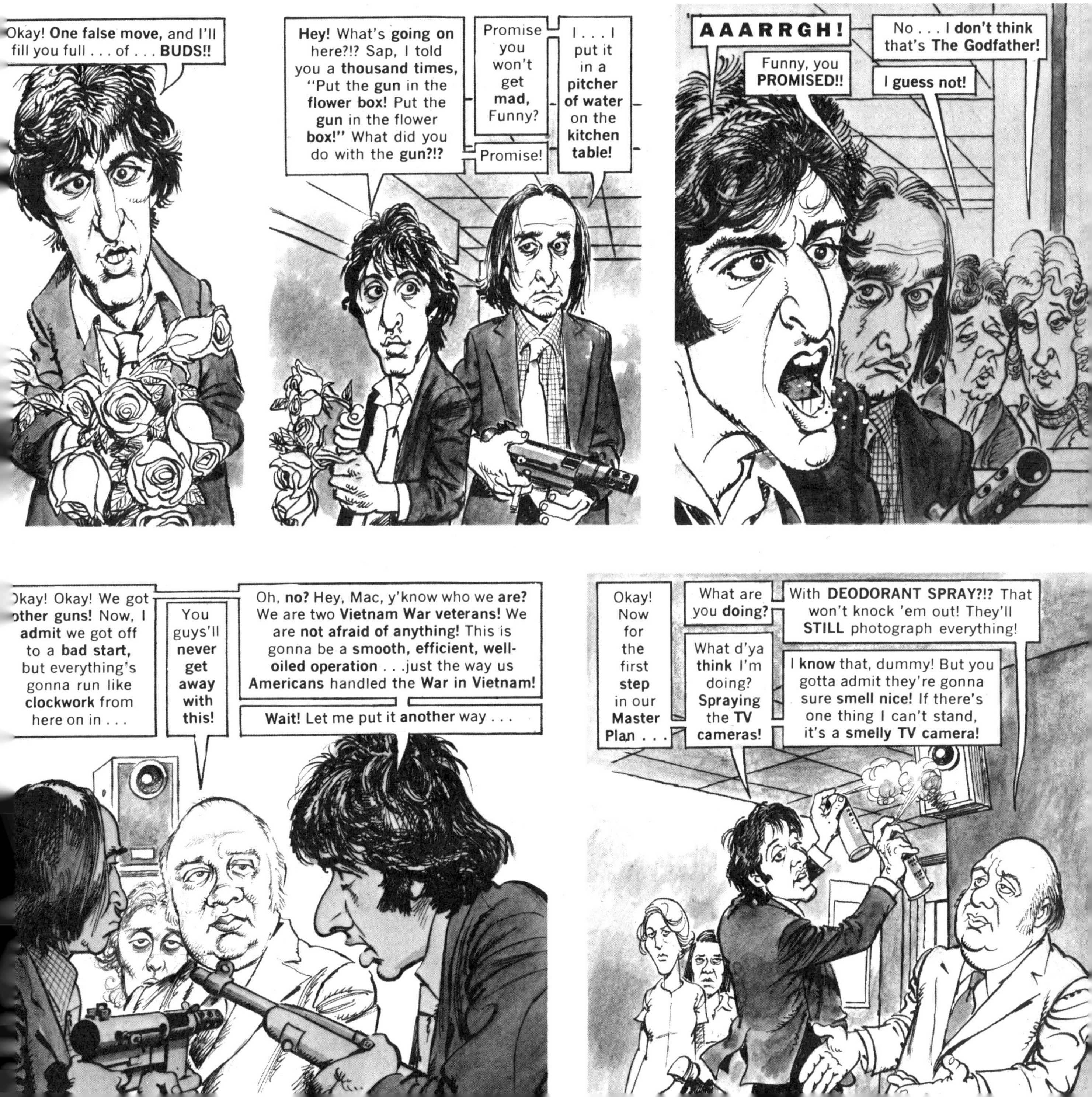
Okay! One false move, and I'll fill you full . . . of . . . BUDS!!
Hey! What's going on here?!? Sap, I told you a thousand times, "Put the gun in the flower box! Put the gun in the flower box!" What did you do with the gun?!?
Promise you won't get mad, Funny?
Promise!
I . . . I put it in a pitcher of water on the kitchen table!
AAARRGH!
Funny, you PROMISED!!
No . . . I don't think that's The Godfather!
I guess not!
Okay! Okay! We got other guns! Now, I admit we got off to a bad start, but everything's gonna run like clockwork from here on in . . .
You guys'll never get away with this!
Oh, no? Hey, Mac, y'know who we are? We are two Vietnam War veterans! We are not afraid of anything! This is gonna be a smooth, efficient, well-oiled operation . . .just the way us Americans handled the War in Vietnam!
Wait! Let me put it another way . . .
Okay! Now for the first step in our Master Plan . . .
What are you doing?
What d'ya think I'm doing? Spraying the TV cameras!
With DEODORANT SPRAY?!? That won't knock 'em out! They'll STILL photograph everything!
I know that, dummy! But you gotta admit they're gonna sure smell nice! If there's one thing I can't stand, it's a smelly TV camera!

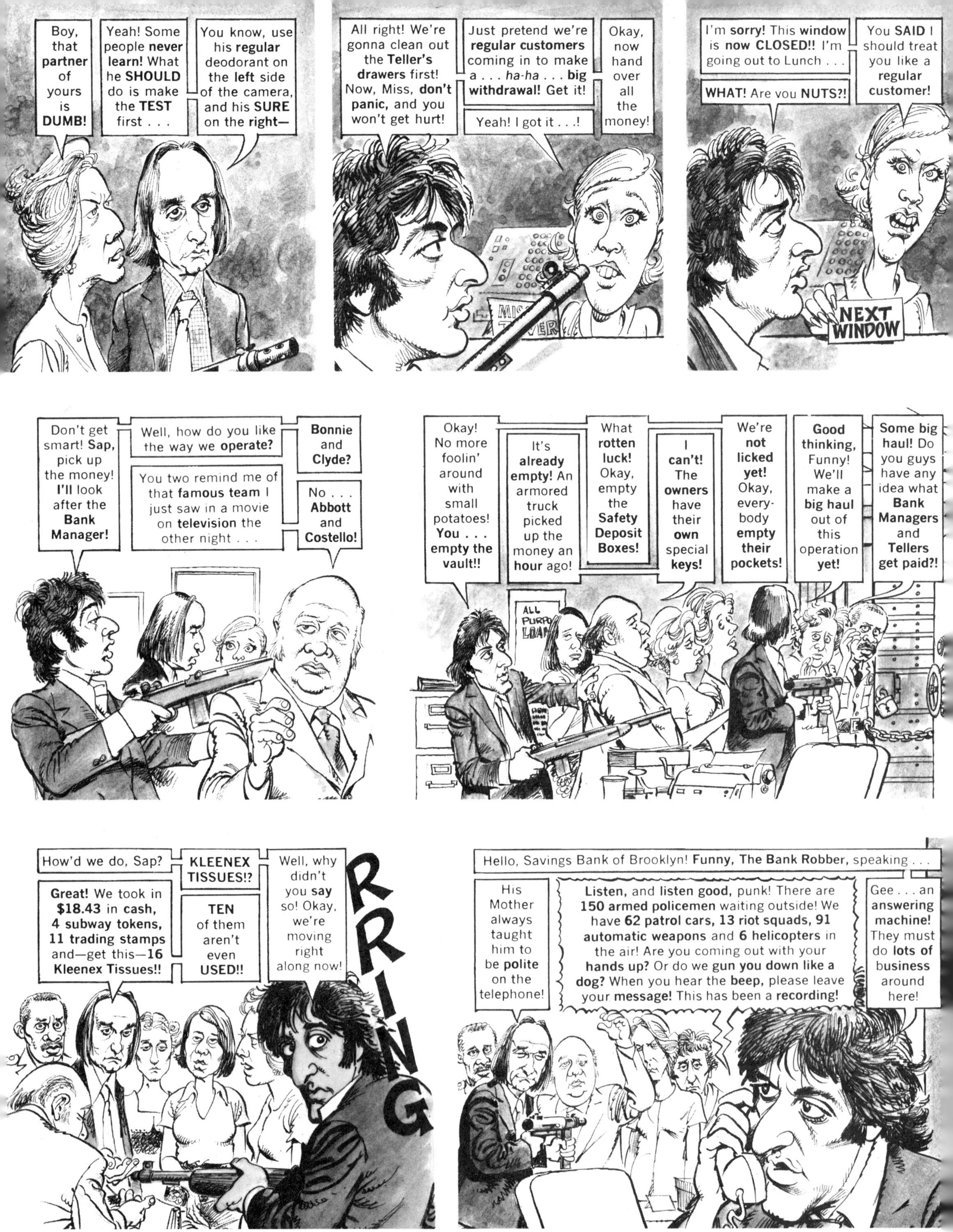

Boy, that partner of yours is DUMB!
Yeah! Some people never learn! What he SHOULD do is make the TEST first . . .
You know, use his regular deodorant on the left side of the camera, and his SURE on the right—
All right! We're gonna clean out the Teller's drawers first! Now, Miss, don't panic, and you won't get hurt!
Just pretend we're regular customers coming in to make a . . . ha-ha . . . big withdrawal! Get it!
Yeah! I got it . . .!
Okay, now hand over all the money!
I'm sorry! This window is now CLOSED!! I'm going out to Lunch . . .
WHAT! Are you NUTS?!
You SAID I should treat you like a regular customer!
NEXT WINDOW
Don't get smart! Sap, pick up the money! I'll look after the Bank Manager!
Well, how do you like the way we operate?
You two remind me of that famous team I just saw in a movie on television the other night . . .
Bonnie and Clyde?
No . . . Abbott and Costello!
Okay! No more foolin' around with small potatoes! You . . . empty the vault!!
It's already empty! An armored truck picked up the money an hour ago!
What rotten luck! Okay, empty the Safety Deposit Boxes!
I can't! The owners have their own special keys!
We're not licked yet! Okay, everybody empty their pockets!
Good thinking, Funny! We'll make a big haul out of this operation yet!
Some big haul! Do you guys have any idea what Bank Managers and Tellers get paid?!
ALL PURPO LOAN
How'd we do, Sap?
Great! We took in $18.43 in cash, 4 subway tokens, 11 trading stamps and—get this—16 Kleenex Tissues!!
KLEENEX TISSUES!?
TEN of them aren't even USED!!
Well, why didn't you say so! Okay, we're moving right along now!
RRING
Hello, Savings Bank of Brooklyn! Funny, The Bank Robber, speaking . . .
His Mother always taught him to be polite on the telephone!
Listen, and listen good, punk! There are 150 armed policemen waiting outside! We have 62 patrol cars, 13 riot squads, 91 automatic weapons and 6 helicopters in the air! Are you coming out with your hands up? Or do we gun you down like a dog? When you hear the beep, please leave your message! This has been a recording!
Gee . . . an answering machine! They must do lots of business around here!


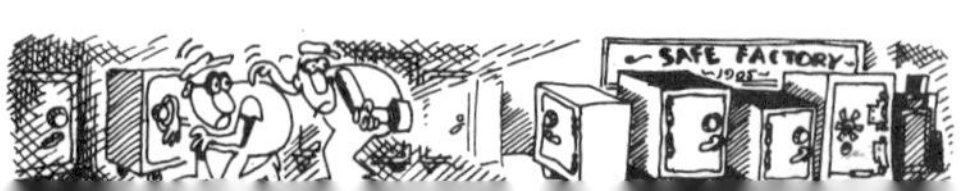

SAFE FACTORY

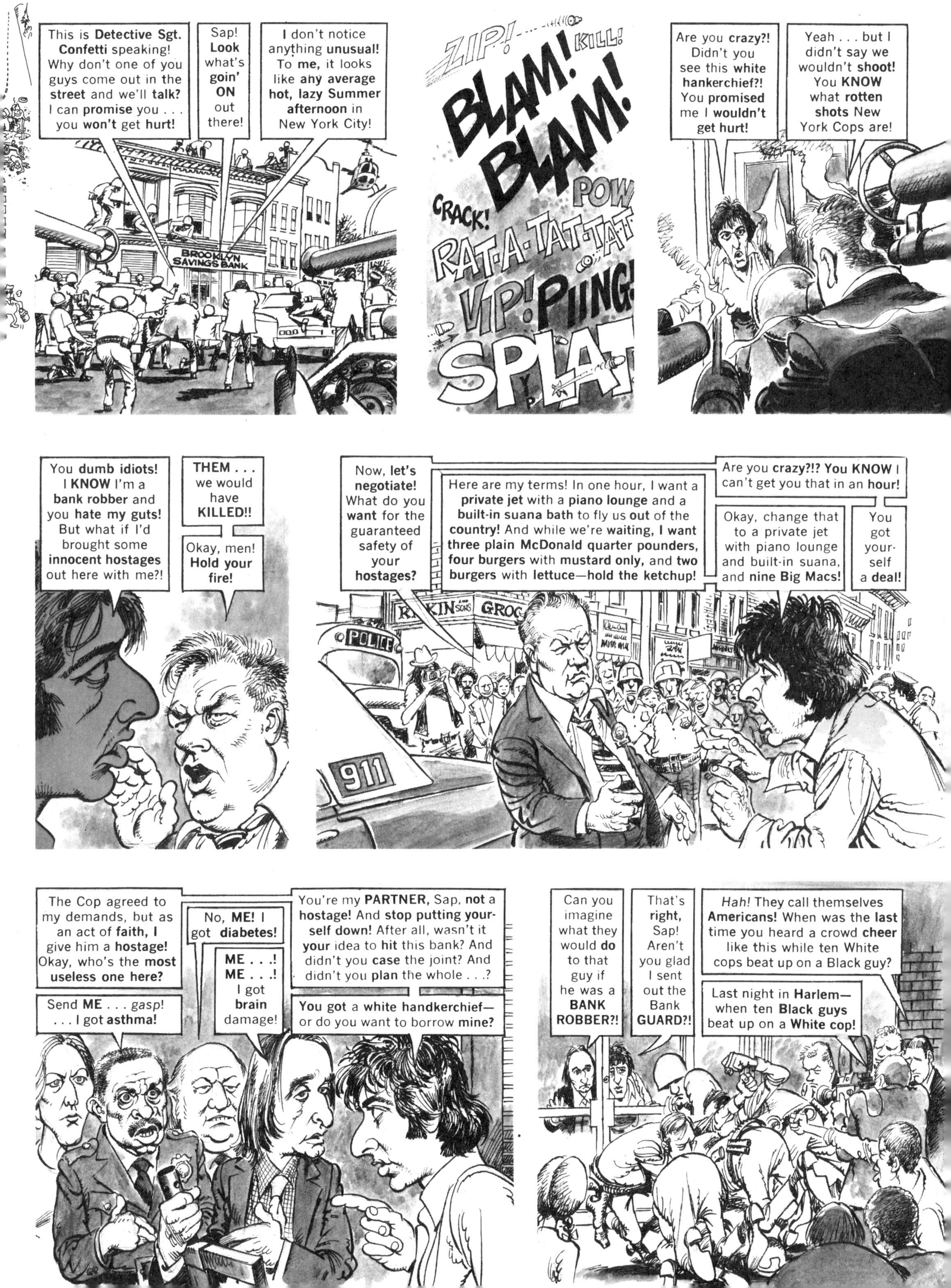
This is Detective Sgt. Confetti speaking! Why don't one of you guys come out in the street and we'll talk? I can promise you . . . you won't get hurt!
Sap! Look what's goin' ON out there!
I don't notice anything unusual! To me, it looks like any average hot, lazy Summer afternoon in New York City!
BROOKLYN SAVINGS BANK
ZIP! KILL!
BLAM! BLAM!
CRACK! POW
RAT-A-TAT-TAT-TAT
VIP! PIING!
SPLAT
Are you crazy?! Didn't you see this white hankerchief?! You promised me I wouldn't get hurt!
Yeah . . . but I didn't say we wouldn't shoot! You KNOW what rotten shots New York Cops are!
You dumb idiots! I KNOW I'm a bank robber and you hate my guts! But what if I'd brought some innocent hostages out here with me?!
THEM . . . we would have KILLED!!
Okay, men! Hold your fire!
Now, let's negotiate! What do you want for the guaranteed safety of your hostages?
Here are my terms! In one hour, I want a private jet with a piano lounge and a built-in suana bath to fly us out of the country! And while we're waiting, I want three plain McDonald quarter pounders, four burgers with mustard only, and two burgers with lettuce—hold the ketchup!
Are you crazy?!? You KNOW I can't get you that in an hour!
Okay, change that to a private jet with piano lounge and built-in suana, and nine Big Macs!
You got your-self a deal!
POLICE
911
The Cop agreed to my demands, but as an act of faith, I give him a hostage! Okay, who's the most useless one here?
No, ME! I got diabetes!
Send ME . . . gasp! . . . I got asthma!
ME . . .! ME . . .! I got brain damage!
You're my PARTNER, Sap, not a hostage! And stop putting your-self down! After all, wasn't it your idea to hit this bank? And didn't you case the joint? And didn't you plan the whole . . .?
You got a white handkerchief—or do you want to borrow mine?
Can you imagine what they would do to that guy if he was a BANK ROBBER?!
That's right, Sap! Aren't you glad I sent out the Bank GUARD?!
Hah! They call themselves Americans! When was the last time you heard a crowd cheer like this while ten White cops beat up on a Black guy?
Last night in Harlem—when ten Black guys beat up on a White cop!

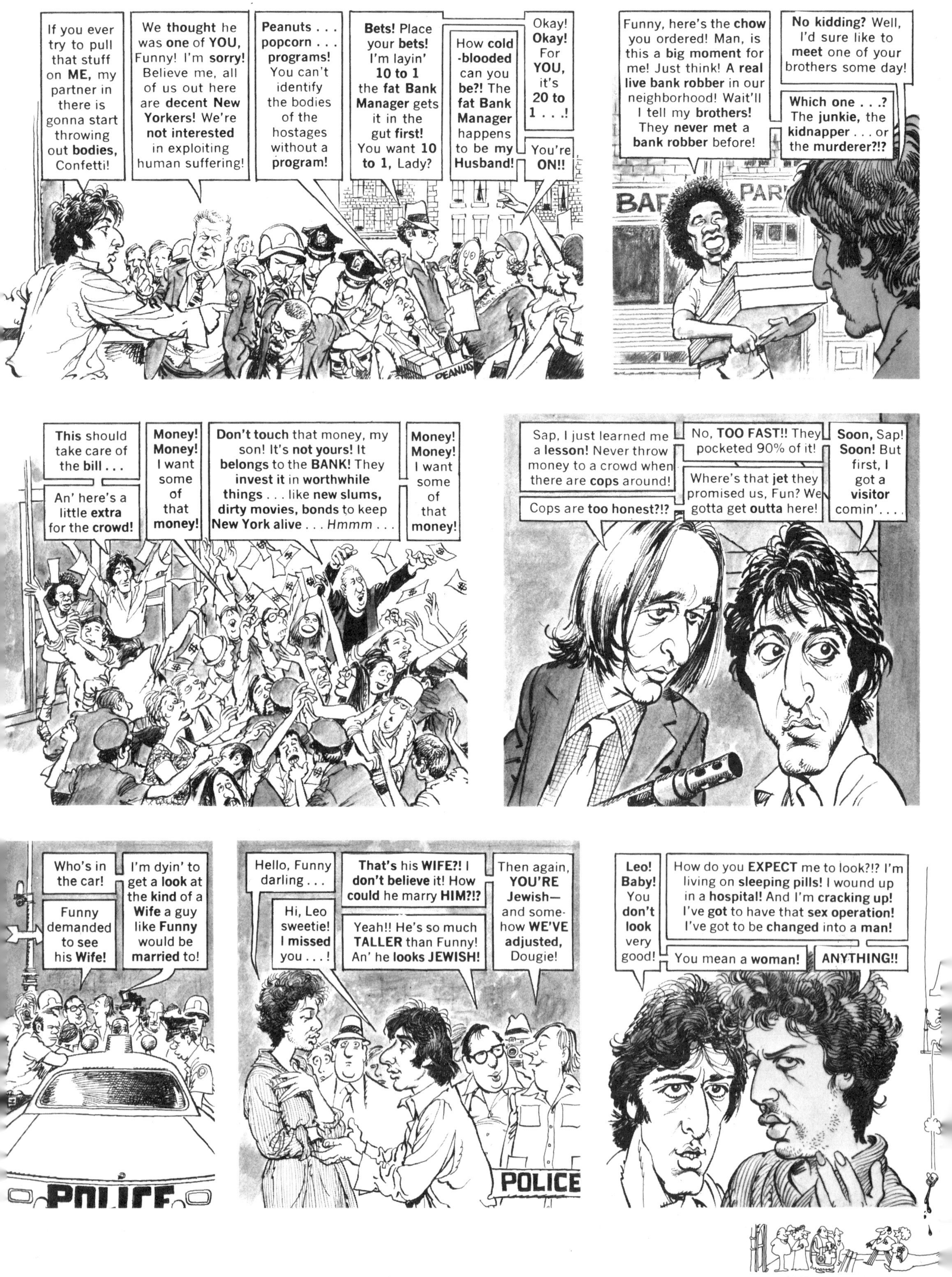

If you ever try to pull that stuff on ME, my partner in there is gonna start throwing out bodies, Confetti!
We thought he was one of YOU, Funny! I'm sorry! Believe me, all of us out here are decent New Yorkers! We're not interested in exploiting human suffering!
Peanuts . . . popcorn . . . programs! You can't identify the bodies of the hostages without a program!
PEANUTS
Bets! Place your bets! I'm layin' 10 to 1 the fat Bank Manager gets it in the gut first! You want 10 to 1, Lady?
How cold-blooded can you be?! The fat Bank Manager happens to be my Husband!
Okay! Okay! For YOU, it's 20 to 1 . . .!
You're ON!!
Funny, here's the chow you ordered! Man, is this a big moment for me! Just think! A real live bank robber in our neighborhood! Wait'll I tell my brothers! They never met a bank robber before!
No kidding? Well, I'd sure like to meet one of your brothers some day!
Which one . . .? The junkie, the kidnapper . . . or the murderer?!?
This should take care of the bill . . .
An' here's a little extra for the crowd!
Money! Money! I want some of that money!
Don't touch that money, my son! It's not yours! It belongs to the BANK! They invest it in worthwhile things . . . like new slums, dirty movies, bonds to keep New York alive . . . Hmmm . . .
Money! Money! I want some of that money!
Sap, I just learned me a lesson! Never throw money to a crowd when there are cops around!
Cops are too honest?!?
No, TOO FAST!! They pocketed 90% of it!
Where's that jet they promised us, Fun? We gotta get outta here!
Soon, Sap! Soon! But first, I got a visitor comin'. . . .
Who's in the car!
Funny demanded to see his Wife!
I'm dyin' to get a look at the kind of a Wife a guy like Funny would be married to!
POLICE
Hello, Funny darling . . .
Hi, Leo sweetie! I missed you . . .!
That's his WIFE?! I don't believe it! How could he marry HIM?!?
Yeah!! He's so much TALLER than Funny! An' he looks JEWISH!
Then again, YOU'RE Jewish—and somehow WE'VE adjusted, Dougie!
POLICE
Leo! Baby! You don't look very good!
How do you EXPECT me to look?!? I'm living on sleeping pills! I wound up in a hospital! And I'm cracking up! I've got to have that sex operation! I've got to be changed into a man!
You mean a woman!
ANYTHING!!

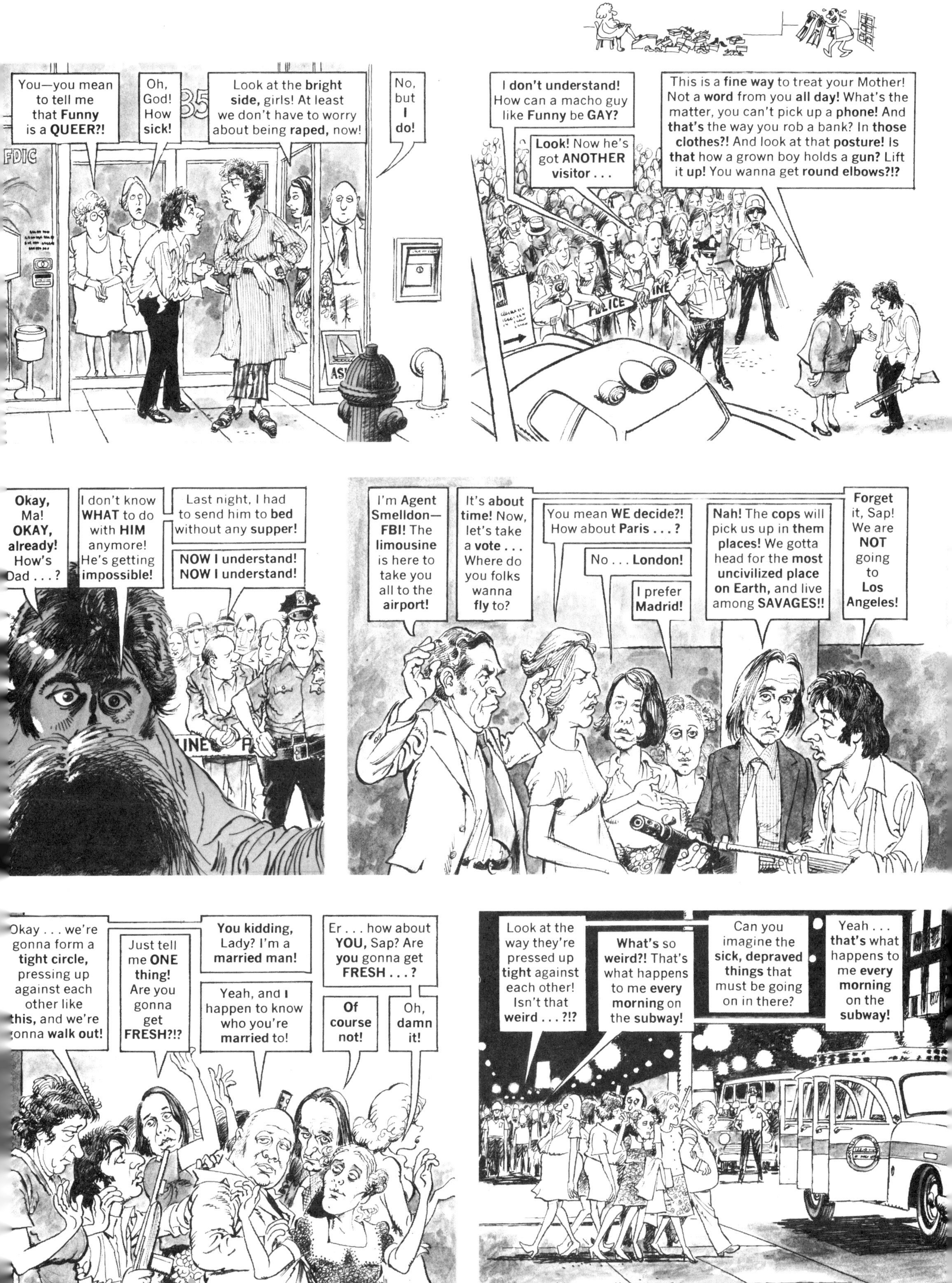
You—you mean to tell me that Funny is a QUEER?!
Oh, God! How sick!
Look at the bright side, girls! At least we don't have to worry about being raped, now!
No, but I do!
FDIC
I don't understand! How can a macho guy like Funny be GAY?
Look! Now he's got ANOTHER visitor . . .
This is a fine way to treat your Mother! Not a word from you all day! What's the matter, you can't pick up a phone! And that's the way you rob a bank? In those clothes?! And look at that posture! Is that how a grown boy holds a gun? Lift it up! You wanna get round elbows?!?
POLICE
Okay, Ma! OKAY, already! How's Dad . . . ?
I don't know WHAT to do with HIM anymore! He's getting impossible!
Last night, I had to send him to bed without any supper!
NOW I understand! NOW I understand!
I'm Agent Smelldon—FBI! The limousine is here to take you all to the airport!
It's about time! Now, let's take a vote . . . Where do you folks wanna fly to?
You mean WE decide?! How about Paris . . . ?
No . . . London!
I prefer Madrid!
Nah! The cops will pick us up in them places! We gotta head for the most uncivilized place on Earth, and live among SAVAGES!!
Forget it, Sap! We are NOT going to Los Angeles!
Okay . . . we're gonna form a tight circle, pressing up against each other like this, and we're gonna walk out!
Just tell me ONE thing! Are you gonna get FRESH?!?
You kidding, Lady? I'm a married man!
Yeah, and I happen to know who you're married to!
Er . . . how about YOU, Sap? Are you gonna get FRESH . . . ?
Of course not!
Oh, damn it!
Look at the way they're pressed up tight against each other! Isn't that weird . . . ?!?
What's so weird?! That's what happens to me every morning on the subway!
Can you imagine the sick, depraved things that must be going on in there?
Yeah . . . that's what happens to me every morning on the subway!

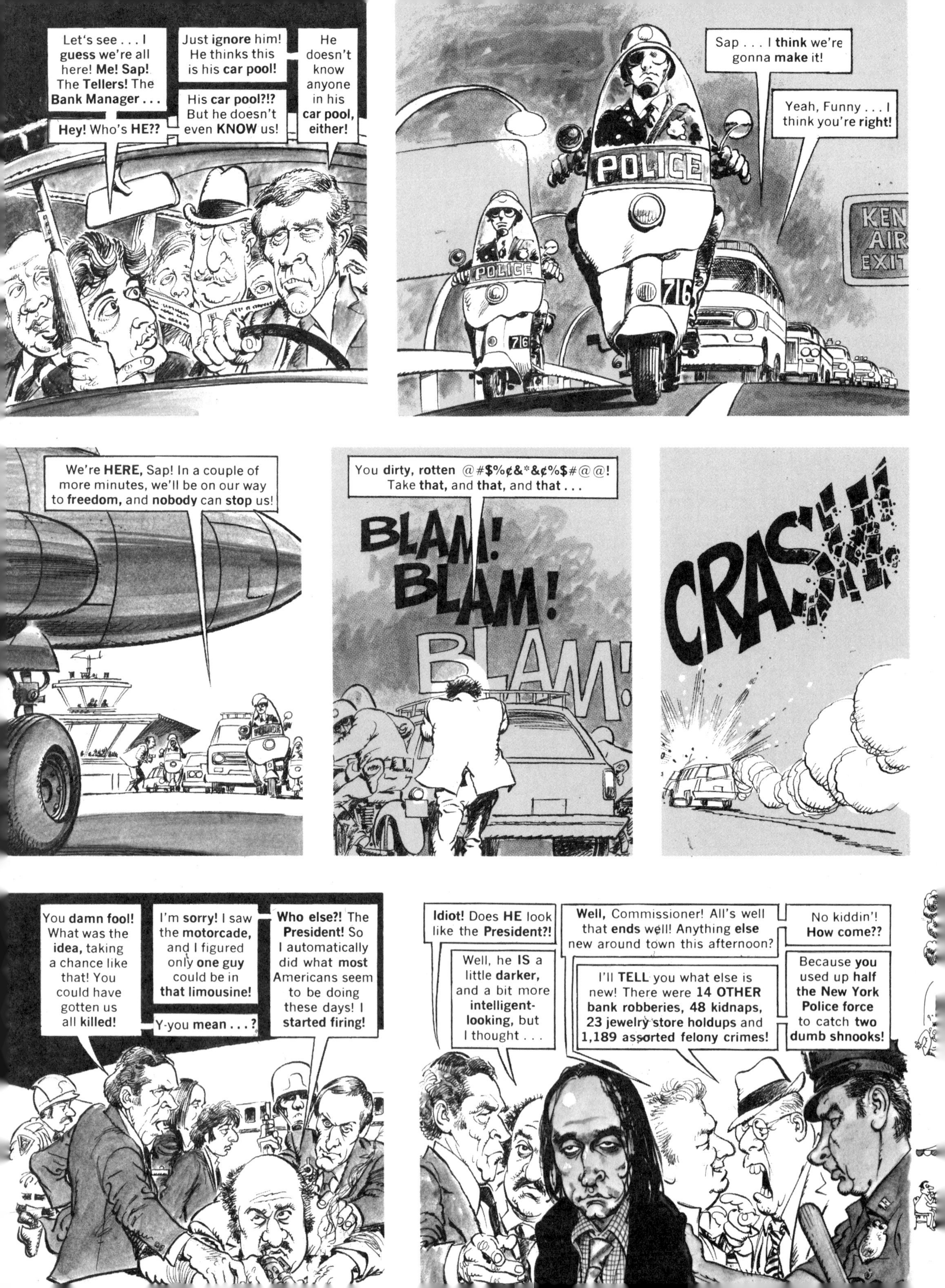

Let's see . . . I guess we're all here! Me! Sap! The Tellers! The Bank Manager . . .
Hey! Who's HE??
Just ignore him! He thinks this is his car pool!
His car pool?!? But he doesn't even KNOW us!
He doesn't know anyone in his car pool, either!
Sap . . . I think we're gonna make it!
Yeah, Funny . . . I think you're right!
POLICE
POLICE
716
716
KEN
AIR
EXIT
We're HERE, Sap! In a couple of more minutes, we'll be on our way to freedom, and nobody can stop us!
You dirty, rotten @#$%¢&*&¢%$#@@! Take that, and that, and that . . .
BLAM! BLAM! BLAM!
CRASH!!
You damn fool! What was the idea, taking a chance like that! You could have gotten us all killed!
I'm sorry! I saw the motorcade, and I figured only one guy could be in that limousine!
Y-you mean . . . ?
Who else?! The President! So I automatically did what most Americans seem to be doing these days! I started firing!
Idiot! Does HE look like the President?!
Well, he IS a little darker, and a bit more intelligent-looking, but I thought . . .
Well, Commissioner! All's well that ends well! Anything else new around town this afternoon?
I'll TELL you what else is new! There were 14 OTHER bank robberies, 48 kidnaps, 23 jewelry store holdups and 1,189 assorted felony crimes!
No kiddin'! How come??
Because you used up half the New York Police force to catch two dumb shnooks!

# Scenes We'd Like to See

## The Human Shield

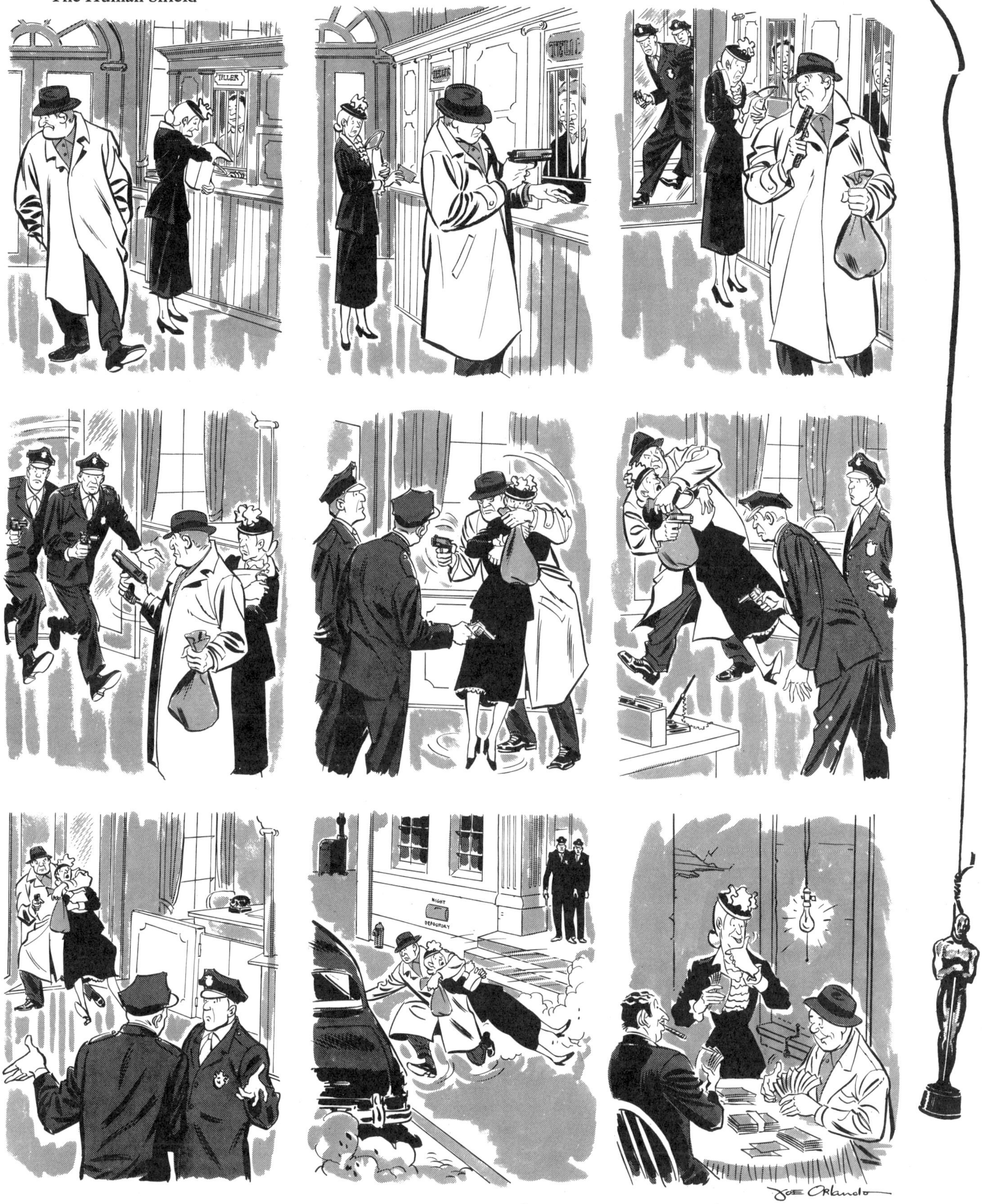
TELLER
NIGHT DEPOSITORY
Joe Orlando

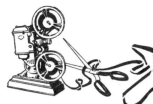

**WASHINGTON POST-MORTEM DEPT.**

For more than four years, we've all read about "Watergate" in newspapers, we've watched it on television, we've heard about it on radio and we've read about it in best-seller books! Now, before it becomes a TV Series with a different law-breaker indicted every week (and no need for Summer re-runs because there's plenty of crooks to go around for years!), here's MAD's version of the smash-hit "WATERGATE MOVIE"! The time is 1972, the place is Washington, D.C., and we are about to discover the unmitigated . . .

# GALL
# PRESI

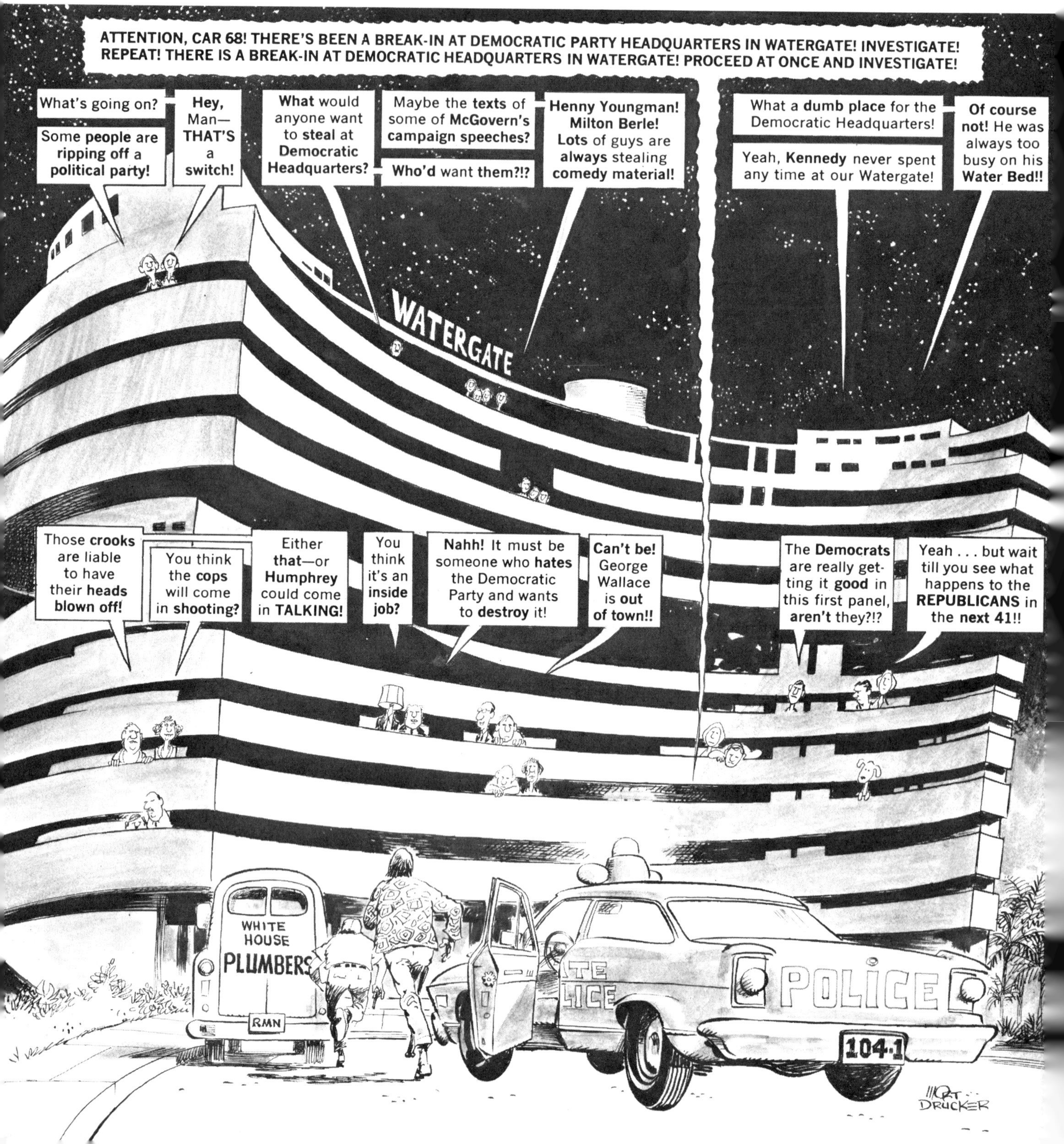

ATTENTION, CAR 68! THERE'S BEEN A BREAK-IN AT DEMOCRATIC PARTY HEADQUARTERS IN WATERGATE! INVESTIGATE! REPEAT! THERE IS A BREAK-IN AT DEMOCRATIC HEADQUARTERS IN WATERGATE! PROCEED AT ONCE AND INVESTIGATE!
What's going on?
Some people are ripping off a political party!
Hey, Man—THAT'S a switch!
What would anyone want to steal at Democratic Headquarters?
Maybe the texts of some of McGovern's campaign speeches?
Who'd want them?!?
Henny Youngman! Milton Berle! Lots of guys are always stealing comedy material!
What a dumb place for the Democratic Headquarters!
Yeah, Kennedy never spent any time at our Watergate!
Of course not! He was always too busy on his Water Bed!!
WATERGATE
Those crooks are liable to have their heads blown off!
You think the cops will come in shooting?
Either that—or Humphrey could come in TALKING!
You think it's an inside job?
Nahh! It must be someone who hates the Democratic Party and wants to destroy it!
Can't be! George Wallace is out of town!!
The Democrats are really getting it good in this first panel, aren't they?!?
Yeah . . . but wait till you see what happens to the REPUBLICANS in the next 41!!
WHITE HOUSE PLUMBERS
RMN
POLICE
104·1
MORT DRUCKER

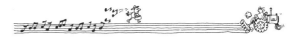

# OF THE
# DENT'S MEN

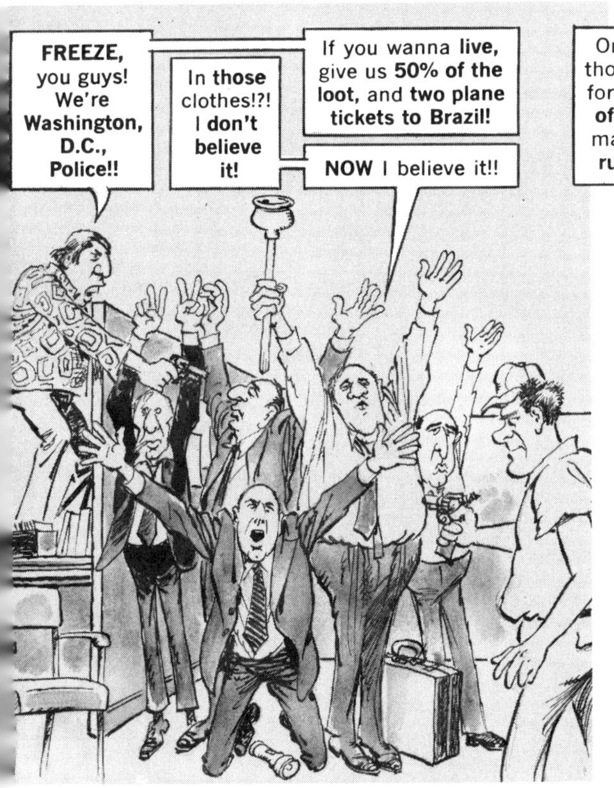
FREEZE, you guys! We're Washington, D.C., Police!!
In those clothes!?! I don't believe it!
If you wanna live, give us 50% of the loot, and two plane tickets to Brazil!
NOW I believe it!!

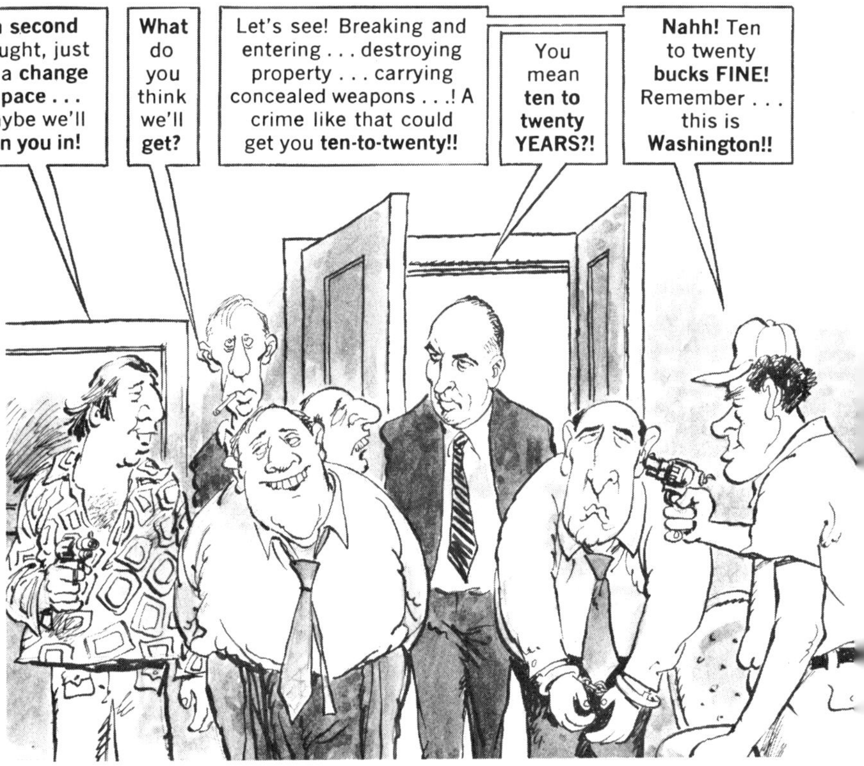
On second thought, just for a change of pace . . . maybe we'll run you in!
What do you think we'll get?
Let's see! Breaking and entering . . . destroying property . . . carrying concealed weapons . . .! A crime like that could get you ten-to-twenty!!
You mean ten to twenty YEARS?!
Nahh! Ten to twenty bucks FINE! Remember . . . this is Washington!!

ARTIST: MORT DRUCKER WRITER: LARRY SIEGEL

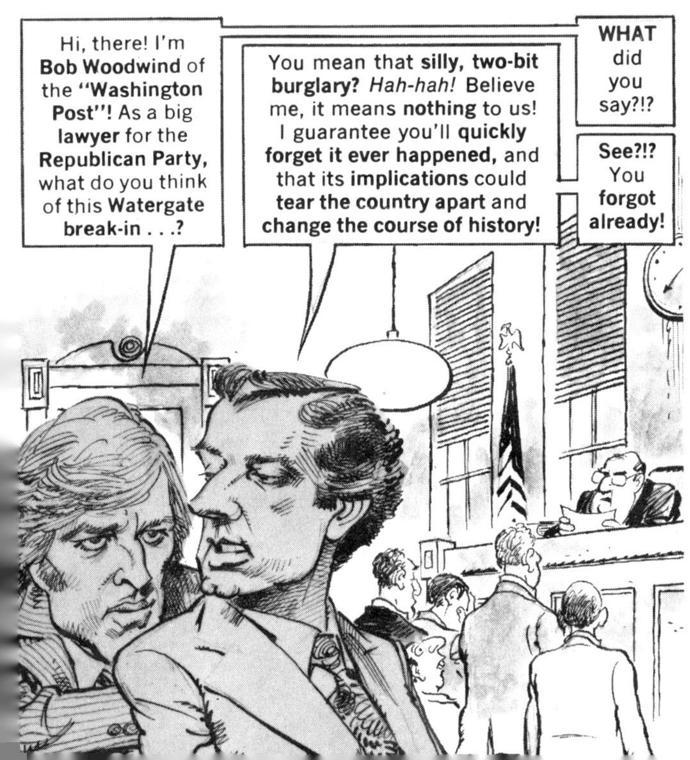
Hi, there! I'm Bob Woodwind of the "Washington Post"! As a big lawyer for the Republican Party, what do you think of this Watergate break-in . . .?
You mean that silly, two-bit burglary? Hah-hah! Believe me, it means nothing to us! I guarantee you'll quickly forget it ever happened, and that its implications could tear the country apart and change the course of history!
WHAT did you say?!?
See?!? You forgot already!

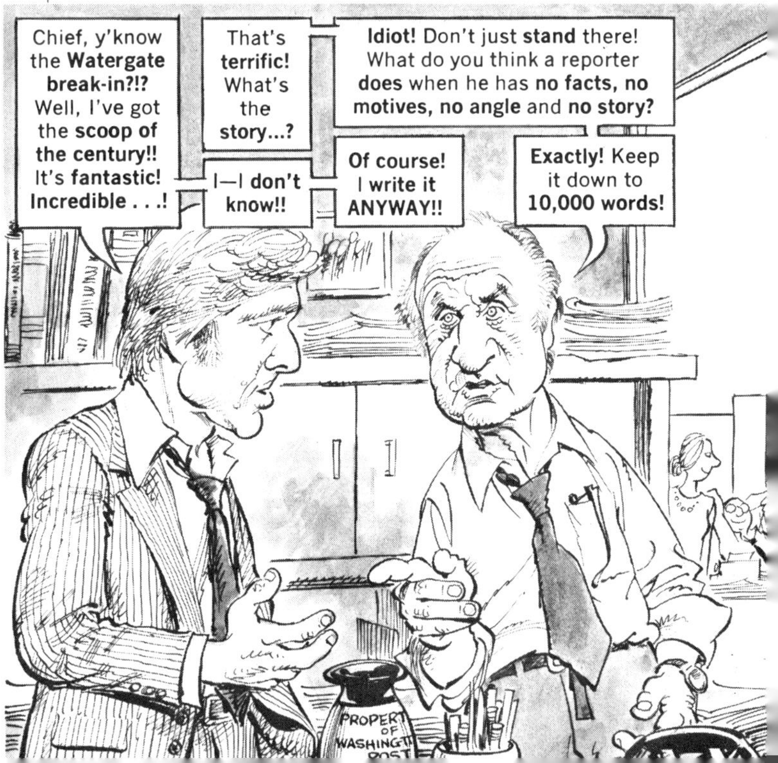
Chief, y'know the Watergate break-in?!? Well, I've got the scoop of the century!! It's fantastic! Incredible . . .!
That's terrific! What's the story...?
I—I don't know!!
Idiot! Don't just stand there! What do you think a reporter does when he has no facts, no motives, no angle and no story?
Of course! I write it ANYWAY!!
Exactly! Keep it down to 10,000 words!
PROPERTY OF WASHINGTON POST

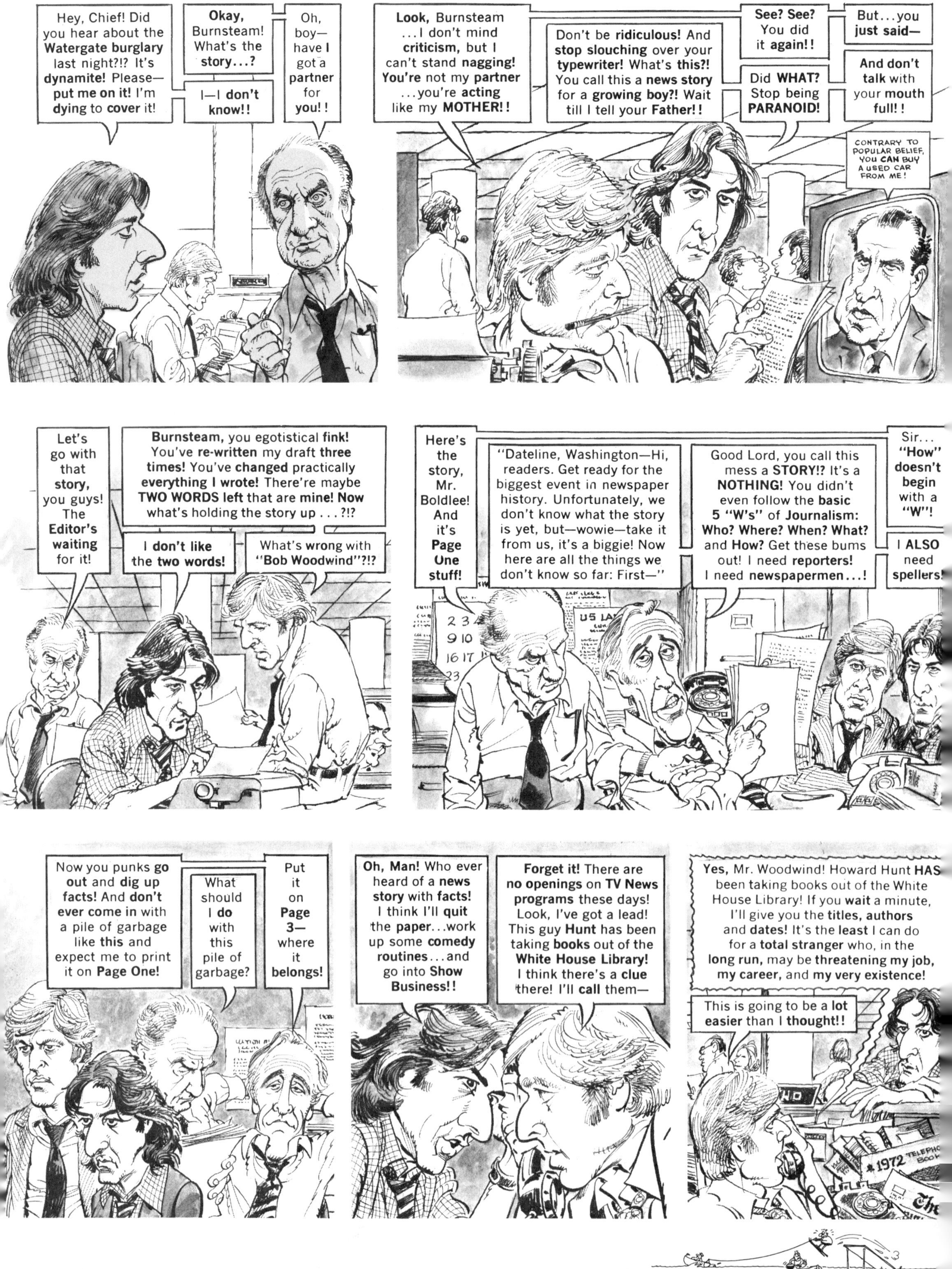

Hey, Chief! Did you hear about the Watergate burglary last night?!? It's dynamite! Please— put me on it! I'm dying to cover it!
Okay, Burnsteam! What's the story...?
I—I don't know!!
Oh, boy— have I got a partner for you!!
Look, Burnsteam ...I don't mind criticism, but I can't stand nagging! You're not my partner ...you're acting like my MOTHER!!
Don't be ridiculous! And stop slouching over your typewriter! What's this?! You call this a news story for a growing boy?! Wait till I tell your Father!!
See? See? You did it again!!
Did WHAT? Stop being PARANOID!
But...you just said—
And don't talk with your mouth full!!
CONTRARY TO POPULAR BELIEF, YOU CAN BUY A USED CAR FROM ME!
Let's go with that story, you guys! The Editor's waiting for it!
Burnsteam, you egotistical fink! You've re-written my draft three times! You've changed practically everything I wrote! There're maybe TWO WORDS left that are mine! Now what's holding the story up...?!?
I don't like the two words!
What's wrong with "Bob Woodwind"?!?
Here's the story, Mr. Boldlee! And it's Page One stuff!
"Dateline, Washington—Hi, readers. Get ready for the biggest event in newspaper history. Unfortunately, we don't know what the story is yet, but—wowie—take it from us, it's a biggie! Now here are all the things we don't know so far: First—"
Good Lord, you call this mess a STORY!? It's a NOTHING! You didn't even follow the basic 5 "W's" of Journalism: Who? Where? When? What? and How? Get these bums out! I need reporters! I need newspapermen...!
Sir... "How" doesn't begin with a "W"!
I ALSO need spellers!
Now you punks go out and dig up facts! And don't ever come in with a pile of garbage like this and expect me to print it on Page One!
What should I do with this pile of garbage?
Put it on Page 3— where it belongs!
Oh, Man! Who ever heard of a news story with facts! I think I'll quit the paper...work up some comedy routines...and go into Show Business!!
Forget it! There are no openings on TV News programs these days! Look, I've got a lead! This guy Hunt has been taking books out of the White House Library! I think there's a clue there! I'll call them—
Yes, Mr. Woodwind! Howard Hunt HAS been taking books out of the White House Library! If you wait a minute, I'll give you the titles, authors and dates! It's the least I can do for a total stranger who, in the long run, may be threatening my job, my career, and my very existence!
This is going to be a lot easier than I thought!!
1972 TELEPHONE BOOK

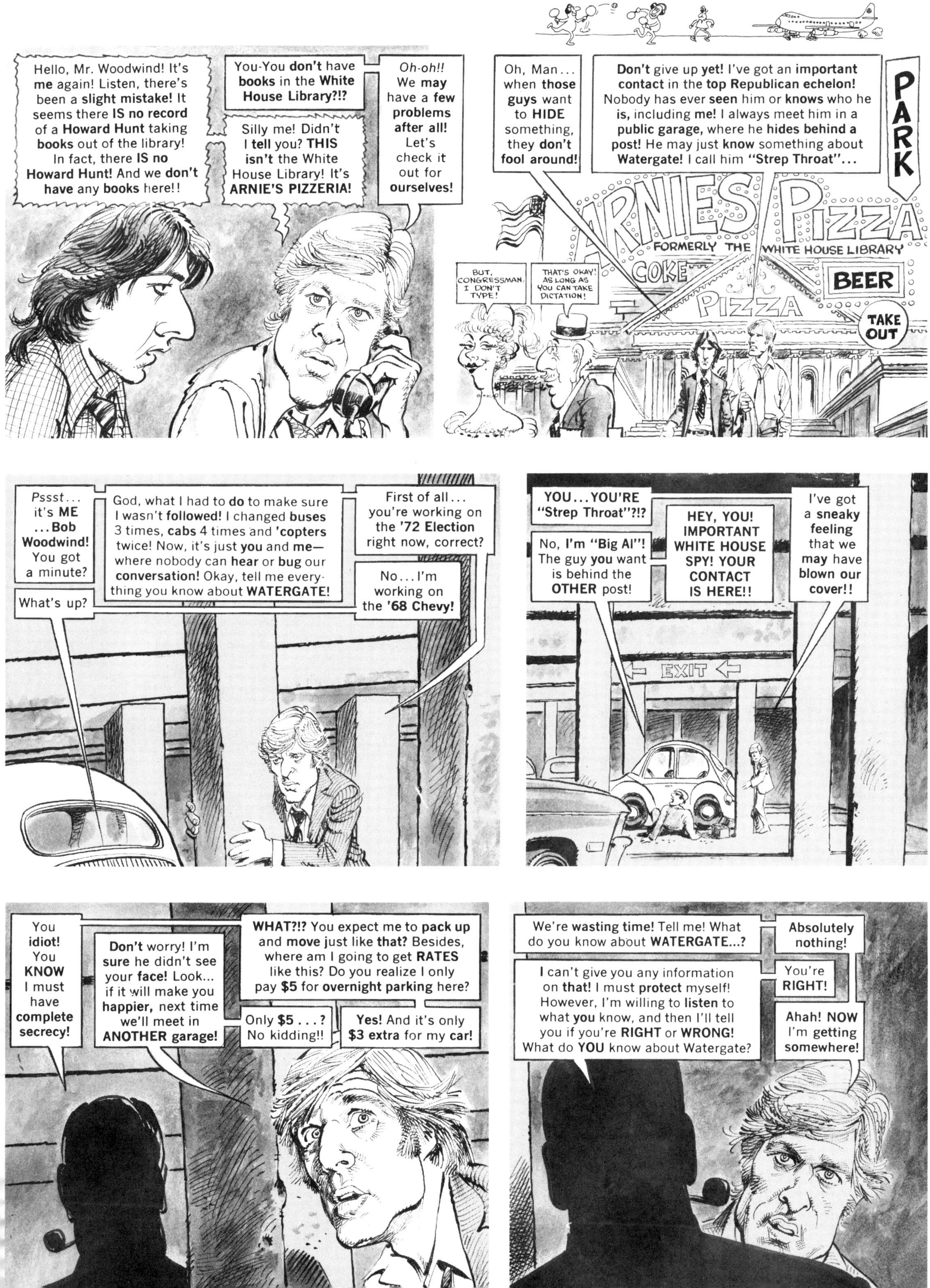
Hello, Mr. Woodwind! It's me again! Listen, there's been a slight mistake! It seems there IS no record of a Howard Hunt taking books out of the library! In fact, there IS no Howard Hunt! And we don't have any books here!!
You-You don't have books in the White House Library?!?
Silly me! Didn't I tell you? THIS isn't the White House Library! It's ARNIE'S PIZZERIA!
Oh-oh!! We may have a few problems after all! Let's check it out for ourselves!
Oh, Man... when those guys want to HIDE something, they don't fool around!
Don't give up yet! I've got an important contact in the top Republican echelon! Nobody has ever seen him or knows who he is, including me! I always meet him in a public garage, where he hides behind a post! He may just know something about Watergate! I call him "Strep Throat"...
PARK
ARNIES PIZZA
FORMERLY THE WHITE HOUSE LIBRARY
COKE
BEER
PIZZA
TAKE OUT
BUT, CONGRESSMAN, I DON'T TYPE!
THAT'S OKAY! AS LONG AS YOU CAN TAKE DICTATION!
Pssst... it's ME ...Bob Woodwind! You got a minute?
What's up?
God, what I had to do to make sure I wasn't followed! I changed buses 3 times, cabs 4 times and 'copters twice! Now, it's just you and me— where nobody can hear or bug our conversation! Okay, tell me everything you know about WATERGATE!
First of all... you're working on the '72 Election right now, correct?
No... I'm working on the '68 Chevy!
YOU... YOU'RE "Strep Throat"?!?
No, I'm "Big Al"! The guy you want is behind the OTHER post!
HEY, YOU! IMPORTANT WHITE HOUSE SPY! YOUR CONTACT IS HERE!!
I've got a sneaky feeling that we may have blown our cover!!
EXIT
You idiot! You KNOW I must have complete secrecy!
Don't worry! I'm sure he didn't see your face! Look... if it will make you happier, next time we'll meet in ANOTHER garage!
WHAT?!? You expect me to pack up and move just like that? Besides, where am I going to get RATES like this? Do you realize I only pay $5 for overnight parking here?
Only $5 . . . ? No kidding!!
Yes! And it's only $3 extra for my car!
We're wasting time! Tell me! What do you know about WATERGATE...?
Absolutely nothing!
I can't give you any information on that! I must protect myself! However, I'm willing to listen to what you know, and then I'll tell you if you're RIGHT or WRONG! What do YOU know about Watergate?
You're RIGHT!
Ahah! NOW I'm getting somewhere!

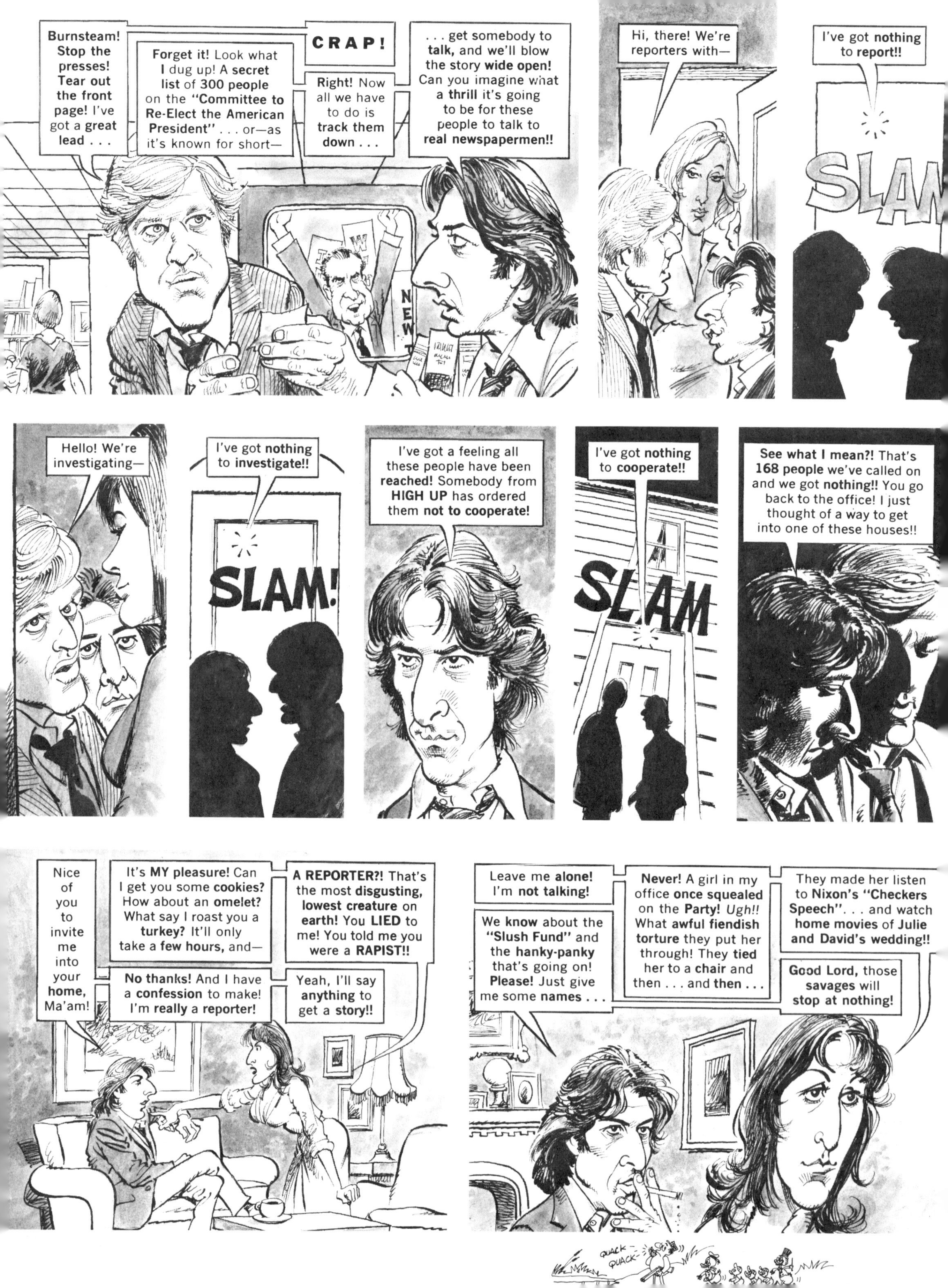

Burnsteam! Stop the presses! Tear out the front page! I've got a great lead . . .
Forget it! Look what I dug up! A secret list of 300 people on the "Committee to Re-Elect the American President" . . . or—as it's known for short—
CRAP!
Right! Now all we have to do is track them down . . .
. . . get somebody to talk, and we'll blow the story wide open! Can you imagine what a thrill it's going to be for these people to talk to real newspapermen!!
Hi, there! We're reporters with—
I've got nothing to report!!
SLAM
Hello! We're investigating—
I've got nothing to investigate!!
SLAM!
I've got a feeling all these people have been reached! Somebody from HIGH UP has ordered them not to cooperate!
I've got nothing to cooperate!!
SLAM
See what I mean?! That's 168 people we've called on and we got nothing!! You go back to the office! I just thought of a way to get into one of these houses!!
Nice of you to invite me into your home, Ma'am!
It's MY pleasure! Can I get you some cookies? How about an omelet? What say I roast you a turkey? It'll only take a few hours, and—
No thanks! And I have a confession to make! I'm really a reporter!
A REPORTER?! That's the most disgusting, lowest creature on earth! You LIED to me! You told me you were a RAPIST!!
Yeah, I'll say anything to get a story!!
Leave me alone! I'm not talking!
We know about the "Slush Fund" and the hanky-panky that's going on! Please! Just give me some names . . .
Never! A girl in my office once squealed on the Party! Ugh!! What awful fiendish torture they put her through! They tied her to a chair and then . . . and then . . .
They made her listen to Nixon's "Checkers Speech". . . and watch home movies of Julie and David's wedding!!
Good Lord, those savages will stop at nothing!
QUACK-QUACK

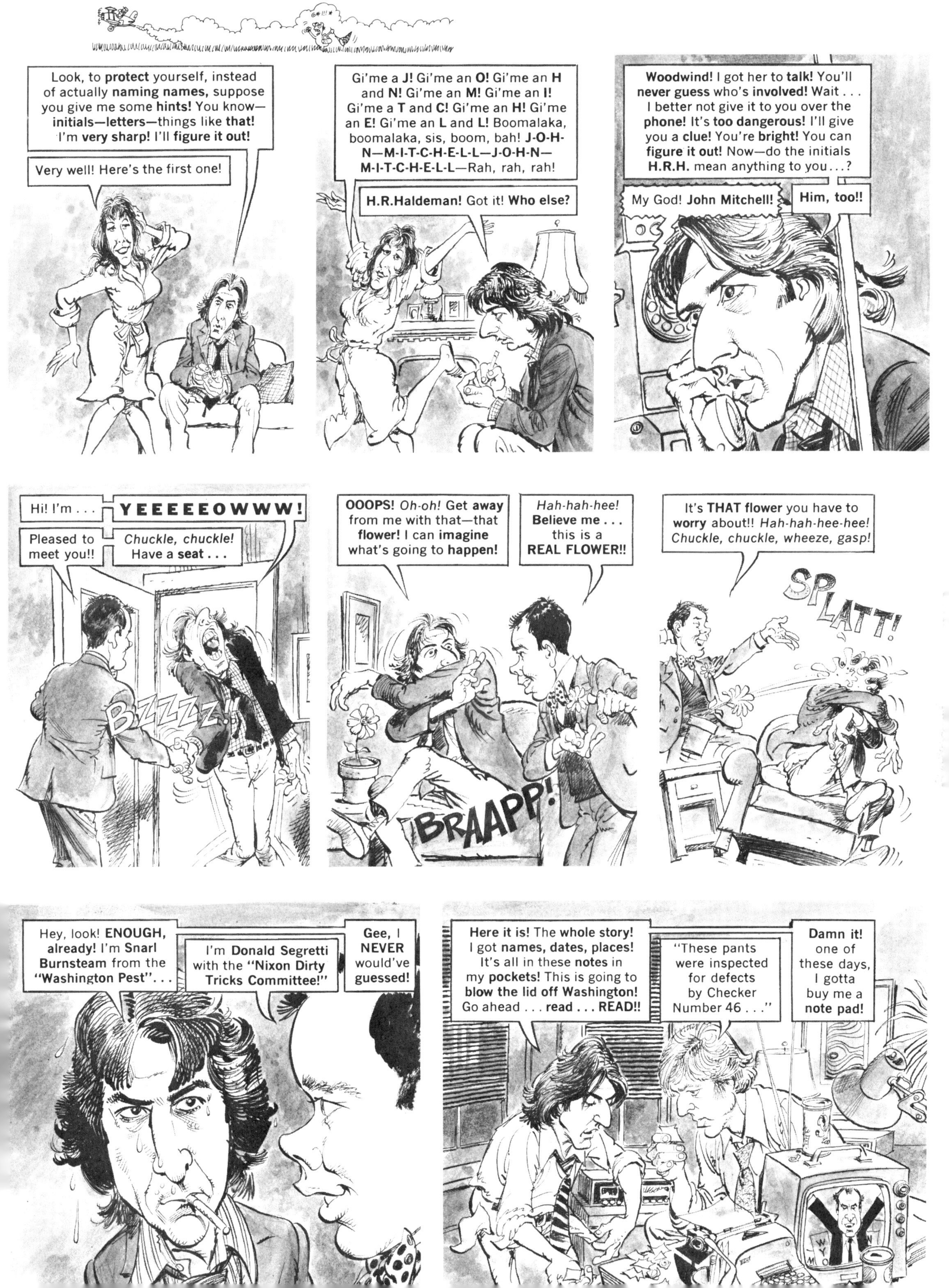

Look, to protect yourself, instead of actually naming names, suppose you give me some hints! You know—initials—letters—things like that! I'm very sharp! I'll figure it out!
Very well! Here's the first one!
Gi'me a J! Gi'me an O! Gi'me an H and N! Gi'me an M! Gi'me an I! Gi'me a T and C! Gi'me an H! Gi'me an E! Gi'me an L and L! Boomalaka, boomalaka, sis, boom, bah! J-O-H-N—M-I-T-C-H-E-L-L—J-O-H-N—M-I-T-C-H-E-L-L—Rah, rah, rah!
H.R.Haldeman! Got it! Who else?
Woodwind! I got her to talk! You'll never guess who's involved! Wait . . . I better not give it to you over the phone! It's too dangerous! I'll give you a clue! You're bright! You can figure it out! Now—do the initials H.R.H. mean anything to you . . .?
My God! John Mitchell!
Him, too!!
Hi! I'm . . .
YEEEEEOWWW!
Pleased to meet you!!
Chuckle, chuckle! Have a seat . . .
BZZZZZ
OOOPS! Oh-oh! Get away from me with that—that flower! I can imagine what's going to happen!
Hah-hah-hee! Believe me . . . this is a REAL FLOWER!!
BRAAPP!
It's THAT flower you have to worry about!! Hah-hah-hee-hee! Chuckle, chuckle, wheeze, gasp!
SPLATT!
Hey, look! ENOUGH, already! I'm Snarl Burnsteam from the "Washington Pest" . . .
I'm Donald Segretti with the "Nixon Dirty Tricks Committee!"
Gee, I NEVER would've guessed!
Here it is! The whole story! I got names, dates, places! It's all in these notes in my pockets! This is going to blow the lid off Washington! Go ahead . . . read . . . READ!!
"These pants were inspected for defects by Checker Number 46 . . ."
Damn it! one of these days, I gotta buy me a note pad!

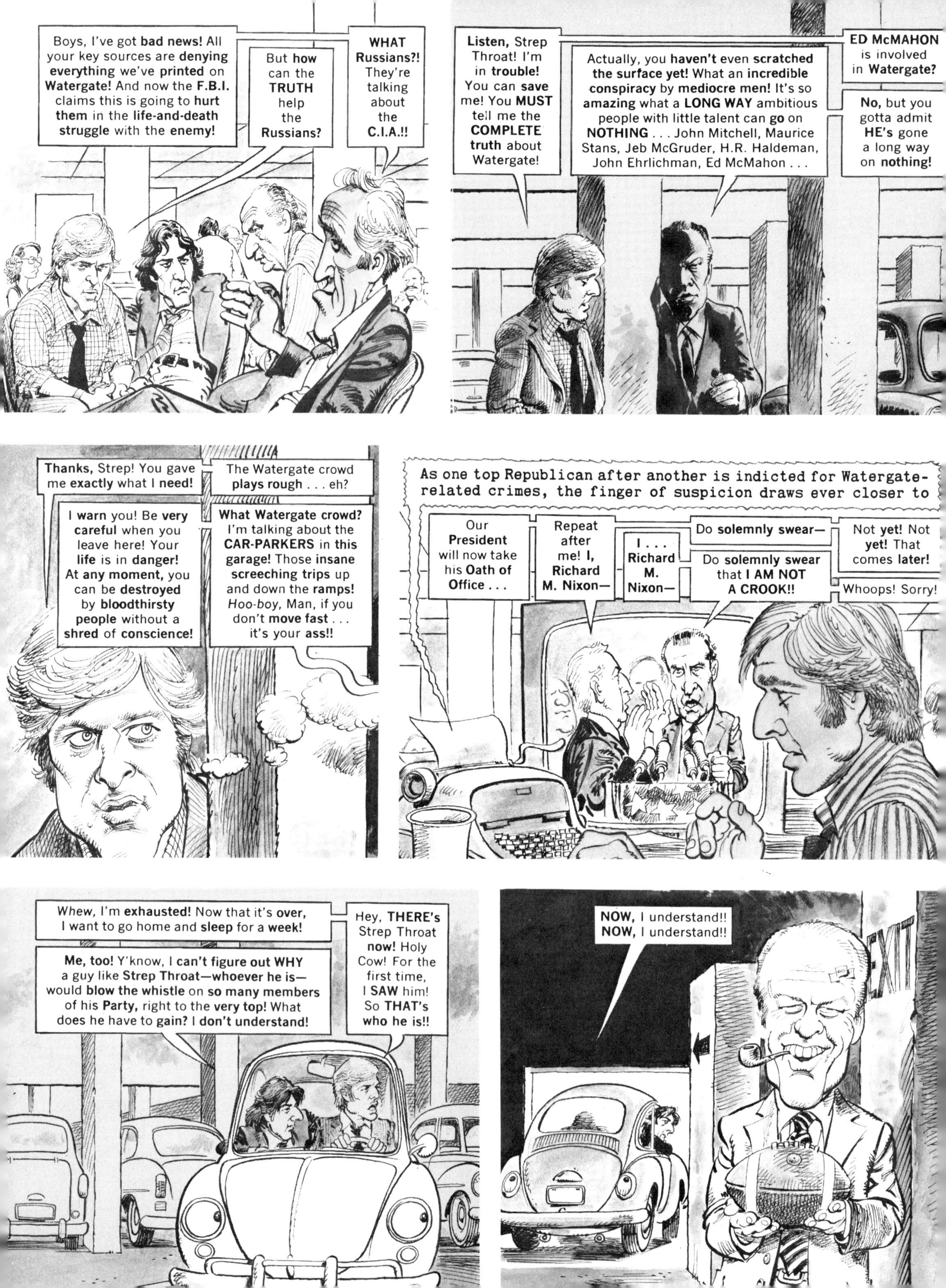
Boys, I've got bad news! All your key sources are denying everything we've printed on Watergate! And now the F.B.I. claims this is going to hurt them in the life-and-death struggle with the enemy!
But how can the TRUTH help the Russians?
WHAT Russians?! They're talking about the C.I.A.!!
Listen, Strep Throat! I'm in trouble! You can save me! You MUST tell me the COMPLETE truth about Watergate!
Actually, you haven't even scratched the surface yet! What an incredible conspiracy by mediocre men! It's so amazing what a LONG WAY ambitious people with little talent can go on NOTHING . . . John Mitchell, Maurice Stans, Jeb McGruder, H.R. Haldeman, John Ehrlichman, Ed McMahon . . .
ED McMAHON is involved in Watergate?
No, but you gotta admit HE's gone a long way on nothing!
Thanks, Strep! You gave me exactly what I need!
I warn you! Be very careful when you leave here! Your life is in danger! At any moment, you can be destroyed by bloodthirsty people without a shred of conscience!
The Watergate crowd plays rough . . . eh?
What Watergate crowd? I'm talking about the CAR-PARKERS in this garage! Those insane screeching trips up and down the ramps! Hoo-boy, Man, if you don't move fast . . . it's your ass!!
As one top Republican after another is indicted for Watergate-related crimes, the finger of suspicion draws ever closer to
Our President will now take his Oath of Office . . .
Repeat after me! I, Richard M. Nixon—
I . . . Richard M. Nixon—
Do solemnly swear—
Do solemnly swear that I AM NOT A CROOK!!
Not yet! Not yet! That comes later!
Whoops! Sorry!
Whew, I'm exhausted! Now that it's over, I want to go home and sleep for a week!
Me, too! Y'know, I can't figure out WHY a guy like Strep Throat—whoever he is—would blow the whistle on so many members of his Party, right to the very top! What does he have to gain? I don't understand!
Hey, THERE's Strep Throat now! Holy Cow! For the first time, I SAW him! So THAT's who he is!!
NOW, I understand!! NOW, I understand!!
EXIT

TRITE & TRUE DEPT.

# MAD'S "LATE SHOW" CLICHÉ MOVIE SCRIPT

ARTIST: BRUCE STARK WRITER: HARRY PURVIS

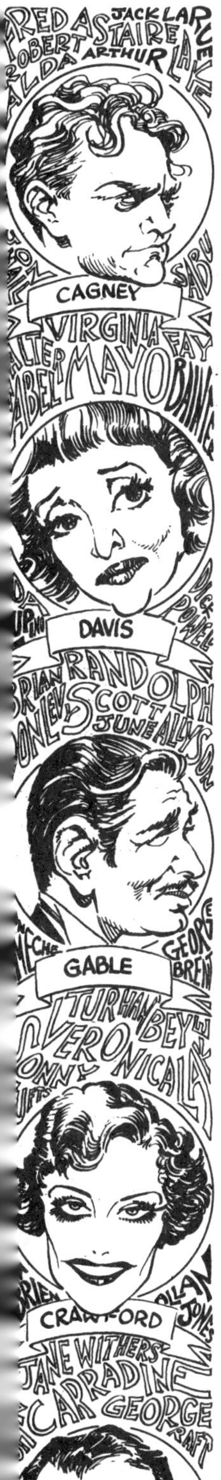
CAGNEY
DAVIS
GABLE
CRAWFORD

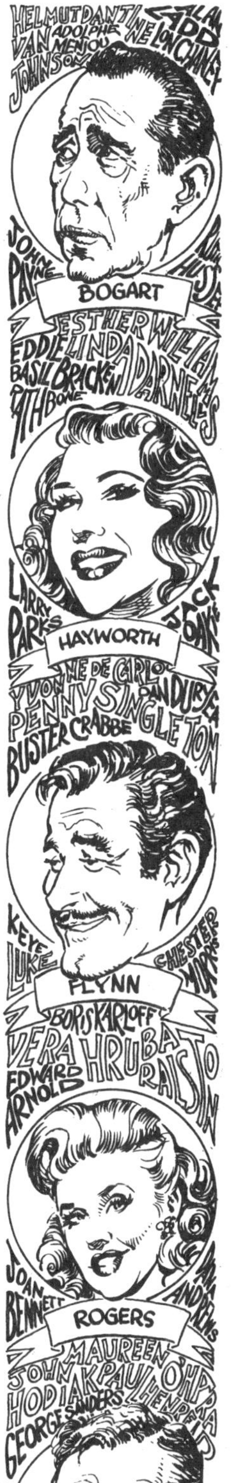
BOGART
HAYWORTH
FLYNN
ROGERS

## THE "OPERA" MOVIE

"You have a charming little voice, my dear. However, it needs training--a great deal of training! You understand that if I, Vittorio Calamare, take you on as my protegee, it will mean years of hard work. There will be no time for the unimportant things that most girls dream about--things like love and marriage."

* * * * * * *

"Don't you see, Mike? It's my big chance. You can't ask me to give it up. Not now! Not after I've worked so hard!"

* * * * * * *

"Signore e Signori, it is with regret that I must make the following announcement. Due to illness, Mme. Lucia Maledizione will not sing tonight. However, in her place, I am pleased to present--in her debut performance--Miss Irene Fairly..."

* * * * * * *

"Go ahead, my dear, and do not be nervous. They will love you!"

* * * * * * *

"Poor kid, they're not giving her a chance. This crowd came to hear the great Maledizione, and no one else. Wait--isn't that Vittorio Calamare himself, walking out onto the stage?"

* * * * * * *

"You call yourselves opera lovers? Then ACT like it! This girl is my pupil! Would I consent to this appearance if I did not believe she could sing the role of 'Zuccini' as it has never been sung before?!"

* * * * * * *

"Listen to that applause! Even Maledizione at her best never received such an ovation! We are watching opera history being made tonight!"

* * * * * * *

"Yes, I was there tonight! Mike, the cow hand, in his forty dollar suit, standing among the white ties and tails. But even I saw it, Irene--even I know now that you've been given a great gift...a gift that belongs to the world! I have no right to ask you to waste it on some little cattle ranch in the middle of nowhere!"

* * * * * * *

"...and after London, Irene--we go to Milan! Think of it! No American coloratura has ever sing the role of 'Fettucine' at 'La Scala' before!"

* * * * * * *

"But, Vittorio! You promised that when this tour was over I could have a vacation! I want to go home, Vittorio! I'm...tired...<u>sob</u>..."

* * * * * * *

"Ladies and gentlemen, thank you. You are much too kind. To sing at 'The Met' is privilege enough...but my statue at the entrance--well, what can I say?! It makes it even harder for me to tell you...that...that this was my LAST PERFORMANCE! No--no, please--you mustn't! You see, after tonight, Irene Fairly will be no more! She will become, instead, just plain Mrs. Mike Nolan of Butte, Montana! That is--if he'll still have me! I hope you're listening, Mike...because this is my farewell aria--and I dedicate it to you..."

* * * * * * *

"Maestro...would you please play "Home On The Range" in the key of High C...?"

THE END

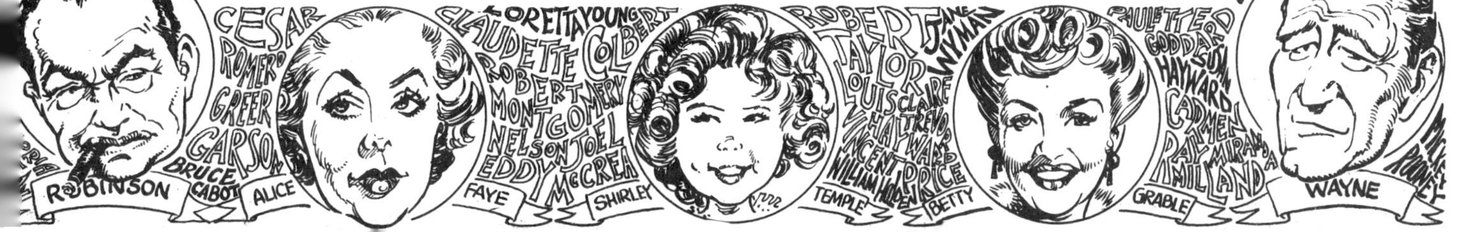
STARK
ROBINSON
ALICE
FAYE
SHIRLEY
TEMPLE
BETTY
GRABLE
WAYNE

## ROCK OF AGED DEPT.

Forty years ago, Hollywood made a film about an unknown girl from a small town who comes to Hollywood and becomes a movie star. The film was a huge success. A few years later, they decided to make the same picture over... and again it was a hit. Now, they've made the picture for the third time, only it's not about an actress, but a singer; and the background isn't the movies, but the Rock Music scene. Well, you know how Hollywood works: Keep doing something until you get it wrong! Which is what they did! Yep, even with a Superstar like Barbra Streisand in full control of production, this new version clearly demonstrates once again that, most of the time, when a Superstar with a super ego attempts to step beyond her talent as a performer

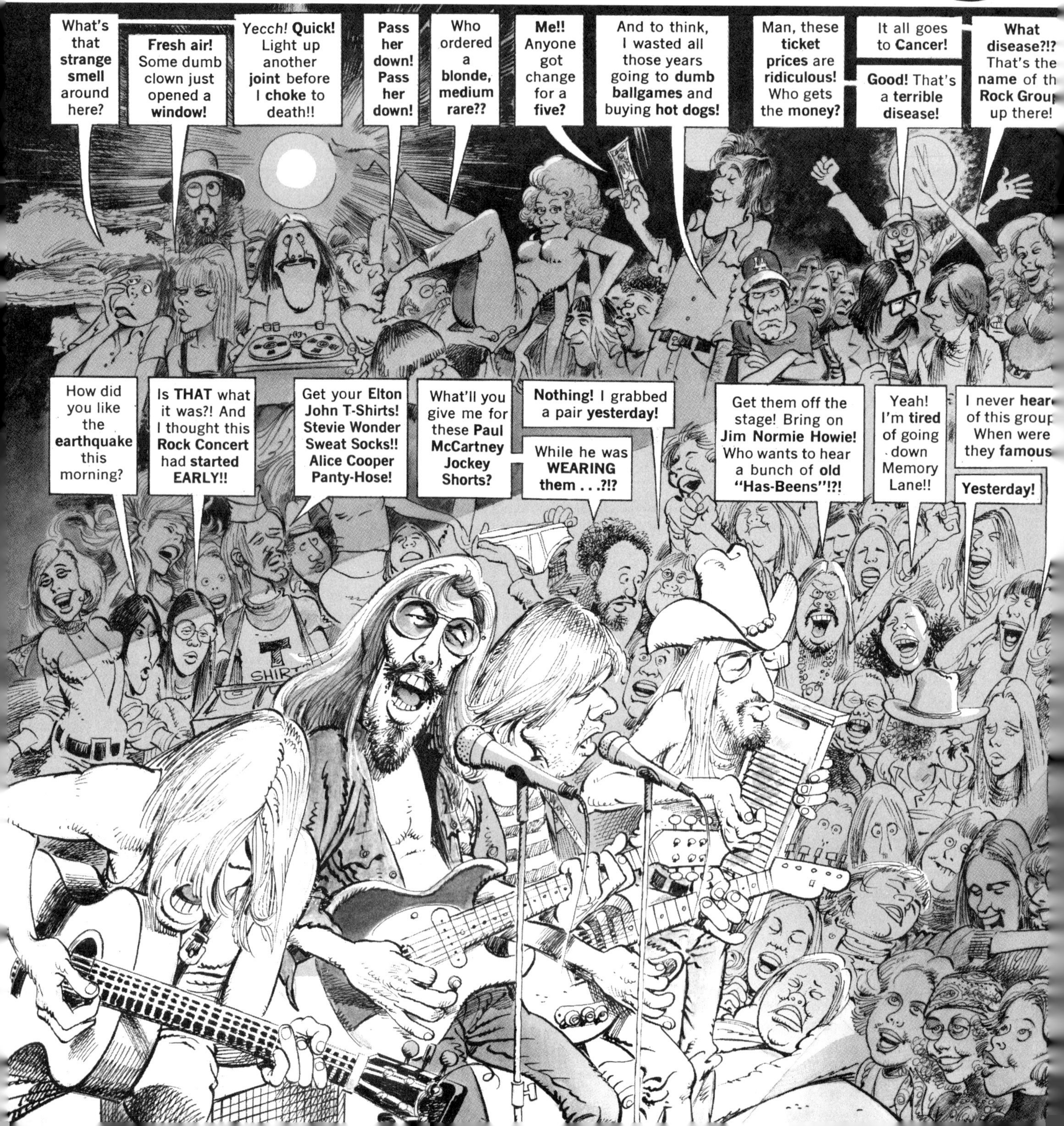

What's that strange smell around here?
Fresh air! Some dumb clown just opened a window!
Yecch! Quick! Light up another joint before I choke to death!!
Pass her down! Pass her down!
Who ordered a blonde, medium rare??
Me!! Anyone got change for a five?
And to think, I wasted all those years going to dumb ballgames and buying hot dogs!
Man, these ticket prices are ridiculous! Who gets the money?
It all goes to Cancer!
Good! That's a terrible disease!
What disease?!? That's the name of th Rock Grou up there!
How did you like the earthquake this morning?
Is THAT what it was?! And I thought this Rock Concert had started EARLY!!
Get your Elton John T-Shirts! Stevie Wonder Sweat Socks!! Alice Cooper Panty-Hose!
What'll you give me for these Paul McCartney Jockey Shorts?
Nothing! I grabbed a pair yesterday!
While he was WEARING them . . .?!?
Get them off the stage! Bring on Jim Normie Howie! Who wants to hear a bunch of old "Has-Beens"!?!
Yeah! I'm tired of going down Memory Lane!!
I never hear of this group When were they famous
Yesterday!

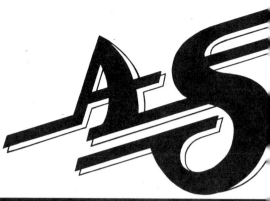

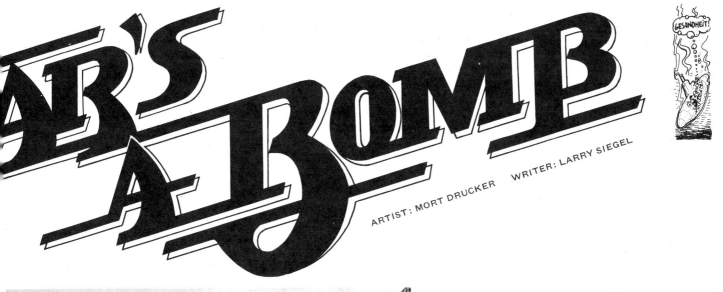

# AR'S A BOMB

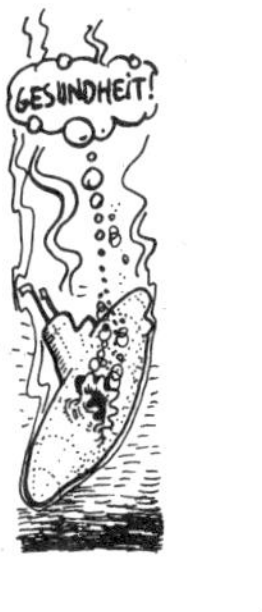
GESUNDHEIT!

ARTIST: MORT DRUCKER WRITER: LARRY SIEGEL

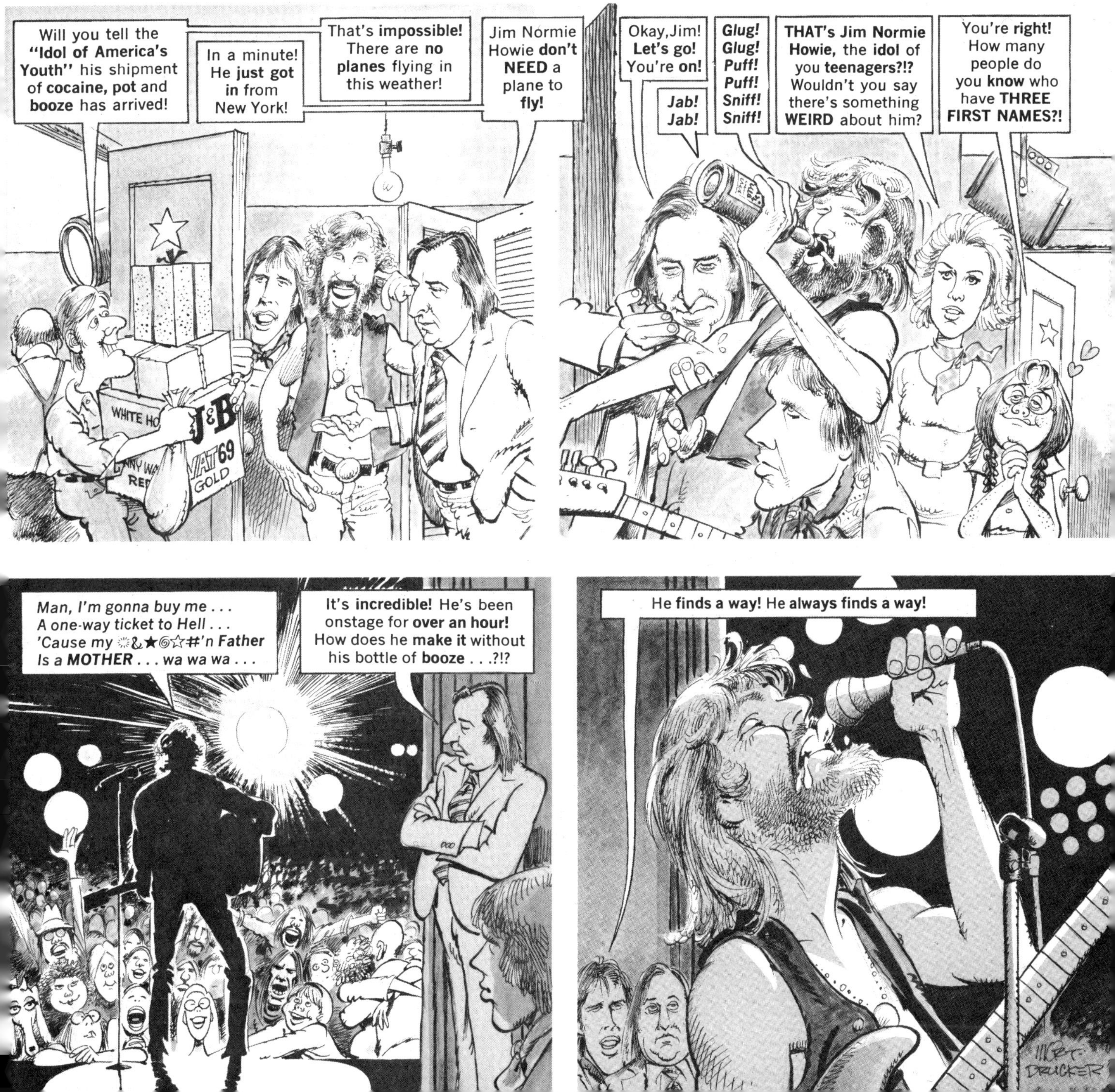
Will you tell the **"Idol of America's Youth"** his shipment of **cocaine, pot** and **booze** has arrived!
In a minute! He **just got in** from New York!
That's **impossible!** There are **no planes** flying in this weather!
Jim Normie Howie **don't NEED** a plane to **fly!**
Okay, Jim! **Let's go!** You're **on!**
**Jab! Jab!**
**Glug! Glug! Puff! Puff! Sniff! Sniff!**
**THAT's Jim Normie Howie,** the **idol** of you **teenagers?!?** Wouldn't you say there's something **WEIRD** about him?
You're **right!** How many people do you **know** who have **THREE FIRST NAMES?!**
WHITE HO
J&B
VAT 69 GOLD
Man, I'm gonna buy me . . . A one-way ticket to Hell . . . 'Cause my ☼&★@☆#'n **Father** Is a **MOTHER** . . . wa wa wa . . .
It's **incredible!** He's been onstage for **over an hour!** How does he **make it** without his bottle of **booze** . . .?!?
He **finds a way!** He **always finds a way!**
MORT DRUCKER

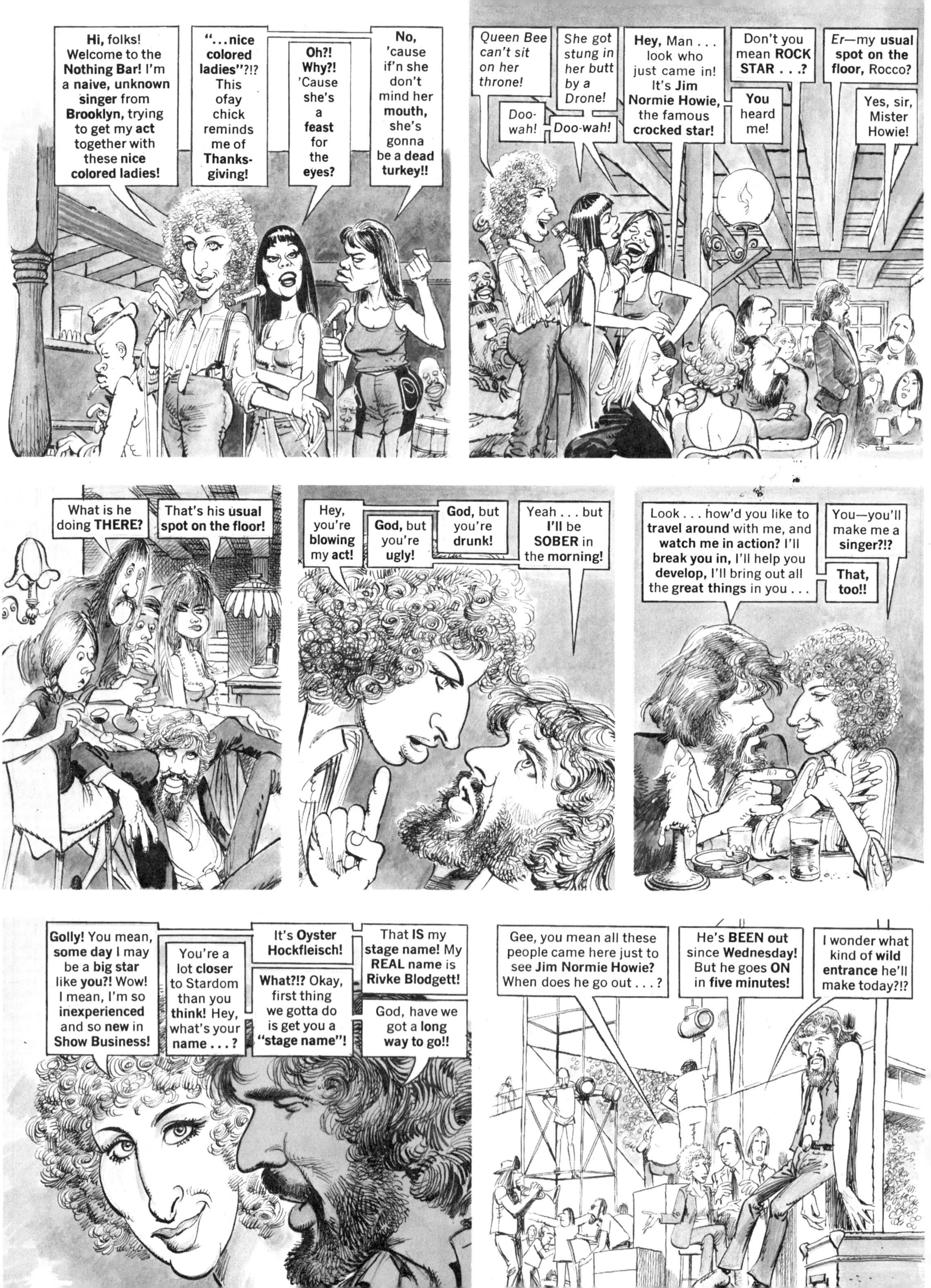
Hi, folks! Welcome to the Nothing Bar! I'm a naive, unknown singer from Brooklyn, trying to get my act together with these nice colored ladies!
"...nice colored ladies"?!? This ofay chick reminds me of Thanksgiving!
Oh?! Why?! 'Cause she's a feast for the eyes?
No, 'cause if'n she don't mind her mouth, she's gonna be a dead turkey!!
Queen Bee can't sit on her throne!
Doo-wah!
She got stung in her butt by a Drone!
Doo-wah!
Hey, Man . . . look who just came in! It's Jim Normie Howie, the famous crocked star!
Don't you mean ROCK STAR . . .?
You heard me!
Er—my usual spot on the floor, Rocco?
Yes, sir, Mister Howie!
What is he doing THERE?
That's his usual spot on the floor!
Hey, you're blowing my act!
God, but you're drunk!
God, but you're ugly!
Yeah . . . but I'll be SOBER in the morning!
Look . . . how'd you like to travel around with me, and watch me in action? I'll break you in, I'll help you develop, I'll bring out all the great things in you . . .
You—you'll make me a singer?!?
That, too!!
Golly! You mean, some day I may be a big star like you?! Wow! I mean, I'm so inexperienced and so new in Show Business!
You're a lot closer to Stardom than you think! Hey, what's your name . . . ?
It's Oyster Hockfleisch!
What?!? Okay, first thing we gotta do is get you a "stage name"!
That IS my stage name! My REAL name is Rivke Blodgett!
God, have we got a long way to go!!
Gee, you mean all these people came here just to see Jim Normie Howie? When does he go out . . . ?
He's BEEN out since Wednesday! But he goes ON in five minutes!
I wonder what kind of wild entrance he'll make today?!?

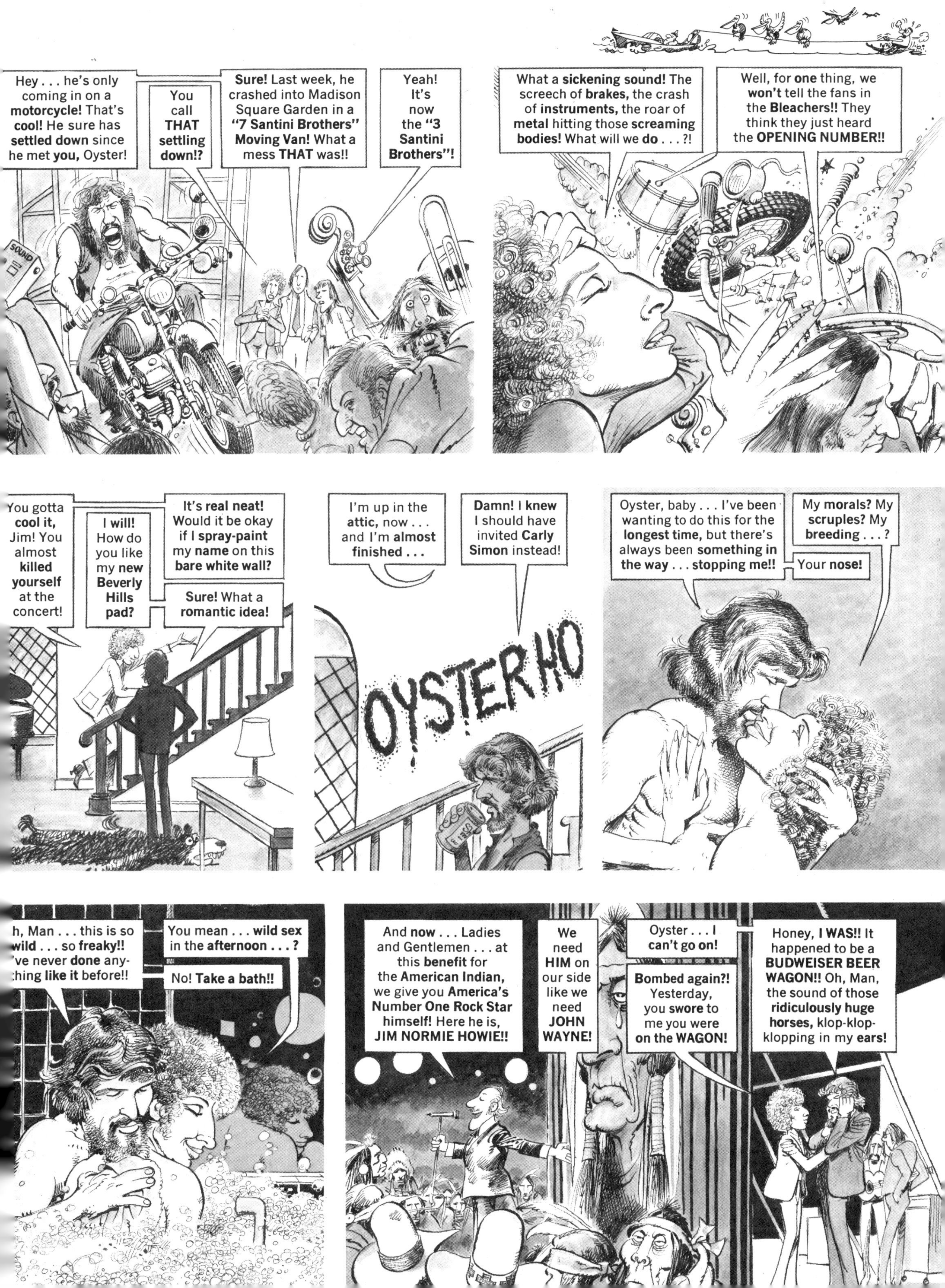
Hey . . . he's only coming in on a motorcycle! That's cool! He sure has settled down since he met you, Oyster!
You call THAT settling down!?
Sure! Last week, he crashed into Madison Square Garden in a "7 Santini Brothers" Moving Van! What a mess THAT was!!
Yeah! It's now the "3 Santini Brothers"!
SOUND
What a sickening sound! The screech of brakes, the crash of instruments, the roar of metal hitting those screaming bodies! What will we do . . . ?!
Well, for one thing, we won't tell the fans in the Bleachers!! They think they just heard the OPENING NUMBER!!
You gotta cool it, Jim! You almost killed yourself at the concert!
I will! How do you like my new Beverly Hills pad?
It's real neat! Would it be okay if I spray-paint my name on this bare white wall?
Sure! What a romantic idea!
I'm up in the attic, now . . . and I'm almost finished . . .
Damn! I knew I should have invited Carly Simon instead!
OYSTER HO
Oyster, baby . . . I've been wanting to do this for the longest time, but there's always been something in the way . . . stopping me!!
My morals? My scruples? My breeding . . . ?
Your nose!
h, Man . . . this is so wild . . . so freaky!! 've never done anything like it before!!
You mean . . . wild sex in the afternoon . . . ?
No! Take a bath!!
And now . . . Ladies and Gentlemen . . . at this benefit for the American Indian, we give you America's Number One Rock Star himself! Here he is, JIM NORMIE HOWIE!!
We need HIM on our side like we need JOHN WAYNE!
Oyster . . . I can't go on!
Bombed again?! Yesterday, you swore to me you were on the WAGON!
Honey, I WAS!! It happened to be a BUDWEISER BEER WAGON!! Oh, Man, the sound of those ridiculously huge horses, klop-klop-klopping in my ears!

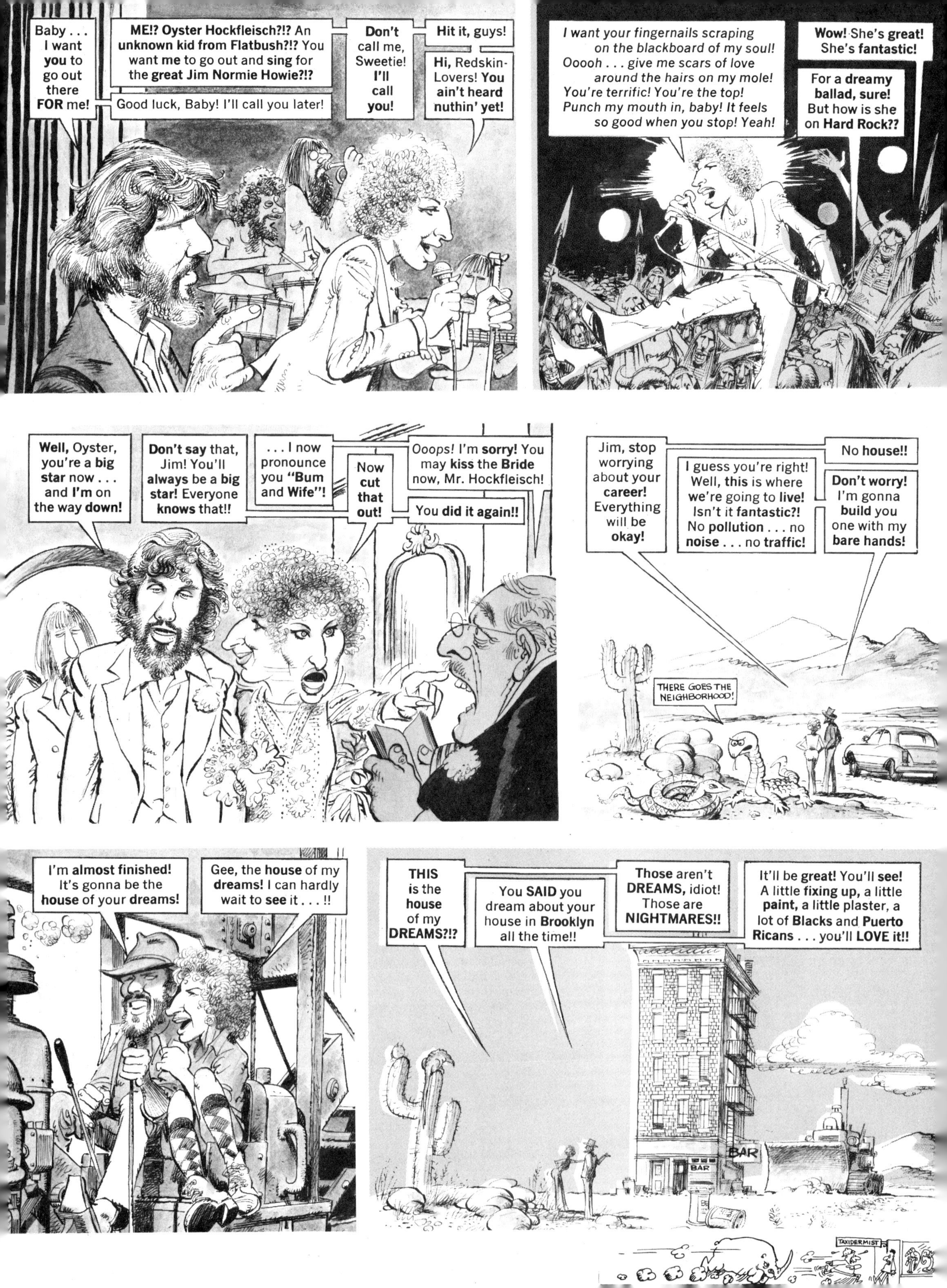

Baby . . . I want you to go out there FOR me!
ME!? Oyster Hockfleisch?!? An unknown kid from Flatbush?!? You want me to go out and sing for the great Jim Normie Howie?!?
Good luck, Baby! I'll call you later!
Don't call me, Sweetie! I'll call you!
Hit it, guys!
Hi, Redskin-Lovers! You ain't heard nuthin' yet!
I want your fingernails scraping on the blackboard of my soul! Ooooh . . . give me scars of love around the hairs on my mole! You're terrific! You're the top! Punch my mouth in, baby! It feels so good when you stop! Yeah!
Wow! She's great! She's fantastic!
For a dreamy ballad, sure! But how is she on Hard Rock??
Well, Oyster, you're a big star now . . . and I'm on the way down!
Don't say that, Jim! You'll always be a big star! Everyone knows that!!
. . . I now pronounce you "Bum and Wife"!
Now cut that out!
Ooops! I'm sorry! You may kiss the Bride now, Mr. Hockfleisch!
You did it again!!
Jim, stop worrying about your career! Everything will be okay!
I guess you're right! Well, this is where we're going to live! Isn't it fantastic?! No pollution . . . no noise . . . no traffic!
No house!!
Don't worry! I'm gonna build you one with my bare hands!
THERE GOES THE NEIGHBORHOOD!
I'm almost finished! It's gonna be the house of your dreams!
Gee, the house of my dreams! I can hardly wait to see it . . . !!
THIS is the house of my DREAMS?!?
You SAID you dream about your house in Brooklyn all the time!!
Those aren't DREAMS, idiot! Those are NIGHTMARES!!
It'll be great! You'll see! A little fixing up, a little paint, a little plaster, a lot of Blacks and Puerto Ricans . . . you'll LOVE it!!
BAR
BAR
TAXIDERMIST

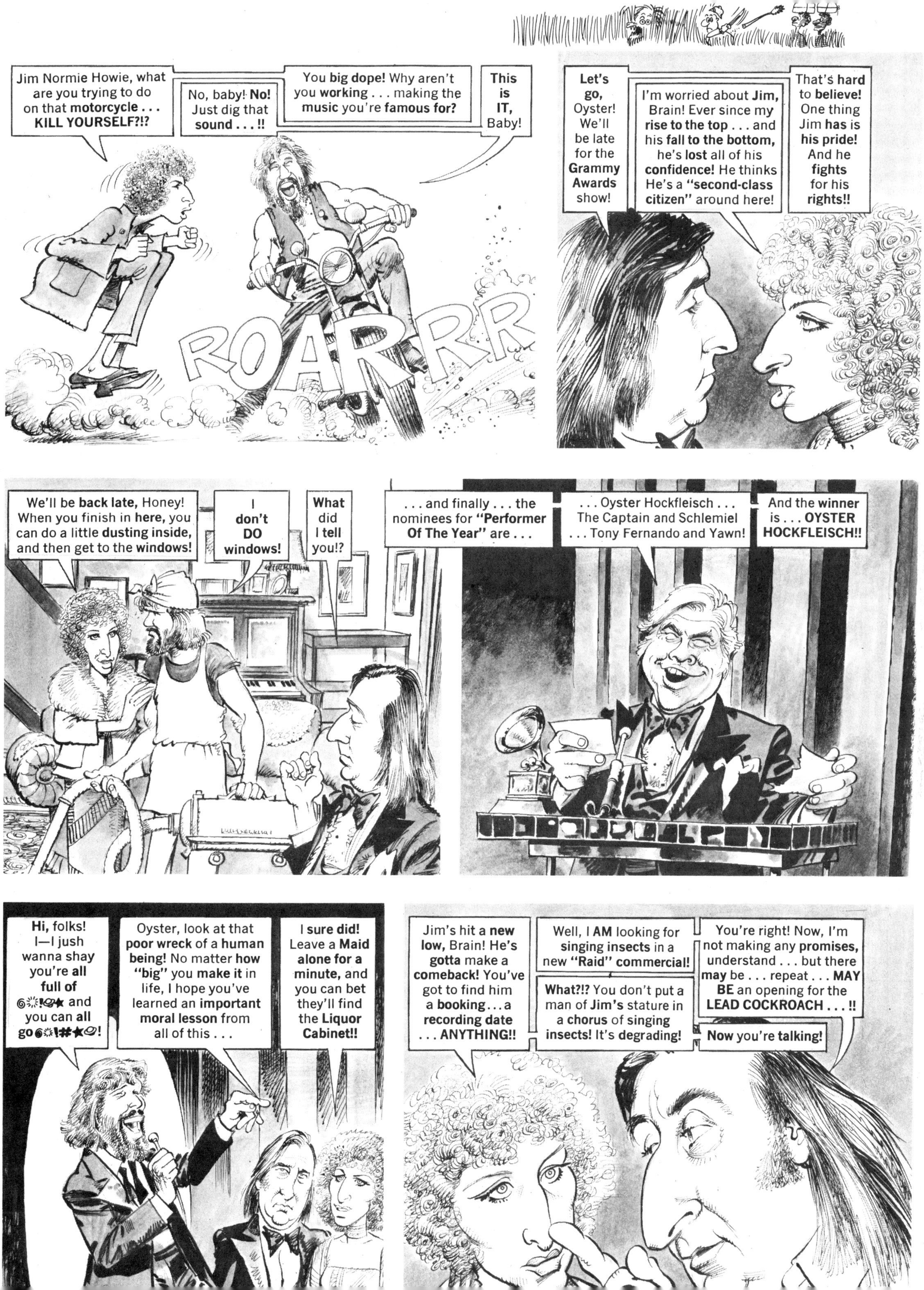

Jim Normie Howie, what are you trying to do on that motorcycle . . . KILL YOURSELF?!?
No, baby! No! Just dig that sound . . . !!
You big dope! Why aren't you working . . . making the music you're famous for?
This is IT, Baby!
ROARRR
Let's go, Oyster! We'll be late for the Grammy Awards show!
I'm worried about Jim, Brain! Ever since my rise to the top . . . and his fall to the bottom, he's lost all of his confidence! He thinks He's a "second-class citizen" around here!
That's hard to believe! One thing Jim has is his pride! And he fights for his rights!!
We'll be back late, Honey! When you finish in here, you can do a little dusting inside, and then get to the windows!
I don't DO windows!
What did I tell you!?
. . . and finally . . . the nominees for "Performer Of The Year" are . . .
. . . Oyster Hockfleisch . . . The Captain and Schlemiel . . . Tony Fernando and Yawn!
And the winner is . . . OYSTER HOCKFLEISCH!!
Hi, folks! I—I jush wanna shay you're all full of @$!@★ and you can all go @$!#★@!
Oyster, look at that poor wreck of a human being! No matter how "big" you make it in life, I hope you've learned an important moral lesson from all of this . . .
I sure did! Leave a Maid alone for a minute, and you can bet they'll find the Liquor Cabinet!!
Jim's hit a new low, Brain! He's gotta make a comeback! You've got to find him a booking . . . a recording date . . . ANYTHING!!
Well, I AM looking for singing insects in a new "Raid" commercial!
What?!? You don't put a man of Jim's stature in a chorus of singing insects! It's degrading!
You're right! Now, I'm not making any promises, understand . . . but there may be . . . repeat . . . MAY BE an opening for the LEAD COCKROACH . . . !!
Now you're talking!

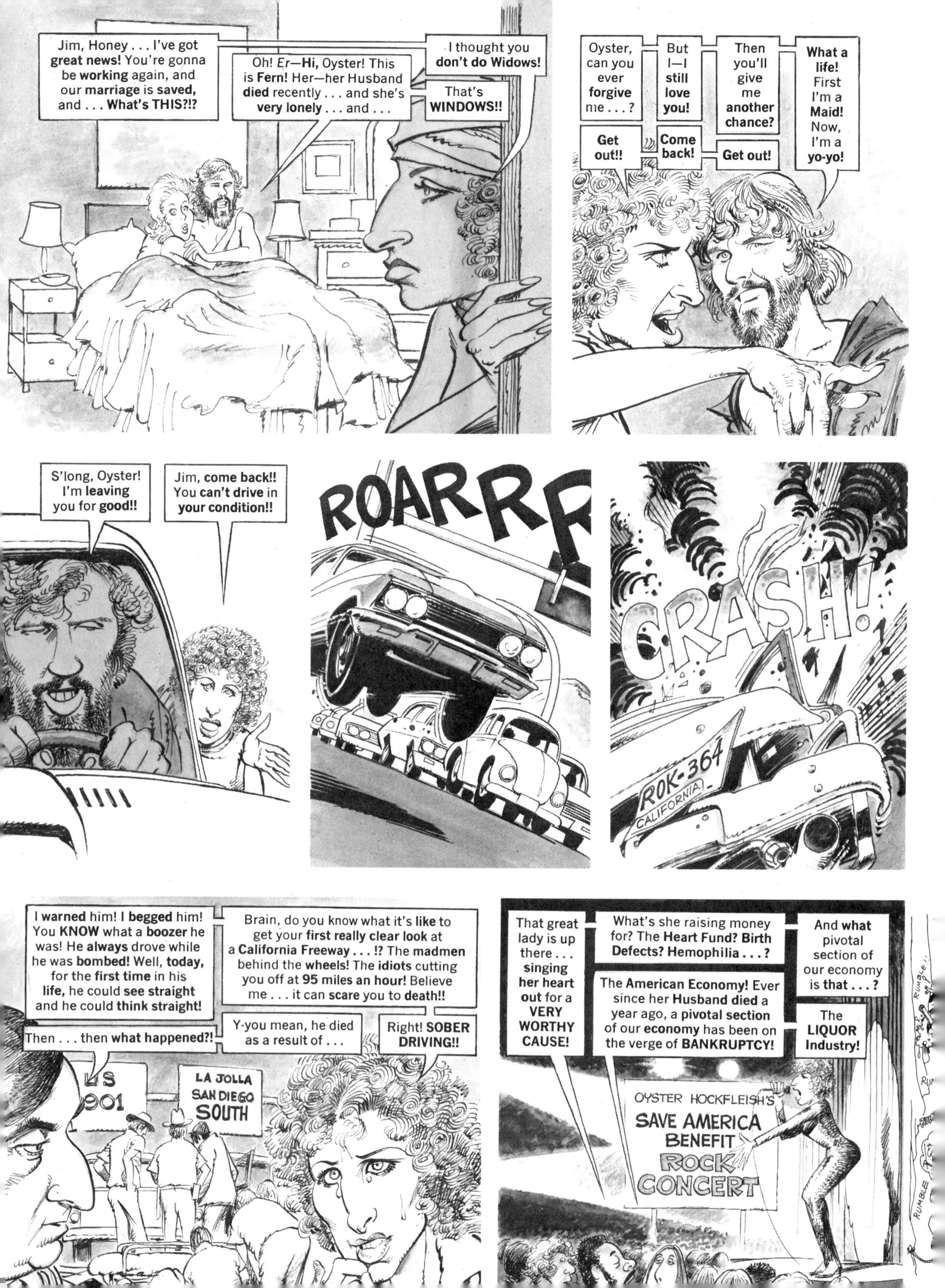

Jim, Honey . . . I've got **great news!** You're gonna be **working** again, and our **marriage** is **saved,** and . . . **What's THIS?!?**
I thought you **don't do Widows!**
Oh! *Er*—**Hi,** Oyster! This is **Fern!** Her—her Husband **died** recently . . . and she's **very lonely** . . . and . . .
That's **WINDOWS!!**
Oyster, can you ever **forgive** me . . . ?
**Get out!!**
But I—I **still love you!**
**Come back!**
Then you'll give me **another chance?**
**Get out!**
**What a life!** First I'm a **Maid!** Now, I'm a **yo-yo!**
S'long, Oyster! I'm **leaving** you for **good!!**
Jim, **come back!!** You **can't drive** in **your condition!!**
ROARRR
CRASH!
ROK-364
CALIFORNIA
I **warned** him! I **begged** him! You **KNOW** what a **boozer** he was! He **always** drove while he was **bombed!** Well, **today,** for the **first time** in his **life,** he could **see straight** and he could **think straight!**
Brain, do you know what it's **like** to get your **first really clear look** at a **California Freeway . . . !?** The **madmen** behind the **wheels!** The **idiots** cutting you off at **95 miles an hour!** Believe me . . . it can **scare** you to **death!!**
Then . . . then **what happened?!**
Y-you mean, he died as a result of . . .
Right! **SOBER DRIVING!!**
LA JOLLA
SAN DIEGO
SOUTH
That great lady is up there . . . **singing her heart out** for a **VERY WORTHY CAUSE!**
What's she raising money for? The **Heart Fund? Birth Defects? Hemophilia . . . ?**
And **what** pivotal section of our economy is **that . . . ?**
The **American Economy!** Ever since her **Husband died** a year ago, a **pivotal section** of our **economy** has been on the verge of **BANKRUPTCY!**
The **LIQUOR Industry!**
OYSTER HOCKFLEISH'S
SAVE AMERICA BENEFIT
ROCK CONCERT
RUMBLE

# Scenes We'd Like to See

## The Big Break

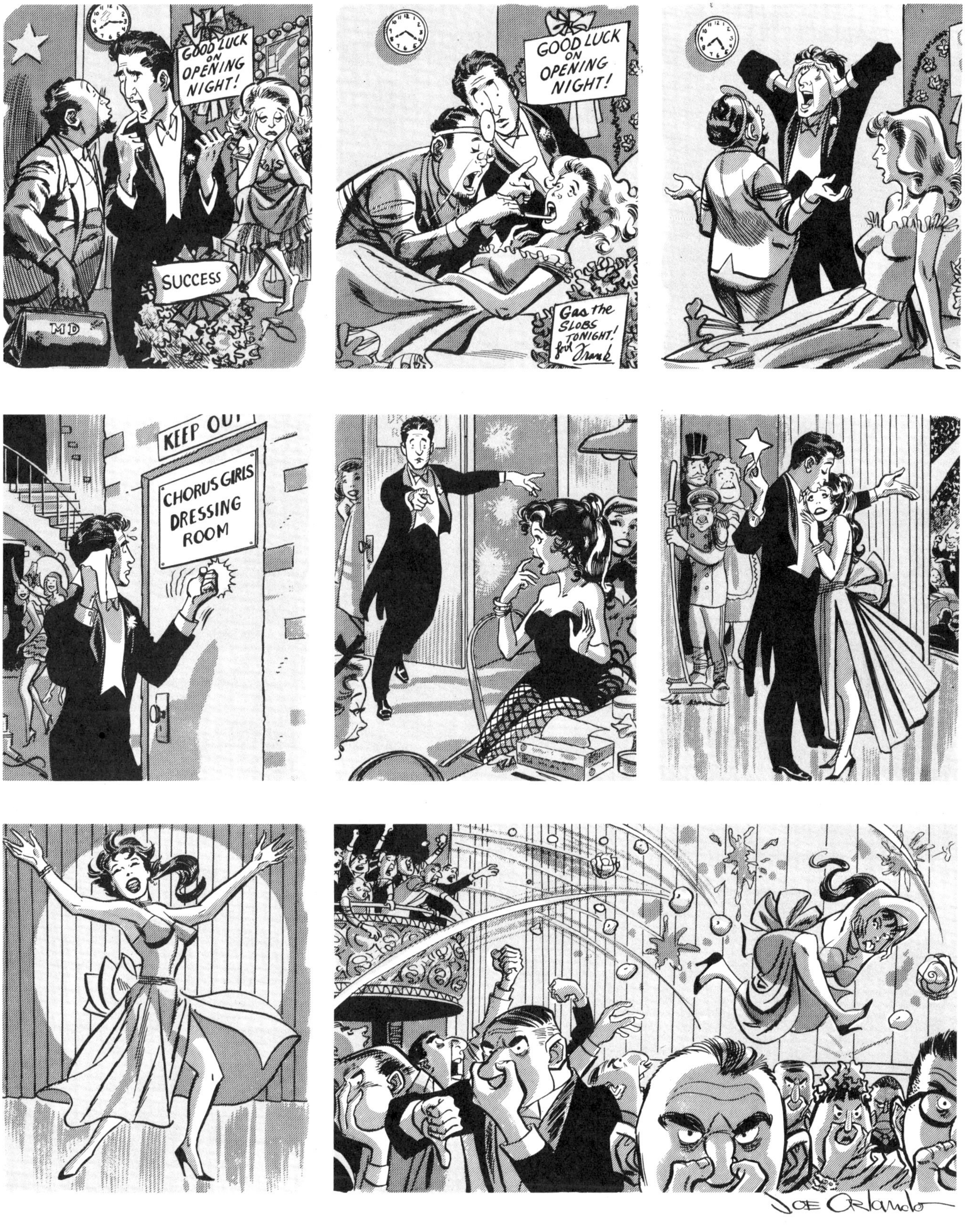
GOOD LUCK ON OPENING NIGHT!
SUCCESS
MD
GOOD LUCK ON OPENING NIGHT!
Gas the SLOBS TONIGHT! Frank
KEEP OUT
CHORUS GIRLS DRESSING ROOM
JOE ORLANDO

**SUPER MARKETING DEPT.**

**He started out in the Thirties as a comic book hero. Then, he became the star of a movie serial, a radio show, a television series, a Broadway musical, and now...at last...he's the star of a multi-million dollar full-length feature motion picture! Look...up in the sky! It's a gold mine! It's a bonanza! It's**

# SUPER

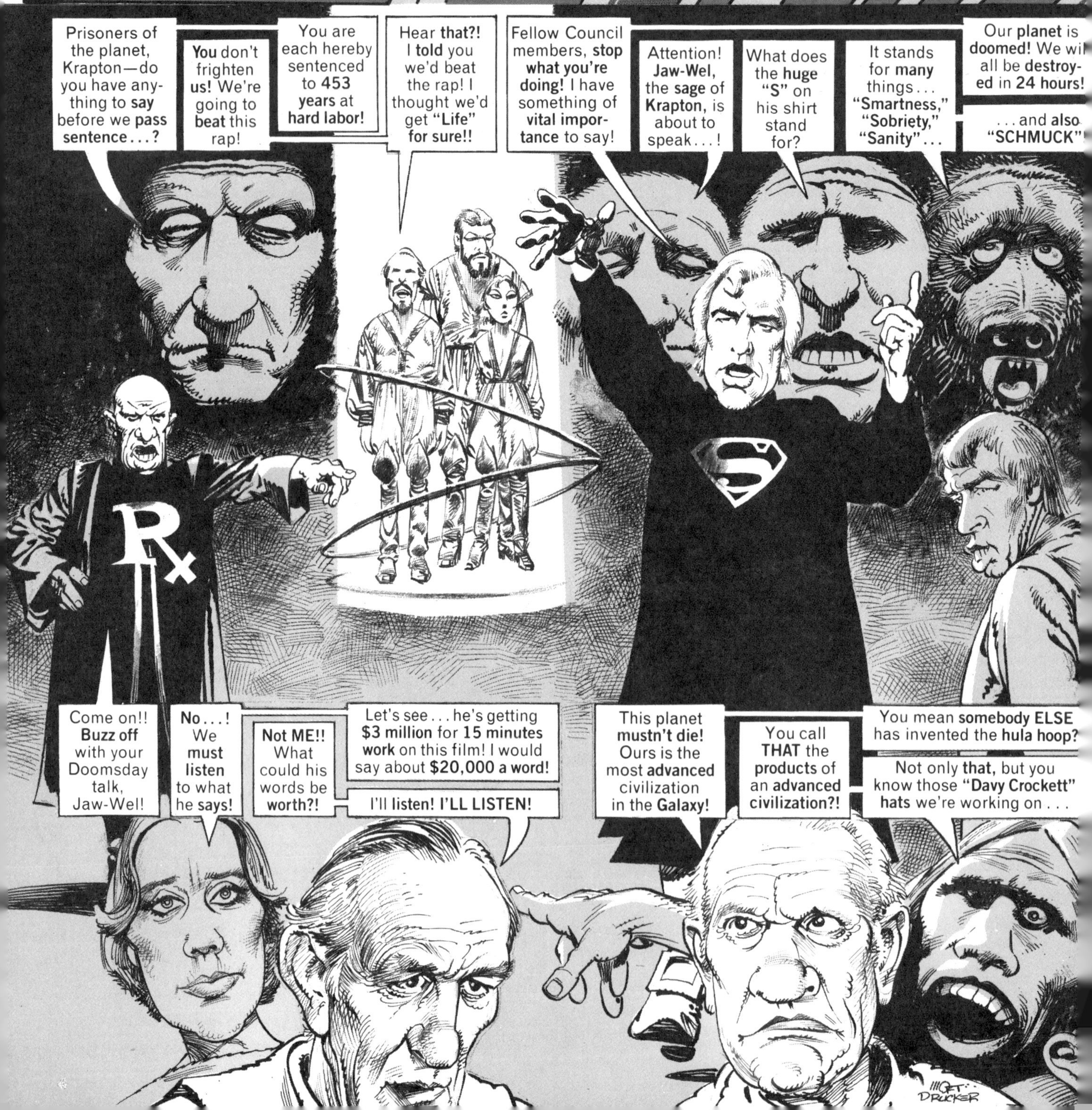

Prisoners of the planet, Krapton—do you have anything to say before we pass sentence...?
You don't frighten us! We're going to beat this rap!
You are each hereby sentenced to 453 years at hard labor!
Hear that?! I told you we'd beat the rap! I thought we'd get "Life" for sure!!
Fellow Council members, stop what you're doing! I have something of vital importance to say!
Attention! Jaw-Wel, the sage of Krapton, is about to speak...!
What does the huge "S" on his shirt stand for?
It stands for many things... "Smartness," "Sobriety," "Sanity"...
Our planet is doomed! We wi all be destroyed in 24 hours!
...and also "SCHMUCK"
Come on!! Buzz off with your Doomsday talk, Jaw-Wel!
No...! We must listen to what he says!
Not ME!! What could his words be worth?!
Let's see...he's getting $3 million for 15 minutes work on this film! I would say about $20,000 a word!
I'll listen! I'LL LISTEN!
This planet mustn't die! Ours is the most advanced civilization in the Galaxy!
You call THAT the products of an advanced civilization?!
You mean somebody ELSE has invented the hula hoop?
Not only that, but you know those "Davy Crockett" hats we're working on...
MORT DRUCKER

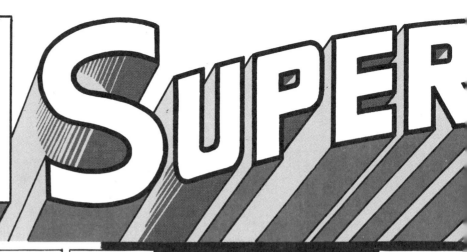

# DUPERMAN

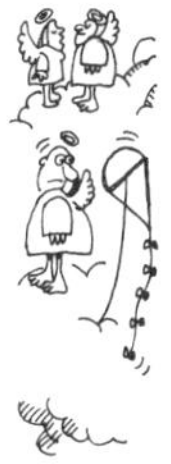

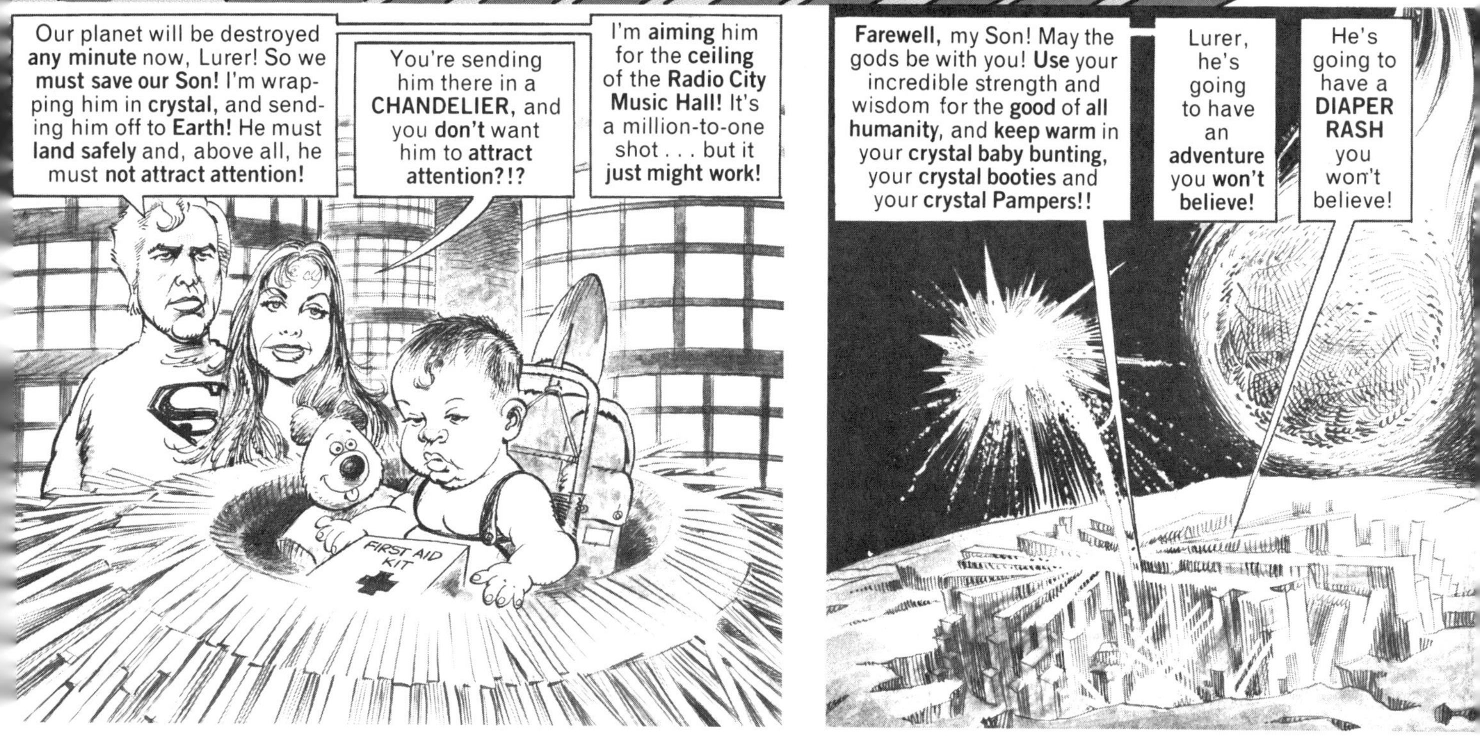
Our planet will be destroyed any minute now, Lurer! So we must save our Son! I'm wrapping him in crystal, and sending him off to Earth! He must land safely and, above all, he must not attract attention!
You're sending him there in a CHANDELIER, and you don't want him to attract attention?!?
I'm aiming him for the ceiling of the Radio City Music Hall! It's a million-to-one shot . . . but it just might work!
FIRST AID KIT
Farewell, my Son! May the gods be with you! Use your incredible strength and wisdom for the good of all humanity, and keep warm in your crystal baby bunting, your crystal booties and your crystal Pampers!!
Lurer, he's going to have an adventure you won't believe!
He's going to have a DIAPER RASH you won't believe!

ARTIST: MORT DRUCKER WRITER: LARRY SIEGEL

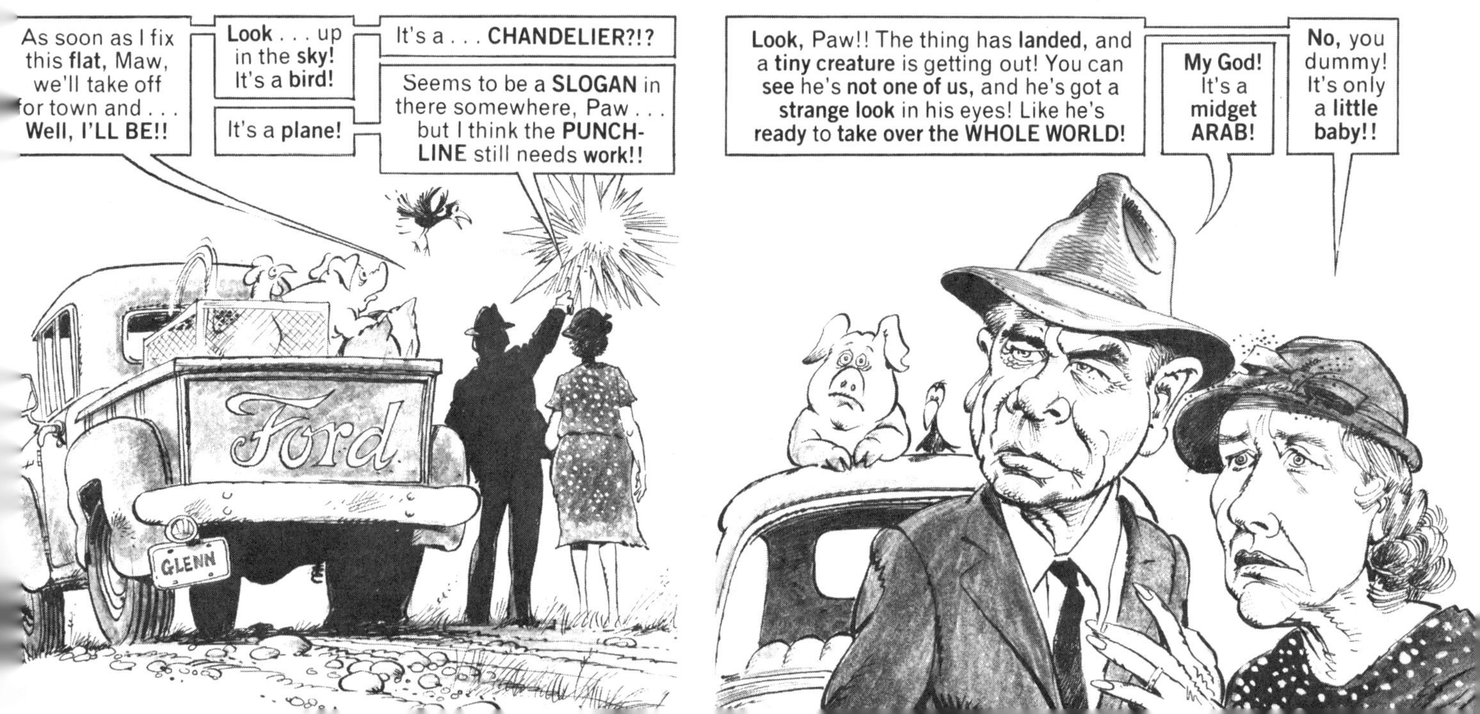
As soon as I fix this flat, Maw, we'll take off for town and . . . Well, I'LL BE!!
Look . . . up in the sky! It's a bird!
It's a plane!
It's a . . . CHANDELIER?!?
Seems to be a SLOGAN in there somewhere, Paw . . . but I think the PUNCH-LINE still needs work!!
Ford
GLENN
Look, Paw!! The thing has landed, and a tiny creature is getting out! You can see he's not one of us, and he's got a strange look in his eyes! Like he's ready to take over the WHOLE WORLD!
My God! It's a midget ARAB!
No, you dummy! It's only a little baby!!

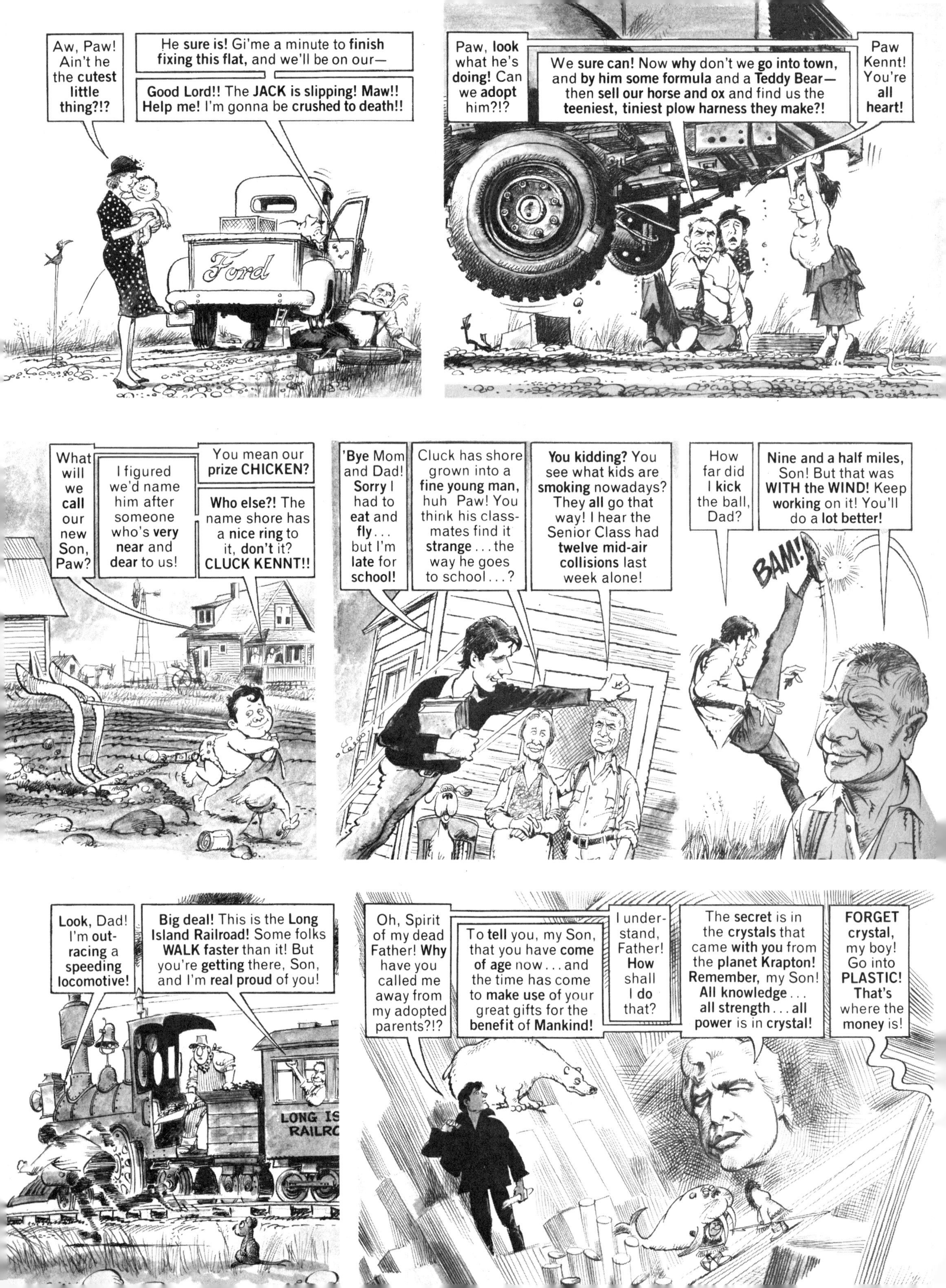
Aw, Paw! Ain't he the cutest little thing?!?
He sure is! Gi'me a minute to finish fixing this flat, and we'll be on our—
Good Lord!! The JACK is slipping! Maw!! Help me! I'm gonna be crushed to death!!
Ford
Paw, look what he's doing! Can we adopt him?!?
We sure can! Now why don't we go into town, and by him some formula and a Teddy Bear—then sell our horse and ox and find us the teeniest, tiniest plow harness they make?!
Paw Kennt! You're all heart!
What will we call our new Son, Paw?
I figured we'd name him after someone who's very near and dear to us!
You mean our prize CHICKEN?
Who else?! The name shore has a nice ring to it, don't it? CLUCK KENNT!!
'Bye Mom and Dad! Sorry I had to eat and fly . . . but I'm late for school!
Cluck has shore grown into a fine young man, huh Paw! You think his classmates find it strange . . . the way he goes to school . . . ?
You kidding? You see what kids are smoking nowadays? They all go that way! I hear the Senior Class had twelve mid-air collisions last week alone!
How far did I kick the ball, Dad?
Nine and a half miles, Son! But that was WITH the WIND! Keep working on it! You'll do a lot better!
BAM!
Look, Dad! I'm out-racing a speeding locomotive!
Big deal! This is the Long Island Railroad! Some folks WALK faster than it! But you're getting there, Son, and I'm real proud of you!
Oh, Spirit of my dead Father! Why have you called me away from my adopted parents?!?
To tell you, my Son, that you have come of age now . . . and the time has come to make use of your great gifts for the benefit of Mankind!
I understand, Father! How shall I do that?
The secret is in the crystals that came with you from the planet Krapton! Remember, my Son! All knowledge . . . all strength . . . all power is in crystal!
FORGET crystal, my boy! Go into PLASTIC! That's where the money is!

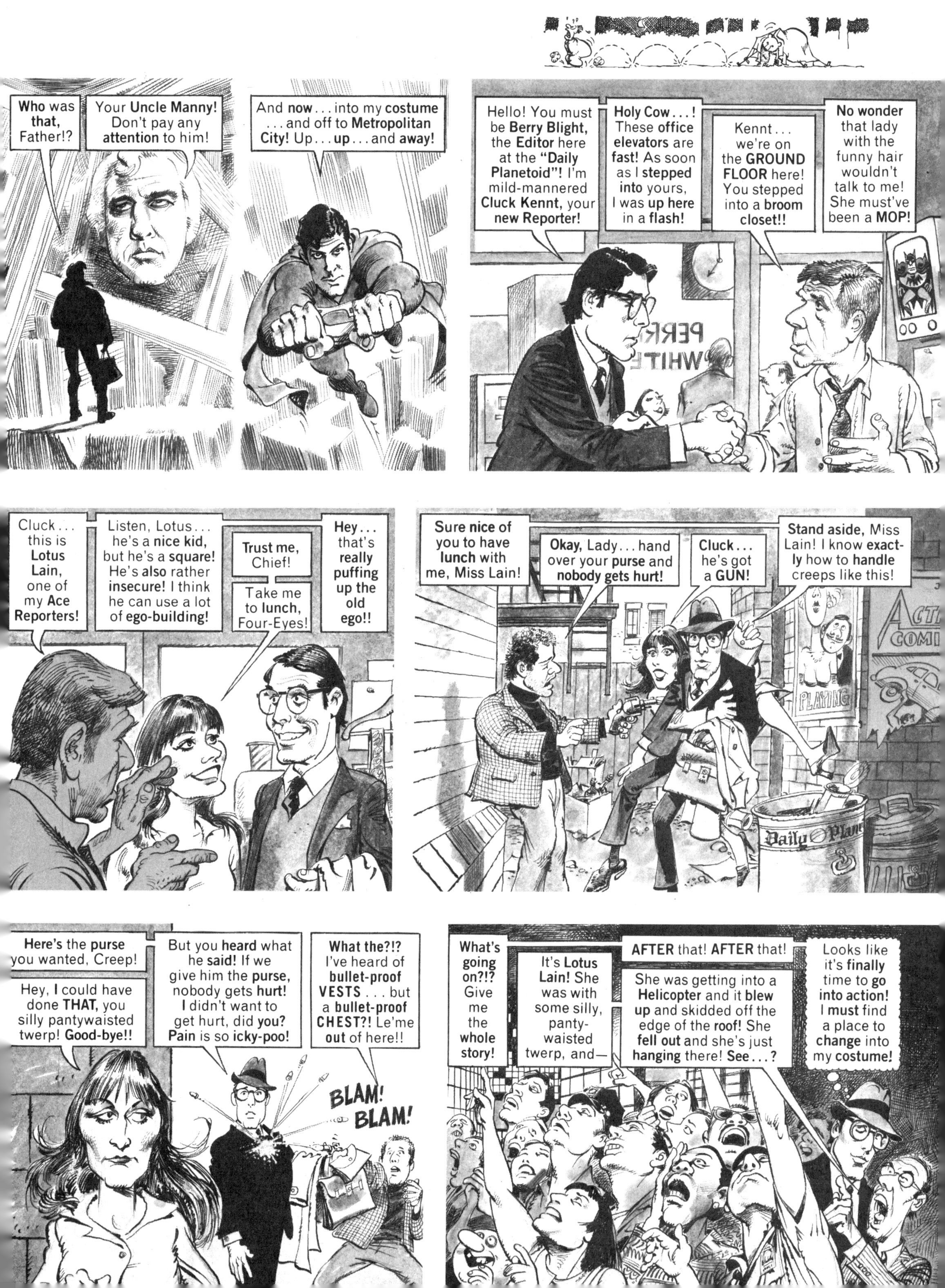
Who was that, Father!?
Your Uncle Manny! Don't pay any attention to him!
And now . . . into my costume . . . and off to Metropolitan City! Up . . . up . . . and away!
Hello! You must be Berry Blight, the Editor here at the "Daily Planetoid"! I'm mild-mannered Cluck Kennt, your new Reporter!
Holy Cow . . .! These office elevators are fast! As soon as I stepped into yours, I was up here in a flash!
Kennt . . . we're on the GROUND FLOOR here! You stepped into a broom closet!!
No wonder that lady with the funny hair wouldn't talk to me! She must've been a MOP!
PERR WHITE
Cluck . . . this is Lotus Lain, one of my Ace Reporters!
Listen, Lotus . . . he's a nice kid, but he's a square! He's also rather insecure! I think he can use a lot of ego-building!
Trust me, Chief!
Take me to lunch, Four-Eyes!
Hey . . . that's really puffing up the old ego!!
Sure nice of you to have lunch with me, Miss Lain!
Okay, Lady . . . hand over your purse and nobody gets hurt!
Cluck . . . he's got a GUN!
Stand aside, Miss Lain! I know exactly how to handle creeps like this!
PLAYING
Daily Plane
Here's the purse you wanted, Creep!
Hey, I could have done THAT, you silly pantywaisted twerp! Good-bye!!
But you heard what he said! If we give him the purse, nobody gets hurt! I didn't want to get hurt, did you? Pain is so icky-poo!
What the?!? I've heard of bullet-proof VESTS . . . but a bullet-proof CHEST?! Le'me out of here!!
BLAM! BLAM!
What's going on?!? Give me the whole story!
It's Lotus Lain! She was with some silly, panty-waisted twerp, and—
AFTER that! AFTER that!
She was getting into a Helicopter and it blew up and skidded off the edge of the roof! She fell out and she's just hanging there! See . . .?
Looks like it's finally time to go into action! I must find a place to change into my costume!

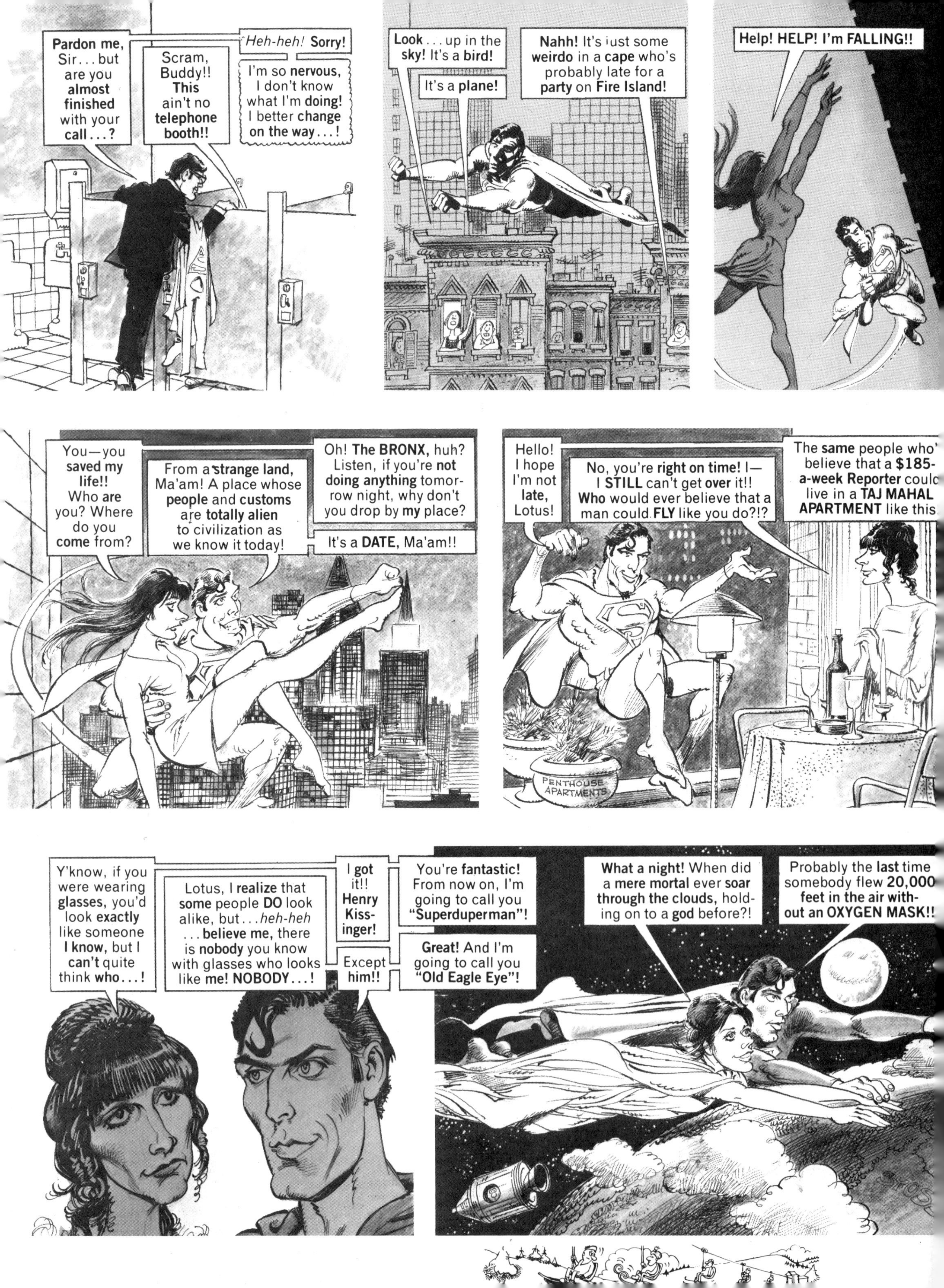

Pardon me, Sir... but are you almost finished with your call...?
Scram, Buddy!! This ain't no telephone booth!!
Heh-heh! Sorry!
I'm so nervous, I don't know what I'm doing! I better change on the way...!
Look... up in the sky! It's a bird!
It's a plane!
Nahh! It's just some weirdo in a cape who's probably late for a party on Fire Island!
Help! HELP! I'm FALLING!!
You—you saved my life!! Who are you? Where do you come from?
From a strange land, Ma'am! A place whose people and customs are totally alien to civilization as we know it today!
Oh! The BRONX, huh? Listen, if you're not doing anything tomorrow night, why don't you drop by my place?
It's a DATE, Ma'am!!
Hello! I hope I'm not late, Lotus!
No, you're right on time! I—I STILL can't get over it!! Who would ever believe that a man could FLY like you do?!?
The same people who believe that a $185-a-week Reporter could live in a TAJ MAHAL APARTMENT like this
PENTHOUSE APARTMENTS
Y'know, if you were wearing glasses, you'd look exactly like someone I know, but I can't quite think who...!
Lotus, I realize that some people DO look alike, but...heh-heh ...believe me, there is nobody you know with glasses who looks like me! NOBODY...!
I got it!! Henry Kissinger!
Except him!!
You're fantastic! From now on, I'm going to call you "Superduperman"!
Great! And I'm going to call you "Old Eagle Eye"!
What a night! When did a mere mortal ever soar through the clouds, holding on to a god before?!
Probably the last time somebody flew 20,000 feet in the air without an OXYGEN MASK!!

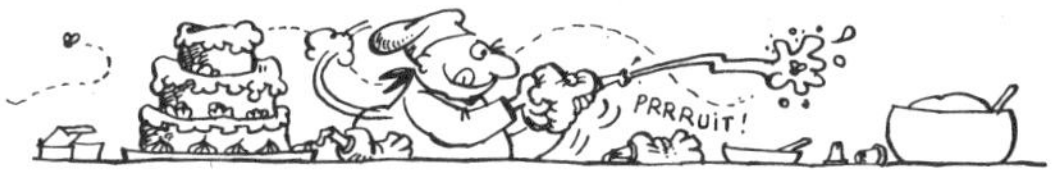

PRRRUIT!


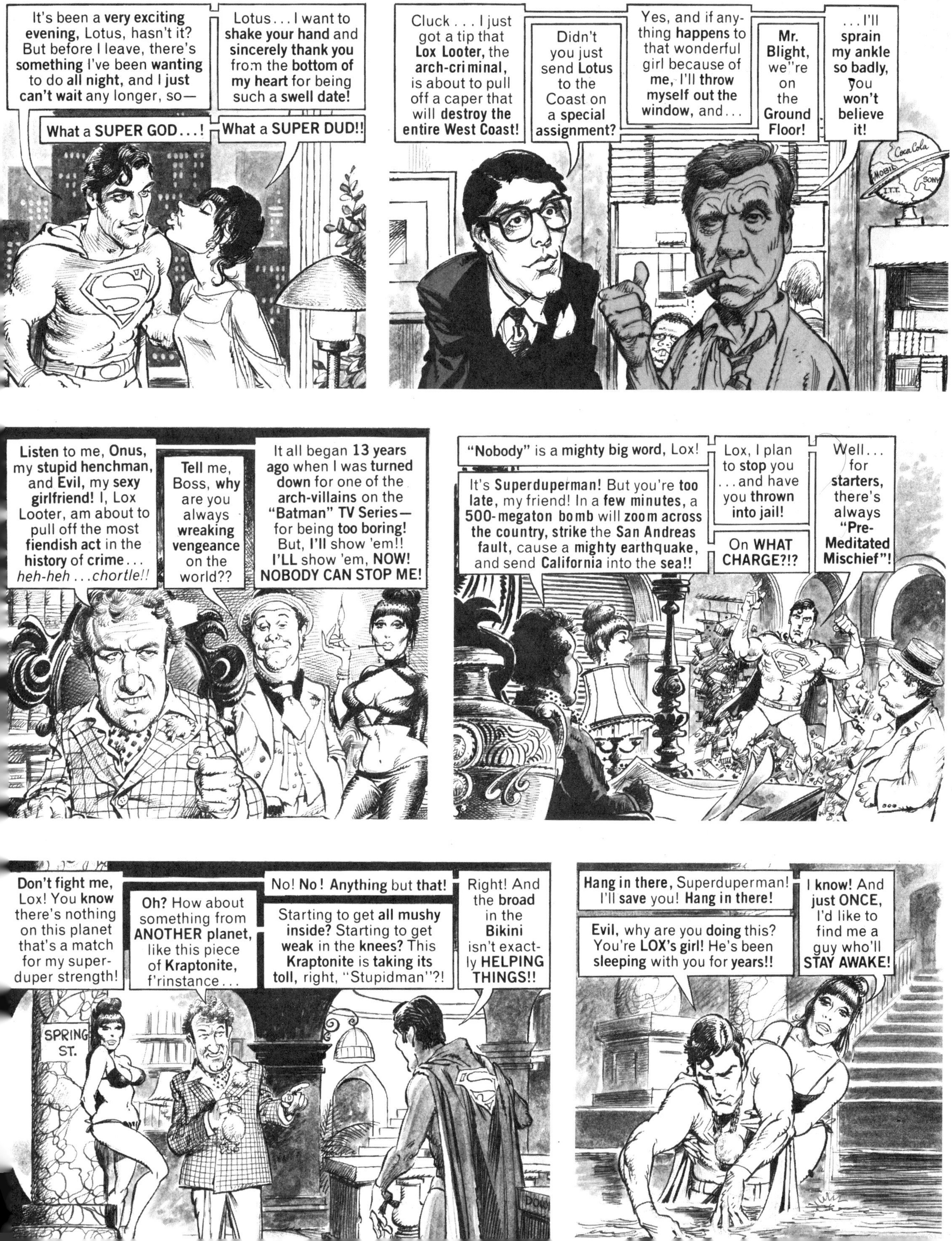

It's been a **very exciting evening,** Lotus, hasn't it? But before I leave, there's **something** I've been **wanting** to do **all night,** and I **just can't wait** any longer, so—
**What a SUPER GOD . . . !**
Lotus . . . I want to **shake your hand** and **sincerely thank you** from the **bottom of my heart** for being such a **swell date!**
**What a SUPER DUD!!**
Cluck . . . I just got a tip that **Lox Looter,** the **arch-criminal,** is about to pull off a caper that will **destroy the entire West Coast!**
Didn't you just send **Lotus** to the Coast on a **special assignment?**
Yes, and if anything **happens** to that wonderful girl because of **me,** I'll **throw myself out the window,** and . . .
**Mr. Blight,** we"re on the **Ground Floor!**
. . . I'll **sprain my ankle so badly,** you **won't believe** it!
Coca Cola
MOBIL
I.T.T.
**Listen** to me, **Onus,** my **stupid henchman,** and **Evil,** my **sexy girlfriend!** I, Lox Looter, am about to pull off the most **fiendish act** in the **history** of **crime** . . . *heh-heh . . . chortle!!*
**Tell** me, Boss, **why** are you always **wreaking vengeance** on the world??
It all began **13 years** ago when I was **turned down** for one of the **arch-villains** on the **"Batman" TV Series**—for being **too boring!** But, **I'll** show 'em!! **I'LL** show 'em, **NOW! NOBODY CAN STOP ME!**
**"Nobody"** is a **mighty big word,** Lox!
It's **Superduperman!** But you're **too late,** my friend! In a **few minutes,** a **500-megaton bomb** will **zoom across the country, strike** the **San Andreas fault,** cause a **mighty earthquake,** and send **California** into the **sea!!**
Lox, I plan to **stop** you . . . and have you **thrown into jail!**
On **WHAT CHARGE?!?**
Well . . . for **starters,** there's always **"Pre-Meditated Mischief"!**
**Don't fight me,** Lox! You **know** there's nothing on this planet that's a match for my super-duper strength!
**Oh?** How about something from **ANOTHER planet,** like this piece of **Kraptonite,** f'rinstance . . .
No! **No! Anything** but **that!**
Starting to get **all mushy inside?** Starting to get **weak** in the **knees?** This **Kraptonite** is **taking its toll,** right, "Stupidman"?!
Right! And the **broad** in the **Bikini** isn't exactly **HELPING THINGS!!**
SPRING ST.
**Hang in there,** Superduperman! I'll **save** you! **Hang in there!**
**Evil,** why are you **doing** this? You're **LOX's girl!** He's been **sleeping** with you for **years!!**
**I know!** And **just ONCE,** I'd like to find me a guy who'll **STAY AWAKE!**

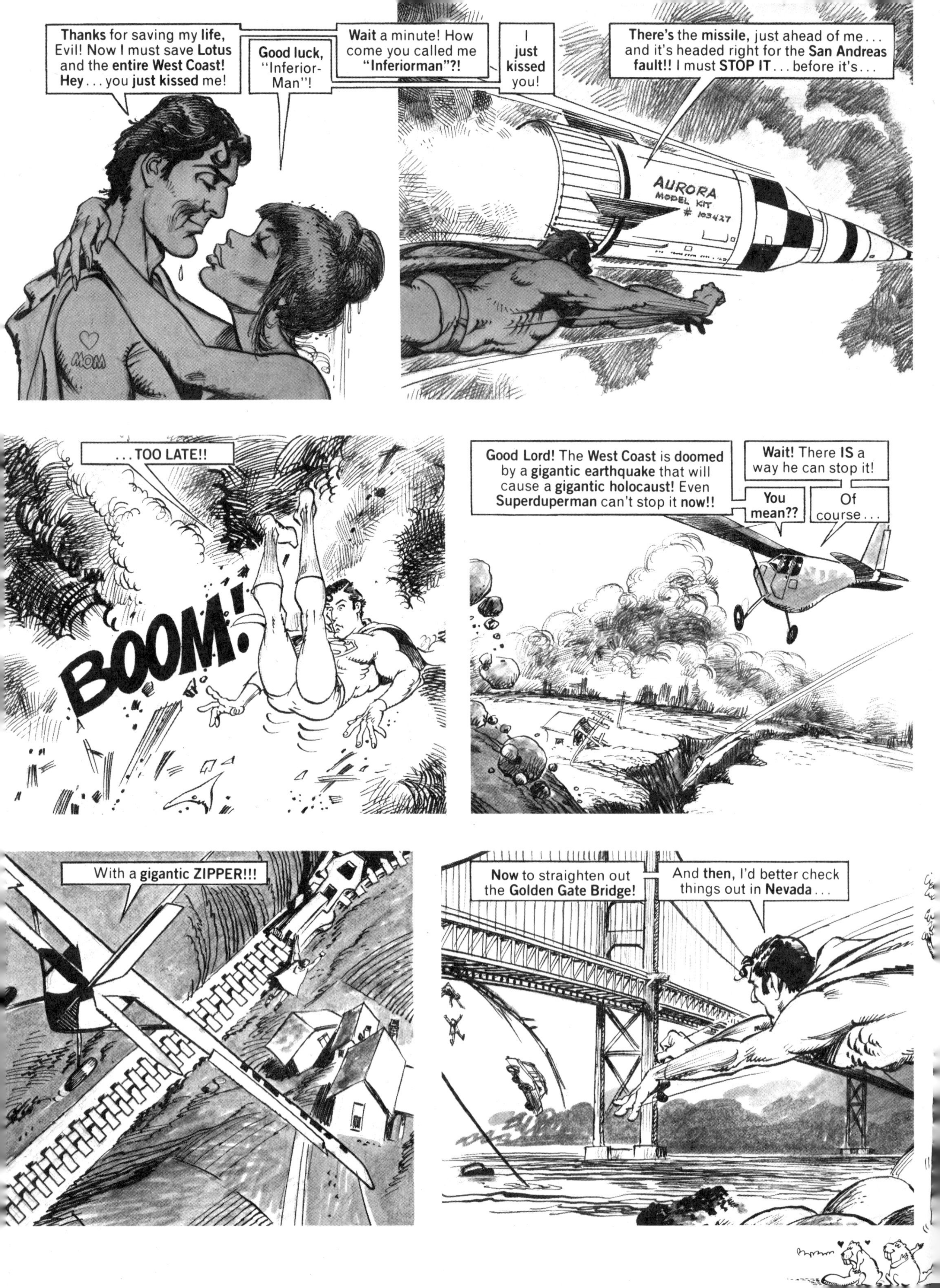
Thanks for saving my life, Evil! Now I must save Lotus and the entire West Coast! Hey . . . you just kissed me!
Good luck, "Inferior-Man"!
Wait a minute! How come you called me "Inferiorman"?!
I just kissed you!
There's the missile, just ahead of me . . . and it's headed right for the San Andreas fault!! I must STOP IT . . . before it's . . .
AURORA MODEL KIT # 103427
MOM
. . . TOO LATE!!
BOOM!
Good Lord! The West Coast is doomed by a gigantic earthquake that will cause a gigantic holocaust! Even Superduperman can't stop it now!!
Wait! There IS a way he can stop it!
You mean??
Of course . . .
With a gigantic ZIPPER!!!
Now to straighten out the Golden Gate Bridge!
And then, I'd better check things out in Nevada . . .

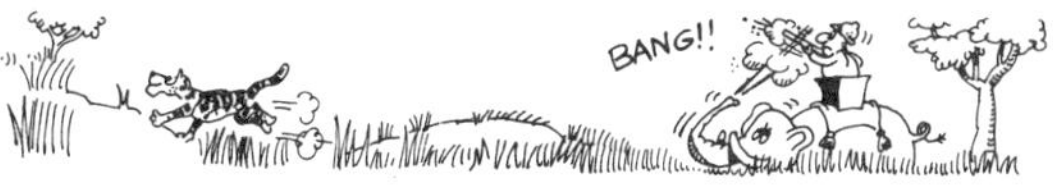
BANG!!

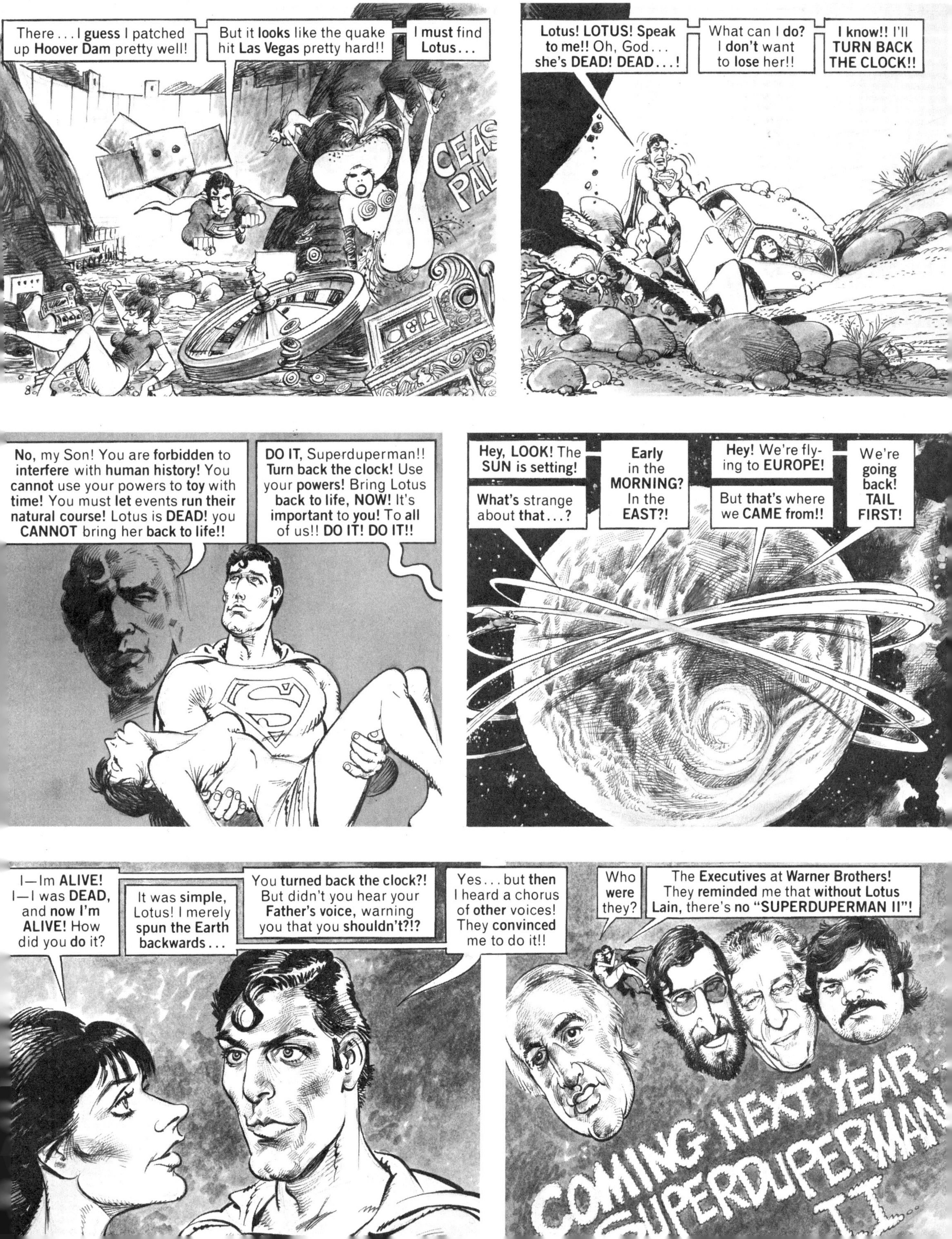
There . . . I guess I patched up Hoover Dam pretty well!
But it looks like the quake hit Las Vegas pretty hard!!
I must find Lotus . . .
Lotus! LOTUS! Speak to me!! Oh, God . . . she's DEAD! DEAD . . . !
What can I do? I don't want to lose her!!
I know!! I'll TURN BACK THE CLOCK!!
No, my Son! You are forbidden to interfere with human history! You cannot use your powers to toy with time! You must let events run their natural course! Lotus is DEAD! you CANNOT bring her back to life!!
DO IT, Superduperman!! Turn back the clock! Use your powers! Bring Lotus back to life, NOW! It's important to you! To all of us!! DO IT! DO IT!!
Hey, LOOK! The SUN is setting!
What's strange about that . . .?
Early in the MORNING? In the EAST?!
Hey! We're fly-ing to EUROPE!
But that's where we CAME from!!
We're going back! TAIL FIRST!
I—Im ALIVE! I—I was DEAD, and now I'm ALIVE! How did you do it?
It was simple, Lotus! I merely spun the Earth backwards . . .
You turned back the clock?! But didn't you hear your Father's voice, warning you that you shouldn't?!?
Yes . . . but then I heard a chorus of other voices! They convinced me to do it!!
Who were they?
The Executives at Warner Brothers! They reminded me that without Lotus Lain, there's no "SUPERDUPERMAN II"!
COMING NEXT YEAR...
SUPERDUPERMAN II

UP THE BRASS DEPT

**Once upon a time, there was a Publisher of a magazine. He was a happy man, publishing his magazine. But one day, he said, "Wouldn't it be swell if they made a movie and my magazine sponsored it?! It would help sales! Isn't that a wonderful idea?" All of his Yes-Men agreed that it was a wonderful idea, and so the smart people in Hollywood made a movie, and the magazine sponsored it. But did the Publisher live**

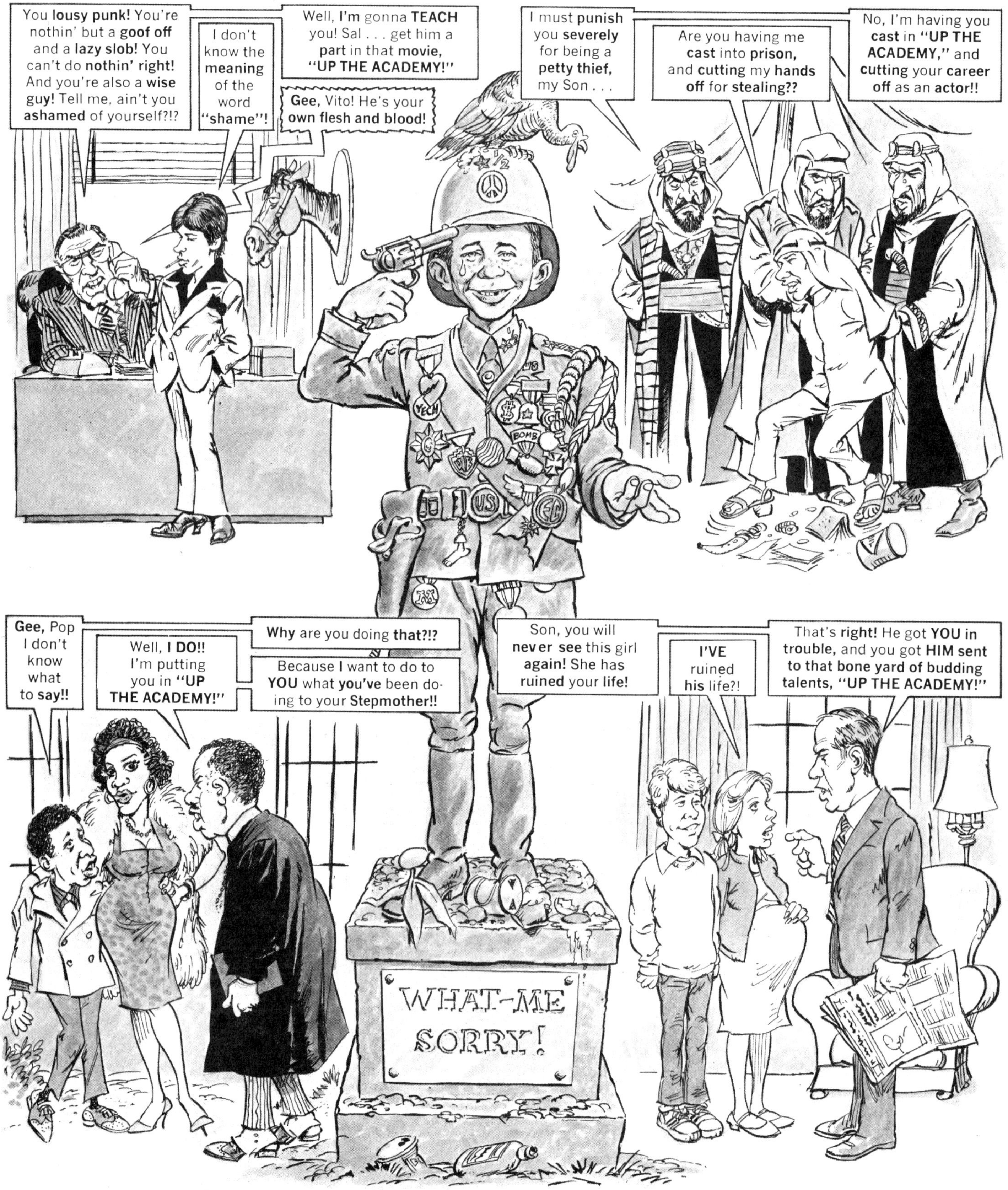
You lousy punk! You're nothin' but a goof off and a lazy slob! You can't do nothin' right! And you're also a wise guy! Tell me, ain't you ashamed of yourself?!?
I don't know the meaning of the word "shame"!
Well, I'm gonna TEACH you! Sal . . . get him a part in that movie, "UP THE ACADEMY!"
Gee, Vito! He's your own flesh and blood!
I must punish you severely for being a petty thief, my Son . . .
Are you having me cast into prison, and cutting my hands off for stealing??
No, I'm having you cast in "UP THE ACADEMY," and cutting your career off as an actor!!
Gee, Pop I don't know what to say!!
Well, I DO!! I'm putting you in "UP THE ACADEMY!"
Why are you doing that?!?
Because I want to do to YOU what you've been doing to your Stepmother!!
Son, you will never see this girl again! She has ruined your life!
I'VE ruined his life?!
That's right! He got YOU in trouble, and you got HIM sent to that bone yard of budding talents, "UP THE ACADEMY!"
WHAT-ME SORRY!

appily ever after? Not on your life! Because he overlooked one little thing while e was summoning up images of millions of people rushing to see the movie and then ushing to newsstands to buy his magazine. The thing he overlooked was to find out the movie was any good! Well? Was it? If you've seen it, you already know the nswer to that question! And if you haven't seen it, let us save you the money as

# MAD MAGAZINE RESENTS
# THROW UP THE ACADEMY

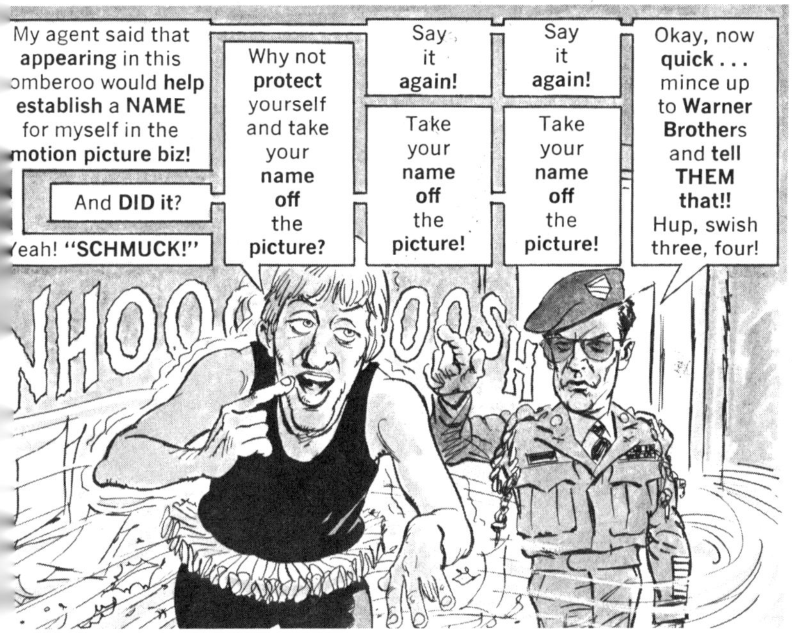

My agent said that appearing in this omberoo would help establish a NAME for myself in the motion picture biz!
And DID it?
Yeah! "SCHMUCK!"
Why not protect yourself and take your name off the picture?
Say it again!
Take your name off the picture!
Say it again!
Take your name off the picture!
Okay, now quick . . . mince up to Warner Brothers and tell THEM that!! Hup, swish three, four!
WHOOSH WOOSH


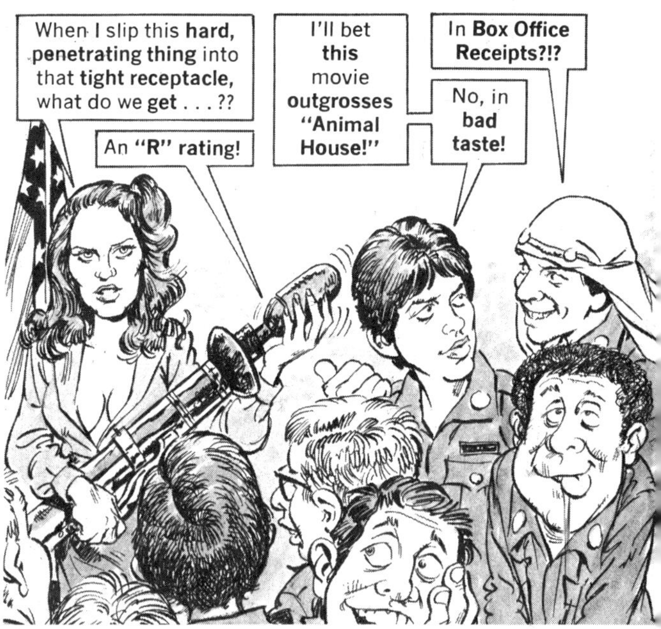

When I slip this hard, penetrating thing into that tight receptacle, what do we get . . . ??
An "R" rating!
I'll bet this movie outgrosses "Animal House!"
In Box Office Receipts?!?
No, in bad taste!


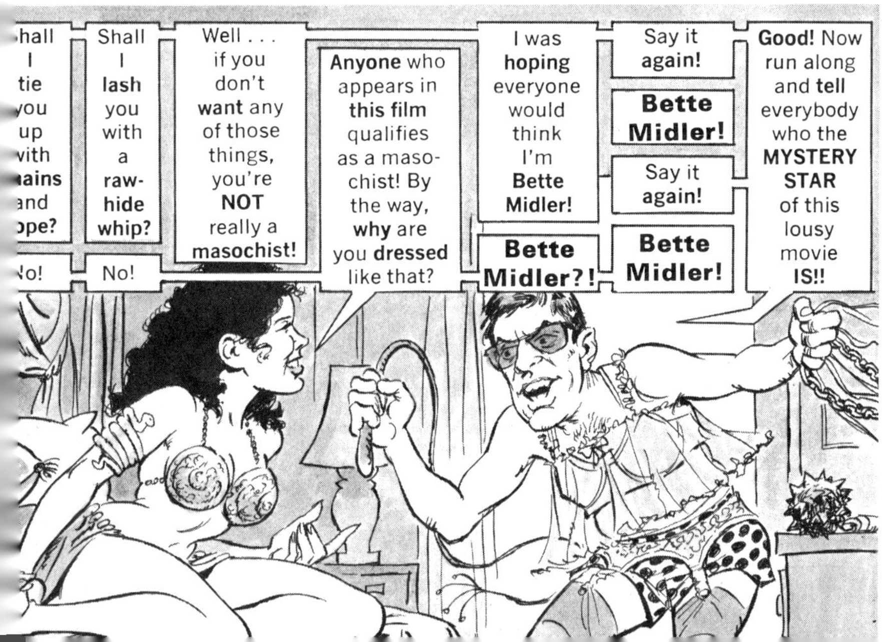

Shall I tie you up with chains and rope?
No!
Shall I lash you with a raw-hide whip?
No!
Well . . . if you don't want any of those things, you're NOT really a masochist!
Anyone who appears in this film qualifies as a maso-chist! By the way, why are you dressed like that?
I was hoping everyone would think I'm Bette Midler!
Bette Midler?!
Say it again!
Bette Midler!
Say it again!
Bette Midler!
Good! Now run along and tell everybody who the MYSTERY STAR of this lousy movie IS!!


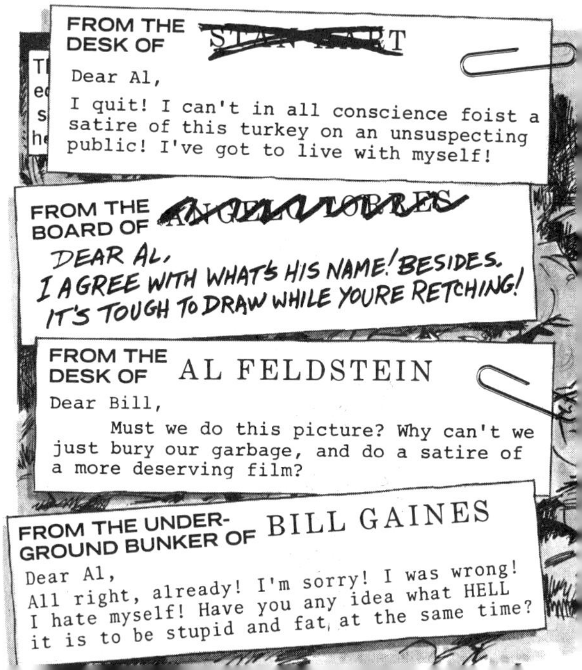

FROM THE DESK OF ~~STAN HART~~
Dear Al,
I quit! I can't in all conscience foist a satire of this turkey on an unsuspecting public! I've got to live with myself!
FROM THE BOARD OF ~~ANGELO TORRES~~
DEAR AL,
I AGREE WITH WHAT'S HIS NAME! BESIDES. IT'S TOUGH TO DRAW WHILE YOU'RE RETCHING!
FROM THE DESK OF AL FELDSTEIN
Dear Bill,
Must we do this picture? Why can't we just bury our garbage, and do a satire of a more deserving film?
FROM THE UNDER-GROUND BUNKER OF BILL GAINES
Dear Al,
All right, already! I'm sorry! I was wrong! I hate myself! Have you any idea what HELL it is to be stupid and fat at the same time?

HATCHET JOB DEPT.

**A talented writer named Steven King once wrote a terrifying book called "The Shining." Now, a famous Director named Stanley Kubrick has made a movie out of it. Unfortunately, his film has given Mr. King's book, and all the other great horror films of the past, a black eye! Which is why we at MAD call our version:**

# THE

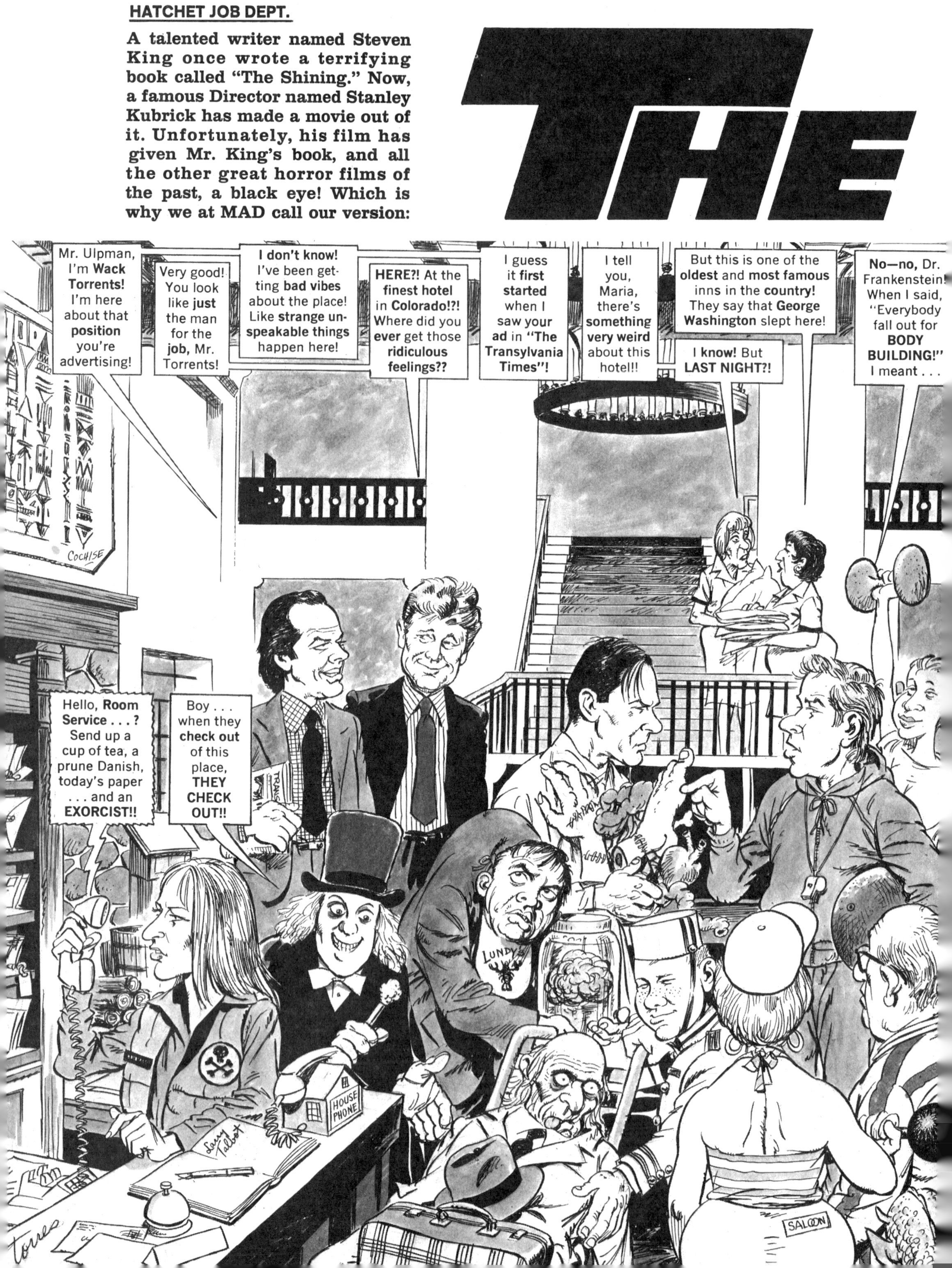

Mr. Ulpman, I'm Wack Torrents! I'm here about that position you're advertising!
Very good! You look like just the man for the job, Mr. Torrents!
I don't know! I've been getting bad vibes about the place! Like strange unspeakable things happen here!
HERE?! At the finest hotel in Colorado!?! Where did you ever get those ridiculous feelings??
I guess it first started when I saw your ad in "The Transylvania Times"!
I tell you, Maria, there's something very weird about this hotel!!
But this is one of the oldest and most famous inns in the country! They say that George Washington slept here!
I know! But LAST NIGHT?!
No—no, Dr. Frankenstein! When I said, "Everybody fall out for BODY BUILDING!" I meant . . .
Hello, Room Service . . . ? Send up a cup of tea, a prune Danish, today's paper . . . and an EXORCIST!!
Boy . . . when they check out of this place, THEY CHECK OUT!!
COCHISE
LUNDY'S
HOUSE PHONE
Larry Talbot
SALOON

# SHINER

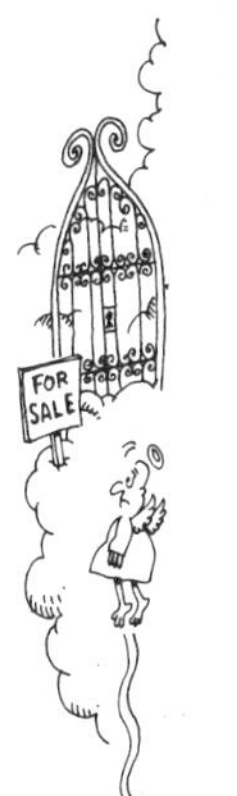
FOR SALE

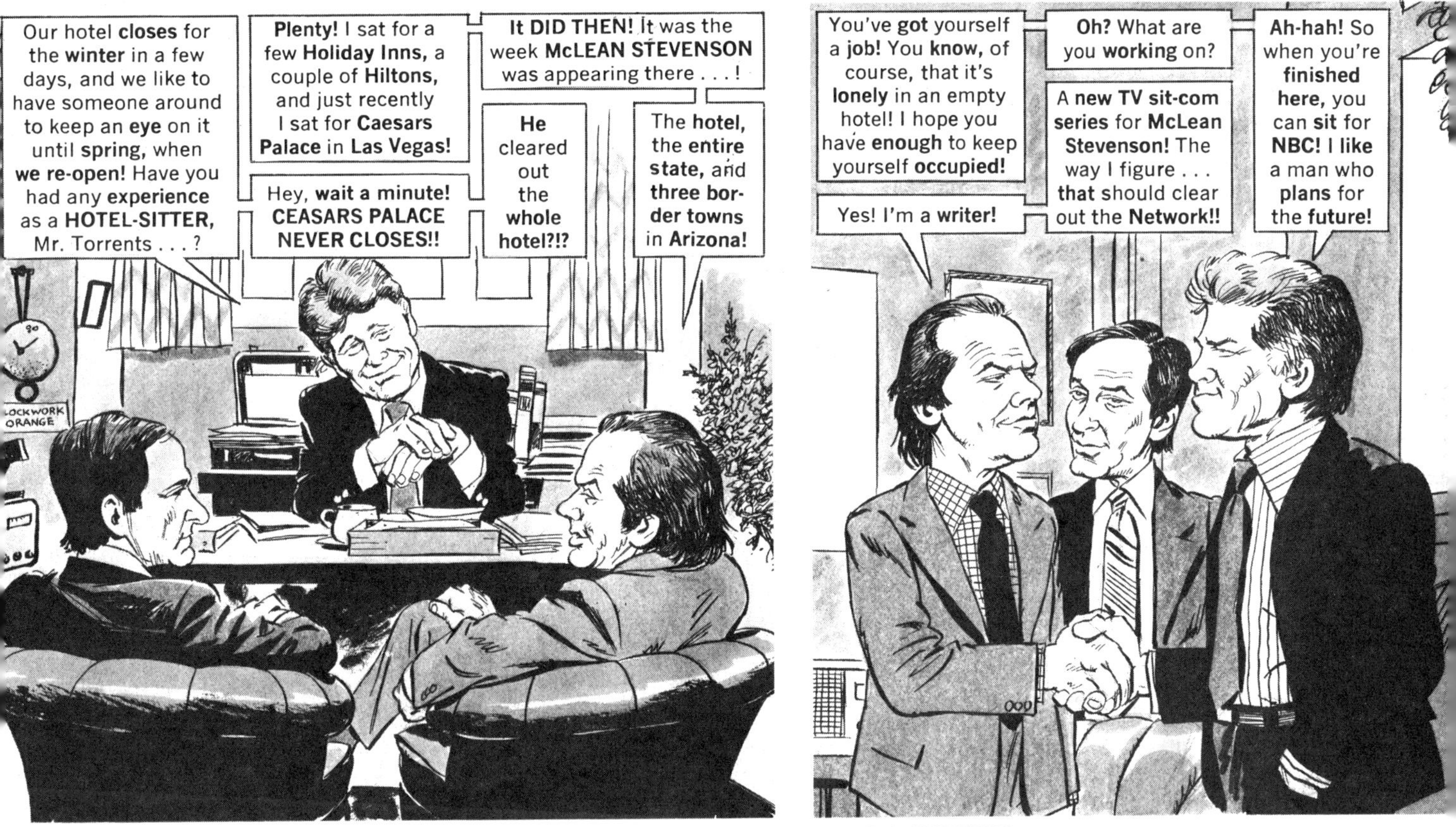
Our hotel closes for the winter in a few days, and we like to have someone around to keep an eye on it until spring, when we re-open! Have you had any experience as a HOTEL-SITTER, Mr. Torrents . . . ?
Plenty! I sat for a few Holiday Inns, a couple of Hiltons, and just recently I sat for Caesars Palace in Las Vegas!
Hey, wait a minute! CEASARS PALACE NEVER CLOSES!!
It DID THEN! It was the week McLEAN STEVENSON was appearing there . . . !
He cleared out the whole hotel?!?
The hotel, the entire state, and three border towns in Arizona!
LOCKWORK ORANGE
You've got yourself a job! You know, of course, that it's lonely in an empty hotel! I hope you have enough to keep yourself occupied!
Yes! I'm a writer!
Oh? What are you working on?
A new TV sit-com series for McLean Stevenson! The way I figure . . . that should clear out the Network!!
Ah-hah! So when you're finished here, you can sit for NBC! I like a man who plans for the future!

ARTIST: ANGELO TORRES WRITER: LARRY SIEGEL

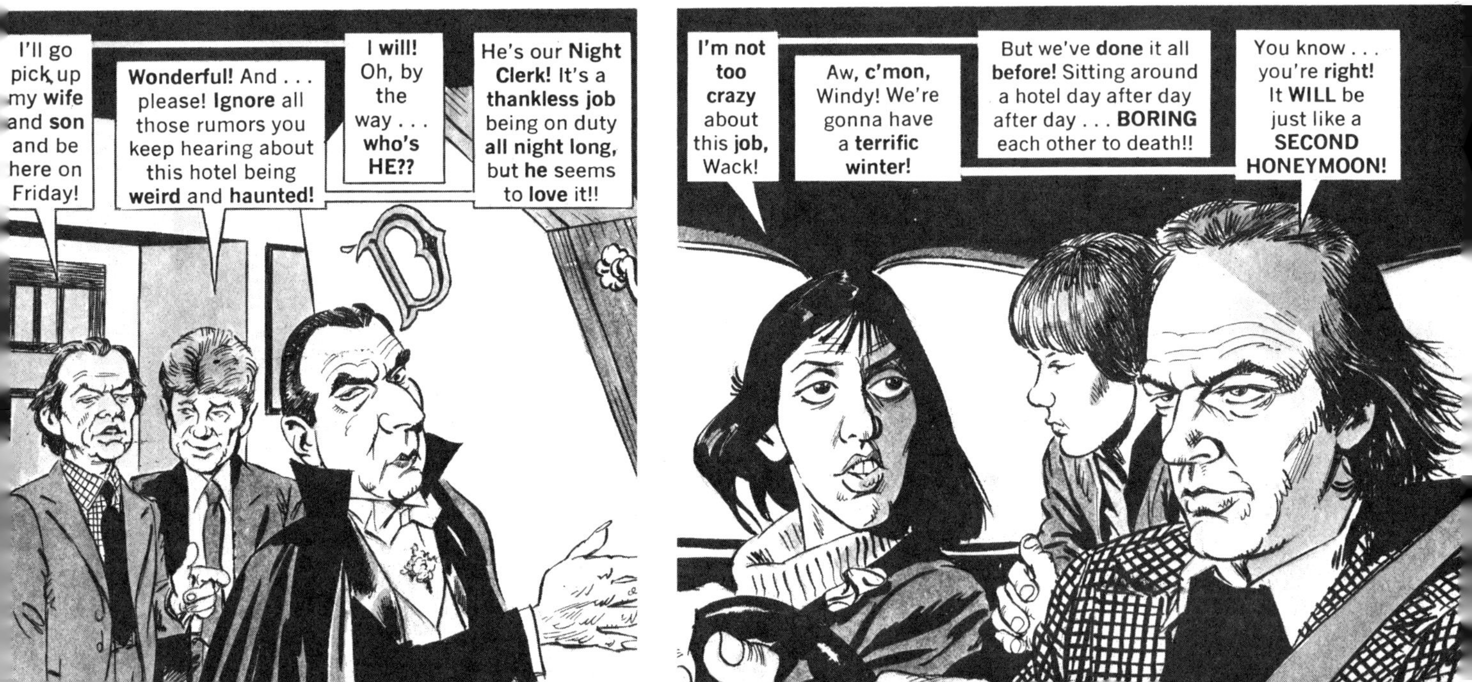
I'll go pick up my wife and son and be here on Friday!
Wonderful! And . . . please! Ignore all those rumors you keep hearing about this hotel being weird and haunted!
I will! Oh, by the way . . . who's HE??
He's our Night Clerk! It's a thankless job being on duty all night long, but he seems to love it!!
I'm not too crazy about this job, Wack!
Aw, c'mon, Windy! We're gonna have a terrific winter!
But we've done it all before! Sitting around a hotel day after day after day . . . BORING each other to death!!
You know . . . you're right! It WILL be just like a SECOND HONEYMOON!

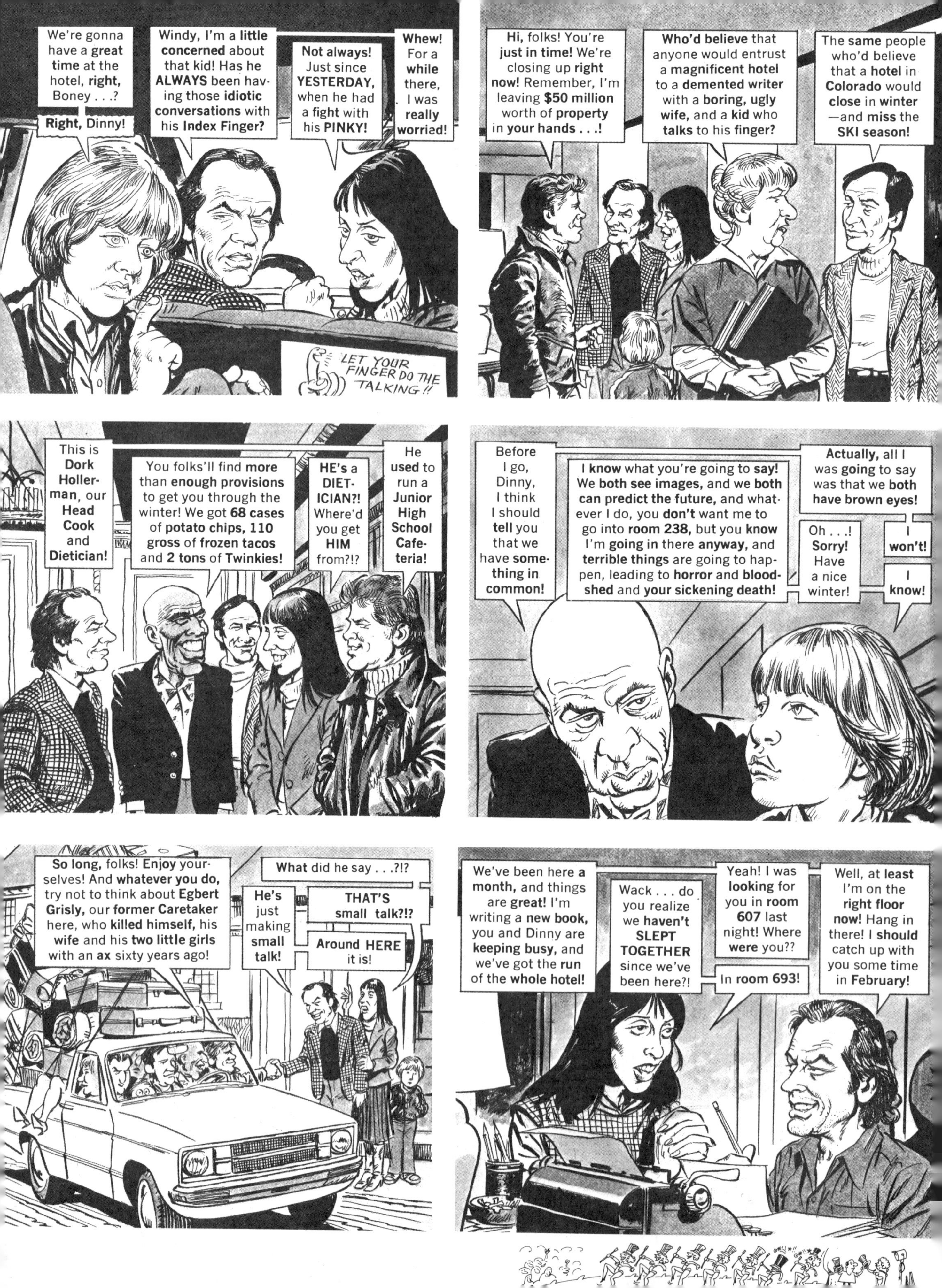

We're gonna have a great time at the hotel, right, Boney . . .?
Right, Dinny!
Windy, I'm a little concerned about that kid! Has he ALWAYS been having those idiotic conversations with his Index Finger?
Not always! Just since YESTERDAY, when he had a fight with his PINKY!
Whew! For a while there, I was really worried!
LET YOUR FINGER DO THE TALKING!!
Hi, folks! You're just in time! We're closing up right now! Remember, I'm leaving $50 million worth of property in your hands . . .!
Who'd believe that anyone would entrust a magnificent hotel to a demented writer with a boring, ugly wife, and a kid who talks to his finger?
The same people who'd believe that a hotel in Colorado would close in winter —and miss the SKI season!
This is Dork Hollerman, our Head Cook and Dietician!
You folks'll find more than enough provisions to get you through the winter! We got 68 cases of potato chips, 110 gross of frozen tacos and 2 tons of Twinkies!
HE's a DIETICIAN?! Where'd you get HIM from?!?
He used to run a Junior High School Cafeteria!
Before I go, Dinny, I think I should tell you that we have something in common!
I know what you're going to say! We both see images, and we both can predict the future, and whatever I do, you don't want me to go into room 238, but you know I'm going in there anyway, and terrible things are going to happen, leading to horror and bloodshed and your sickening death!
Actually, all I was going to say was that we both have brown eyes!
Oh . . .! Sorry! Have a nice winter!
I won't!
I know!
So long, folks! Enjoy yourselves! And whatever you do, try not to think about Egbert Grisly, our former Caretaker here, who killed himself, his wife and his two little girls with an ax sixty years ago!
What did he say . . .?!?
He's just making small talk!
THAT'S small talk?!?
Around HERE it is!
We've been here a month, and things are great! I'm writing a new book, you and Dinny are keeping busy, and we've got the run of the whole hotel!
Wack . . . do you realize we haven't SLEPT TOGETHER since we've been here?!
Yeah! I was looking for you in room 607 last night! Where were you??
In room 693!
Well, at least I'm on the right floor now! Hang in there! I should catch up with you some time in February!

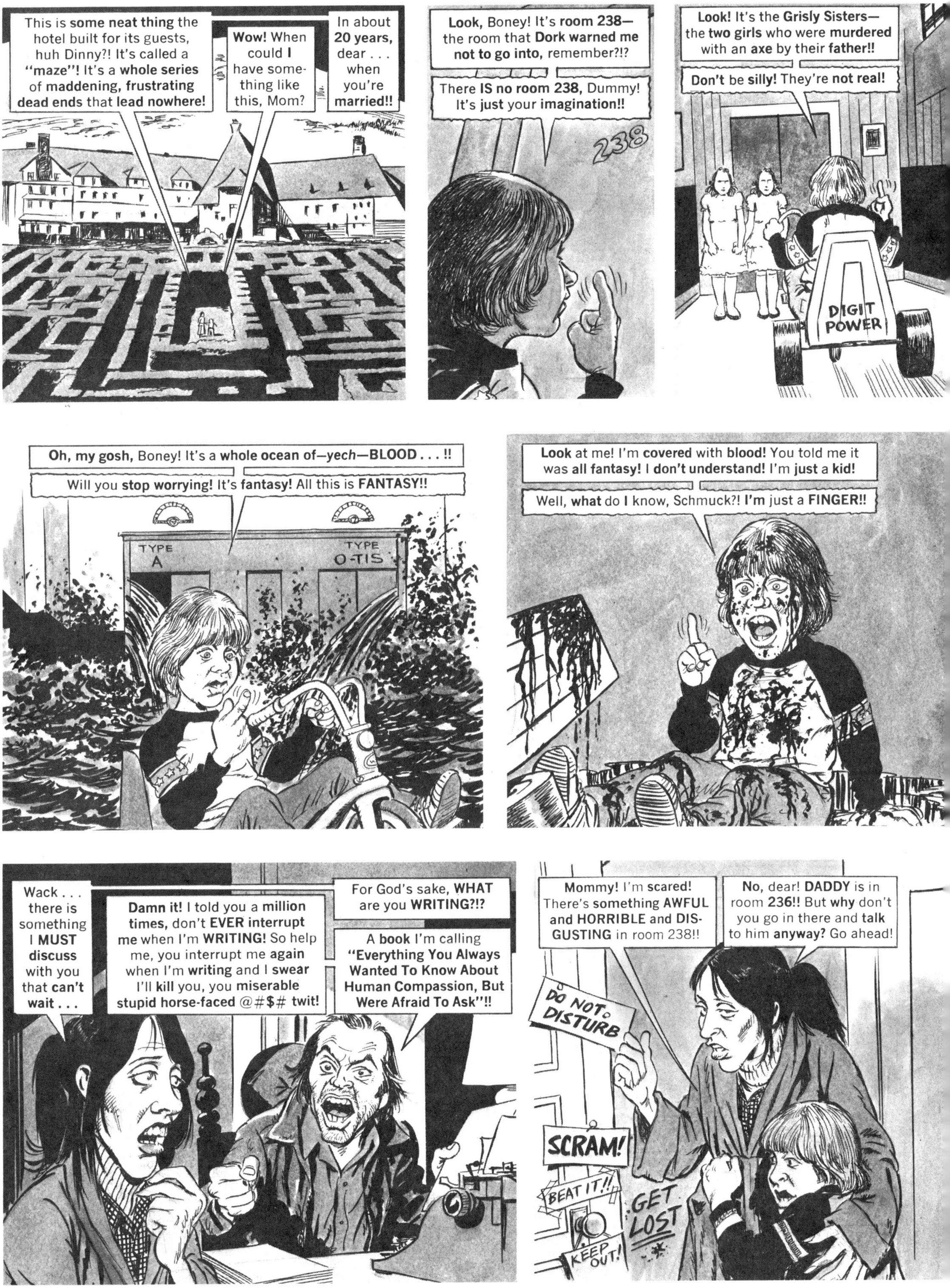

This is some neat thing the hotel built for its guests, huh Dinny?! It's called a "maze"! It's a whole series of maddening, frustrating dead ends that lead nowhere!
Wow! When could I have something like this, Mom?
In about 20 years, dear . . . when you're married!!
Look, Boney! It's room 238—the room that Dork warned me not to go into, remember?!?
There IS no room 238, Dummy! It's just your imagination!!
238
Look! It's the Grisly Sisters—the two girls who were murdered with an axe by their father!!
Don't be silly! They're not real!
DIGIT POWER
Oh, my gosh, Boney! It's a whole ocean of—*yech*—BLOOD . . . !!
Will you stop worrying! It's fantasy! All this is FANTASY!!
TYPE A
TYPE O-TIS
Look at me! I'm covered with blood! You told me it was all fantasy! I don't understand! I'm just a kid!
Well, what do I know, Schmuck?! I'm just a FINGER!!
Wack . . . there is something I MUST discuss with you that can't wait . . .
Damn it! I told you a million times, don't EVER interrupt me when I'm WRITING! So help me, you interrupt me again when I'm writing and I swear I'll kill you, you miserable stupid horse-faced @#$# twit!
For God's sake, WHAT are you WRITING?!?
A book I'm calling "Everything You Always Wanted To Know About Human Compassion, But Were Afraid To Ask"!!
Mommy! I'm scared! There's something AWFUL and HORRIBLE and DISGUSTING in room 238!!
No, dear! DADDY is in room 236!! But why don't you go in there and talk to him anyway? Go ahead!
DO NOT DISTURB
SCRAM!
BEAT IT!!
GET LOST
KEEP OUT!

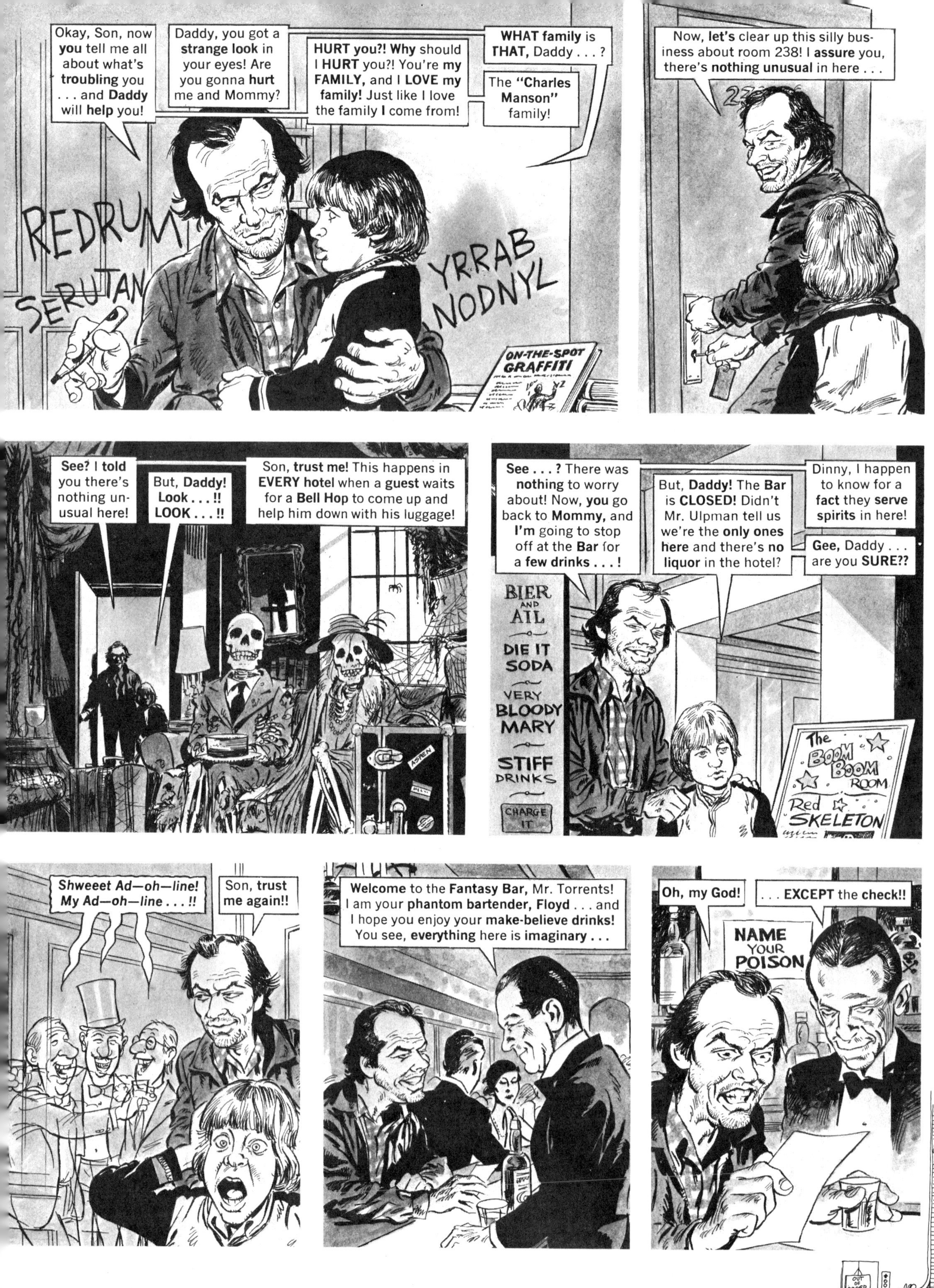
Okay, Son, now you tell me all about what's troubling you . . . and Daddy will help you!
Daddy, you got a strange look in your eyes! Are you gonna hurt me and Mommy?
HURT you?! Why should I HURT you?! You're my FAMILY, and I LOVE my family! Just like I love the family I come from!
WHAT family is THAT, Daddy . . . ?
The "Charles Manson" family!
REDRUM
SERUTAN
YRRAB
NODNYL
ON-THE-SPOT GRAFFITI
Now, let's clear up this silly business about room 238! I assure you, there's nothing unusual in here . . .
See? I told you there's nothing unusual here!
But, Daddy! Look . . . !! LOOK . . . !!
Son, trust me! This happens in EVERY hotel when a guest waits for a Bell Hop to come up and help him down with his luggage!
ASPEN
See . . . ? There was nothing to worry about! Now, you go back to Mommy, and I'm going to stop off at the Bar for a few drinks . . . !
But, Daddy! The Bar is CLOSED! Didn't Mr. Ulpman tell us we're the only ones here and there's no liquor in the hotel?
Dinny, I happen to know for a fact they serve spirits in here!
Gee, Daddy . . . are you SURE??
BIER AND AIL
DIE IT SODA
VERY BLOODY MARY
STIFF DRINKS
CHARGE IT
The BOOM BOOM ROOM
Red SKELETON
Shweeet Ad—oh—line! My Ad—oh—line . . . !!
Son, trust me again!!
Welcome to the Fantasy Bar, Mr. Torrents! I am your phantom bartender, Floyd . . . and I hope you enjoy your make-believe drinks! You see, everything here is imaginary . . .
Oh, my God!
. . . EXCEPT the check!!
NAME YOUR POISON
OUT OF ORDER

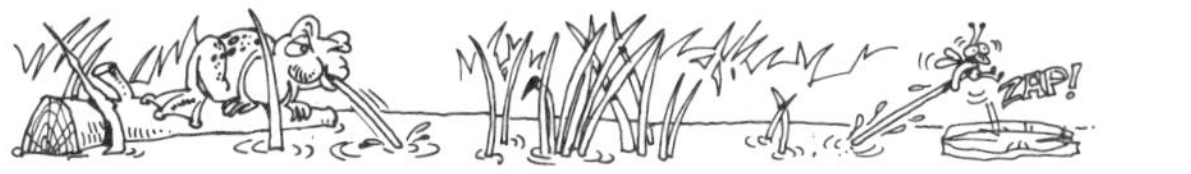
ZAP!

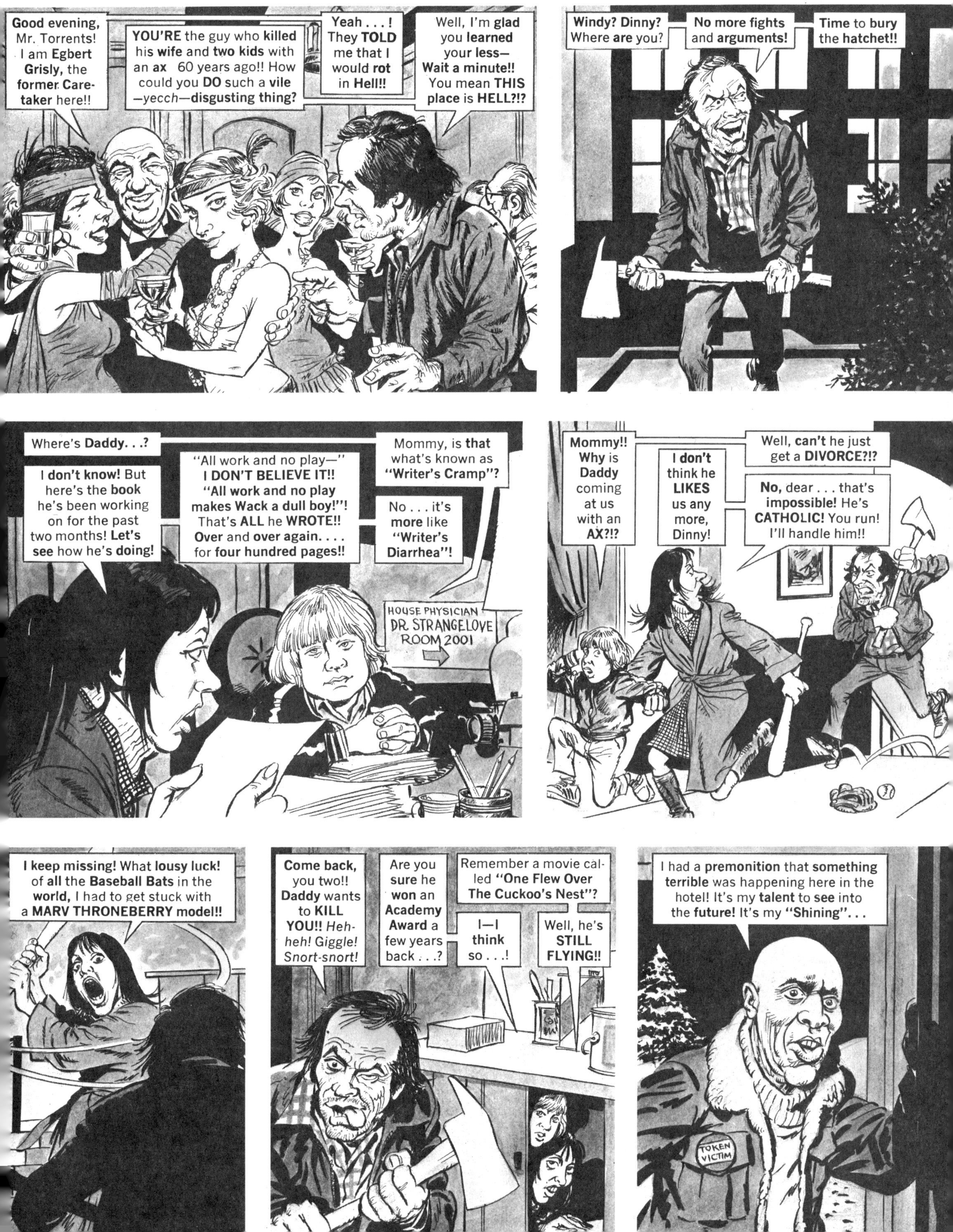
Good evening, Mr. Torrents! I am Egbert Grisly, the former Caretaker here!!
YOU'RE the guy who killed his wife and two kids with an ax 60 years ago!! How could you DO such a vile —yecch—disgusting thing?
Yeah . . . ! They TOLD me that I would rot in Hell!!
Well, I'm glad you learned your less— Wait a minute!! You mean THIS place is HELL?!?
Windy? Dinny? Where are you?
No more fights and arguments!
Time to bury the hatchet!!
Where's Daddy. . .?
I don't know! But here's the book he's been working on for the past two months! Let's see how he's doing!
"All work and no play—" I DON'T BELIEVE IT!! "All work and no play makes Wack a dull boy!"! That's ALL he WROTE!! Over and over again. . . . for four hundred pages!!
Mommy, is that what's known as "Writer's Cramp"?
No . . . it's more like "Writer's Diarrhea"!
HOUSE PHYSICIAN
DR. STRANGELOVE
ROOM 2001
Mommy!! Why is Daddy coming at us with an AX?!?
I don't think he LIKES us any more, Dinny!
Well, can't he just get a DIVORCE?!?
No, dear . . . that's impossible! He's CATHOLIC! You run! I'll handle him!!
I keep missing! What lousy luck! of all the Baseball Bats in the world, I had to get stuck with a MARV THRONEBERRY model!!
Come back, you two!! Daddy wants to KILL YOU!! Heh-heh! Giggle! Snort-snort!
Are you sure he won an Academy Award a few years back . . .?
I—I think so . . .!
Remember a movie called "One Flew Over The Cuckoo's Nest"?
Well, he's STILL FLYING!!
I had a premonition that something terrible was happening here in the hotel! It's my talent to see into the future! It's my "Shining". . .
TOKEN VICTIM

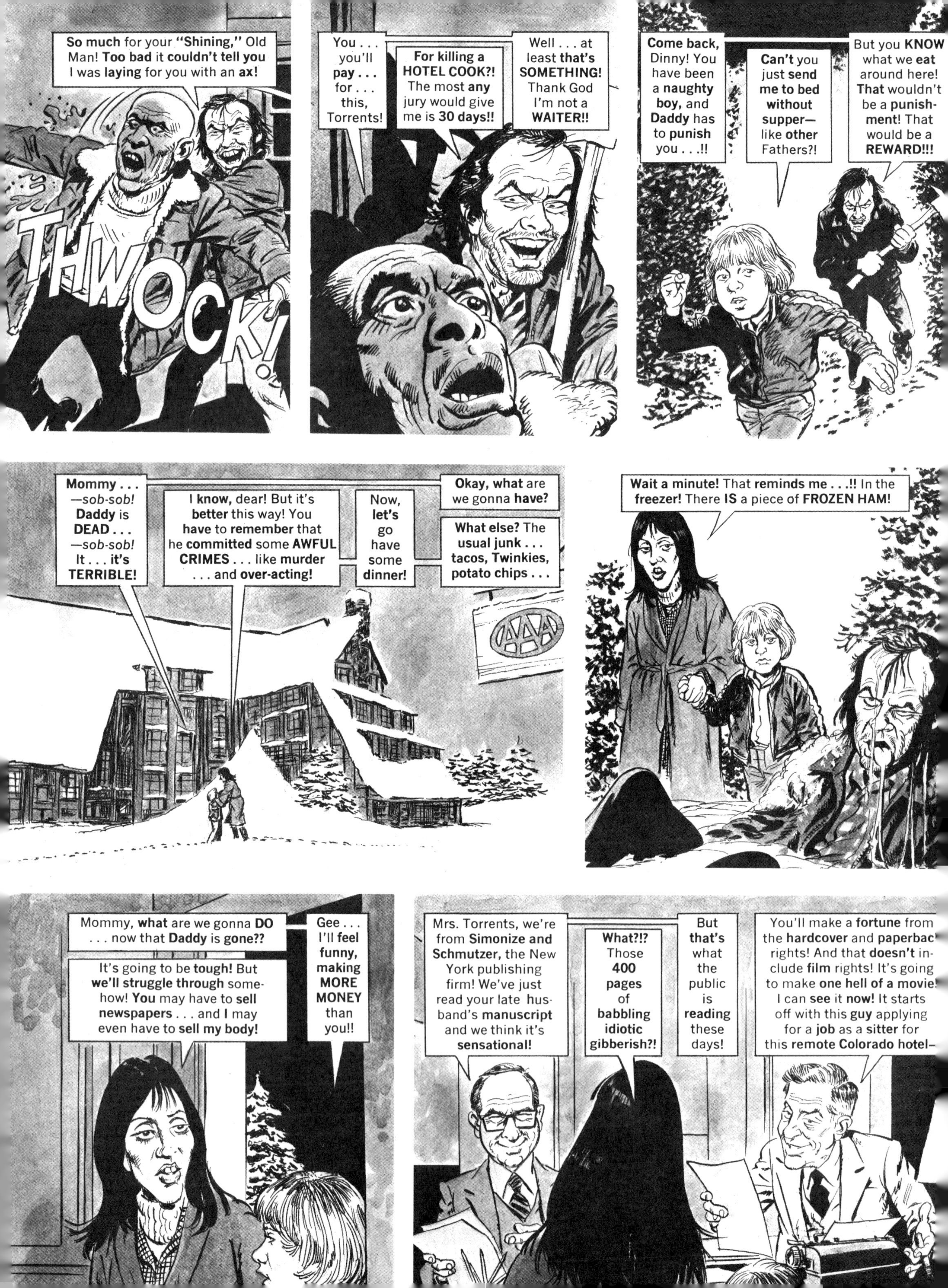
So much for your "Shining," Old Man! Too bad it couldn't tell you I was laying for you with an ax!
THWOCK!
You . . . you'll pay . . . for . . . this, Torrents!
For killing a HOTEL COOK?! The most any jury would give me is 30 days!!
Well . . . at least that's SOMETHING! Thank God I'm not a WAITER!!
Come back, Dinny! You have been a naughty boy, and Daddy has to punish you . . .!!
Can't you just send me to bed without supper— like other Fathers?!
But you KNOW what we eat around here! That wouldn't be a punishment! That would be a REWARD!!!
Mommy . . . —sob-sob! Daddy is DEAD . . . —sob-sob! It . . . it's TERRIBLE!
I know, dear! But it's better this way! You have to remember that he committed some AWFUL CRIMES . . . like murder . . . and over-acting!
Now, let's go have some dinner!
Okay, what are we gonna have?
What else? The usual junk . . . tacos, Twinkies, potato chips . . .
Wait a minute! That reminds me . . .!! In the freezer! There IS a piece of FROZEN HAM!
Mommy, what are we gonna DO . . . now that Daddy is gone??
It's going to be tough! But we'll struggle through somehow! You may have to sell newspapers . . . and I may even have to sell my body!
Gee . . . I'll feel funny, making MORE MONEY than you!!
Mrs. Torrents, we're from Simonize and Schmutzer, the New York publishing firm! We've just read your late husband's manuscript and we think it's sensational!
What?!? Those 400 pages of babbling idiotic gibberish?!
But that's what the public is reading these days!
You'll make a fortune from the hardcover and paperbac rights! And that doesn't include film rights! It's going to make one hell of a movie! I can see it now! It starts off with this guy applying for a job as a sitter for this remote Colorado hotel—

HOLLYWOOD DEPT.

# Scenes We'd Like to See

The Doctor's Pronouncement.

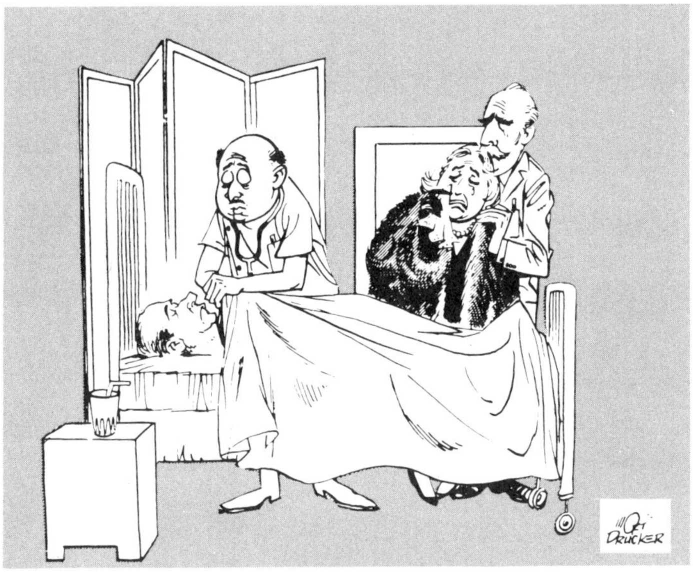
DRUCKER

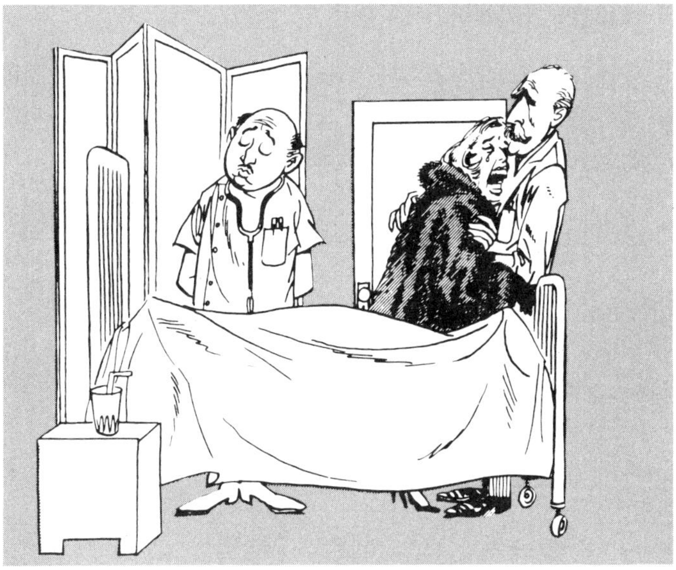

WRITER: AL JAFFEE

ARTIST: MORT DRUCKER

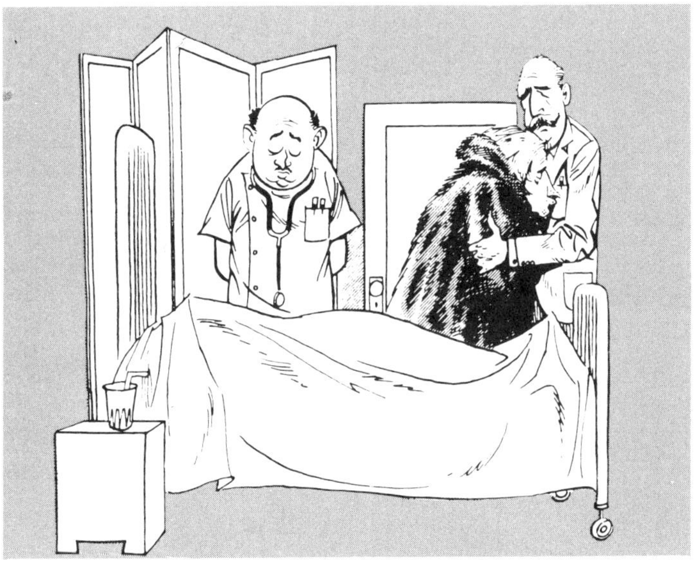

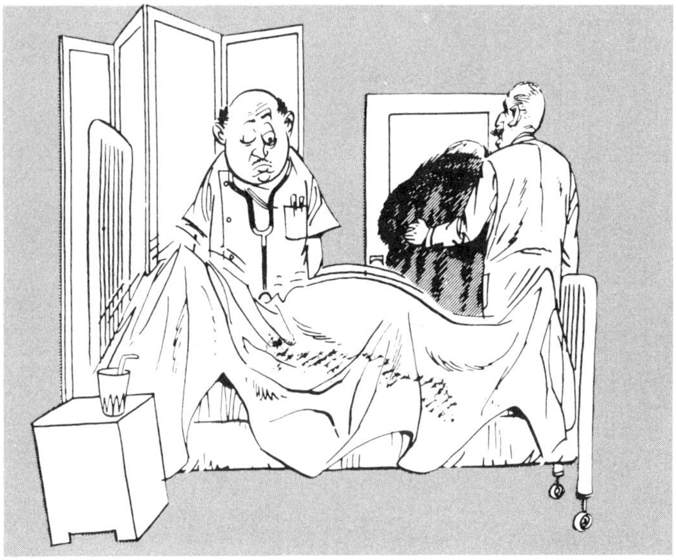

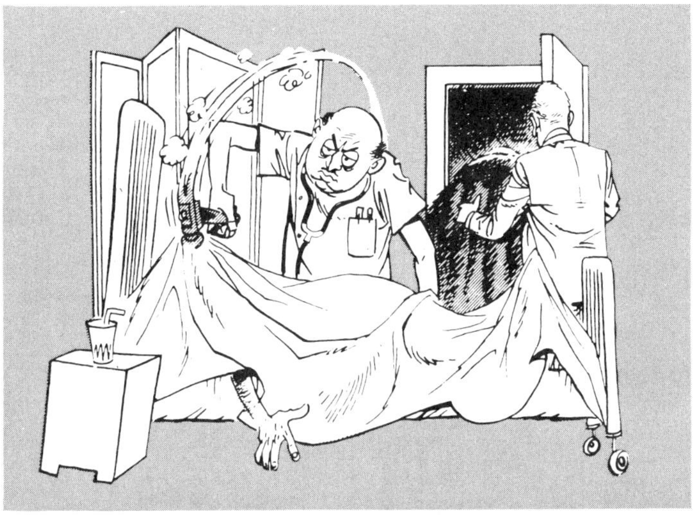

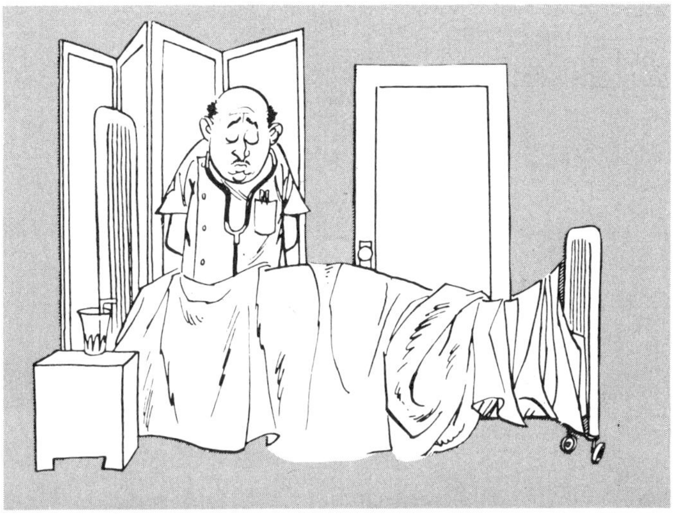

**A Play about Pavlov's Experiments with Dogs called "Bell, Bark and Kennel"

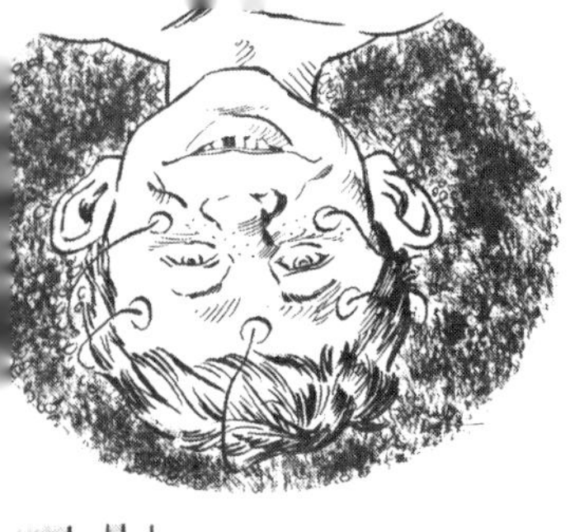

**FROM "SOUP" TO "NUTS" DEPT.**

Every once in a while, a motion picture comes along that exhilarates the senses expands the imagination, and explores the unknown. Unfortunately, this is not on of those movies! The only new technique this movie employs is to have the actor all speak their lines at the same time. MAD applauds said new technique in thi movie. The stars don't have to know their lines well, and the audience hears al that boring dialogue in ⅓ the normal time. And when all that pseudo-scientifi mumbo-jumbo and all those drug trips are thrown at you, the film leaves you in a

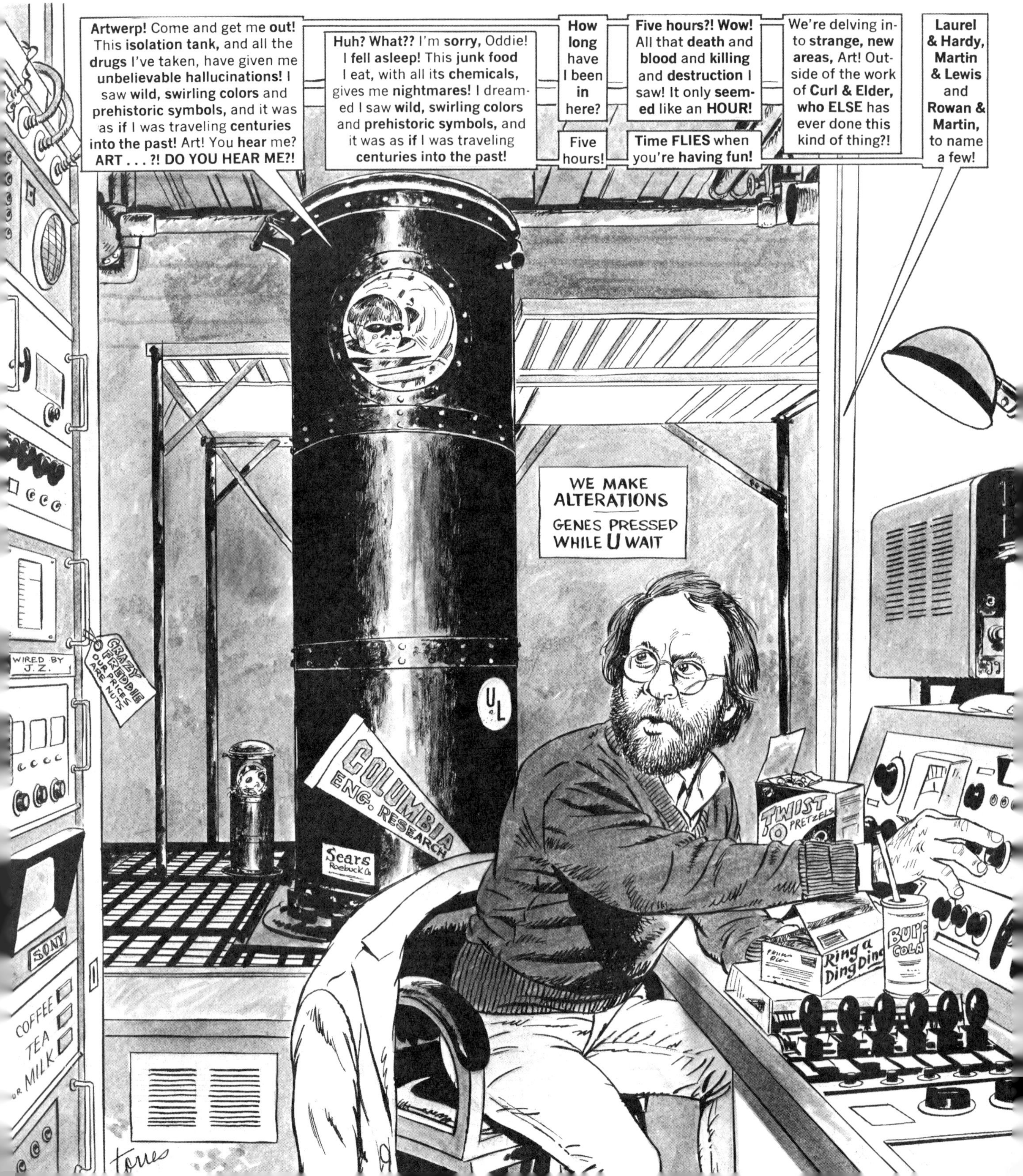

Artwerp! Come and get me out! This isolation tank, and all the drugs I've taken, have given me unbelievable hallucinations! I saw wild, swirling colors and prehistoric symbols, and it was as if I was traveling centuries into the past! Art! You hear me? ART . . . ?! DO YOU HEAR ME?!
Huh? What?? I'm sorry, Oddie! I fell asleep! This junk food I eat, with all its chemicals, gives me nightmares! I dreamed I saw wild, swirling colors and prehistoric symbols, and it was as if I was traveling centuries into the past!
How long have I been in here?
Five hours!
Five hours?! Wow! All that death and blood and killing and destruction I saw! It only seemed like an HOUR!
Time FLIES when you're having fun!
We're delving into strange, new areas, Art! Outside of the work of Curl & Elder, who ELSE has ever done this kind of thing?!
Laurel & Hardy, Martin & Lewis and Rowan & Martin, to name a few!
WE MAKE ALTERATIONS
GENES PRESSED WHILE U WAIT
WIRED BY J.Z.
CRAZY FREDDIE OUR PRICES ARE NUTS
COLUMBIA ENG. RESEARCH
Sears Roebuck Co
UL
TWIST PRETZELS
Ring a Ding Ding
BURP COLA
SONY
COFFEE TEA OR MILK
torres

# ASSAULTED STATE

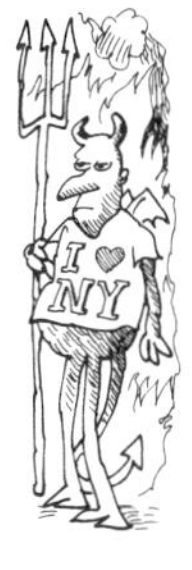

I ♥ NY


ARTIST: ANGELO TORRES WRITER: DICK DE BARTOLO

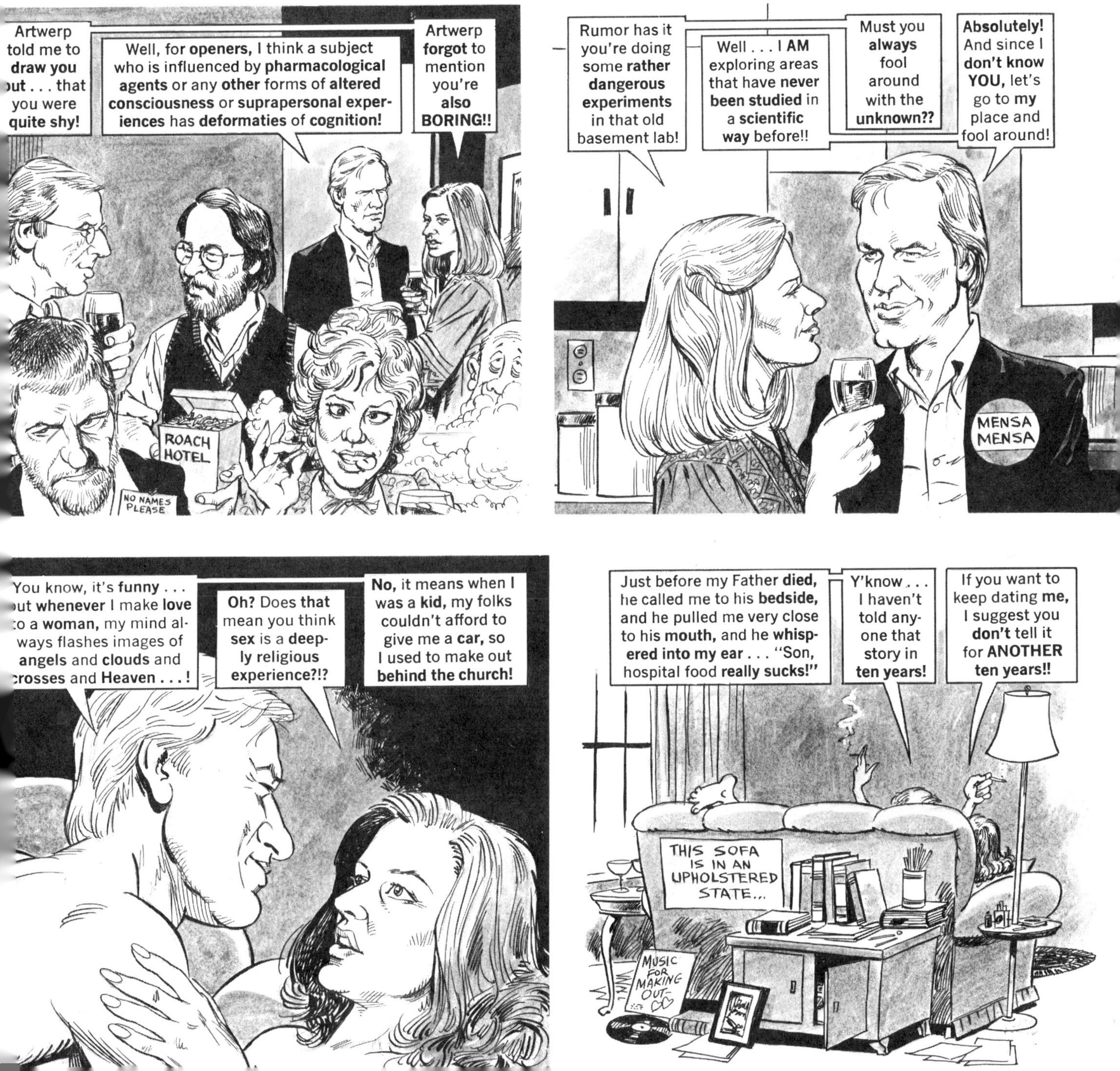

Artwerp told me to draw you ut . . . that you were quite shy!
Well, for openers, I think a subject who is influenced by pharmacological agents or any other forms of altered consciousness or suprapersonal experiences has deformaties of cognition!
Artwerp forgot to mention you're also BORING!!
ROACH HOTEL
NO NAMES PLEASE
Rumor has it you're doing some rather dangerous experiments in that old basement lab!
Well . . . I AM exploring areas that have never been studied in a scientific way before!!
Must you always fool around with the unknown??
Absolutely! And since I don't know YOU, let's go to my place and fool around!
MENSA MENSA
You know, it's funny . . . ut whenever I make love o a woman, my mind always flashes images of angels and clouds and rosses and Heaven . . . !
Oh? Does that mean you think sex is a deeply religious experience?!?
No, it means when I was a kid, my folks couldn't afford to give me a car, so I used to make out behind the church!
Just before my Father died, he called me to his bedside, and he pulled me very close to his mouth, and he whispered into my ear . . . "Son, hospital food really sucks!"
Y'know . . . I haven't told anyone that story in ten years!
If you want to keep dating me, I suggest you don't tell it for ANOTHER ten years!!
THIS SOFA IS IN AN UPHOLSTERED STATE...
MUSIC FOR MAKING OUT

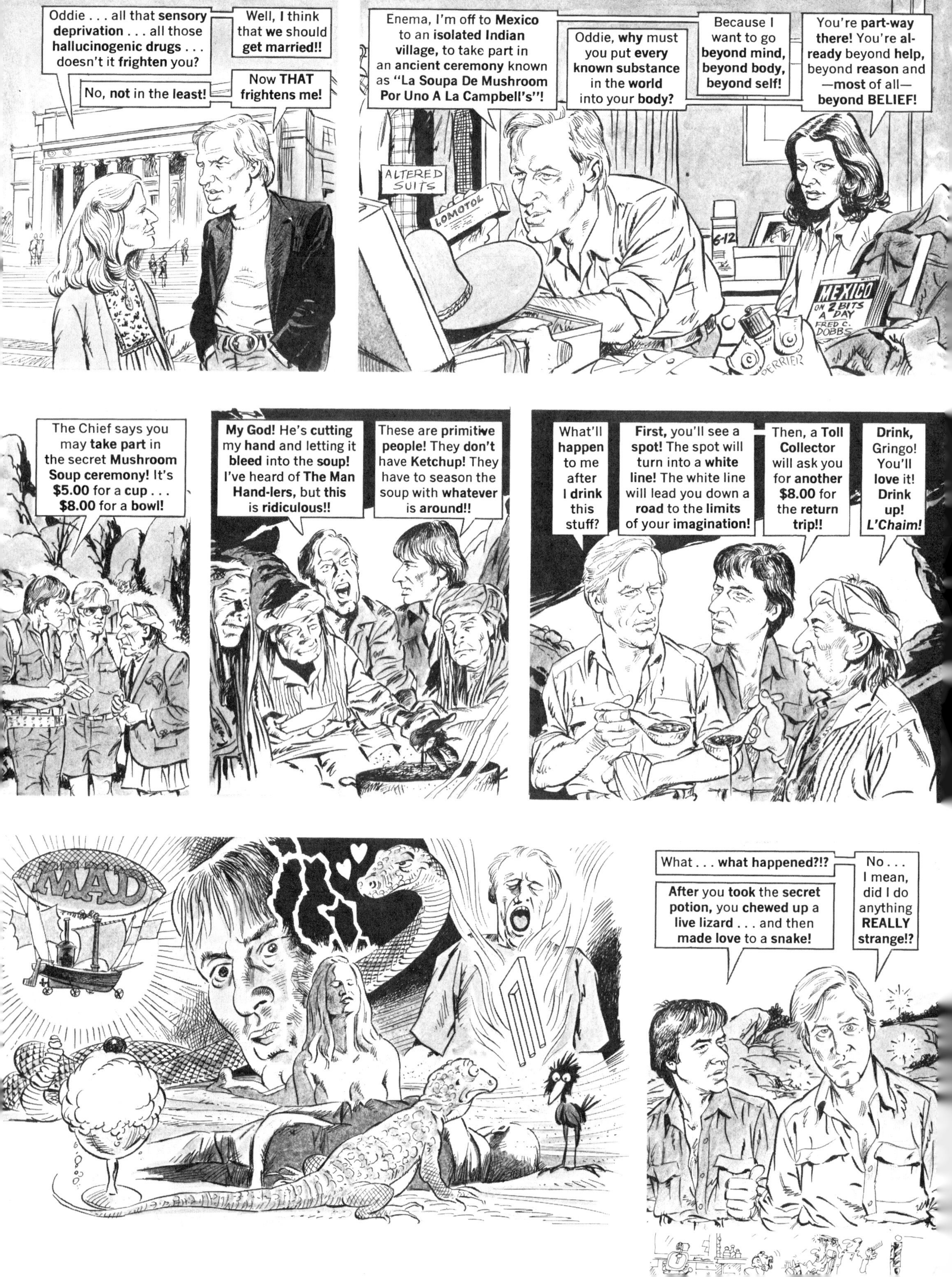
Oddie . . . all that sensory deprivation . . . all those hallucinogenic drugs . . . doesn't it frighten you?
No, not in the least!
Well, I think that we should get married!!
Now THAT frightens me!
Enema, I'm off to Mexico to an isolated Indian village, to take part in an ancient ceremony known as "La Soupa De Mushroom Por Uno A La Campbell's"!
Oddie, why must you put every known substance in the world into your body?
Because I want to go beyond mind, beyond body, beyond self!
You're part-way there! You're already beyond help, beyond reason and —most of all— beyond BELIEF!
ALTERED SUITS
LOMOTOL
6-12
MEXICO ON 2 BITS A DAY
FRED C. DOBBS
PERRIER
The Chief says you may take part in the secret Mushroom Soup ceremony! It's $5.00 for a cup . . . $8.00 for a bowl!
My God! He's cutting my hand and letting it bleed into the soup! I've heard of The Man Hand-lers, but this is ridiculous!!
These are primitive people! They don't have Ketchup! They have to season the soup with whatever is around!!
What'll happen to me after I drink this stuff?
First, you'll see a spot! The spot will turn into a white line! The white line will lead you down a road to the limits of your imagination!
Then, a Toll Collector will ask you for another $8.00 for the return trip!!
Drink, Gringo! You'll love it! Drink up! L'Chaim!
MAD
What . . . what happened?!?
After you took the secret potion, you chewed up a live lizard . . . and then made love to a snake!
No . . . I mean, did I do anything REALLY strange!?

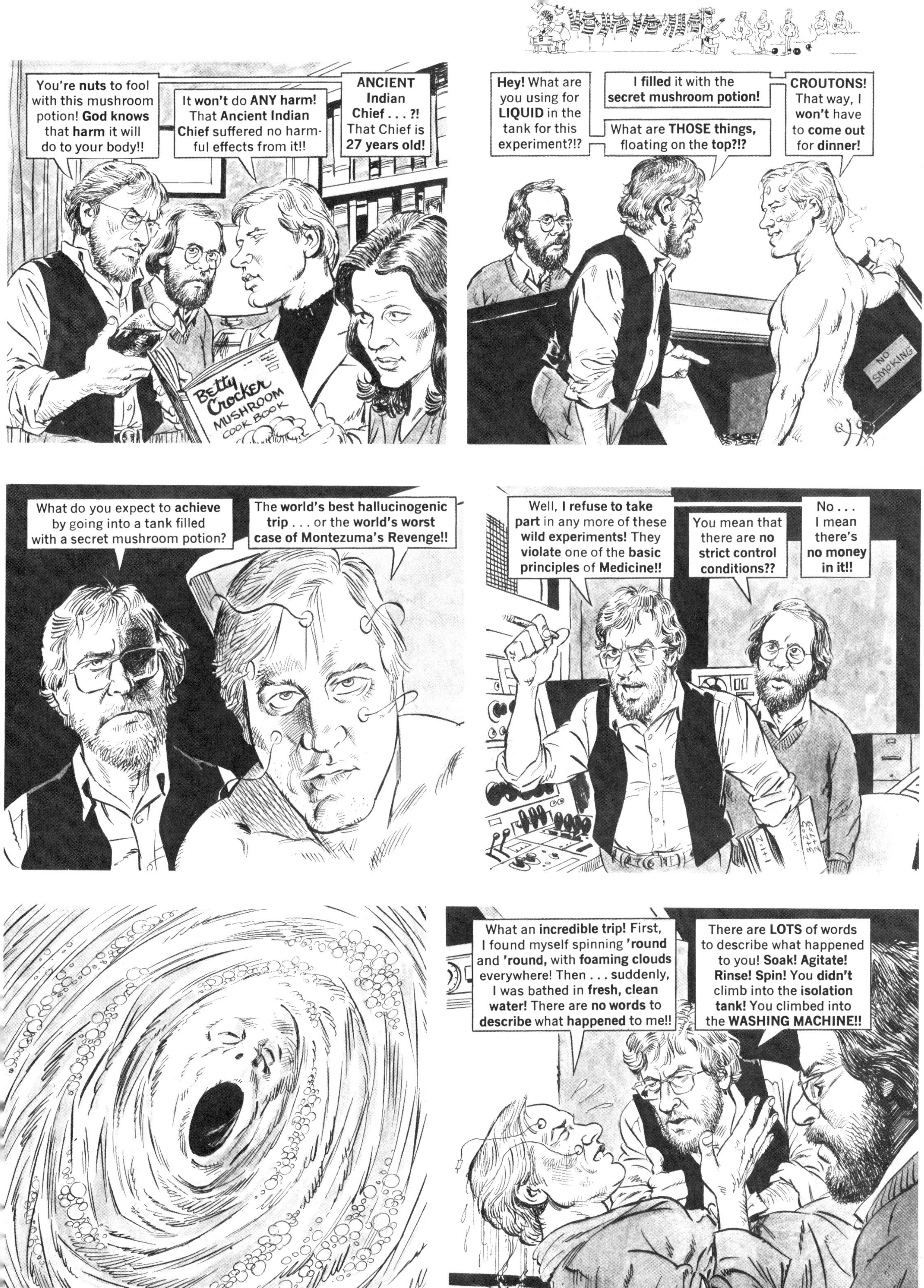
You're nuts to fool with this mushroom potion! God knows that harm it will do to your body!!
It won't do ANY harm! That Ancient Indian Chief suffered no harmful effects from it!!
ANCIENT Indian Chief . . . ?! That Chief is 27 years old!
Betty Crocker MUSHROOM COOK BOOK
Hey! What are you using for LIQUID in the tank for this experiment?!?
I filled it with the secret mushroom potion!
What are THOSE things, floating on the top?!?
CROUTONS! That way, I won't have to come out for dinner!
NO SMOKING
What do you expect to achieve by going into a tank filled with a secret mushroom potion?
The world's best hallucinogenic trip . . . or the world's worst case of Montezuma's Revenge!!
Well, I refuse to take part in any more of these wild experiments! They violate one of the basic principles of Medicine!!
You mean that there are no strict control conditions??
No . . . I mean there's no money in it!!
What an incredible trip! First, I found myself spinning 'round and 'round, with foaming clouds everywhere! Then . . . suddenly, I was bathed in fresh, clean water! There are no words to describe what happened to me!!
There are LOTS of words to describe what happened to you! Soak! Agitate! Rinse! Spin! You didn't climb into the isolation tank! You climbed into the WASHING MACHINE!!

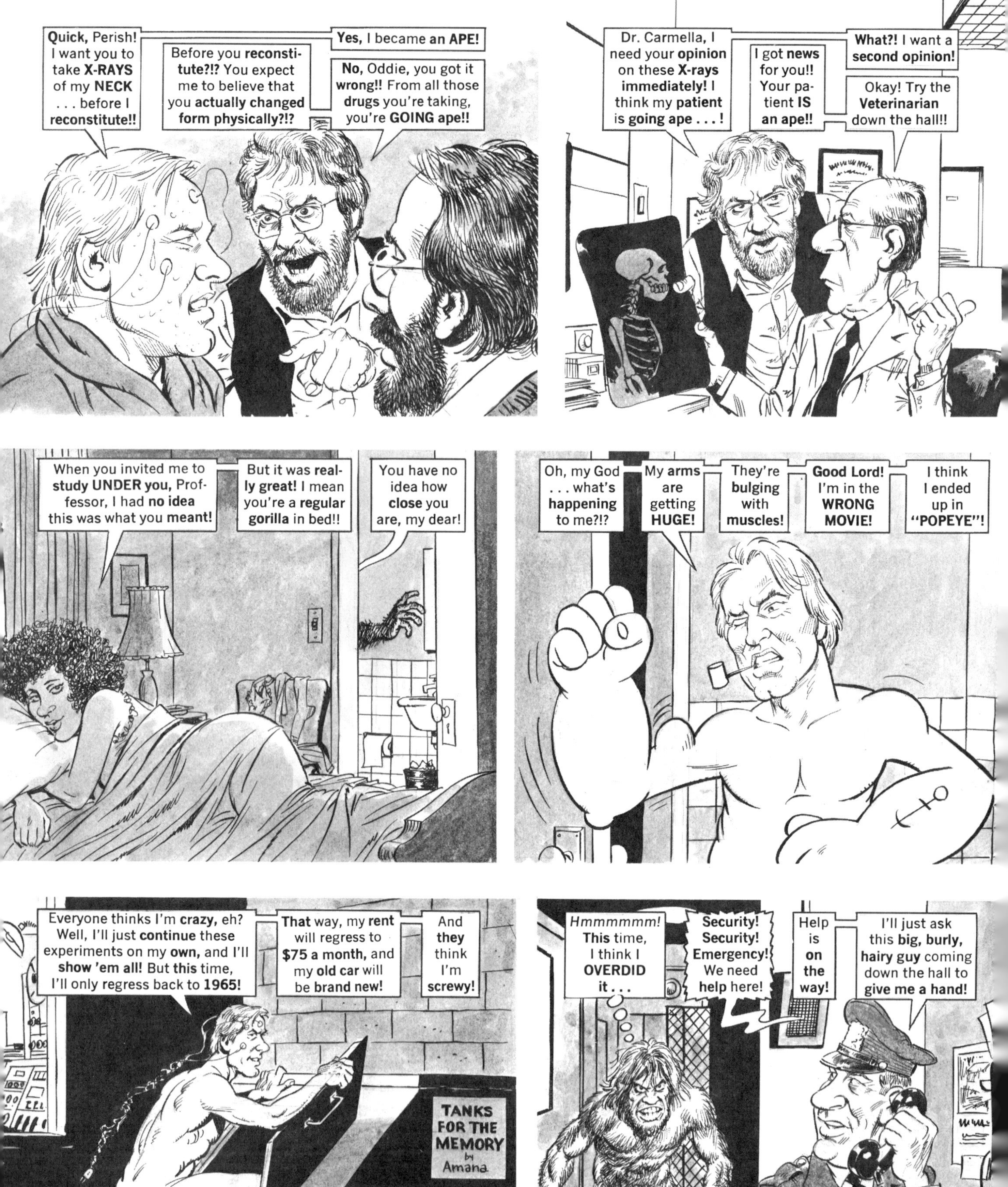
Quick, Perish! I want you to take X-RAYS of my NECK . . . before I reconstitute!!
Yes, I became an APE!
Before you reconstitute?!? You expect me to believe that you actually changed form physically?!?
No, Oddie, you got it wrong!! From all those drugs you're taking, you're GOING ape!!
Dr. Carmella, I need your opinion on these X-rays immediately! I think my patient is going ape . . . !
What?! I want a second opinion!
I got news for you!! Your patient IS an ape!!
Okay! Try the Veterinarian down the hall!!
When you invited me to study UNDER you, Professor, I had no idea this was what you meant!
But it was really great! I mean you're a regular gorilla in bed!!
You have no idea how close you are, my dear!
Oh, my God . . . what's happening to me?!?
My arms are getting HUGE!
They're bulging with muscles!
Good Lord! I'm in the WRONG MOVIE!
I think I ended up in "POPEYE"!
Everyone thinks I'm crazy, eh? Well, I'll just continue these experiments on my own, and I'll show 'em all! But this time, I'll only regress back to 1965!
That way, my rent will regress to $75 a month, and my old car will be brand new!
And they think I'm screwy!
TANKS FOR THE MEMORY by Amana
Hmmmmmm! This time, I think I OVERDID it . . .
Security! Security! Emergency! We need help here!
Help is on the way!
I'll just ask this big, burly, hairy guy coming down the hall to give me a hand!

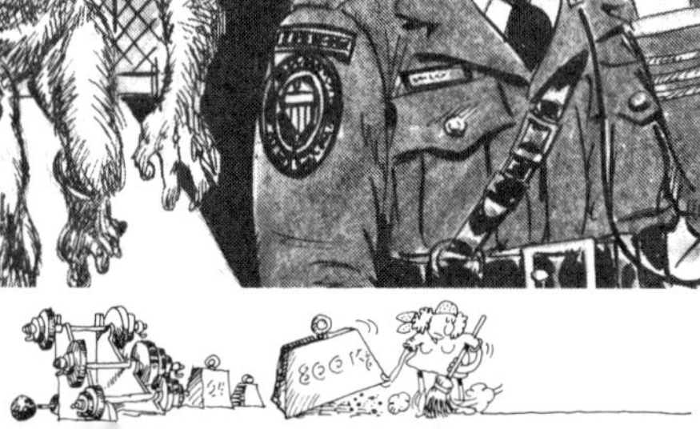

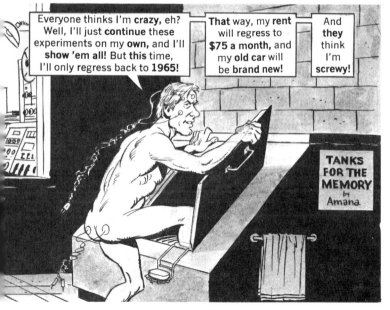

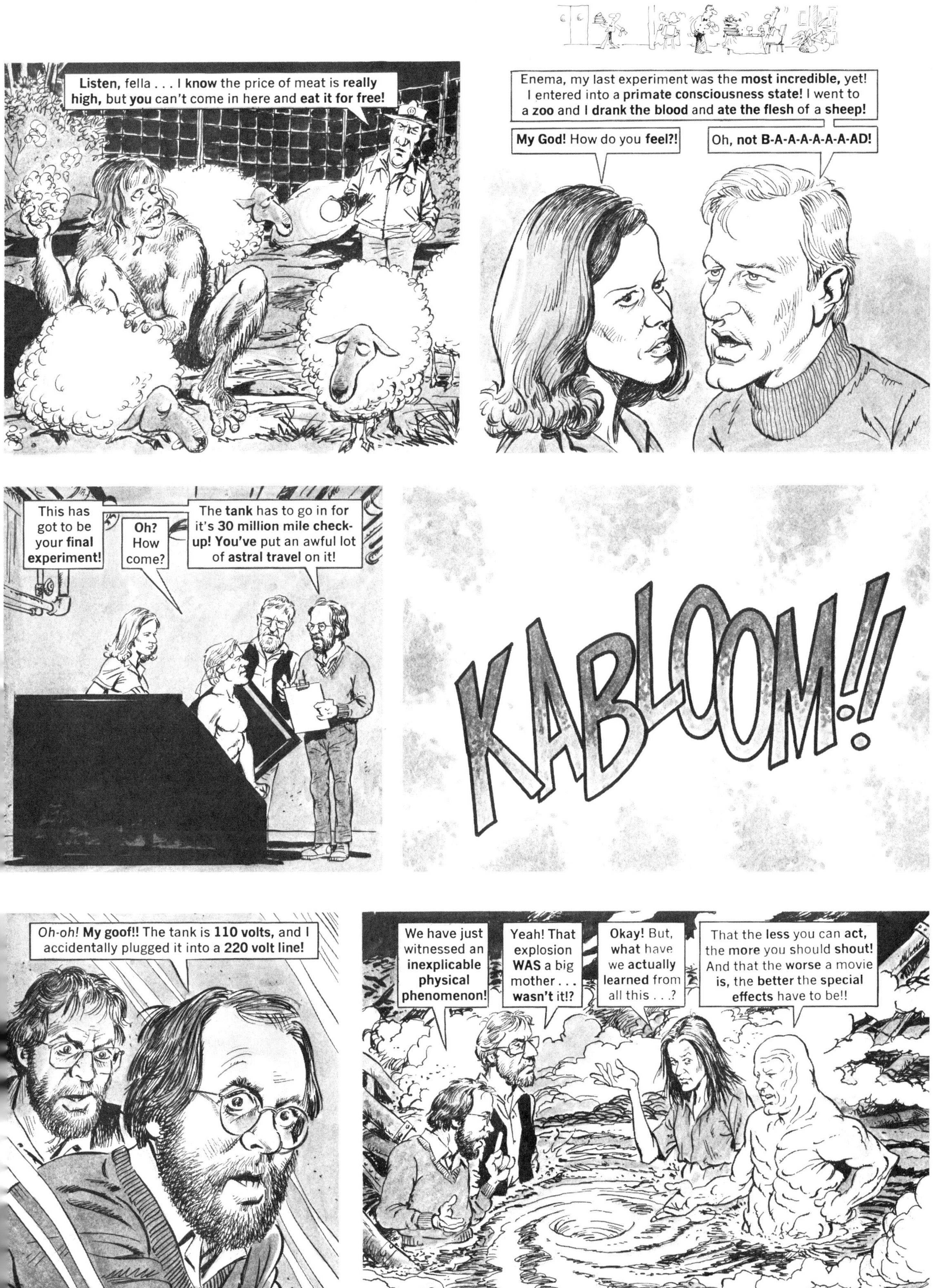

**Listen,** fella . . . I **know** the price of meat is **really high,** but **you** can't come in here and **eat it for free!**
Enema, my last experiment was the **most incredible,** yet! I entered into a **primate consciousness state!** I went to a **zoo** and I **drank the blood** and **ate the flesh** of a **sheep!**
**My God!** How do you **feel?!**
Oh, **not B-A-A-A-A-A-A-AD!**
This has got to be your **final experiment!**
**Oh?** How come?
The **tank** has to go in for it's **30 million mile check-up! You've** put an awful lot of **astral travel** on it!
KABLOOM!!
*Oh-oh!* **My goof!!** The tank is **110 volts,** and I accidentally plugged it into a **220 volt line!**
We have just witnessed an **inexplicable physical phenomenon!**
Yeah! That explosion **WAS** a big mother . . . **wasn't** it!?
**Okay!** But, **what** have we **actually learned** from all this . . .?
That the **less** you can **act,** the **more** you should **shout!** And that the **worse** a movie **is,** the **better** the **special effects** have to be!!

**ALL MEN ARE CREATING SEQUELS DEPT.**

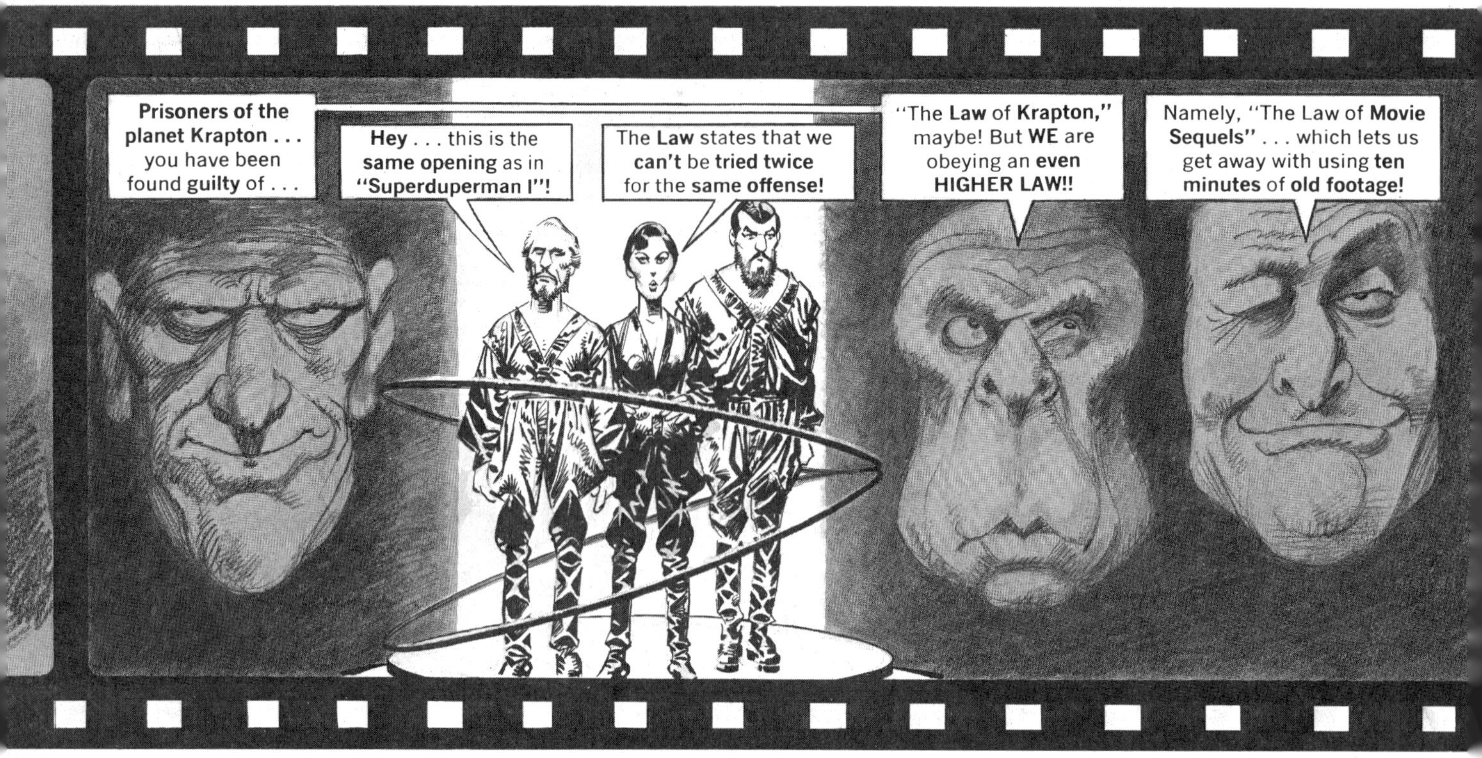

Prisoners of the planet Krapton . . . you have been found guilty of . . .
Hey . . . this is the same opening as in "Superduperman I"!
The Law states that we can't be tried twice for the same offense!
"The Law of Krapton," maybe! But WE are obeying an even HIGHER LAW!!
Namely, "The Law of Movie Sequels" . . . which lets us get away with using ten minutes of old footage!


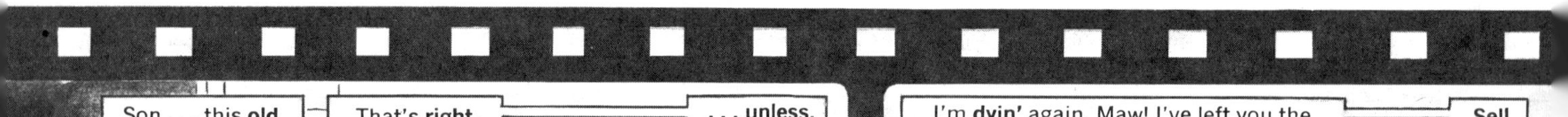

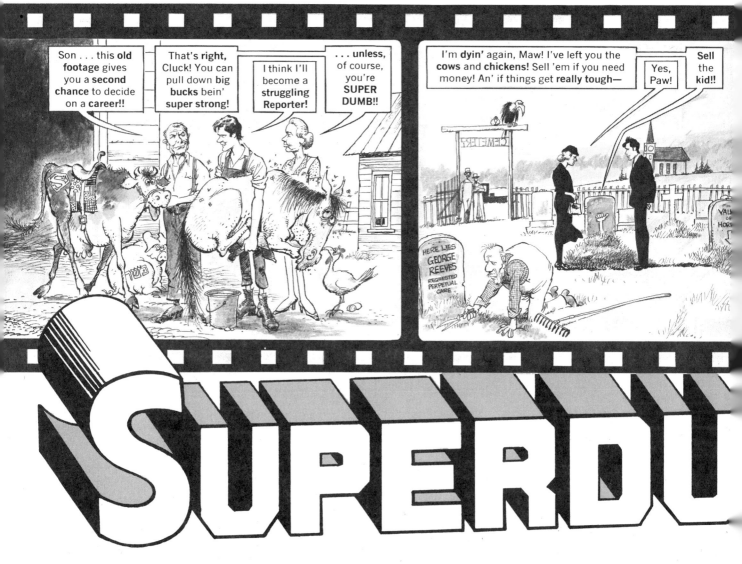

Son . . . this old footage gives you a second chance to decide on a career!!
That's right, Cluck! You can pull down big bucks bein' super strong!
I think I'll become a struggling Reporter!
. . . unless, of course, you're SUPER DUMB!!
I'm dyin' again, Maw! I've left you the cows and chickens! Sell 'em if you need money! An' if things get really tough—
Yes, Paw!
Sell the kid!!
HERE LIES GEORGE REEVES REQUESTED PERPETUAL CARE


# SUPERDU

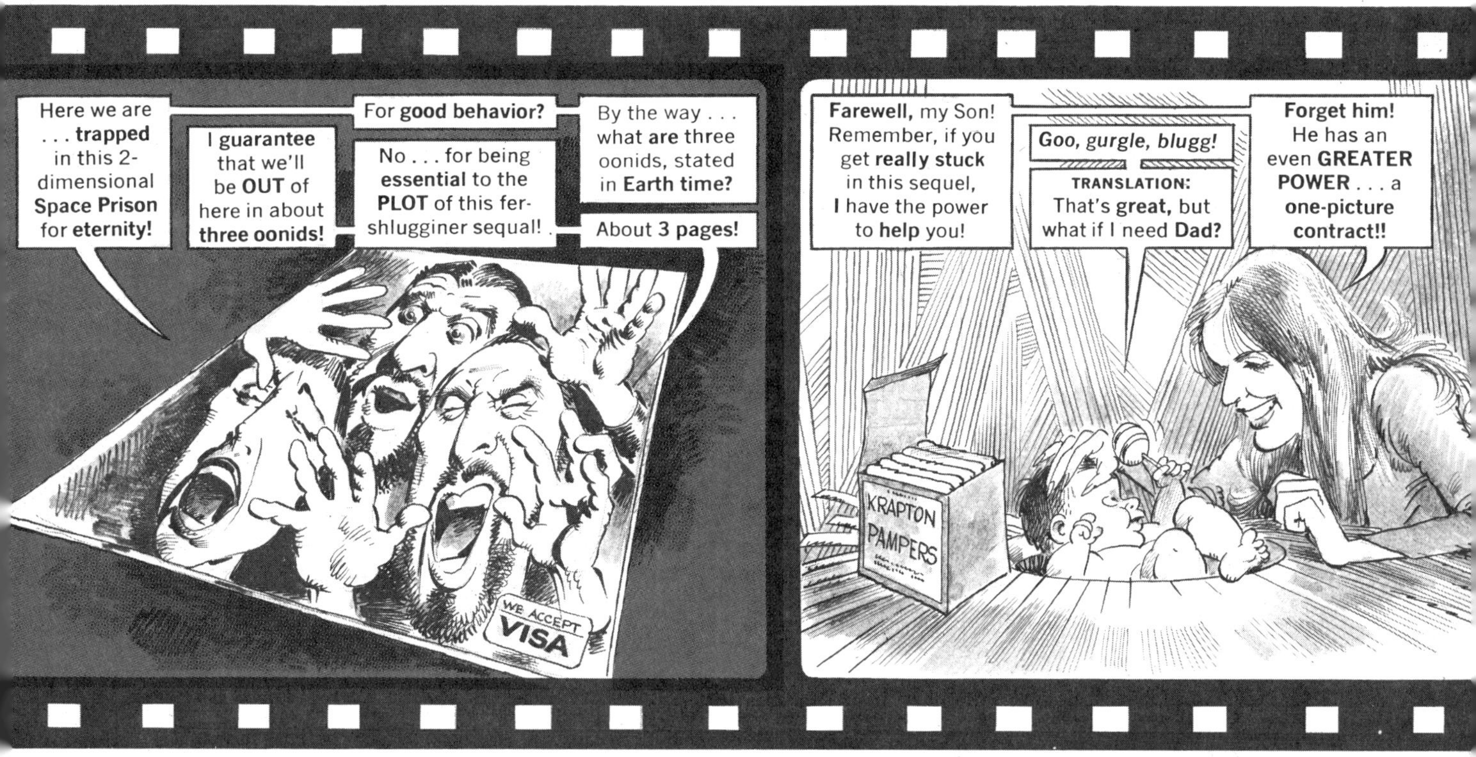
Here we are . . . trapped in this 2-dimensional Space Prison for eternity!
For good behavior?
I guarantee that we'll be OUT of here in about three oonids!
No . . . for being essential to the PLOT of this fershlugginer sequal!
By the way . . . what are three oonids, stated in Earth time?
About 3 pages!
WE ACCEPT VISA
Farewell, my Son! Remember, if you get really stuck in this sequel, I have the power to help you!
Goo, gurgle, blugg!
TRANSLATION: That's great, but what if I need Dad?
Forget him! He has an even GREATER POWER . . . a one-picture contract!!
KRAPTON PAMPERS

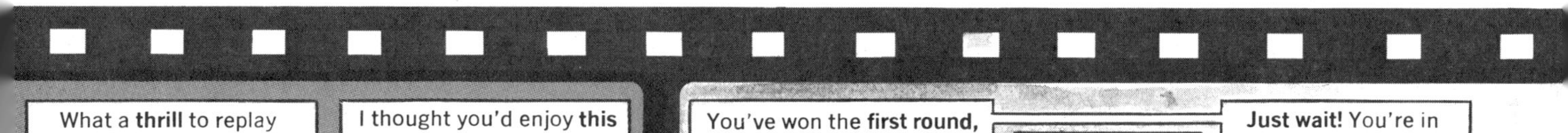
What a thrill to replay my first date with Superduperman! He's still as strong . . . still as manly . . . still as powerful . . .
I thought you'd enjoy this a lot more than going out to dinner and the theater!
. . . and still as cheap!!
IT'S A BIRD?
You've won the first round, Superduperman! But don't put that cape in mothballs!
You don't scare me, Lox Looter!
Just wait! You're in for even bigger, more terrible trouble in—
MORT DRUCKER

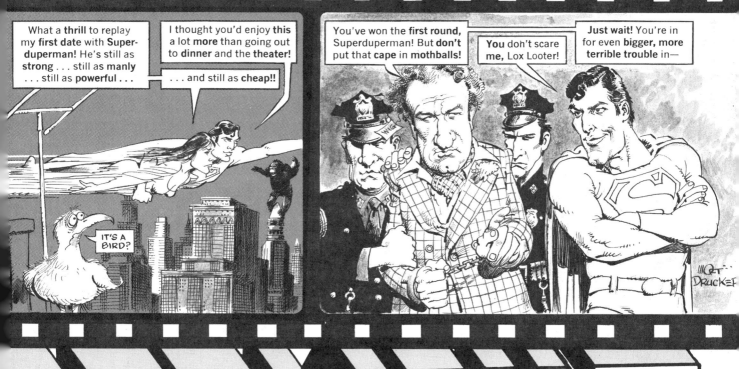

# PERMAN II

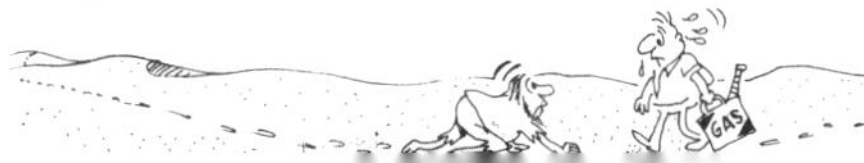

ARTIST: MORT DRUCKER

WRITER: FRANK JACOBS

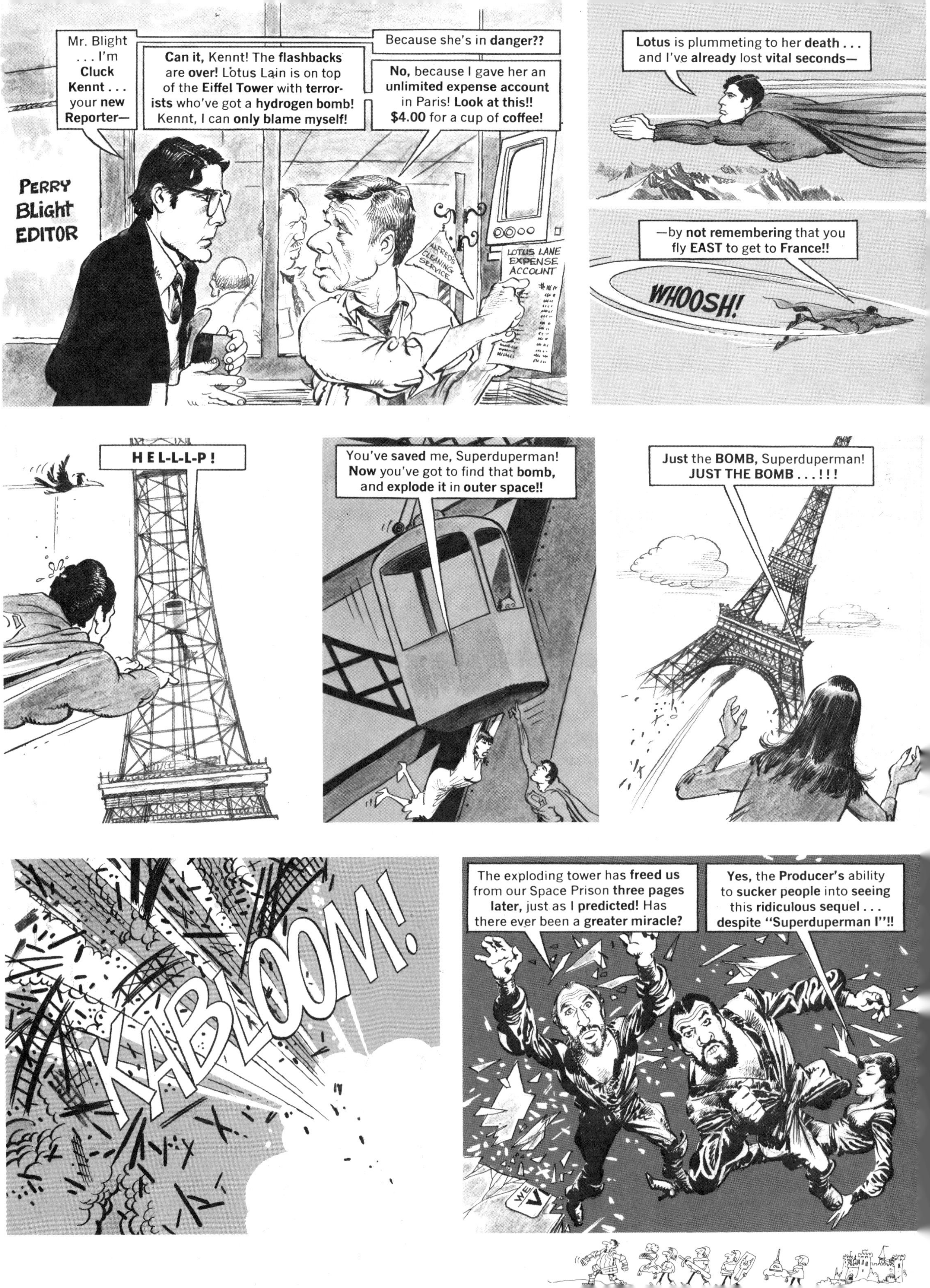
Mr. Blight . . . I'm Cluck Kennt . . . your new Reporter—
PERRY BLIGHT EDITOR
Can it, Kennt! The flashbacks are over! Lotus Lain is on top of the Eiffel Tower with terrorists who've got a hydrogen bomb! Kennt, I can only blame myself!
Because she's in danger??
No, because I gave her an unlimited expense account in Paris! Look at this!! $4.00 for a cup of coffee!
ALFRED'S CLEANING SERVICE
LOTUS LANE EXPENSE ACCOUNT
Lotus is plummeting to her death . . . and I've already lost vital seconds—
—by not remembering that you fly EAST to get to France!!
WHOOSH!
HEL-L-L-P!
You've saved me, Superduperman! Now you've got to find that bomb, and explode it in outer space!!
Just the BOMB, Superduperman! JUST THE BOMB . . . !!!
KABLOOM!
The exploding tower has freed us from our Space Prison three pages later, just as I predicted! Has there ever been a greater miracle?
Yes, the Producer's ability to sucker people into seeing this ridiculous sequel . . . despite "Superduperman I"!!

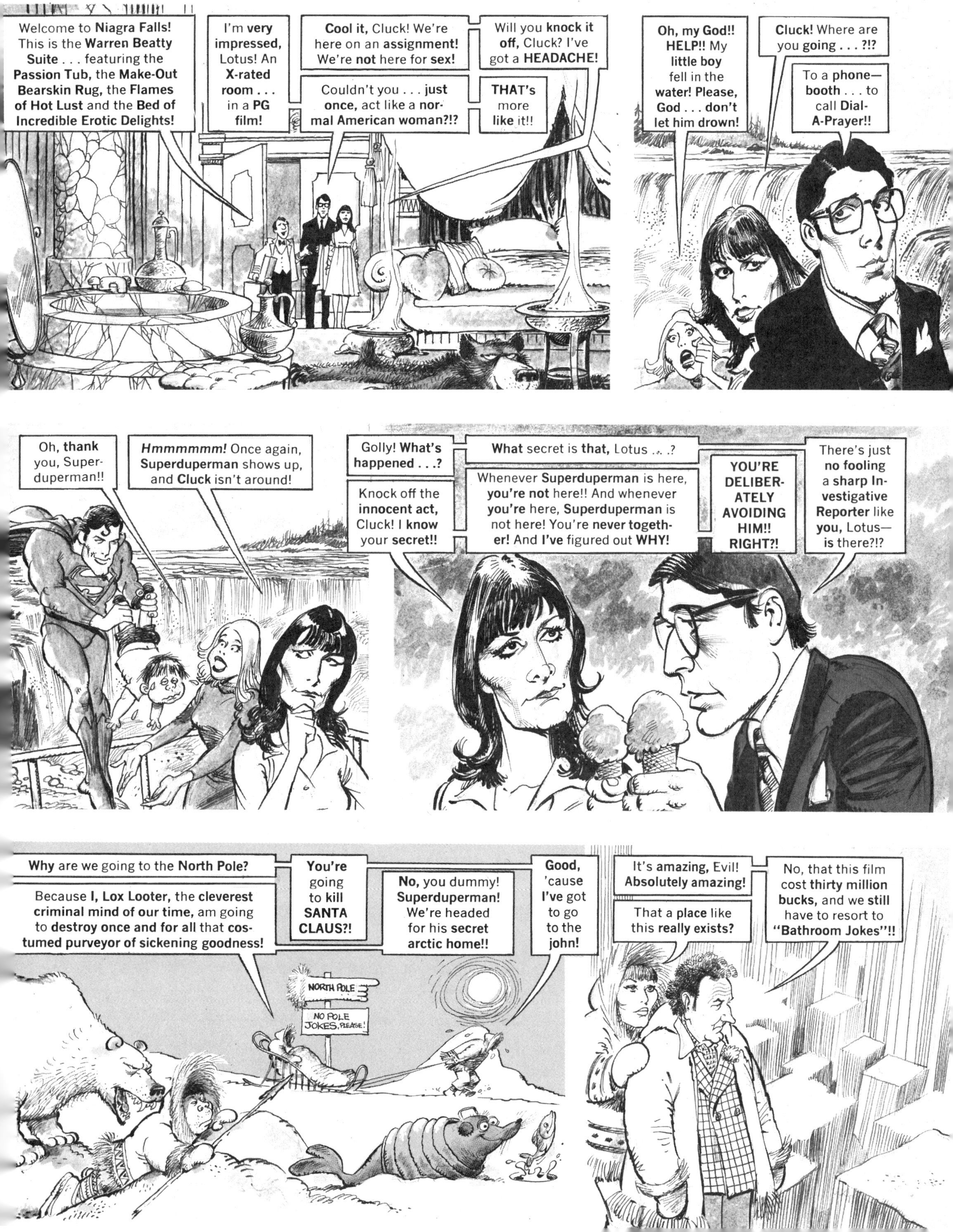

Welcome to Niagra Falls! This is the Warren Beatty Suite . . . featuring the Passion Tub, the Make-Out Bearskin Rug, the Flames of Hot Lust and the Bed of Incredible Erotic Delights!
I'm very impressed, Lotus! An X-rated room . . . in a PG film!
Cool it, Cluck! We're here on an assignment! We're not here for sex!
Couldn't you . . . just once, act like a normal American woman?!?
Will you knock it off, Cluck? I've got a HEADACHE!
THAT's more like it!!
Oh, my God!! HELP!! My little boy fell in the water! Please, God . . . don't let him drown!
Cluck! Where are you going . . . ?!?
To a phone-booth . . . to call Dial-A-Prayer!!
Oh, thank you, Superduperman!!
Hmmmmmm! Once again, Superduperman shows up, and Cluck isn't around!
Golly! What's happened . . .?
Knock off the innocent act, Cluck! I know your secret!!
What secret is that, Lotus . . .?
Whenever Superduperman is here, you're not here!! And whenever you're here, Superduperman is not here! You're never together! And I've figured out WHY!
YOU'RE DELIBERATELY AVOIDING HIM!! RIGHT?!
There's just no fooling a sharp Investigative Reporter like you, Lotus—is there?!?
Why are we going to the North Pole?
Because I, Lox Looter, the cleverest criminal mind of our time, am going to destroy once and for all that costumed purveyor of sickening goodness!
You're going to kill SANTA CLAUS?!
No, you dummy! Superduperman! We're headed for his secret arctic home!!
Good, 'cause I've got to go to the john!
NORTH POLE
NO POLE JOKES, PLEASE!
It's amazing, Evil! Absolutely amazing!
That a place like this really exists?
No, that this film cost thirty million bucks, and we still have to resort to "Bathroom Jokes"!!

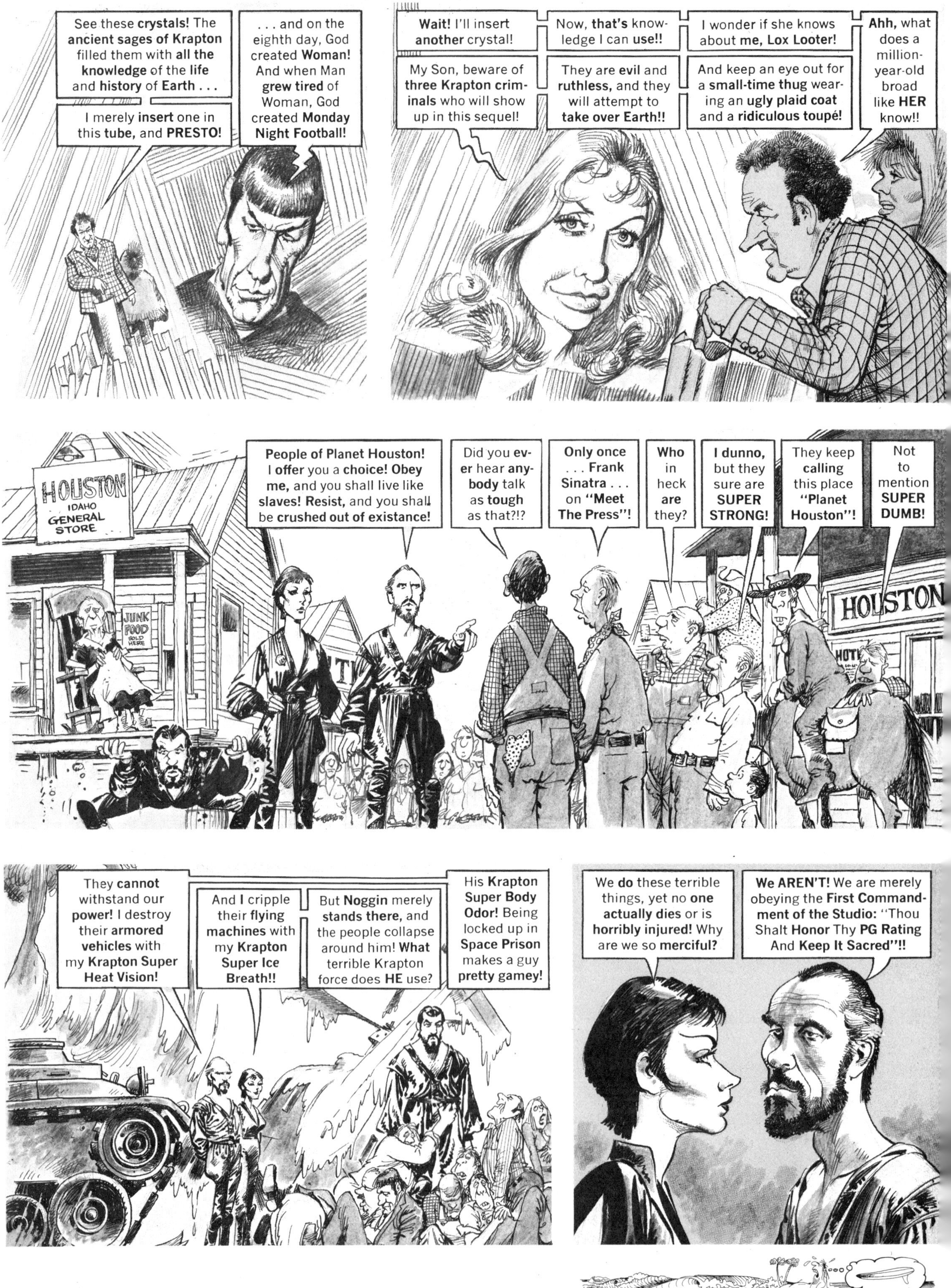
See these crystals! The ancient sages of Krapton filled them with all the knowledge of the life and history of Earth . . .
I merely insert one in this tube, and PRESTO!
. . . and on the eighth day, God created Woman! And when Man grew tired of Woman, God created Monday Night Football!
Wait! I'll insert another crystal!
My Son, beware of three Krapton criminals who will show up in this sequel!
Now, that's knowledge I can use!!
They are evil and ruthless, and they will attempt to take over Earth!!
I wonder if she knows about me, Lox Looter!
And keep an eye out for a small-time thug wearing an ugly plaid coat and a ridiculous toupé!
Ahh, what does a million-year-old broad like HER know!!
HOUSTON IDAHO GENERAL STORE
JUNK FOOD SOLD HERE
People of Planet Houston! I offer you a choice! Obey me, and you shall live like slaves! Resist, and you shall be crushed out of existance!
Did you ever hear anybody talk as tough as that?!?
Only once . . . Frank Sinatra . . . on "Meet The Press"!
Who in heck are they?
I dunno, but they sure are SUPER STRONG!
They keep calling this place "Planet Houston"!
Not to mention SUPER DUMB!
HOUSTON
HOTE
They cannot withstand our power! I destroy their armored vehicles with my Krapton Super Heat Vision!
And I cripple their flying machines with my Krapton Super Ice Breath!!
But Noggin merely stands there, and the people collapse around him! What terrible Krapton force does HE use?
His Krapton Super Body Odor! Being locked up in Space Prison makes a guy pretty gamey!
We do these terrible things, yet no one actually dies or is horribly injured! Why are we so merciful?
We AREN'T! We are merely obeying the First Commandment of the Studio: "Thou Shalt Honor Thy PG Rating And Keep It Sacred"!!

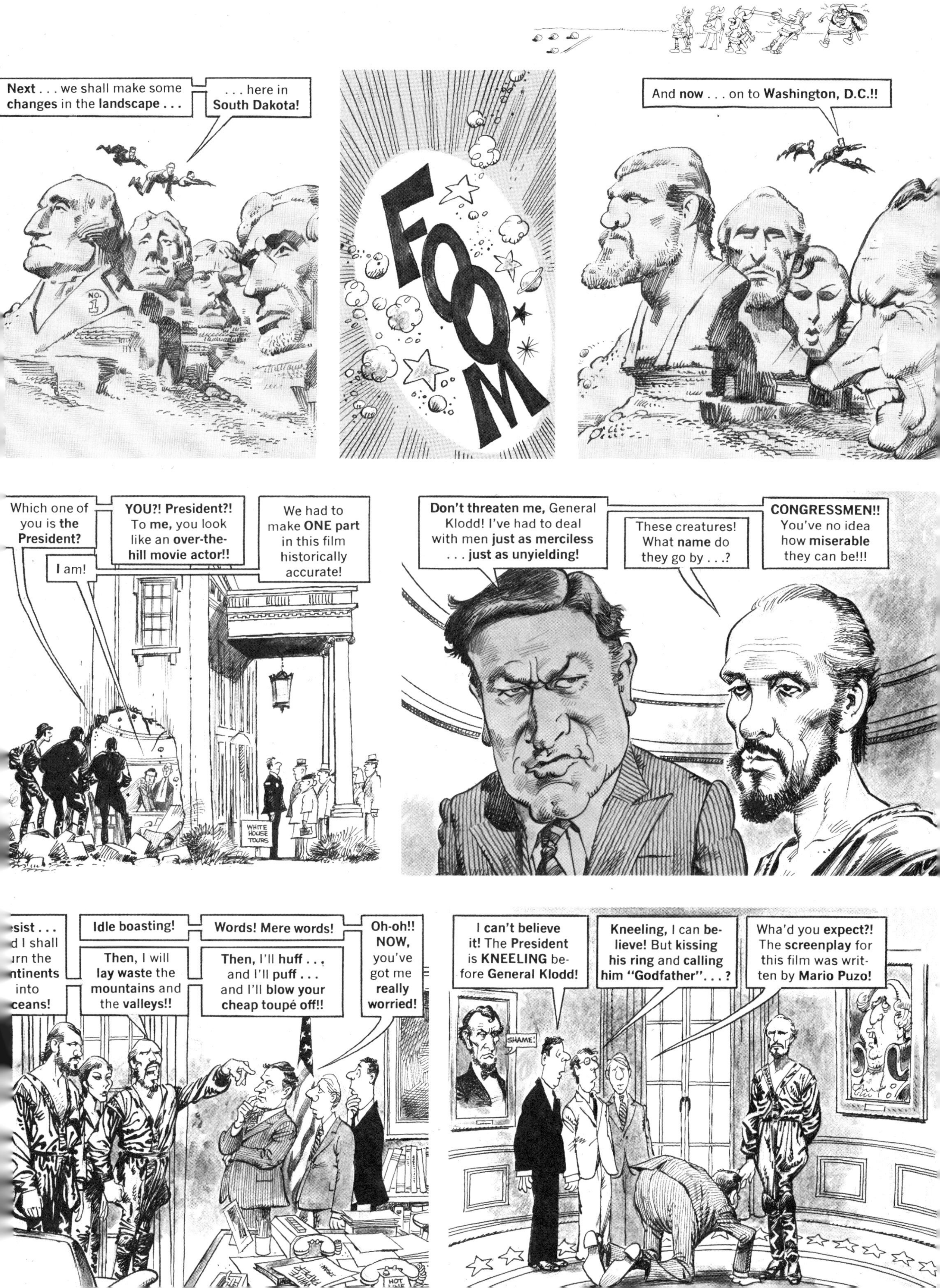
Next . . . we shall make some changes in the landscape . . .
. . . here in South Dakota!
NO. 1
FOOM
And now . . . on to Washington, D.C.!!
Which one of you is the President?
YOU?! President?! To me, you look like an over-the-hill movie actor!!
I am!
We had to make ONE part in this film historically accurate!
WHITE HOUSE TOURS
Don't threaten me, General Klodd! I've had to deal with men just as merciless . . . just as unyielding!
These creatures! What name do they go by . . .?
CONGRESSMEN!! You've no idea how miserable they can be!!!
esist . . . d I shall urn the ntinents into ceans!
Idle boasting!
Then, I will lay waste the mountains and the valleys!!
Words! Mere words!
Then, I'll huff . . . and I'll puff . . . and I'll blow your cheap toupé off!!
Oh-oh!! NOW, you've got me really worried!
I can't believe it! The President is KNEELING before General Klodd!
SHAME!
Kneeling, I can believe! But kissing his ring and calling him "Godfather". . . ?
Wha'd you expect?! The screenplay for this film was written by Mario Puzo!

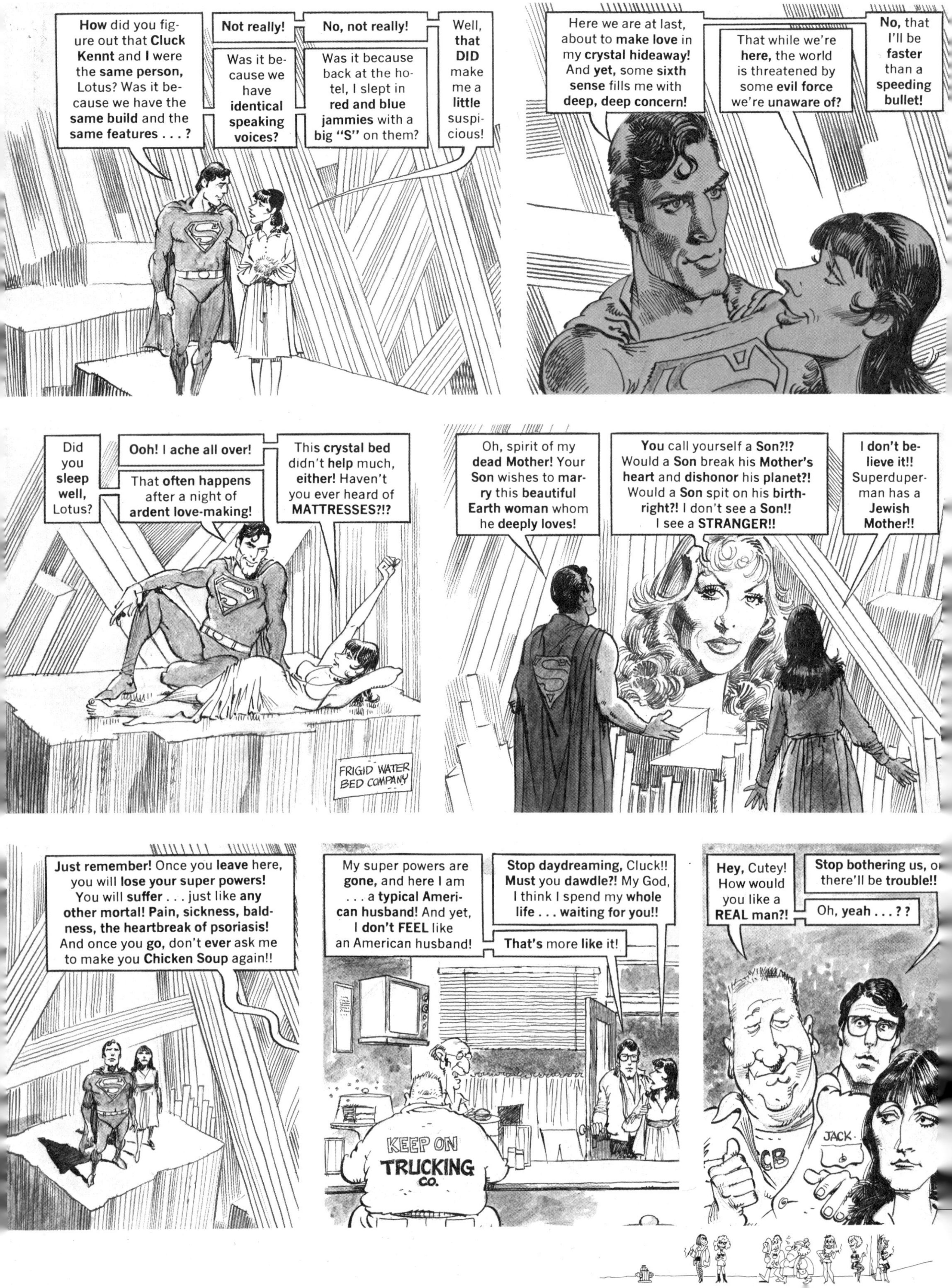

How did you figure out that Cluck Kennt and I were the same person, Lotus? Was it because we have the same build and the same features . . . ?
Not really!
Was it because we have identical speaking voices?
No, not really!
Was it because back at the hotel, I slept in red and blue jammies with a big "S" on them?
Well, that DID make me a little suspicious!
Here we are at last, about to make love in my crystal hideaway! And yet, some sixth sense fills me with deep, deep concern!
That while we're here, the world is threatened by some evil force we're unaware of?
No, that I'll be faster than a speeding bullet!
Did you sleep well, Lotus?
Ooh! I ache all over!
That often happens after a night of ardent love-making!
This crystal bed didn't help much, either! Haven't you ever heard of MATTRESSES?!?
FRIGID WATER BED COMPANY
Oh, spirit of my dead Mother! Your Son wishes to marry this beautiful Earth woman whom he deeply loves!
You call yourself a Son?!? Would a Son break his Mother's heart and dishonor his planet?! Would a Son spit on his birthright?! I don't see a Son!! I see a STRANGER!!
I don't believe it!! Superduperman has a Jewish Mother!!
Just remember! Once you leave here, you will lose your super powers! You will suffer . . . just like any other mortal! Pain, sickness, baldness, the heartbreak of psoriasis! And once you go, don't ever ask me to make you Chicken Soup again!!
My super powers are gone, and here I am . . . a typical American husband! And yet, I don't FEEL like an American husband!
Stop daydreaming, Cluck!! Must you dawdle?! My God, I think I spend my whole life . . . waiting for you!!
That's more like it!
KEEP ON TRUCKING CO.
Hey, Cutey! How would you like a REAL man?!
Stop bothering us, o
there'll be trouble!!
Oh, yeah . . . ??
CB
JACK

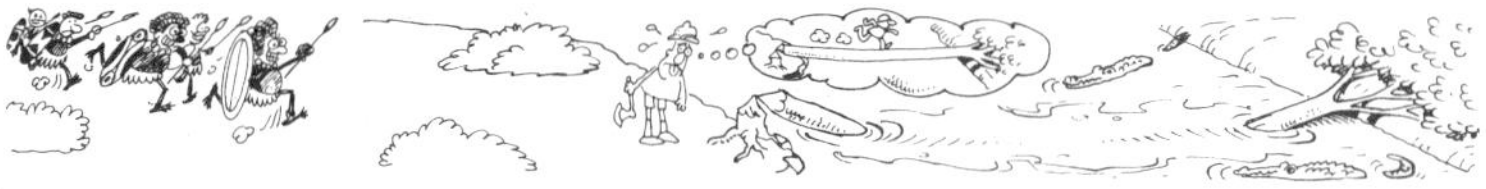

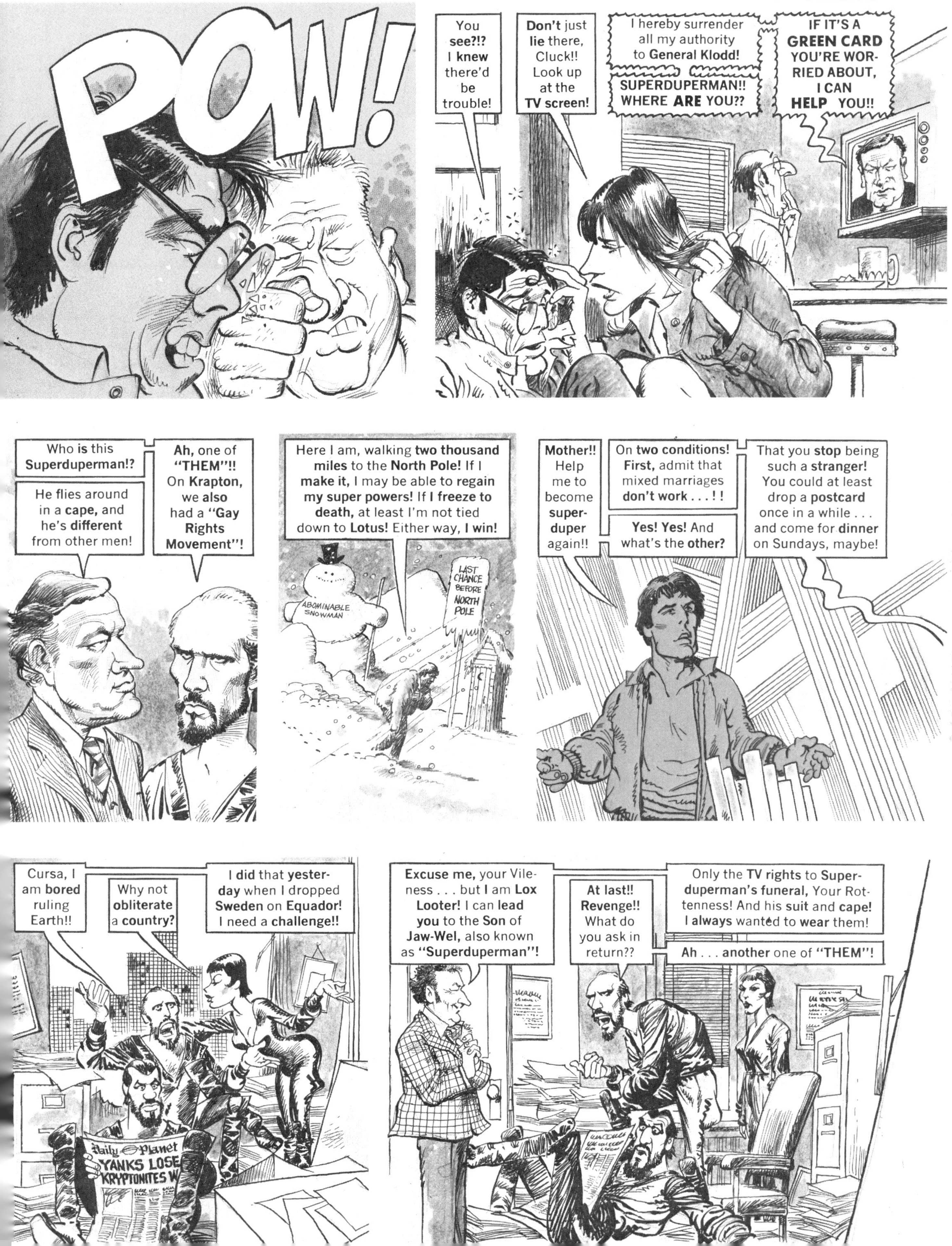

POW!
You see?!? I knew there'd be trouble!
Don't just lie there, Cluck!! Look up at the TV screen!
I hereby surrender all my authority to General Klodd!
SUPERDUPERMAN!! WHERE ARE YOU??
IF IT'S A GREEN CARD YOU'RE WORRIED ABOUT, I CAN HELP YOU!!
Who is this Superduperman!?
He flies around in a cape, and he's different from other men!
Ah, one of "THEM"!! On Krapton, we also had a "Gay Rights Movement"!
Here I am, walking two thousand miles to the North Pole! If I make it, I may be able to regain my super powers! If I freeze to death, at least I'm not tied down to Lotus! Either way, I win!
ABOMINABLE SNOWMAN
LAST CHANCE BEFORE NORTH POLE
Mother!! Help me to become superduper again!!
On two conditions! First, admit that mixed marriages don't work . . . ! !
Yes! Yes! And what's the other?
That you stop being such a stranger! You could at least drop a postcard once in a while . . . and come for dinner on Sundays, maybe!
Cursa, I am bored ruling Earth!!
Why not obliterate a country?
I did that yesterday when I dropped Sweden on Equador! I need a challenge!!
Daily Planet
YANKS LOSE
KRYPTONITES W
Excuse me, your Vileness . . . but I am Lox Looter! I can lead you to the Son of Jaw-Wel, also known as "Superduperman"!
At last!! Revenge!! What do you ask in return??
Only the TV rights to Superduperman's funeral, Your Rottenness! And his suit and cape! I always wanted to wear them!
Ah . . . another one of "THEM"!

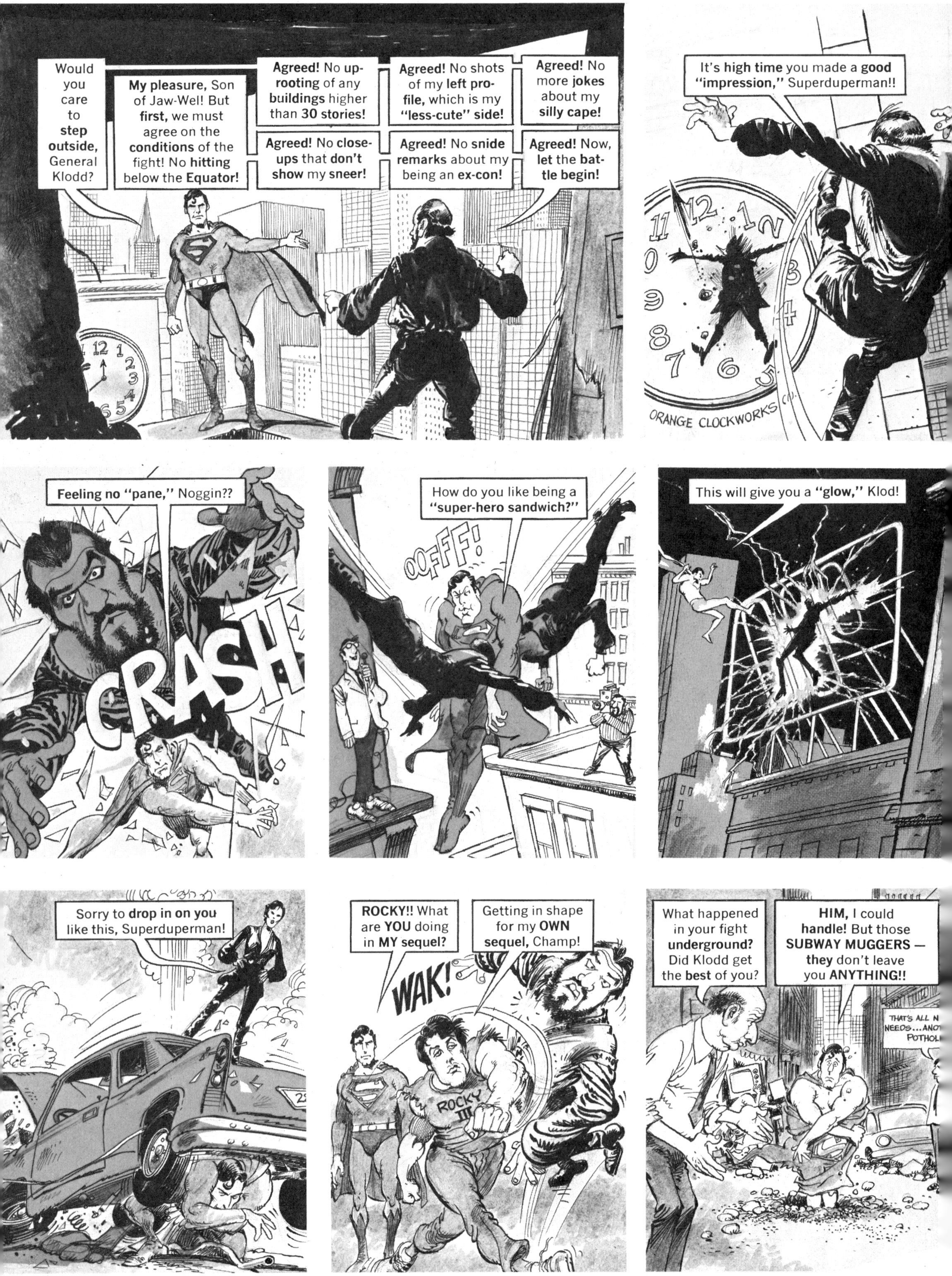
Would you care to step outside, General Klodd?
My pleasure, Son of Jaw-Wel! But first, we must agree on the conditions of the fight! No hitting below the Equator!
Agreed! No up-rooting of any buildings higher than 30 stories!
Agreed! No shots of my left pro-file, which is my "less-cute" side!
Agreed! No more jokes about my silly cape!
Agreed! No close-ups that don't show my sneer!
Agreed! No snide remarks about my being an ex-con!
Agreed! Now, let the bat-tle begin!
It's high time you made a good "impression," Superduperman!!
ORANGE CLOCKWORKS CO.
Feeling no "pane," Noggin??
CRASH
How do you like being a "super-hero sandwich?"
OOFFF!
This will give you a "glow," Klod!
Sorry to drop in on you like this, Superduperman!
ROCKY!! What are YOU doing in MY sequel?
Getting in shape for my OWN sequel, Champ!
WAK!
ROCKY III
What happened in your fight underground? Did Klodd get the best of you?
HIM, I could handle! But those SUBWAY MUGGERS — they don't leave you ANYTHING!!

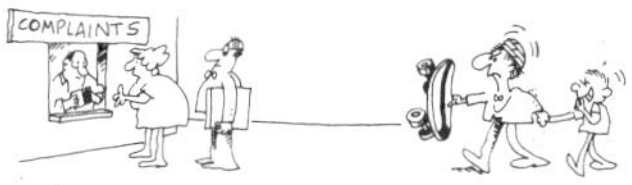
COMPLAINTS

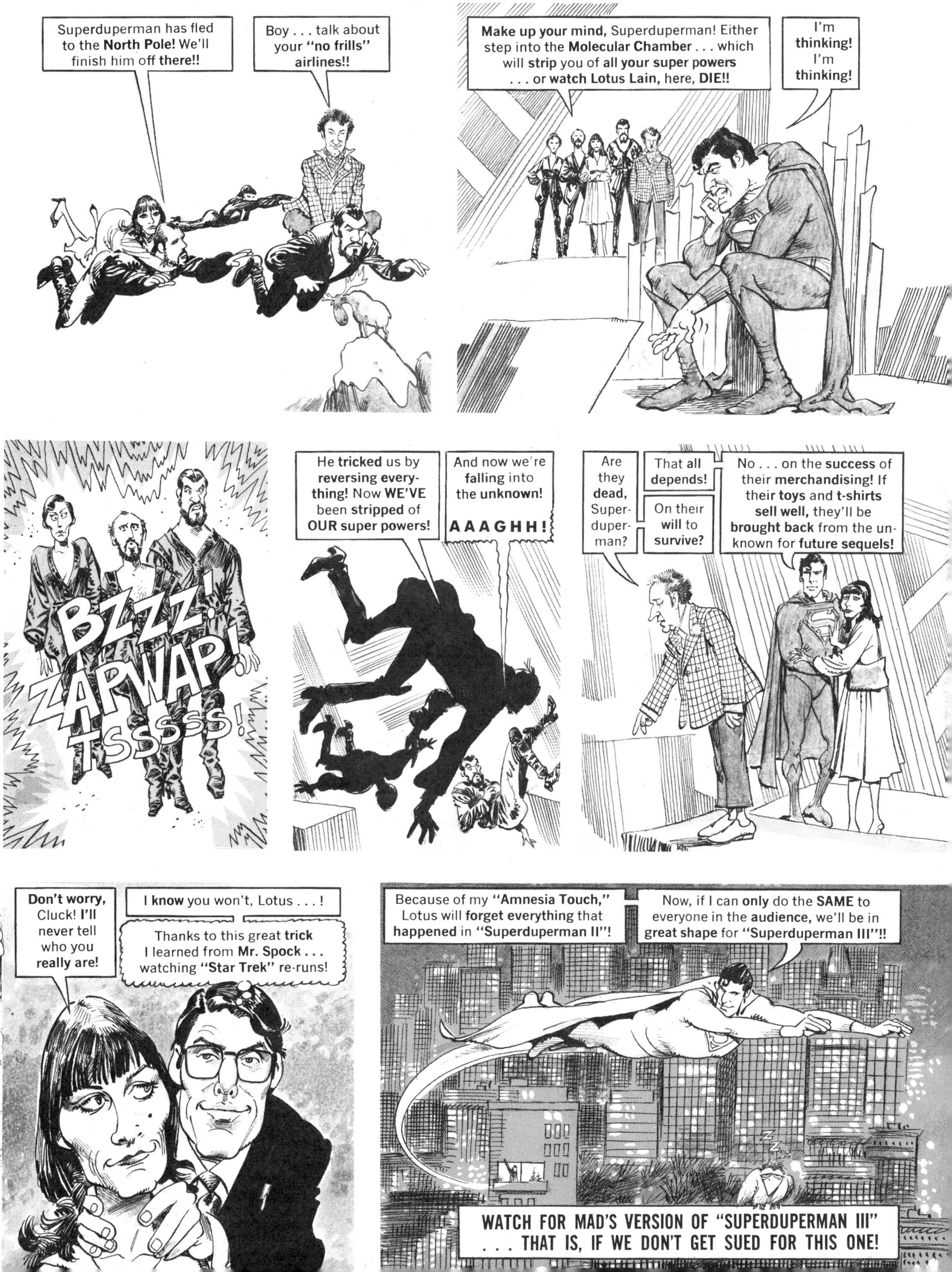
Superduperman has fled to the North Pole! We'll finish him off there!!
Boy . . . talk about your "no frills" airlines!!
Make up your mind, Superduperman! Either step into the Molecular Chamber . . . which will strip you of all your super powers . . . or watch Lotus Lain, here, DIE!!
I'm thinking! I'm thinking!
BZZZ! ZAPWAP! TSSSSSS!
He tricked us by reversing everything! Now WE'VE been stripped of OUR super powers!
And now we're falling into the unknown!
AAAGHH!
Are they dead, Superduperman?
That all depends!
On their will to survive?
No . . . on the success of their merchandising! If their toys and t-shirts sell well, they'll be brought back from the unknown for future sequels!
Don't worry, Cluck! I'll never tell who you really are!
I know you won't, Lotus . . . !
Thanks to this great trick I learned from Mr. Spock . . . watching "Star Trek" re-runs!
Because of my "Amnesia Touch," Lotus will forget everything that happened in "Superduperman II"!
Now, if I can only do the SAME to everyone in the audience, we'll be in great shape for "Superduperman III"!!
WATCH FOR MAD'S VERSION OF "SUPERDUPERMAN III" . . . THAT IS, IF WE DON'T GET SUED FOR THIS ONE!

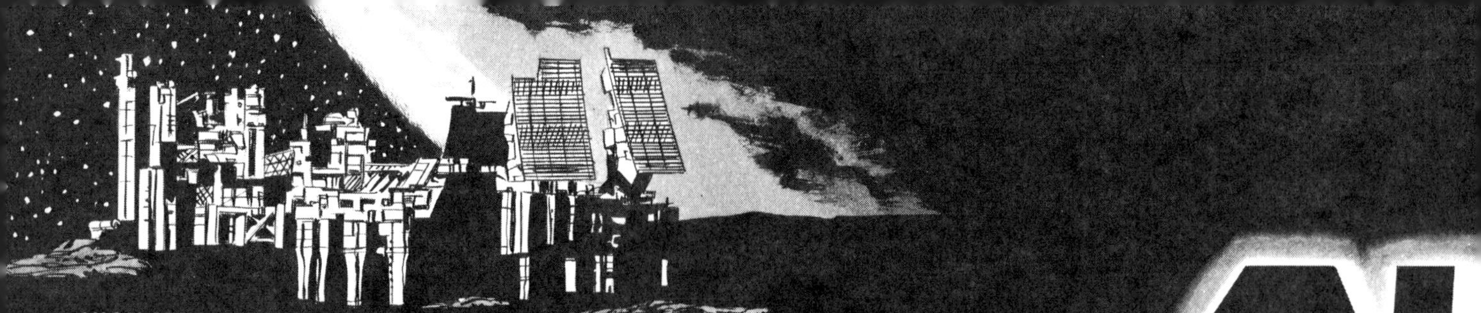

HIGH MOON DEPT.

Movie Location: HiHo, Sixth Moon Of Jupiter.

Distance From Nearest Place You Can Find A Parking Place: 345,675 Miles.

Principle Product: Soapy Melodrama With Very Thin Plot.

Running Time Of Movie: 1 hour and 45 minutes. Seems Like: 2 light years.

Entire Plot Stolen From: "High Noon"

Title Of This Idiotic MAD Version:

# OU

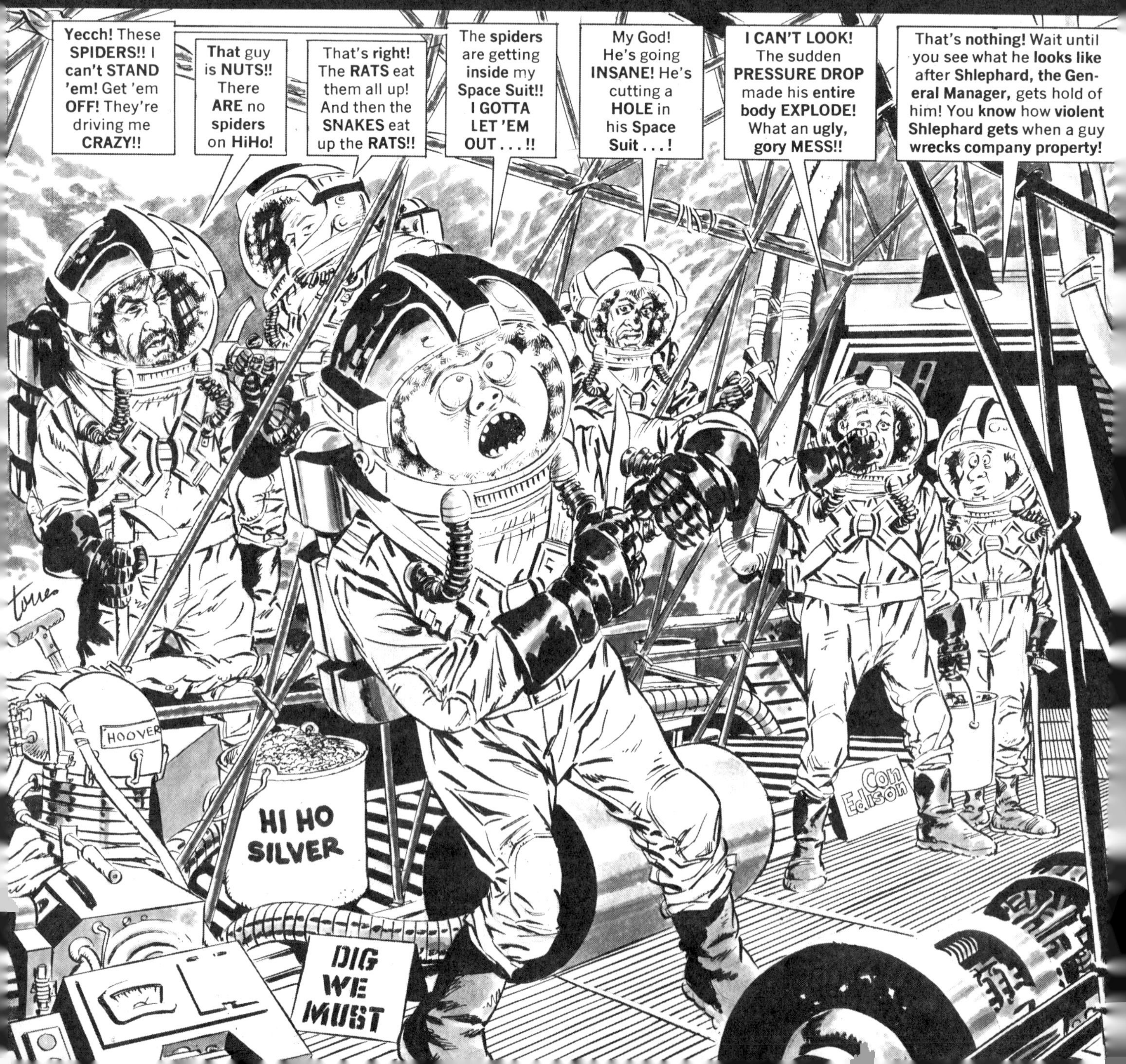

**Yecch!** These **SPIDERS!!** I **can't STAND 'em!** Get 'em **OFF!** They're driving me **CRAZY!!**
**That** guy is **NUTS!!** There **ARE** no **spiders** on **HiHo!**
That's **right!** The **RATS** eat them all up! And then the **SNAKES** eat up the **RATS!!**
The **spiders** are getting **inside** my **Space Suit!! I GOTTA LET 'EM OUT . . . !!**
My God! He's going **INSANE!** He's cutting a **HOLE** in his **Space Suit . . . !**
**I CAN'T LOOK!** The sudden **PRESSURE DROP** made his **entire body EXPLODE!** What an ugly, **gory MESS!!**
That's **nothing!** Wait until you see what he **looks like** after **Shlephard, the General Manager,** gets hold of him! You **know** how **violent Shlephard gets** when a guy **wrecks company property!**
HOOVER
HI HO SILVER
Con Edison
DIG WE MUST
torres

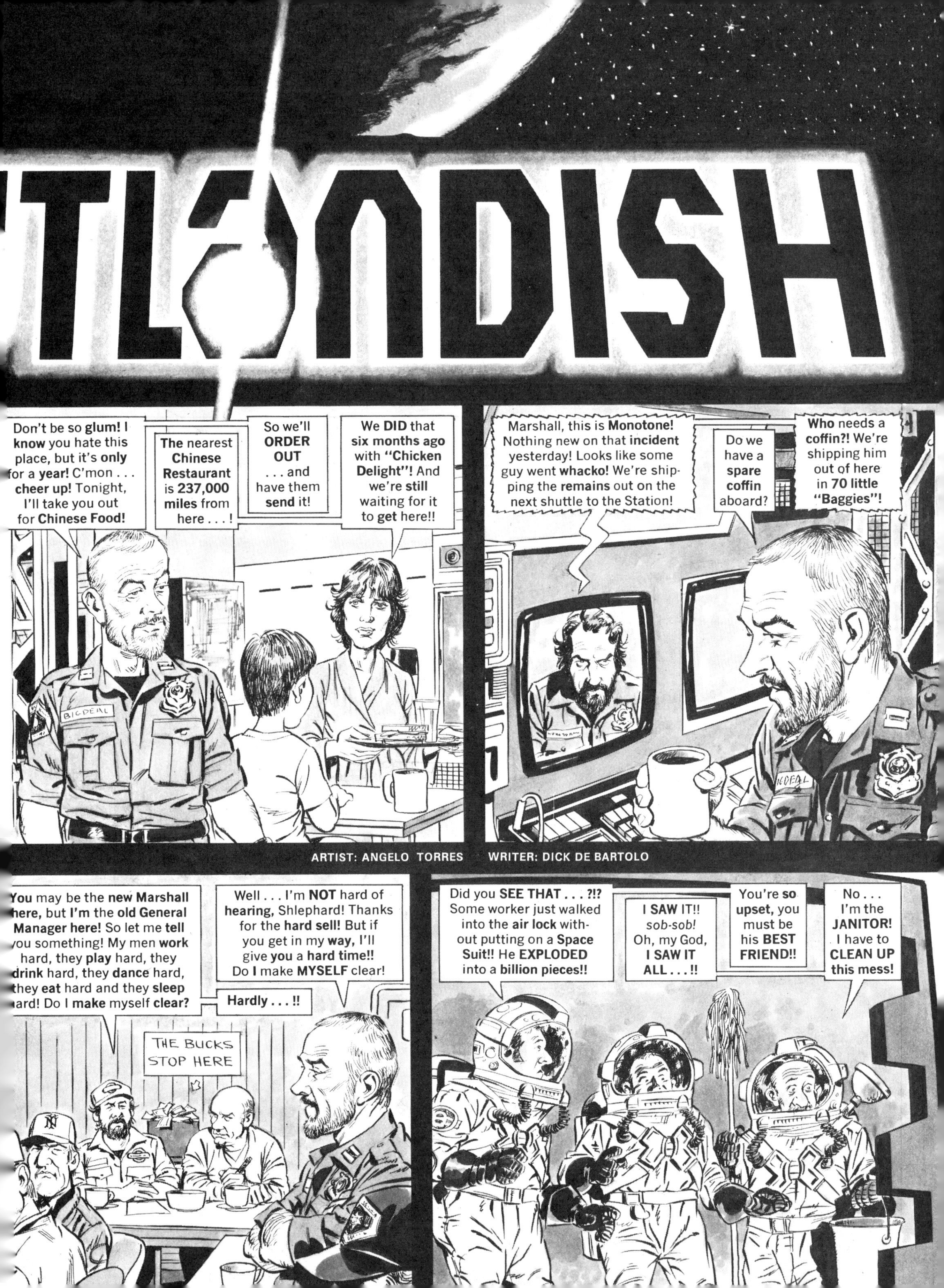
TLANDISH
Don't be so glum! I know you hate this place, but it's only for a year! C'mon . . . cheer up! Tonight, I'll take you out for Chinese Food!
The nearest Chinese Restaurant is 237,000 miles from here . . . !
So we'll ORDER OUT . . . and have them send it!
We DID that six months ago with "Chicken Delight"! And we're still waiting for it to get here!!
BIGDEAL
Marshall, this is Monotone! Nothing new on that incident yesterday! Looks like some guy went whacko! We're shipping the remains out on the next shuttle to the Station!
Do we have a spare coffin aboard?
Who needs a coffin?! We're shipping him out of here in 70 little "Baggies"!
ARTIST: ANGELO TORRES WRITER: DICK DE BARTOLO
You may be the new Marshall here, but I'm the old General Manager here! So let me tell you something! My men work hard, they play hard, they drink hard, they dance hard, they eat hard and they sleep hard! Do I make myself clear?
Well . . . I'm NOT hard of hearing, Shlephard! Thanks for the hard sell! But if you get in my way, I'll give you a hard time!! Do I make MYSELF clear!
Hardly . . . !!
THE BUCKS STOP HERE
Did you SEE THAT . . . ?!? Some worker just walked into the air lock without putting on a Space Suit!! He EXPLODED into a billion pieces!!
I SAW IT!! sob-sob! Oh, my God, I SAW IT ALL . . . !!
You're so upset, you must be his BEST FRIEND!!
No . . . I'm the JANITOR! I have to CLEAN UP this mess!

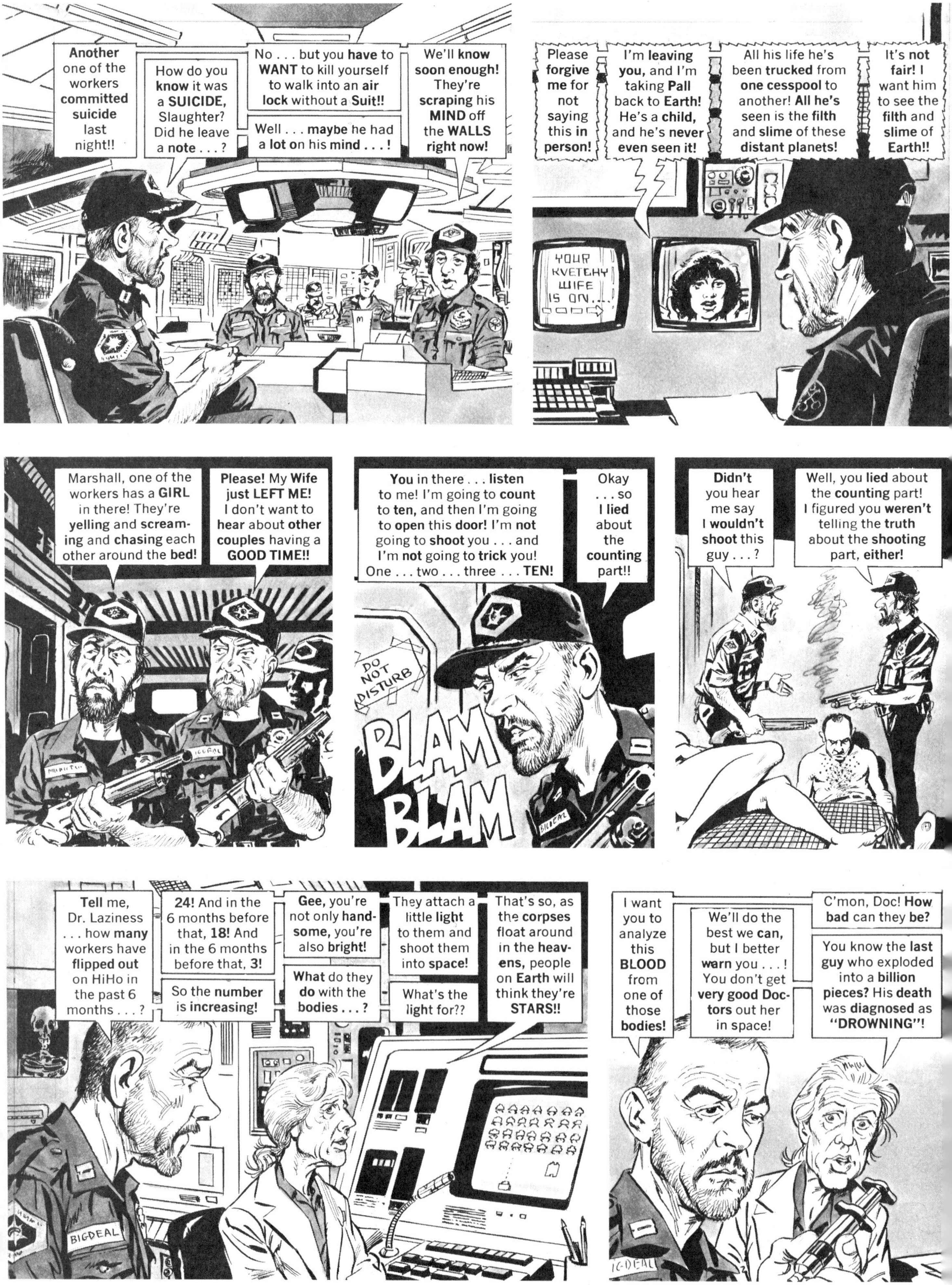
Another one of the workers committed suicide last night!!
How do you know it was a SUICIDE, Slaughter? Did he leave a note . . . ?
No . . . but you have to WANT to kill yourself to walk into an air lock without a Suit!!
Well . . . maybe he had a lot on his mind . . . !
We'll know soon enough! They're scraping his MIND off the WALLS right now!
Please forgive me for not saying this in person!
I'm leaving you, and I'm taking Pall back to Earth! He's a child, and he's never even seen it!
All his life he's been trucked from one cesspool to another! All he's seen is the filth and slime of these distant planets!
It's not fair! I want him to see the filth and slime of Earth!!
YOUR KVETCHY WIFE IS ON...
Marshall, one of the workers has a GIRL in there! They're yelling and screaming and chasing each other around the bed!
Please! My Wife just LEFT ME! I don't want to hear about other couples having a GOOD TIME!!
You in there . . . listen to me! I'm going to count to ten, and then I'm going to open this door! I'm not going to shoot you . . . and I'm not going to trick you! One . . . two . . . three . . . TEN!
Okay . . . so I lied about the counting part!!
DO NOT DISTURB
BLAM
BLAM
Didn't you hear me say I wouldn't shoot this guy . . . ?
Well, you lied about the counting part! I figured you weren't telling the truth about the shooting part, either!
Tell me, Dr. Laziness . . . how many workers have flipped out on HiHo in the past 6 months . . . ?
24! And in the 6 months before that, 18! And in the 6 months before that, 3!
So the number is increasing!
Gee, you're not only handsome, you're also bright!
What do they do with the bodies . . . ?
They attach a little light to them and shoot them into space!
What's the light for??
That's so, as the corpses float around in the heavens, people on Earth will think they're STARS!!
BIGDEAL
I want you to analyze this BLOOD from one of those bodies!
We'll do the best we can, but I better warn you . . . ! You don't get very good Doctors out her in space!
C'mon, Doc! How bad can they be?
You know the last guy who exploded into a billion pieces? His death was diagnosed as "DROWNING"!

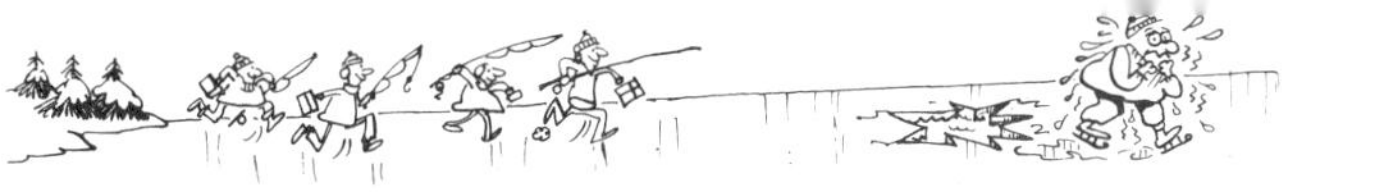

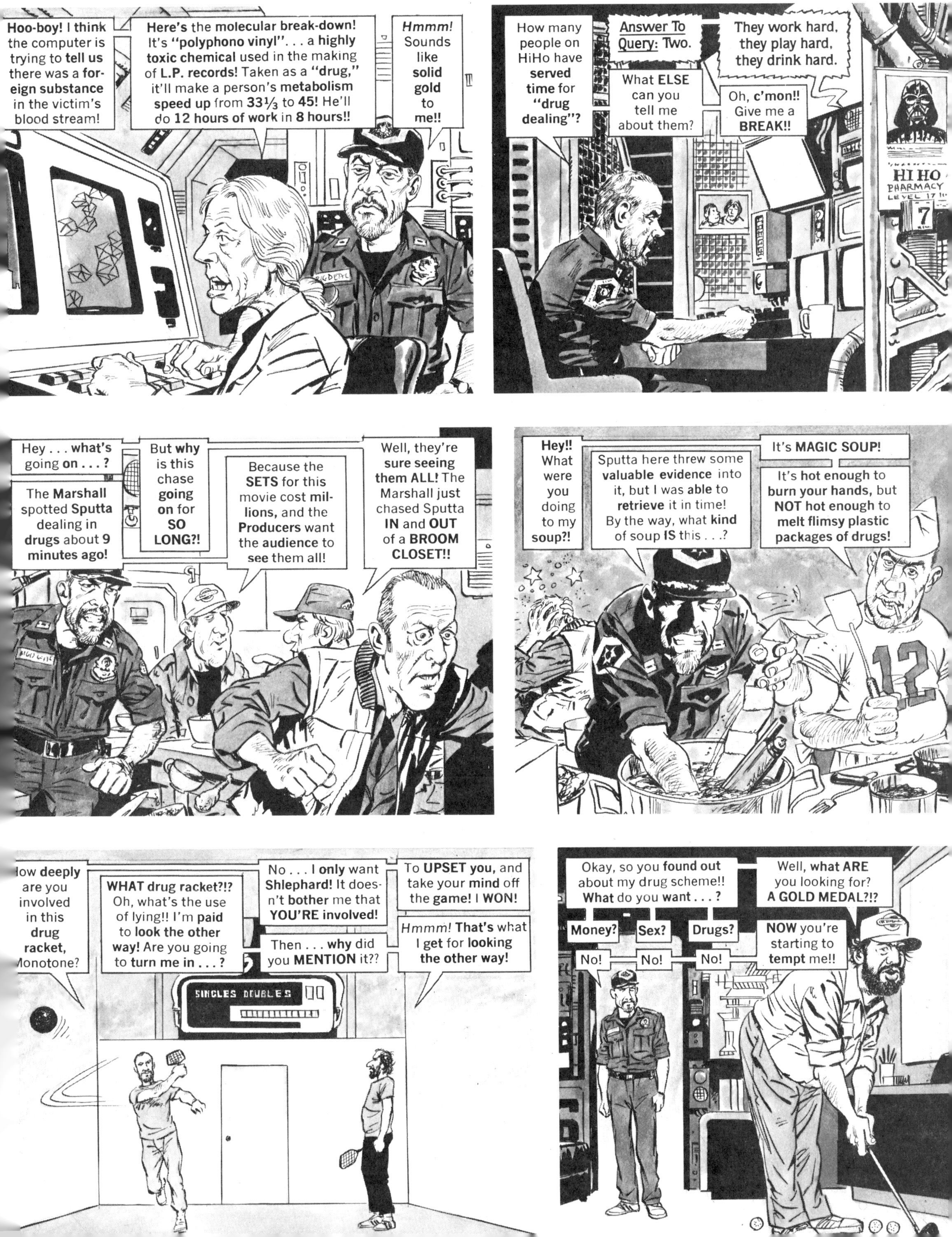
Hoo-boy! I think the computer is trying to tell us there was a foreign substance in the victim's blood stream!
Here's the molecular break-down! It's "polyphono vinyl". . . a highly toxic chemical used in the making of L.P. records! Taken as a "drug," it'll make a person's metabolism speed up from 33⅓ to 45! He'll do 12 hours of work in 8 hours!!
Hmmm! Sounds like solid gold to me!!
How many people on HiHo have served time for "drug dealing"?
Answer To Query: Two.
What ELSE can you tell me about them?
They work hard, they play hard, they drink hard.
Oh, c'mon!! Give me a BREAK!!
HI HO
PHARMACY
LEVEL 17
7
Hey . . . what's going on . . . ?
The Marshall spotted Sputta dealing in drugs about 9 minutes ago!
But why is this chase going on for SO LONG?!
Because the SETS for this movie cost millions, and the Producers want the audience to see them all!
Well, they're sure seeing them ALL! The Marshall just chased Sputta IN and OUT of a BROOM CLOSET!!
Hey!! What were you doing to my soup?!
Sputta here threw some valuable evidence into it, but I was able to retrieve it in time! By the way, what kind of soup IS this . . .?
It's MAGIC SOUP!
It's hot enough to burn your hands, but NOT hot enough to melt flimsy plastic packages of drugs!
12
How deeply are you involved in this drug racket, Monotone?
WHAT drug racket?!? Oh, what's the use of lying!! I'm paid to look the other way! Are you going to turn me in . . . ?
No . . . I only want Shlephard! It doesn't bother me that YOU'RE involved!
Then . . . why did you MENTION it??
To UPSET you, and take your mind off the game! I WON!
Hmmm! That's what I get for looking the other way!
SINGLES DOUBLES
Okay, so you found out about my drug scheme!! What do you want . . . ?
Money?
No!
Sex?
No!
Drugs?
No!
Well, what ARE you looking for? A GOLD MEDAL?!?
NOW you're starting to tempt me!!

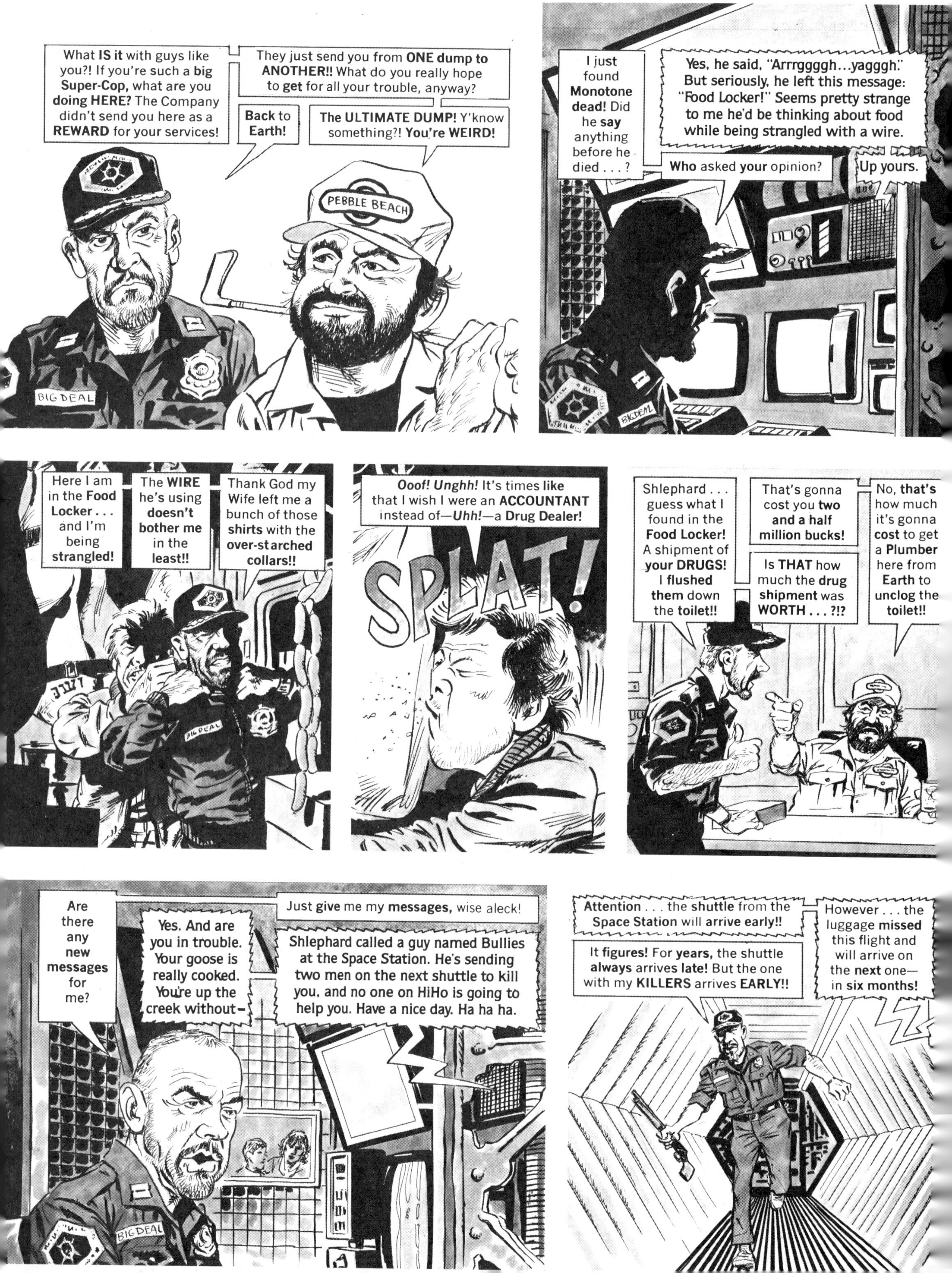

What IS it with guys like you?! If you're such a big Super-Cop, what are you doing HERE? The Company didn't send you here as a REWARD for your services!
They just send you from ONE dump to ANOTHER!! What do you really hope to get for all your trouble, anyway?
Back to Earth!
The ULTIMATE DUMP! Y'know something?! You're WEIRD!
PEBBLE BEACH
BIG DEAL
I just found Monotone dead! Did he say anything before he died . . . ?
Yes, he said, "Arrrggggh…yagggh." But seriously, he left this message: "Food Locker!" Seems pretty strange to me he'd be thinking about food while being strangled with a wire.
Who asked your opinion?
Up yours.
BIG DEAL
Here I am in the Food Locker . . . and I'm being strangled!
The WIRE he's using doesn't bother me in the least!!
Thank God my Wife left me a bunch of those shirts with the over-starched collars!!
BIG DEAL
Ooof! Unghh! It's times like that I wish I were an ACCOUNTANT instead of—Uhh!—a Drug Dealer!
SPLAT!
Shlephard . . . guess what I found in the Food Locker! A shipment of your DRUGS! I flushed them down the toilet!!
That's gonna cost you two and a half million bucks!
Is THAT how much the drug shipment was WORTH . . . ?!?
No, that's how much it's gonna cost to get a Plumber here from Earth to unclog the toilet!!
Are there any new messages for me?
Just give me my messages, wise aleck!
Yes. And are you in trouble. Your goose is really cooked. You're up the creek without-
Shlephard called a guy named Bullies at the Space Station. He's sending two men on the next shuttle to kill you, and no one on HiHo is going to help you. Have a nice day. Ha ha ha.
BIG DEAL
Attention . . . the shuttle from the Space Station will arrive early!!
However . . . the luggage missed this flight and will arrive on the next one—in six months!
It figures! For years, the shuttle always arrives late! But the one with my KILLERS arrives EARLY!!

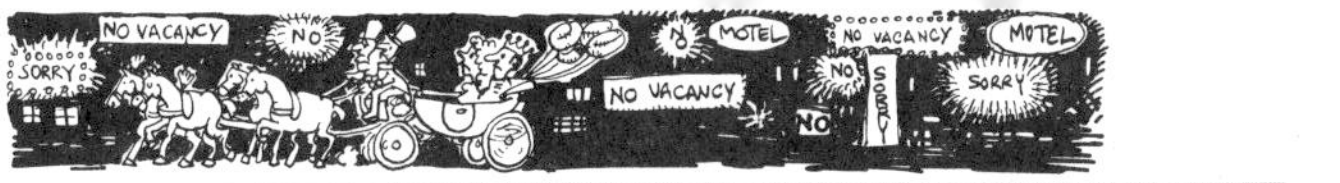
NO VACANCY
NO
SORRY
MOTEL
NO VACANCY
MOTEL
SORRY
NO VACANCY
NO

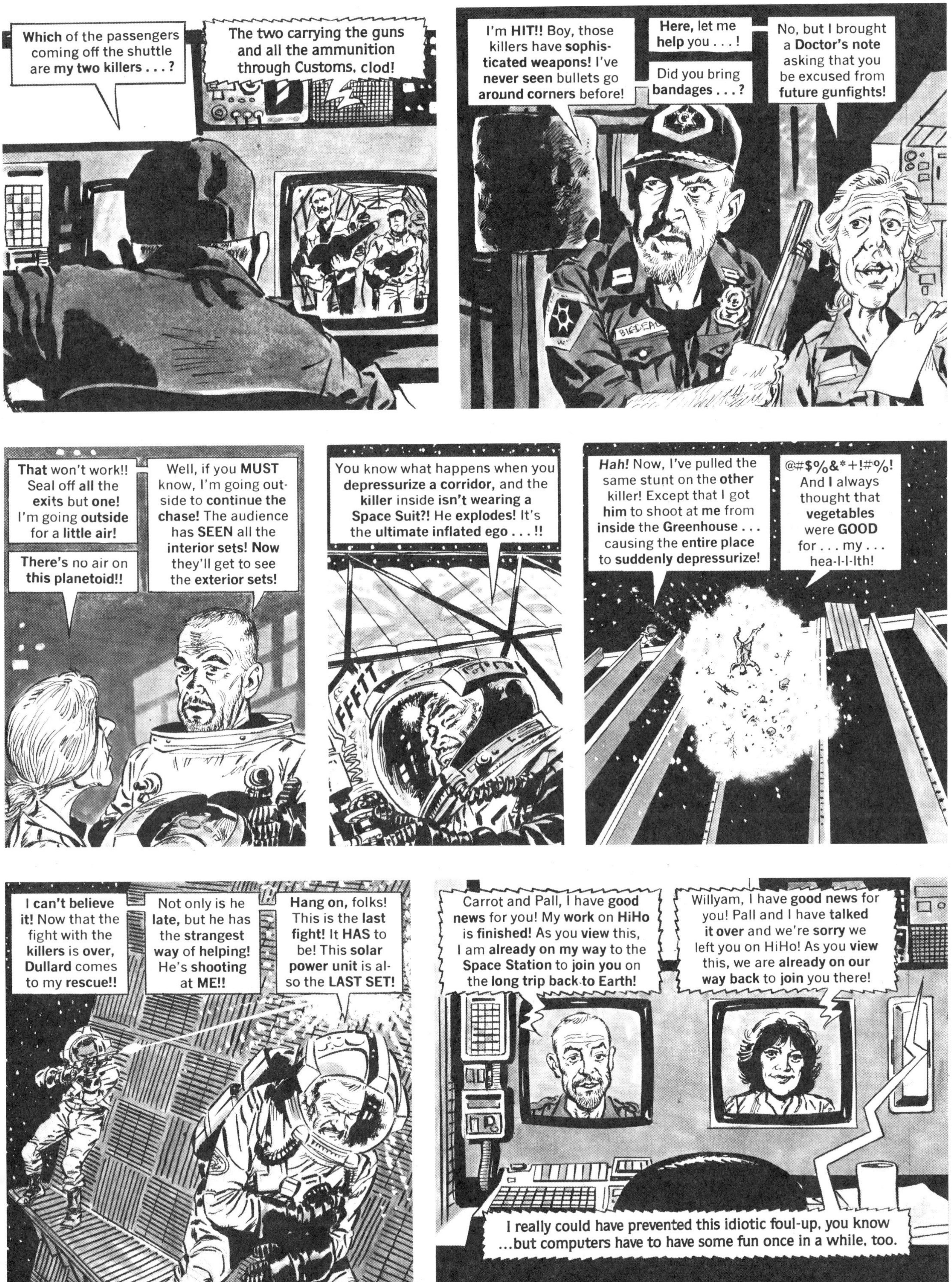
**Which** of the passengers coming off the shuttle are **my two killers . . . ?**
The two carrying the guns and all the ammunition through Customs, clod!
I'm **HIT!!** Boy, those killers have **sophisticated weapons!** I've **never seen** bullets go **around corners** before!
**Here,** let me **help** you . . . !
Did you bring **bandages . . . ?**
No, but I brought a **Doctor's note** asking that you be excused from **future gunfights!**
**That** won't work!! Seal off **all** the **exits** but **one!** I'm going **outside** for a **little air!**
**There's** no air on **this planetoid!!**
Well, if you **MUST** know, I'm going outside to **continue the chase!** The audience has **SEEN** all the **interior sets! Now** they'll get to see the **exterior sets!**
You know what happens when you **depressurize a corridor,** and the **killer** inside **isn't wearing a Space Suit?!** He **explodes!** It's the **ultimate inflated ego . . . !!**
FFFTT
*Hah!* Now, I've pulled the same stunt on the **other** killer! Except that I got **him** to shoot at **me** from **inside** the **Greenhouse . . .** causing the **entire place** to **suddenly depressurize!**
@#$%&*+!#%! And **I** always thought that **vegetables** were **GOOD** for . . . my . . . hea-l-l-lth!
I **can't believe it!** Now that the fight with the **killers** is **over, Dullard** comes to my **rescue!!**
Not only is he **late,** but he has the **strangest way** of **helping!** He's **shooting** at **ME!!**
**Hang on,** folks! This is the **last fight!** It **HAS** to be! This **solar power unit** is also the **LAST SET!**
Carrot and Pall, I have **good news** for you! My **work** on **HiHo** is **finished!** As you **view** this, I am **already on my way** to the **Space Station** to **join you** on the **long trip back to Earth!**
Willyam, I have **good news** for you! Pall and I have **talked it over** and we're **sorry** we left you on HiHo! As you **view** this, we are **already on our way back** to **join** you there!
I really could have prevented this idiotic foul-up, you know ...but computers have to have some fun once in a while, too.

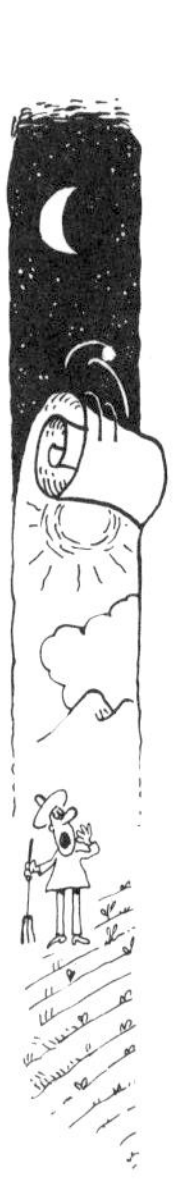

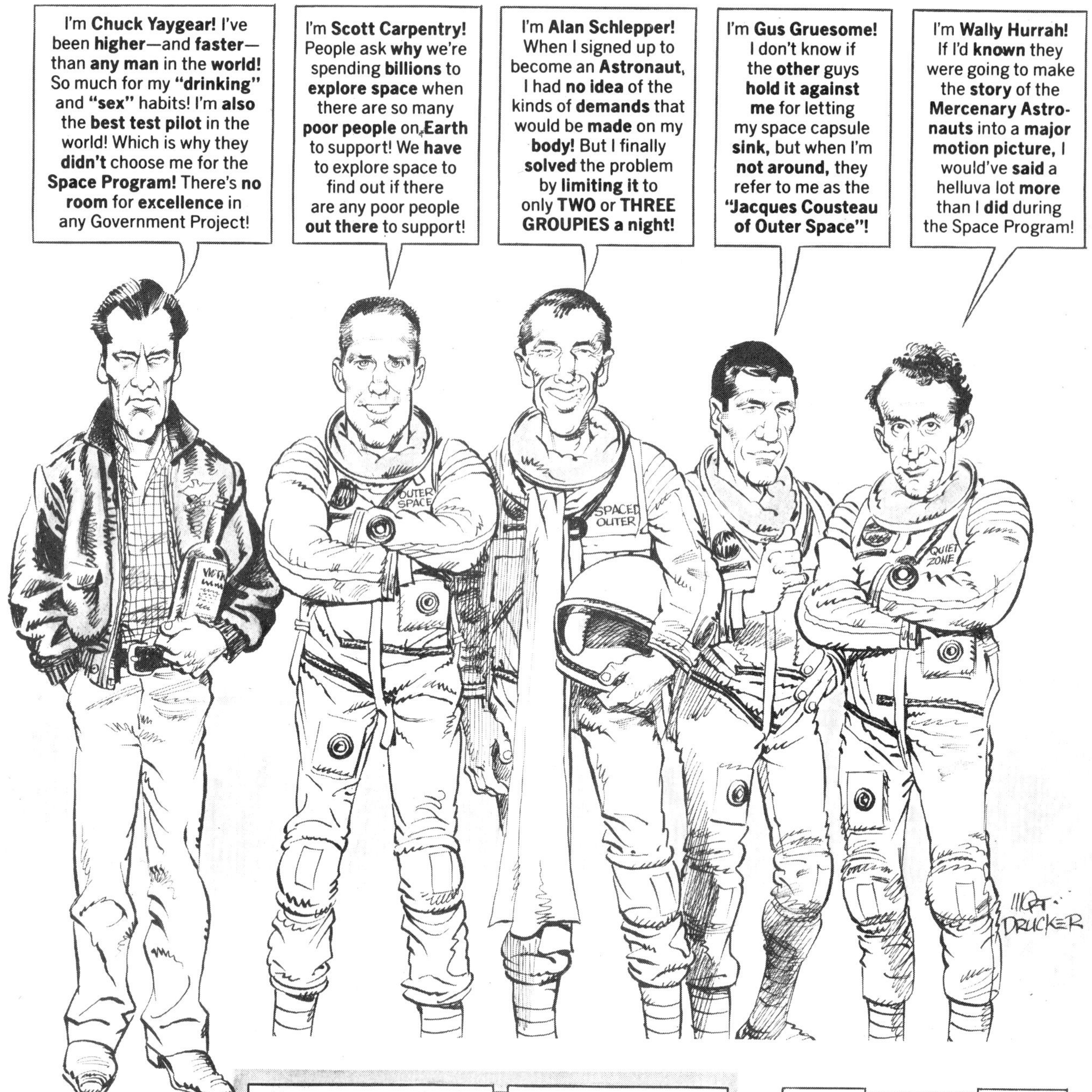

I'm Chuck Yaygear! I've been higher—and faster—than any man in the world! So much for my "drinking" and "sex" habits! I'm also the best test pilot in the world! Which is why they didn't choose me for the Space Program! There's no room for excellence in any Government Project!
I'm Scott Carpentry! People ask why we're spending billions to explore space when there are so many poor people on Earth to support! We have to explore space to find out if there are any poor people out there to support!
I'm Alan Schlepper! When I signed up to become an Astronaut, I had no idea of the kinds of demands that would be made on my body! But I finally solved the problem by limiting it to only TWO or THREE GROUPIES a night!
I'm Gus Gruesome! I don't know if the other guys hold it against me for letting my space capsule sink, but when I'm not around, they refer to me as the "Jacques Cousteau of Outer Space"!
I'm Wally Hurrah! If I'd known they were going to make the story of the Mercenary Astronauts into a major motion picture, I would've said a helluva lot more than I did during the Space Program!
OUTER SPACE
SPACED OUTER
QUIET ZONE


THE VERY FIRST JET PILOTS BELIEVED THAT A DEMON LIVED IN THE SKY, AND THAT WHEN YOU CAME FACE TO FACE WITH IT, YOUR CONTROLS WOULD FREEZE UP, YOUR INSTRUMENTS WOULD SHATTER AND YOU WOULD POOP IN YOUR PANTS. THEY BELIEVED THAT THIS CREATURE LIVED BEHIND A BRICK WALL CALLED THE "SOUND BARRIER." BUT SOME WERE BRAVE ENOUGH TO GO LOOKING FOR THE DEMON. THESE MEN WERE GIVEN SPECIAL EQUIPMENT CALLED "TEST PLANES" AND SPECIAL INSTRUMENTS CALLED "TEST GAUGES." AND THESE MEN WERE CALLED SPECIAL NAMES—LIKE "IDIOT" AND "SCHMUCK"!

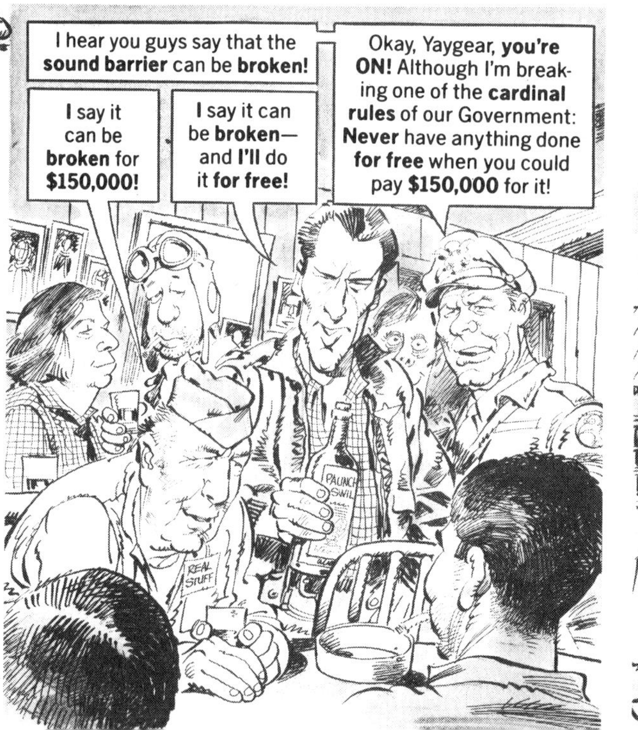

I hear you guys say that the sound barrier can be broken!
I say it can be broken for $150,000!
I say it can be broken—and I'll do it for free!
Okay, Yaygear, you're ON! Although I'm breaking one of the cardinal rules of our Government: Never have anything done for free when you could pay $150,000 for it!
REAL STUFF


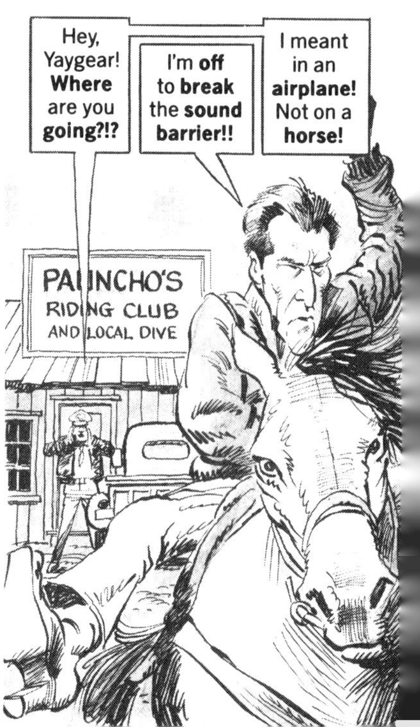

Hey, Yaygear! Where are you going?!?
I'm off to break the sound barrier!!
I meant in an airplane! Not on a horse!
PAUNCHO'S RIDING CLUB AND LOCAL DIVE

BLAST-OFFUL DEPT.

# THESE ARE THE MEN THAT THE GOVERNMENT PICKED WHEN THEY WENT LOOKING FOR...

# THE RIGHT STIFF

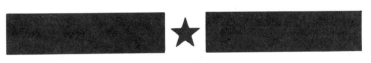

ARTIST: MORT DRUCKER WRITER: DICK DE BARTOLO

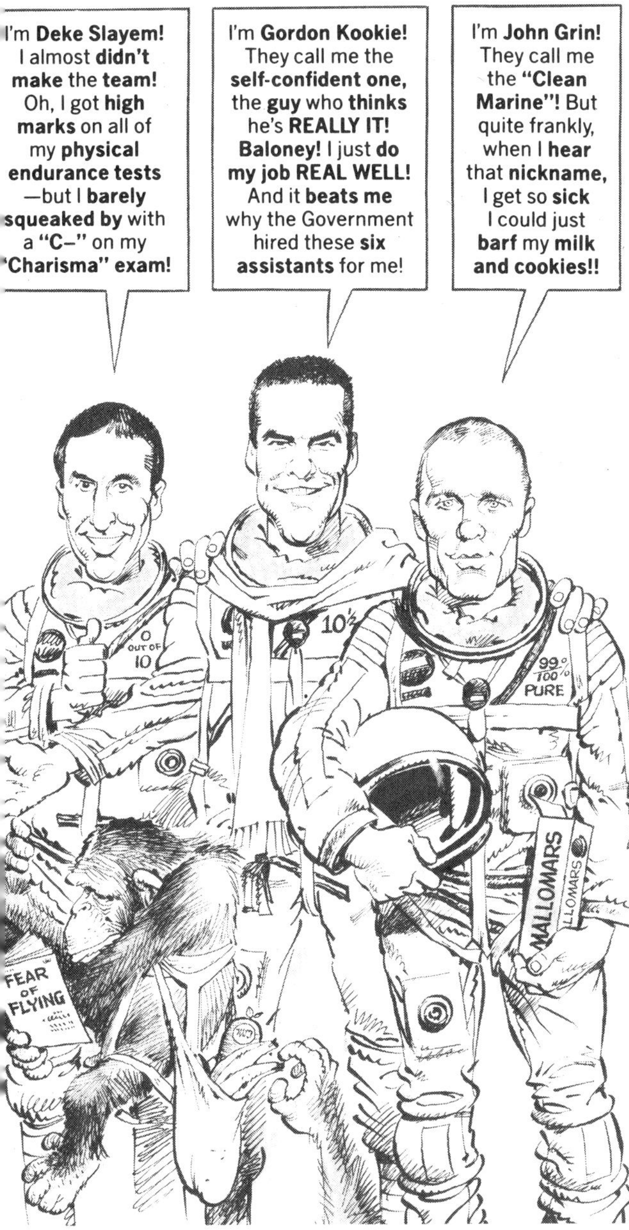

I'm Deke Slayem! I almost didn't make the team! Oh, I got high marks on all of my physical endurance tests—but I barely squeaked by with a "C–" on my "Charisma" exam!
I'm Gordon Kookie! They call me the self-confident one, the guy who thinks he's REALLY IT! Baloney! I just do my job REAL WELL! And it beats me why the Government hired these six assistants for me!
I'm John Grin! They call me the "Clean Marine"! But quite frankly, when I hear that nickname, I get so sick I could just barf my milk and cookies!!
0 OUT OF 10
10½
99 9/10 /100 PURE
MALLOMARS
FEAR OF FLYING


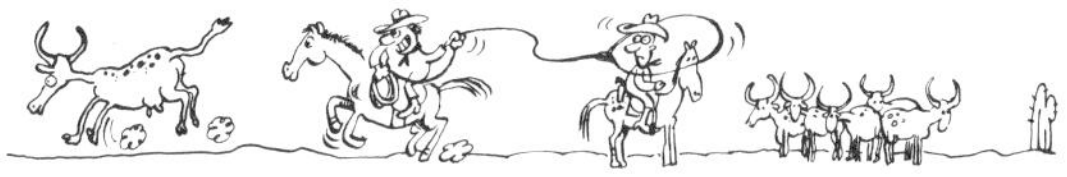

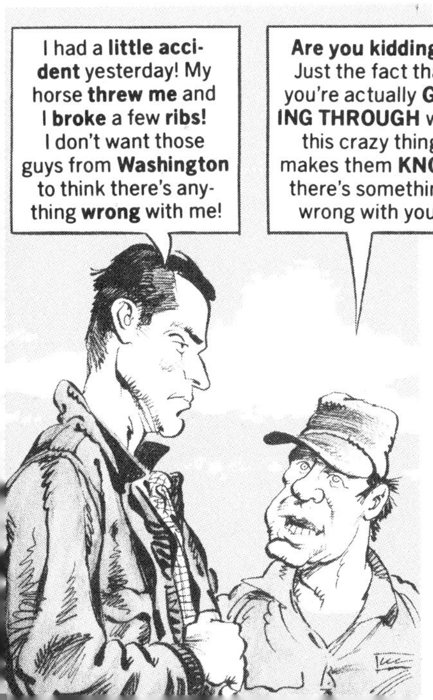

I had a little accident yesterday! My horse threw me and I broke a few ribs! I don't want those guys from Washington to think there's anything wrong with me!
Are you kidding?! Just the fact that you're actually GOING THROUGH with this crazy thing makes them KNOW there's something wrong with you!


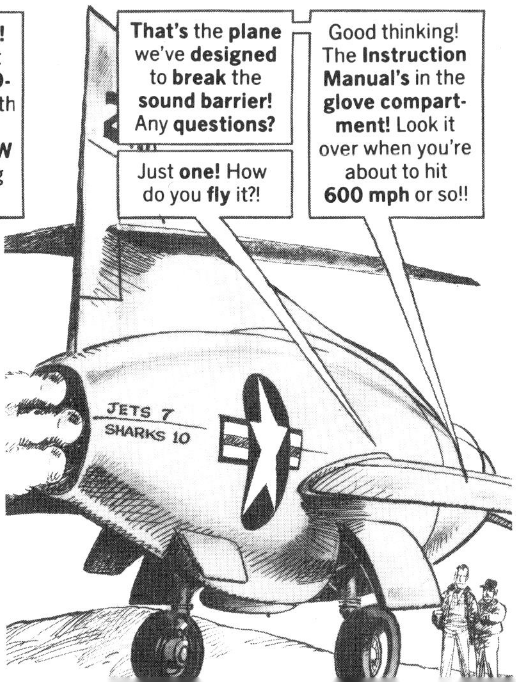

That's the plane we've designed to break the sound barrier! Any questions?
Just one! How do you fly it?!
Good thinking! The Instruction Manual's in the glove compartment! Look it over when you're about to hit 600 mph or so!!
JETS 7
SHARKS 10


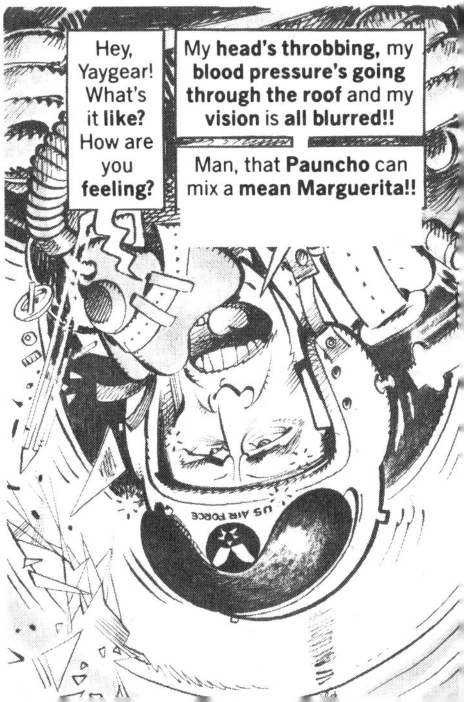

Hey, Yaygear! What's it like? How are you feeling?
My head's throbbing, my blood pressure's going through the roof and my vision is all blurred!!
Man, that Pauncho can mix a mean Marguerita!!
US AIR FORCE

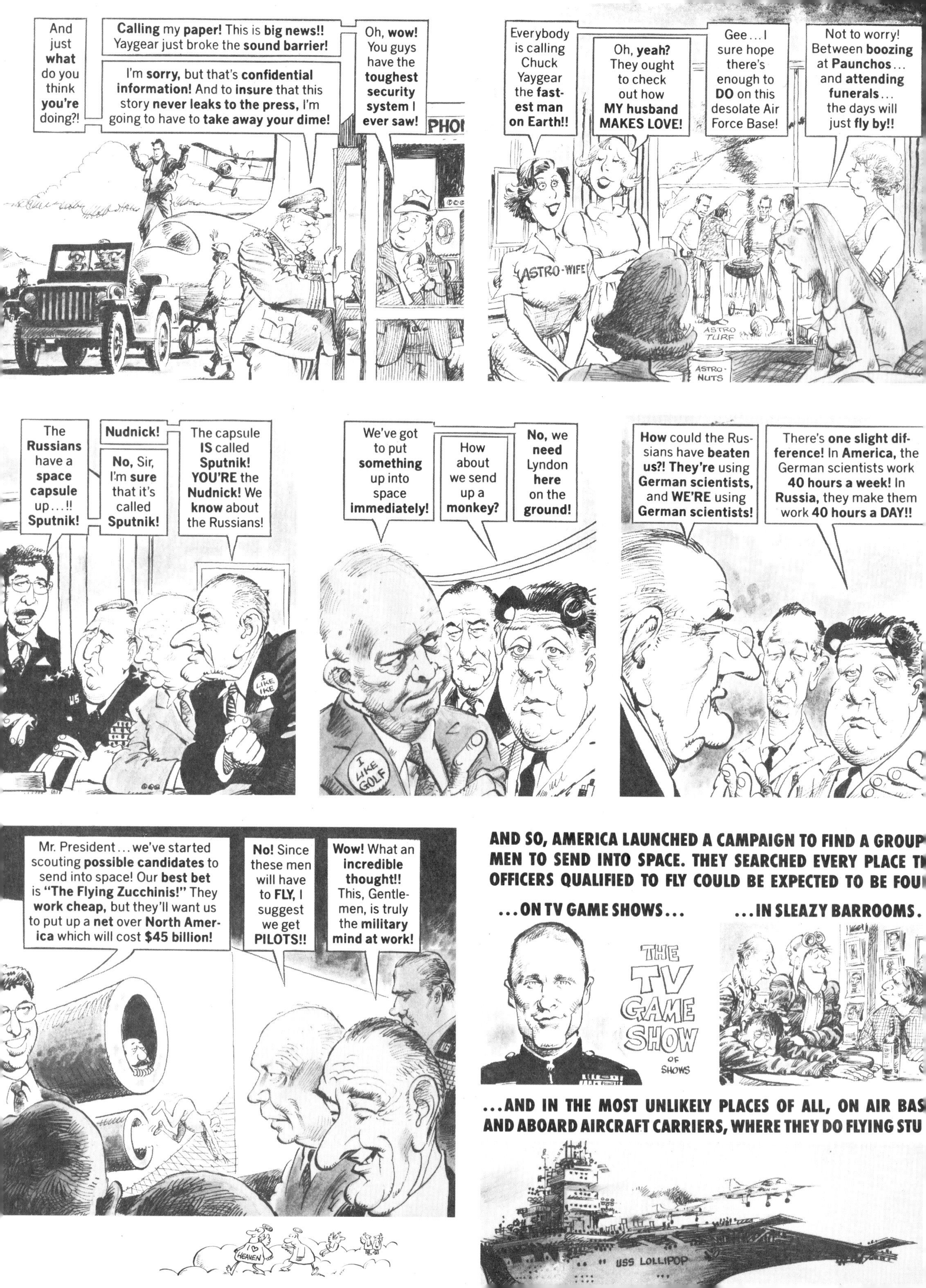
And just what do you think you're doing?!
Calling my paper! This is big news!! Yaygear just broke the sound barrier!
I'm sorry, but that's confidential information! And to insure that this story never leaks to the press, I'm going to have to take away your dime!
Oh, wow! You guys have the toughest security system I ever saw!
PHON
Everybody is calling Chuck Yaygear the fast-est man on Earth!!
Oh, yeah? They ought to check out how MY husband MAKES LOVE!
Gee... I sure hope there's enough to DO on this desolate Air Force Base!
Not to worry! Between boozing at Paunchos... and attending funerals... the days will just fly by!!
ASTRO-WIFE
ASTRO TURF
ASTRO-NUTS
The Russians have a space capsule up...!! Sputnik!
Nudnick!
No, Sir, I'm sure that it's called Sputnik!
The capsule IS called Sputnik! YOU'RE the Nudnick! We know about the Russians!
US
I LIKE IKE
We've got to put something up into space immediately!
How about we send up a monkey?
No, we need Lyndon here on the ground!
I LIKE GOLF
How could the Russians have beaten us?! They're using German scientists, and WE'RE using German scientists!
There's one slight difference! In America, the German scientists work 40 hours a week! In Russia, they make them work 40 hours a DAY!!
Mr. President... we've started scouting possible candidates to send into space! Our best bet is "The Flying Zucchinis!" They work cheap, but they'll want us to put up a net over North America which will cost $45 billion!
No! Since these men will have to FLY, I suggest we get PILOTS!!
Wow! What an incredible thought!! This, Gentlemen, is truly the military mind at work!
US
I ♥ HEAVEN
AND SO, AMERICA LAUNCHED A CAMPAIGN TO FIND A GROUP
MEN TO SEND INTO SPACE. THEY SEARCHED EVERY PLACE TH
OFFICERS QUALIFIED TO FLY COULD BE EXPECTED TO BE FOU
...ON TV GAME SHOWS...
...IN SLEAZY BARROOMS.
THE TV GAME SHOW OF SHOWS
...AND IN THE MOST UNLIKELY PLACES OF ALL, ON AIR BAS
AND ABOARD AIRCRAFT CARRIERS, WHERE THEY DO FLYING STU
USS LOLLIPOP

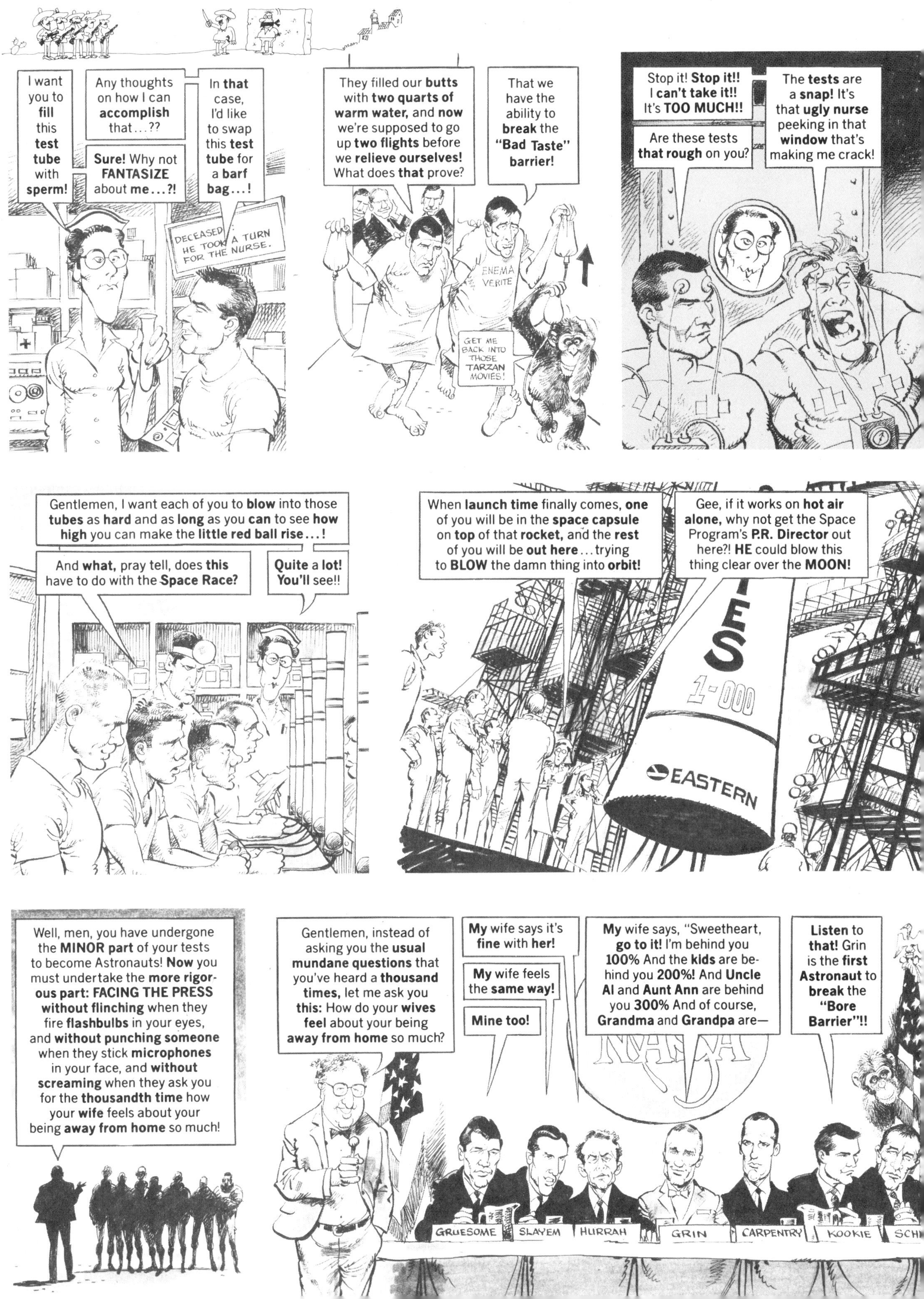

I want you to **fill** this **test tube** with **sperm!**
Any thoughts on how I can **accomplish** that...??
Sure! Why not **FANTASIZE** about **me...?!**
In **that** case, I'd like to swap this **test tube** for a **barf bag...!**
DECEASED: HE TOOK A TURN FOR THE NURSE.
They filled our **butts** with **two quarts of warm water,** and **now** we're supposed to go up **two flights** before we **relieve ourselves!** What does **that** prove?
That we have the ability to **break** the **"Bad Taste" barrier!**
ENEMA VERITE
GET ME BACK INTO THOSE TARZAN MOVIES!
Stop it! **Stop it!!** I **can't take it!!** It's **TOO MUCH!!**
Are these tests **that rough** on you?
The **tests** are a **snap!** It's that **ugly nurse** peeking in that **window** that's making me crack!
Gentlemen, I want each of you to **blow** into those **tubes** as **hard** and as **long** as you **can** to see **how high** you can make the **little red ball rise...!**
And **what,** pray tell, does **this** have to do with the **Space Race?**
**Quite** a **lot! You'll** see!!
When **launch time** finally comes, **one** of you will be in the **space capsule** on **top** of that **rocket,** and the **rest** of you will be **out here**... trying to **BLOW** the damn thing into **orbit!**
Gee, if it works on **hot air alone,** why not get the Space Program's **P.R. Director** out here?! **HE** could blow this thing clear over the **MOON!**
1-000
EASTERN
Well, men, you have undergone the **MINOR part** of your tests to become Astronauts! **Now** you must undertake the **more rigorous part: FACING THE PRESS without flinching** when they fire **flashbulbs** in your eyes, and **without punching someone** when they stick **microphones** in your face, and **without screaming** when they ask you for the **thousandth time** how your **wife** feels about your being **away from home** so much!
Gentlemen, instead of asking you the **usual mundane questions** that you've heard a **thousand times,** let me ask you **this:** How do your **wives feel** about your being **away from home** so much?
**My** wife says it's **fine** with **her!**
**My** wife feels the **same way!**
**Mine too!**
**My** wife says, "Sweetheart, **go to it!** I'm behind you **100%** And the **kids** are behind you **200%!** And **Uncle Al** and **Aunt Ann** are behind you **300%** And of course, **Grandma** and **Grandpa** are—
**Listen** to **that!** Grin is the **first Astronaut** to **break** the **"Bore Barrier"!!**
NASA
GRUESOME
SLAYEM
HURRAH
GRIN
CARPENTRY
KOOKIE

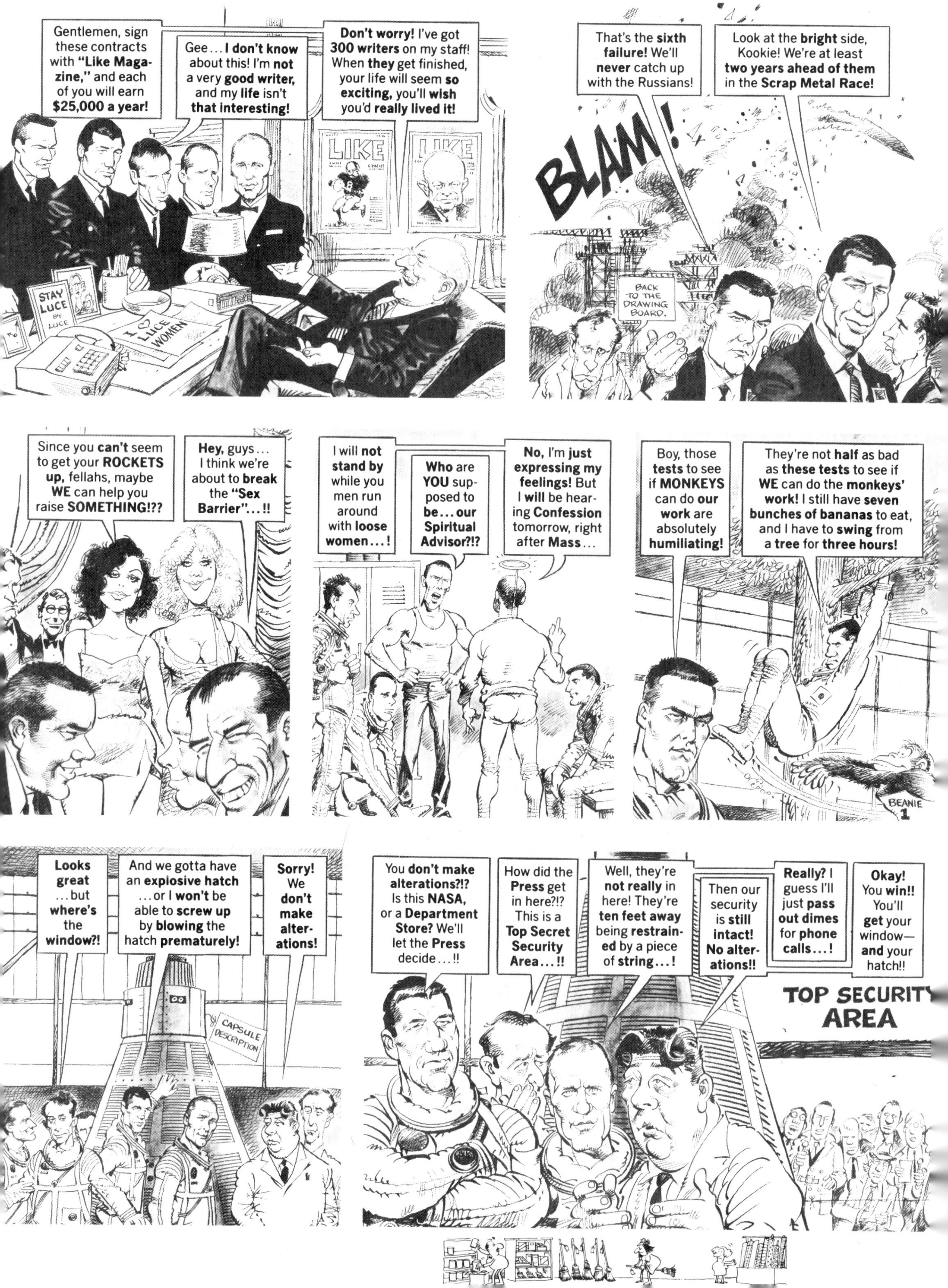

Gentlemen, sign these contracts with "Like Magazine," and each of you will earn $25,000 a year!
Gee... I don't know about this! I'm not a very good writer, and my life isn't that interesting!
Don't worry! I've got 300 writers on my staff! When they get finished, your life will seem so exciting, you'll wish you'd really lived it!
LIKE
LIKE
STAY LUCE BY LUCE
I ♥ LUCE WOMEN
That's the sixth failure! We'll never catch up with the Russians!
Look at the bright side, Kookie! We're at least two years ahead of them in the Scrap Metal Race!
BLAM!
BACK TO THE DRAWING BOARD.
Since you can't seem to get your ROCKETS up, fellahs, maybe WE can help you raise SOMETHING!??
Hey, guys... I think we're about to break the "Sex Barrier"...!!
I will not stand by while you men run around with loose women...!
Who are YOU supposed to be... our Spiritual Advisor?!?
No, I'm just expressing my feelings! But I will be hearing Confession tomorrow, right after Mass...
Boy, those tests to see if MONKEYS can do our work are absolutely humiliating!
They're not half as bad as these tests to see if WE can do the monkeys' work! I still have seven bunches of bananas to eat, and I have to swing from a tree for three hours!
BEANIE 1
Looks great ...but where's the window?!
And we gotta have an explosive hatch ...or I won't be able to screw up by blowing the hatch prematurely!
Sorry! We don't make alterations!
CAPSULE DESCRIPTION
You don't make alterations?!? Is this NASA, or a Department Store? We'll let the Press decide...!!
How did the Press get in here?!? This is a Top Secret Security Area...!!
Well, they're not really in here! They're ten feet away being restrained by a piece of string...!
Then our security is still intact! No alterations!!
Really? I guess I'll just pass out dimes for phone calls...!
Okay! You win!! You'll get your window—and your hatch!!
TOP SECURITY AREA

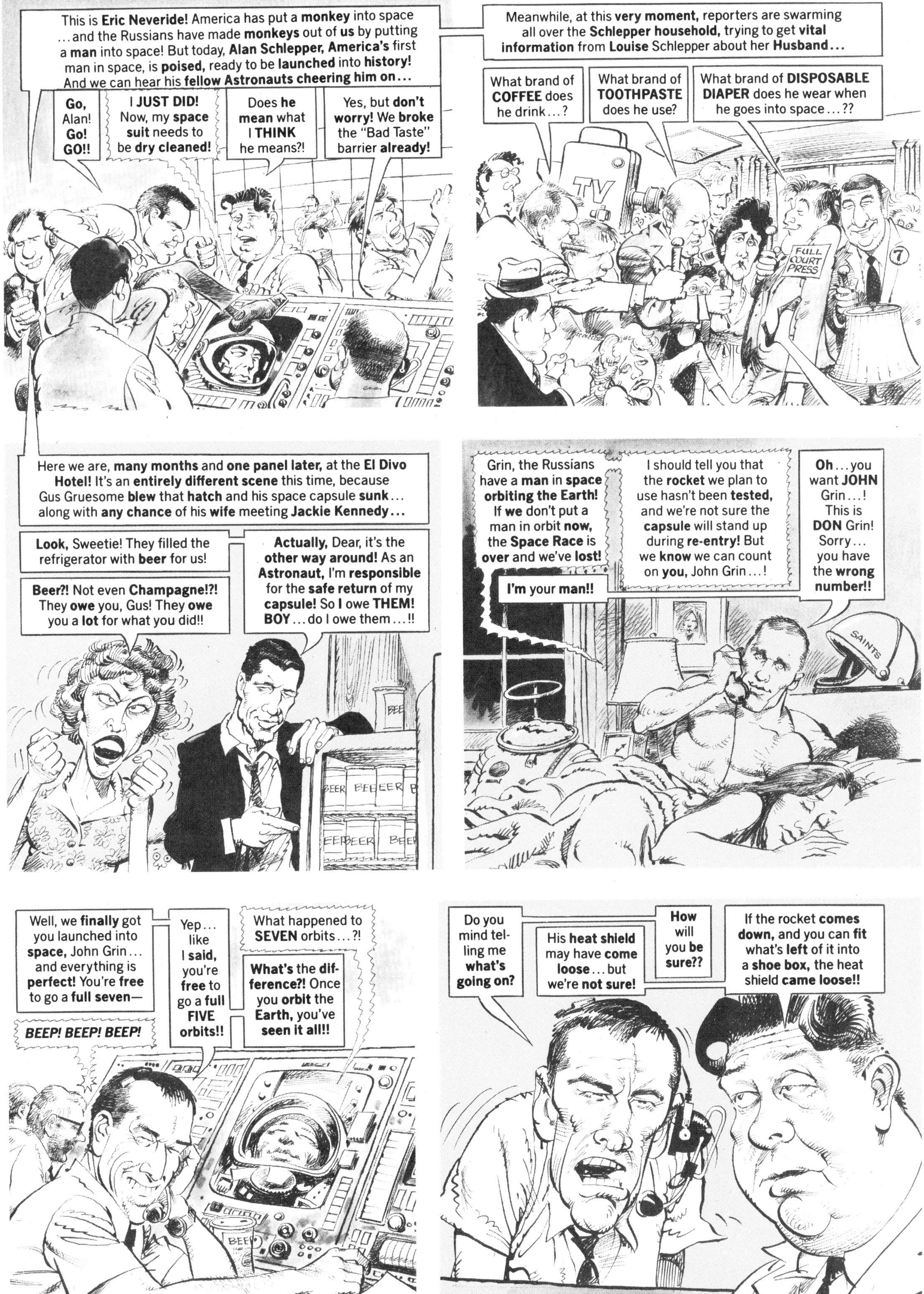
This is **Eric Neveride!** America has put a **monkey** into space . . . and the Russians have made **monkeys** out of **us** by putting a **man** into space! But today, **Alan Schlepper, America's** first man in space, is **poised,** ready to be **launched** into **history!** And we can hear his **fellow Astronauts cheering him on . . .**
**Go,** Alan! **Go! GO!!**
I **JUST DID!** Now, my **space suit** needs to be **dry cleaned!**
Does **he mean** what I **THINK** he means?!
Yes, but **don't worry!** We **broke** the "Bad Taste" barrier **already!**
Meanwhile, at this **very moment,** reporters are swarming all over the **Schlepper household,** trying to get **vital information** from **Louise** Schlepper about her **Husband . . .**
What brand of **COFFEE** does he drink . . . ?
What brand of **TOOTHPASTE** does he use?
What brand of **DISPOSABLE DIAPER** does he wear when he goes into space . . . ??
TV
FULL COURT PRESS
7
Here we are, **many months** and **one panel later,** at the **El Divo Hotel!** It's an **entirely different scene** this time, because Gus Gruesome **blew** that **hatch** and his space capsule **sunk . . .** along with **any chance** of his **wife** meeting **Jackie Kennedy . . .**
**Look,** Sweetie! They filled the refrigerator with **beer** for us!
**Beer?!** Not even **Champagne!?!** They **owe** you, Gus! They **owe** you a **lot** for what you did!!
**Actually,** Dear, it's the **other way around!** As an **Astronaut,** I'm **responsible** for the **safe return** of my **capsule!** So **I** owe **THEM! BOY . . .** do I owe them . . . !!
BEER
Grin, the Russians have a **man** in **space orbiting the Earth!** If **we** don't put a man in orbit **now,** the **Space Race** is **over** and we've **lost!**
I should tell you that the **rocket** we plan to use hasn't been **tested,** and we're not sure the **capsule** will stand up during **re-entry!** But we **know** we can count on **you,** John Grin . . . !
**I'm** your **man!!**
**Oh . . .** you want **JOHN** Grin . . . ! This is **DON** Grin! Sorry . . . you have the **wrong number!!**
SAINTS
Well, we **finally** got you launched into **space,** John Grin . . . and everything is **perfect!** You're **free** to go a **full seven—**
***BEEP! BEEP! BEEP!***
Yep . . . like **I said,** you're **free** to go a **full FIVE orbits!!**
What happened to **SEVEN** orbits . . . ?!
**What's** the **difference?!** Once you **orbit** the **Earth,** you've **seen it all!!**
Do you mind telling me **what's going on?**
His **heat shield** may have **come loose . . .** but we're **not sure!**
**How** will you **be sure??**
If the rocket **comes down,** and you can **fit** what's **left** of it into a **shoe box,** the heat shield **came loose!!**

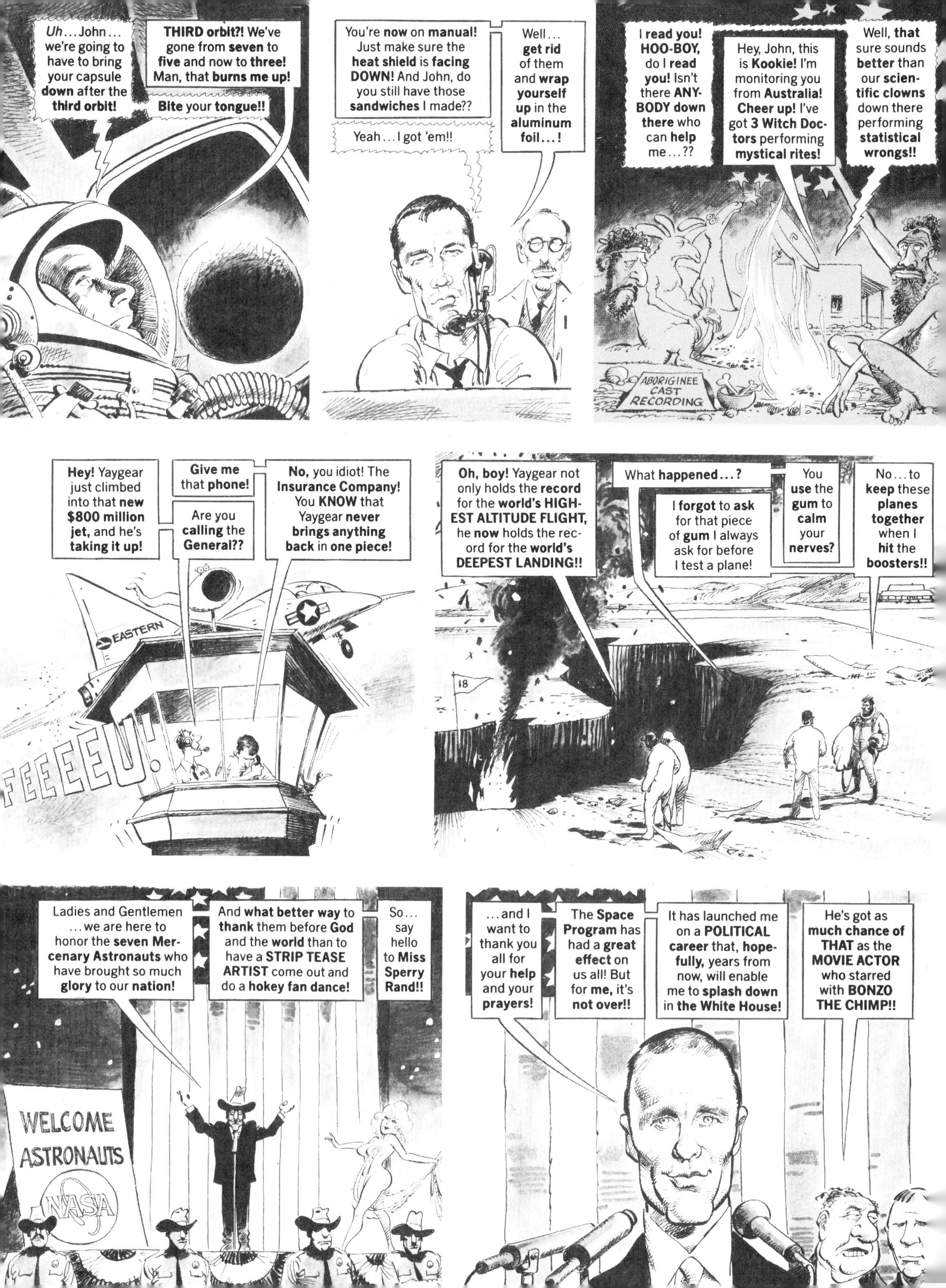
Uh... John... we're going to have to bring your capsule down after the third orbit!
THIRD orbit?! We've gone from seven to five and now to three! Man, that burns me up!
Bite your tongue!!
You're now on manual! Just make sure the heat shield is facing DOWN! And John, do you still have those sandwiches I made??
Yeah... I got 'em!!
Well... get rid of them and wrap yourself up in the aluminum foil...!
I read you! HOO-BOY, do I read you! Isn't there ANYBODY down there who can help me...??
Hey, John, this is Kookie! I'm monitoring you from Australia! Cheer up! I've got 3 Witch Doctors performing mystical rites!
Well, that sure sounds better than our scientific clowns down there performing statistical wrongs!!
ABORIGINEE CAST RECORDING
Hey! Yaygear just climbed into that new $800 million jet, and he's taking it up!
Are you calling the General??
Give me that phone!
No, you idiot! The Insurance Company! You KNOW that Yaygear never brings anything back in one piece!
EASTERN
FEEEEU!
Oh, boy! Yaygear not only holds the record for the world's HIGHEST ALTITUDE FLIGHT, he now holds the record for the world's DEEPEST LANDING!!
18
What happened...?
I forgot to ask for that piece of gum I always ask for before I test a plane!
You use the gum to calm your nerves?
No... to keep these planes together when I hit the boosters!!
Ladies and Gentlemen ...we are here to honor the seven Mercenary Astronauts who have brought so much glory to our nation!
And what better way to thank them before God and the world than to have a STRIP TEASE ARTIST come out and do a hokey fan dance!
So... say hello to Miss Sperry Rand!!
WELCOME ASTRONAUTS
NASA
...and I want to thank you all for your help and your prayers!
The Space Program has had a great effect on us all! But for me, it's not over!!
It has launched me on a POLITICAL career that, hopefully, years from now, will enable me to splash down in the White House!
He's got as much chance of THAT as the MOVIE ACTOR who starred with BONZO THE CHIMP!!

TRITE & TRUE DEPT.

# MAD'S "LATE SHOW" CLICHÉ MOVIE SCRIPT

ARTIST: BRUCE STARK    WRITER: HARRY PURVIS

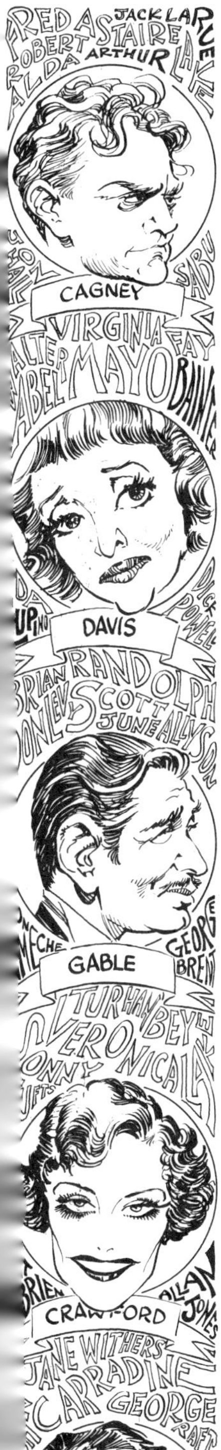
CAGNEY
DAVIS
GABLE
CRAWFORD

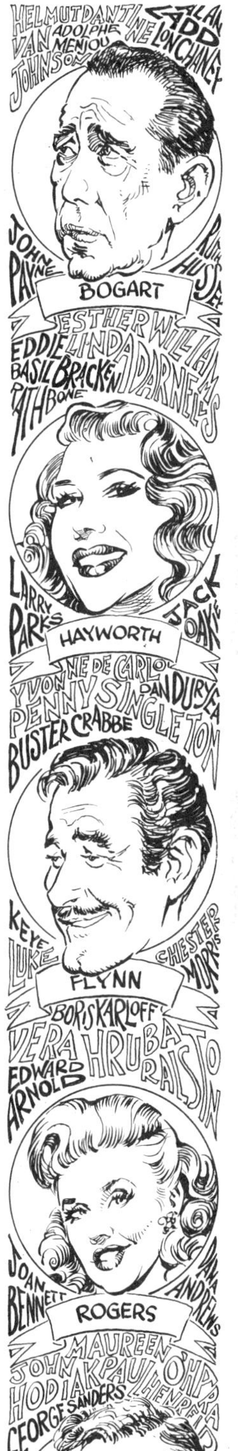
BOGART
HAYWORTH
FLYNN
ROGERS

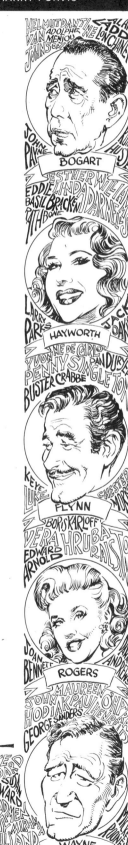

## THE "WAR" MOVIE

"Before this training period is over, you guys are gonna hate my guts! But if you live through it . . . someday, you'll thank me for it!"

* * * * * *

"We're not running this war for your personal pleasure, Bradshaw! Tonight, by disobeying orders, you endangered the life of every man in this company! Maybe back in Civilian life you could pull things like that, being Senator Bradshaw's son! But here in this Boot Camp, you're just plain PRIVATE Bradshaw!"

* * * * * *

"Any of you guys got any letters to write, you got exactly two minutes! Because we're shipping out!"

* * * * * *

"Don't let 'im get your goat, kid. She'll wait. Not all dames are like that. Simpson's just sore 'cause he ain't got no one to come back to."

* * * * * *

"I'll go crazy if I don't see some action soon!"

* * * * * *

"Men, we're up against an enemy who'll stop at nothing to hold this island! So, good luck! And . . . give 'em hell!"

* * * * * *

"Okay, I need some volunteers for this mission . . . Anderson, Brown, Cowznofski, DeGrazzo, Hanlon, MacNutt, O'Reilly and Silverstein! Now, let's see . . . <u>what</u> have I missed? Oh, yeah--you, too, Sun Luck Chow!"

* * * * * *

"I know you didn't ask to come out here, Bradshaw--but by God, now that you ARE here, you'll fight! Now <u>I'll</u> tell YOU something . . . first time out, <u>I</u> was afraid, too! Yeah, ME! Does that surprise you?"

* * * * * *

"You can't ask them to do it, Colonel! They've been looking forward to this leave for months! It's all that's kept them going! Now, to tell them they've been ordered back into action . . . it--it just isn't fair!"

* * * * * *

"I wish Arkansas would learn a new tune! That one's driving me nuts!"

* * * * * *

"Boy, what I wouldn't give to be back on Flatbush Avenue, watchin' all the blondes go by! How about you, Bradshaw? Any real-stacked blondes up on Snob Hill? Hey . . . where ya goin' . . . ?"

* * * * * *

"The last thing he said was--'Tell the Sarge this one's for Benny!'"

* * * * * *

"He wiped out that machine gun nest single-handed! And to think I once called him 'yellow'!"

* * * * * *

"When I see those fresh green kids coming up, eager to fight, it makes me want to cry. I was like that once. It seems like so many years ago. It's hard to believe we've only been on this island 5 days!"

* * * * * *

"Think it'll do any good, Padre? All this killing and dying, I mean . . ."

* * * * * *

". . . and the generations to come will remember what it was like, and what it was all for! Have no fear of that, my son!"

THE END

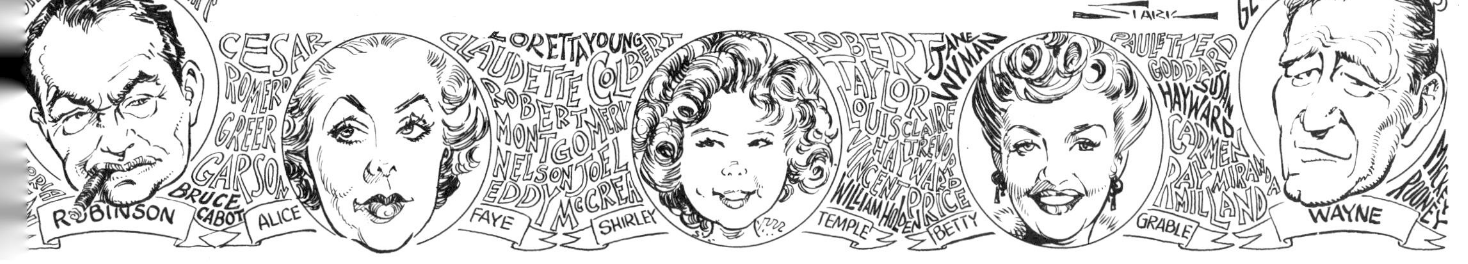
ROBINSON
ALICE
FAYE
SHIRLEY
TEMPLE
BETTY
GRABLE
WAYNE

**OUR CREATURES PRESENTATION DEPT.**

**Two summers ago, Steven Spielberg gave us "E.T.", a smash-hit film about a cuddly alien who has to withstand the villainies of us humans to get back home. This summer, Steven's come up with another smash-hit film—with an extra-added wrinkle. Oh, sure, there's a cuddly creature in it again! Why give up a good thing? But now, there are also a lot of evil creatures, too. And they're attacking us humans! But enough of this prose. Look at the pictures...and try reading MAD's version of...**

# GRI

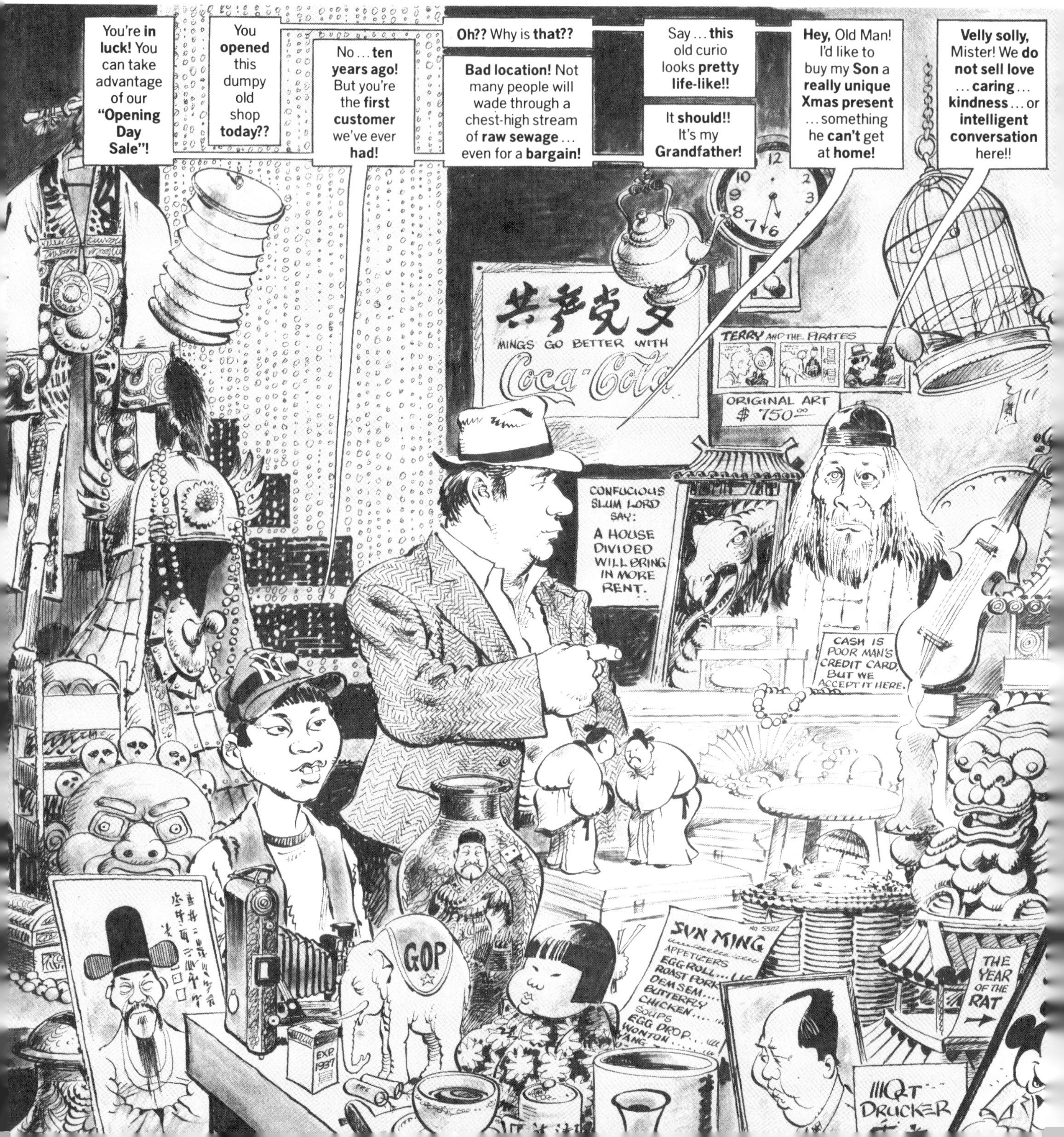

You're in luck! You can take advantage of our "Opening Day Sale"!
You opened this dumpy old shop today??
No... ten years ago! But you're the first customer we've ever had!
Oh?? Why is that??
Bad location! Not many people will wade through a chest-high stream of raw sewage... even for a bargain!
Say... this old curio looks pretty life-like!!
It should!! It's my Grandfather!
Hey, Old Man! I'd like to buy my Son a really unique Xmas present ...something he can't get at home!
Velly solly, Mister! We do not sell love ...caring... kindness... or intelligent conversation here!!
MINGS GO BETTER WITH
Coca-Cola
TERRY AND THE PIRATES
ORIGINAL ART $ 750.00
CONFUCIOUS SLUM LORD SAY: A HOUSE DIVIDED WILL BRING IN MORE RENT.
CASH IS POOR MAN'S CREDIT CARD, BUT WE ACCEPT IT HERE.
GOP
EXP. 1937
SUN MING
APPETIZERS
EGG ROLL...
ROAST PORK...
DEM SEM...
BUTTERFLY CHICKEN...
SOUPS
EGG DROP...
WONTON
THE YEAR OF THE RAT
DRUCKER

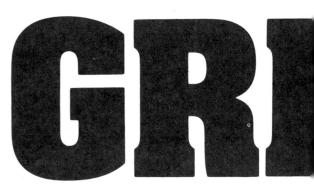

# MLINS

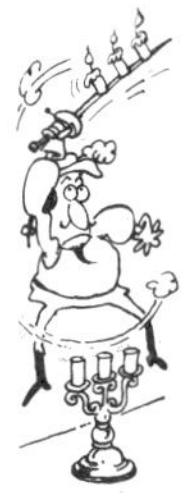

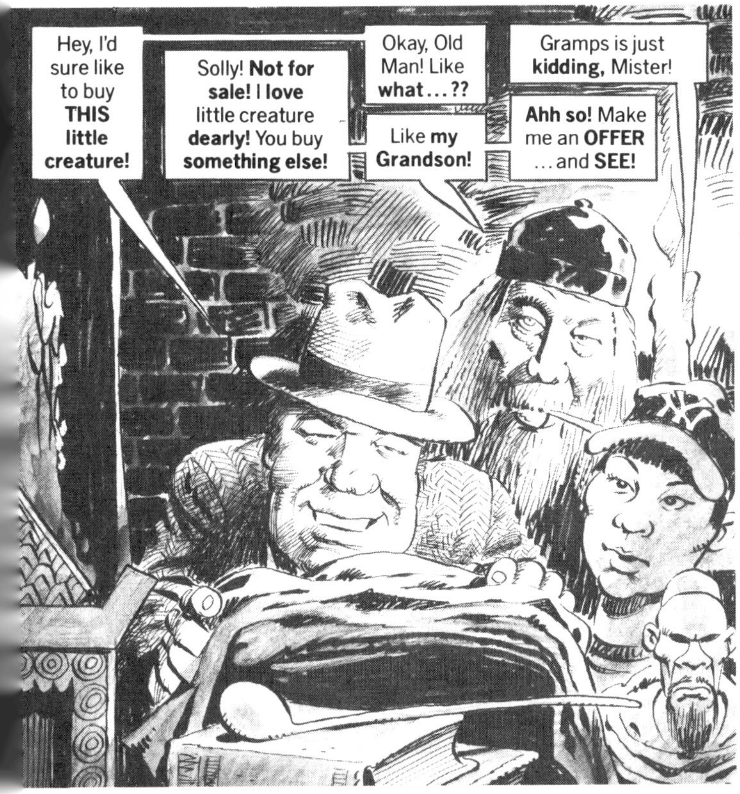

Hey, I'd sure like to buy **THIS little creature!**
Solly! **Not for sale! I love** little creature **dearly!** You buy **something else!**
Okay, Old Man! Like **what . . . ??**
Like **my Grandson!**
Gramps is just **kidding,** Mister!
**Ahh so!** Make me an **OFFER . . . and SEE!**


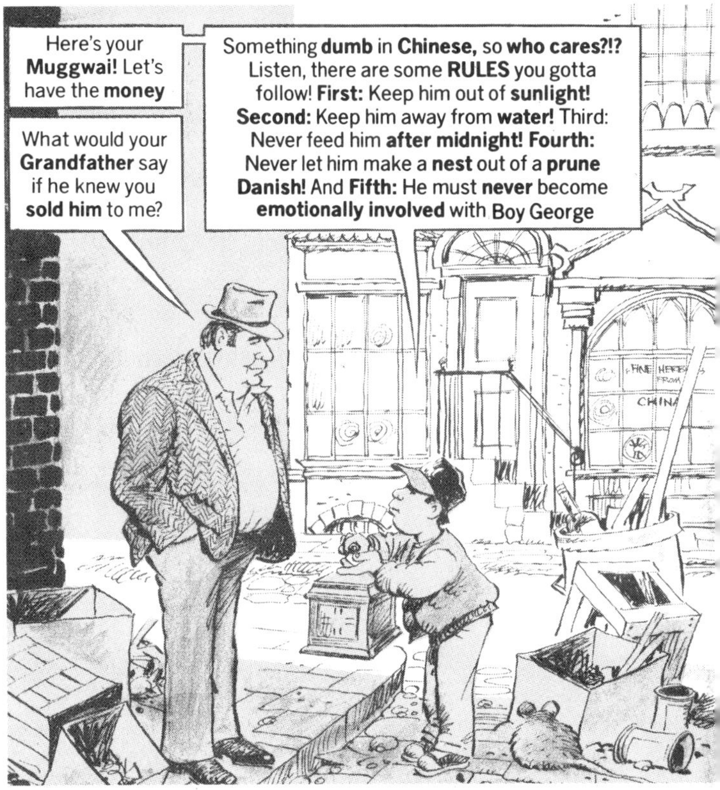

Here's your **Muggwai!** Let's have the **money**
What would your **Grandfather** say if he knew you **sold him** to me?
Something **dumb** in **Chinese,** so **who cares?!?** Listen, there are some **RULES** you gotta follow! **First:** Keep him out of **sunlight! Second:** Keep him away from **water!** Third: Never feed him **after midnight! Fourth:** Never let him make a **nest** out of a **prune Danish!** And **Fifth:** He must **never** become **emotionally involved** with Boy George
FINE HERBS FROM CHINA


**ARTIST: MORT DRUCKER** **WRITER: STAN HART**

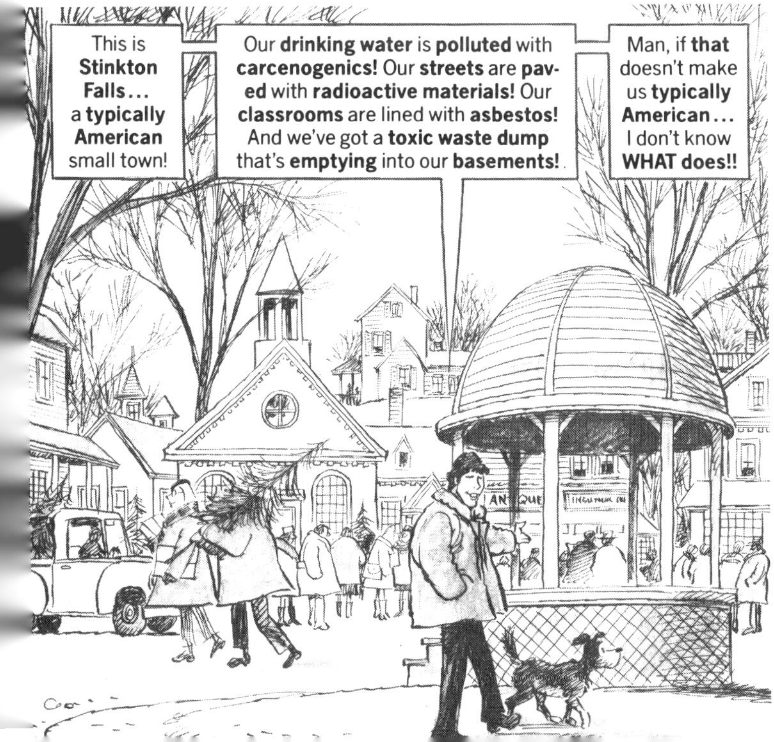

This is **Stinkton Falls . . .** a **typically American** small town!
Our **drinking water** is **polluted** with **carcenogenics!** Our **streets** are **paved** with **radioactive materials!** Our **classrooms** are lined with **asbestos!** And we've got a **toxic waste dump** that's **emptying** into our **basements!**
Man, if **that** doesn't make us **typically American . . .** I don't know **WHAT does!!**


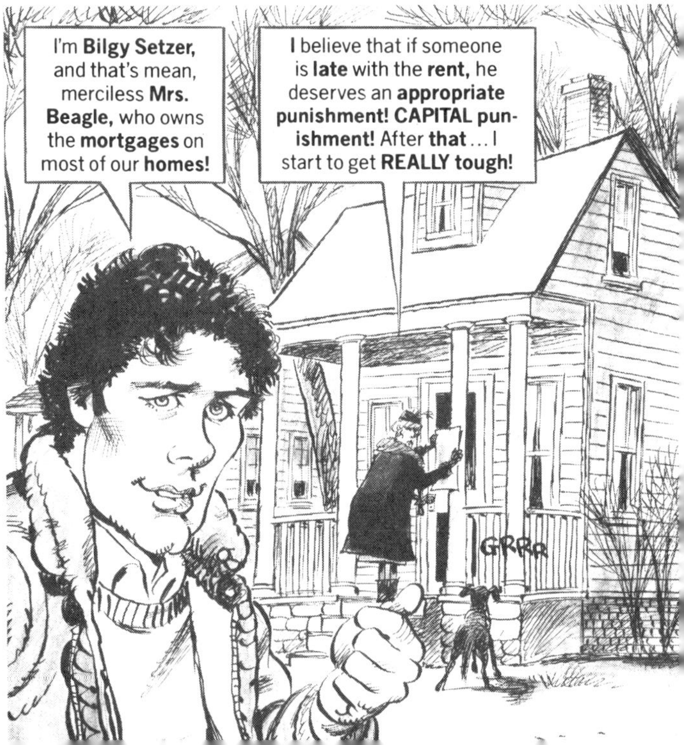

I'm **Bilgy Setzer,** and that's mean, merciless **Mrs. Beagle,** who owns the **mortgages** on most of our **homes!**
**I** believe that if someone is **late** with the **rent,** he deserves an **appropriate punishment! CAPITAL punishment!** After **that . . .** I start to get **REALLY tough!**
GRRR

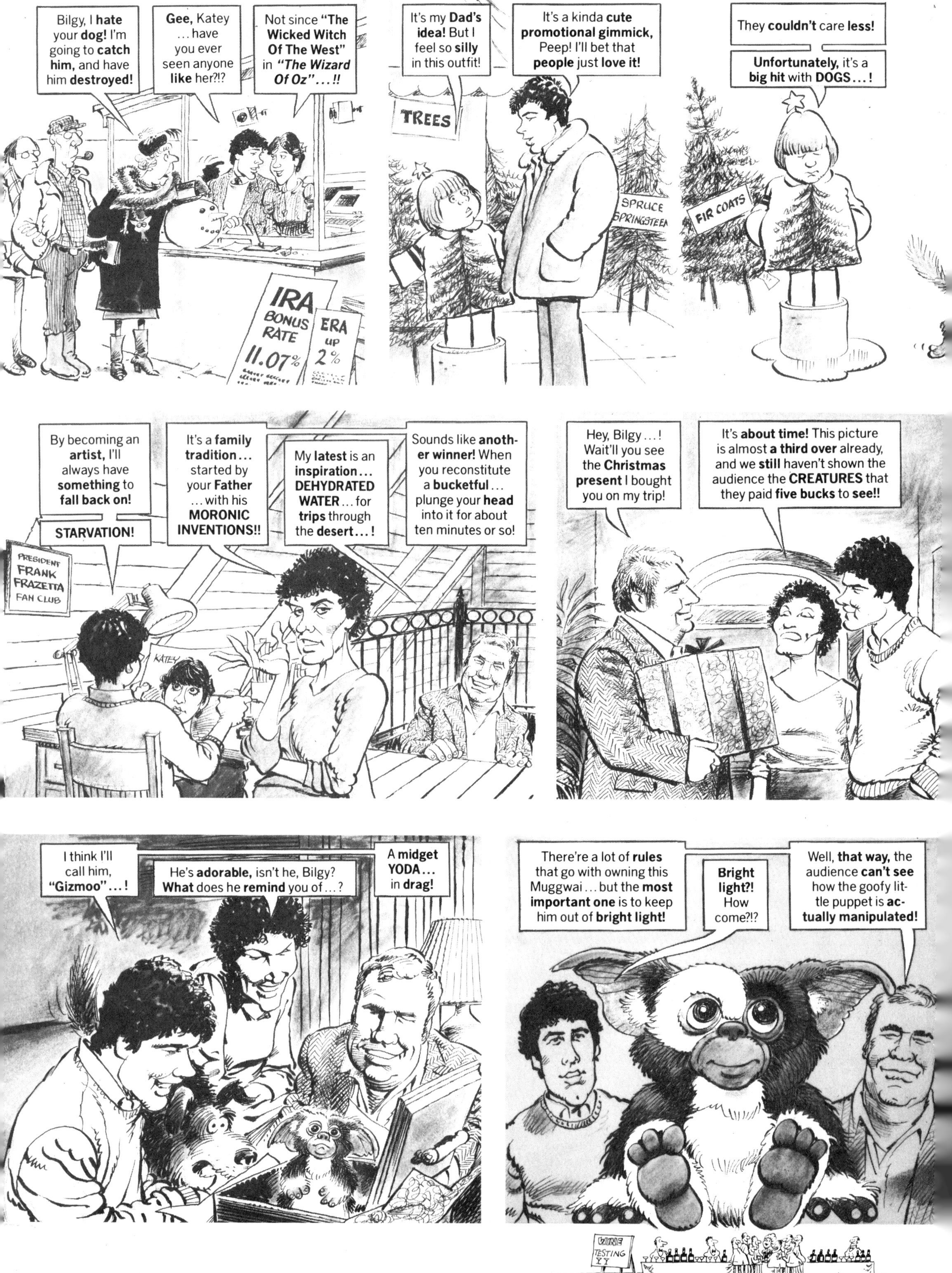

Bilgy, I hate your dog! I'm going to catch him, and have him destroyed!
Gee, Katey ... have you ever seen anyone like her?!?
Not since "The Wicked Witch Of The West" in "The Wizard Of Oz"...!!
IRA BONUS RATE 11.07%
ERA up 2%
It's my Dad's idea! But I feel so silly in this outfit!
It's a kinda cute promotional gimmick, Peep! I'll bet that people just love it!
TREES
SPRUCE SPRINGSTEEN
They couldn't care less!
Unfortunately, it's a big hit with DOGS...!
FIR COATS
By becoming an artist, I'll always have something to fall back on!
STARVATION!
It's a family tradition... started by your Father ... with his MORONIC INVENTIONS!!
My latest is an inspiration... DEHYDRATED WATER... for trips through the desert...!
Sounds like another winner! When you reconstitute a bucketful... plunge your head into it for about ten minutes or so!
PRESIDENT FRANK FRAZETTA FAN CLUB
KATEY
Hey, Bilgy...! Wait'll you see the Christmas present I bought you on my trip!
It's about time! This picture is almost a third over already, and we still haven't shown the audience the CREATURES that they paid five bucks to see!!
I think I'll call him, "Gizmoo"...!
He's adorable, isn't he, Bilgy? What does he remind you of...?
A midget YODA... in drag!
There're a lot of rules that go with owning this Muggwai... but the most important one is to keep him out of bright light!
Bright light?! How come?!?
Well, that way, the audience can't see how the goofy little puppet is actually manipulated!
WINE TESTING

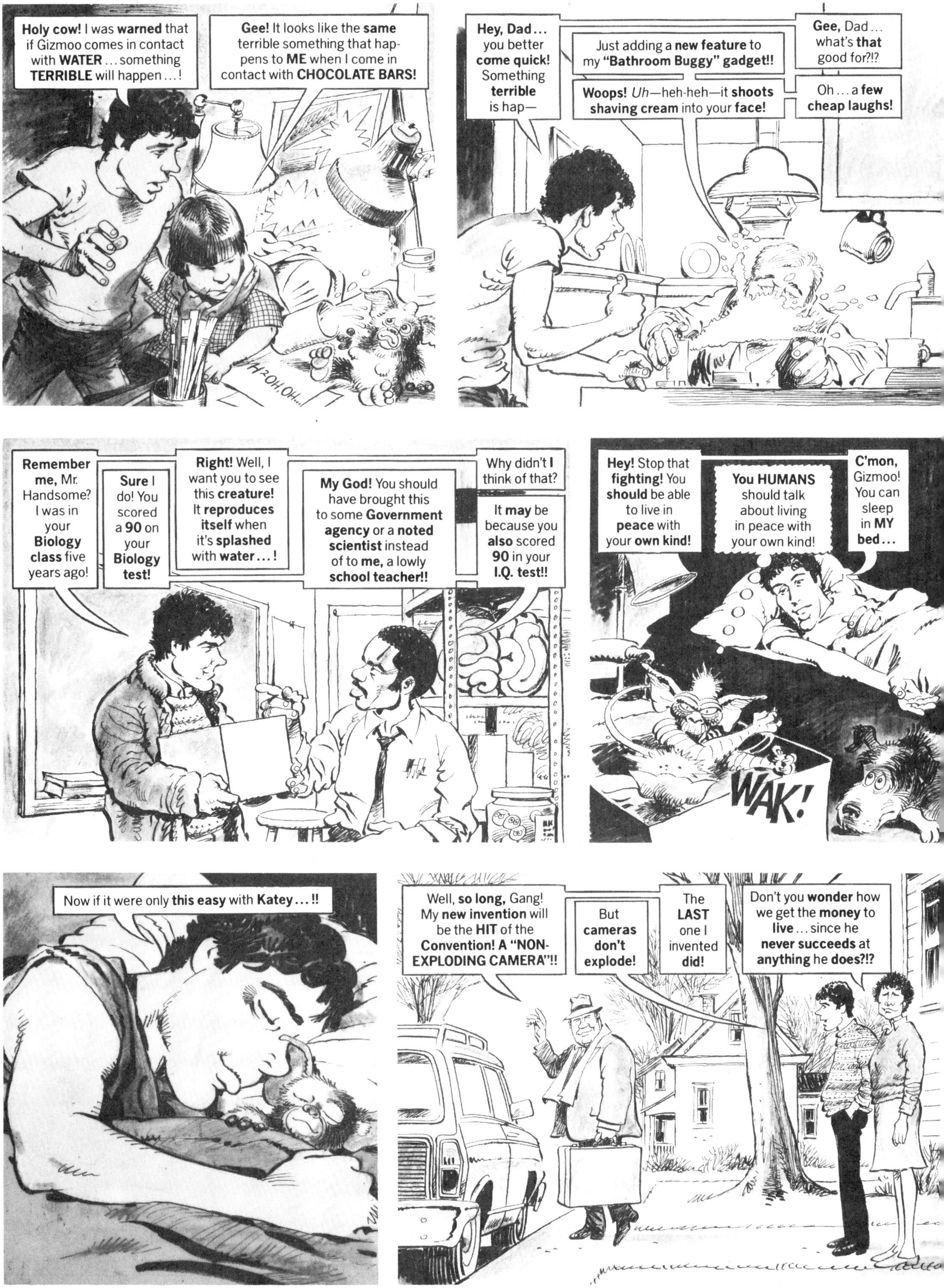

Holy cow! I was warned that if Gizmoo comes in contact with WATER ... something TERRIBLE will happen ...!
Gee! It looks like the same terrible something that happens to ME when I come in contact with CHOCOLATE BARS!
H2OH,OH...
Hey, Dad ... you better come quick! Something terrible is hap—
Just adding a new feature to my "Bathroom Buggy" gadget!!
Woops! Uh—heh-heh—it shoots shaving cream into your face!
Gee, Dad ... what's that good for?!?
Oh ... a few cheap laughs!
Remember me, Mr. Handsome? I was in your Biology class five years ago!
Sure I do! You scored a 90 on your Biology test!
Right! Well, I want you to see this creature! It reproduces itself when it's splashed with water ...!
My God! You should have brought this to some Government agency or a noted scientist instead of to me, a lowly school teacher!!
Why didn't I think of that?
It may be because you also scored 90 in your I.Q. test!!
Hey! Stop that fighting! You should be able to live in peace with your own kind!
You HUMANS should talk about living in peace with your own kind!
C'mon, Gizmoo! You can sleep in MY bed ...
WAK!
Now if it were only this easy with Katey ... !!
Well, so long, Gang! My new invention will be the HIT of the Convention! A "NON-EXPLODING CAMERA"!!
But cameras don't explode!
The LAST one I invented did!
Don't you wonder how we get the money to live ... since he never succeeds at anything he does?!?

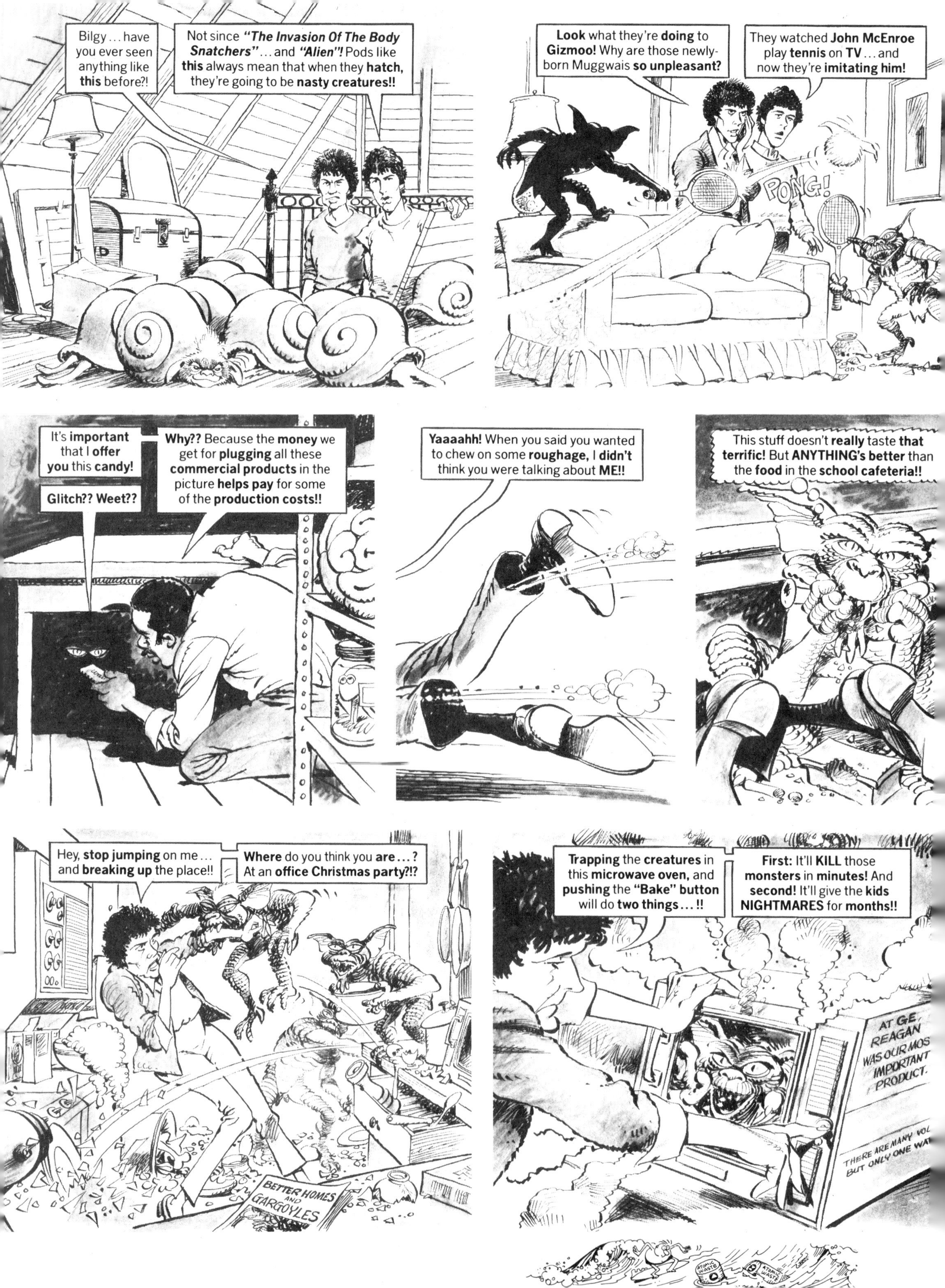

Bilgy... have you ever seen anything like **this** before?!
Not since ***"The Invasion Of The Body Snatchers"***... and ***"Alien"!*** Pods like **this** always mean that when they **hatch,** they're going to be **nasty creatures!!**
**Look** what they're **doing** to **Gizmoo!** Why are those newly-born Muggwais **so unpleasant?**
They watched **John McEnroe** play **tennis** on **TV**... and now they're **imitating him!**
PONG!
It's **important** that I **offer you** this **candy!**
**Why??** Because the **money** we get for **plugging** all these **commercial products** in the picture **helps pay** for some of the **production costs!!**
**Glitch?? Weet??**
**Yaaaahh!** When you said you wanted to chew on some **roughage,** I **didn't** think you were talking about **ME!!**
This stuff doesn't **really** taste **that terrific!** But **ANYTHING's better** than the **food** in the **school cafeteria!!**
Hey, **stop jumping** on me... and **breaking up** the place!!
**Where** do you think you **are...?** At an **office Christmas party?!?**
BETTER HOMES AND GARGOYLES
**Trapping** the **creatures** in this **microwave oven,** and **pushing** the **"Bake"** button will do **two things...!!**
**First:** It'll **KILL** those **monsters** in **minutes!** And **second!** It'll give the **kids NIGHTMARES** for **months!!**
AT G.E. REAGAN WAS OUR MOS IMPORTANT PRODUCT.
THERE ARE MANY VOL BUT ONLY ONE WAT

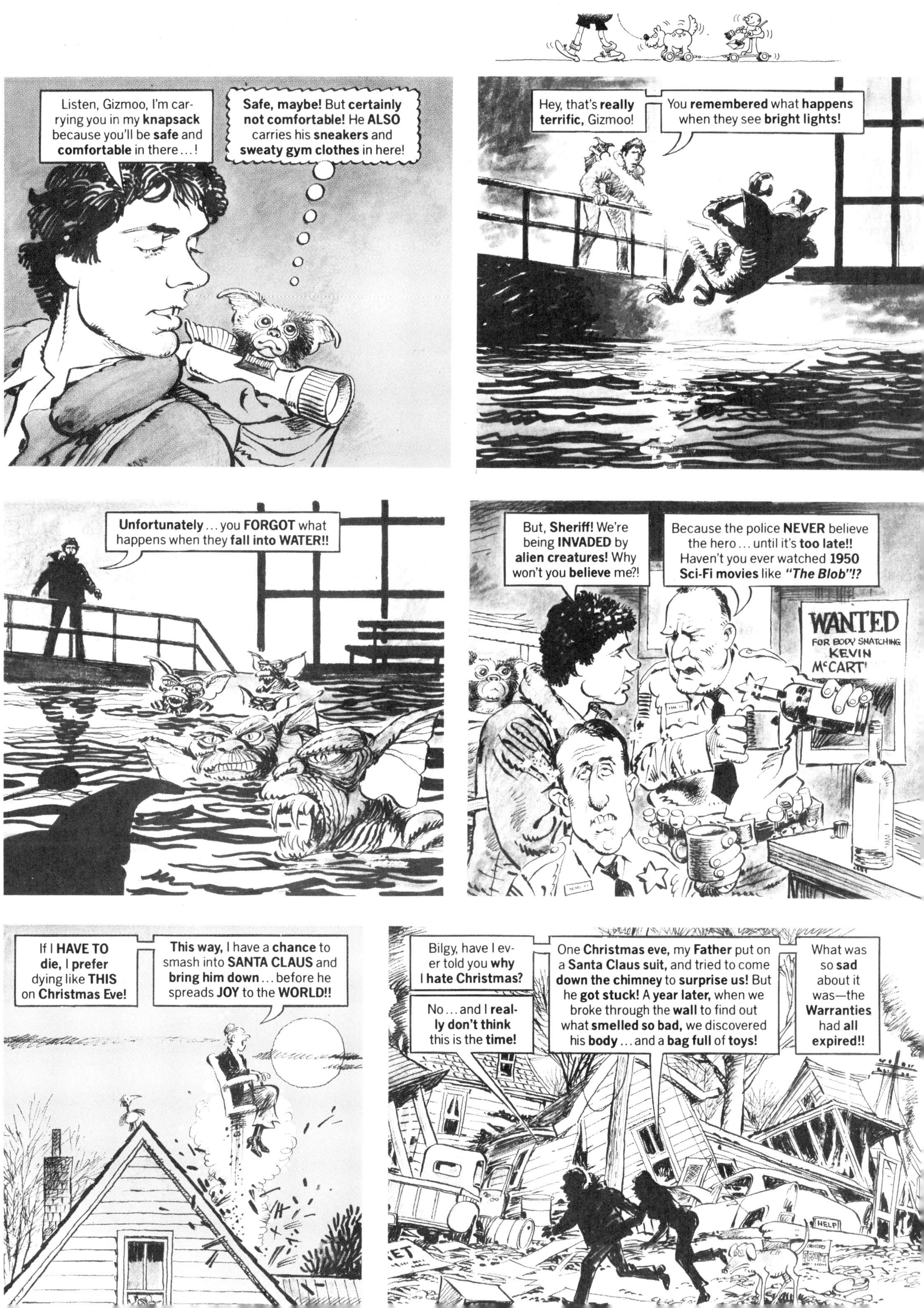
Listen, Gizmoo, I'm carrying you in my **knapsack** because you'll be **safe** and **comfortable** in there . . . !
**Safe, maybe!** But **certainly not comfortable!** He **ALSO** carries his **sneakers** and **sweaty gym clothes** in here!
Hey, that's **really terrific,** Gizmoo!
You **remembered** what **happens** when they see **bright lights!**
**Unfortunately** . . . you **FORGOT** what happens when they **fall into WATER!!**
But, **Sheriff!** We're being **INVADED** by **alien creatures!** Why won't you **believe** me?!
Because the police **NEVER** believe the hero . . . until it's **too late!!** Haven't you ever watched **1950 Sci-Fi movies** like ***"The Blob"!?***
WANTED
FOR BODY SNATCHING
KEVIN
McCART'
If I **HAVE TO die,** I **prefer** dying like **THIS** on **Christmas Eve!**
**This way,** I have a **chance** to smash into **SANTA CLAUS** and **bring him down** . . . before he spreads **JOY** to the **WORLD!!**
Bilgy, have I ever told you **why I hate Christmas?**
No . . . and I **really don't think** this is the **time!**
One **Christmas eve,** my **Father** put on a **Santa Claus suit,** and tried to come **down the chimney** to **surprise us!** But he **got stuck!** **A year later,** when we broke through the **wall** to find out what **smelled so bad,** we discovered his **body** . . . and a **bag full** of **toys!**
What was so **sad** about it was—the **Warranties** had **all expired!!**
HELP

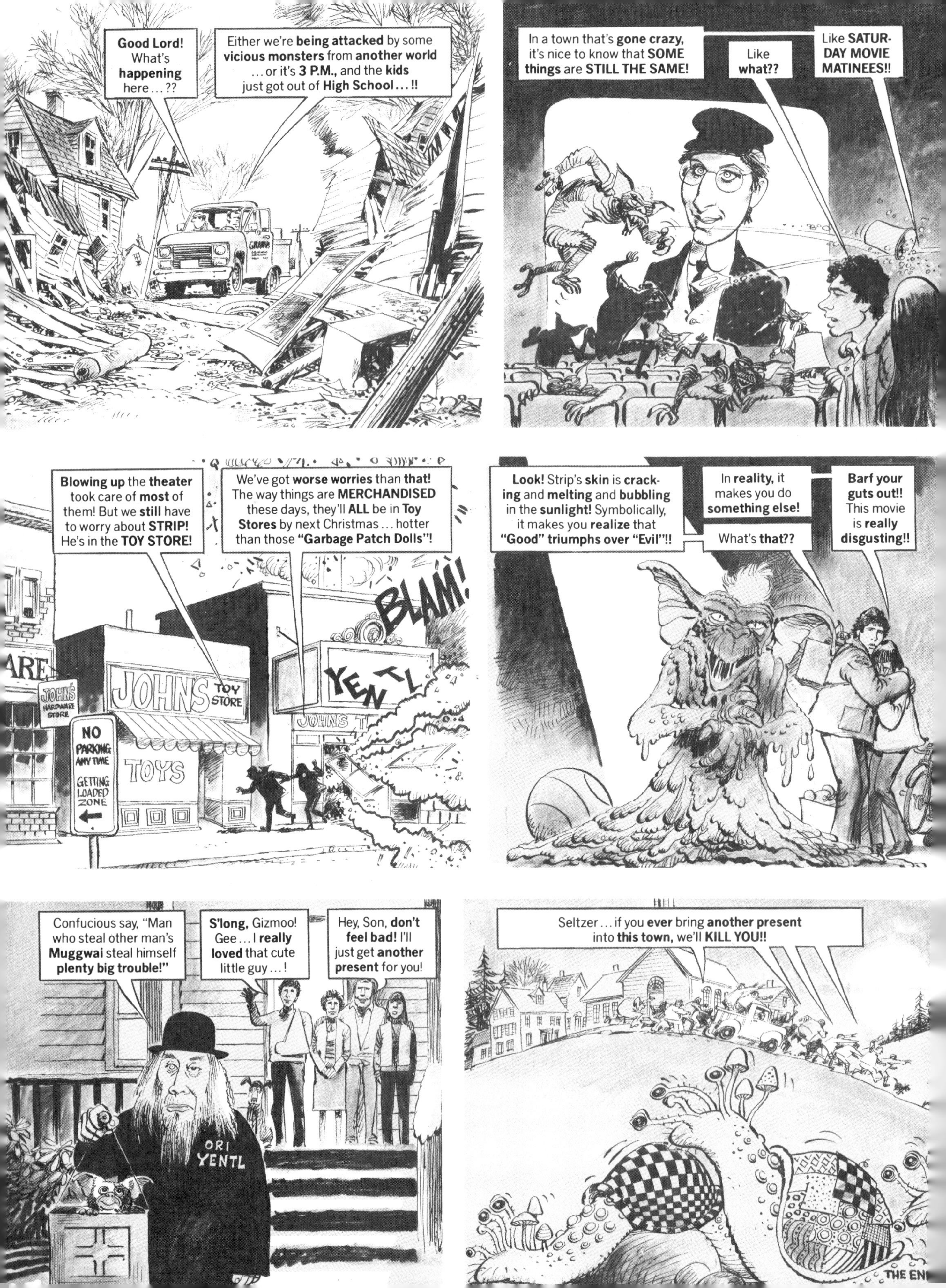

Good Lord! What's happening here ... ??
Either we're being attacked by some vicious monsters from another world ... or it's 3 P.M., and the kids just got out of High School ... !!
In a town that's gone crazy, it's nice to know that SOME things are STILL THE SAME!
Like what??
Like SATURDAY MOVIE MATINEES!!
Blowing up the theater took care of most of them! But we still have to worry about STRIP! He's in the TOY STORE!
We've got worse worries than that! The way things are MERCHANDISED these days, they'll ALL be in Toy Stores by next Christmas ... hotter than those "Garbage Patch Dolls"!
BLAM!
JOHNS TOY STORE
TOYS
JOHN'S HARDWARE STORE
NO PARKING ANY TIME GETTING LOADED ZONE
YENTL
Look! Strip's skin is cracking and melting and bubbling in the sunlight! Symbolically, it makes you realize that "Good" triumphs over "Evil"!!
In reality, it makes you do something else!
What's that??
Barf your guts out!! This movie is really disgusting!!
Confucious say, "Man who steal other man's Muggwai steal himself plenty big trouble!"
S'long, Gizmoo! Gee ... I really loved that cute little guy ... !
Hey, Son, don't feel bad! I'll just get another present for you!
ORI YENTL
Seltzer ... if you ever bring another present into this town, we'll KILL YOU!!
THE END

GRINDING OUT THE SAME OLD SPIEL-BERG DEPT.

Take a bunch of klutzy kids, a deep dark cave, hidden treasure and a giant ogre and what have you got? Our Gang's "Mamma's Little Pirates"? Right? Wrongs! You've got the 1980's rip-off...

ARTIST: JACK DAVIS

WRITER: STAN HART

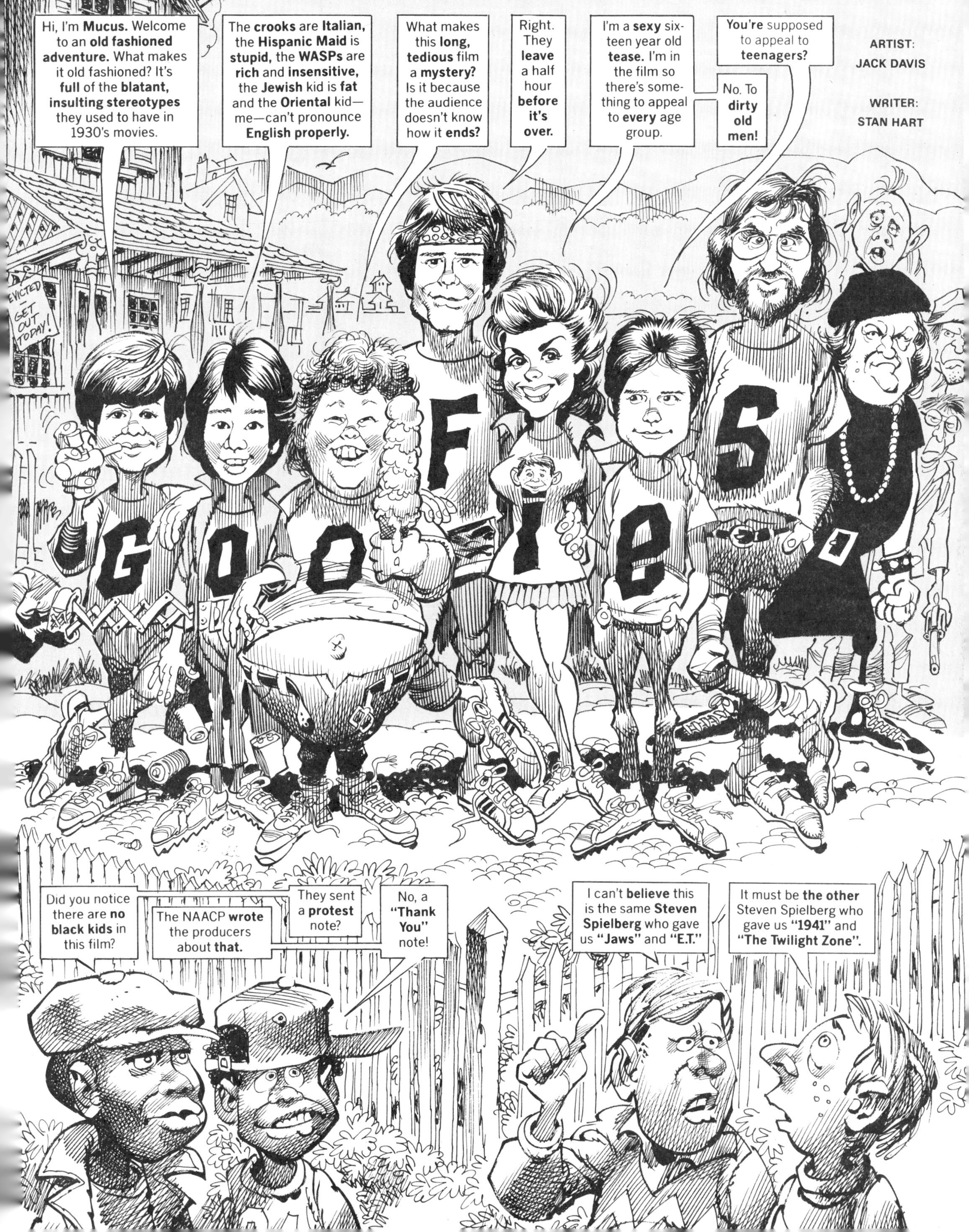

Hi, I'm Mucus. Welcome to an old fashioned adventure. What makes it old fashioned? It's full of the blatant, insulting stereotypes they used to have in 1930's movies.
The crooks are Italian, the Hispanic Maid is stupid, the WASPs are rich and insensitive, the Jewish kid is fat and the Oriental kid—me—can't pronounce English properly.
What makes this long, tedious film a mystery? Is it because the audience doesn't know how it ends?
Right. They leave a half hour before it's over.
I'm a sexy sixteen year old tease. I'm in the film so there's something to appeal to every age group.
You're supposed to appeal to teenagers?
No. To dirty old men!
EVICTED — GET OUT TODAY!
GOOFIES
Did you notice there are no black kids in this film?
The NAACP wrote the producers about that.
They sent a protest note?
No, a "Thank You" note!
I can't believe this is the same Steven Spielberg who gave us "Jaws" and "E.T."
It must be the other Steven Spielberg who gave us "1941" and "The Twilight Zone".

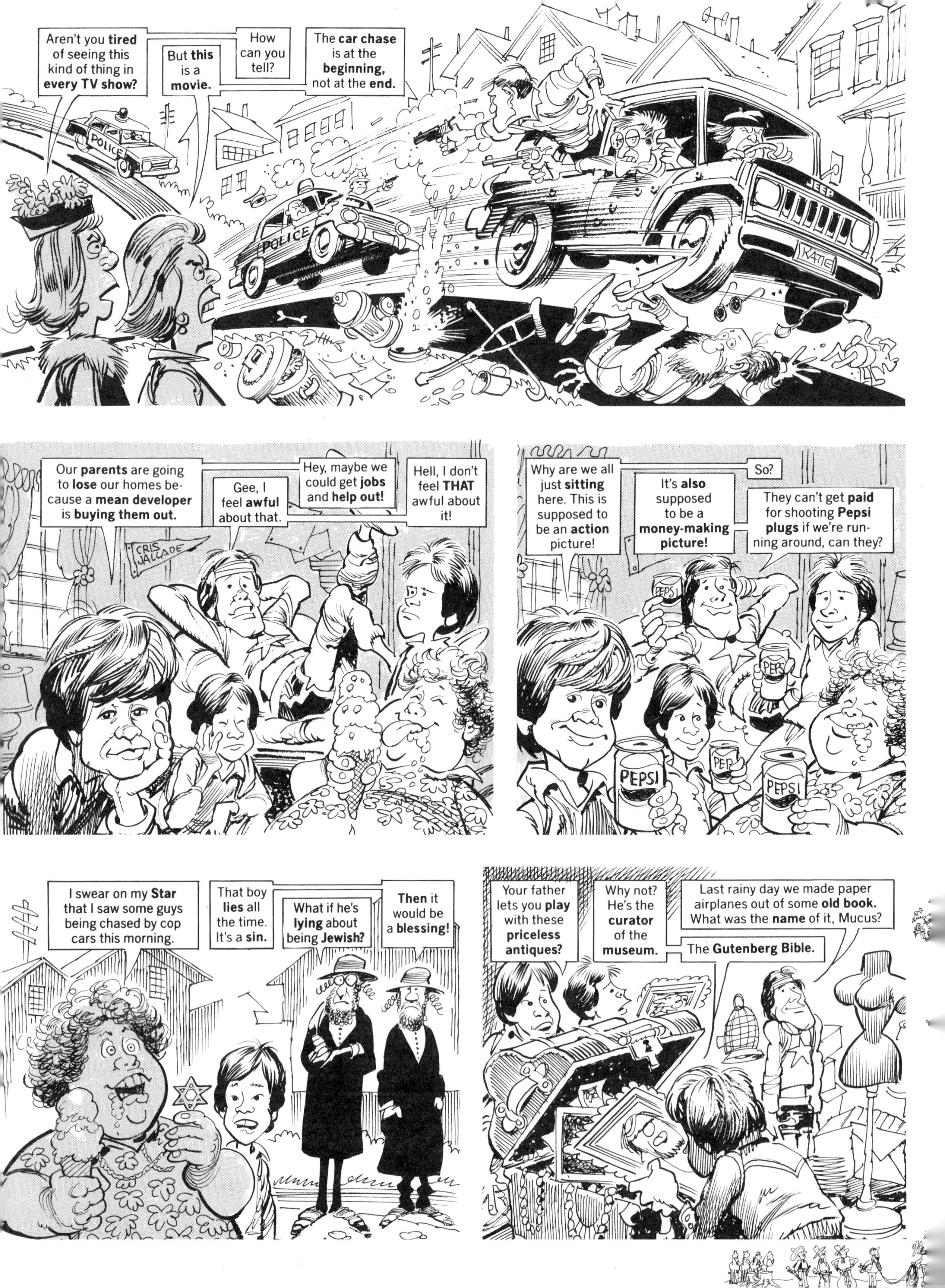

Aren't you **tired** of seeing this kind of thing in **every TV show?**
But **this** is a **movie.**
How can you tell?
The **car chase** is at the **beginning,** not at the **end.**
POLICE
POLICE
JEEP
KATIE
Our **parents** are going to **lose** our homes because a **mean developer** is **buying them out.**
Gee, I feel **awful** about that.
Hey, maybe we could get **jobs** and **help out!**
Hell, I don't feel **THAT** awful about it!
CRIS JALLADE
Why are we all just **sitting** here. This is supposed to be an **action** picture!
It's **also** supposed to be a **money-making picture!**
So?
They can't get **paid** for shooting **Pepsi plugs** if we're running around, can they?
PEPSI
PEPSI
PEPSI
I swear on my **Star** that I saw some guys being chased by cop cars this morning.
That boy **lies** all the time. It's a **sin.**
What if he's **lying** about being **Jewish?**
**Then** it would be a **blessing!**
Your father lets you **play** with these **priceless antiques?**
Why not? He's the **curator** of the **museum.**
Last rainy day we made paper airplanes out of some **old book.** What was the **name** of it, Mucus?
The **Gutenberg Bible.**

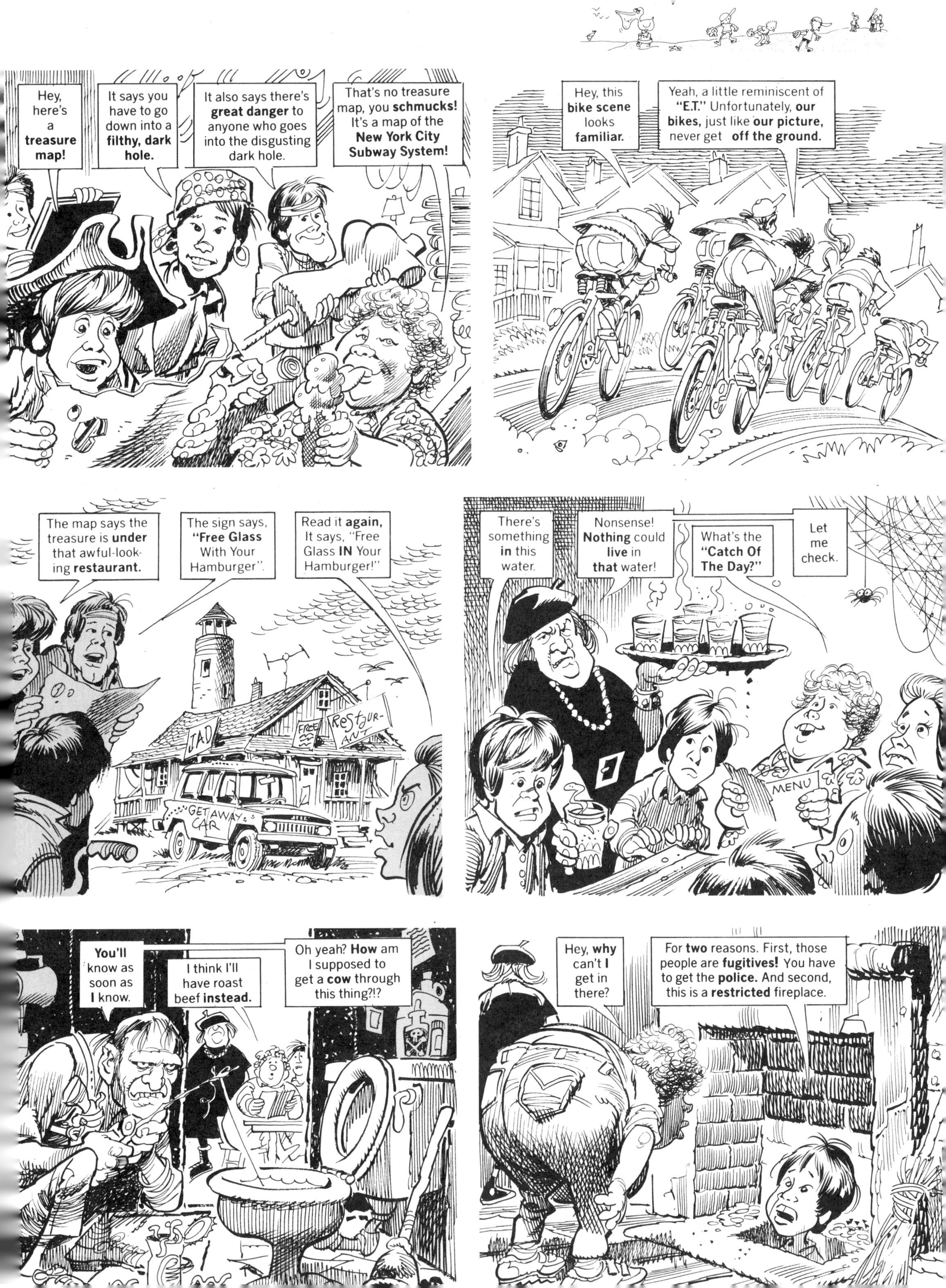
Hey, here's a treasure map!
It says you have to go down into a filthy, dark hole.
It also says there's great danger to anyone who goes into the disgusting dark hole.
That's no treasure map, you schmucks! It's a map of the New York City Subway System!
Hey, this bike scene looks familiar.
Yeah, a little reminiscent of "E.T." Unfortunately, our bikes, just like our picture, never get off the ground.
The map says the treasure is under that awful-looking restaurant.
The sign says, "Free Glass With Your Hamburger".
Read it again, It says, "Free Glass IN Your Hamburger!"
JAD
FREE
RESTURANT
GET AWAY CAR
There's something in this water.
Nonsense! Nothing could live in that water!
What's the "Catch Of The Day?"
Let me check.
MENU
You'll know as soon as I know.
I think I'll have roast beef instead.
Oh yeah? How am I supposed to get a cow through this thing?!?
Hey, why can't I get in there?
For two reasons. First, those people are fugitives! You have to get the police. And second, this is a restricted fireplace.

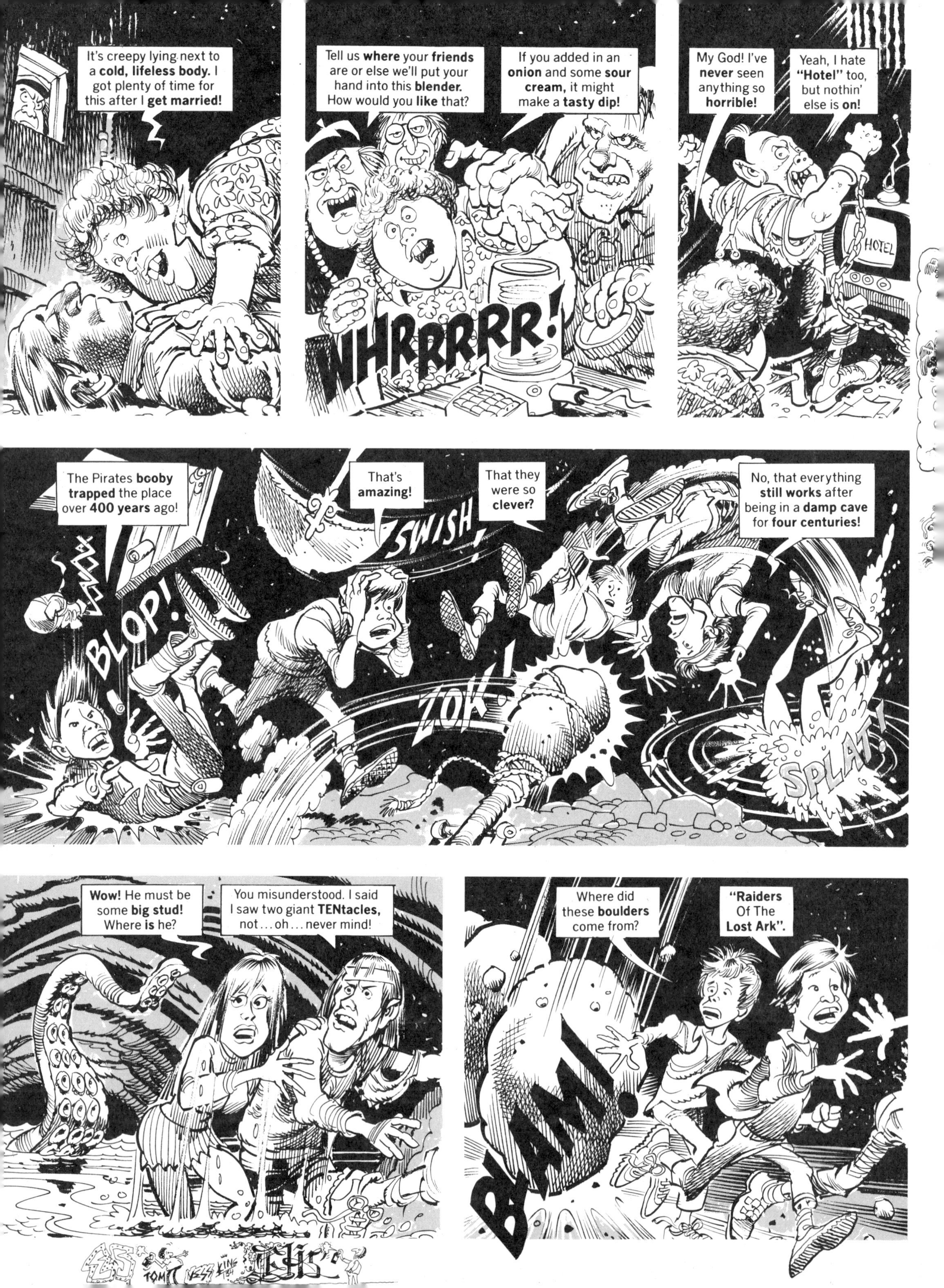

It's creepy lying next to a cold, lifeless body. I got plenty of time for this after I get married!
Tell us where your friends are or else we'll put your hand into this blender. How would you like that?
If you added in an onion and some sour cream, it might make a tasty dip!
WHRRRRR!
My God! I've never seen anything so horrible!
Yeah, I hate "Hotel" too, but nothin' else is on!
HOTEL
The Pirates booby trapped the place over 400 years ago!
That's amazing!
That they were so clever?
No, that everything still works after being in a damp cave for four centuries!
SWISH!
BLOP!
ZOK!
SPLAT!
Wow! He must be some big stud! Where is he?
You misunderstood. I said I saw two giant TENtacles, not . . . oh . . . never mind!
Where did these boulders come from?
"Raiders Of The Lost Ark".
BLAM!

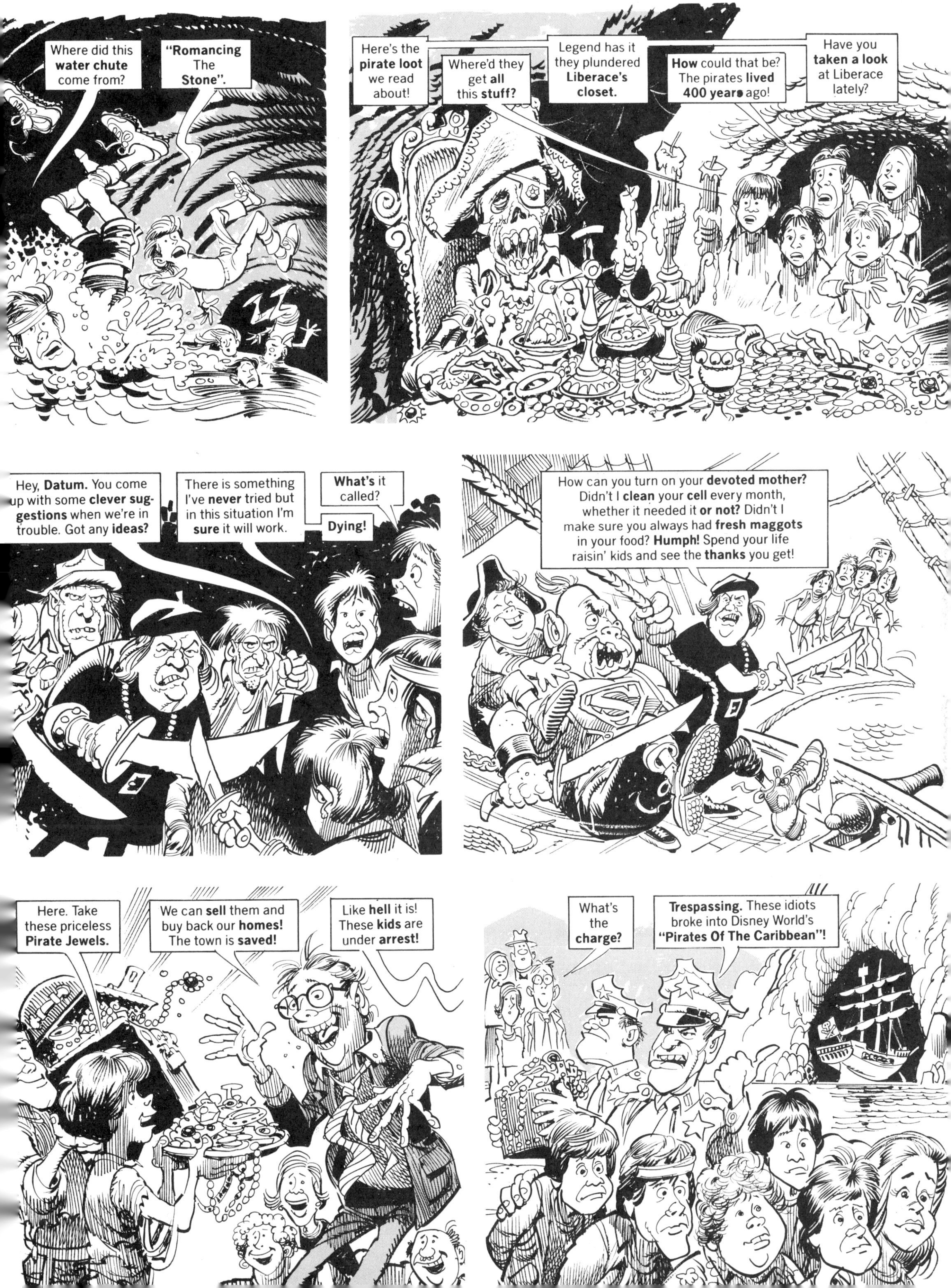
Where did this water chute come from?
"Romancing The Stone".
Here's the pirate loot we read about!
Where'd they get all this stuff?
Legend has it they plundered Liberace's closet.
How could that be? The pirates lived 400 years ago!
Have you taken a look at Liberace lately?
Hey, Datum. You come up with some clever suggestions when we're in trouble. Got any ideas?
There is something I've never tried but in this situation I'm sure it will work.
What's it called?
Dying!
How can you turn on your devoted mother? Didn't I clean your cell every month, whether it needed it or not? Didn't I make sure you always had fresh maggots in your food? Humph! Spend your life raisin' kids and see the thanks you get!
Here. Take these priceless Pirate Jewels.
We can sell them and buy back our homes! The town is saved!
Like hell it is! These kids are under arrest!
What's the charge?
Trespassing. These idiots broke into Disney World's "Pirates Of The Caribbean"!

LAW AND SLAUGHTER DEPT.

**Statute 4, Paragraph 1 of the State Penal Code concerns itself with the intentional destruction of life, while Para. 3 deals with the willful destruction of property. Unfortunately it doesn't seem to pertain to the cops, mainly the ones in the following movie, who do a bang-up job of…**

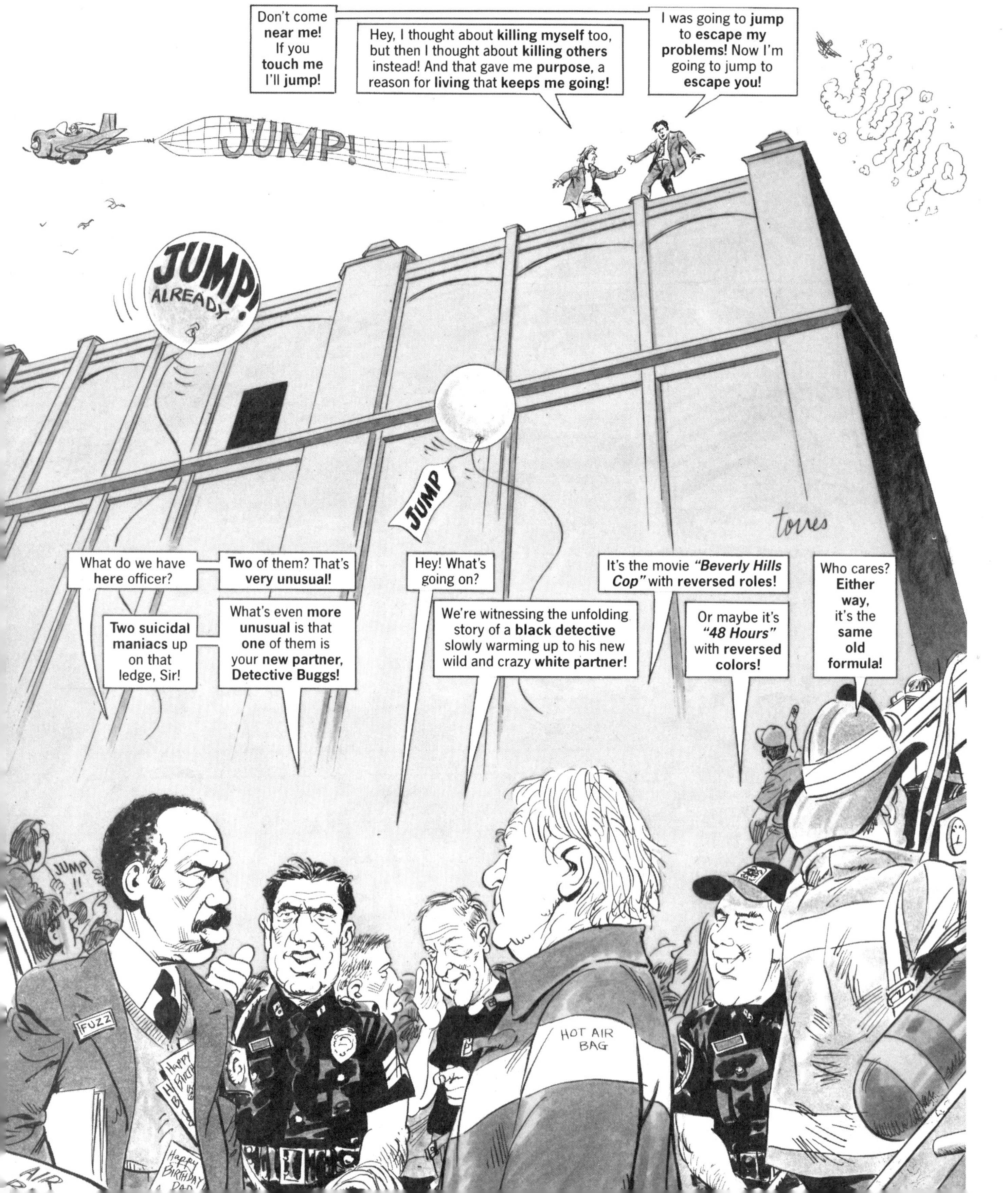
Don't come near me! If you touch me I'll jump!
Hey, I thought about killing myself too, but then I thought about killing others instead! And that gave me purpose, a reason for living that keeps me going!
I was going to jump to escape my problems! Now I'm going to jump to escape you!
JUMP!
JUMP
JUMP ALREADY!
JUMP
torres
What do we have here officer?
Two of them? That's very unusual!
Two suicidal maniacs up on that ledge, Sir!
What's even more unusual is that one of them is your new partner, Detective Buggs!
Hey! What's going on?
We're witnessing the unfolding story of a black detective slowly warming up to his new wild and crazy white partner!
It's the movie "Beverly Hills Cop" with reversed roles!
Or maybe it's "48 Hours" with reversed colors!
Who cares? Either way, it's the same old formula!
JUMP !!
FUZZ
HOT AIR BAG
Happy Birthday Dad

# LEGAL WRECKIN'

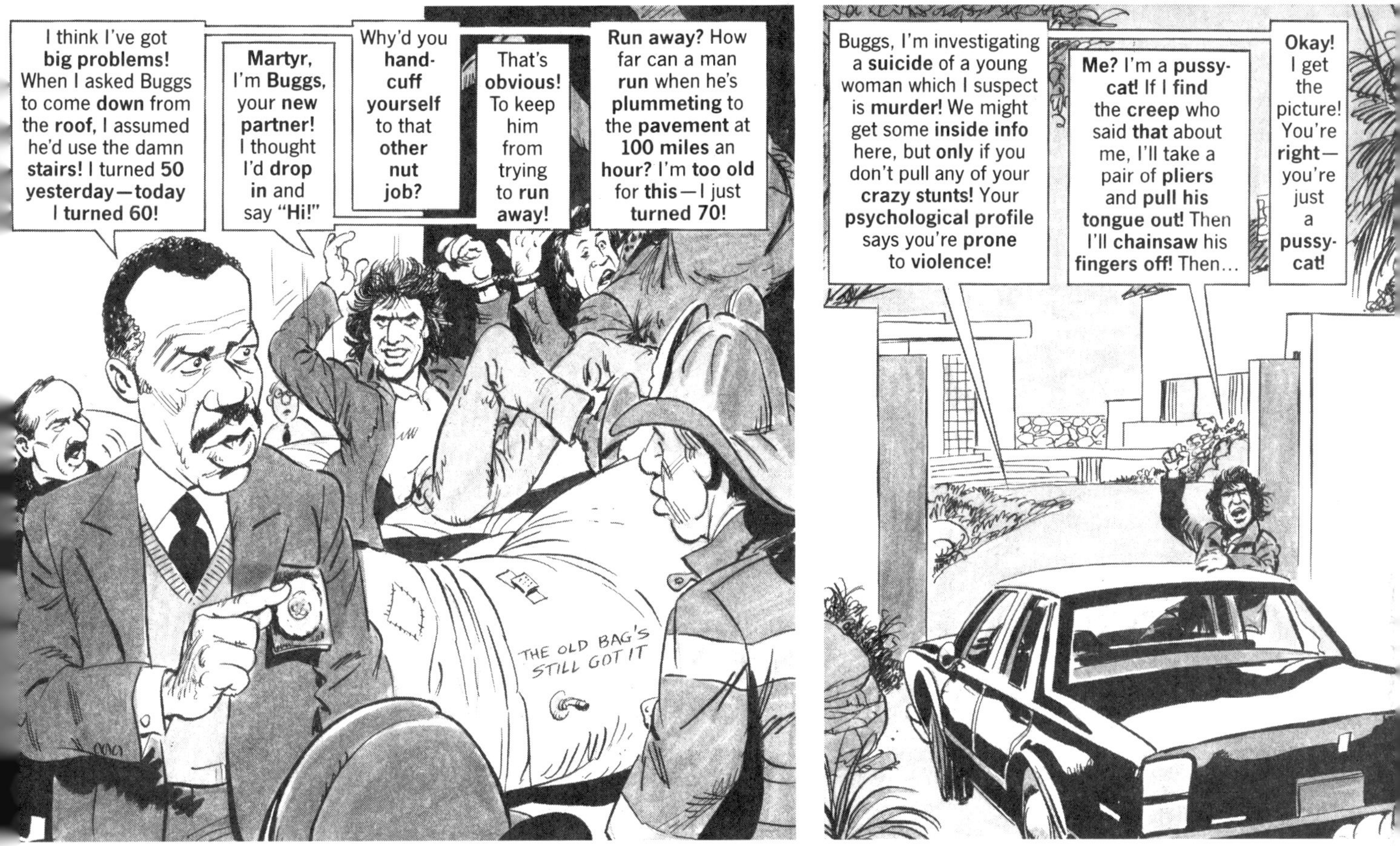
I think I've got **big problems!** When I asked Buggs to come **down** from the **roof**, I assumed he'd use the damn **stairs!** I turned **50 yesterday—today** I **turned 60!**
**Martyr,** I'm **Buggs,** your **new partner!** I thought I'd **drop in** and say **"Hi!"**
Why'd you **hand-cuff yourself** to that **other nut job?**
That's **obvious!** To keep him from trying to **run away!**
**Run away?** How far can a man **run** when he's **plummeting** to the **pavement** at **100 miles** an **hour?** I'm **too old** for **this**—I just **turned 70!**
THE OLD BAG'S STILL GOT IT
Buggs, I'm investigating a **suicide** of a young woman which I suspect is **murder!** We might get some **inside info** here, but **only** if you don't pull any of your **crazy stunts!** Your **psychological profile** says you're **prone** to **violence!**
**Me?** I'm a **pussy-cat!** If I **find** the **creep** who said **that** about me, I'll take a pair of **pliers** and **pull his tongue out!** Then I'll **chainsaw** his **fingers off!** Then…
**Okay!** I get the picture! You're **right**—you're just a **pussy-cat!**

ARTIST: ANGELO TORRES  WRITER: DICK DeBARTOLO

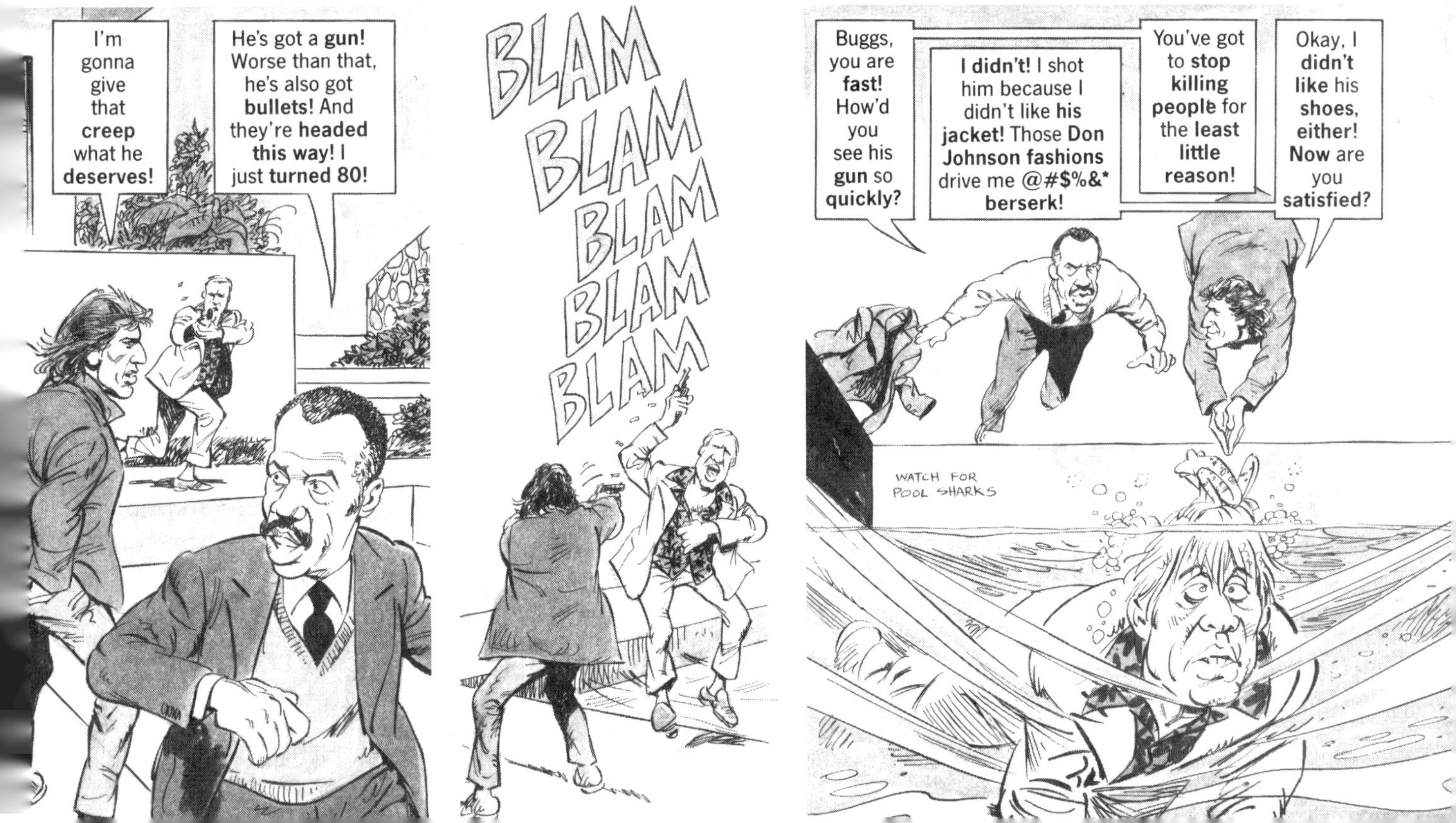
I'm gonna give that **creep** what he **deserves!**
He's got a **gun!** Worse than that, he's also got **bullets!** And they're **headed this way!** I just **turned 80!**
BLAM
BLAM
BLAM
BLAM
BLAM
Buggs, you are **fast!** How'd you see his **gun** so **quickly?**
**I didn't!** I shot him because I didn't like **his jacket!** Those **Don Johnson fashions** drive me @#$%&* **berserk!**
You've got to **stop killing people** for the **least little reason!**
Okay, I **didn't like** his **shoes, either! Now** are you **satisfied?**
WATCH FOR POOL SHARKS

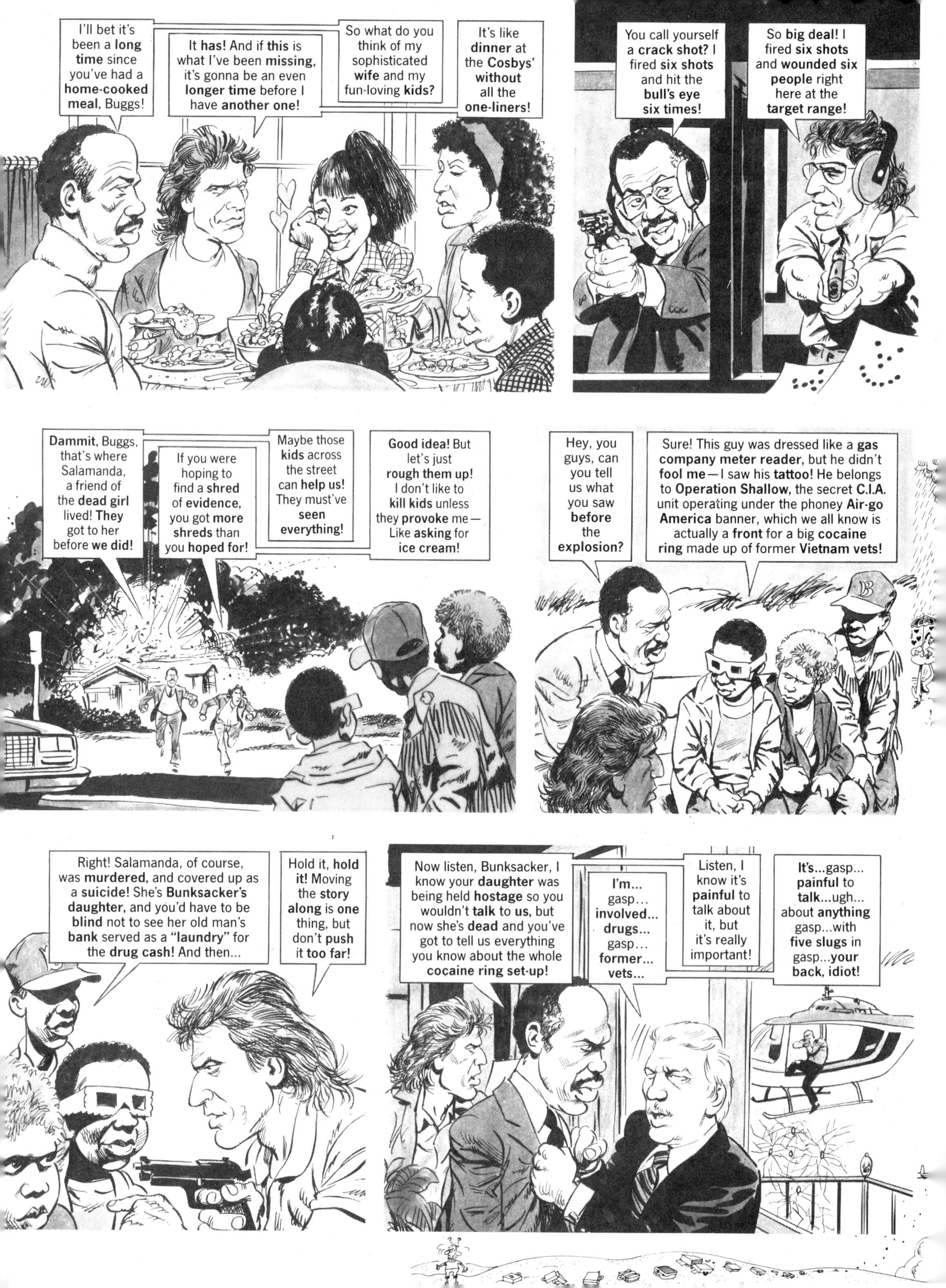
I'll bet it's been a long time since you've had a home-cooked meal, Buggs!
It has! And if this is what I've been missing, it's gonna be an even longer time before I have another one!
So what do you think of my sophisticated wife and my fun-loving kids?
It's like dinner at the Cosbys' without all the one-liners!
You call yourself a crack shot? I fired six shots and hit the bull's eye six times!
So big deal! I fired six shots and wounded six people right here at the target range!
Dammit, Buggs, that's where Salamanda, a friend of the dead girl lived! They got to her before we did!
If you were hoping to find a shred of evidence, you got more shreds than you hoped for!
Maybe those kids across the street can help us! They must've seen everything!
Good idea! But let's just rough them up! I don't like to kill kids unless they provoke me— Like asking for ice cream!
Hey, you guys, can you tell us what you saw before the explosion?
Sure! This guy was dressed like a gas company meter reader, but he didn't fool me—I saw his tattoo! He belongs to Operation Shallow, the secret C.I.A. unit operating under the phoney Air-go America banner, which we all know is actually a front for a big cocaine ring made up of former Vietnam vets!
Right! Salamanda, of course, was murdered, and covered up as a suicide! She's Bunksacker's daughter, and you'd have to be blind not to see her old man's bank served as a "laundry" for the drug cash! And then...
Hold it, hold it! Moving the story along is one thing, but don't push it too far!
Now listen, Bunksacker, I know your daughter was being held hostage so you wouldn't talk to us, but now she's dead and you've got to tell us everything you know about the whole cocaine ring set-up!
I'm... gasp... involved... drugs... gasp... former... vets...
Listen, I know it's painful to talk about it, but it's really important!
It's...gasp... painful to talk...ugh... about anything gasp...with five slugs in gasp...your back, idiot!

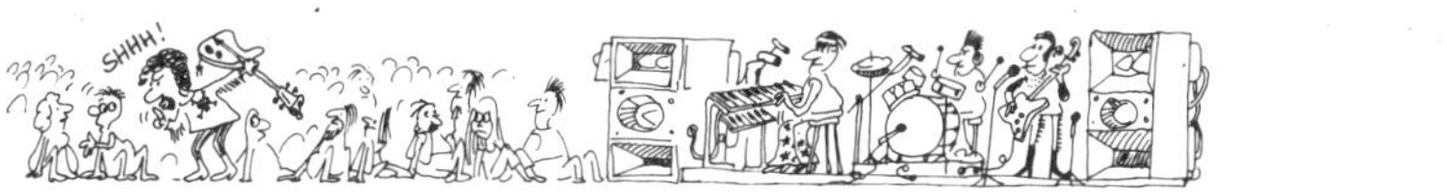
SHHH!

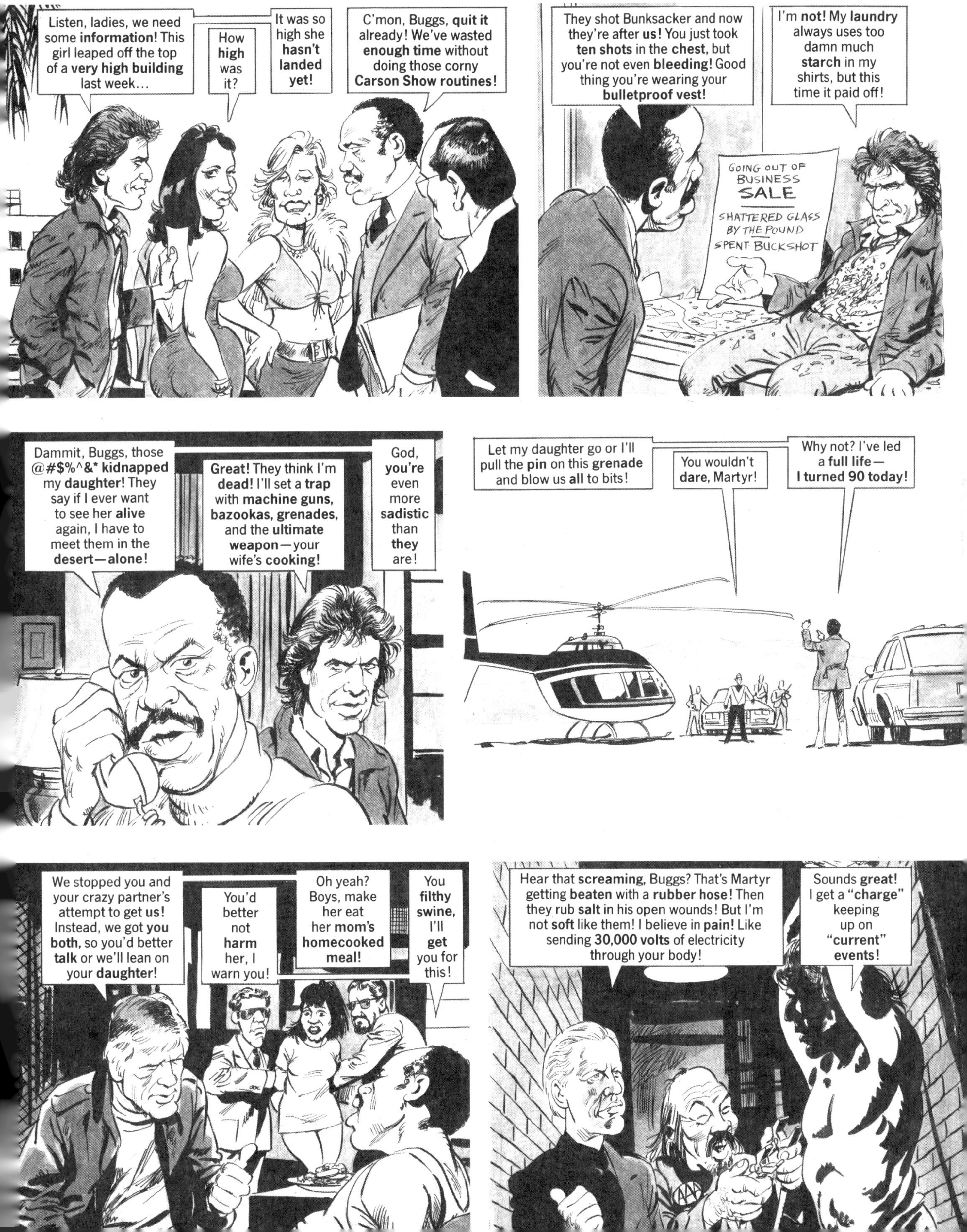
Listen, ladies, we need some **information!** This girl leaped off the top of a **very high building** last week…
How **high** was it?
It was so high she **hasn't landed** yet!
C'mon, Buggs, **quit it** already! We've wasted **enough time** without doing those corny **Carson Show routines!**
They shot Bunksacker and now they're after **us!** You just took **ten shots** in the **chest,** but you're not even **bleeding!** Good thing you're wearing your **bulletproof vest!**
I'm **not!** My **laundry** always uses too damn much **starch** in my shirts, but this time it paid off!
GOING OUT OF BUSINESS SALE
SHATTERED GLASS BY THE POUND
SPENT BUCKSHOT
Dammit, Buggs, those **@#$%^&*** **kidnapped** my **daughter!** They say if I ever want to see her **alive** again, I have to meet them in the **desert—alone!**
**Great!** They think I'm **dead!** I'll set a **trap** with **machine guns, bazookas, grenades,** and the **ultimate weapon**—your wife's **cooking!**
God, **you're** even more **sadistic** than **they** are!
Let my daughter go or I'll pull the **pin** on this **grenade** and blow us **all** to bits!
You wouldn't **dare,** Martyr!
Why not? I've led a **full life— I turned 90 today!**
We stopped you and your crazy partner's attempt to get **us!** Instead, we got **you both,** so you'd better **talk** or we'll lean on your **daughter!**
You'd better not **harm** her, I warn you!
Oh yeah? Boys, make her eat her **mom's homecooked meal!**
You **filthy swine,** I'll **get** you for this!
Hear that **screaming,** Buggs? That's Martyr getting **beaten** with a **rubber hose!** Then they rub **salt** in his open wounds! But I'm not **soft** like them! I believe in **pain!** Like sending **30,000 volts** of electricity through your body!
Sounds **great!** I get a **"charge"** keeping up on **"current" events!**

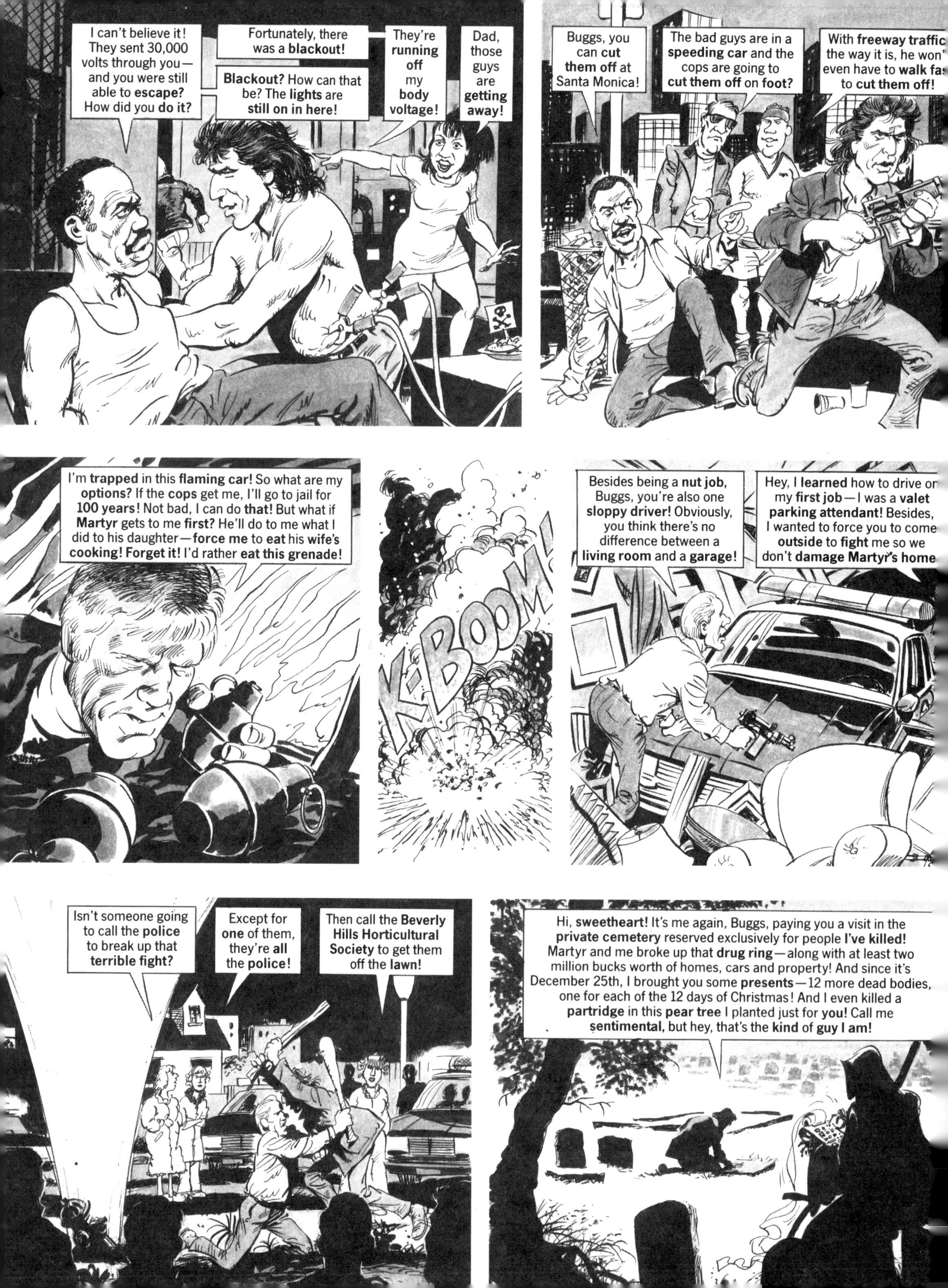
I can't believe it! They sent 30,000 volts through you—and you were still able to escape? How did you do it?
Fortunately, there was a blackout!
Blackout? How can that be? The lights are still on in here!
They're running off my body voltage!
Dad, those guys are getting away!
Buggs, you can cut them off at Santa Monica!
The bad guys are in a speeding car and the cops are going to cut them off on foot?
With freeway traffic the way it is, he won' even have to walk fas to cut them off!
I'm trapped in this flaming car! So what are my options? If the cops get me, I'll go to jail for 100 years! Not bad, I can do that! But what if Martyr gets to me first? He'll do to me what I did to his daughter—force me to eat his wife's cooking! Forget it! I'd rather eat this grenade!
K-BOOM!
Besides being a nut job, Buggs, you're also one sloppy driver! Obviously, you think there's no difference between a living room and a garage!
Hey, I learned how to drive o my first job—I was a valet parking attendant! Besides, I wanted to force you to come outside to fight me so we don't damage Martyr's home
Isn't someone going to call the police to break up that terrible fight?
Except for one of them, they're all the police!
Then call the Beverly Hills Horticultural Society to get them off the lawn!
Hi, sweetheart! It's me again, Buggs, paying you a visit in the private cemetery reserved exclusively for people I've killed! Martyr and me broke up that drug ring—along with at least two million bucks worth of homes, cars and property! And since it's December 25th, I brought you some presents—12 more dead bodies, one for each of the 12 days of Christmas! And I even killed a partridge in this pear tree I planted just for you! Call me sentimental, but hey, that's the kind of guy I am!

# A MAD LOOK AT MOVIE MAKING

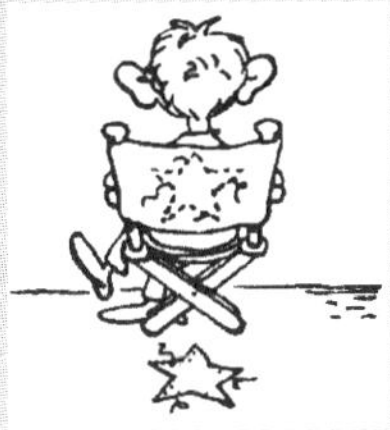

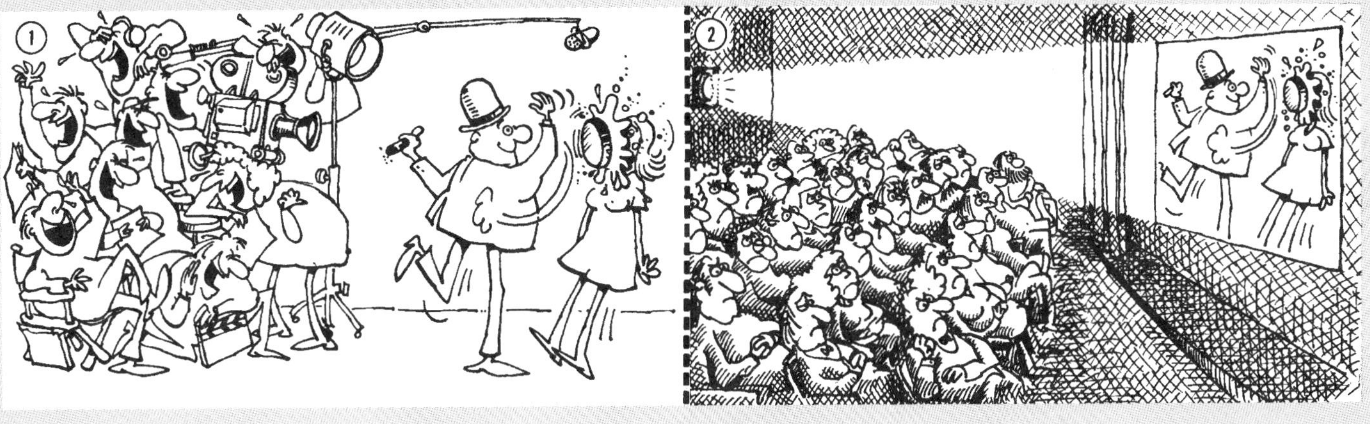

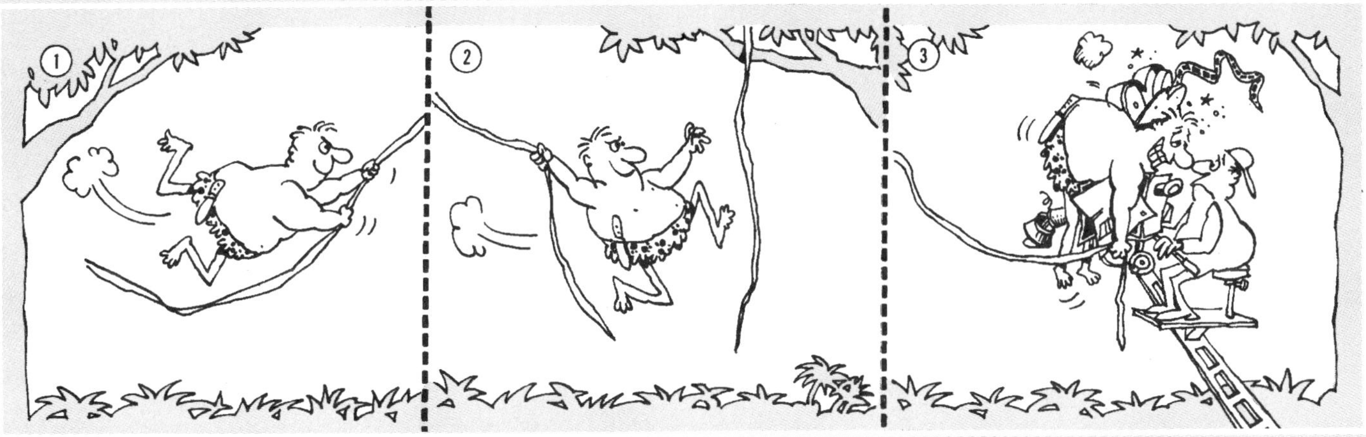

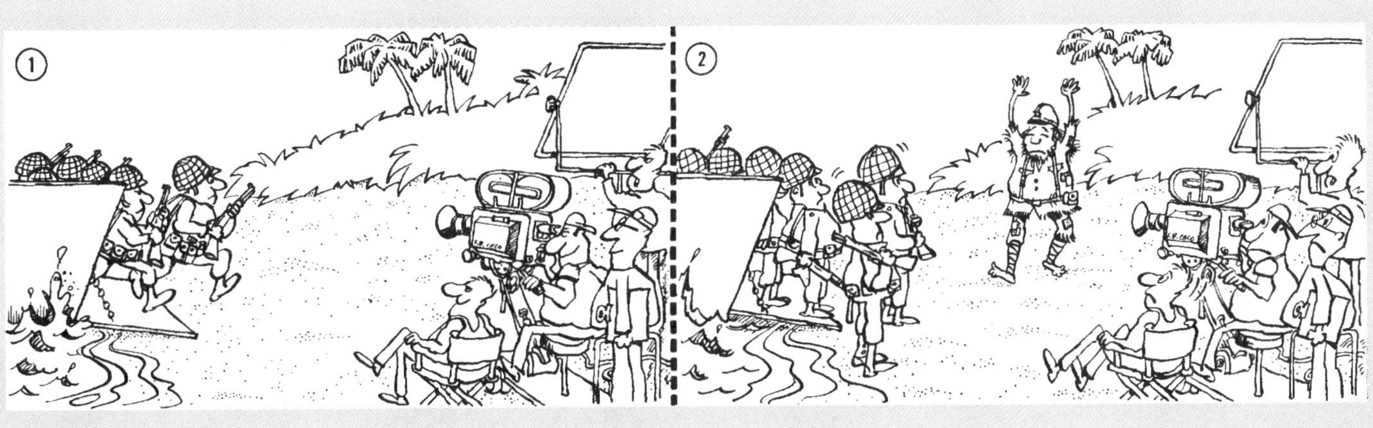

ARTIST AND WRITER: SERGIO ARAGONES

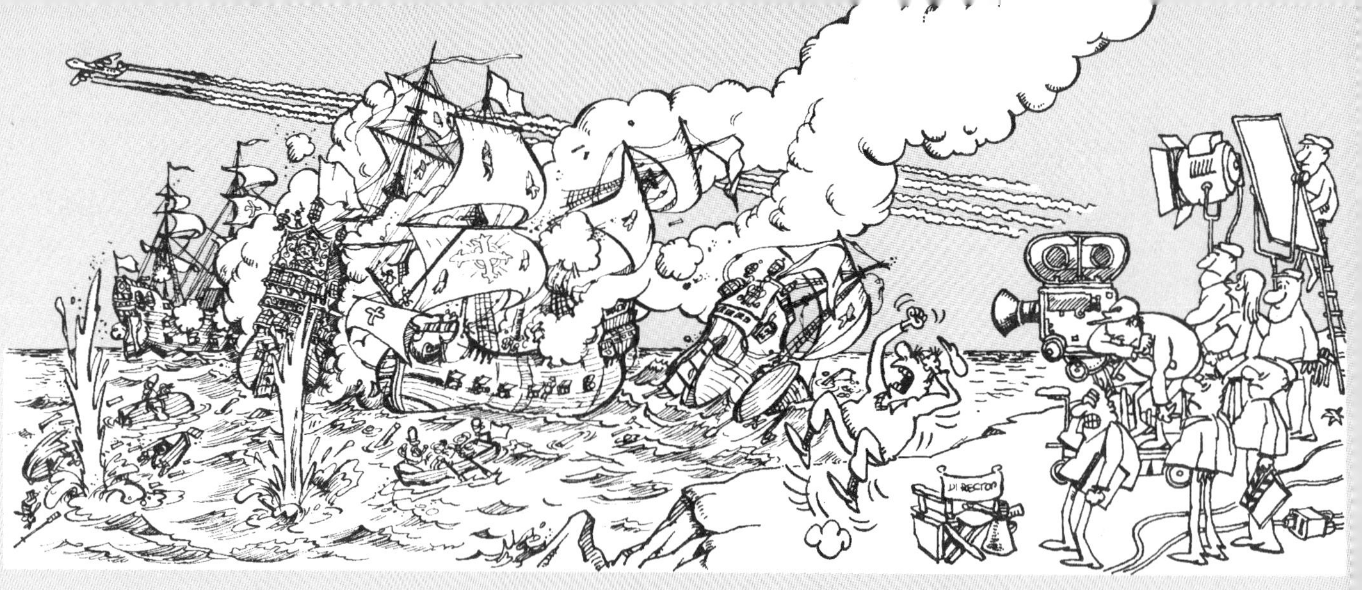
DIRECTOR

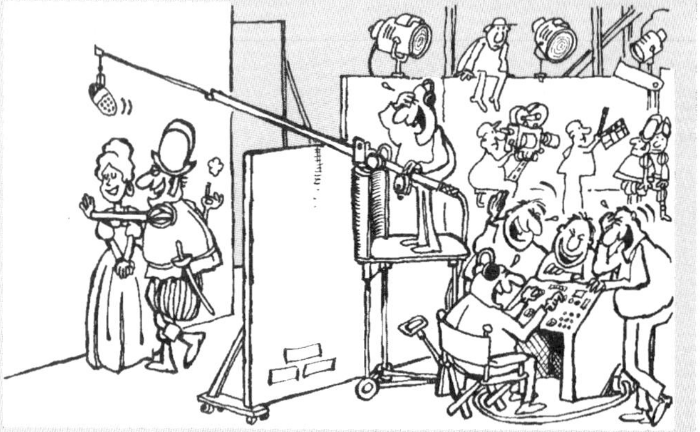

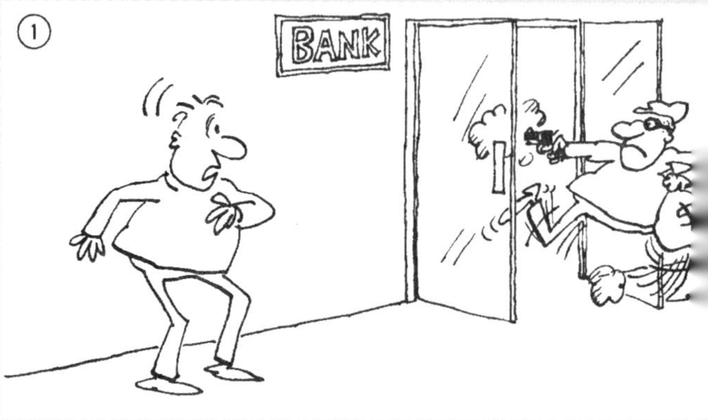
1
BANK

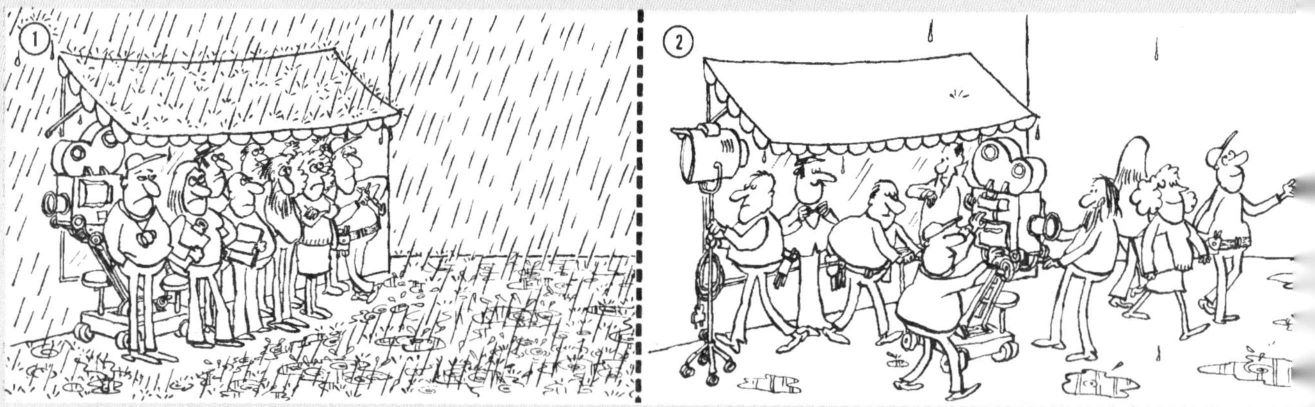
1
2

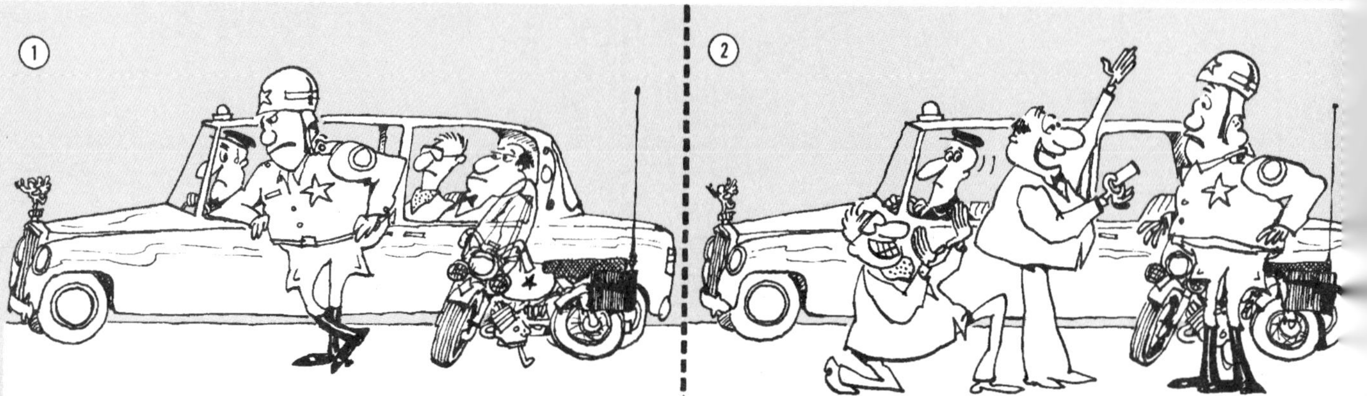
1
2

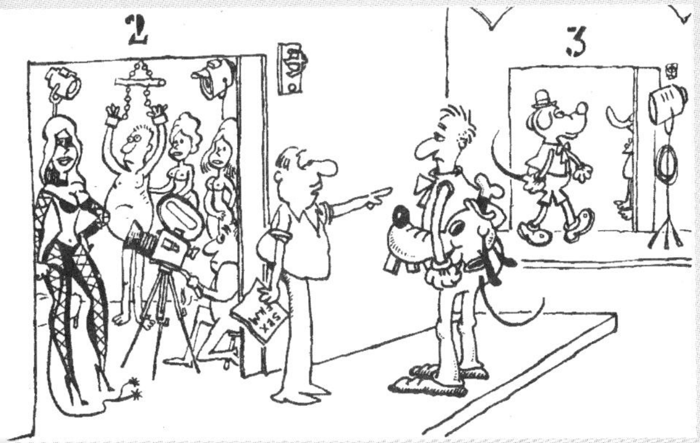
2
3

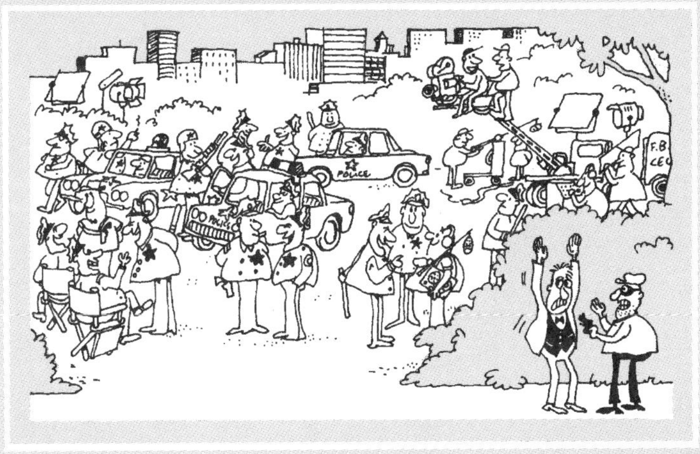
POLICE

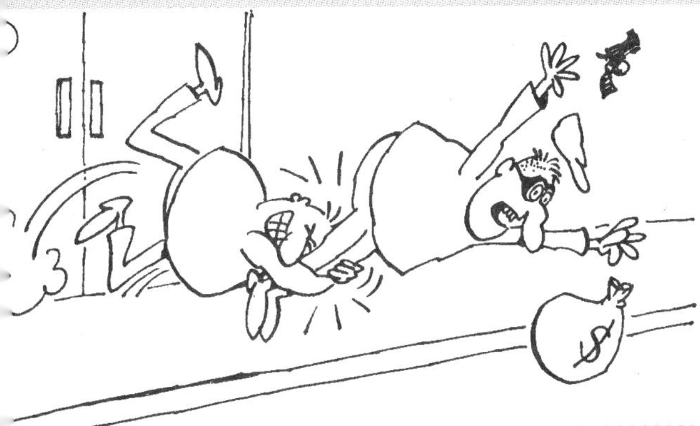

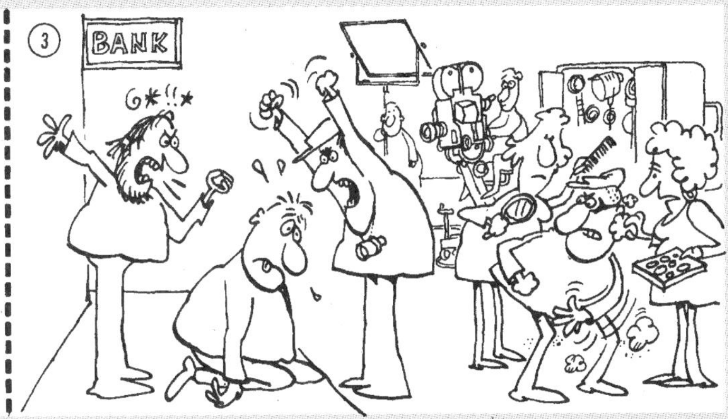
3
BANK
G*!!*

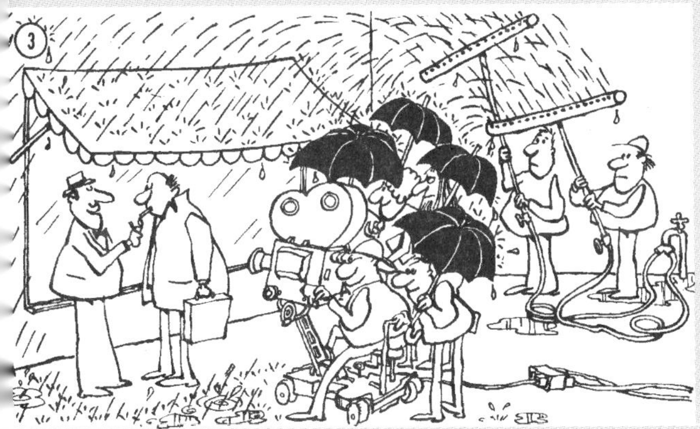
3

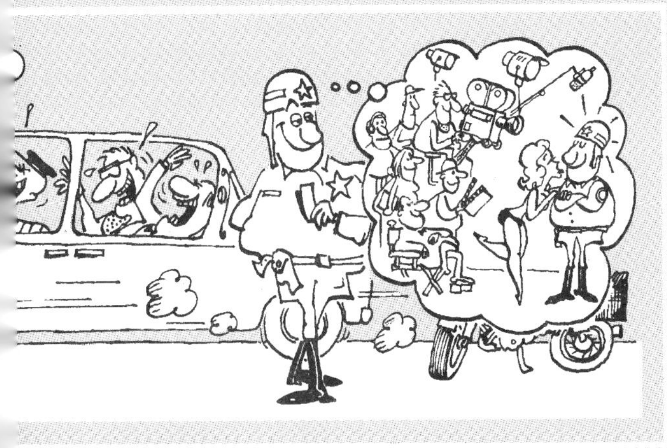

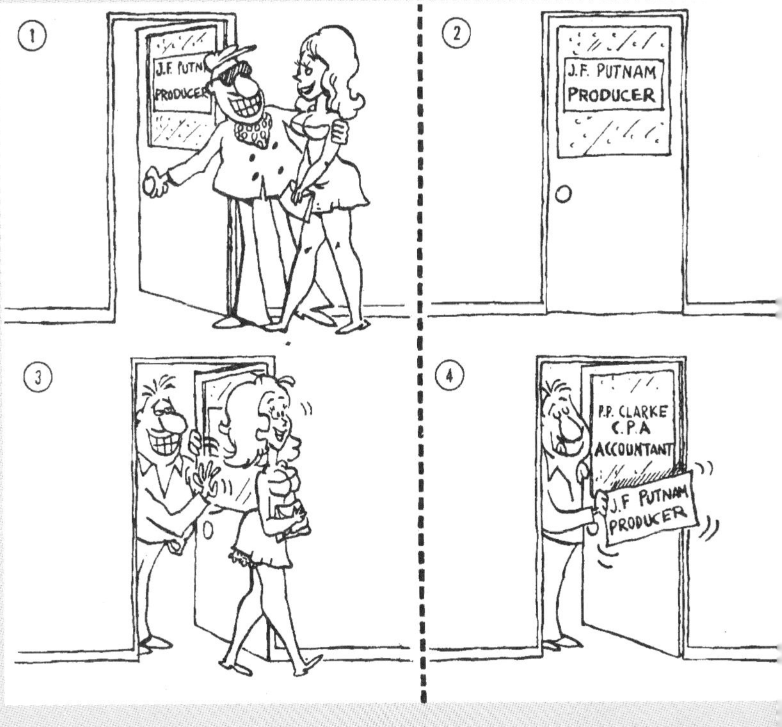
1
J.F. PUTNAM PRODUCER
2
J.F. PUTNAM PRODUCER
3
4
P.P. CLARKE C.P.A ACCOUNTANT
J.F. PUTNAM PRODUCER

**DEVILED HAM AND SCRAMBLED LEGS DEPT.**

Every once in a while, a new movie comes along that's funny, clever and in good taste. Maybe one day we'll be lucky enough to see one! Until then, we'll just have to take whatever Hollywood throws up to us as we try to stomach...

# THE WRETCHES OF ECCHFLICK

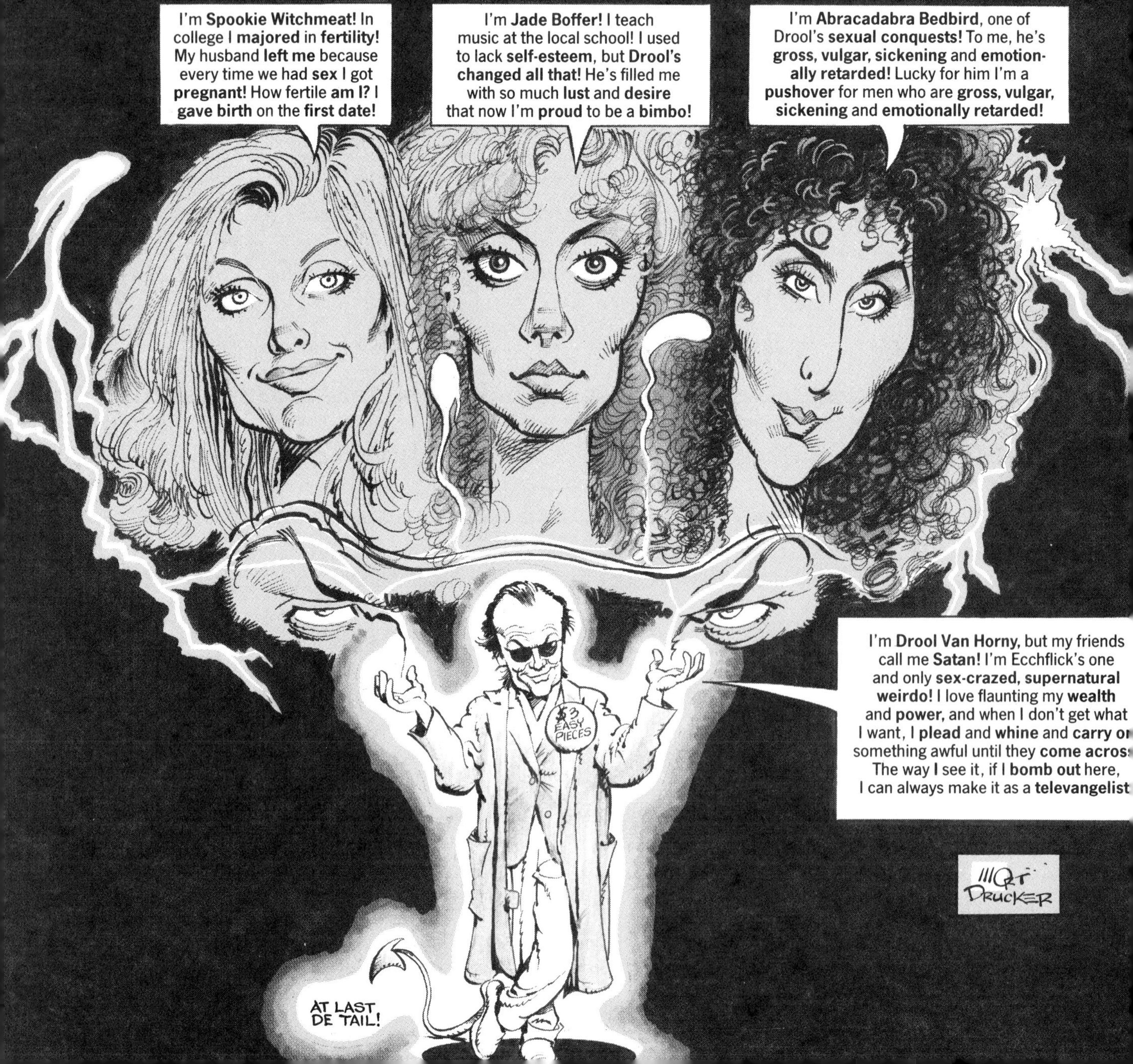
I'm Spookie Witchmeat! In college I majored in fertility! My husband left me because every time we had sex I got pregnant! How fertile am I? I gave birth on the first date!
I'm Jade Boffer! I teach music at the local school! I used to lack self-esteem, but Drool's changed all that! He's filled me with so much lust and desire that now I'm proud to be a bimbo!
I'm Abracadabra Bedbird, one of Drool's sexual conquests! To me, he's gross, vulgar, sickening and emotionally retarded! Lucky for him I'm a pushover for men who are gross, vulgar, sickening and emotionally retarded!
I'm Drool Van Horny, but my friends call me Satan! I'm Ecchflick's one and only sex-crazed, supernatural weirdo! I love flaunting my wealth and power, and when I don't get what I want, I plead and whine and carry o something awful until they come acros The way I see it, if I bomb out here, I can always make it as a televangelist
$3 EASY PIECES
MORT DRUCKER
AT LAST DE TAIL!

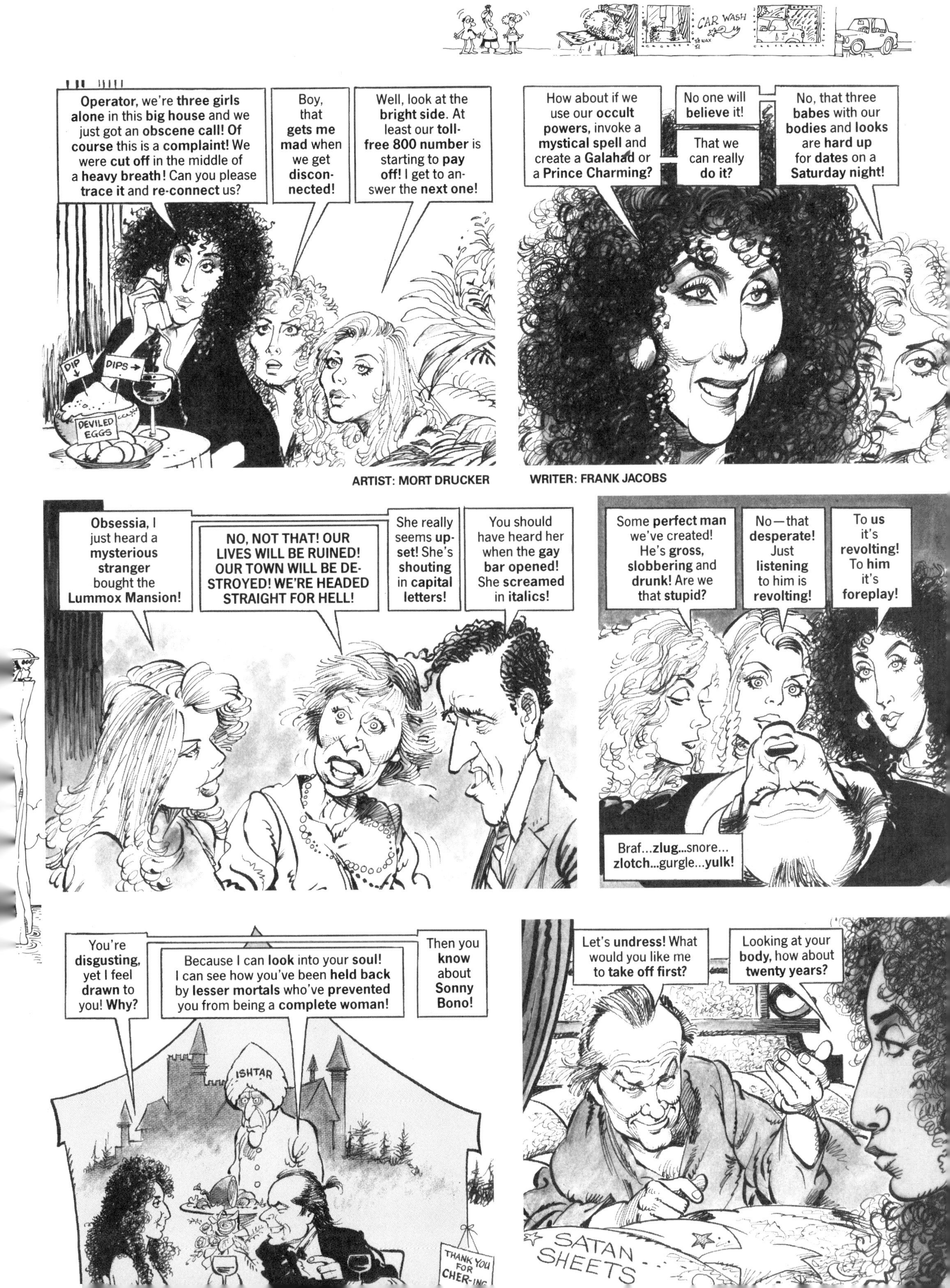
CAR WASH
WAX
Operator, we're three girls alone in this big house and we just got an obscene call! Of course this is a complaint! We were cut off in the middle of a heavy breath! Can you please trace it and re-connect us?
Boy, that gets me mad when we get discon-nected!
Well, look at the bright side. At least our toll-free 800 number is starting to pay off! I get to an-swer the next one!
DIP
DIPS
DEVILED EGGS
How about if we use our occult powers, invoke a mystical spell and create a Galahad or a Prince Charming?
No one will believe it!
That we can really do it?
No, that three babes with our bodies and looks are hard up for dates on a Saturday night!
ARTIST: MORT DRUCKER
WRITER: FRANK JACOBS
Obsessia, I just heard a mysterious stranger bought the Lummox Mansion!
NO, NOT THAT! OUR LIVES WILL BE RUINED! OUR TOWN WILL BE DE-STROYED! WE'RE HEADED STRAIGHT FOR HELL!
She really seems up-set! She's shouting in capital letters!
You should have heard her when the gay bar opened! She screamed in italics!
Some perfect man we've created! He's gross, slobbering and drunk! Are we that stupid?
No—that desperate! Just listening to him is revolting!
To us it's revolting! To him it's foreplay!
Braf...zlug...snore... zlotch...gurgle...yulk!
You're disgusting, yet I feel drawn to you! Why?
Because I can look into your soul! I can see how you've been held back by lesser mortals who've prevented you from being a complete woman!
Then you know about Sonny Bono!
ISHTAR
THANK YOU FOR CHER-ING
Let's undress! What would you like me to take off first?
Looking at your body, how about twenty years?
SATAN SHEETS

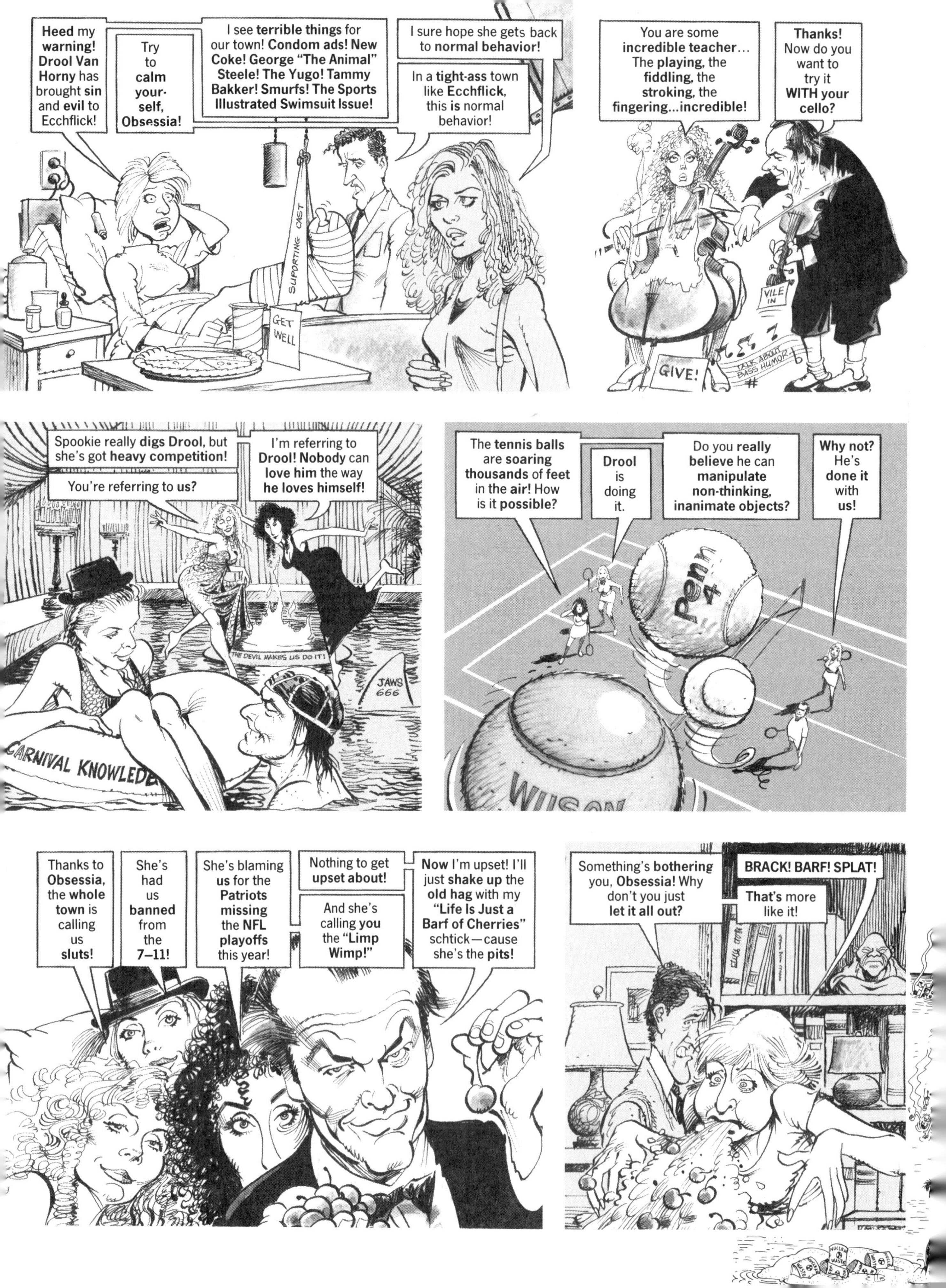

Heed my warning! Drool Van Horny has brought sin and evil to Ecchflick!
Try to calm yourself, Obsessia!
I see terrible things for our town! Condom ads! New Coke! George "The Animal" Steele! The Yugo! Tammy Bakker! Smurfs! The Sports Illustrated Swimsuit Issue!
I sure hope she gets back to normal behavior!
In a tight-ass town like Ecchflick, this is normal behavior!
SUPPORTING CAST
GET WELL
You are some incredible teacher… The playing, the fiddling, the stroking, the fingering…incredible!
Thanks! Now do you want to try it WITH your cello?
VILE IN
GIVE!
TALK ABOUT BASS HUMOR
Spookie really digs Drool, but she's got heavy competition!
You're referring to us?
I'm referring to Drool! Nobody can love him the way he loves himself!
THE DEVIL MAKES US DO IT!
JAWS 666
The tennis balls are soaring thousands of feet in the air! How is it possible?
Drool is doing it.
Do you really believe he can manipulate non-thinking, inanimate objects?
Why not? He's done it with us!
Penn 4
Thanks to Obsessia, the whole town is calling us sluts!
She's had us banned from the 7–11!
She's blaming us for the Patriots missing the NFL playoffs this year!
Nothing to get upset about!
And she's calling you the "Limp Wimp!"
Now I'm upset! I'll just shake up the old hag with my "Life Is Just a Barf of Cherries" schtick—cause she's the pits!
Something's bothering you, Obsessia! Why don't you just let it all out?
BRACK! BARF! SPLAT!
That's more like it!
NUCLEAR WASTE

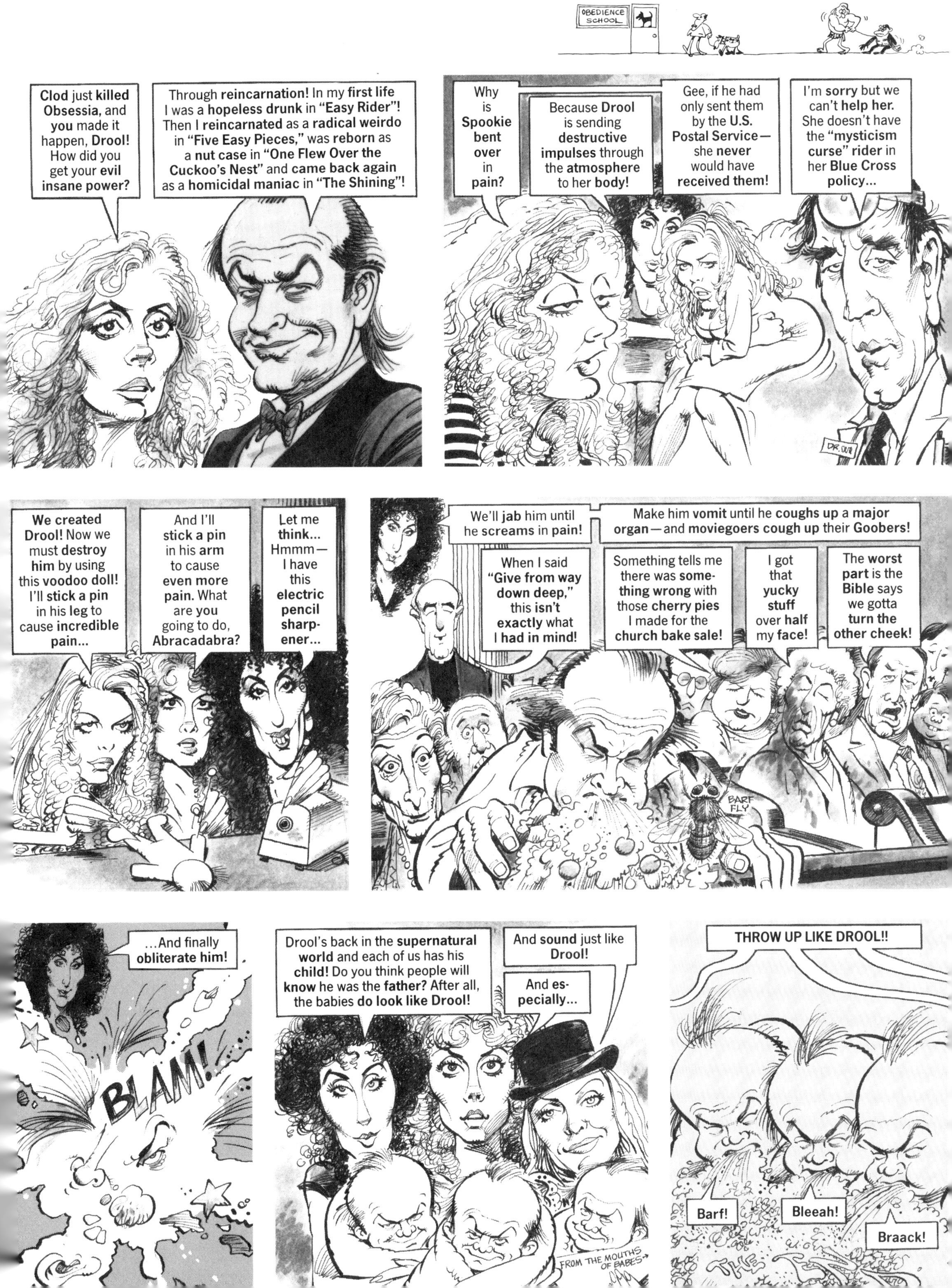

OBEDIENCE SCHOOL
Clod just killed Obsessia, and you made it happen, Drool! How did you get your evil insane power?
Through reincarnation! In my first life I was a hopeless drunk in "Easy Rider"! Then I reincarnated as a radical weirdo in "Five Easy Pieces," was reborn as a nut case in "One Flew Over the Cuckoo's Nest" and came back again as a homicidal maniac in "The Shining"!
Why is Spookie bent over in pain?
Because Drool is sending destructive impulses through the atmosphere to her body!
Gee, if he had only sent them by the U.S. Postal Service — she never would have received them!
I'm sorry but we can't help her. She doesn't have the "mysticism curse" rider in her Blue Cross policy...
We created Drool! Now we must destroy him by using this voodoo doll! I'll stick a pin in his leg to cause incredible pain...
And I'll stick a pin in his arm to cause even more pain. What are you going to do, Abracadabra?
Let me think... Hmmm — I have this electric pencil sharpener...
We'll jab him until he screams in pain!
Make him vomit until he coughs up a major organ — and moviegoers cough up their Goobers!
When I said "Give from way down deep," this isn't exactly what I had in mind!
Something tells me there was something wrong with those cherry pies I made for the church bake sale!
I got that yucky stuff over half my face!
The worst part is the Bible says we gotta turn the other cheek!
BARF FLY
...And finally obliterate him!
BLAM!
Drool's back in the supernatural world and each of us has his child! Do you think people will know he was the father? After all, the babies do look like Drool!
And sound just like Drool!
And especially...
FROM THE MOUTHS OF BABES
THROW UP LIKE DROOL!!
Barf!
Bleeah!
Braack!

THE DYNAMIC UNO DEPT.

**What's the hot-action, feel-good hit of the summer that people are flocking to see? *Ghostbusters II*, of course! Which is why MAD now proudly presents its satire of...**

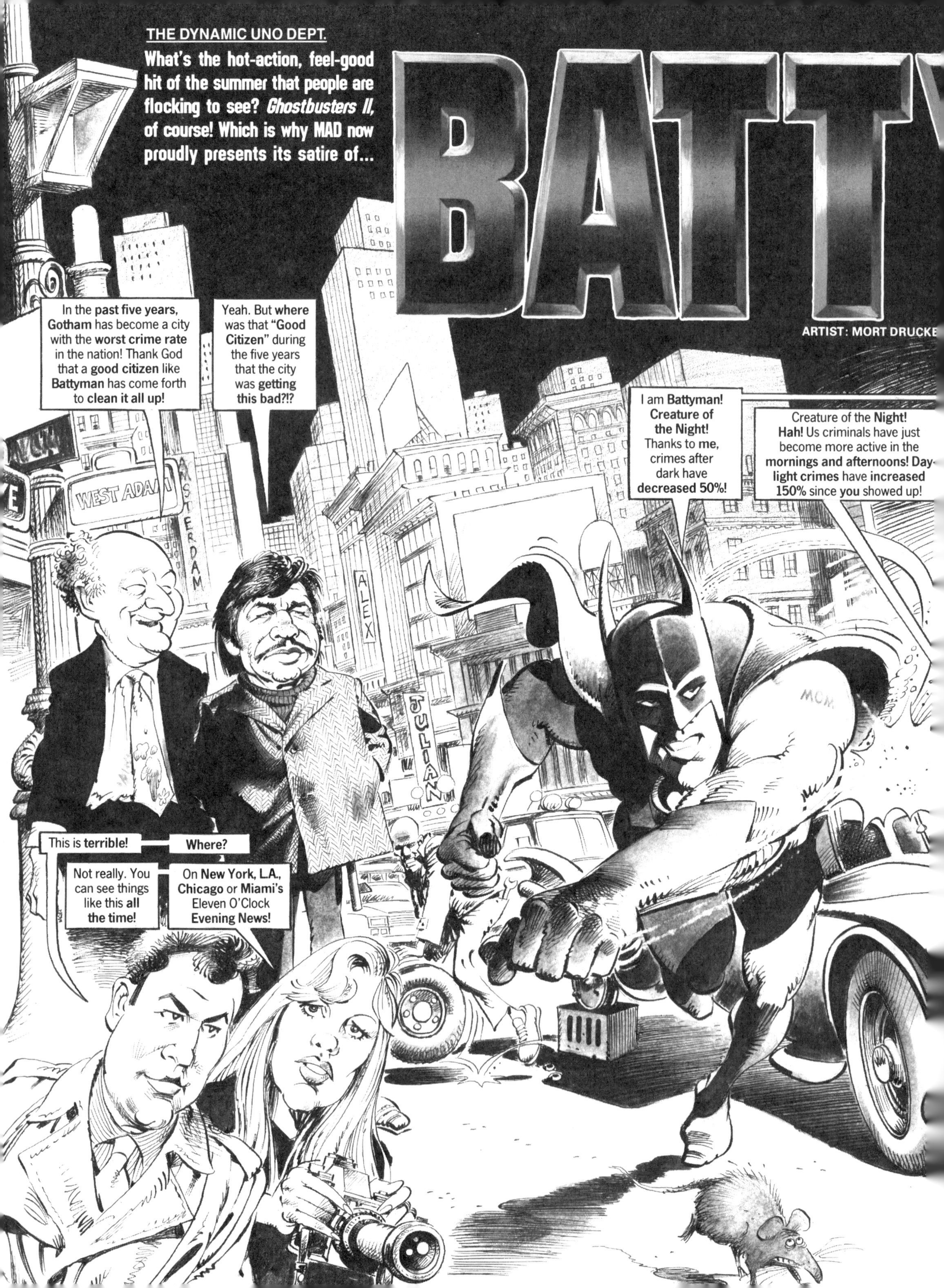

BATT
ARTIST: MORT DRUCKE
In the past five years, Gotham has become a city with the worst crime rate in the nation! Thank God that a good citizen like Battyman has come forth to clean it all up!
Yeah. But where was that "Good Citizen" during the five years that the city was getting this bad?!?
I am Battyman! Creature of the Night! Thanks to me, crimes after dark have decreased 50%!
Creature of the Night! Hah! Us criminals have just become more active in the mornings and afternoons! Daylight crimes have increased 150% since you showed up!
This is terrible!
Where?
Not really. You can see things like this all the time!
On New York, L.A., Chicago or Miami's Eleven O'Clock Evening News!
WEST ADAM
ASTERDAM
ALEX
JULIAN
MOM

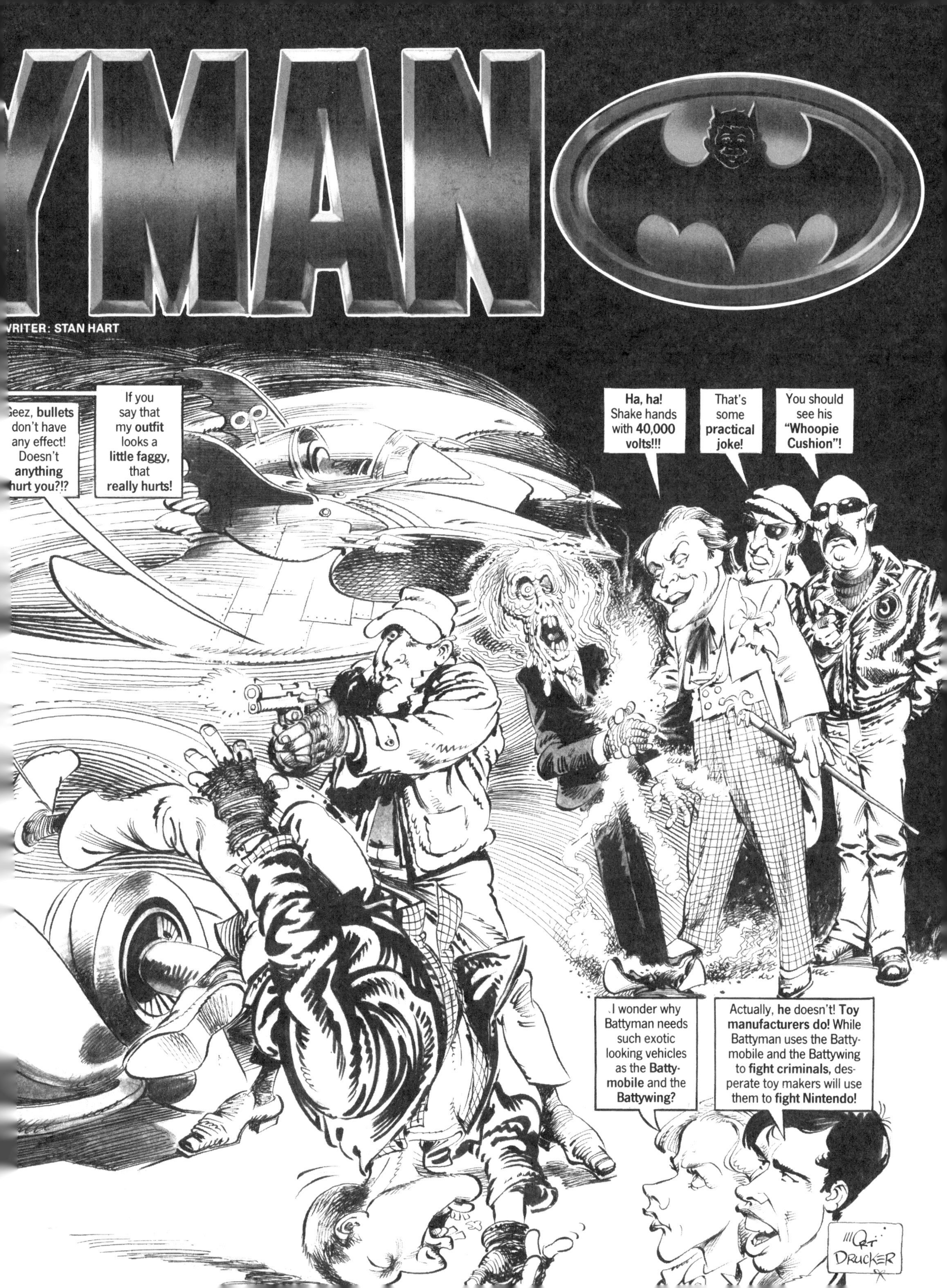

YMAN
WRITER: STAN HART
Geez, bullets don't have any effect! Doesn't anything hurt you?!?
If you say that my outfit looks a little faggy, that really hurts!
Ha, ha! Shake hands with 40,000 volts!!!
That's some practical joke!
You should see his "Whoopie Cushion"!
I wonder why Battyman needs such exotic looking vehicles as the Batty-mobile and the Battywing?
Actually, he doesn't! Toy manufacturers do! While Battyman uses the Batty-mobile and the Battywing to fight criminals, desperate toy makers will use them to fight Nintendo!
ART DRUCKER

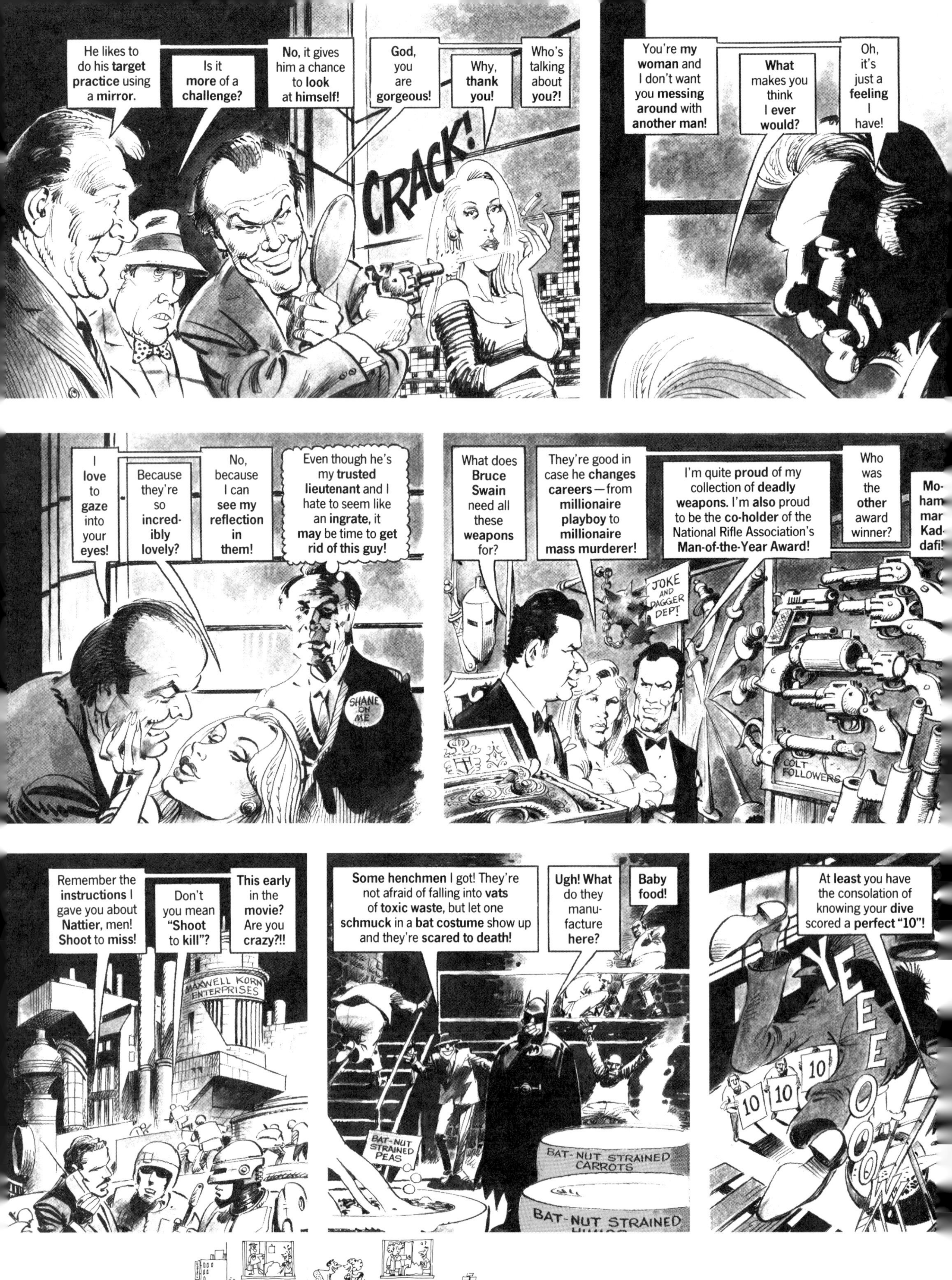
He likes to do his **target practice** using a **mirror.**
Is it **more** of a **challenge?**
**No,** it gives him a chance to **look** at **himself!**
CRACK!
**God,** you are **gorgeous!**
Why, **thank you!**
Who's talking about **you?!**
You're **my woman** and I don't want you **messing around** with **another man!**
**What** makes you think I **ever would?**
Oh, it's just a **feeling** I have!
I **love** to **gaze** into your **eyes!**
Because they're so **incredibly lovely?**
No, because I can **see my reflection in them!**
Even though he's my **trusted lieutenant** and I hate to seem like an **ingrate,** it **may** be time to **get rid of this guy!**
SHANE ON ME
What does **Bruce Swain** need all these **weapons** for?
They're good in case he **changes careers** — from **millionaire playboy** to **millionaire mass murderer!**
I'm quite **proud** of my collection of **deadly weapons.** I'm **also** proud to be the **co-holder** of the National Rifle Association's **Man-of-the-Year Award!**
Who was the **other** award winner?
**Mohammar Kaddafi!**
JOKE AND DAGGER DEPT
COLT FOLLOWERS
Remember the **instructions** I gave you about **Nattier,** men! **Shoot** to **miss!**
Don't you mean **"Shoot to kill"?**
**This early** in the **movie?** Are you **crazy?!!**
MAXWELL KORN ENTERPRISES
**Some henchmen** I got! They're not afraid of falling into **vats** of **toxic waste,** but let one **schmuck** in a **bat costume** show up and they're **scared to death!**
**Ugh! What** do they manufacture **here?**
**Baby food!**
BAT-NUT STRAINED PEAS
BAT-NUT STRAINED CARROTS
BAT-NUT STRAINED
At **least** you have the consolation of knowing your **dive** scored a **perfect "10"!**
10
10
10
YEEEOOOW

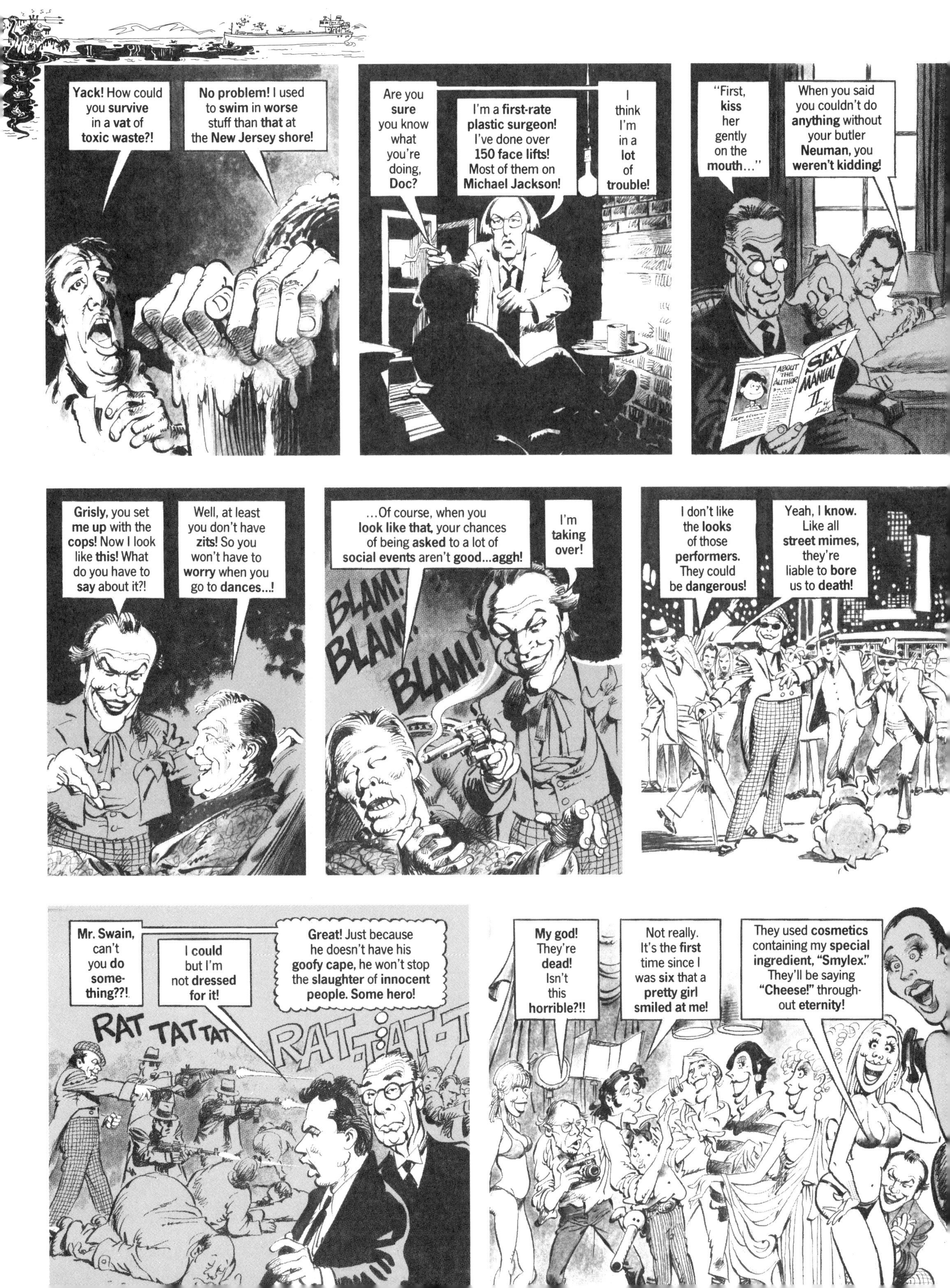

Yack! How could you survive in a vat of toxic waste?!
No problem! I used to swim in worse stuff than that at the New Jersey shore!
Are you sure you know what you're doing, Doc?
I'm a first-rate plastic surgeon! I've done over 150 face lifts! Most of them on Michael Jackson!
I think I'm in a lot of trouble!
"First, kiss her gently on the mouth..."
When you said you couldn't do anything without your butler Neuman, you weren't kidding!
SEX MANUAL II
ABOUT THE AUTHOR
Grisly, you set me up with the cops! Now I look like this! What do you have to say about it?!
Well, at least you don't have zits! So you won't have to worry when you go to dances...!
...Of course, when you look like that, your chances of being asked to a lot of social events aren't good...aggh!
I'm taking over!
BLAM! BLAM! BLAM!
I don't like the looks of those performers. They could be dangerous!
Yeah, I know. Like all street mimes, they're liable to bore us to death!
Mr. Swain, can't you do something??!
I could but I'm not dressed for it!
Great! Just because he doesn't have his goofy cape, he won't stop the slaughter of innocent people. Some hero!
RAT TAT TAT
RAT-TAT-T
My god! They're dead! Isn't this horrible?!!
Not really. It's the first time since I was six that a pretty girl smiled at me!
They used cosmetics containing my special ingredient, "Smylex." They'll be saying "Cheese!" throughout eternity!

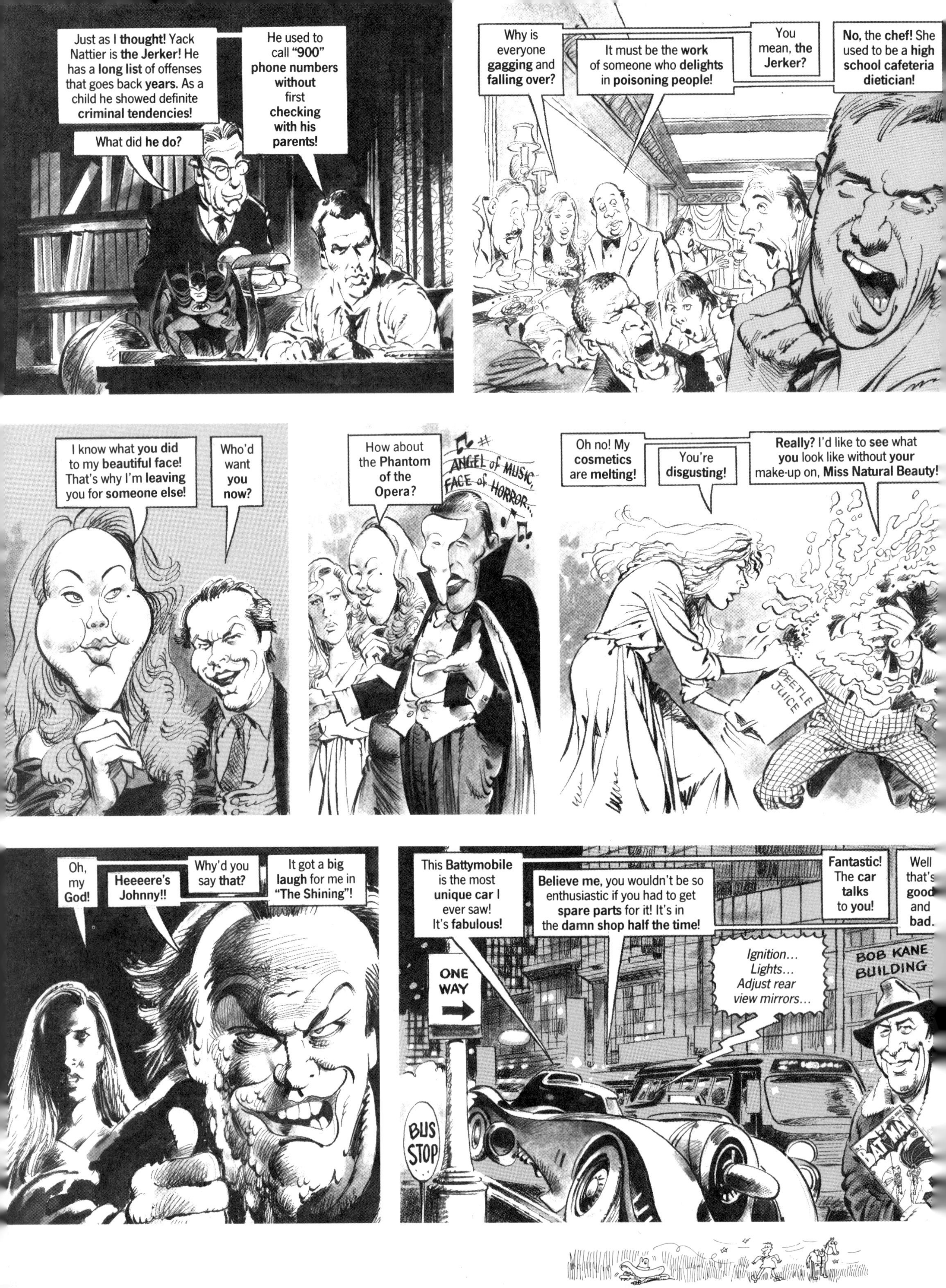

Just as I **thought!** Yack Nattier is **the Jerker!** He has a **long list** of offenses that goes back **years.** As a child he showed definite **criminal tendencies!**
What did **he do?**
He used to call **"900" phone numbers without** first **checking with his parents!**
Why is everyone **gagging** and **falling over?**
It must be the **work** of someone who **delights** in **poisoning people!**
You mean, **the Jerker?**
**No,** the **chef!** She used to be a **high school cafeteria dietician!**
I know what **you did** to my **beautiful face!** That's why I'm **leaving** you for **someone else!**
Who'd want **you** now?
How about the **Phantom of the Opera?**
ANGEL of MUSIC, FACE of HORROR...
Oh no! My **cosmetics** are **melting!**
You're **disgusting!**
**Really?** I'd like to **see** what **you** look like without **your** make-up on, **Miss Natural Beauty!**
BEETLE JUICE
Oh, my **God!**
**Heeeere's Johnny!!**
Why'd you say **that?**
It got a **big laugh** for me in **"The Shining"!**
This **Battymobile** is the most **unique car** I ever saw! It's **fabulous!**
**Believe me,** you wouldn't be so enthusiastic if you had to get **spare parts** for it! It's in the **damn shop half the time!**
**Fantastic!** The **car talks** to **you!**
Well that's **good** and **bad.**
*Ignition... Lights... Adjust rear view mirrors...*
ONE WAY
BUS STOP
BOB KANE BUILDING
BATMAN

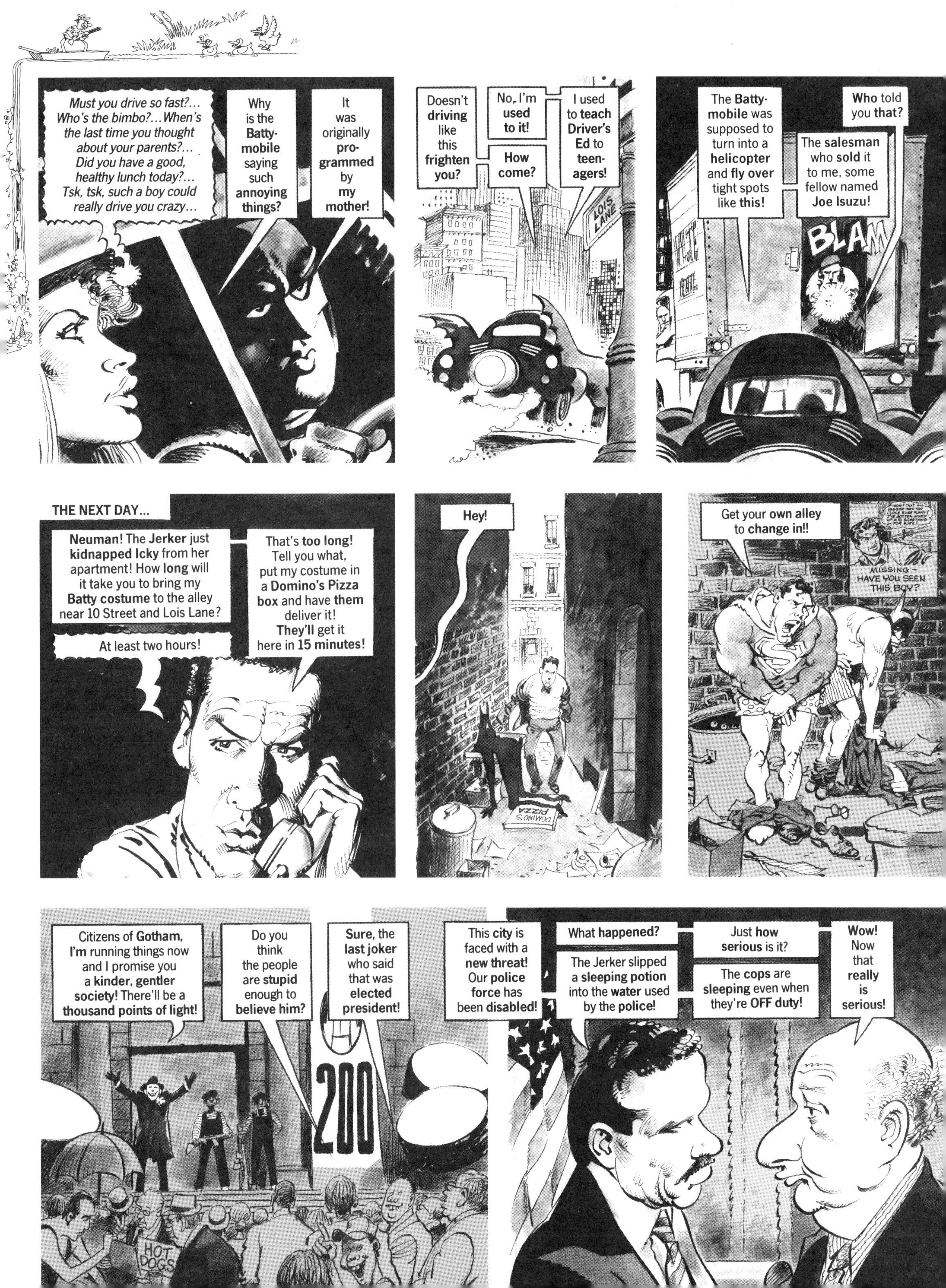
Must you drive so fast?... Who's the bimbo?... When's the last time you thought about your parents?... Did you have a good, healthy lunch today?... Tsk, tsk, such a boy could really drive you crazy...
Why is the Batty-mobile saying such annoying things?
It was originally pro-grammed by my mother!
Doesn't driving like this frighten you?
No, I'm used to it!
How come?
I used to teach Driver's Ed to teen-agers!
LOIS LANE
The Batty-mobile was supposed to turn into a helicopter and fly over tight spots like this!
Who told you that?
The salesman who sold it to me, some fellow named Joe Isuzu!
BLAM
THE NEXT DAY...
Neuman! The Jerker just kidnapped Icky from her apartment! How long will it take you to bring my Batty costume to the alley near 10 Street and Lois Lane?
At least two hours!
That's too long! Tell you what, put my costume in a Domino's Pizza box and have them deliver it! They'll get it here in 15 minutes!
Hey!
DOMINO'S PIZZA
Get your own alley to change in!!
MISSING – HAVE YOU SEEN THIS BOY?
Citizens of Gotham, I'm running things now and I promise you a kinder, gentler society! There'll be a thousand points of light!
Do you think the people are stupid enough to believe him?
Sure, the last joker who said that was elected president!
200
HOT DOGS
This city is faced with a new threat! Our police force has been disabled!
What happened?
The Jerker slipped a sleeping potion into the water used by the police!
Just how serious is it?
The cops are sleeping even when they're OFF duty!
Wow! Now that really is serious!

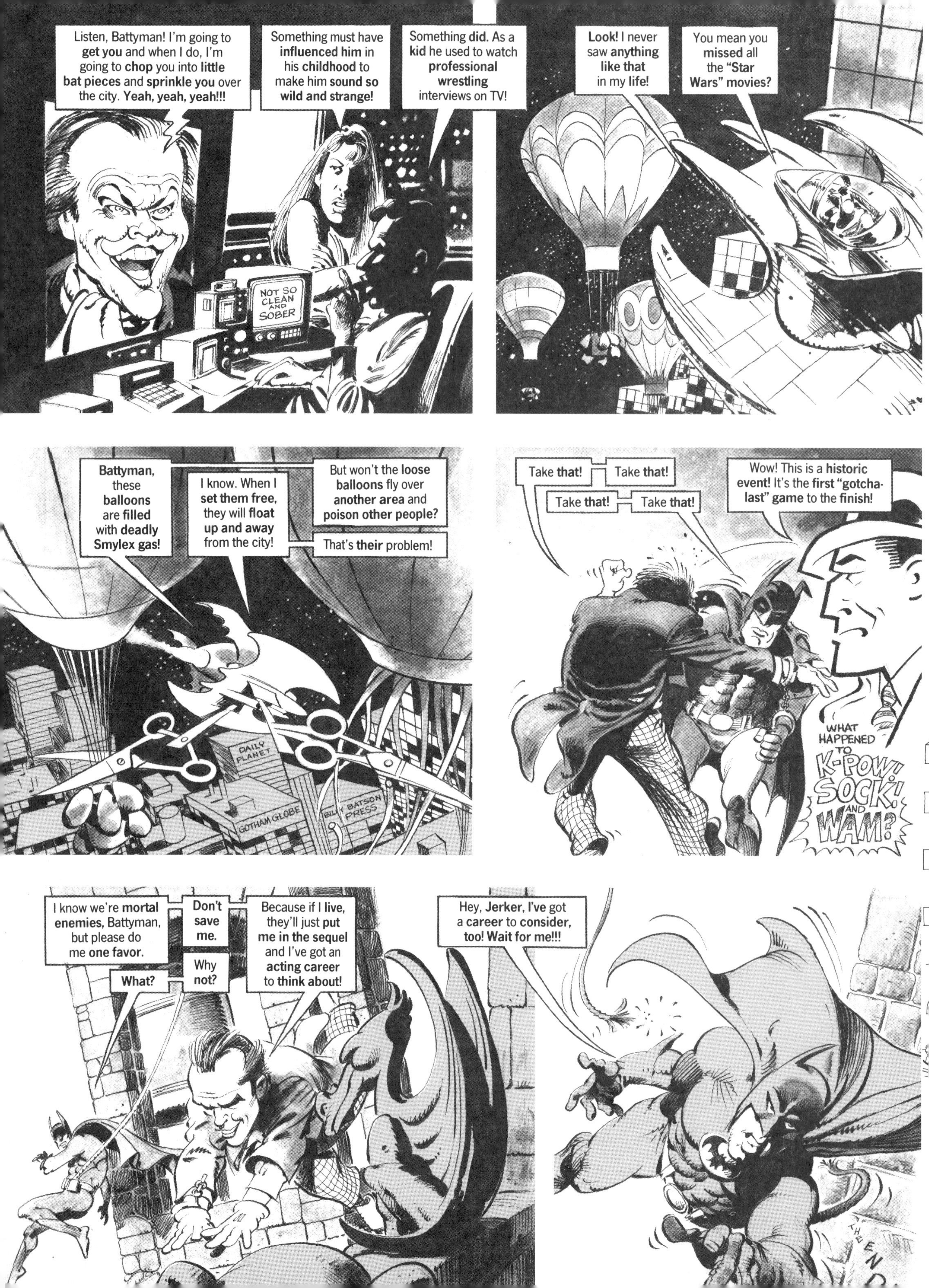

Listen, Battyman! I'm going to get you and when I do, I'm going to chop you into little bat pieces and sprinkle you over the city. Yeah, yeah, yeah!!!
Something must have influenced him in his childhood to make him sound so wild and strange!
Something did. As a kid he used to watch professional wrestling interviews on TV!
NOT SO CLEAN AND SOBER
Look! I never saw anything like that in my life!
You mean you missed all the "Star Wars" movies?
Battyman, these balloons are filled with deadly Smylex gas!
I know. When I set them free, they will float up and away from the city!
But won't the loose balloons fly over another area and poison other people?
That's their problem!
DAILY PLANET
GOTHAM GLOBE
BILLY BATSON PRESS
Take that!
Take that!
Take that!
Take that!
Wow! This is a historic event! It's the first "gotcha-last" game to the finish!
WHAT HAPPENED TO K-POW! SOCK! AND WAM?
I know we're mortal enemies, Battyman, but please do me one favor.
What?
Don't save me.
Why not?
Because if I live, they'll just put me in the sequel and I've got an acting career to think about!
Hey, Jerker, I've got a career to consider, too! Wait for me!!!
THE END

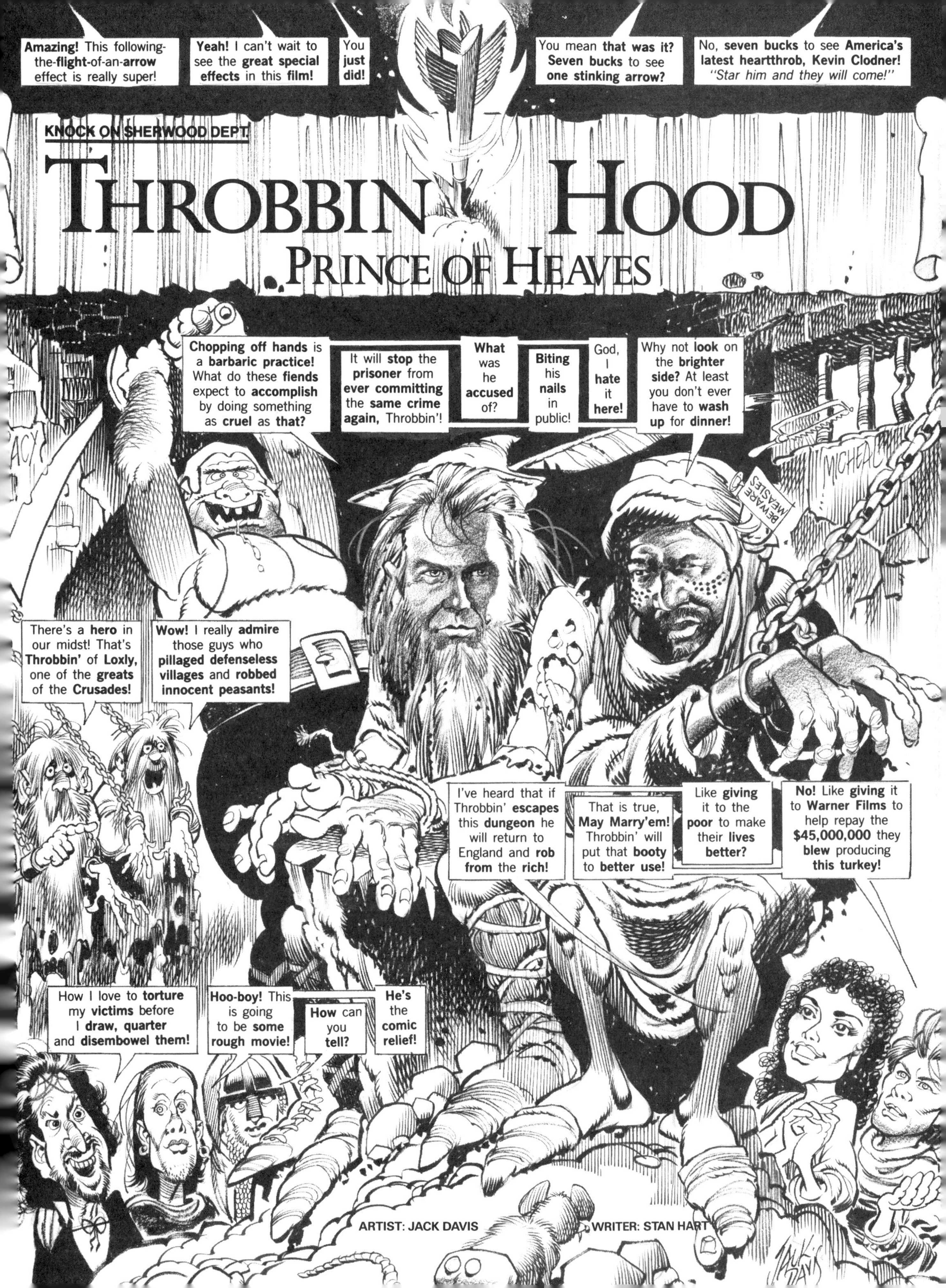

Amazing! This following-the-flight-of-an-arrow effect is really super!
Yeah! I can't wait to see the great special effects in this film!
You just did!
You mean that was it? Seven bucks to see one stinking arrow?
No, seven bucks to see America's latest heartthrob, Kevin Clodner! "Star him and they will come!"
KNOCK ON SHERWOOD DEPT.
THROBBIN HOOD
PRINCE OF HEAVES
Chopping off hands is a barbaric practice! What do these fiends expect to accomplish by doing something as cruel as that?
It will stop the prisoner from ever committing the same crime again, Throbbin'!
What was he accused of?
Biting his nails in public!
God, I hate it here!
Why not look on the brighter side? At least you don't ever have to wash up for dinner!
BEWARE MEASLES
There's a hero in our midst! That's Throbbin' of Loxly, one of the greats of the Crusades!
Wow! I really admire those guys who pillaged defenseless villages and robbed innocent peasants!
I've heard that if Throbbin' escapes this dungeon he will return to England and rob from the rich!
That is true, May Marry'em! Throbbin' will put that booty to better use!
Like giving it to the poor to make their lives better?
No! Like giving it to Warner Films to help repay the $45,000,000 they blew producing this turkey!
How I love to torture my victims before I draw, quarter and disembowel them!
Hoo-boy! This is going to be some rough movie!
How can you tell?
He's the comic relief!
ARTIST: JACK DAVIS
WRITER: STAN HART

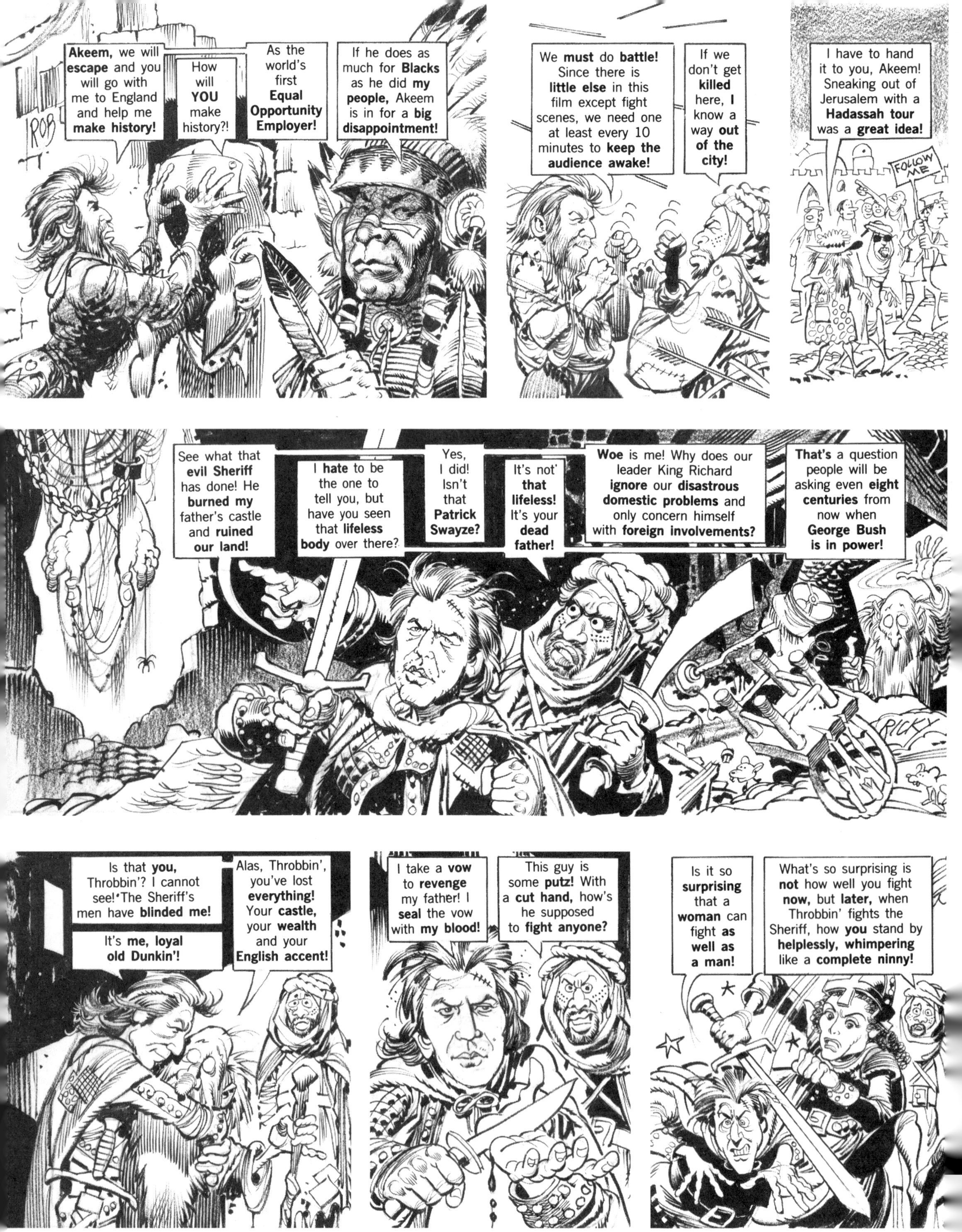
Akeem, we will escape and you will go with me to England and help me make history!
How will YOU make history?!
As the world's first Equal Opportunity Employer!
If he does as much for Blacks as he did my people, Akeem is in for a big disappointment!
We must do battle! Since there is little else in this film except fight scenes, we need one at least every 10 minutes to keep the audience awake!
If we don't get killed here, I know a way out of the city!
I have to hand it to you, Akeem! Sneaking out of Jerusalem with a Hadassah tour was a great idea!
FOLLOW ME
See what that evil Sheriff has done! He burned my father's castle and ruined our land!
I hate to be the one to tell you, but have you seen that lifeless body over there?
Yes, I did! Isn't that Patrick Swayze?
It's not' that lifeless! It's your dead father!
Woe is me! Why does our leader King Richard ignore our disastrous domestic problems and only concern himself with foreign involvements?
That's a question people will be asking even eight centuries from now when George Bush is in power!
Is that you, Throbbin'? I cannot see! The Sheriff's men have blinded me!
It's me, loyal old Dunkin'!
Alas, Throbbin', you've lost everything! Your castle, your wealth and your English accent!
I take a vow to revenge my father! I seal the vow with my blood!
This guy is some putz! With a cut hand, how's he supposed to fight anyone?
Is it so surprising that a woman can fight as well as a man!
What's so surprising is not how well you fight now, but later, when Throbbin' fights the Sheriff, how you stand by helplessly, whimpering like a complete ninny!

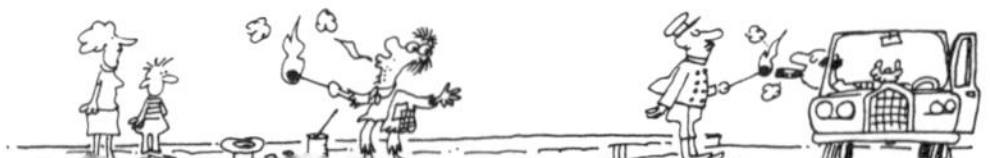

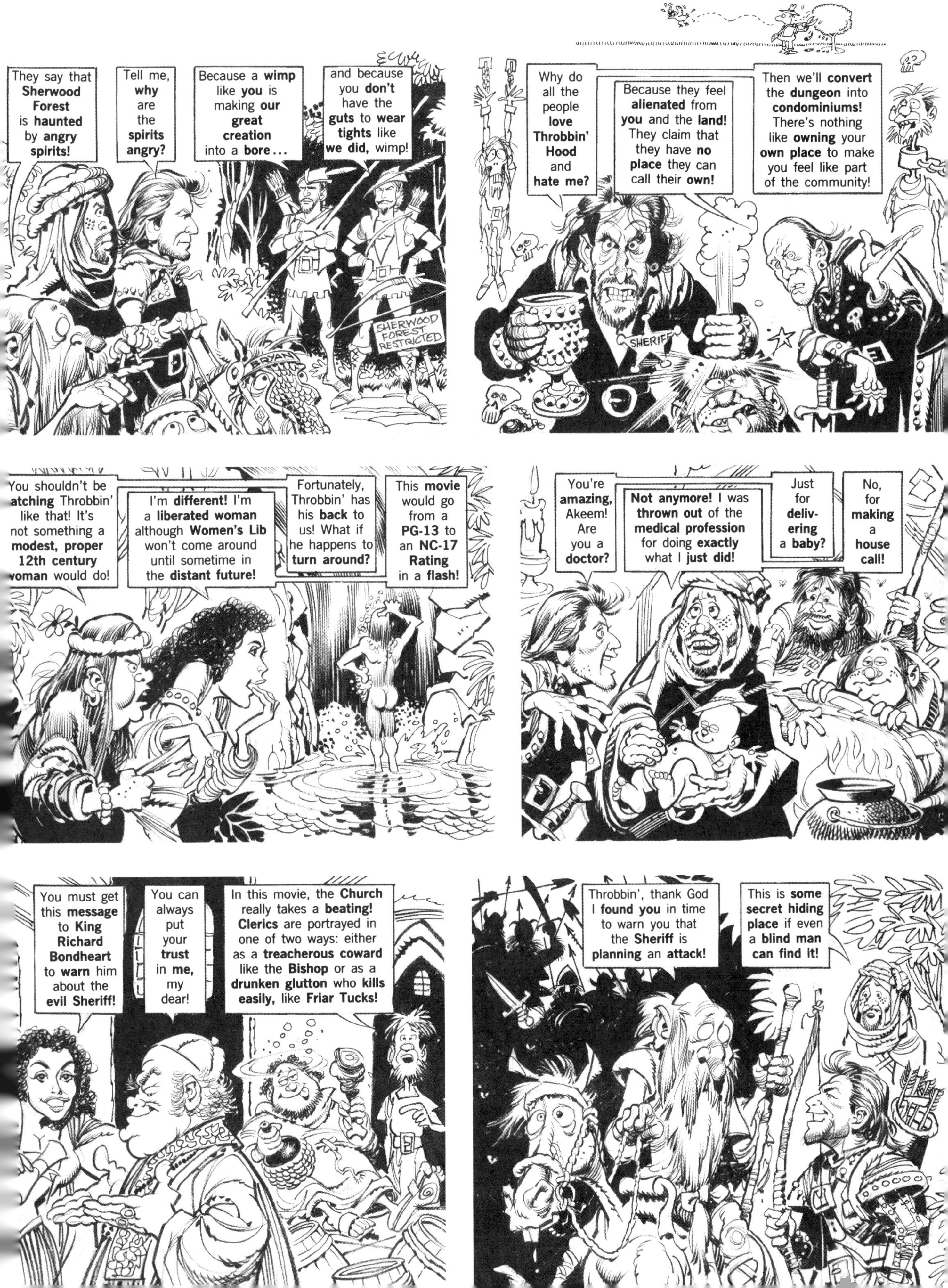

They say that **Sherwood Forest** is **haunted** by **angry spirits!**
Tell me, **why** are the **spirits angry?**
Because a **wimp** like **you** is making **our great creation** into a **bore . . .**
and because you **don't** have the **guts** to **wear tights** like **we did,** wimp!
SHERWOOD FOREST RESTRICTED
BRYAN
Why do all the people **love Throbbin' Hood** and **hate me?**
Because they feel **alienated** from **you** and the **land!** They claim that they have **no place** they can call their **own!**
Then we'll **convert** the **dungeon** into **condominiums!** There's nothing like **owning** your **own place** to make you feel like part of the community!
SHERIFF
You shouldn't be **atching** Throbbin' like that! It's not something a **modest, proper 12th century oman** would do!
I'm **different!** I'm a **liberated woman** although **Women's Lib** won't come around until sometime in the **distant future!**
Fortunately, Throbbin' has his **back** to us! What if he happens to **turn around?**
This **movie** would go from a **PG-13** to an **NC-17 Rating** in a **flash!**
You're **amazing,** Akeem! Are you a **doctor?**
**Not anymore!** I was **thrown out** of the **medical profession** for doing **exactly** what I **just did!**
Just for **deliv-ering** a **baby?**
No, for **making** a **house call!**
You must get this **message** to **King Richard Bondheart** to **warn** him about the **evil Sheriff!**
You can always put your **trust** in **me,** my dear!
In this movie, the **Church** really takes a **beating! Clerics** are portrayed in one of two ways: either as a **treacherous coward** like the **Bishop** or as a **drunken glutton** who **kills easily,** like **Friar Tucks!**
Throbbin', thank God I **found you** in time to warn you that the **Sheriff** is **planning** an **attack!**
This is **some secret hiding place** if even a **blind man can find it!**

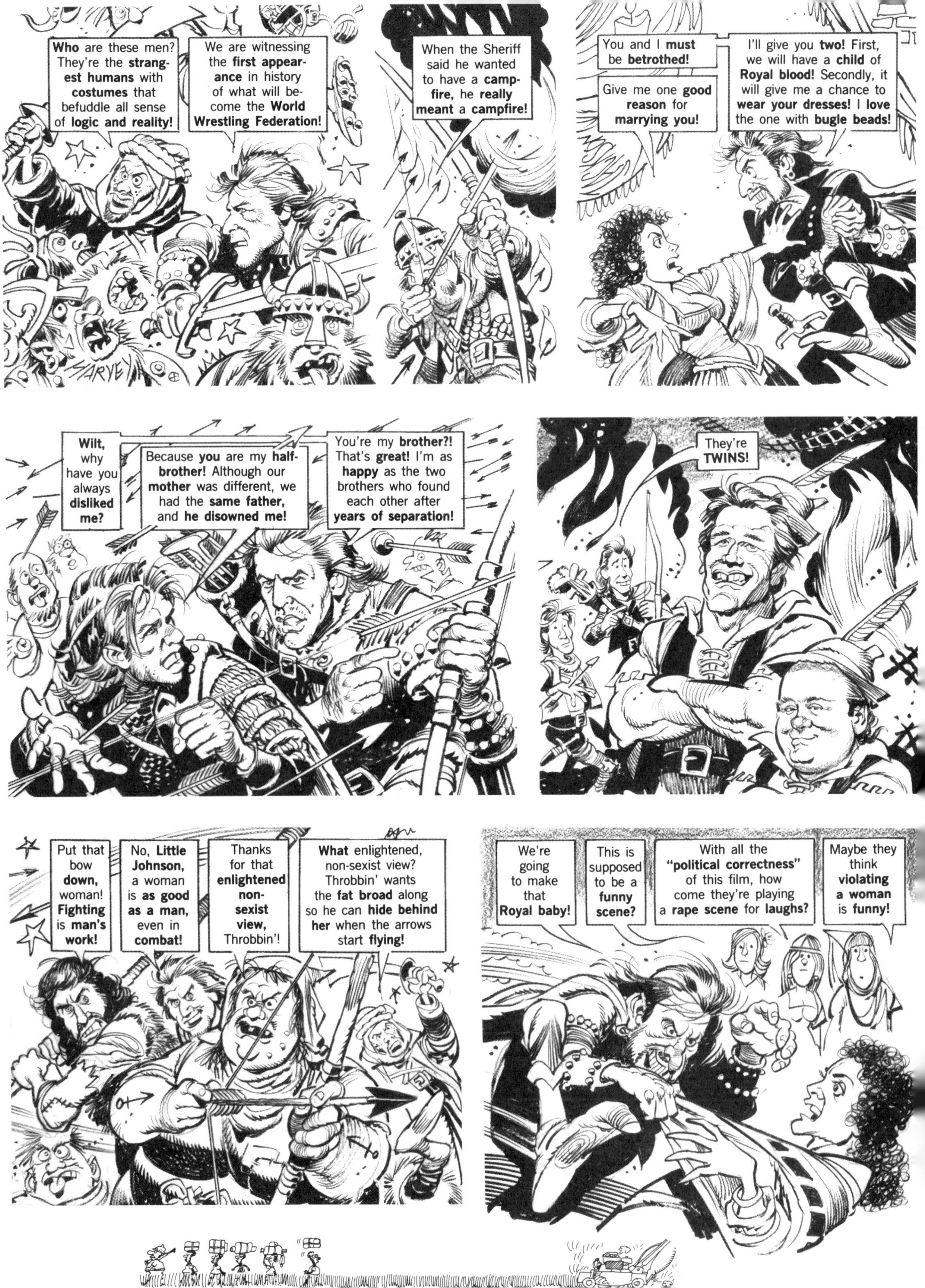
Who are these men? They're the strangest humans with costumes that befuddle all sense of logic and reality!
We are witnessing the first appearance in history of what will become the World Wrestling Federation!
When the Sheriff said he wanted to have a campfire, he really meant a campfire!
You and I must be betrothed!
Give me one good reason for marrying you!
I'll give you two! First, we will have a child of Royal blood! Secondly, it will give me a chance to wear your dresses! I love the one with bugle beads!
Wilt, why have you always disliked me?
Because you are my half-brother! Although our mother was different, we had the same father, and he disowned me!
You're my brother?! That's great! I'm as happy as the two brothers who found each other after years of separation!
They're TWINS!
Put that bow down, woman! Fighting is man's work!
No, Little Johnson, a woman is as good as a man, even in combat!
Thanks for that enlightened non-sexist view, Throbbin'!
What enlightened, non-sexist view? Throbbin' wants the fat broad along so he can hide behind her when the arrows start flying!
We're going to make that Royal baby!
This is supposed to be a funny scene?
With all the "political correctness" of this film, how come they're playing a rape scene for laughs?
Maybe they think violating a woman is funny!

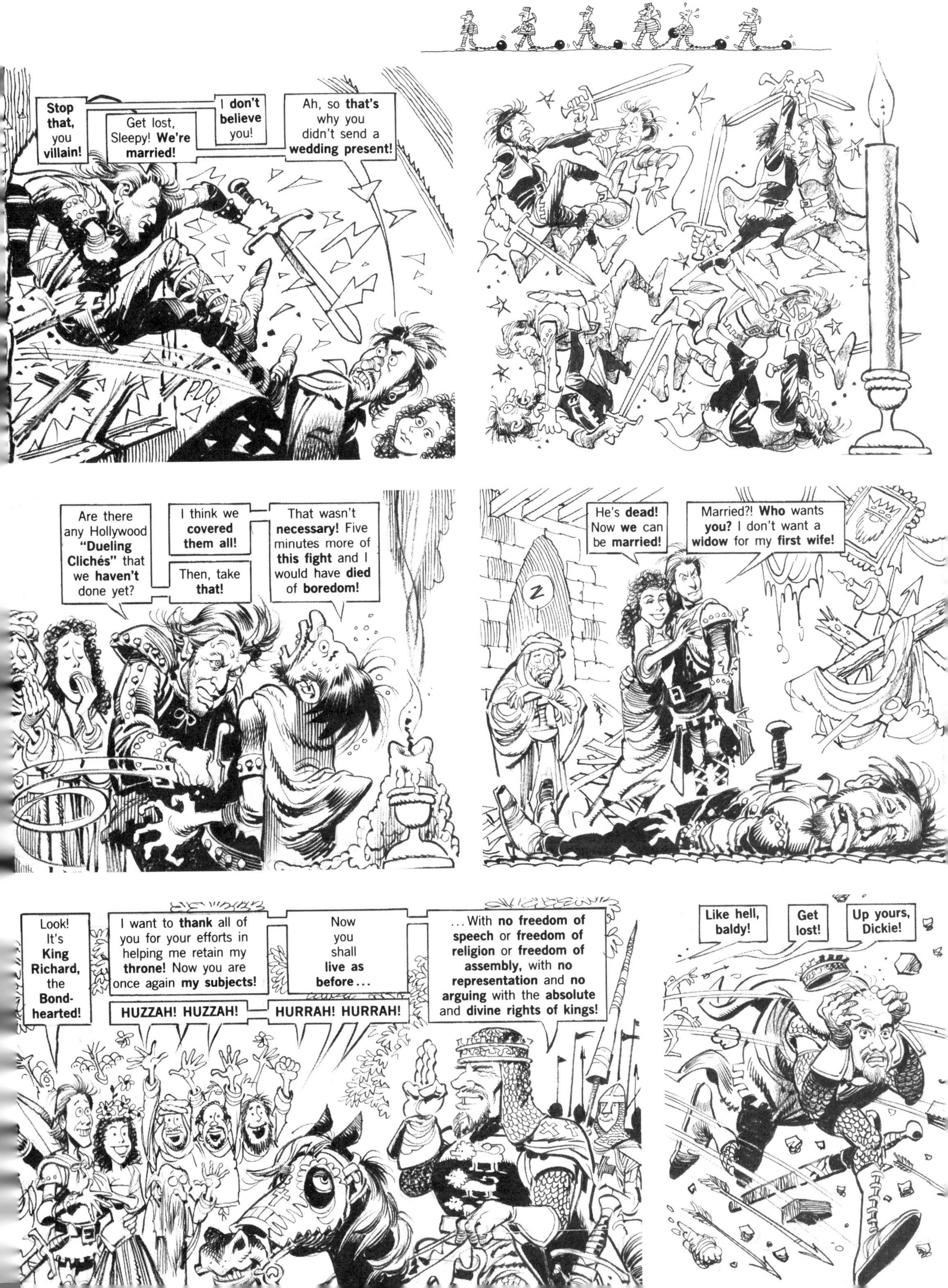
Stop that, you villain!
Get lost, Sleepy! We're married!
I don't believe you!
Ah, so that's why you didn't send a wedding present!
Are there any Hollywood "Dueling Clichés" that we haven't done yet?
I think we covered them all!
Then, take that!
That wasn't necessary! Five minutes more of this fight and I would have died of boredom!
He's dead! Now we can be married!
Married?! Who wants you? I don't want a widow for my first wife!
Look! It's King Richard, the Bond-hearted!
I want to thank all of you for your efforts in helping me retain my throne! Now you are once again my subjects!
HUZZAH! HUZZAH!
Now you shall live as before...
HURRAH! HURRAH!
...With no freedom of speech or freedom of religion or freedom of assembly, with no representation and no arguing with the absolute and divine rights of kings!
Like hell, baldy!
Get lost!
Up yours, Dickie!

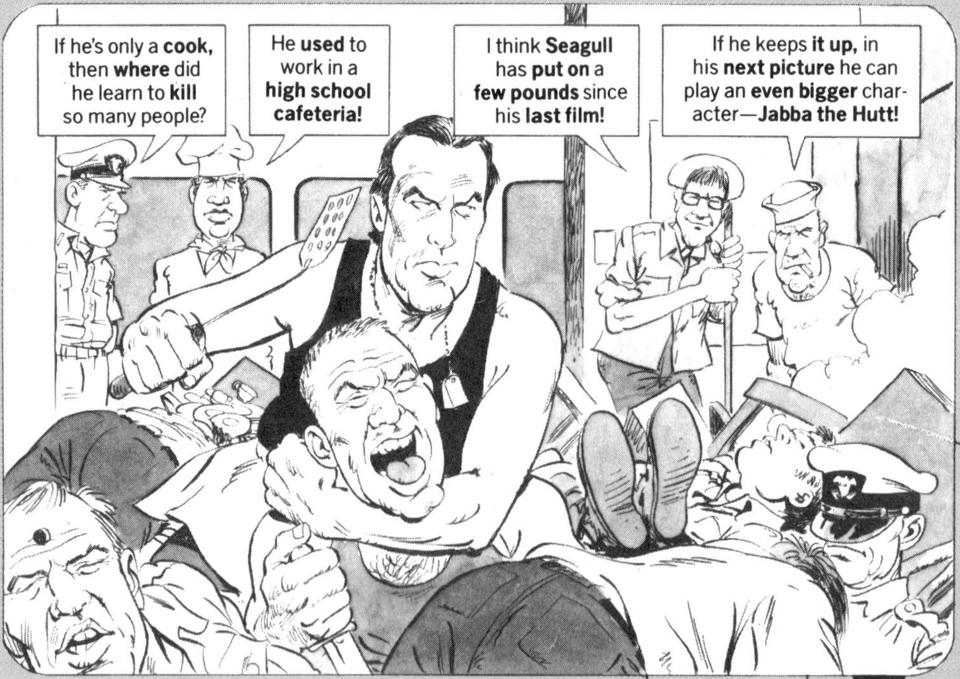
If he's only a cook, then where did he learn to kill so many people?
He used to work in a high school cafeteria!
I think Seagull has put on a few pounds since his last film!
If he keeps it up, in his next picture he can play an even bigger character—Jabba the Hutt!

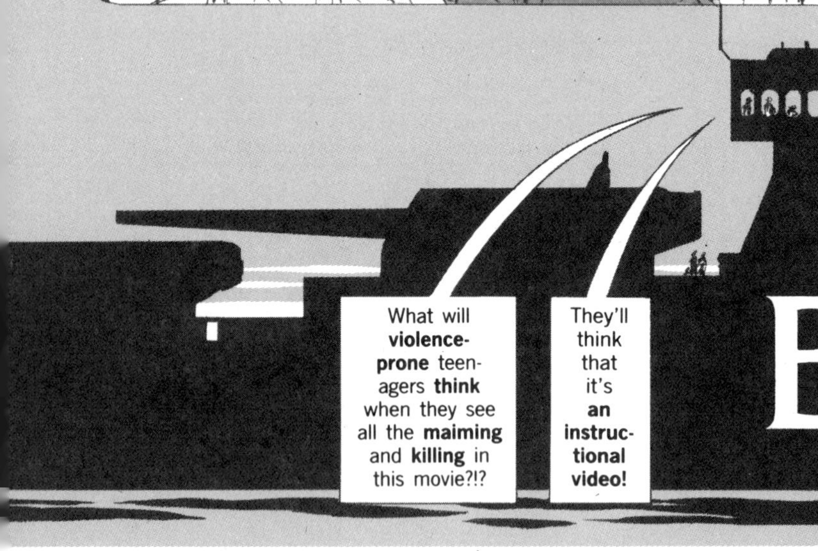
What will violence-prone teenagers think when they see all the maiming and killing in this movie?!?
They'll think that it's an instructional video!

**A MAN FOR ALL SEIZIN'S DEPT.**

Take a psychotic, burnt-out CIA operative, a petty, jealou
naval officer who enjoys dressing up like a woman (now tha
President Clinton says he's going to allow that sort o

# BLUNDE

ARTIST: ANGELO TORRE

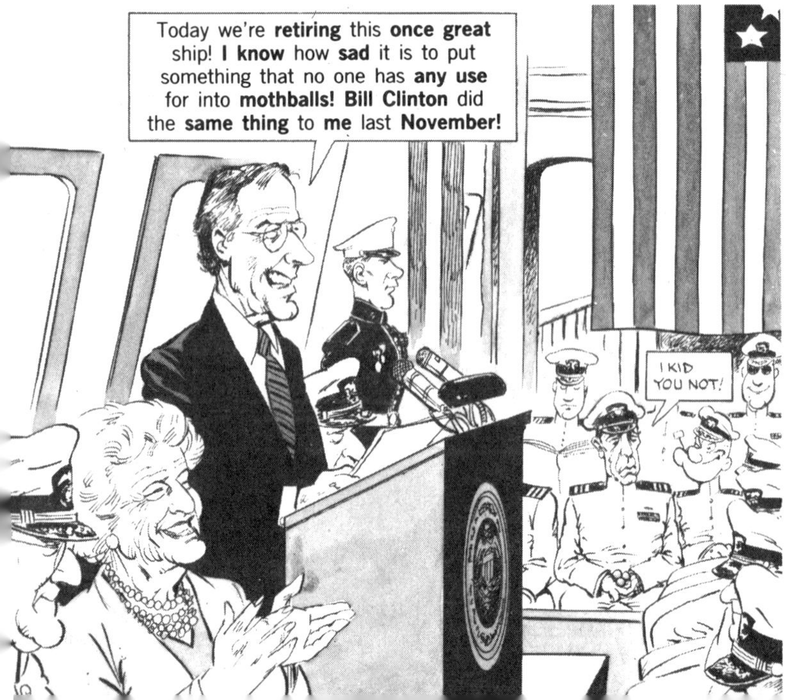
Today we're retiring this once great ship! I know how sad it is to put something that no one has any use for into mothballs! Bill Clinton did the same thing to me last November!
I KID YOU NOT!

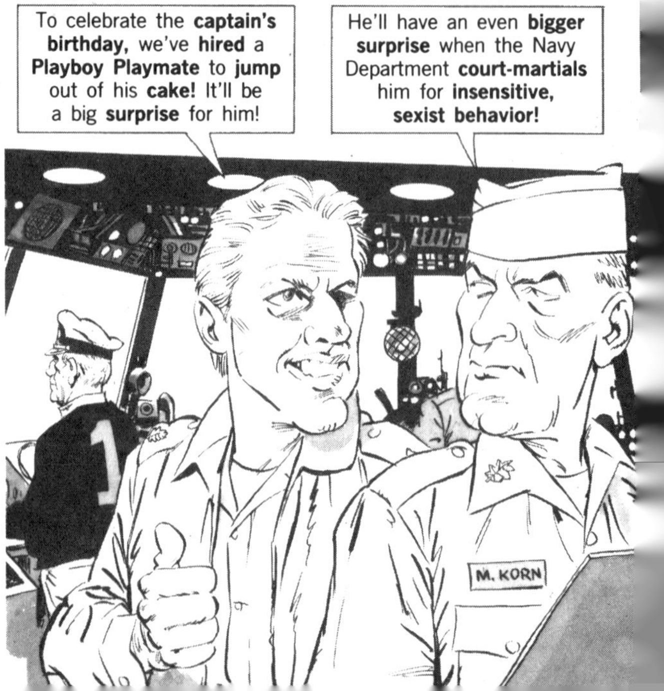
To celebrate the captain's birthday, we've hired a Playboy Playmate to jump out of his cake! It'll be a big surprise for him!
He'll have an even bigger surprise when the Navy Department court-martials him for insensitive, sexist behavior!
M. KORN

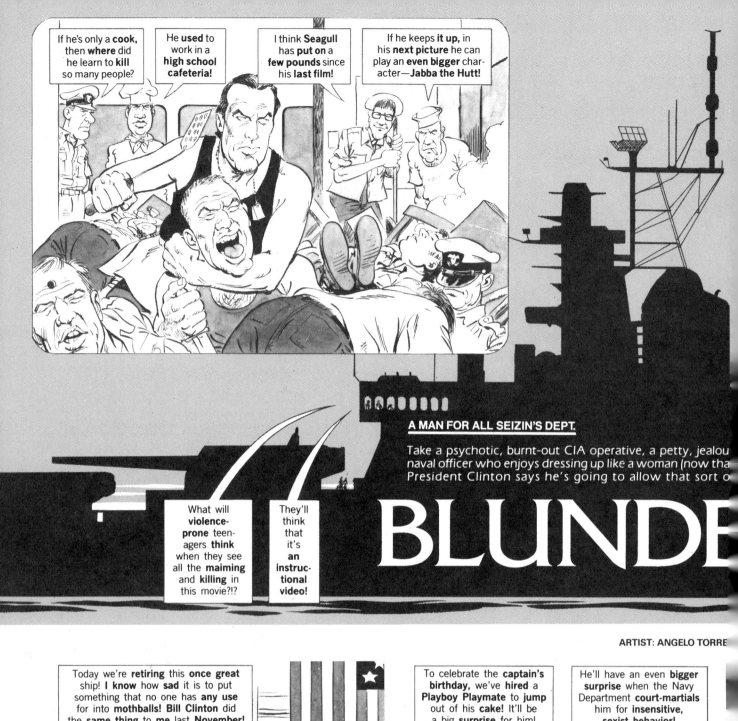

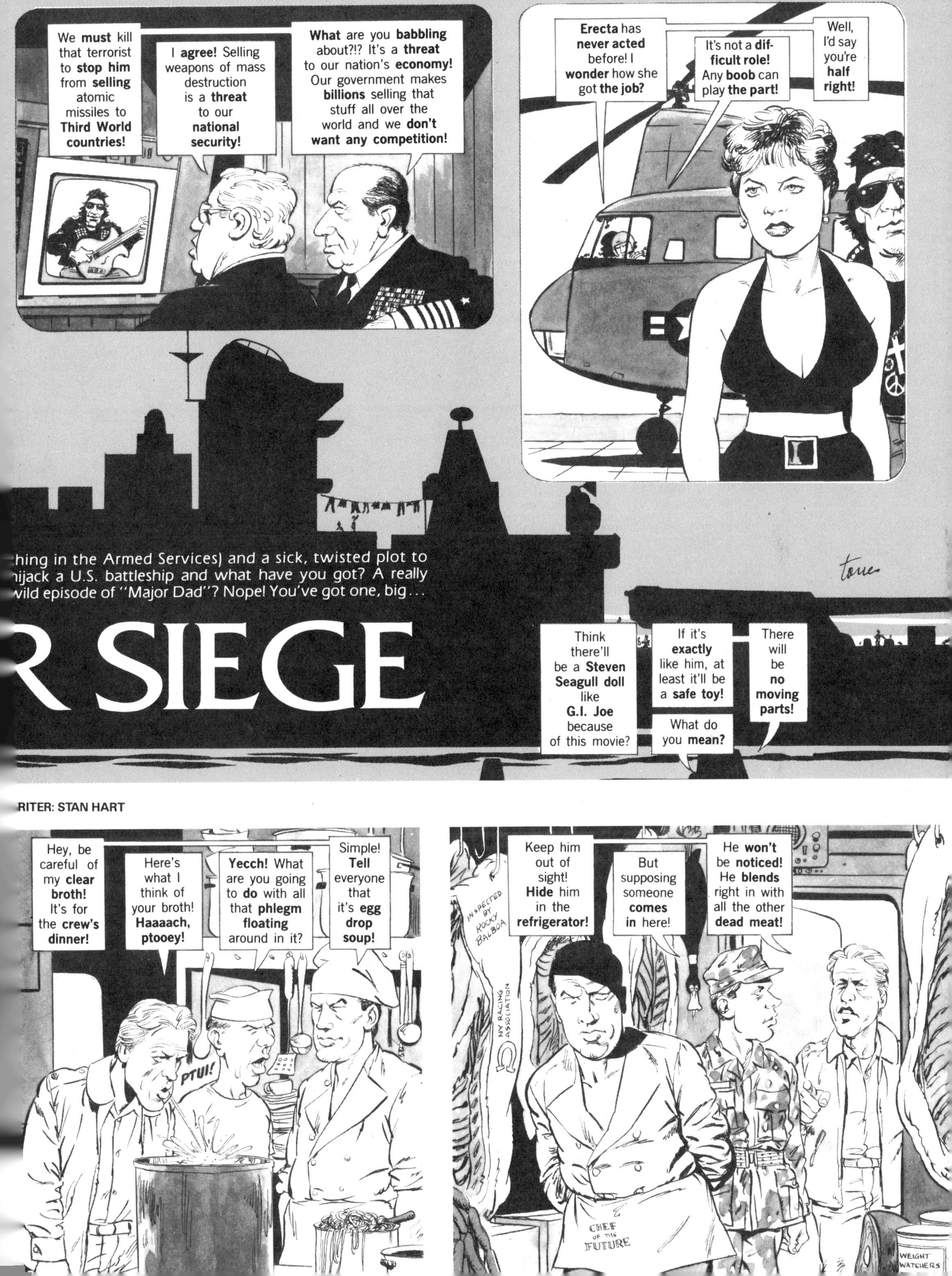
We must kill that terrorist to stop him from selling atomic missiles to Third World countries!
I agree! Selling weapons of mass destruction is a threat to our national security!
What are you babbling about?!? It's a threat to our nation's economy! Our government makes billions selling that stuff all over the world and we don't want any competition!
Erecta has never acted before! I wonder how she got the job?
It's not a difficult role! Any boob can play the part!
Well, I'd say you're half right!
hing in the Armed Services) and a sick, twisted plot to hijack a U.S. battleship and what have you got? A really wild episode of "Major Dad"? Nope! You've got one, big . . .
R SIEGE
Think there'll be a Steven Seagull doll like G.I. Joe because of this movie?
If it's exactly like him, at least it'll be a safe toy!
What do you mean?
There will be no moving parts!
RITER: STAN HART
Hey, be careful of my clear broth! It's for the crew's dinner!
Here's what I think of your broth! Haaaach, ptooey!
PTUI!
Yecch! What are you going to do with all that phlegm floating around in it?
Simple! Tell everyone that it's egg drop soup!
Keep him out of sight! Hide him in the refrigerator!
But supposing someone comes in here!
He won't be noticed! He blends right in with all the other dead meat!
INSPECTED BY ROCKY BALBOA
NY RACING ASSOCIATION
CHEF OF THE FUTURE
WEIGHT WATCHERS

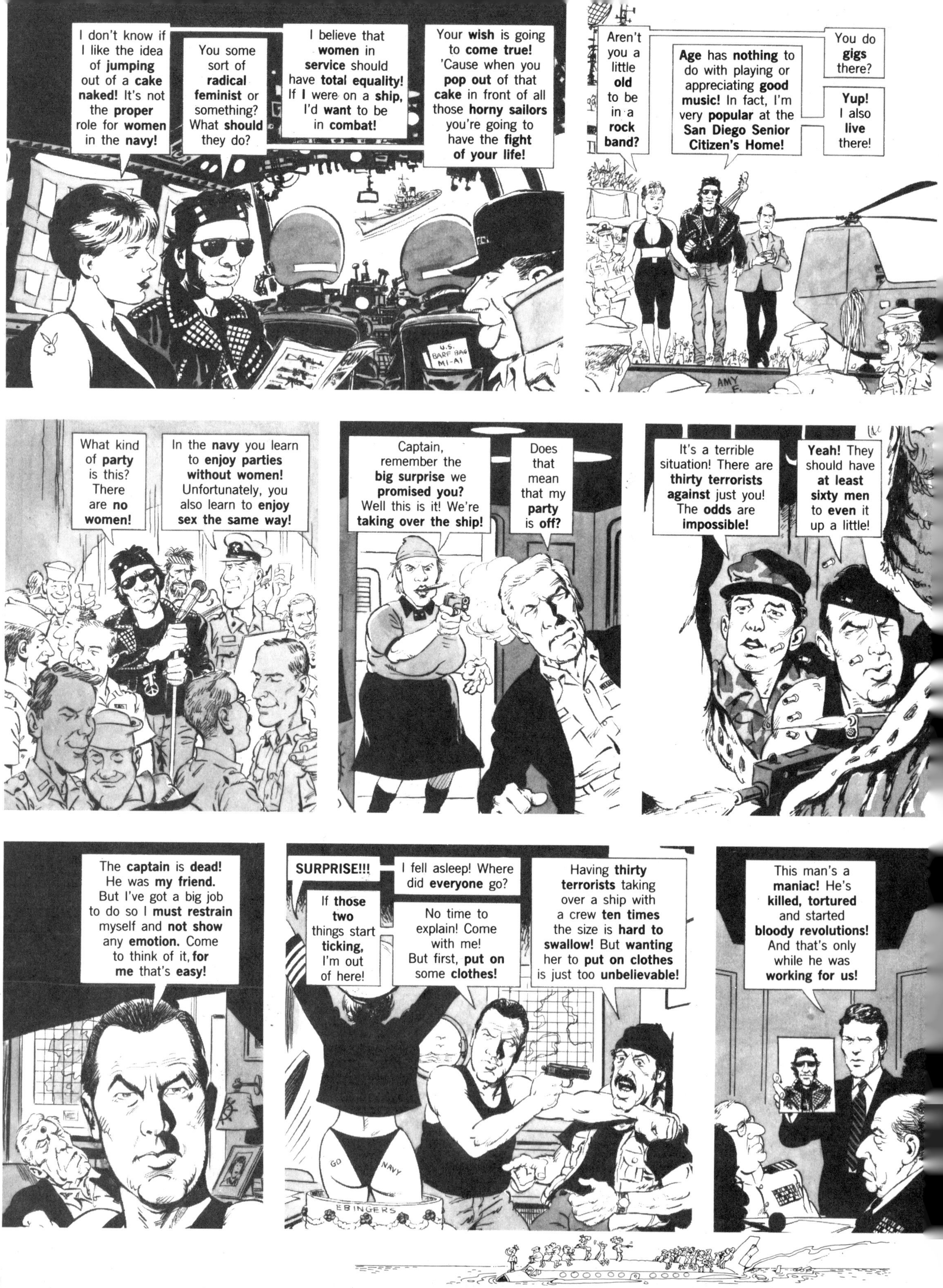
I don't know if I like the idea of **jumping** out of a **cake naked!** It's not the **proper** role for **women** in the **navy!**
You some sort of **radical feminist** or something? What **should** they do?
I believe that **women** in **service** should have **total equality!** If **I** were on a **ship**, I'd **want** to be in **combat!**
Your **wish** is going to **come true!** 'Cause when you **pop out** of that **cake** in front of all those **horny sailors** you're going to have the **fight of your life!**
U.S. BARF BAG MI-AI
Aren't you a little **old** to be in a **rock band?**
**Age** has **nothing** to do with playing or appreciating **good music!** In fact, I'm very **popular** at the **San Diego Senior Citizen's Home!**
You do **gigs** there?
**Yup!** I also **live** there!
AMY F.
What kind of **party** is this? There are **no women!**
In the **navy** you learn to **enjoy parties without women!** Unfortunately, you also learn to **enjoy sex the same way!**
Captain, remember the **big surprise** we **promised you?** Well this is it! We're **taking over the ship!**
Does that mean that my **party** is **off?**
It's a terrible situation! There are **thirty terrorists against** just you! The **odds** are **impossible!**
**Yeah!** They should have **at least sixty men** to **even** it up a little!
The **captain** is **dead!** He was **my friend.** But I've got a big job to do so I **must restrain** myself and **not show** any **emotion.** Come to think of it, **for me** that's **easy!**
**SURPRISE!!!**
I fell asleep! Where did **everyone** go?
If **those two** things start **ticking,** I'm out of here!
No time to explain! Come with me! But first, **put on** some **clothes!**
Having **thirty terrorists** taking over a ship with a crew **ten times** the size is **hard to swallow!** But **wanting** her to **put on clothes** is just too **unbelievable!**
GO NAVY
EBINGERS
This man's a **maniac!** He's **killed, tortured** and started **bloody revolutions!** And that's only while he was **working for us!**

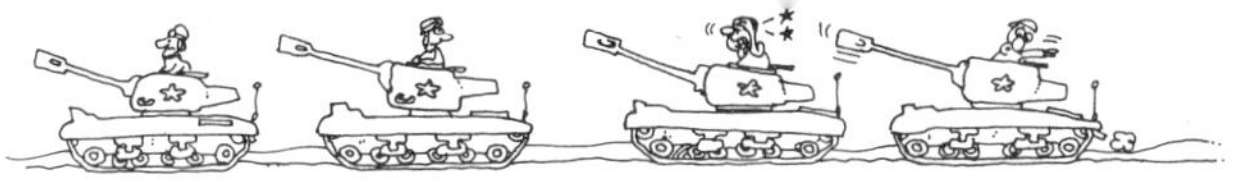

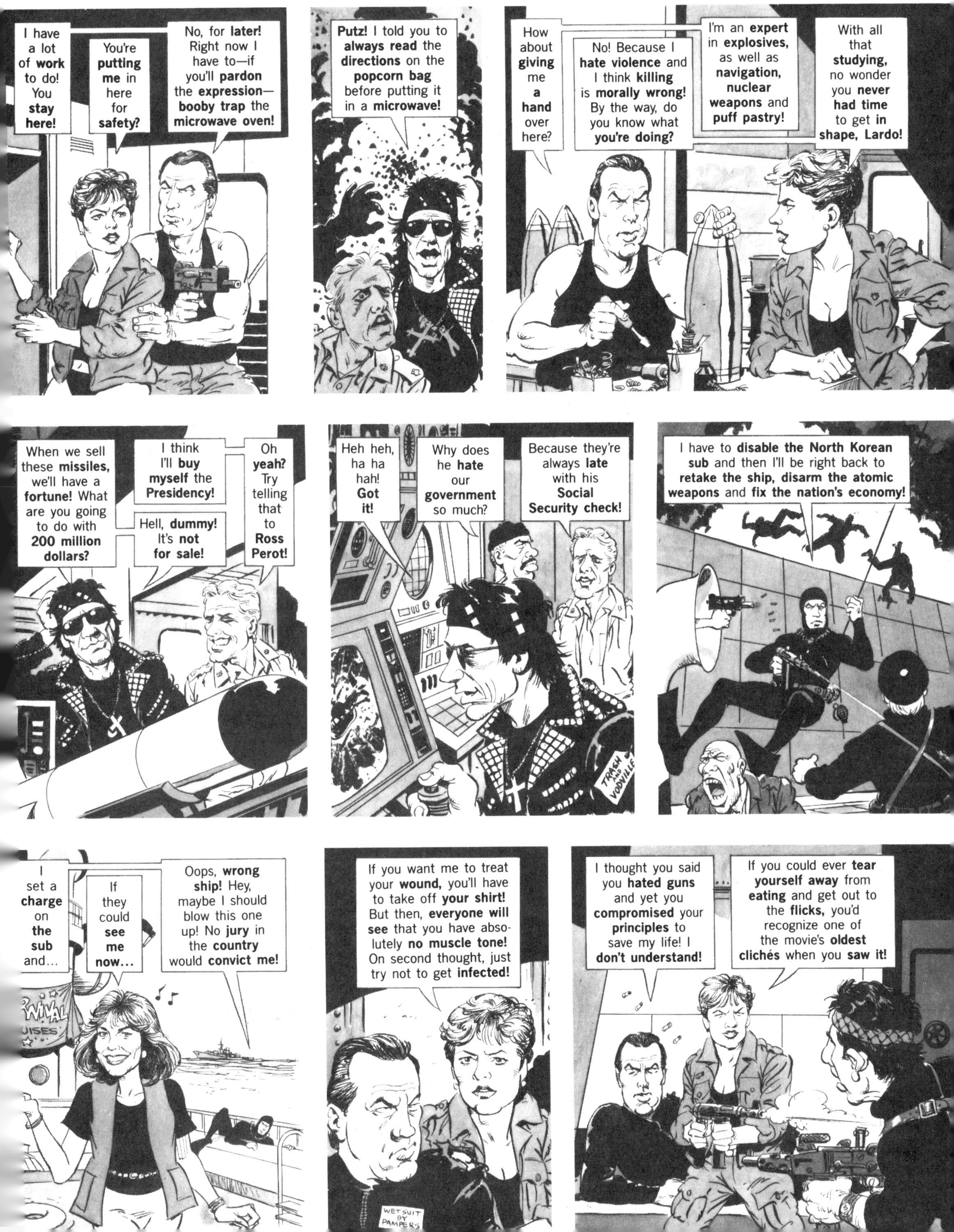

I have a lot of **work** to do! You **stay here!**
You're **putting me** in here for **safety?**
No, for **later!** Right now I have to—if you'll **pardon** the **expression—booby trap** the **microwave oven!**
**Putz!** I told you to **always read** the **directions** on the **popcorn bag** before putting it in a **microwave!**
How about **giving** me **a hand** over here?
No! Because I **hate violence** and I think **killing** is **morally wrong!** By the way, do you know what **you're doing?**
I'm an **expert** in **explosives,** as well as **navigation, nuclear weapons** and **puff pastry!**
With all that **studying,** no wonder you **never had time** to get **in shape, Lardo!**
When we sell these **missiles,** we'll have a **fortune!** What are you going to do with **200 million dollars?**
I think I'll **buy myself** the **Presidency!**
Hell, **dummy!** It's **not for sale!**
Oh **yeah?** Try telling that to **Ross Perot!**
Heh heh, ha ha hah! **Got it!**
Why does he **hate** our **government** so much?
Because they're always **late** with his **Social Security check!**
TRASH AND VODVILLE
I have to **disable the North Korean sub** and then I'll be right back to **retake the ship, disarm the atomic weapons** and **fix the nation's economy!**
I set a **charge** on **the sub** and...
If they could **see me now...**
Oops, **wrong ship!** Hey, maybe I should blow this one up! No **jury** in the **country** would **convict me!**
If you want me to treat your **wound,** you'll have to take off **your shirt!** But then, **everyone will see** that you have absolutely **no muscle tone!** On second thought, just try not to get **infected!**
WET SUIT BY PAMPERS
I thought you said you **hated guns** and yet you **compromised** your **principles** to save my life! I **don't understand!**
If you could ever **tear yourself away** from **eating** and get out to the **flicks,** you'd recognize one of the movie's **oldest clichés** when you **saw it!**

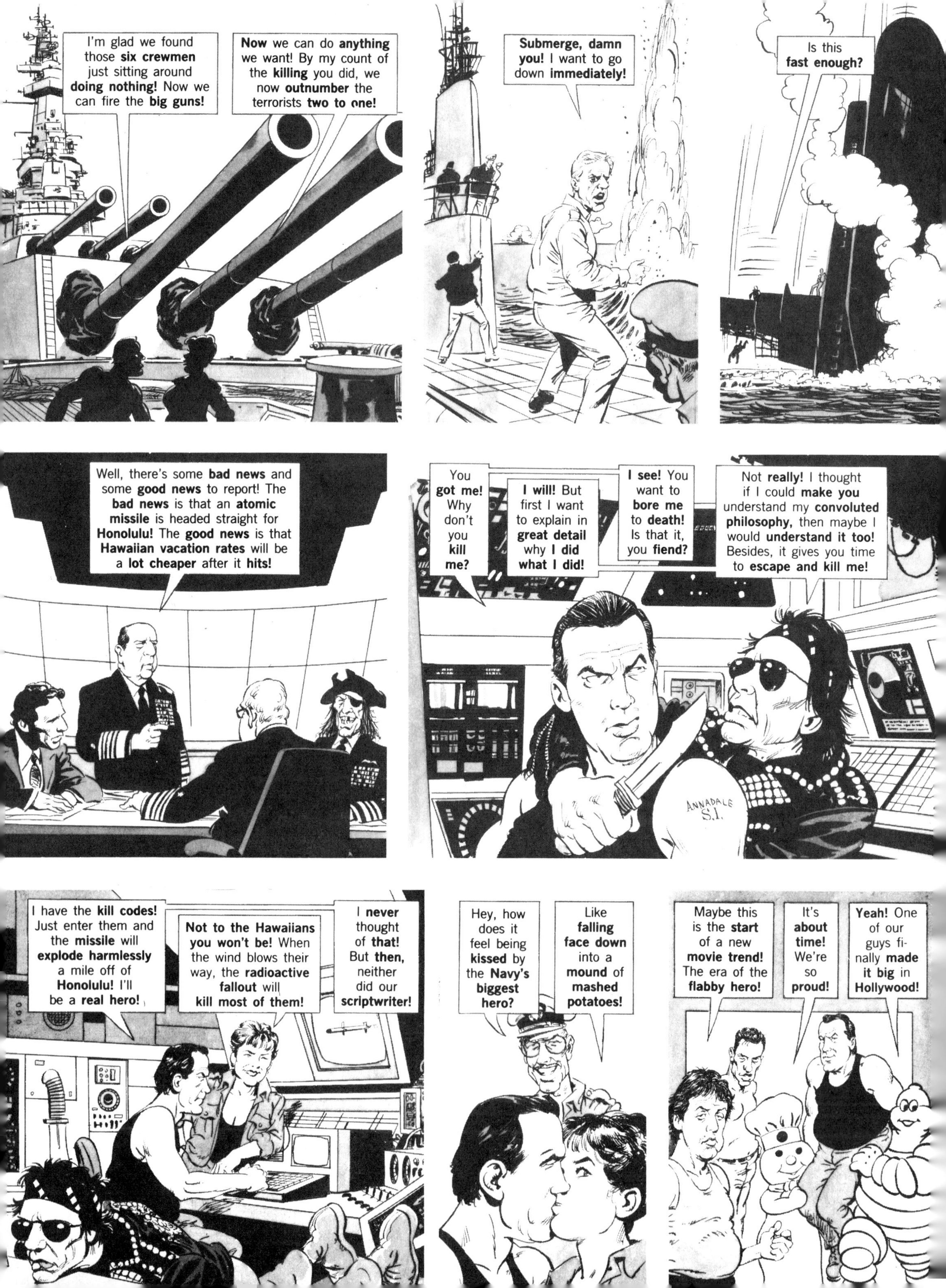
I'm glad we found those six crewmen just sitting around doing nothing! Now we can fire the big guns!
Now we can do anything we want! By my count of the killing you did, we now outnumber the terrorists two to one!
Submerge, damn you! I want to go down immediately!
Is this fast enough?
Well, there's some bad news and some good news to report! The bad news is that an atomic missile is headed straight for Honolulu! The good news is that Hawaiian vacation rates will be a lot cheaper after it hits!
You got me! Why don't you kill me?
I will! But first I want to explain in great detail why I did what I did!
I see! You want to bore me to death! Is that it, you fiend?
Not really! I thought if I could make you understand my convoluted philosophy, then maybe I would understand it too! Besides, it gives you time to escape and kill me!
ANNADALE S.I.
I have the kill codes! Just enter them and the missile will explode harmlessly a mile off of Honolulu! I'll be a real hero!
Not to the Hawaiians you won't be! When the wind blows their way, the radioactive fallout will kill most of them!
I never thought of that! But then, neither did our scriptwriter!
Hey, how does it feel being kissed by the Navy's biggest hero?
Like falling face down into a mound of mashed potatoes!
Maybe this is the start of a new movie trend! The era of the flabby hero!
It's about time! We're so proud!
Yeah! One of our guys finally made it big in Hollywood!

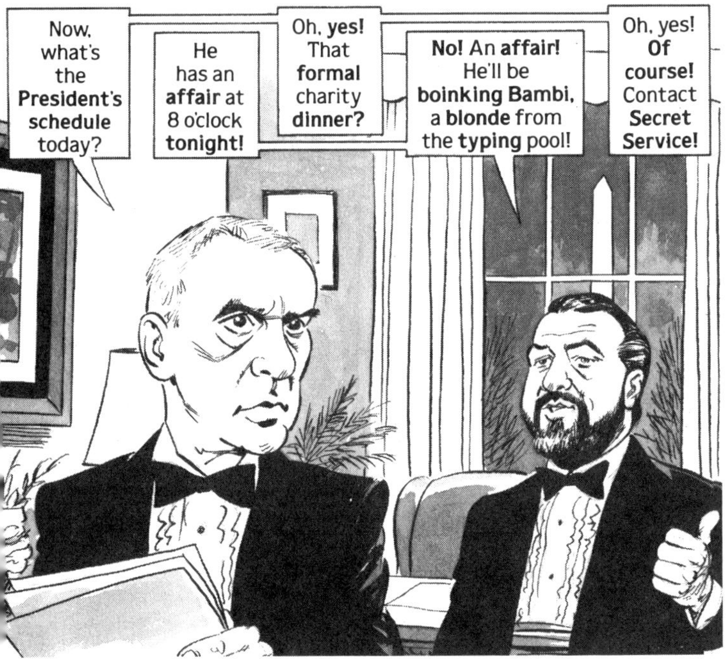

Now, what's the President's schedule today?
He has an affair at 8 o'clock tonight!
Oh, yes! That formal charity dinner?
No! An affair! He'll be boinking Bambi, a blonde from the typing pool!
Oh, yes! Of course! Contact Secret Service!


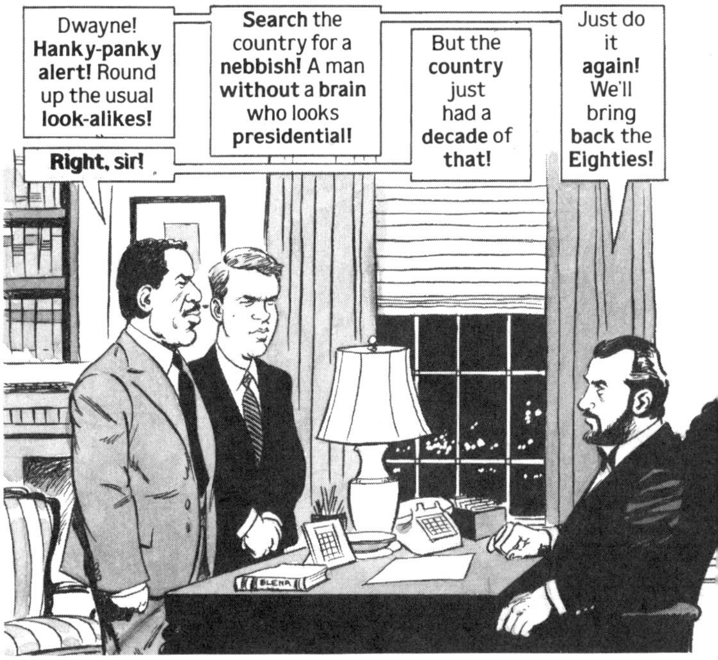

Dwayne! Hanky-panky alert! Round up the usual look-alikes!
Right, sir!
Search the country for a nebbish! A man without a brain who looks presidential!
But the country just had a decade of that!
Just do it again! We'll bring back the Eighties!


**THE FAKING OF THE PRESIDENT DEPT.**

**When a movie comes out in the spring and gets a ton of critical acclaim it usually means one thing: if it came out in the fall along with all the other movies looking to cop an Oscar, nobody would even notice it at all. Unfortunately, the producers of this film have bigger problems at hand. Praised though it may be, once the big summer movies like Jurassic Park and Last Action Hero come out, this film is sure to take a box-office...**

# DIVE


ARTIST: ANGELO TORRES WRITER: ARNIE KOGEN


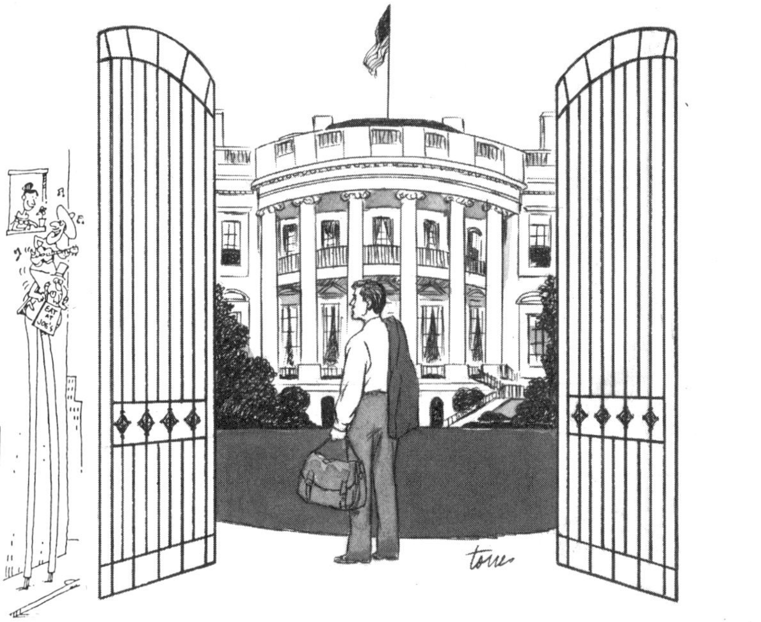

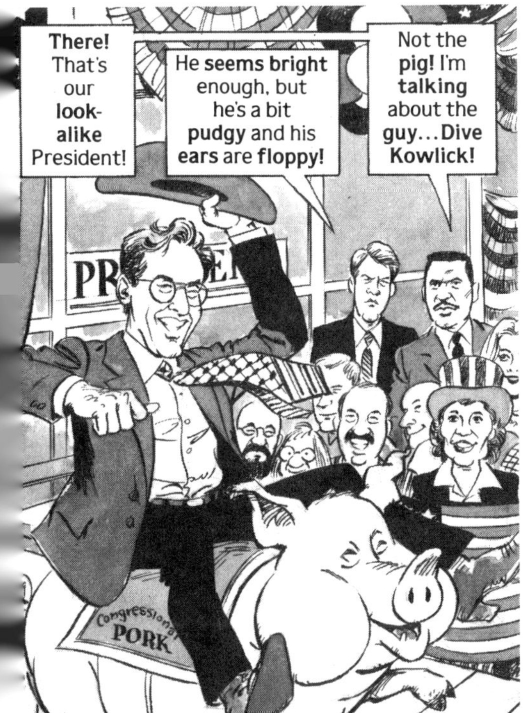

There! That's our look-alike President!
He seems bright enough, but he's a bit pudgy and his ears are floppy!
Not the pig! I'm talking about the guy... Dive Kowlick!
PORK


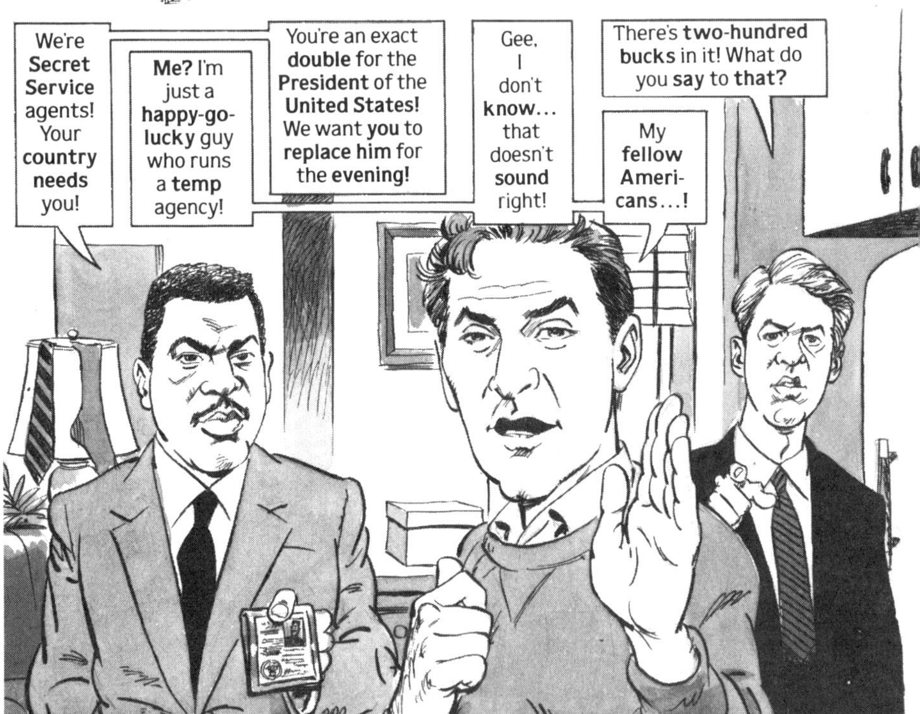

We're Secret Service agents! Your country needs you!
Me? I'm just a happy-go-lucky guy who runs a temp agency!
You're an exact double for the President of the United States! We want you to replace him for the evening!
Gee, I don't know... that doesn't sound right!
There's two-hundred bucks in it! What do you say to that?
My fellow Ameri-cans...!

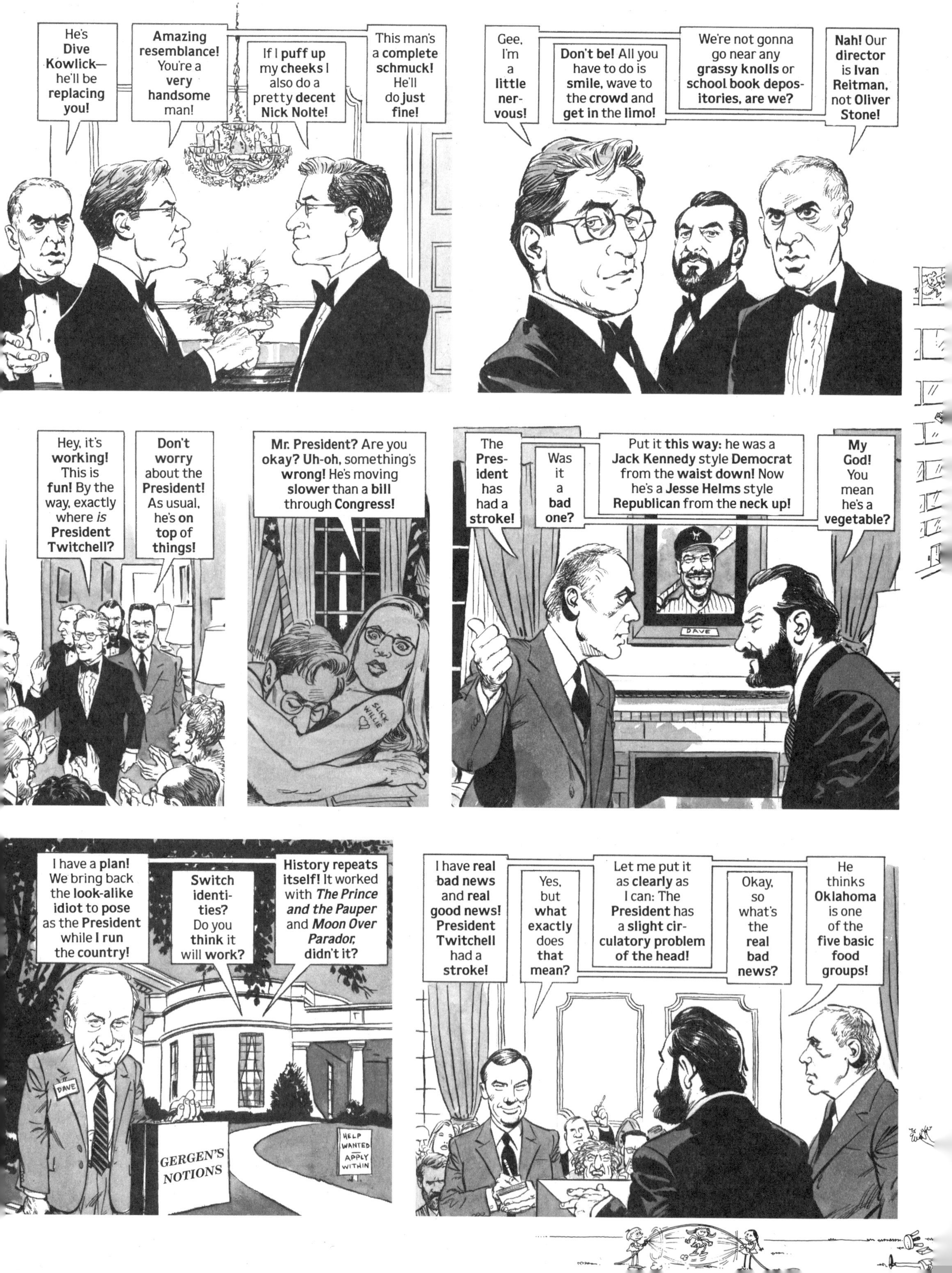
He's Dive Kowlick—he'll be replacing you!
Amazing resemblance! You're a very handsome man!
If I puff up my cheeks I also do a pretty decent Nick Nolte!
This man's a complete schmuck! He'll do just fine!
Gee, I'm a little nervous!
Don't be! All you have to do is smile, wave to the crowd and get in the limo!
We're not gonna go near any grassy knolls or school book depositories, are we?
Nah! Our director is Ivan Reitman, not Oliver Stone!
Hey, it's working! This is fun! By the way, exactly where is President Twitchell?
Don't worry about the President! As usual, he's on top of things!
Mr. President? Are you okay? Uh-oh, something's wrong! He's moving slower than a bill through Congress!
SLICK WILLIE
The President has had a stroke!
Was it a bad one?
Put it this way: he was a Jack Kennedy style Democrat from the waist down! Now he's a Jesse Helms style Republican from the neck up!
My God! You mean he's a vegetable?
DAVE
I have a plan! We bring back the look-alike idiot to pose as the President while I run the country!
Switch identities? Do you think it will work?
History repeats itself! It worked with The Prince and the Pauper and Moon Over Parador, didn't it?
DAVE
GERGEN'S NOTIONS
HELP WANTED APPLY WITHIN
I have real bad news and real good news! President Twitchell had a stroke!
Yes, but what exactly does that mean?
Let me put it as clearly as I can: The President has a slight circulatory problem of the head!
Okay, so what's the real bad news?
He thinks Oklahoma is one of the five basic food groups!

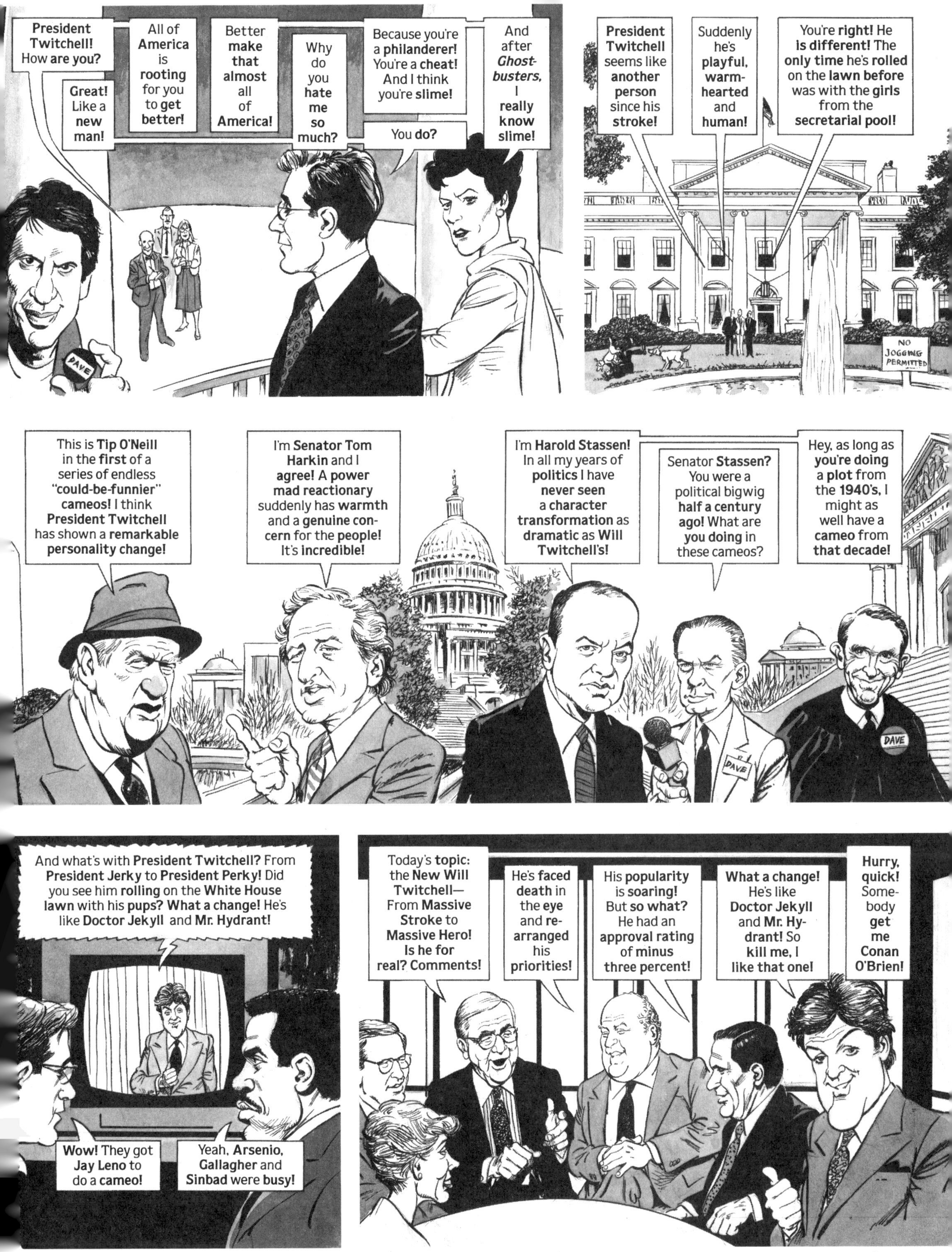

President Twitchell! How are you?
Great! Like a new man!
All of America is rooting for you to get better!
Better make that almost all of America!
Why do you hate me so much?
Because you're a philanderer! You're a cheat! And I think you're slime!
You do?
And after Ghostbusters, I really know slime!
President Twitchell seems like another person since his stroke!
Suddenly he's playful, warm-hearted and human!
You're right! He is different! The only time he's rolled on the lawn before was with the girls from the secretarial pool!
NO JOGGING PERMITTED
This is Tip O'Neill in the first of a series of endless "could-be-funnier" cameos! I think President Twitchell has shown a remarkable personality change!
I'm Senator Tom Harkin and I agree! A power mad reactionary suddenly has warmth and a genuine concern for the people! It's incredible!
I'm Harold Stassen! In all my years of politics I have never seen a character transformation as dramatic as Will Twitchell's!
Senator Stassen? You were a political bigwig half a century ago! What are you doing in these cameos?
Hey, as long as you're doing a plot from the 1940's, I might as well have a cameo from that decade!
DAVE
And what's with President Twitchell? From President Jerky to President Perky! Did you see him rolling on the White House lawn with his pups? What a change! He's like Doctor Jekyll and Mr. Hydrant!
Wow! They got Jay Leno to do a cameo!
Yeah, Arsenio, Gallagher and Sinbad were busy!
Today's topic: the New Will Twitchell— From Massive Stroke to Massive Hero! Is he for real? Comments!
He's faced death in the eye and rearranged his priorities!
His popularity is soaring! But so what? He had an approval rating of minus three percent!
What a change! He's like Doctor Jekyll and Mr. Hydrant! So kill me, I like that one!
Hurry, quick! Somebody get me Conan O'Brien!

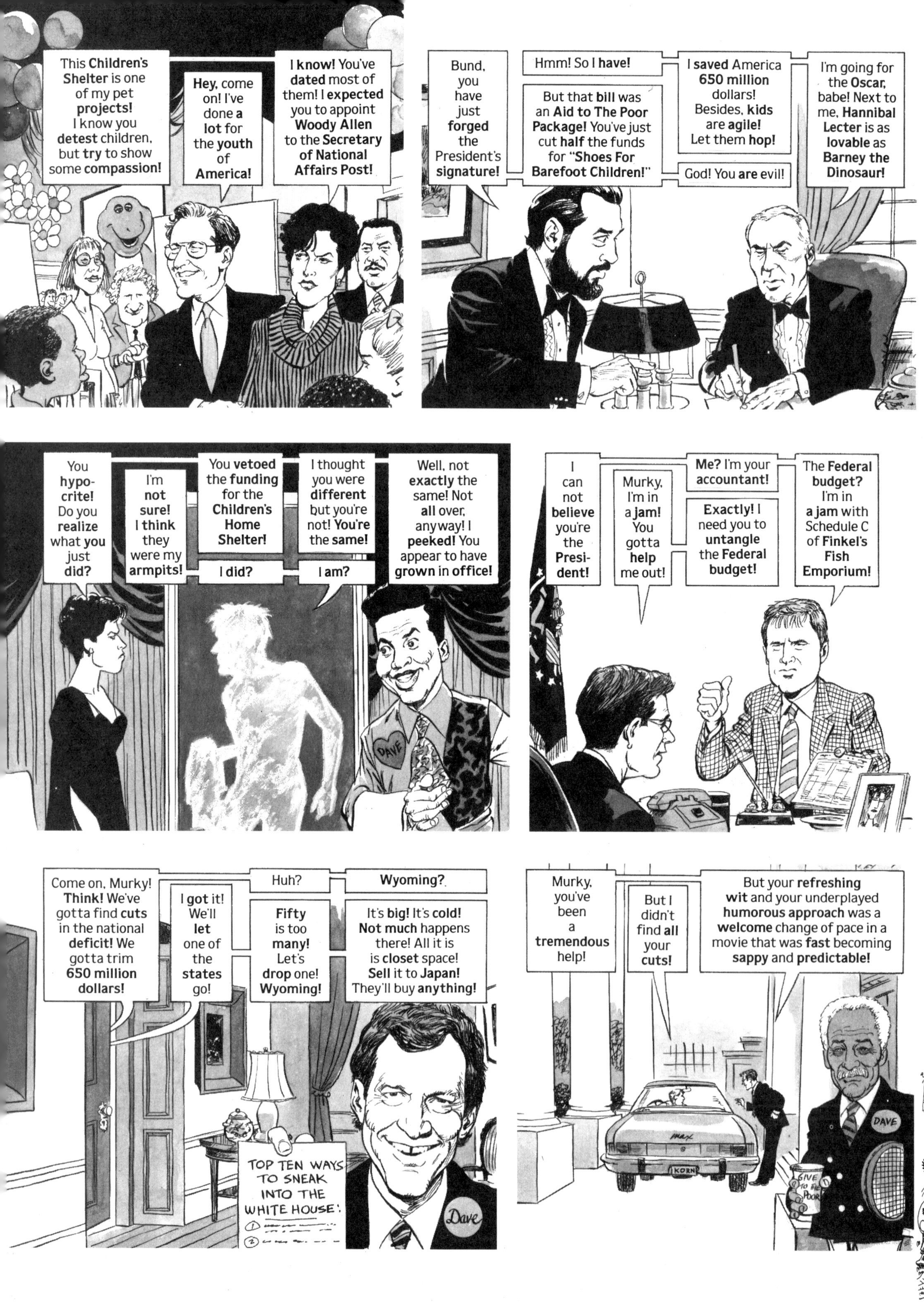
This Children's Shelter is one of my pet projects! I know you detest children, but try to show some compassion!
Hey, come on! I've done a lot for the youth of America!
I know! You've dated most of them! I expected you to appoint Woody Allen to the Secretary of National Affairs Post!
Bund, you have just forged the President's signature!
Hmm! So I have!
But that bill was an Aid to The Poor Package! You've just cut half the funds for "Shoes For Barefoot Children!"
I saved America 650 million dollars! Besides, kids are agile! Let them hop!
God! You are evil!
I'm going for the Oscar, babe! Next to me, Hannibal Lecter is as lovable as Barney the Dinosaur!
You hypo-crite! Do you realize what you just did?
I'm not sure! I think they were my armpits!
You vetoed the funding for the Children's Home Shelter!
I did?
I thought you were different but you're not! You're the same!
I am?
Well, not exactly the same! Not all over, anyway! I peeked! You appear to have grown in office!
DAVE
I can not believe you're the Presi-dent!
Murky, I'm in a jam! You gotta help me out!
Me? I'm your accountant!
Exactly! I need you to untangle the Federal budget!
The Federal budget? I'm in a jam with Schedule C of Finkel's Fish Emporium!
Come on, Murky! Think! We've gotta find cuts in the national deficit! We gotta trim 650 million dollars!
I got it! We'll let one of the states go!
Huh?
Fifty is too many! Let's drop one! Wyoming!
Wyoming?
It's big! It's cold! Not much happens there! All it is is closet space! Sell it to Japan! They'll buy anything!
TOP TEN WAYS TO SNEAK INTO THE WHITE HOUSE:
Dave
Murky, you've been a tremendous help!
But I didn't find all your cuts!
But your refreshing wit and your underplayed humorous approach was a welcome change of pace in a movie that was fast becoming sappy and predictable!
KORN
DAVE

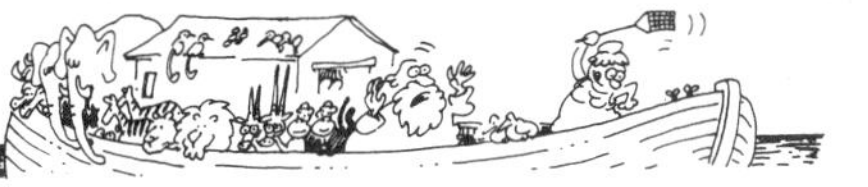

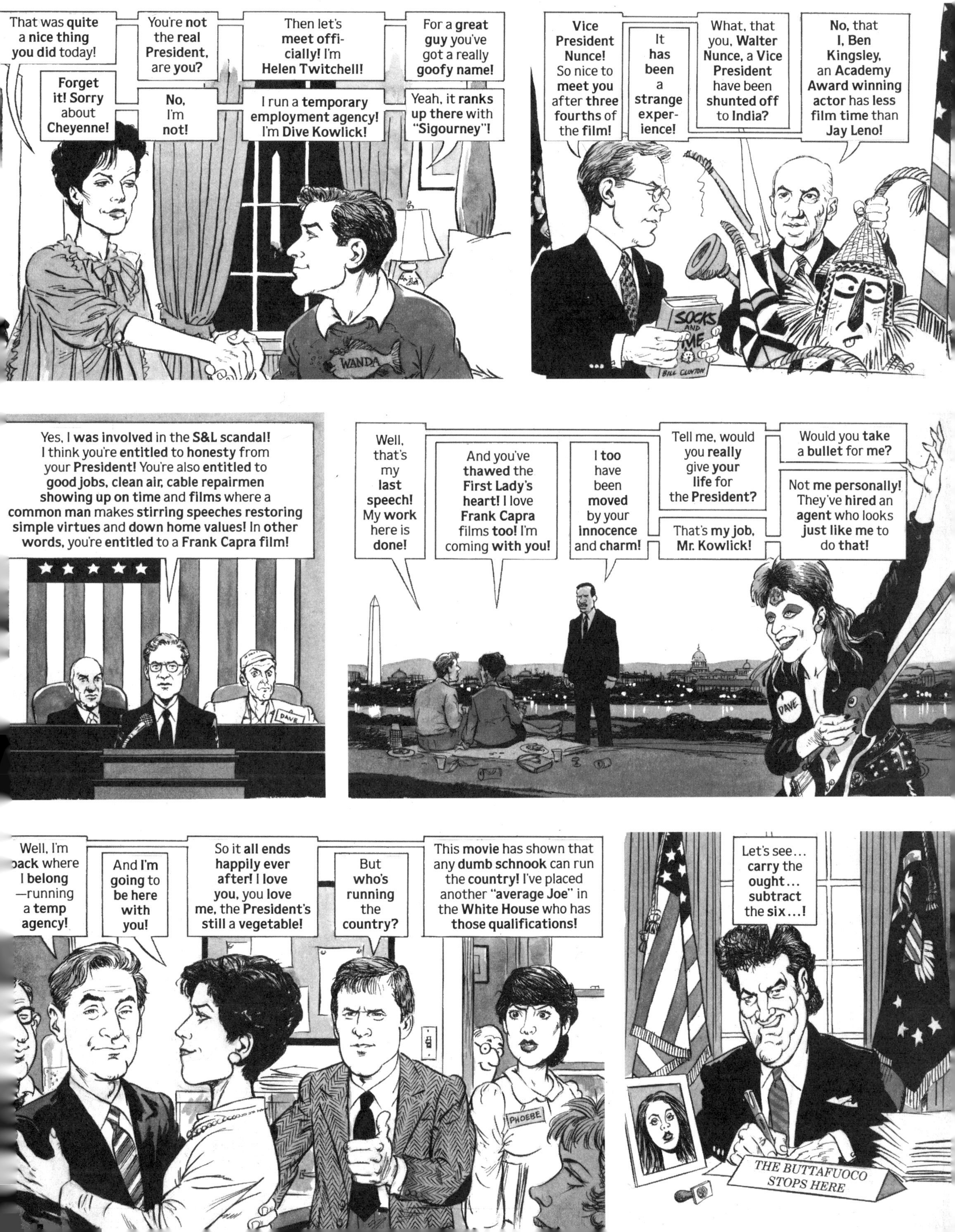

That was quite a nice thing you did today!
Forget it! Sorry about Cheyenne!
You're not the real President, are you?
No, I'm not!
Then let's meet officially! I'm Helen Twitchell!
I run a temporary employment agency! I'm Dive Kowlick!
For a great guy you've got a really goofy name!
Yeah, it ranks up there with "Sigourney"!
WANDA
Vice President Nunce! So nice to meet you after three fourths of the film!
It has been a strange experience!
What, that you, Walter Nunce, a Vice President have been shunted off to India?
No, that I, Ben Kingsley, an Academy Award winning actor has less film time than Jay Leno!
SOCKS AND ME
BILL CLINTON
Yes, I was involved in the S&L scandal! I think you're entitled to honesty from your President! You're also entitled to good jobs, clean air, cable repairmen showing up on time and films where a common man makes stirring speeches restoring simple virtues and down home values! In other words, you're entitled to a Frank Capra film!
DAVE
Well, that's my last speech! My work here is done!
And you've thawed the First Lady's heart! I love Frank Capra films too! I'm coming with you!
I too have been moved by your innocence and charm!
Tell me, would you really give your life for the President?
That's my job, Mr. Kowlick!
Would you take a bullet for me?
Not me personally! They've hired an agent who looks just like me to do that!
DAVE
Well, I'm back where I belong —running a temp agency!
And I'm going to be here with you!
So it all ends happily ever after! I love you, you love me, the President's still a vegetable!
But who's running the country?
This movie has shown that any dumb schnook can run the country! I've placed another "average Joe" in the White House who has those qualifications!
PHOEBE
Let's see… carry the ought… subtract the six…!
THE BUTTAFUOCO STOPS HERE

**FLEE CIRCUS DEPT.**

**Years ago there was a hit TV show about a man always on the move, hounded and persecuted endlessly and living the life of a forlorn nomad—but enough about Gomer Pyle! We're talking about Dr. Richard Cornball, a man with the cunning, intelligence and resourcefulness of three men! Unfortunately, those three men happen to be Moe, Larry and Curly (and occasionally Shemp or Joe Besser!), which is why we call him…**

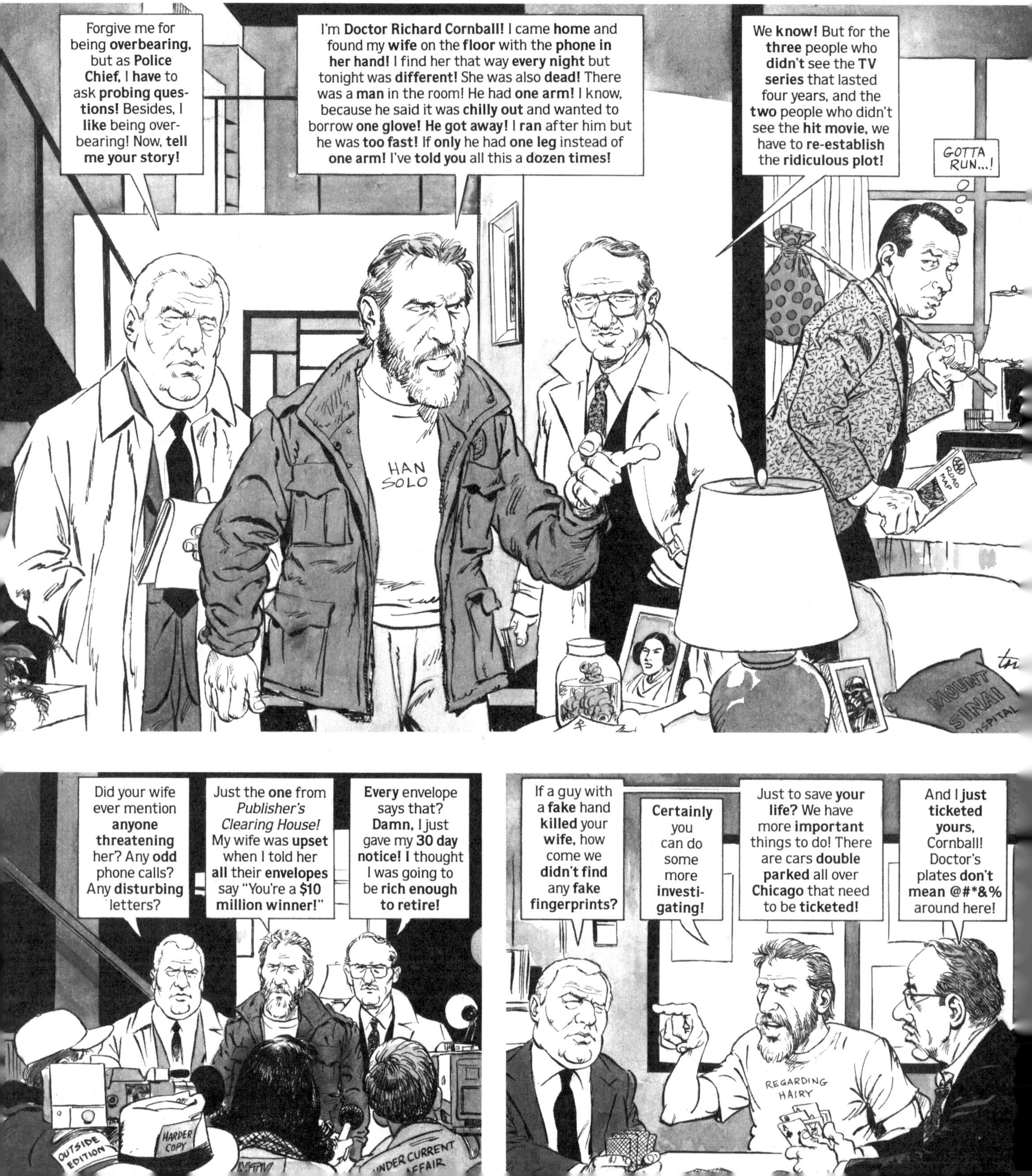

Forgive me for being **overbearing**, but as **Police Chief**, I **have** to ask **probing questions!** Besides, I **like** being overbearing! Now, **tell me your story!**
I'm **Doctor Richard Cornball!** I came **home** and found my **wife** on the **floor** with the **phone in her hand!** I find her that way **every night** but tonight was **different!** She was also **dead!** There was a **man** in the room! He had **one arm!** I know, because he said it was **chilly out** and wanted to borrow **one glove! He got away!** I **ran** after him but he was **too fast!** If **only** he had **one leg** instead of **one arm!** I've **told you** all this a **dozen times!**
We **know!** But for the **three** people who **didn't** see the **TV series** that lasted four years, and the **two** people who didn't see the **hit movie**, we have to **re-establish** the **ridiculous plot!**
GOTTA RUN…!
HAN SOLO
Did your wife ever mention **anyone threatening** her? Any **odd** phone calls? Any **disturbing** letters?
Just the **one** from *Publisher's Clearing House!* My wife was **upset** when I told her **all** their **envelopes** say "You're a **$10 million winner!**"
**Every** envelope says that? **Damn,** I just gave my **30 day notice!** I thought I was going to be **rich enough to retire!**
OUTSIDE EDITION
HARDER COPY
If a guy with a **fake** hand **killed** your **wife**, how come we **didn't find** any **fake fingerprints?**
**Certainly** you can do some more **investigating!**
Just to save **your life?** We have more **important** things to do! There are cars **double parked** all over **Chicago** that need to be **ticketed!**
And I **just ticketed yours**, Cornball! Doctor's plates **don't mean @#*&%** around here!
REGARDING HAIRY

# THE STOOGE-ITIVE

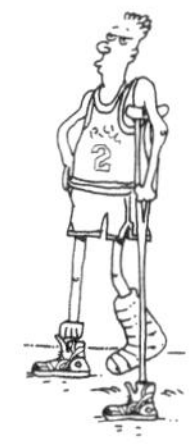

ARTIST: ANGELO TORRES WRITER: DICK DEBARTOLO

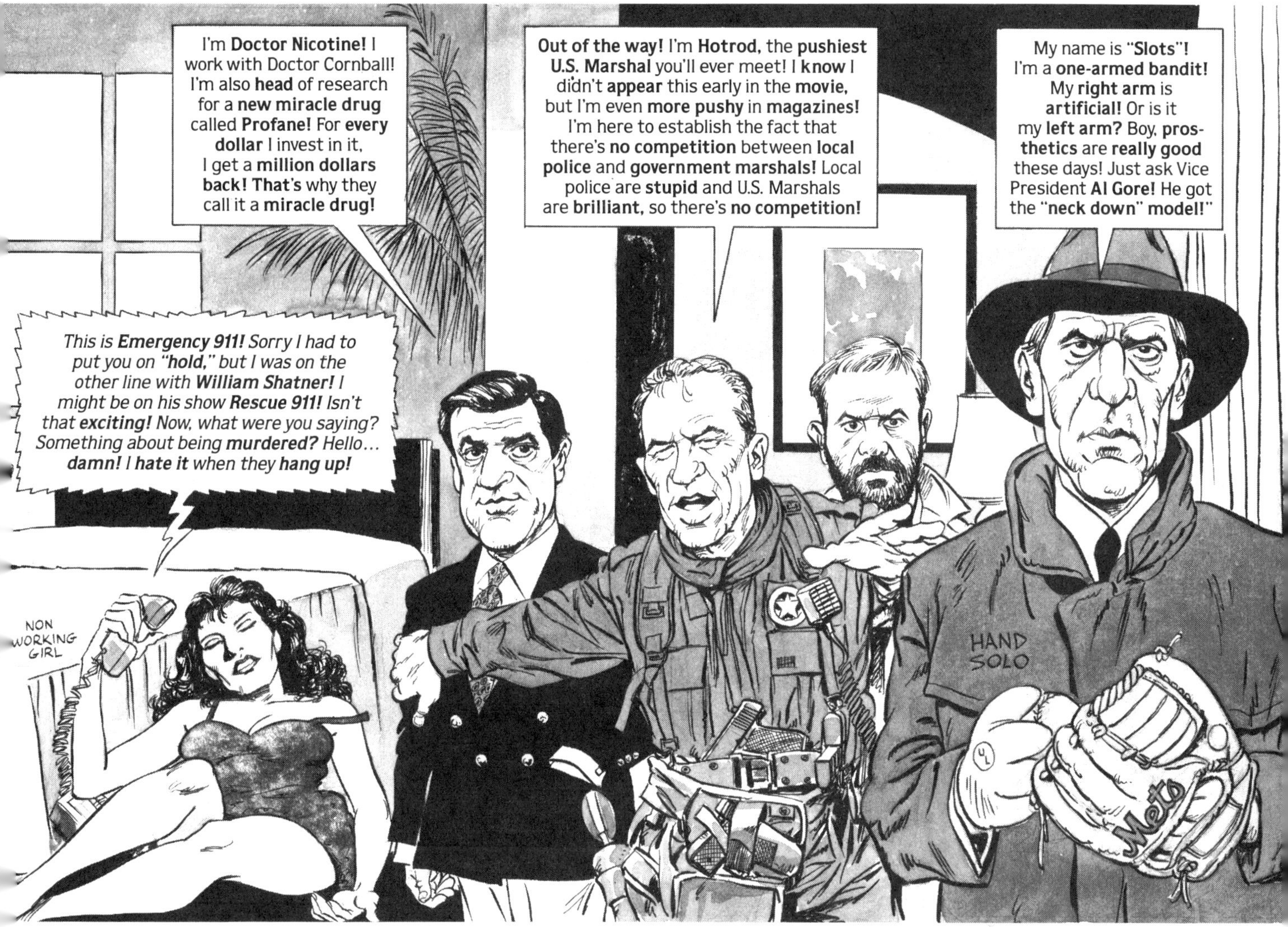

I'm **Doctor Nicotine!** I work with Doctor Cornball! I'm also **head** of research for a **new miracle drug** called **Profane!** For **every dollar** I invest in it, I get a **million dollars back! That's** why they call it a **miracle drug!**
**Out of the way!** I'm **Hotrod,** the **pushiest U.S. Marshal** you'll ever meet! I **know** I didn't **appear** this early in the **movie,** but I'm even **more pushy** in **magazines!** I'm here to establish the fact that there's **no competition** between **local police** and **government marshals!** Local police are **stupid** and U.S. Marshals are **brilliant,** so there's **no competition!**
My name is **"Slots"!** I'm a **one-armed bandit!** My **right arm** is **artificial!** Or is it my **left arm?** Boy, **prosthetics** are **really good** these days! Just ask Vice President **Al Gore!** He got the **"neck down" model!"**
*This is **Emergency 911!** Sorry I had to put you on **"hold,"** but I was on the other line with **William Shatner!** I might be on his show **Rescue 911!** Isn't that **exciting!** Now, what were you saying? Something about being **murdered?** Hello… **damn!** I **hate it** when they **hang up!***
NON WORKING GIRL
HAND SOLO
Mets


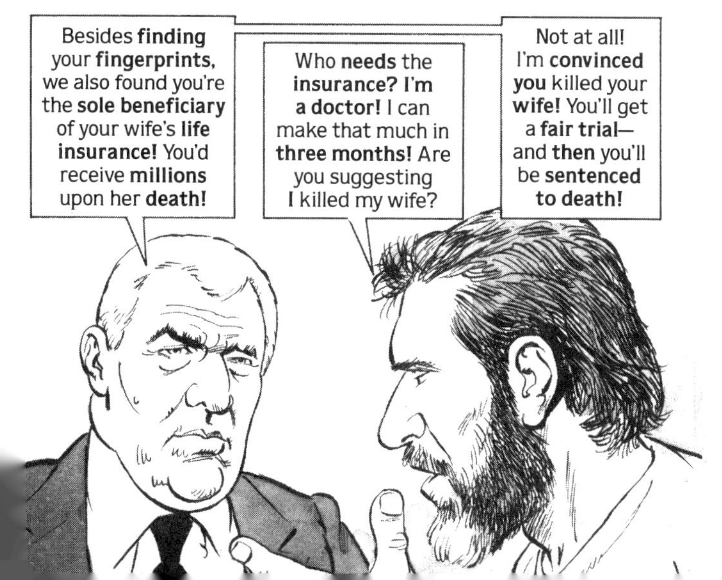

Besides **finding** your **fingerprints,** we also found you're the **sole beneficiary** of your wife's **life insurance!** You'd receive **millions** upon her **death!**
Who **needs** the **insurance? I'm a doctor!** I can make that much in **three months!** Are you suggesting I killed my wife?
Not at all! I'm **convinced you** killed your **wife!** You'll get a **fair trial**—and **then** you'll be **sentenced to death!**


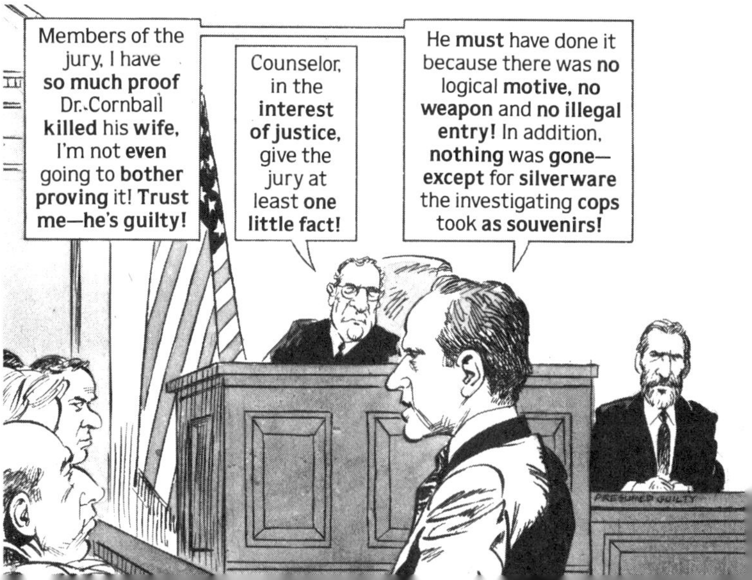

Members of the jury, I have **so much proof** Dr. Cornball **killed** his **wife,** I'm not **even** going to **bother proving** it! **Trust me—he's guilty!**
Counselor, in the **interest of justice,** give the jury at least **one little fact!**
He **must** have done it because there was **no** logical **motive, no weapon** and **no illegal entry!** In addition, **nothing** was **gone—except** for **silverware** the investigating **cops** took **as souvenirs!**
PRESUMED GUILTY

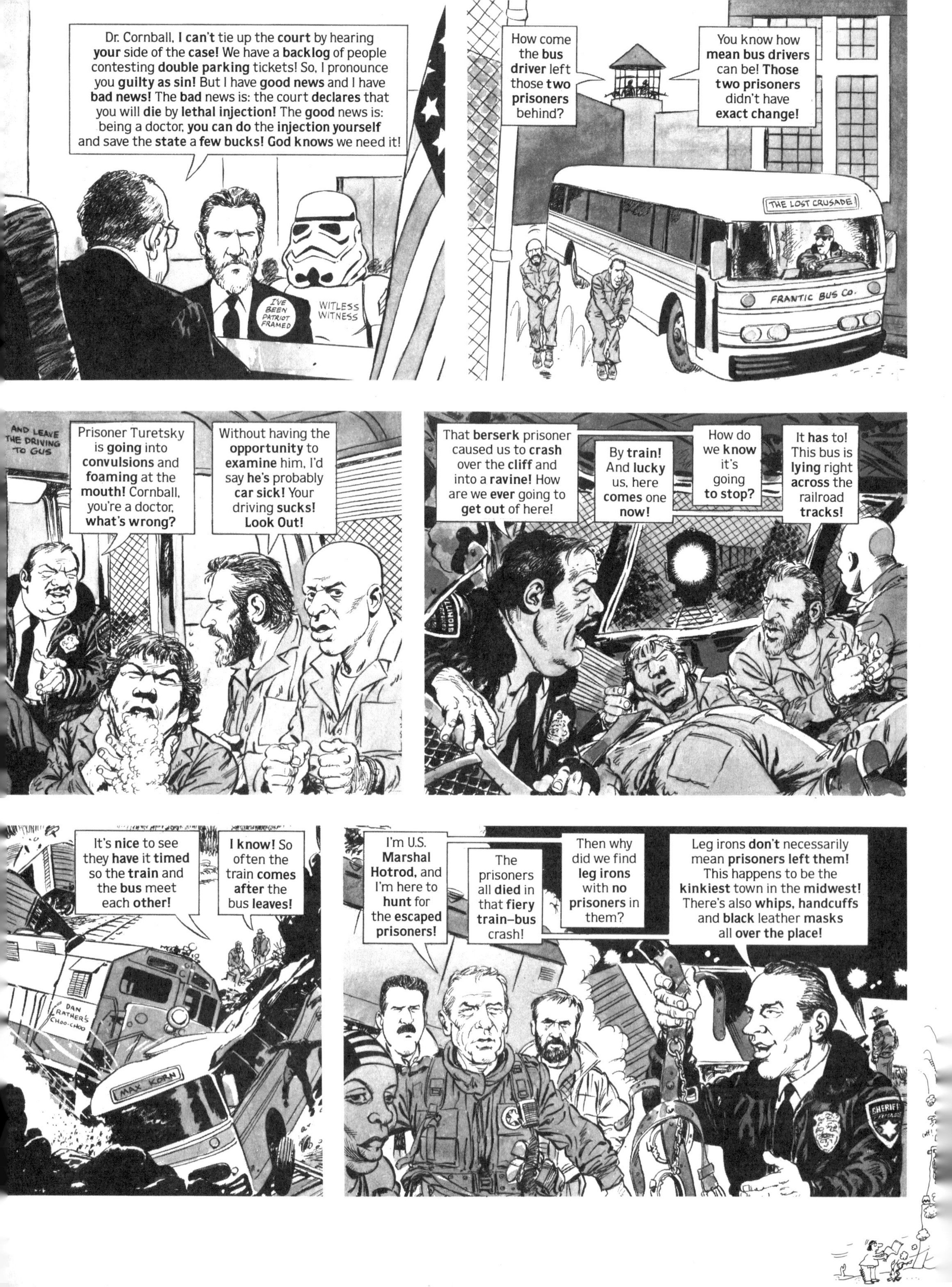
Dr. Cornball, I can't tie up the court by hearing your side of the case! We have a backlog of people contesting double parking tickets! So, I pronounce you guilty as sin! But I have good news and I have bad news! The bad news is: the court declares that you will die by lethal injection! The good news is: being a doctor, you can do the injection yourself and save the state a few bucks! God knows we need it!
I'VE BEEN PATRIOT FRAMED
WITLESS WITNESS
How come the bus driver left those two prisoners behind?
You know how mean bus drivers can be! Those two prisoners didn't have exact change!
THE LOST CRUSADE
FRANTIC BUS CO.
AND LEAVE THE DRIVING TO GUS
Prisoner Turetsky is going into convulsions and foaming at the mouth! Cornball, you're a doctor, what's wrong?
Without having the opportunity to examine him, I'd say he's probably car sick! Your driving sucks! Look Out!
That berserk prisoner caused us to crash over the cliff and into a ravine! How are we ever going to get out of here!
By train! And lucky us, here comes one now!
How do we know it's going to stop?
It has to! This bus is lying right across the railroad tracks!
It's nice to see they have it timed so the train and the bus meet each other!
I know! So often the train comes after the bus leaves!
DAN RATHER'S CHOO-CHOO
MAX KORN
I'm U.S. Marshal Hotrod, and I'm here to hunt for the escaped prisoners!
The prisoners all died in that fiery train–bus crash!
Then why did we find leg irons with no prisoners in them?
Leg irons don't necessarily mean prisoners left them! This happens to be the kinkiest town in the midwest! There's also whips, handcuffs and black leather masks all over the place!
SHERIFF

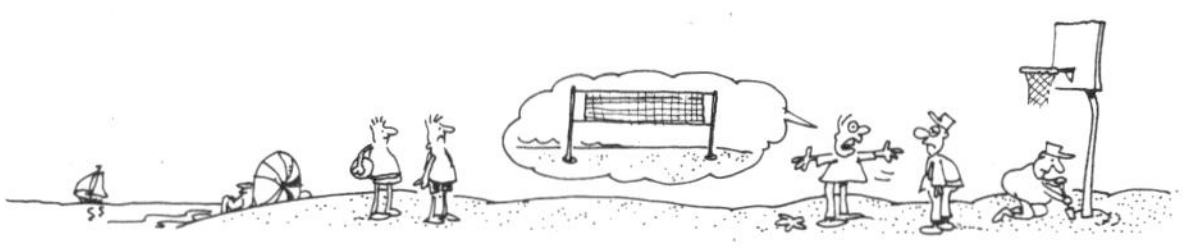

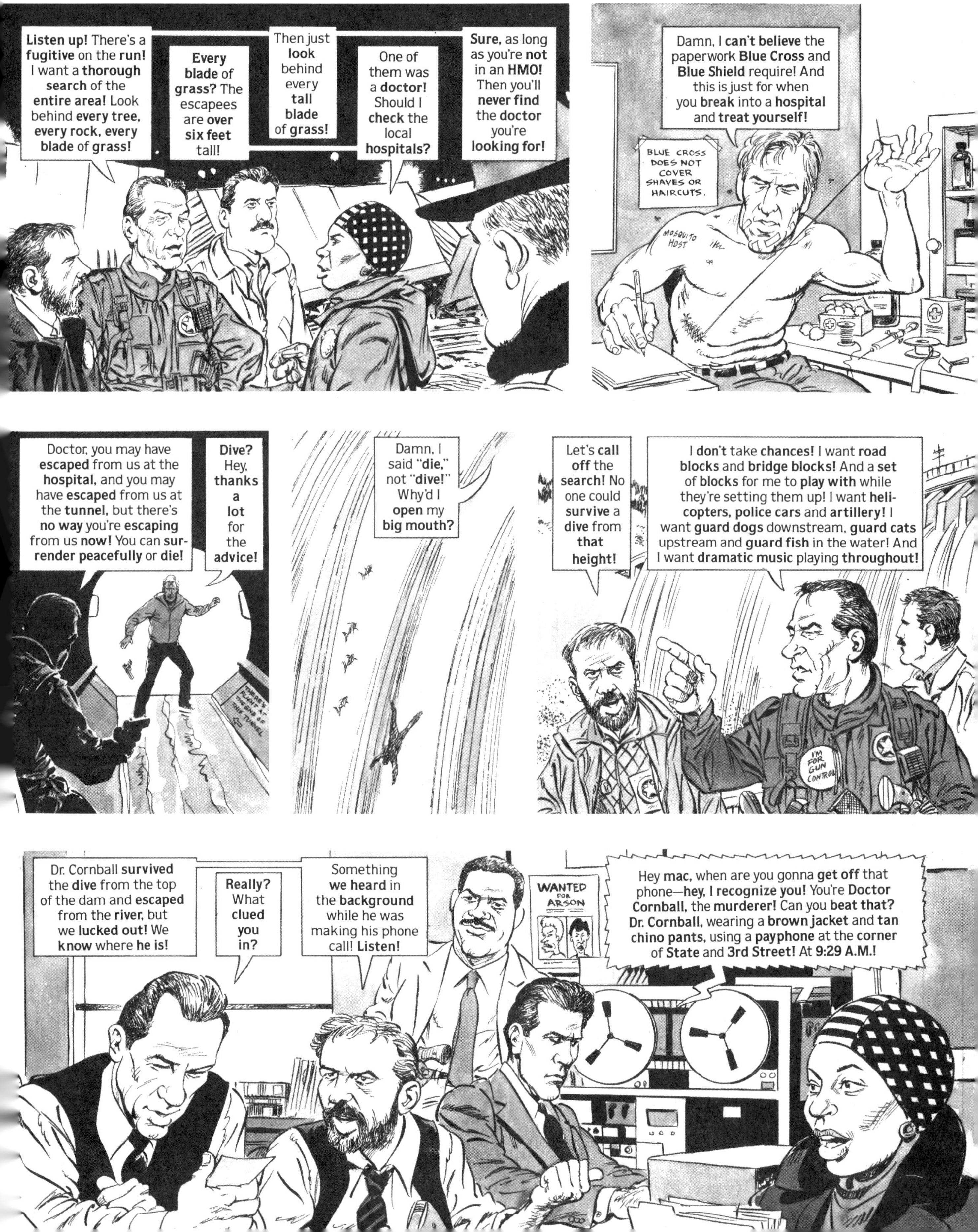

Listen up! There's a fugitive on the run! I want a thorough search of the entire area! Look behind every tree, every rock, every blade of grass!
Every blade of grass? The escapees are over six feet tall!
Then just look behind every tall blade of grass!
One of them was a doctor! Should I check the local hospitals?
Sure, as long as you're not in an HMO! Then you'll never find the doctor you're looking for!
Damn, I can't believe the paperwork Blue Cross and Blue Shield require! And this is just for when you break into a hospital and treat yourself!
BLUE CROSS DOES NOT COVER SHAVES OR HAIRCUTS.
MOSQUITO HOST
Doctor, you may have escaped from us at the hospital, and you may have escaped from us at the tunnel, but there's no way you're escaping from us now! You can surrender peacefully or die!
Dive? Hey, thanks a lot for the advice!
THERE'S PLIGHT AT THE END OF THIS TUNNEL
Damn, I said "die," not "dive!" Why'd I open my big mouth?
Let's call off the search! No one could survive a dive from that height!
I don't take chances! I want road blocks and bridge blocks! And a set of blocks for me to play with while they're setting them up! I want helicopters, police cars and artillery! I want guard dogs downstream, guard cats upstream and guard fish in the water! And I want dramatic music playing throughout!
I'M FOR GUN CONTROL
Dr. Cornball survived the dive from the top of the dam and escaped from the river, but we lucked out! We know where he is!
Really? What clued you in?
Something we heard in the background while he was making his phone call! Listen!
WANTED FOR ARSON
Hey mac, when are you gonna get off that phone—hey, I recognize you! You're Doctor Cornball, the murderer! Can you beat that? Dr. Cornball, wearing a brown jacket and tan chino pants, using a payphone at the corner of State and 3rd Street! At 9:29 A.M.!

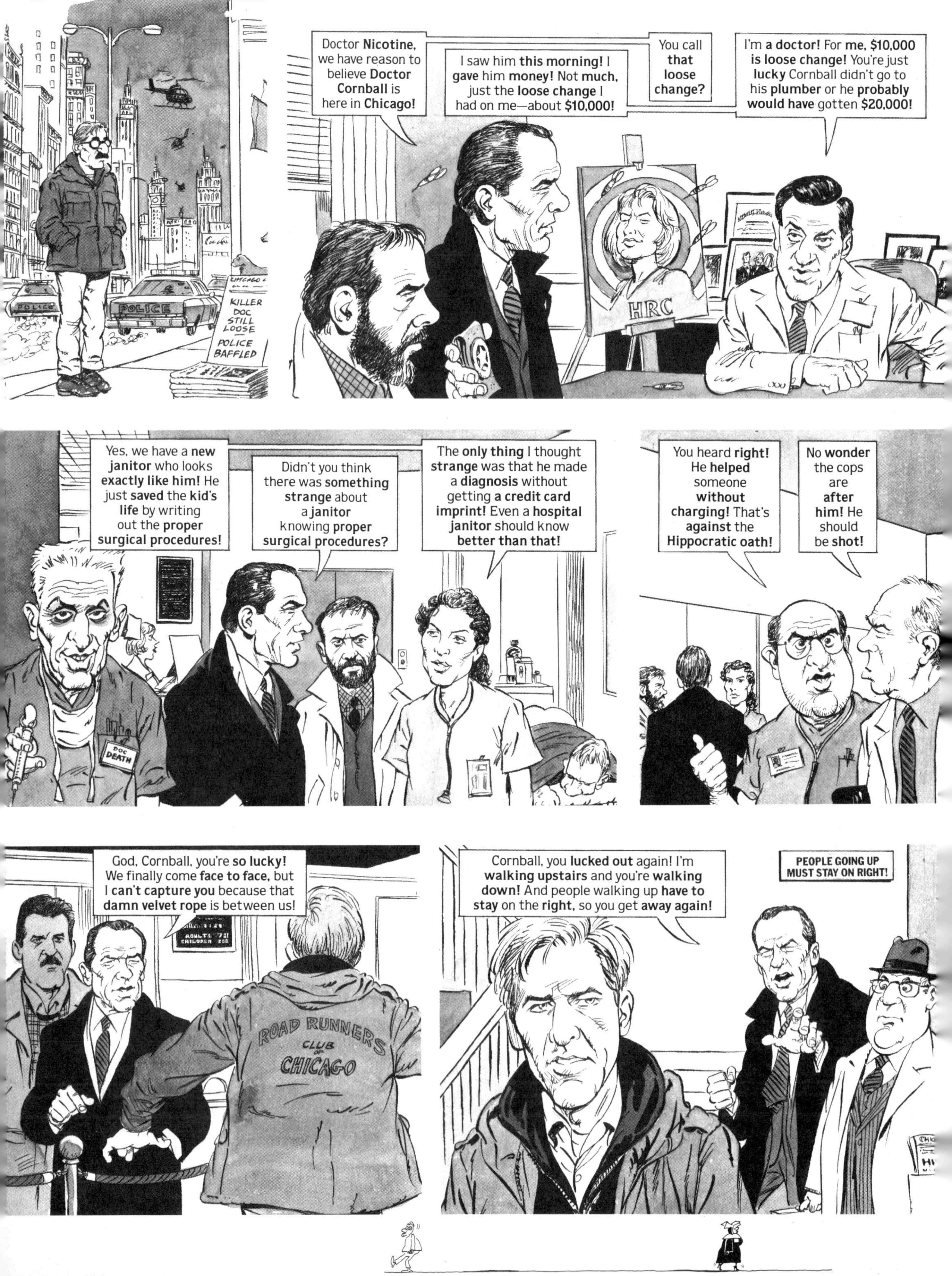

KILLER DOC STILL LOOSE
POLICE BAFFLED
POLICE
Doctor Nicotine, we have reason to believe Doctor Cornball is here in Chicago!
I saw him this morning! I gave him money! Not much, just the loose change I had on me—about $10,000!
You call that loose change?
I'm a doctor! For me, $10,000 is loose change! You're just lucky Cornball didn't go to his plumber or he probably would have gotten $20,000!
HRC
Yes, we have a new janitor who looks exactly like him! He just saved the kid's life by writing out the proper surgical procedures!
DOC DEATH
Didn't you think there was something strange about a janitor knowing proper surgical procedures?
The only thing I thought strange was that he made a diagnosis without getting a credit card imprint! Even a hospital janitor should know better than that!
You heard right! He helped someone without charging! That's against the Hippocratic oath!
No wonder the cops are after him! He should be shot!
God, Cornball, you're so lucky! We finally come face to face, but I can't capture you because that damn velvet rope is between us!
ROAD RUNNERS CLUB OF CHICAGO
Cornball, you lucked out again! I'm walking upstairs and you're walking down! And people walking up have to stay on the right, so you get away again!
PEOPLE GOING UP MUST STAY ON RIGHT!

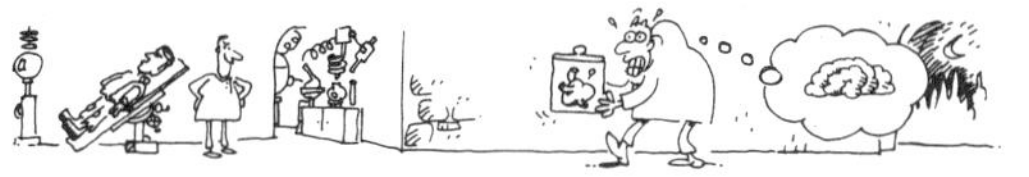

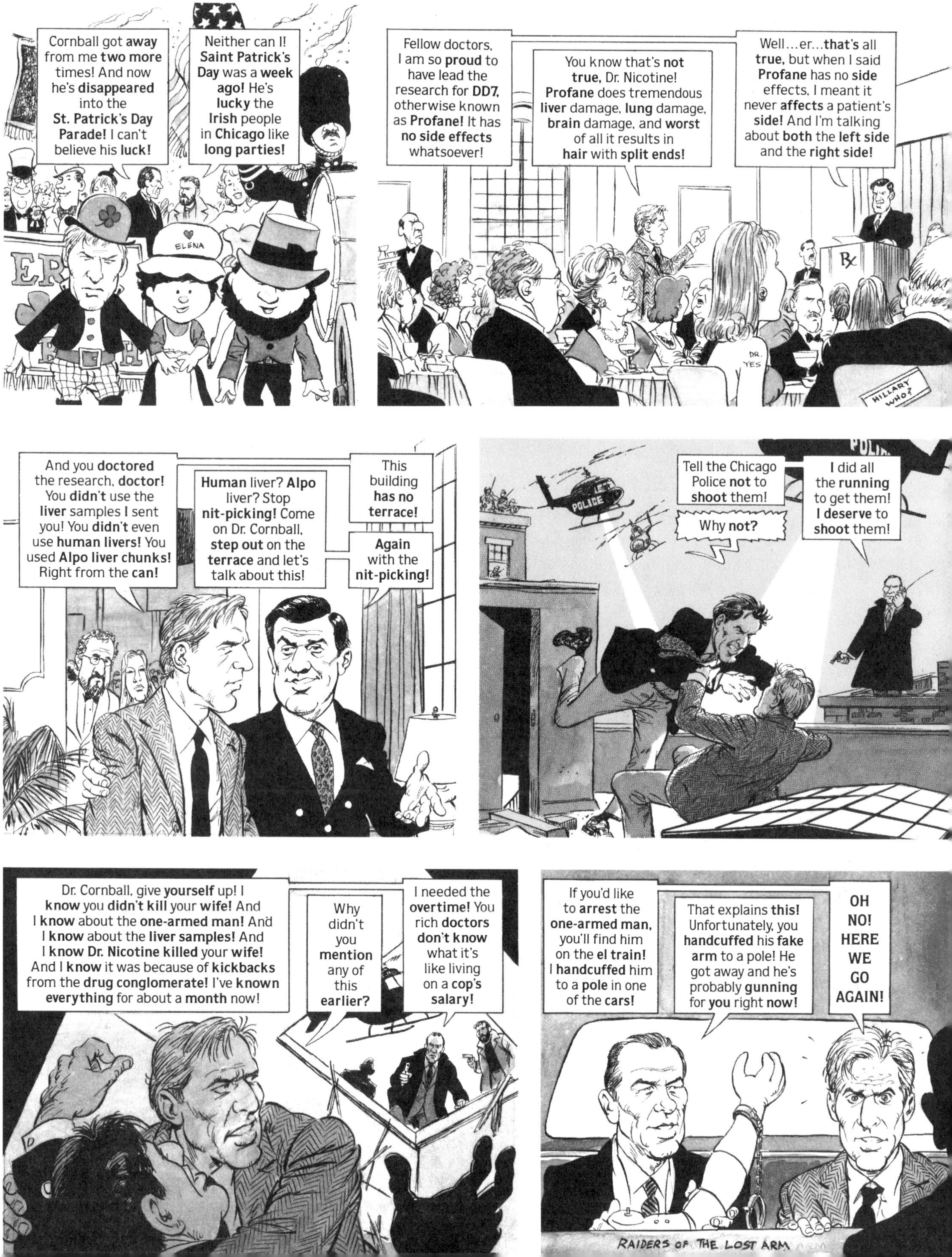

Cornball got away from me two more times! And now he's disappeared into the St. Patrick's Day Parade! I can't believe his luck!
Neither can I! Saint Patrick's Day was a week ago! He's lucky the Irish people in Chicago like long parties!
ELENA
Fellow doctors, I am so proud to have lead the research for DD7, otherwise known as Profane! It has no side effects whatsoever!
You know that's not true, Dr. Nicotine! Profane does tremendous liver damage, lung damage, brain damage, and worst of all it results in hair with split ends!
Well...er...that's all true, but when I said Profane has no side effects, I meant it never affects a patient's side! And I'm talking about both the left side and the right side!
Rx
DR. YES
HILLARY WHO?
And you doctored the research, doctor! You didn't use the liver samples I sent you! You didn't even use human livers! You used Alpo liver chunks! Right from the can!
Human liver? Alpo liver? Stop nit-picking! Come on Dr. Cornball, step out on the terrace and let's talk about this!
This building has no terrace!
Again with the nit-picking!
Tell the Chicago Police not to shoot them!
Why not?
I did all the running to get them! I deserve to shoot them!
POLICE
Dr. Cornball, give yourself up! I know you didn't kill your wife! And I know about the one-armed man! And I know about the liver samples! And I know Dr. Nicotine killed your wife! And I know it was because of kickbacks from the drug conglomerate! I've known everything for about a month now!
Why didn't you mention any of this earlier?
I needed the overtime! You rich doctors don't know what it's like living on a cop's salary!
If you'd like to arrest the one-armed man, you'll find him on the el train! I handcuffed him to a pole in one of the cars!
That explains this! Unfortunately, you handcuffed his fake arm to a pole! He got away and he's probably gunning for you right now!
OH NO! HERE WE GO AGAIN!
RAIDERS OF THE LOST ARM

MEL-ADJUSTED DEPT.

# MAVERSHTICK

ARTIST: MORT DRUCKER WRITER: ARNIE KOGEN

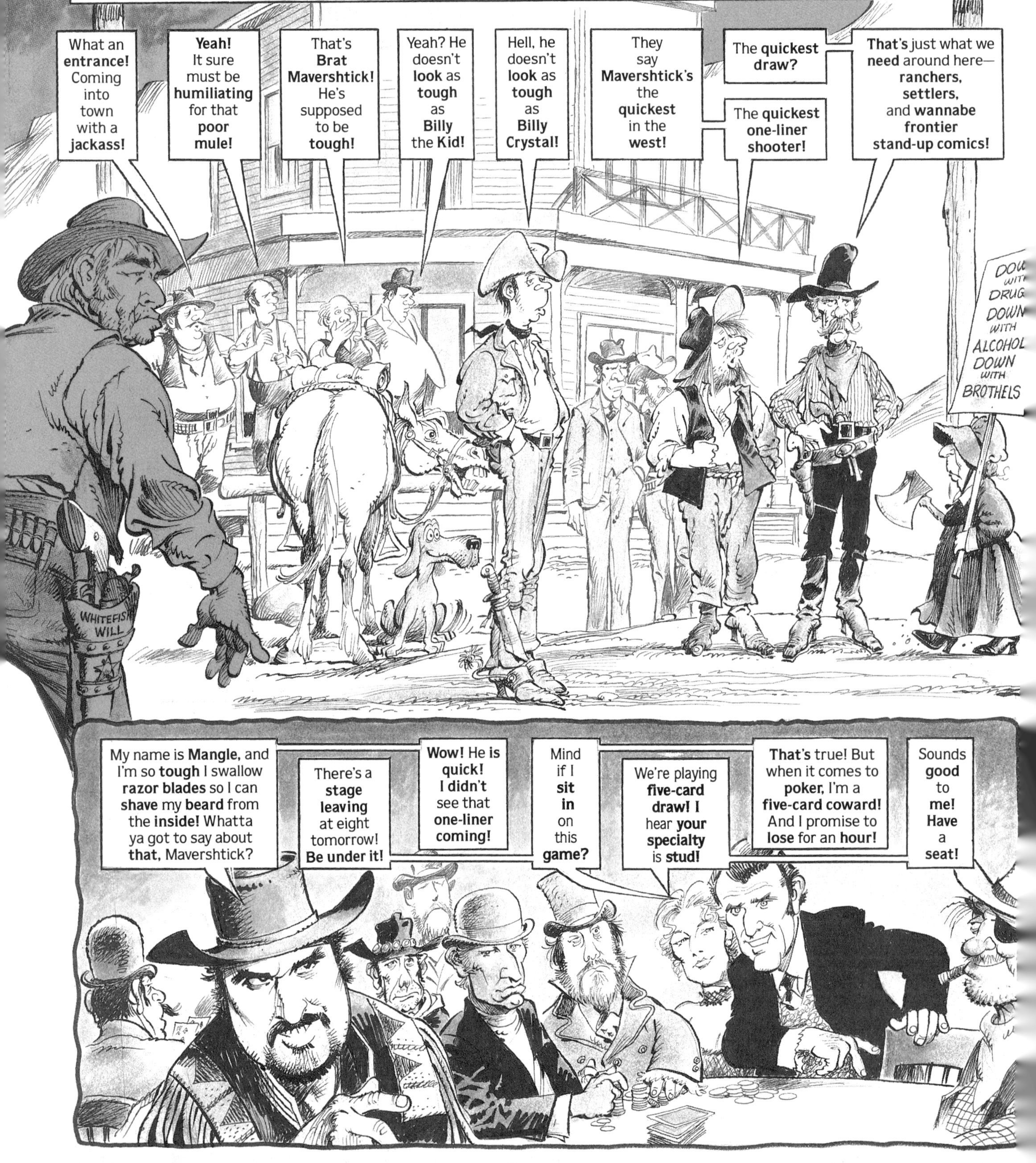
What an entrance! Coming into town with a jackass!
Yeah! It sure must be humiliating for that poor mule!
That's Brat Mavershtick! He's supposed to be tough!
Yeah? He doesn't look as tough as Billy the Kid!
Hell, he doesn't look as tough as Billy Crystal!
They say Mavershtick's the quickest in the west!
The quickest draw?
The quickest one-liner shooter!
That's just what we need around here—ranchers, settlers, and wannabe frontier stand-up comics!
WHITEFISH WILL
DOW WIT DRUG DOWN WITH ALCOHOL DOWN WITH BROTHELS
My name is Mangle, and I'm so tough I swallow razor blades so I can shave my beard from the inside! Whatta ya got to say about that, Mavershtick?
There's a stage leaving at eight tomorrow! Be under it!
Wow! He is quick! I didn't see that one-liner coming!
Mind if I sit in on this game?
We're playing five-card draw! I hear your specialty is stud!
That's true! But when it comes to poker, I'm a five-card coward! And I promise to lose for an hour!
Sounds good to me! Have a seat!

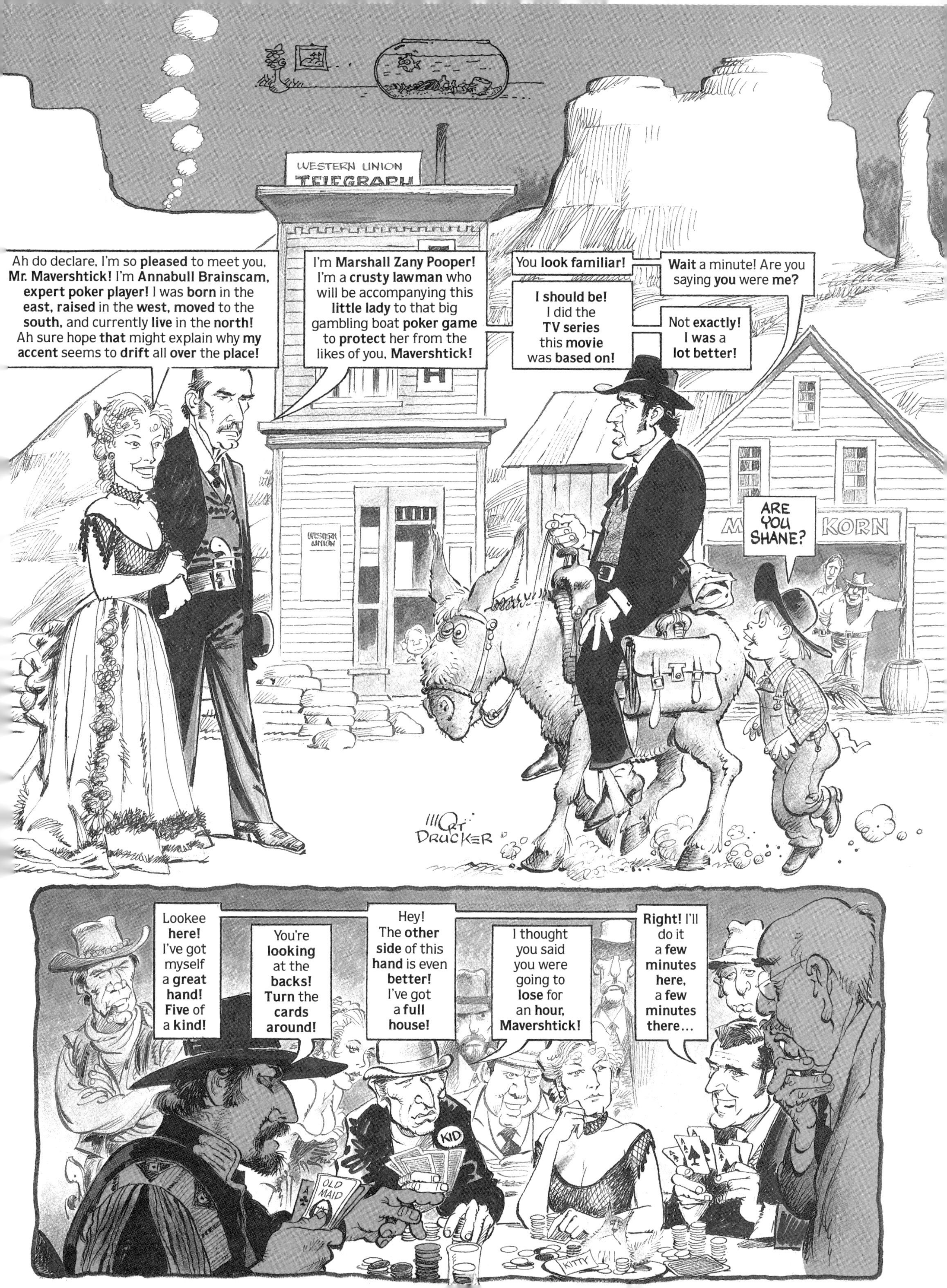
WESTERN UNION TELEGRAPH
Ah do declare, I'm so **pleased** to meet you, **Mr. Mavershtick!** I'm **Annabull Brainscam, expert poker player!** I was **born** in the **east, raised** in the **west, moved** to the **south,** and currently **live** in the **north!** Ah sure hope **that** might explain why **my accent** seems to **drift** all **over** the **place!**
I'm **Marshall Zany Pooper!** I'm a **crusty lawman** who will be accompanying this **little lady** to that big gambling boat **poker game** to **protect** her from the likes of you, **Mavershtick!**
You **look familiar!**
**I should be!** I did the **TV series** this **movie** was **based on!**
**Wait** a minute! Are you saying **you** were **me?**
Not **exactly! I was** a **lot better!**
WESTERN UNION
KORN
ARE YOU SHANE?
ART DRUCKER
Lookee **here!** I've got myself a **great hand! Five** of a **kind!**
You're **looking** at the **backs! Turn** the **cards around!**
Hey! The **other side** of this **hand** is even **better!** I've got a **full house!**
I thought you said you were going to **lose** for an **hour, Mavershtick!**
**Right!** I'll do it a **few minutes here,** a **few minutes there...**
OLD MAID
KID
KITTY

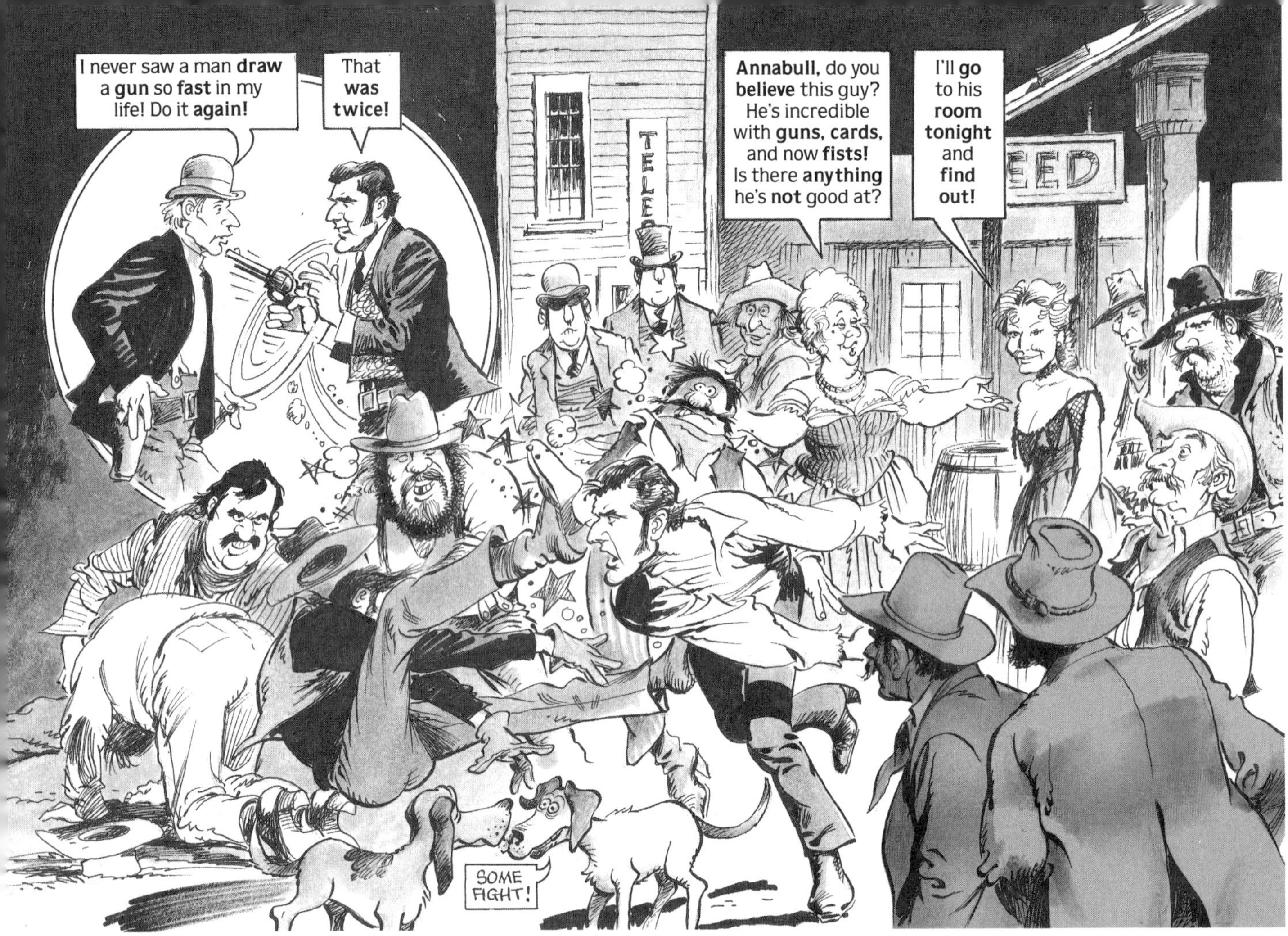

I never saw a man draw a gun so fast in my life! Do it again!
That was twice!
Annabull, do you believe this guy? He's incredible with guns, cards, and now fists! Is there anything he's not good at?
I'll go to his room tonight and find out!
SOME FIGHT!


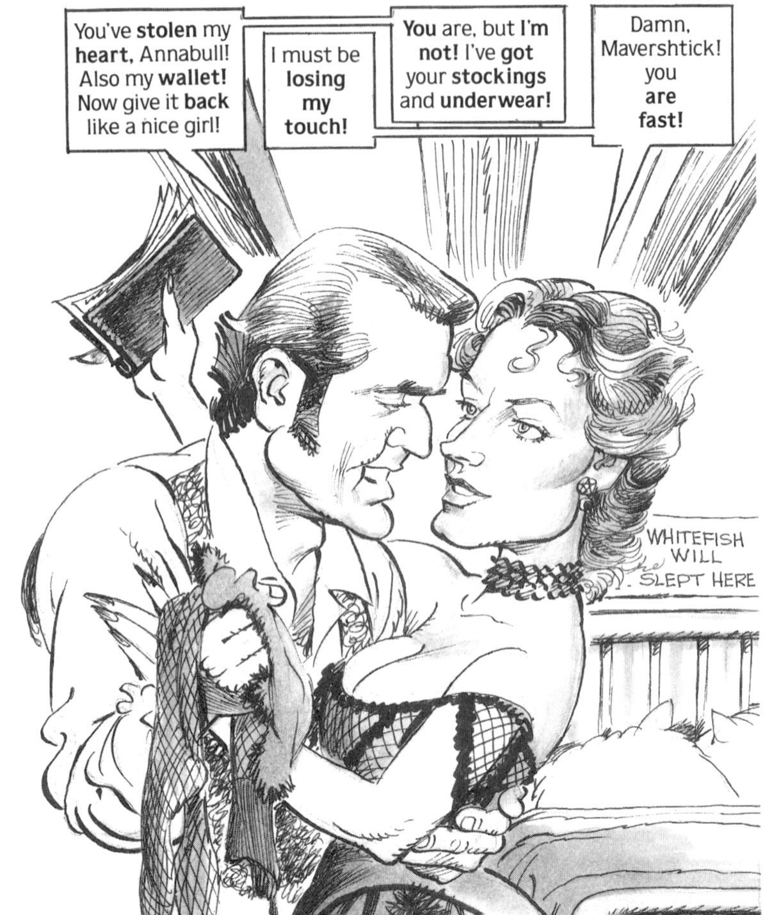

You've stolen my heart, Annabull! Also my wallet! Now give it back like a nice girl!
I must be losing my touch!
You are, but I'm not! I've got your stockings and underwear!
Damn, Mavershtick! you are fast!
WHITEFISH WILL SLEPT HERE


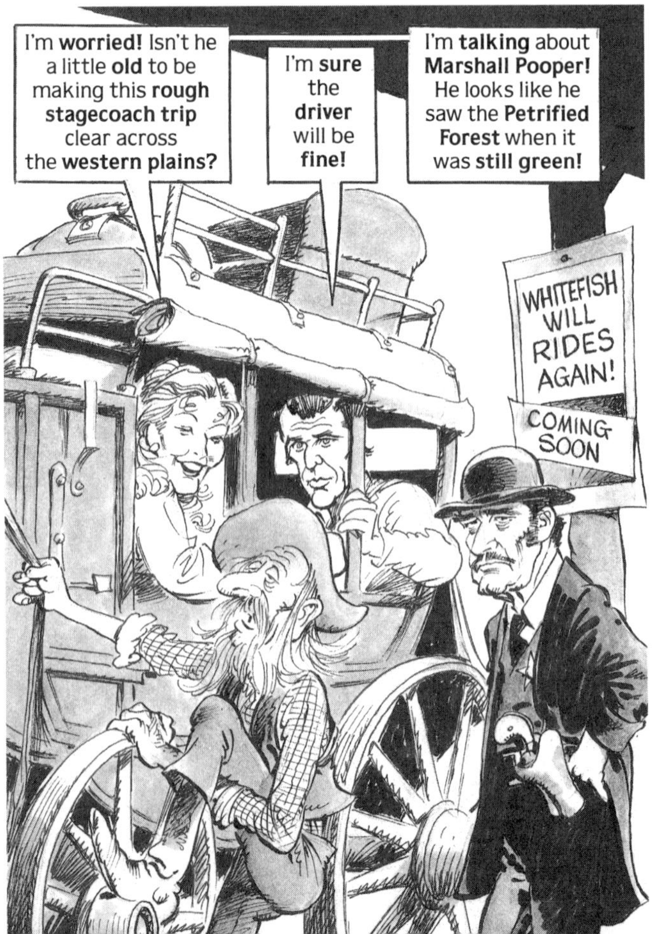

I'm worried! Isn't he a little old to be making this rough stagecoach trip clear across the western plains?
I'm sure the driver will be fine!
I'm talking about Marshall Pooper! He looks like he saw the Petrified Forest when it was still green!
WHITEFISH WILL RIDES AGAIN!
COMING SOON

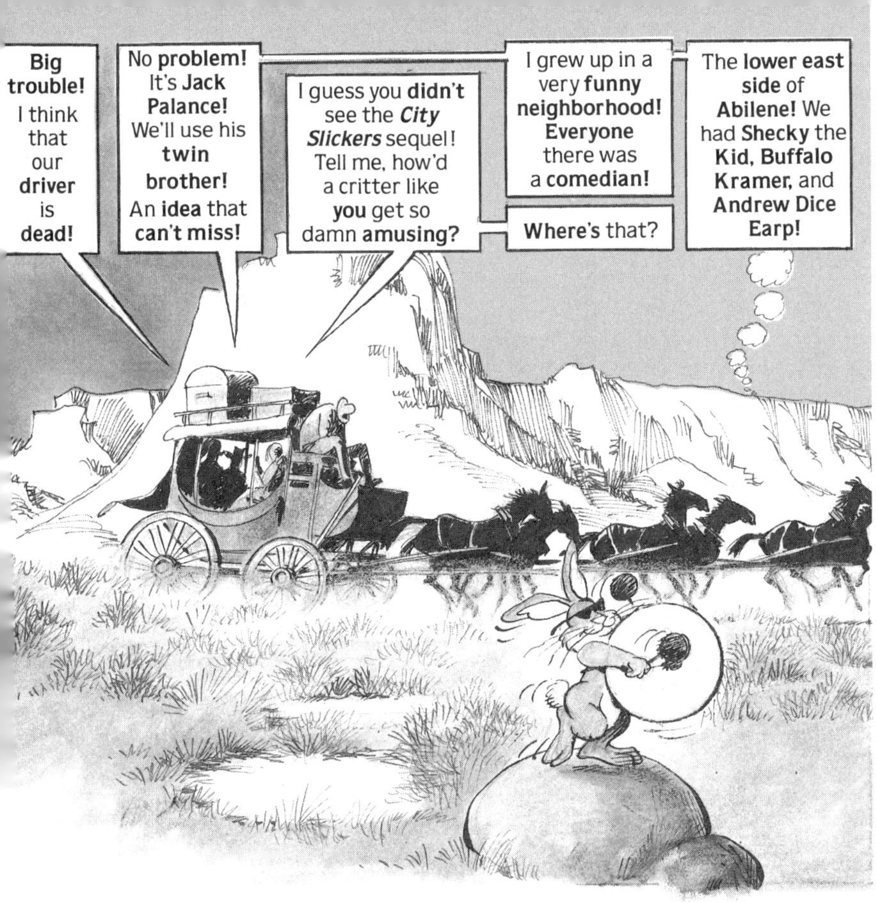
Big trouble! I think that our driver is dead!
No problem! It's Jack Palance! We'll use his twin brother! An idea that can't miss!
I guess you didn't see the City Slickers sequel! Tell me, how'd a critter like you get so damn amusing?
I grew up in a very funny neighborhood! Everyone there was a comedian!
Where's that?
The lower east side of Abilene! We had Shecky the Kid, Buffalo Kramer, and Andrew Dice Earp!

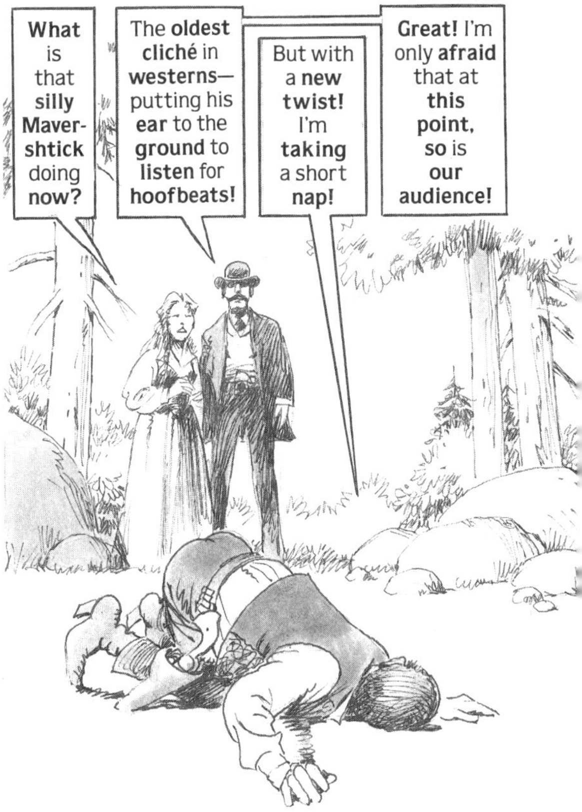
What is that silly Maver-shtick doing now?
The oldest cliché in westerns—putting his ear to the ground to listen for hoofbeats!
But with a new twist! I'm taking a short nap!
Great! I'm only afraid that at this point, so is our audience!

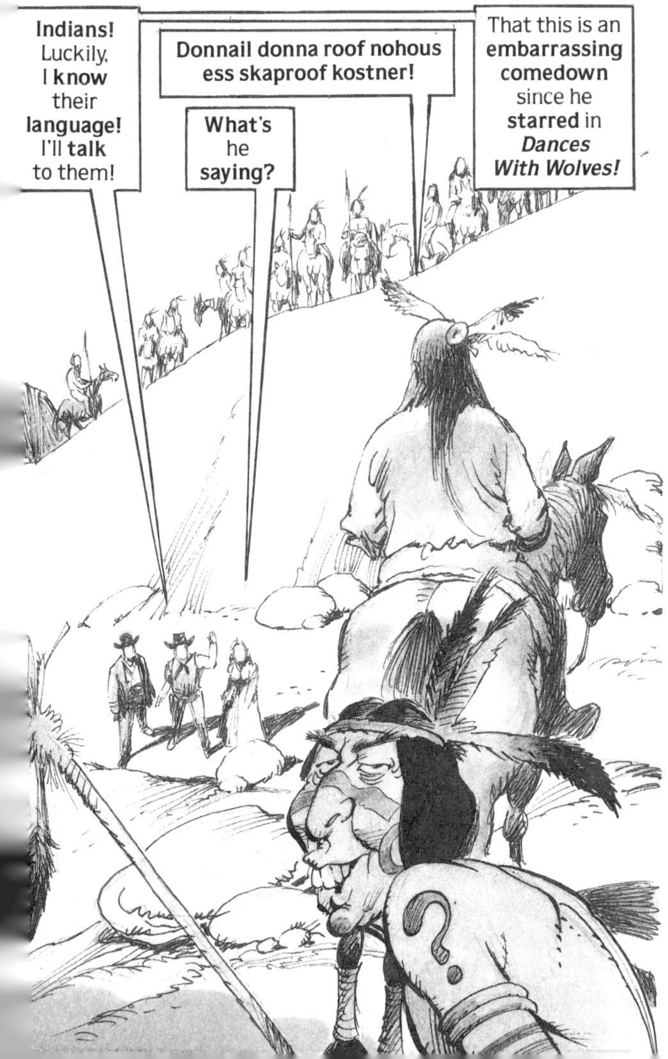
Indians! Luckily, I know their language! I'll talk to them!
Donnail donna roof nohous ess skaproof kostner!
What's he saying?
That this is an embarrassing comedown since he starred in Dances With Wolves!

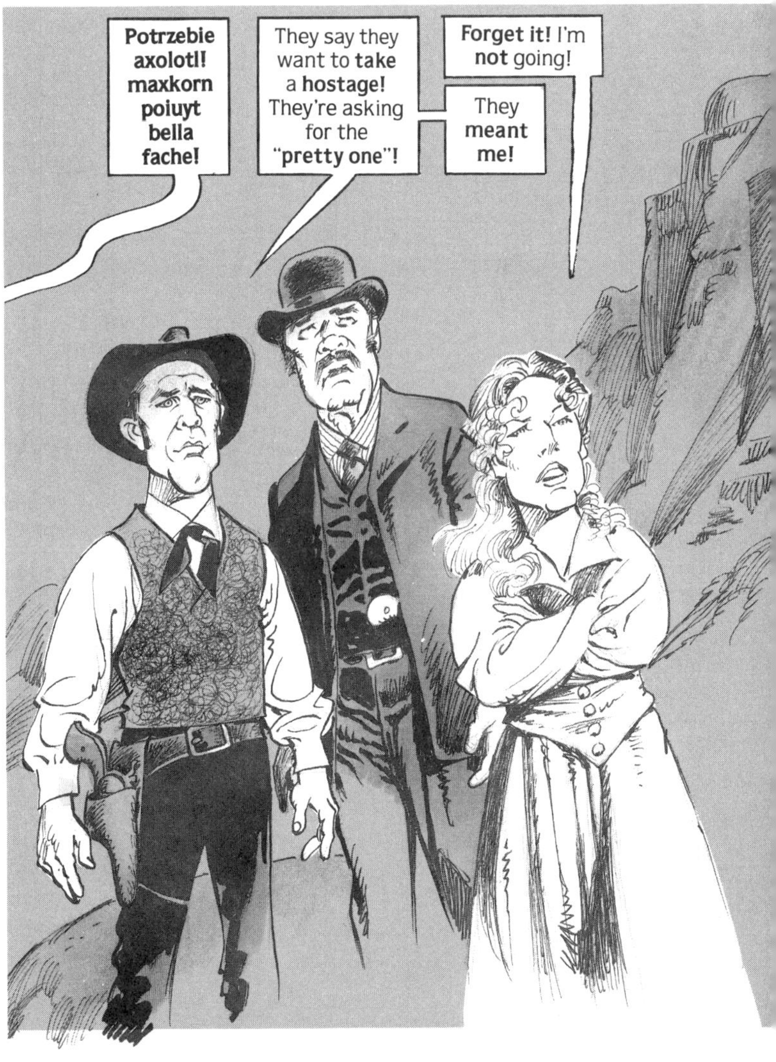
Potrzebie axolotl! maxkorn poiuyt bella fache!
They say they want to take a hostage! They're asking for the "pretty one"!
They meant me!
Forget it! I'm not going!

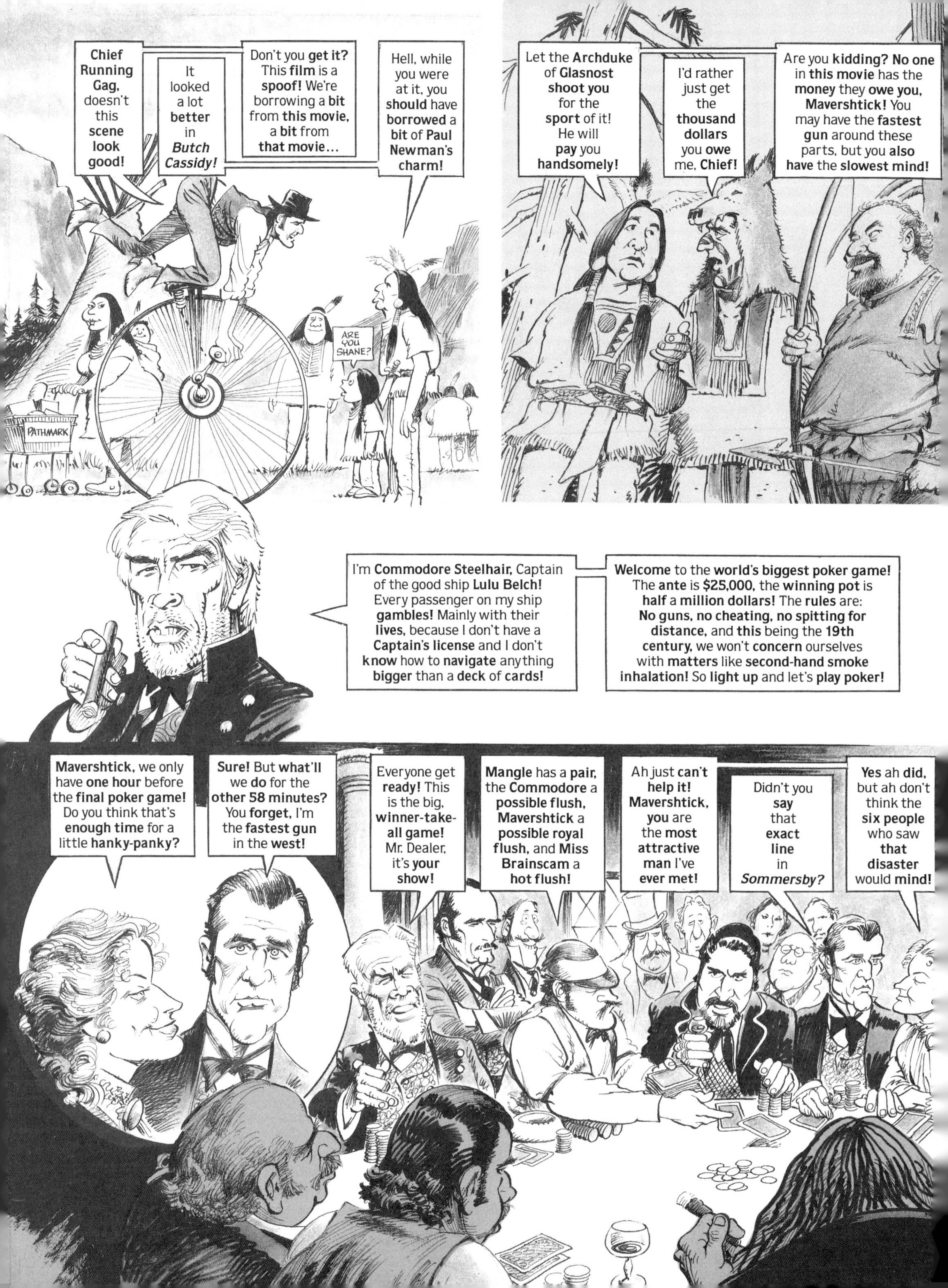
Chief Running Gag, doesn't this scene look good!
It looked a lot better in *Butch Cassidy!*
Don't you get it? This film is a spoof! We're borrowing a bit from this movie, a bit from that movie…
Hell, while you were at it, you should have borrowed a bit of Paul Newman's charm!
ARE YOU SHANE?
PATHMARK
Let the Archduke of Glasnost shoot you for the sport of it! He will pay you handsomely!
I'd rather just get the thousand dollars you owe me, Chief!
Are you kidding? No one in this movie has the money they owe you, Mavershtick! You may have the fastest gun around these parts, but you also have the slowest mind!
I'm Commodore Steelhair, Captain of the good ship Lulu Belch! Every passenger on my ship gambles! Mainly with their lives, because I don't have a Captain's license and I don't know how to navigate anything bigger than a deck of cards!
Welcome to the world's biggest poker game! The ante is $25,000, the winning pot is half a million dollars! The rules are: No guns, no cheating, no spitting for distance, and this being the 19th century, we won't concern ourselves with matters like second-hand smoke inhalation! So light up and let's play poker!
Mavershtick, we only have one hour before the final poker game! Do you think that's enough time for a little hanky-panky?
Sure! But what'll we do for the other 58 minutes? You forget, I'm the fastest gun in the west!
Everyone get ready! This is the big, winner-take-all game! Mr. Dealer, it's your show!
Mangle has a pair, the Commodore a possible flush, Mavershtick a possible royal flush, and Miss Brainscam a hot flush!
Ah just can't help it! Mavershtick, you are the most attractive man I've ever met!
Didn't you say that exact line in *Sommersby?*
Yes ah did, but ah don't think the six people who saw that disaster would mind!

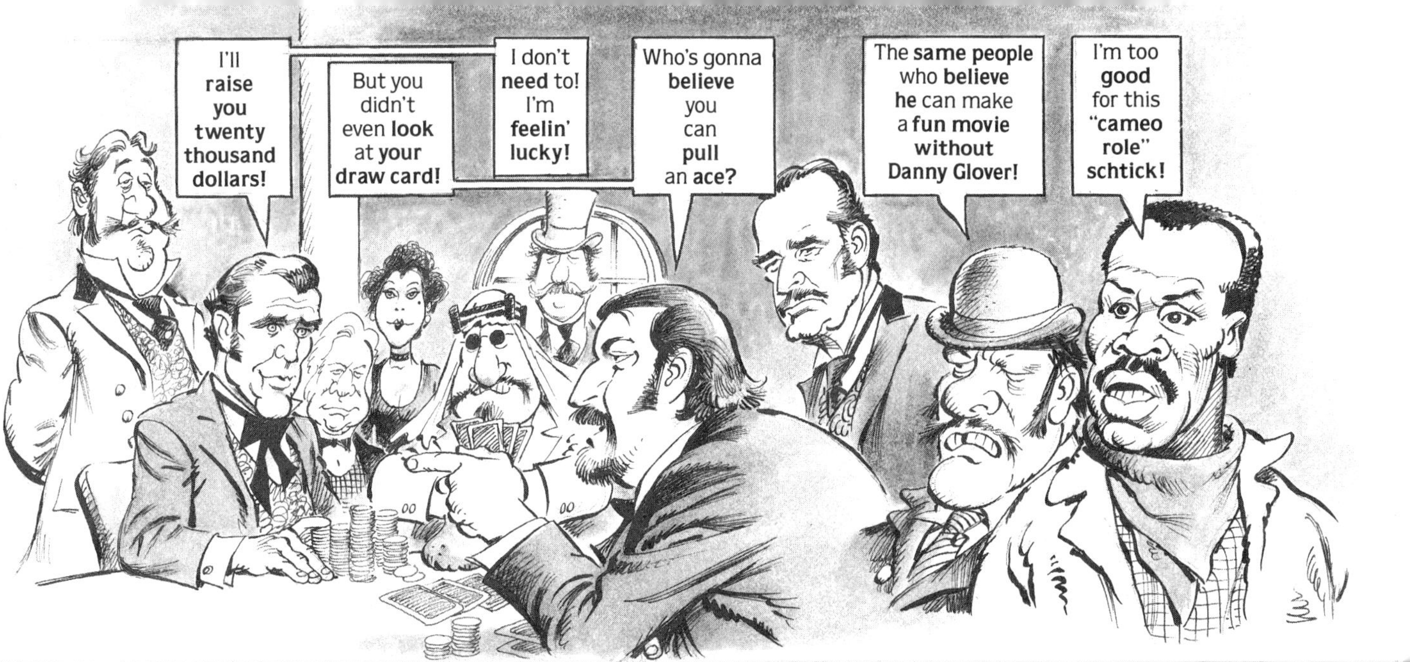
I'll raise you twenty thousand dollars!
But you didn't even look at your draw card!
I don't need to! I'm feelin' lucky!
Who's gonna believe you can pull an ace?
The same people who believe he can make a fun movie without Danny Glover!
I'm too good for this "cameo role" schtick!

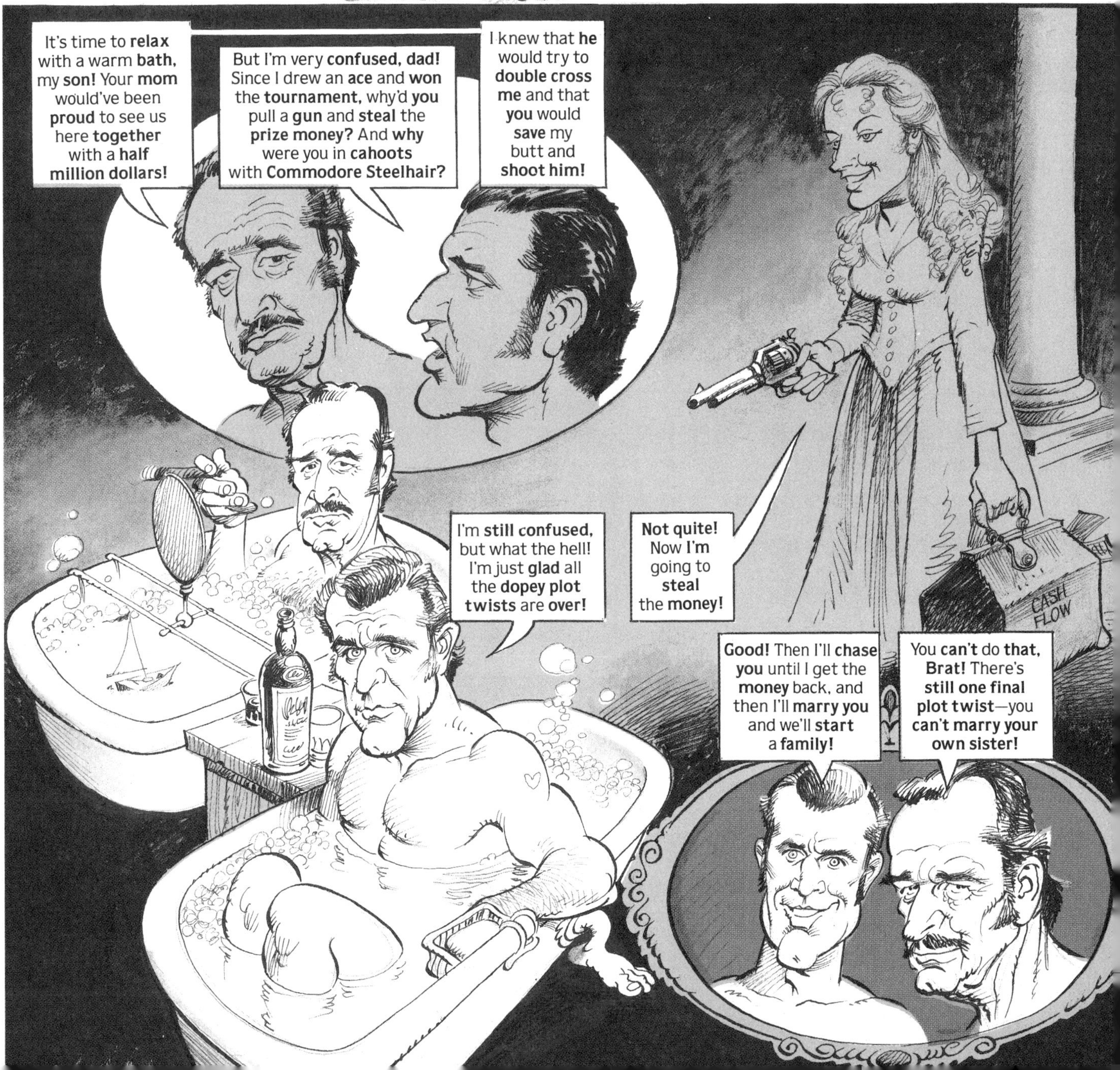
It's time to relax with a warm bath, my son! Your mom would've been proud to see us here together with a half million dollars!
But I'm very confused, dad! Since I drew an ace and won the tournament, why'd you pull a gun and steal the prize money? And why were you in cahoots with Commodore Steelhair?
I knew that he would try to double cross me and that you would save my butt and shoot him!
I'm still confused, but what the hell! I'm just glad all the dopey plot twists are over!
Not quite! Now I'm going to steal the money!
CASH FLOW
Good! Then I'll chase you until I get the money back, and then I'll marry you and we'll start a family!
You can't do that, Brat! There's still one final plot twist—you can't marry your own sister!

(1 CLINTON HEALTH CARE PLAN) + (BOB DOLE) +(RUSH LIMBAUGH) +
("HARRY") + ("LOUISE") = (THE CRAPPY PLAN WE'RE GONNA END UP WITH)

**PLIGHT OF THE LIVING DEAD DEPT.**

**Tom Cruise is a vampire. A 12-year old unknown actress is a vampire. Brad Pitt and Antonio Banderas are vampires. What else can we say about it all, except — he sucks, she sucks, they suck and so does...**

# INTRAVENOUS WITH THE

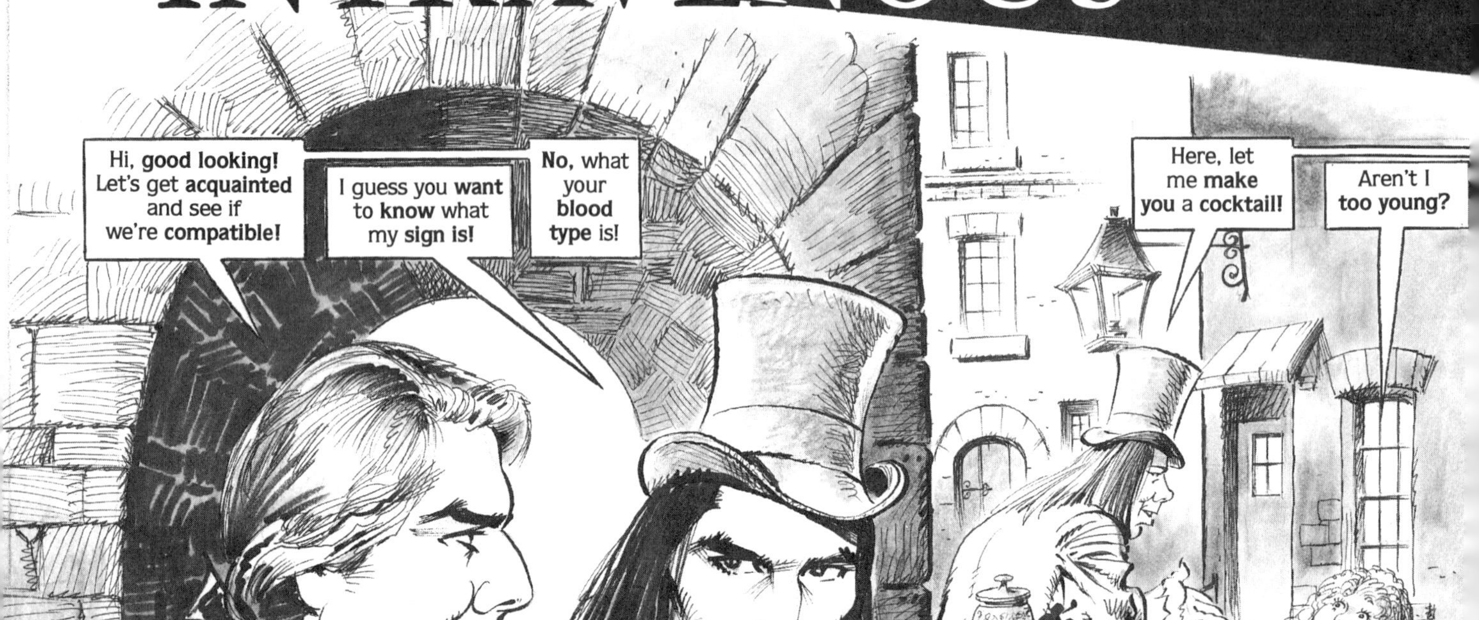


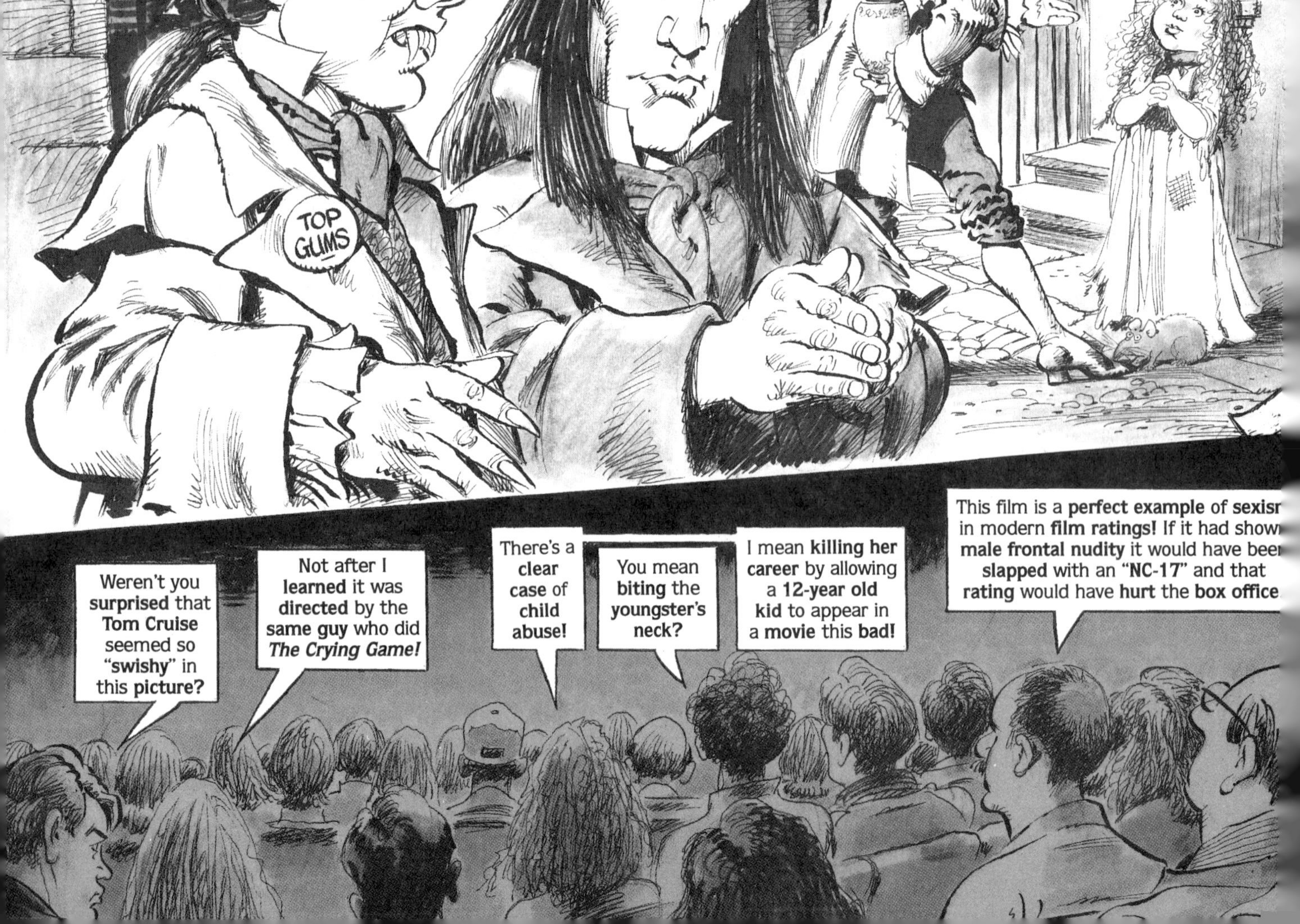

# VAMPIRE

ARTIST: MORT DRUCKER WRITER: STAN HART

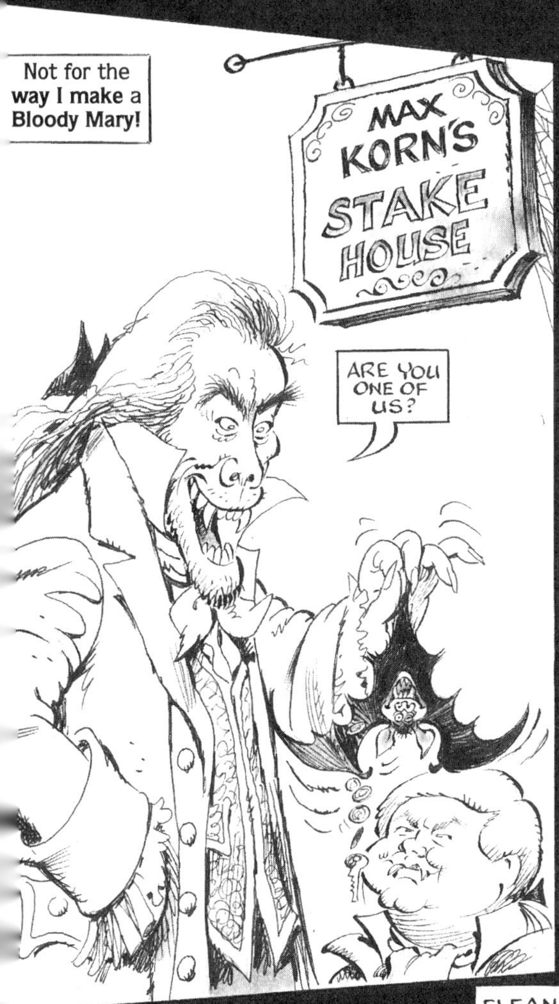
Not for the way I make a Bloody Mary!
MAX KORN'S STAKE HOUSE
ARE YOU ONE OF US?

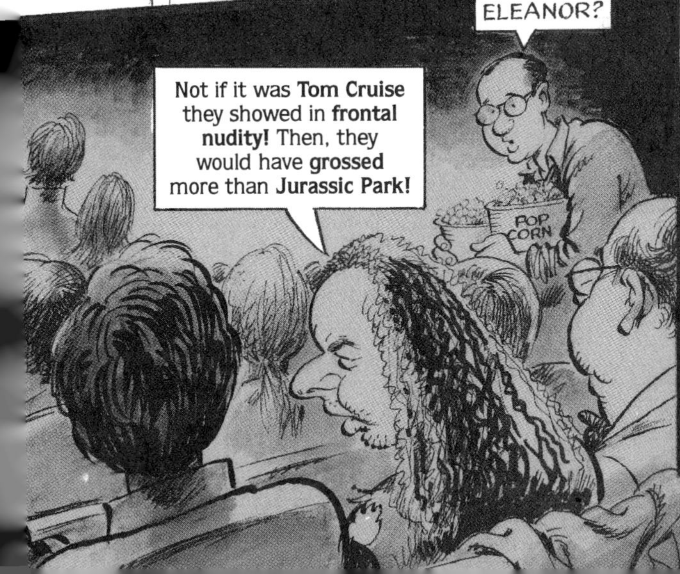
ELEANOR?
Not if it was Tom Cruise they showed in frontal nudity! Then, they would have grossed more than Jurassic Park!
POP CORN

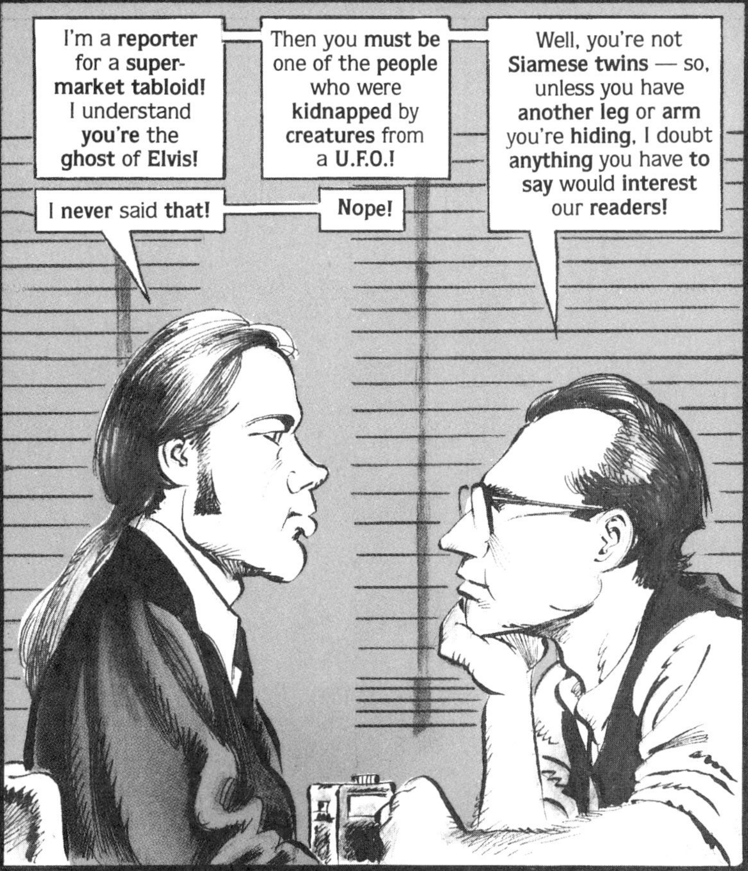
I'm a reporter for a supermarket tabloid! I understand you're the ghost of Elvis!
I never said that!
Then you must be one of the people who were kidnapped by creatures from a U.F.O.!
Nope!
Well, you're not Siamese twins — so, unless you have another leg or arm you're hiding, I doubt anything you have to say would interest our readers!

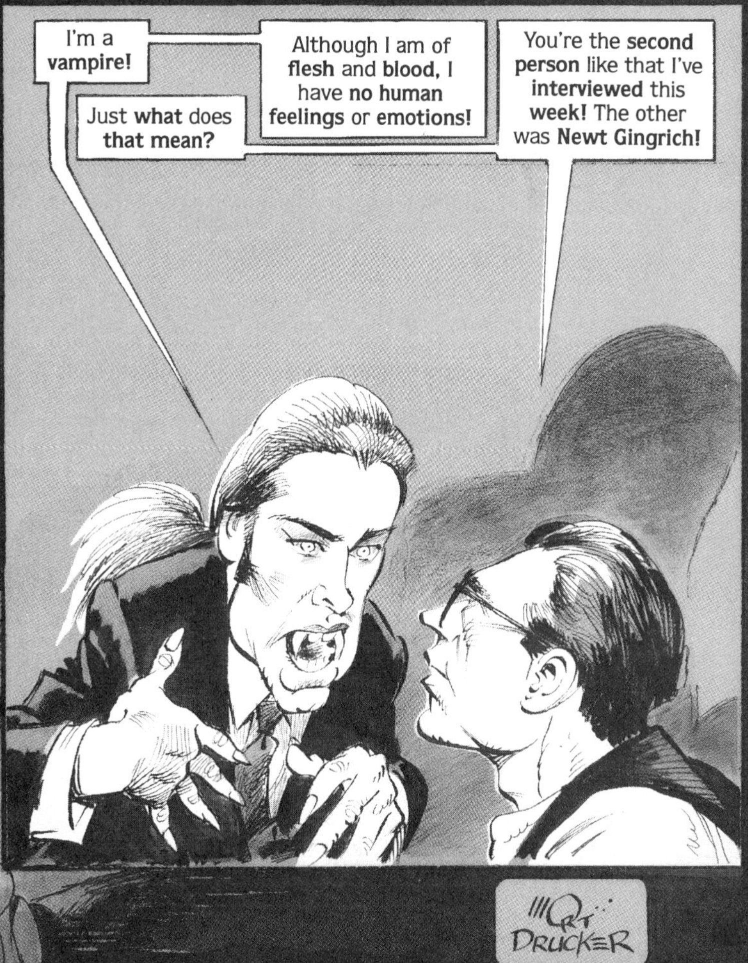
I'm a vampire!
Just what does that mean?
Although I am of flesh and blood, I have no human feelings or emotions!
You're the second person like that I've interviewed this week! The other was Newt Gingrich!
DRUCKER

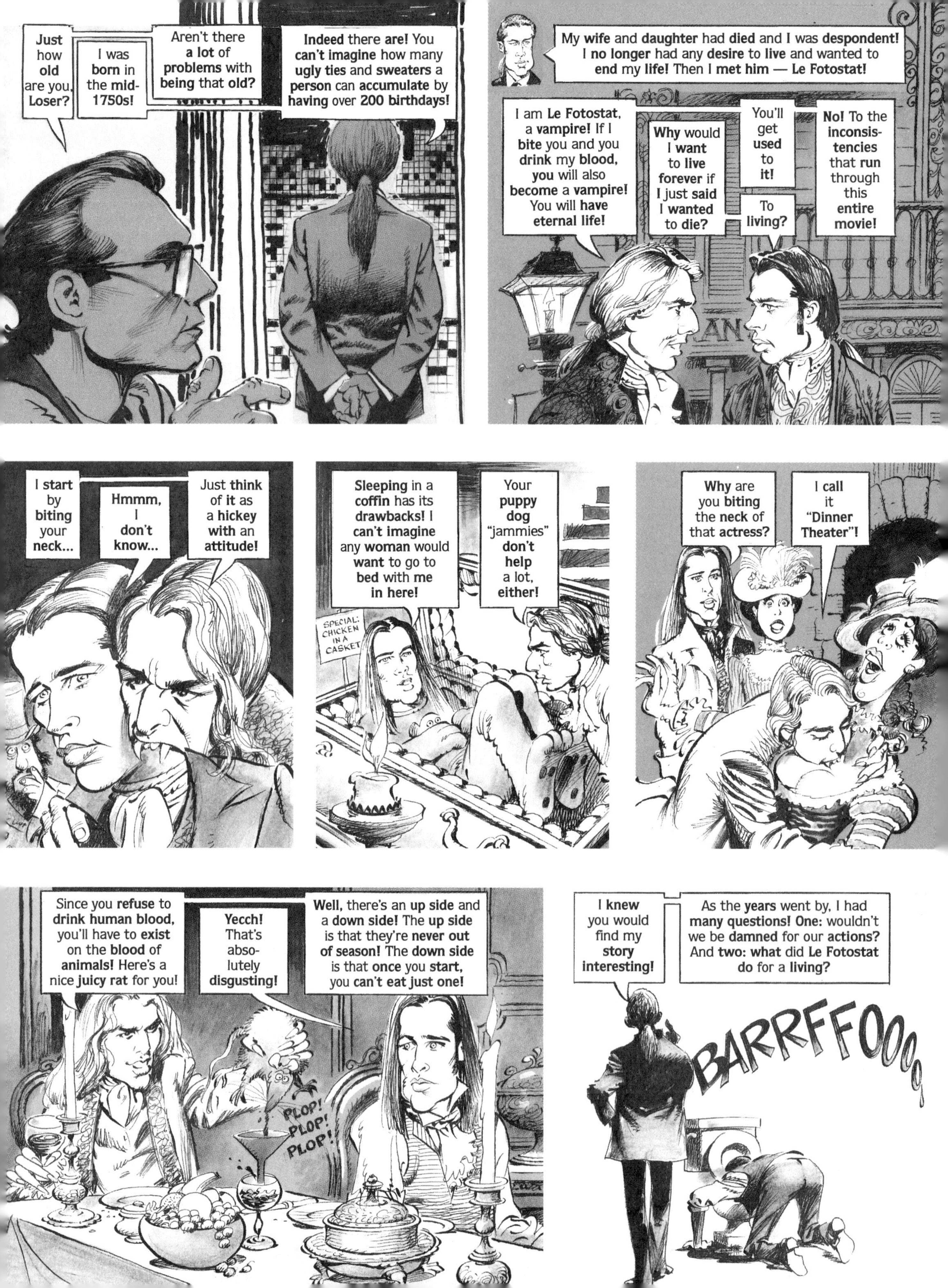

Just how old are you, Loser?
I was born in the mid-1750s!
Aren't there a lot of problems with being that old?
Indeed there are! You can't imagine how many ugly ties and sweaters a person can accumulate by having over 200 birthdays!
My wife and daughter had died and I was despondent! I no longer had any desire to live and wanted to end my life! Then I met him — Le Fotostat!
I am Le Fotostat, a vampire! If I bite you and you drink my blood, you will also become a vampire! You will have eternal life!
Why would I want to live forever if I just said I wanted to die?
You'll get used to it!
To living?
No! To the inconsistencies that run through this entire movie!
I start by biting your neck...
Hmmm, I don't know...
Just think of it as a hickey with an attitude!
Sleeping in a coffin has its drawbacks! I can't imagine any woman would want to go to bed with me in here!
Your puppy dog "jammies" don't help a lot, either!
SPECIAL: CHICKEN IN A CASKET
Why are you biting the neck of that actress?
I call it "Dinner Theater"!
Since you refuse to drink human blood, you'll have to exist on the blood of animals! Here's a nice juicy rat for you!
Yecch! That's absolutely disgusting!
Well, there's an up side and a down side! The up side is that they're never out of season! The down side is that once you start, you can't eat just one!
PLOP! PLOP! PLOP!
I knew you would find my story interesting!
As the years went by, I had many questions! One: wouldn't we be damned for our actions? And two: what did Le Fotostat do for a living?
BARRFFOOOO

MAD FACTOIDS: 4 out of 5 people who said during last year's World Cup that soccer would be "sweeping America" have since changed their phone numbers.

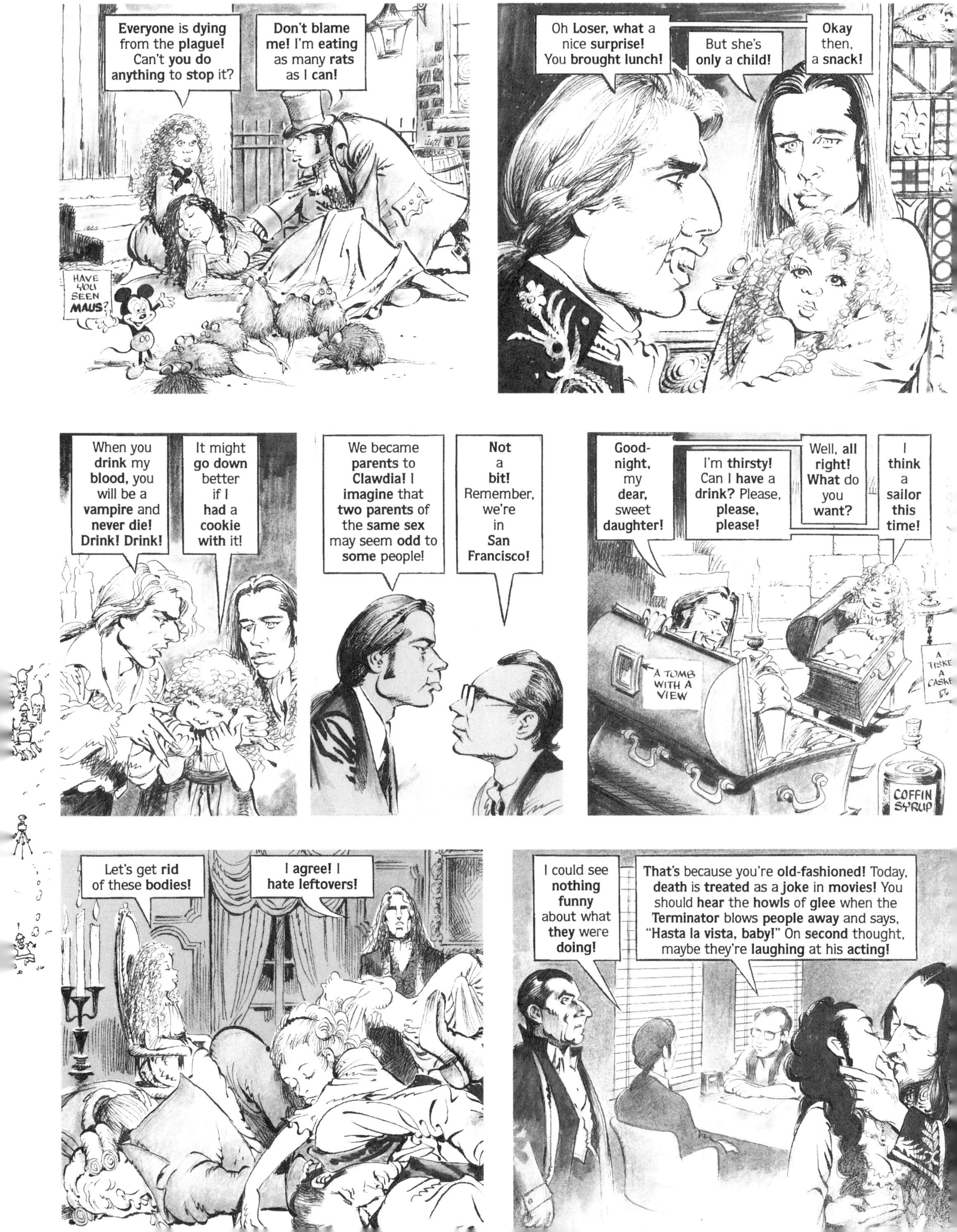
Everyone is dying from the plague! Can't you do anything to stop it?
Don't blame me! I'm eating as many rats as I can!
HAVE YOU SEEN MAUS?
Oh Loser, what a nice surprise! You brought lunch!
But she's only a child!
Okay then, a snack!
When you drink my blood, you will be a vampire and never die! Drink! Drink!
It might go down better if I had a cookie with it!
We became parents to Clawdia! I imagine that two parents of the same sex may seem odd to some people!
Not a bit! Remember, we're in San Francisco!
Good-night, my dear, sweet daughter!
I'm thirsty! Can I have a drink? Please, please, please!
Well, all right! What do you want?
I think a sailor this time!
A TOMB WITH A VIEW
COFFIN SYRUP
Let's get rid of these bodies!
I agree! I hate leftovers!
I could see nothing funny about what they were doing!
That's because you're old-fashioned! Today, death is treated as a joke in movies! You should hear the howls of glee when the Terminator blows people away and says, "Hasta la vista, baby!" On second thought, maybe they're laughing at his acting!

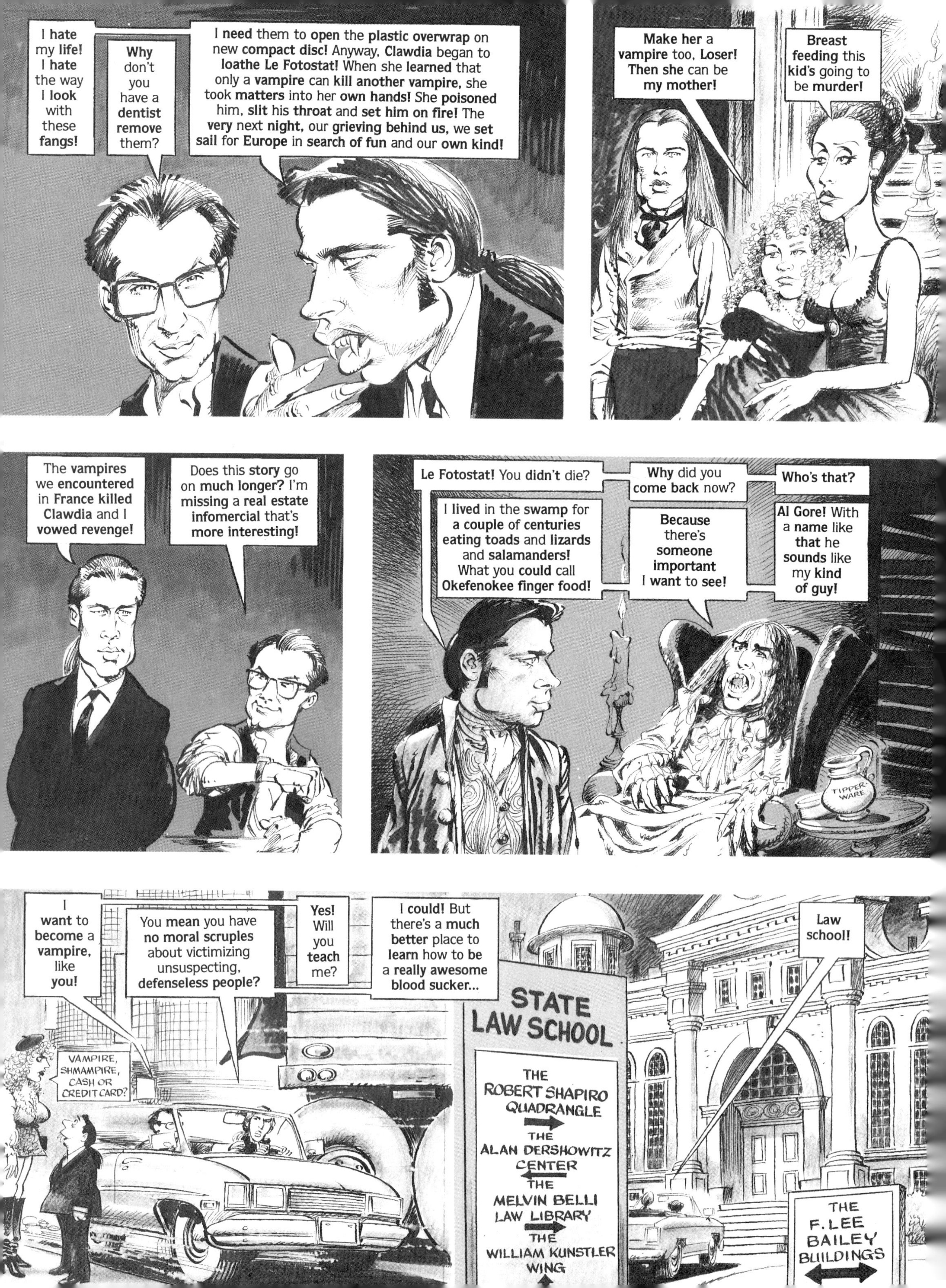

I hate my life! I hate the way I look with these fangs!
Why don't you have a dentist remove them?
I need them to open the plastic overwrap on new compact disc! Anyway, Clawdia began to loathe Le Fotostat! When she learned that only a vampire can kill another vampire, she took matters into her own hands! She poisoned him, slit his throat and set him on fire! The very next night, our grieving behind us, we set sail for Europe in search of fun and our own kind!
Make her a vampire too, Loser! Then she can be my mother!
Breast feeding this kid's going to be murder!
The vampires we encountered in France killed Clawdia and I vowed revenge!
Does this story go on much longer? I'm missing a real estate infomercial that's more interesting!
Le Fotostat! You didn't die?
Why did you come back now?
Who's that?
I lived in the swamp for a couple of centuries eating toads and lizards and salamanders! What you could call Okefenokee finger food!
Because there's someone important I want to see!
Al Gore! With a name like that he sounds like my kind of guy!
TIPPER-WARE
I want to become a vampire, like you!
You mean you have no moral scruples about victimizing unsuspecting, defenseless people?
Yes! Will you teach me?
I could! But there's a much better place to learn how to be a really awesome blood sucker...
Law school!
VAMPIRE, SHMAMPIRE, CASH OR CREDIT CARD?
STATE LAW SCHOOL
THE ROBERT SHAPIRO QUADRANGLE
THE ALAN DERSHOWITZ CENTER
THE MELVIN BELLI LAW LIBRARY
THE WILLIAM KUNSTLER WING
THE F. LEE BAILEY BUILDINGS

# Scenes We'd Like to See

The Race To The Crossing

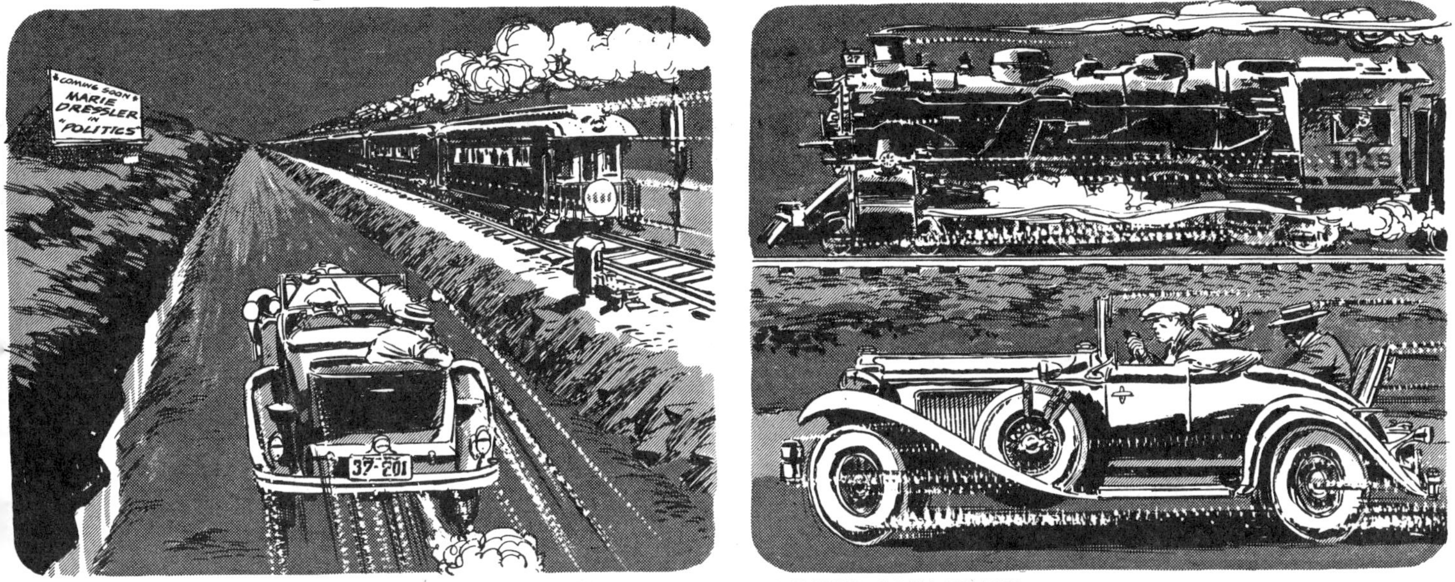
COMING SOON
MARIE
DRESSLER
IN
"POLITICS"
37-201

ARTIST: GEORGE WOODBRIDGE WRITER: GARY BELKIN

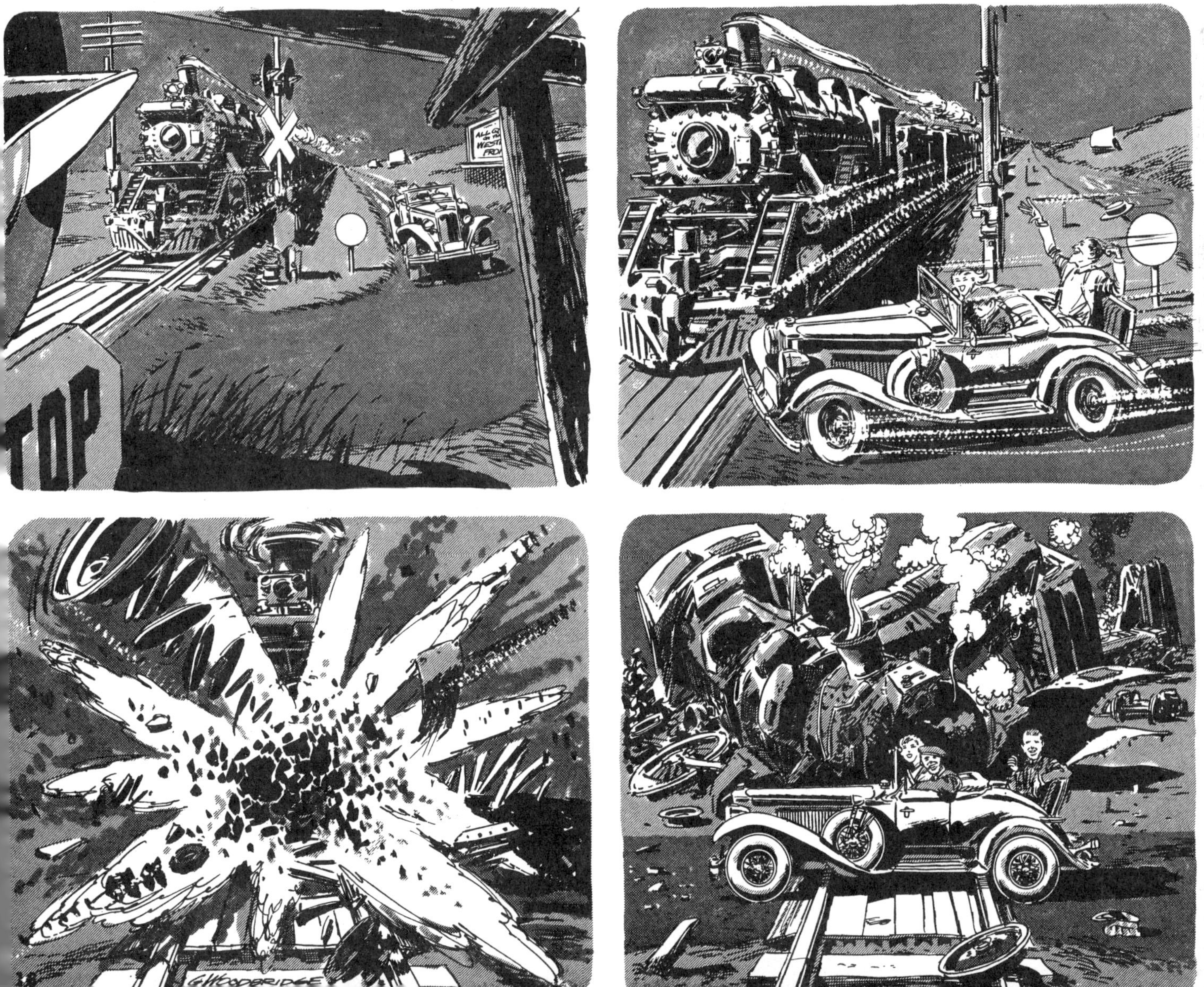
TOP
G.WOODBRIDGE

**STOP THE WHIRL—I WANT TO GET OFF DEPT.**

One of the year's biggest movies is about a group of pinheaded scientists who ran around Oklahoma chasing tornadoes with all the frenzy of Marlon Brando at an all-you-can-eat Polynesian buffet! Why they were trying to catch up with a deadly, whirling cone of air, debris and assorted bovines is too confusing to be explained in a 200-page science book, much less this intro! It begs the question: "Who are the bigger schmucks — the idiot scientists, or the dolts who paid eight bucks to see this dreck?" Hmmm...let's face it, we're ALL a bunch of...

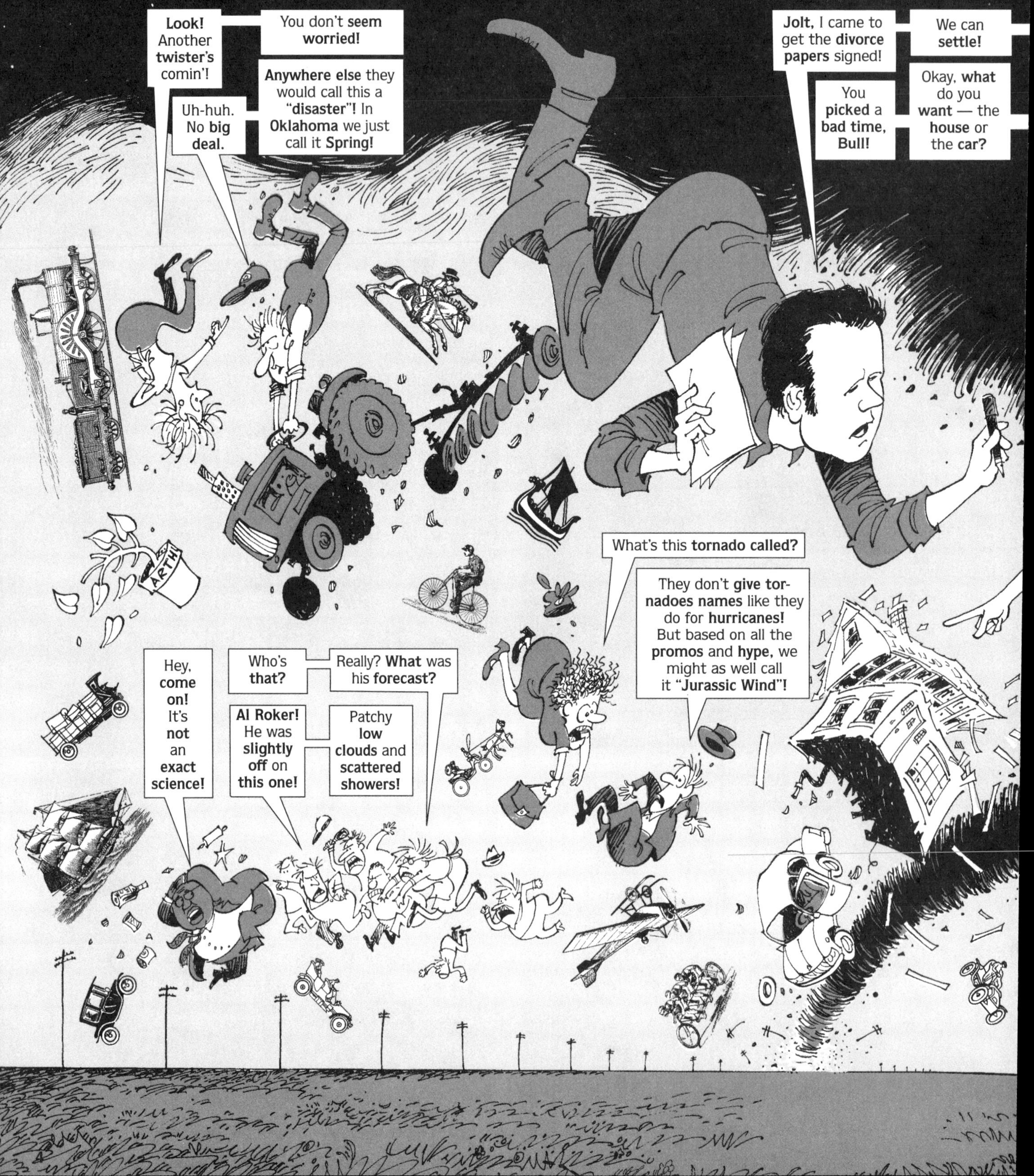
Look! Another twister's comin'!
You don't seem worried!
Uh-huh. No big deal.
Anywhere else they would call this a "disaster"! In Oklahoma we just call it Spring!
Jolt, I came to get the divorce papers signed!
You picked a bad time, Bull!
We can settle!
Okay, what do you want — the house or the car?
What's this tornado called?
They don't give tornadoes names like they do for hurricanes! But based on all the promos and hype, we might as well call it "Jurassic Wind"!
Hey, come on! It's not an exact science!
Who's that?
Al Roker! He was slightly off on this one!
Really? What was his forecast?
Patchy low clouds and scattered showers!
ARTH

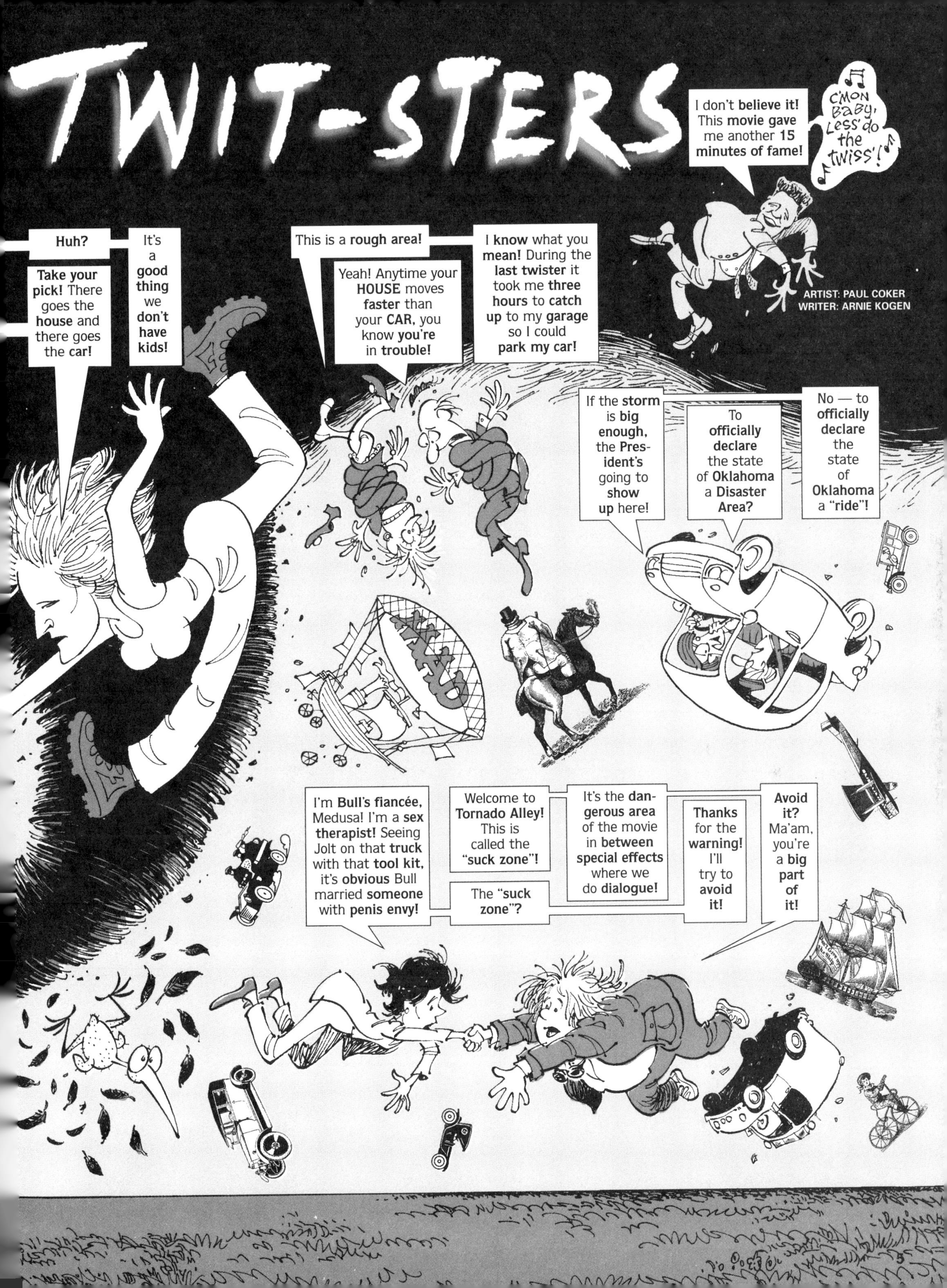
TWIT-STERS
I don't believe it! This movie gave me another 15 minutes of fame!
C'MON BABY, LESS' do the TWISS'!
ARTIST: PAUL COKER
WRITER: ARNIE KOGEN
Huh?
It's a good thing we don't have kids!
Take your pick! There goes the house and there goes the car!
This is a rough area!
Yeah! Anytime your HOUSE moves faster than your CAR, you know you're in trouble!
I know what you mean! During the last twister it took me three hours to catch up to my garage so I could park my car!
If the storm is big enough, the President's going to show up here!
To officially declare the state of Oklahoma a Disaster Area?
No — to officially declare the state of Oklahoma a "ride"!
I'm Bull's fiancée, Medusa! I'm a sex therapist! Seeing Jolt on that truck with that tool kit, it's obvious Bull married someone with penis envy!
Welcome to Tornado Alley! This is called the "suck zone"!
The "suck zone"?
It's the dangerous area of the movie in between special effects where we do dialogue!
Thanks for the warning! I'll try to avoid it!
Avoid it? Ma'am, you're a big part of it!

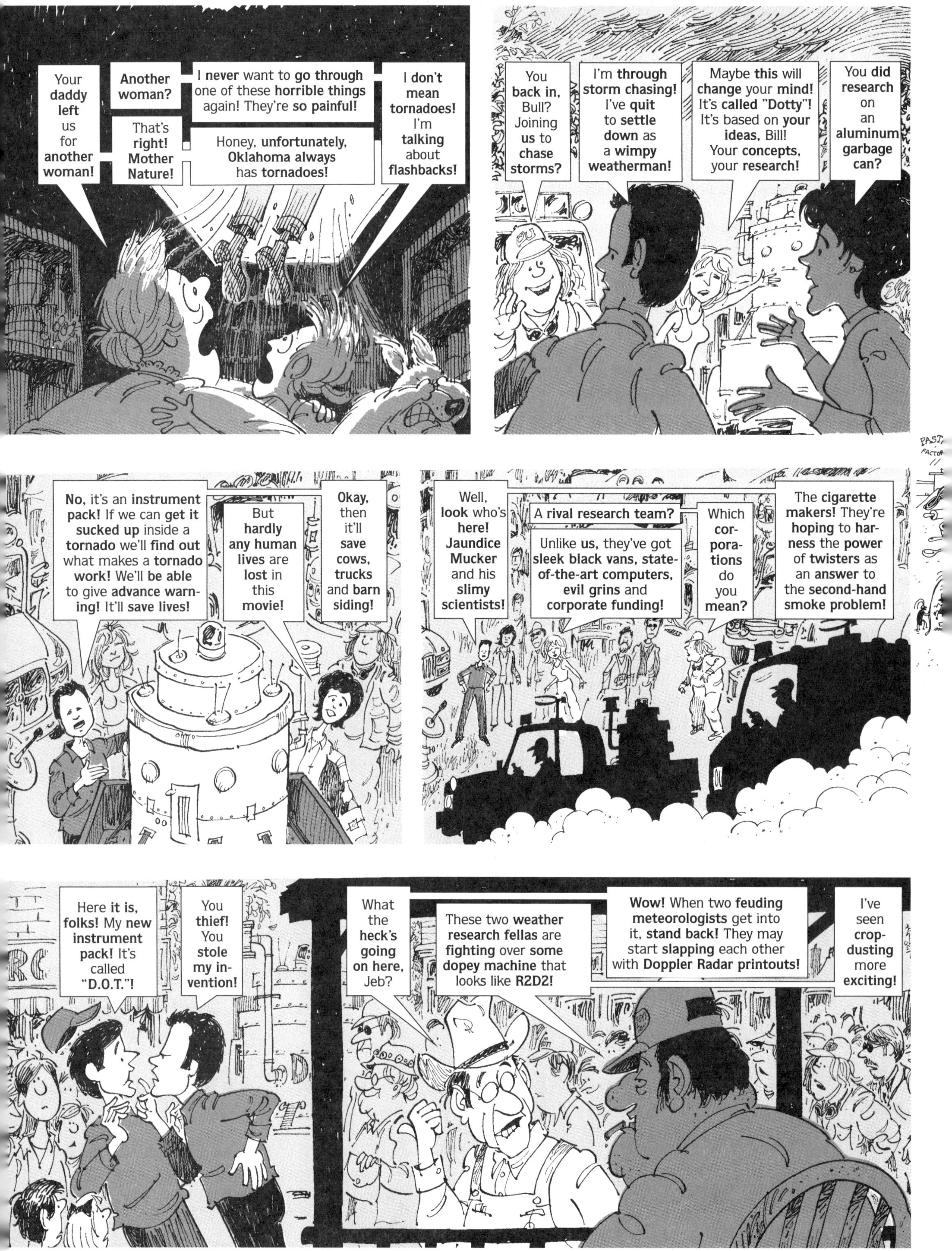

Your daddy left us for another woman!
Another woman?
That's right! Mother Nature!
I never want to go through one of these horrible things again! They're so painful!
Honey, unfortunately, Oklahoma always has tornadoes!
I don't mean tornadoes! I'm talking about flashbacks!
You back in, Bull? Joining us to chase storms?
I'm through storm chasing! I've quit to settle down as a wimpy weatherman!
Maybe this will change your mind! It's called "Dotty"! It's based on your ideas, Bill! Your concepts, your research!
You did research on an aluminum garbage can?
No, it's an instrument pack! If we can get it sucked up inside a tornado we'll find out what makes a tornado work! We'll be able to give advance warning! It'll save lives!
But hardly any human lives are lost in this movie!
Okay, then it'll save cows, trucks and barn siding!
Well, look who's here! Jaundice Mucker and his slimy scientists!
A rival research team?
Unlike us, they've got sleek black vans, state-of-the-art computers, evil grins and corporate funding!
Which corporations do you mean?
The cigarette makers! They're hoping to harness the power of twisters as an answer to the second-hand smoke problem!
Here it is, folks! My new instrument pack! It's called "D.O.T."!
You thief! You stole my invention!
What the heck's going on here, Jeb?
These two weather research fellas are fighting over some dopey machine that looks like R2D2!
Wow! When two feuding meteorologists get into it, stand back! They may start slapping each other with Doppler Radar printouts!
I've seen crop-dusting more exciting!

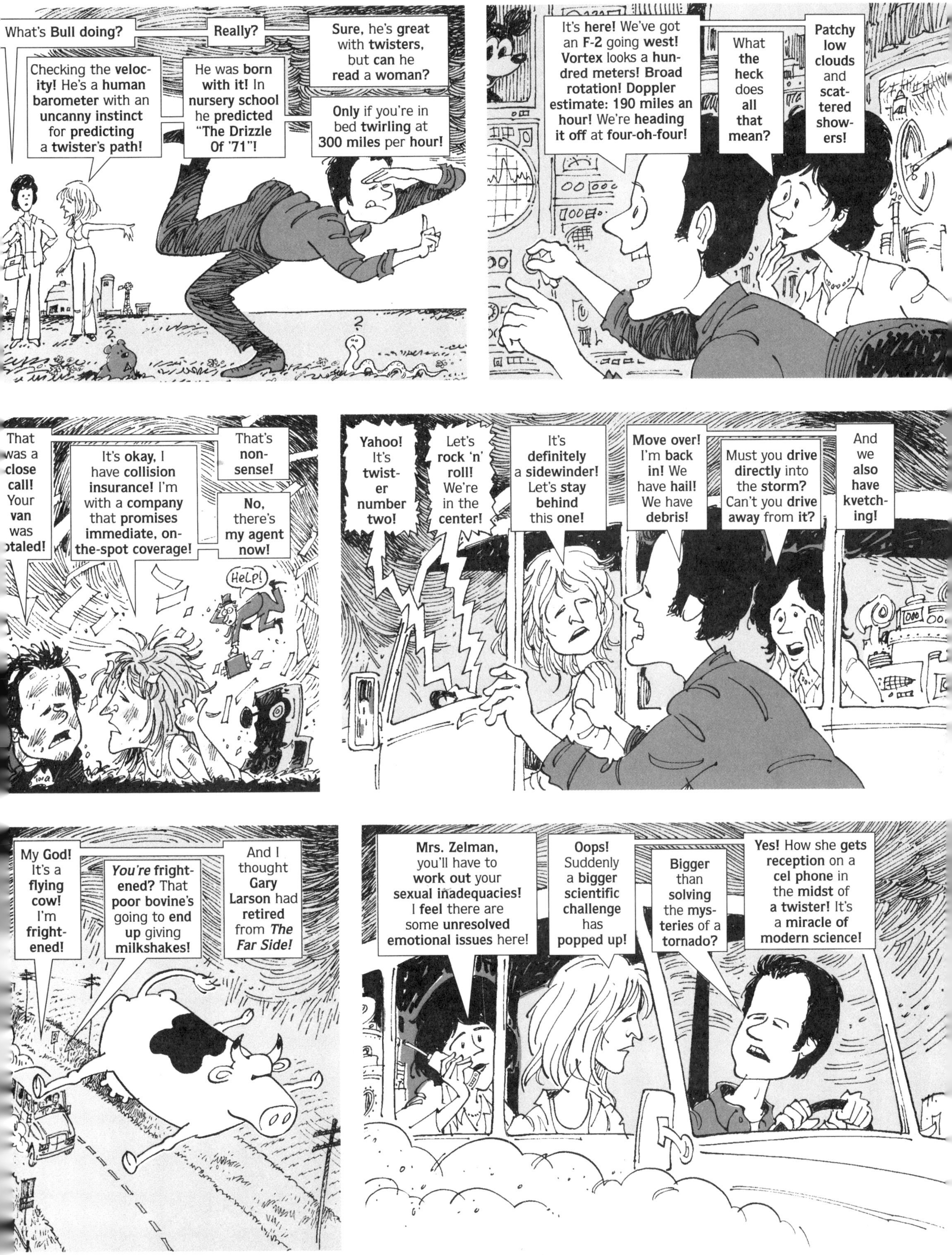

What's Bull doing?
Checking the velocity! He's a human barometer with an uncanny instinct for predicting a twister's path!
Really?
He was born with it! In nursery school he predicted "The Drizzle Of '71"!
Sure, he's great with twisters, but can he read a woman?
Only if you're in bed twirling at 300 miles per hour!
It's here! We've got an F-2 going west! Vortex looks a hundred meters! Broad rotation! Doppler estimate: 190 miles an hour! We're heading it off at four-oh-four!
What the heck does all that mean?
Patchy low clouds and scattered showers!
That was a close call! Your van was otaled!
It's okay, I have collision insurance! I'm with a company that promises immediate, on-the-spot coverage!
That's nonsense!
No, there's my agent now!
HeLp!
Yahoo! It's twister number two!
Let's rock 'n' roll! We're in the center!
It's definitely a sidewinder! Let's stay behind this one!
Move over! I'm back in! We have hail! We have debris!
Must you drive directly into the storm? Can't you drive away from it?
And we also have kvetching!
My God! It's a flying cow! I'm frightened!
You're frightened? That poor bovine's going to end up giving milkshakes!
And I thought Gary Larson had retired from The Far Side!
Mrs. Zelman, you'll have to work out your sexual inadequacies! I feel there are some unresolved emotional issues here!
Oops! Suddenly a bigger scientific challenge has popped up!
Bigger than solving the mysteries of a tornado?
Yes! How she gets reception on a cel phone in the midst of a twister! It's a miracle of modern science!

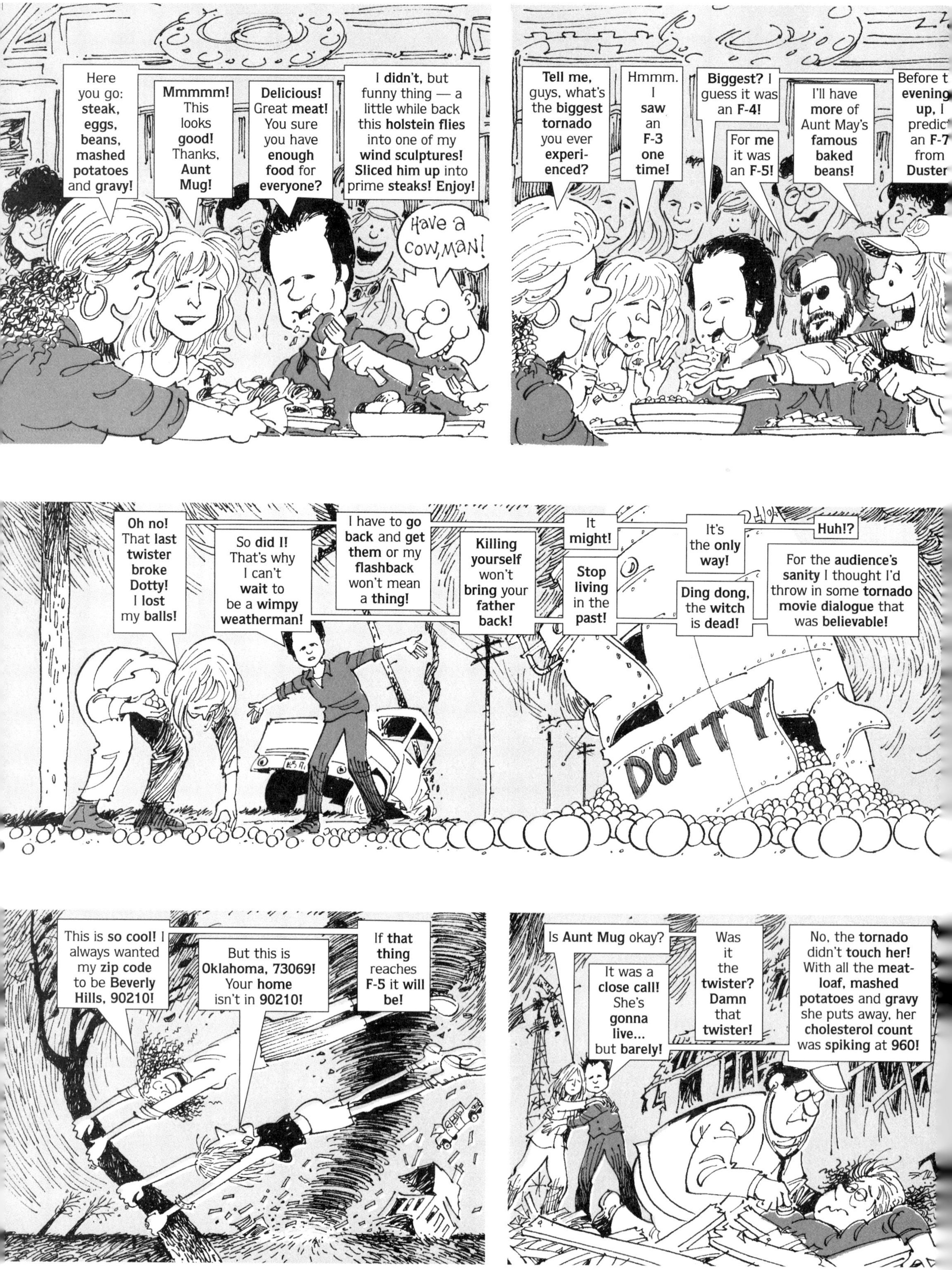
Here you go: steak, eggs, beans, mashed potatoes and gravy!
Mmmmm! This looks good! Thanks, Aunt Mug!
Delicious! Great meat! You sure you have enough food for everyone?
I didn't, but funny thing — a little while back this holstein flies into one of my wind sculptures! Sliced him up into prime steaks! Enjoy!
Have a cow, man!
Tell me, guys, what's the biggest tornado you ever experi-enced?
Hmmm. I saw an F-3 one time!
Biggest? I guess it was an F-4!
For me it was an F-5!
I'll have more of Aunt May's famous baked beans!
Before t evening up, I predic an F-7 from Duster
Oh no! That last twister broke Dotty! I lost my balls!
So did I! That's why I can't wait to be a wimpy weatherman!
I have to go back and get them or my flashback won't mean a thing!
Killing yourself won't bring your father back!
It might!
Stop living in the past!
It's the only way!
Ding dong, the witch is dead!
Huh!?
For the audience's sanity I thought I'd throw in some tornado movie dialogue that was believable!
DOTTY
This is so cool! I always wanted my zip code to be Beverly Hills, 90210!
But this is Oklahoma, 73069! Your home isn't in 90210!
If that thing reaches F-5 it will be!
Is Aunt Mug okay?
It was a close call! She's gonna live... but barely!
Was it the twister? Damn that twister!
No, the tornado didn't touch her! With all the meat-loaf, mashed potatoes and gravy she puts away, her cholesterol count was spiking at 960!

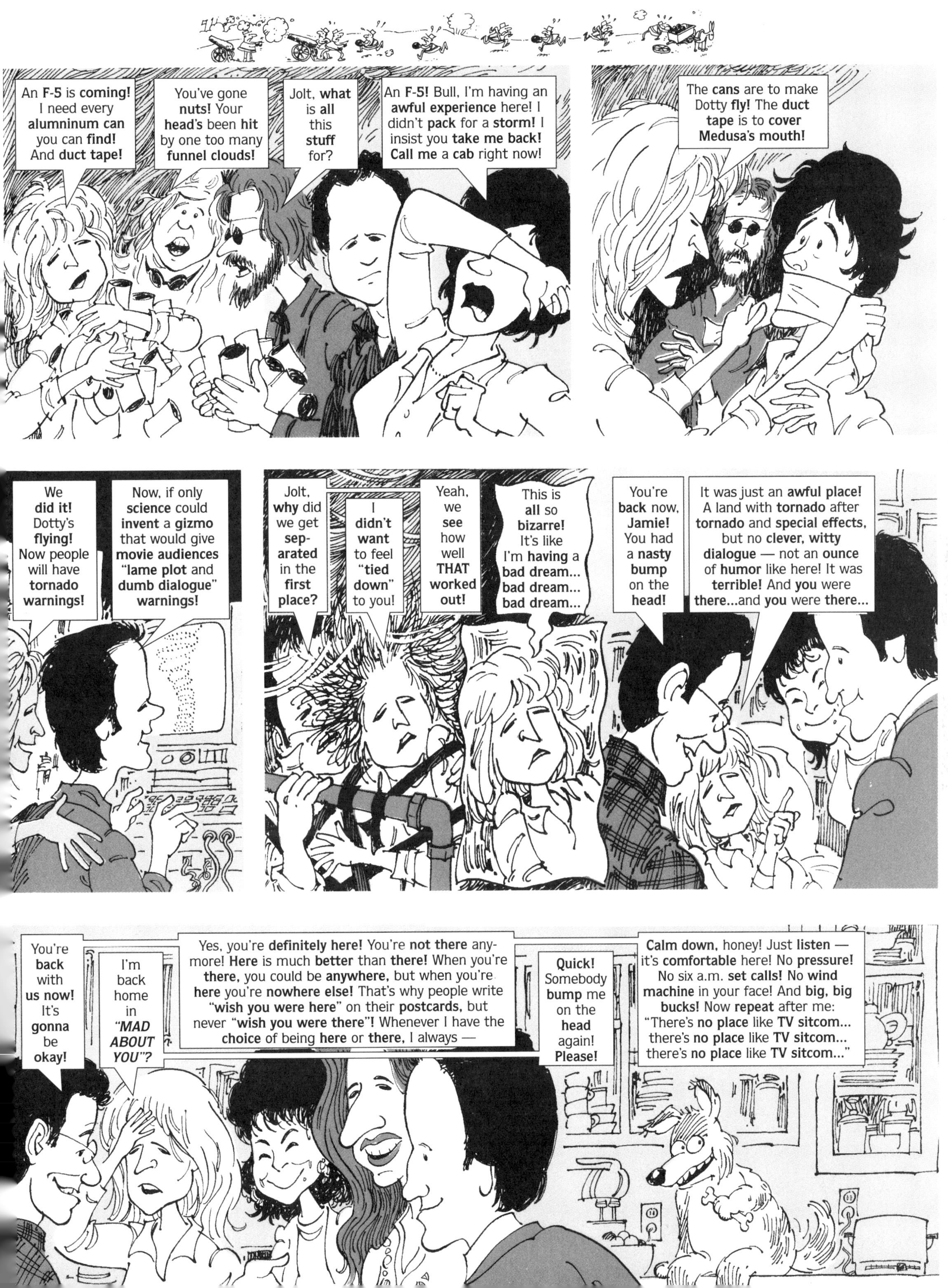
An F-5 is coming! I need every alumninum can you can find! And duct tape!
You've gone nuts! Your head's been hit by one too many funnel clouds!
Jolt, what is all this stuff for?
An F-5! Bull, I'm having an awful experience here! I didn't pack for a storm! I insist you take me back! Call me a cab right now!
The cans are to make Dotty fly! The duct tape is to cover Medusa's mouth!
We did it! Dotty's flying! Now people will have tornado warnings!
Now, if only science could invent a gizmo that would give movie audiences "lame plot and dumb dialogue" warnings!
Jolt, why did we get sep-arated in the first place?
I didn't want to feel "tied down" to you!
Yeah, we see how well THAT worked out!
This is all so bizarre! It's like I'm having a bad dream... bad dream... bad dream...
You're back now, Jamie! You had a nasty bump on the head!
It was just an awful place! A land with tornado after tornado and special effects, but no clever, witty dialogue — not an ounce of humor like here! It was terrible! And you were there...and you were there...
You're back with us now! It's gonna be okay!
I'm back home in "MAD ABOUT YOU"?
Yes, you're definitely here! You're not there any-more! Here is much better than there! When you're there, you could be anywhere, but when you're here you're nowhere else! That's why people write "wish you were here" on their postcards, but never "wish you were there"! Whenever I have the choice of being here or there, I always —
Quick! Somebody bump me on the head again! Please!
Calm down, honey! Just listen — it's comfortable here! No pressure! No six a.m. set calls! No wind machine in your face! And big, big bucks! Now repeat after me: "There's no place like TV sitcom... there's no place like TV sitcom... there's no place like TV sitcom..."

Today's so-called "Movie Villain"—it seems to us—is really quite a nice guy who possesses all of the desirable qualities, while today's so-called "Movie Hero"—on the other hand—is nothing but a rotten louse who possesses all the undesirable traits. And we can prove it. Study these few typical scenes involving typical heroes and villains—with the typical dialogue all foot-noted—and see if you don't agree that:

# MOVIE HEROES are FINKS or

## *"Hey There, Audience, You've Been Booing The Wrong Guy!"*

ARTIST: MORT DRUCKER WRITER: HARRY PURVIS

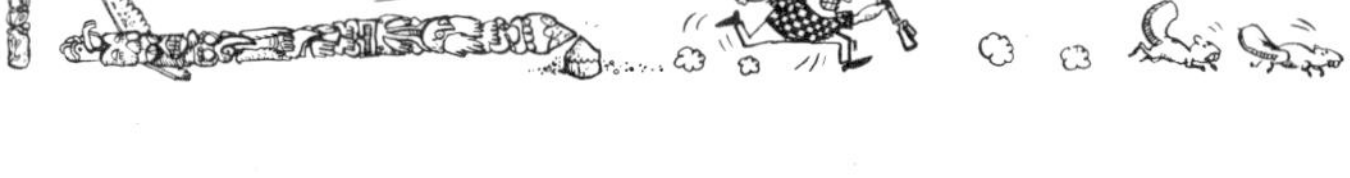

| SO-CALLED VILLAIN | SO-CALLED HERO |
|---|---|

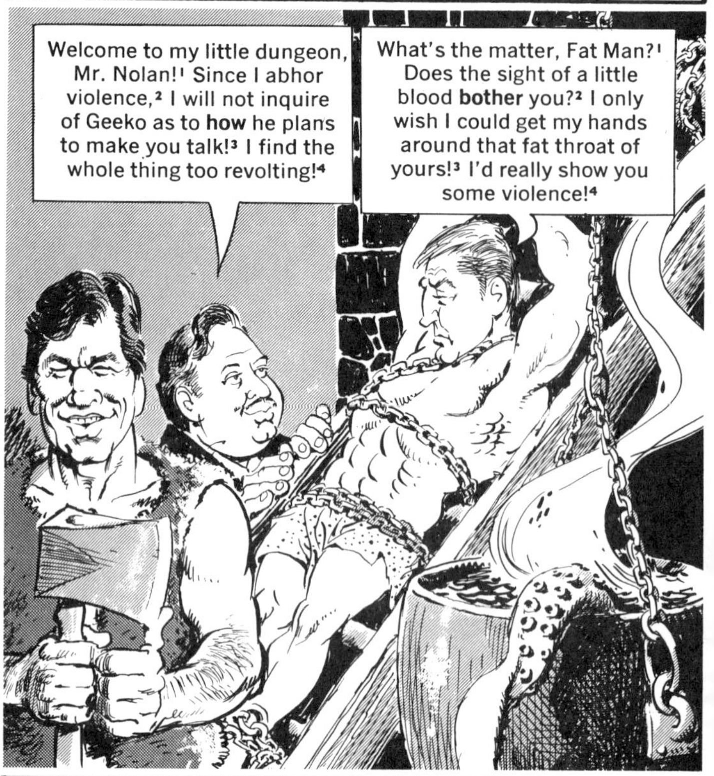
Welcome to my little dungeon, Mr. Nolan![1] Since I abhor violence,[2] I will not inquire of Geeko as to **how** he plans to make you talk![3] I find the whole thing too revolting![4]
What's the matter, Fat Man?[1] Does the sight of a little blood **bother** you?[2] I only wish I could get my hands around that fat throat of yours![3] I'd really show you some violence![4]

| | |
|---|---|
| 1. HOSPITABLE<br>2. PEACE-LOVING<br>3. NOT NOSEY<br>4. SENSITIVE | 1. INSULTING<br>2. SARCASTIC<br>3. VINDICTIVE<br>4. BRUTAL |

| SO-CALLED VILLAIN | SO-CALLED HERO |
|---|---|

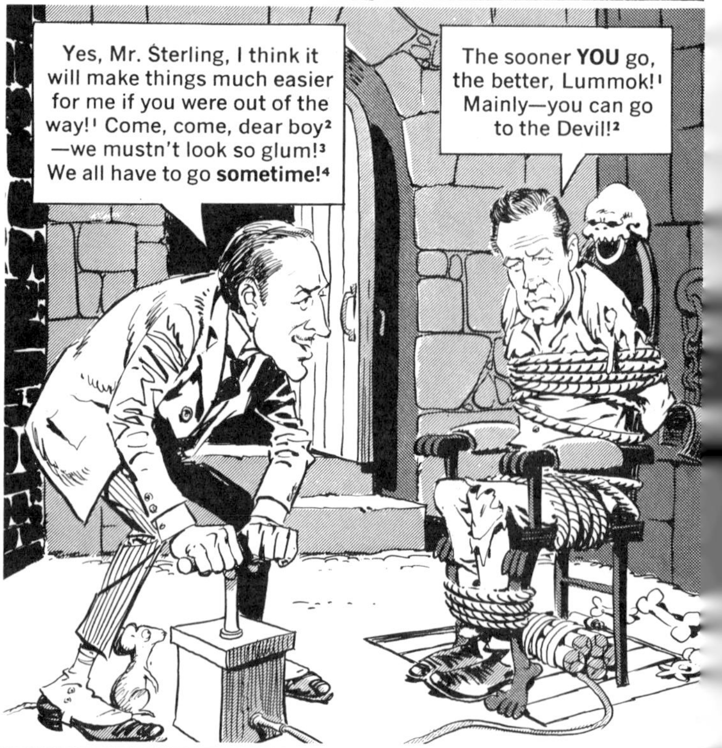
Yes, Mr. Sterling, I think it will make things much easier for me if you were out of the way![1] Come, come, dear boy[2]—we mustn't look so glum![3] We all have to go **sometime**![4]
The sooner **YOU** go, the better, Lummok![1] Mainly—you can go to the Devil![2]

| | |
|---|---|
| 1. EFFICIENT<br>2. AFFECTIONATE<br>3. CHEERFUL<br>4. PHILOSOPHICAL | 1. IMPATIENT AND UNFRIENDLY<br>2. CRUDE AND BLASPHEMOUS |

| SO-CALLED VILLAIN | SO-CALLED HERO |
|---|---|

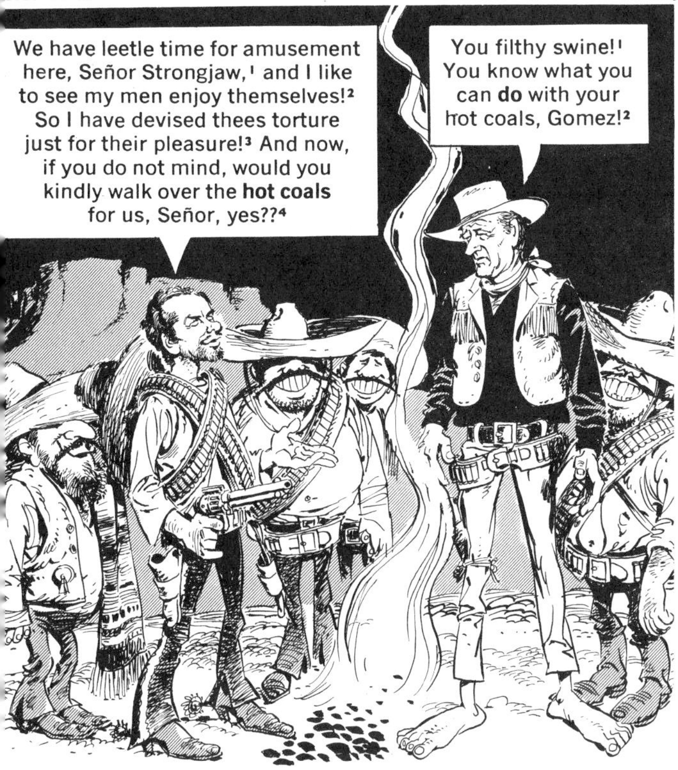
We have leetle time for amusement here, Señor Strongjaw,[1] and I like to see my men enjoy themselves![2] So I have devised thees torture just for their pleasure![3] And now, if you do not mind, would you kindly walk over the **hot coals** for us, Señor, yes??[4]
You filthy swine![1] You know what you can **do** with your hot coals, Gomez![2]

| | |
|---|---|
| . HARDWORKING<br>. BENEVOLENT<br>. INVENTIVE<br>. COURTEOUS | 1. ABRUPT AND DISPARAGING<br>2. UNCOUTH AND SUGGESTIVE |

| SO-CALLED VILLAIN | SO-CALLED HERO |
|---|---|

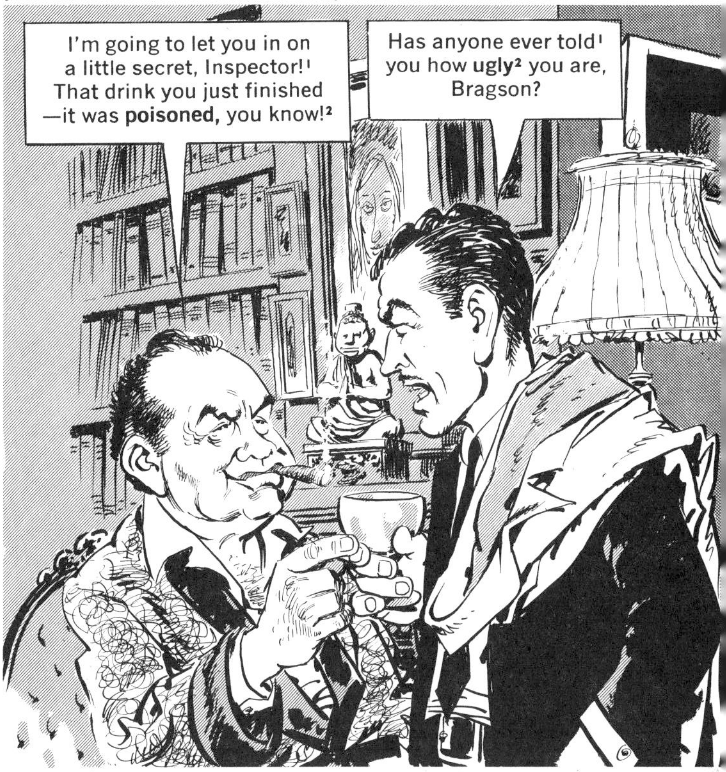
I'm going to let you in on a little secret, Inspector![1] That drink you just finished —it was **poisoned,** you know![2]
Has anyone ever told[1] you how **ugly**[2] you are, Bragson?

| | |
|---|---|
| 1. GENEROUS<br>2. FRANK, CHATTY AND INFORMATIVE | 1. GOSSIPY<br>2. CRITICAL, BLUNT AND TACTLESS |

| SO-CALLED VILLAIN | SO-CALLED HERO |
|---|---|

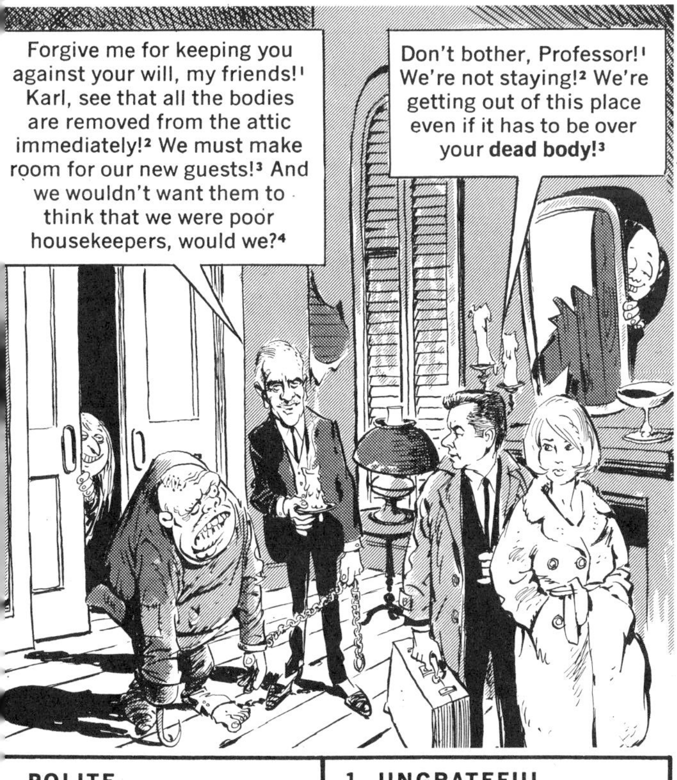
Forgive me for keeping you against your will, my friends![1] Karl, see that all the bodies are removed from the attic immediately![2] We must make room for our new guests![3] And we wouldn't want them to think that we were poor housekeepers, would we?[4]
Don't bother, Professor![1] We're not staying![2] We're getting out of this place even if it has to be over your **dead body!**[3]

| | |
|---|---|
| . POLITE<br>. NEAT<br>. ACCOMMODATING<br>. CONSIDERATE | 1. UNGRATEFUL<br>2. ANTI-SOCIAL<br>3. STUBBORN AND VIOLENT |

| SO-CALLED VILLAIN | SO-CALLED HERO |
|---|---|

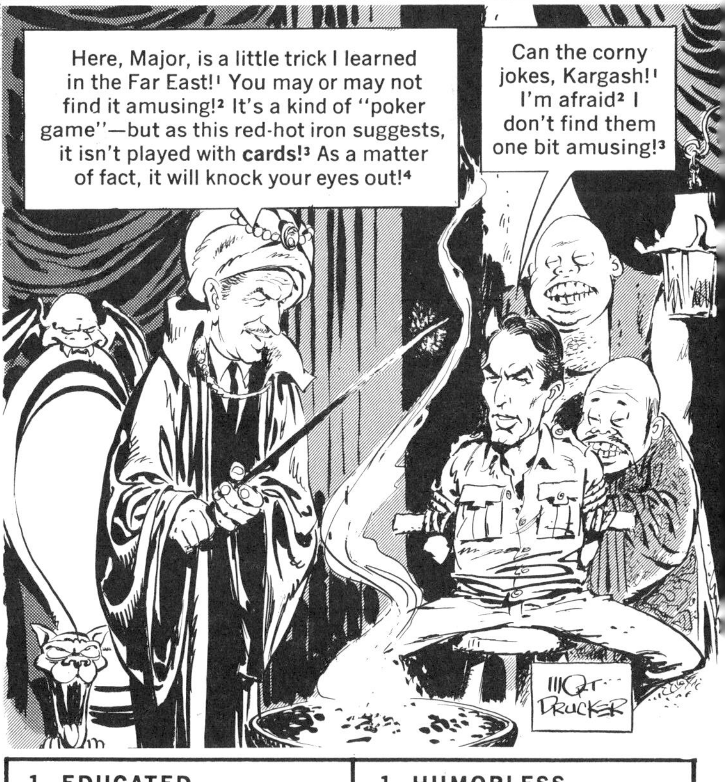
Here, Major, is a little trick I learned in the Far East![1] You may or may not find it amusing![2] It's a kind of "poker game"—but as this red-hot iron suggests, it isn't played with **cards!**[3] As a matter of fact, it will knock your eyes out![4]
Can the corny jokes, Kargash![1] I'm afraid[2] I don't find them one bit amusing![3]
MORT DRUCKER

| | |
|---|---|
| 1. EDUCATED<br>2. MODEST<br>3. ENLIGHTENING<br>4. WITTY | 1. HUMORLESS<br>2. COWARDLY<br>3. SULLEN AND UNAPPRECIATIVE |

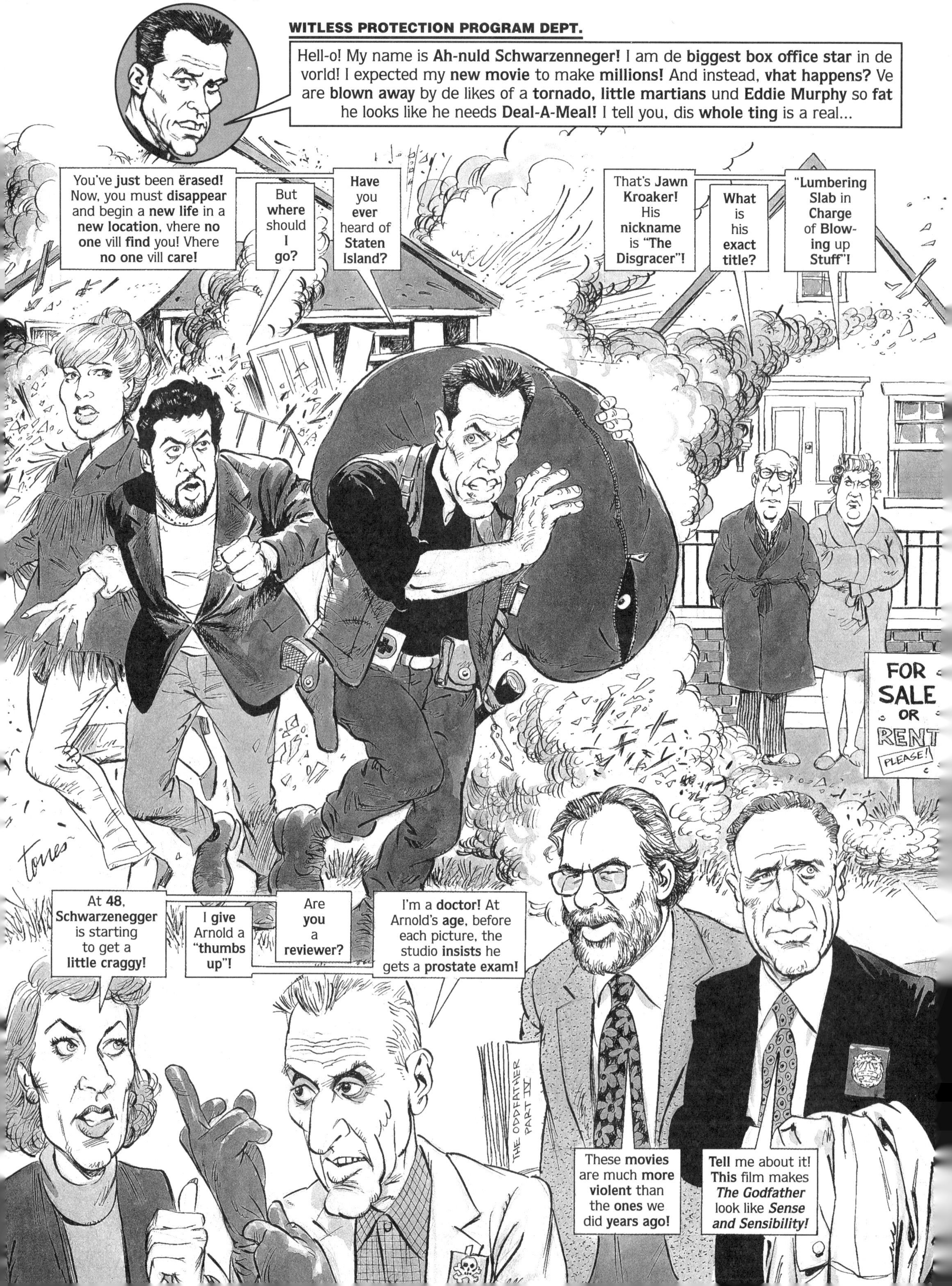
WITLESS PROTECTION PROGRAM DEPT.
Hell-o! My name is Ah-nuld Schwarzenneger! I am de biggest box office star in de vorld! I expected my new movie to make millions! And instead, vhat happens? Ve are blown away by de likes of a tornado, little martians und Eddie Murphy so fat he looks like he needs Deal-A-Meal! I tell you, dis whole ting is a real...
You've just been ërased! Now, you must disappear and begin a new life in a new location, vhere no one vill find you! Vhere no one vill care!
But where should I go?
Have you ever heard of Staten Island?
That's Jawn Kroaker! His nickname is "The Disgracer"!
What is his exact title?
"Lumbering Slab in Charge of Blowing up Stuff"!
FOR SALE OR RENT
PLEASE!
At 48, Schwarzenegger is starting to get a little craggy!
I give Arnold a "thumbs up"!
Are you a reviewer?
I'm a doctor! At Arnold's age, before each picture, the studio insists he gets a prostate exam!
THE ODDFATHER PART IV
These movies are much more violent than the ones we did years ago!
Tell me about it! This film makes The Godfather look like Sense and Sensibility!

# DISGRACER

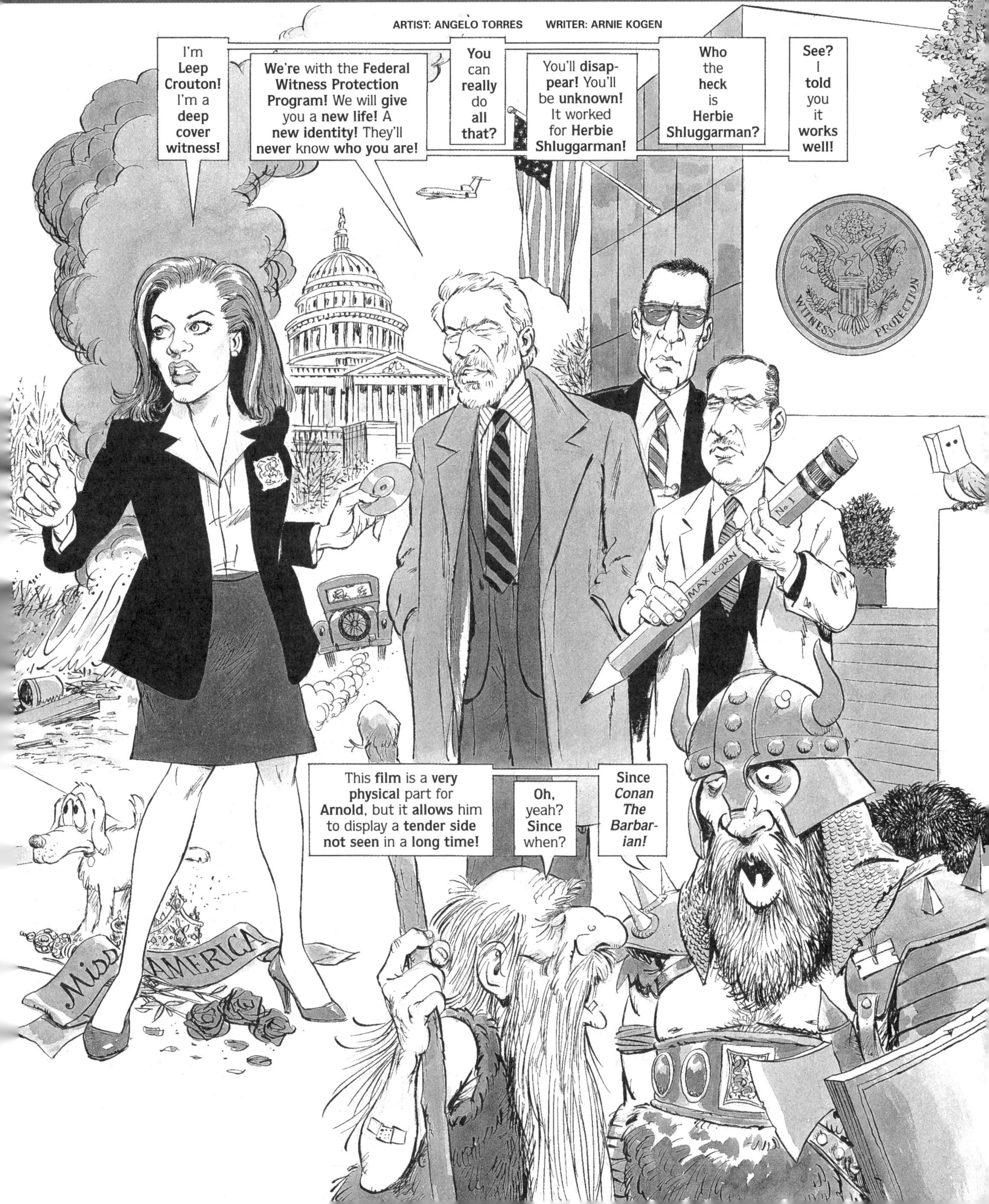

ARTIST: ANGELO TORRES WRITER: ARNIE KOGEN
I'm Leep Crouton! I'm a deep cover witness!
We're with the Federal Witness Protection Program! We will give you a new life! A new identity! They'll never know who you are!
You can really do all that?
You'll disappear! You'll be unknown! It worked for Herbie Shluggarman!
Who the heck is Herbie Shluggarman?
See? I told you it works well!
WITNESS PROTECTION
MAX KORN
No. 1
This film is a very physical part for Arnold, but it allows him to display a tender side not seen in a long time!
Oh, yeah? Since when?
Since Conan The Barbarian!
Miss AMERICA

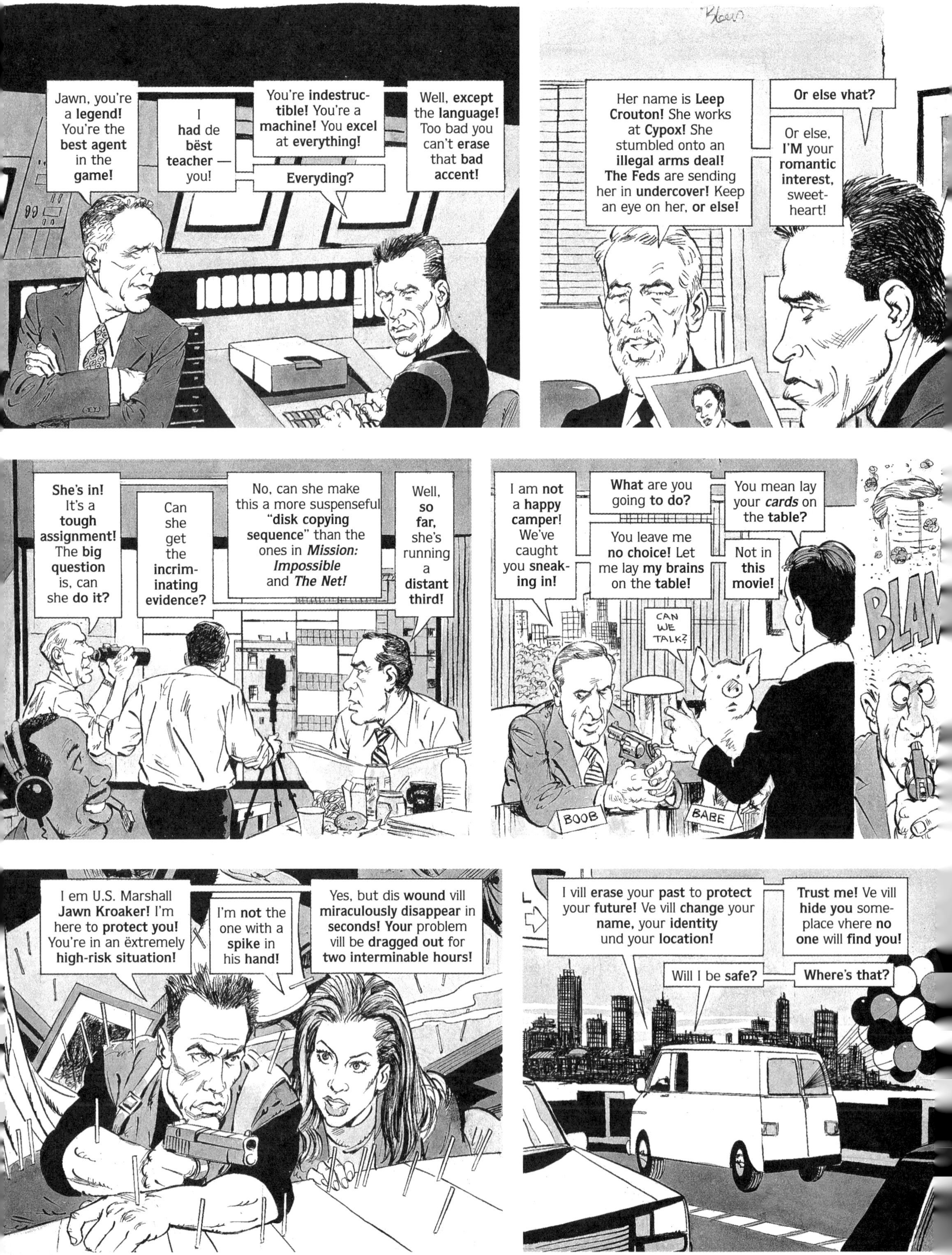

Jawn, you're a **legend!** You're the **best agent** in the **game!**
I **had** de **bëst teacher** — you!
You're **indestructible!** You're a **machine!** You **excel** at **everything!**
**Everyding?**
Well, **except** the **language!** Too bad you can't **erase** that **bad accent!**
Her name is **Leep Crouton!** She works at **Cypox!** She stumbled onto an **illegal arms deal! The Feds** are sending her in **undercover!** Keep an eye on her, **or else!**
**Or else vhat?**
Or else, **I'M** your **romantic interest,** sweet-heart!
**She's in!** It's a **tough assignment!** The **big question** is, can she **do it?**
Can she get the **incriminating evidence?**
No, can she make this a more suspenseful "**disk copying sequence**" than the ones in ***Mission: Impossible*** and ***The Net!***
Well, **so far,** she's running a **distant third!**
I am **not** a **happy camper!** We've caught you **sneaking in!**
**What** are you going **to do?**
You leave me **no choice!** Let me lay **my brains** on the **table!**
CAN WE TALK?
You mean lay your ***cards*** on the **table?**
Not in **this movie!**
BOOB
BABE
BLA
I em U.S. Marshall **Jawn Kroaker!** I'm here to **protect you!** You're in an ëxtremely **high-risk situation!**
I'm **not** the one with a **spike** in his **hand!**
Yes, but dis **wound** vill **miraculously disappear** in **seconds! Your** problem vill be **dragged out** for **two interminable hours!**
I vill **erase** your **past** to **protect** your **future!** Ve vill **change** your **name,** your **identity** und your **location!**
Will I be **safe?**
**Trust me!** Ve vill **hide you** someplace vhere **no one** will **find you!**
**Where's that?**

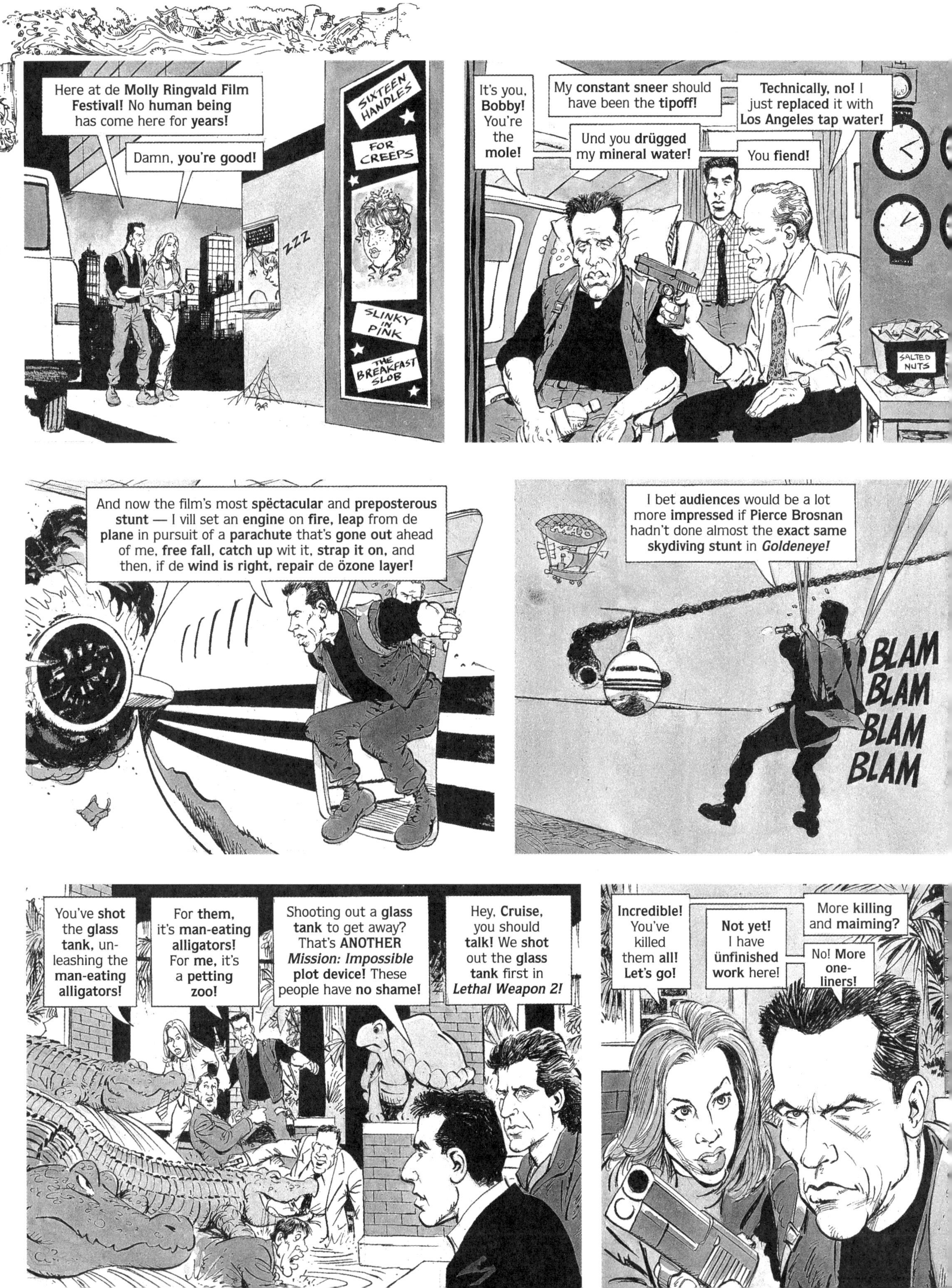
Here at de **Molly Ringvald Film Festival!** No **human being** has come here for **years!**
Damn, **you're good!**
SIXTEEN HANDLES
FOR CREEPS
SLINKY IN PINK
THE BREAKFAST SLOB
ZZZ
It's you, **Bobby!** You're the **mole!**
My **constant sneer** should have been the **tipoff!**
Und you **drügged** my **mineral water!**
**Technically, no!** I just **replaced** it with **Los Angeles tap water!**
You **fiend!**
SALTED NUTS
And now the film's most **spëctacular** and **preposterous stunt** — I vill set an **engine** on **fire, leap** from de **plane** in pursuit of a **parachute** that's **gone out** ahead of me, **free fall, catch up** wit it, **strap it on,** and then, if de **wind is right, repair** de **özone layer!**
I bet **audiences** would be a lot more **impressed** if **Pierce Brosnan** hadn't done almost the **exact same skydiving stunt** in ***Goldeneye!***
BLAM BLAM BLAM BLAM
You've **shot** the **glass tank,** un-leashing the **man-eating alligators!**
For **them,** it's **man-eating alligators!** For **me,** it's a **petting zoo!**
Shooting out a **glass tank** to get away? That's **ANOTHER *Mission: Impossible*** **plot device!** These people have **no shame!**
Hey, **Cruise,** you should **talk!** We **shot** out the **glass tank** first in ***Lethal Weapon 2!***
**Incredible!** You've killed them **all! Let's go!**
**Not yet!** I have **ünfinished work** here!
More **killing** and **maiming?**
No! **More one-liners!**

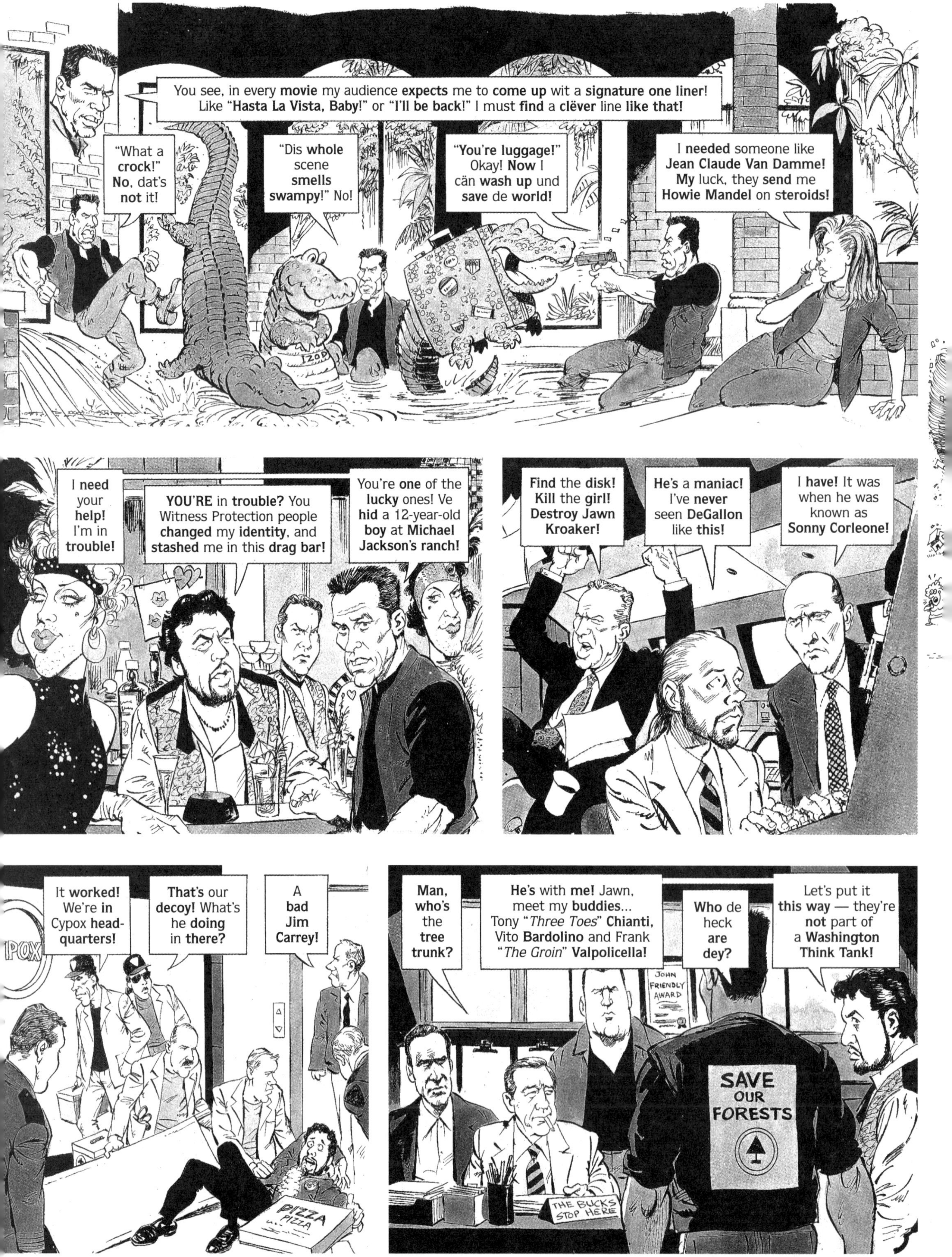

You see, in every **movie** my audience **expects** me to **come up** wit a **signature one liner**! Like "**Hasta La Vista, Baby!**" or "**I'll be back!**" I must **find** a **clëver** line **like that!**
"What a **crock!**" **No**, dat's **not** it!
"Dis **whole** scene **smells swampy!**" No!
"**You're luggage!**" Okay! **Now** I cän **wash up** und **save** de **world!**
I **needed** someone like **Jean Claude Van Damme! My** luck, they **send** me **Howie Mandel** on **steroids!**
IZOD
I **need** your **help!** I'm in **trouble!**
**YOU'RE** in **trouble?** You Witness Protection people **changed** my **identity**, and **stashed** me in this **drag bar!**
You're **one** of the **lucky** ones! Ve **hid** a 12-year-old **boy** at **Michael Jackson's ranch!**
**Find** the **disk! Kill** the **girl! Destroy Jawn Kroaker!**
**He's** a **maniac!** I've **never** seen **DeGallon** like **this!**
I **have!** It was when he was known as **Sonny Corleone!**
It **worked!** We're **in** Cypox **head-quarters!**
**That's** our **decoy!** What's he **doing** in **there?**
A **bad Jim Carrey!**
POX
PIZZA PIZZA
**Man, who's** the **tree trunk?**
**He's** with **me!** Jawn, meet my **buddies**... Tony "*Three Toes*" **Chianti**, Vito **Bardolino** and Frank "*The Groin*" **Valpolicella!**
**Who** de heck **are** dey?
Let's put it **this way** — they're **not** part of a **Washington Think Tank!**
JOHN FRIENDLY AWARD
THE BUCKS STOP HERE
SAVE OUR FORESTS

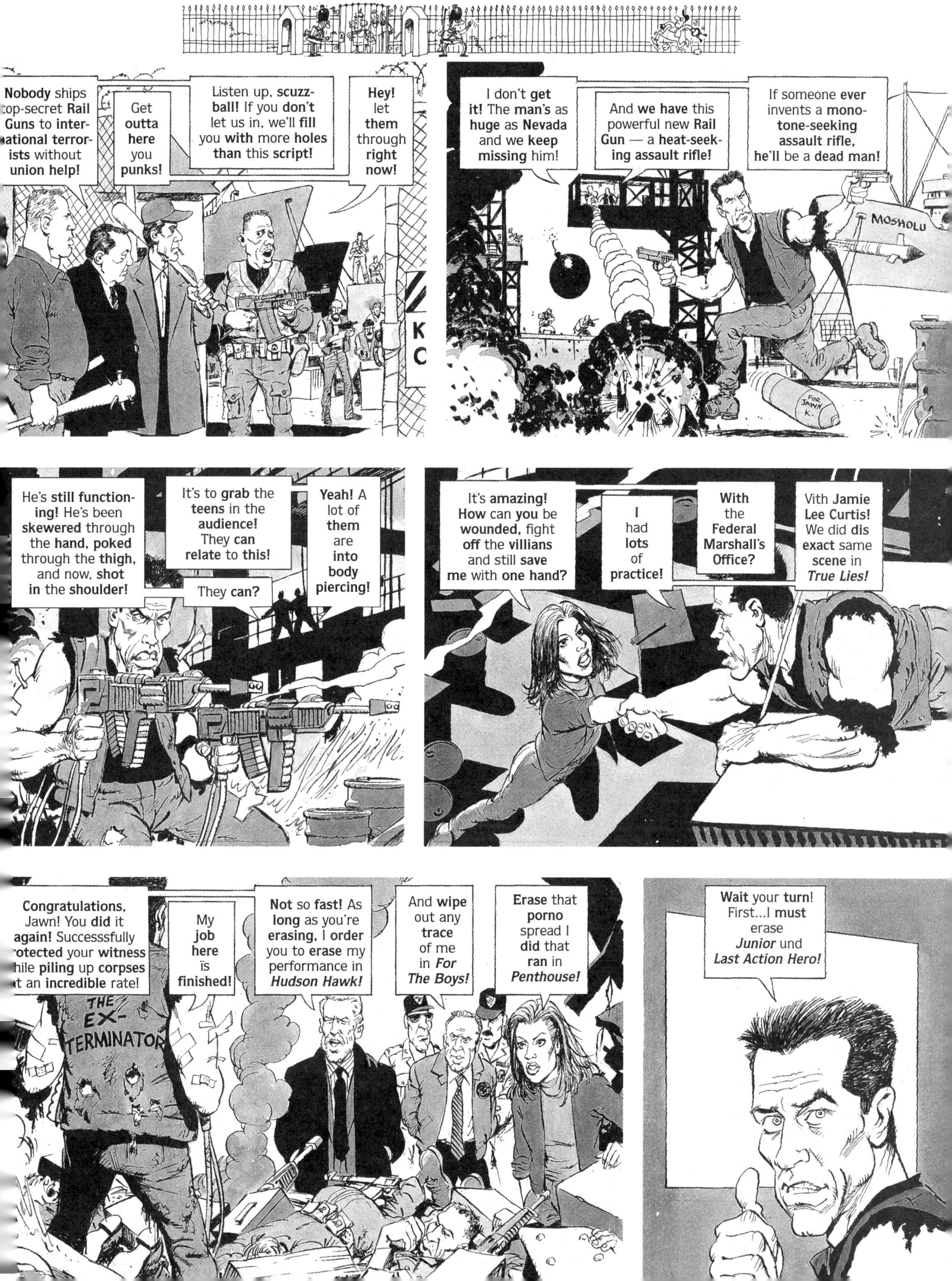

Nobody ships op-secret Rail Guns to inter- ational terror- ists without union help!
Get outta here you punks!
Listen up, scuzz- ball! If you don't let us in, we'll fill you with more holes than this script!
Hey! let them through right now!
KC
I don't get it! The man's as huge as Nevada and we keep missing him!
And we have this powerful new Rail Gun — a heat-seek- ing assault rifle!
If someone ever invents a mono- tone-seeking assault rifle, he'll be a dead man!
MOSHOLU
FOR JAWN K.
He's still function- ing! He's been skewered through the hand, poked through the thigh, and now, shot in the shoulder!
It's to grab the teens in the audience! They can relate to this!
They can?
Yeah! A lot of them are into body piercing!
It's amazing! How can you be wounded, fight off the villians and still save me with one hand?
I had lots of practice!
With the Federal Marshall's Office?
Vith Jamie Lee Curtis! We did dis exact same scene in True Lies!
Congratulations, Jawn! You did it again! Successsfully otected your witness hile piling up corpses t an incredible rate!
THE EX- TERMINATOR
My job here ïs finished!
Not so fast! As long as you're erasing, I order you to erase my performance in Hudson Hawk!
And wipe out any trace of me in For The Boys!
Erase that porno spread I did that ran in Penthouse!
Wait your turn! First...I must erase Junior und Last Action Hero!

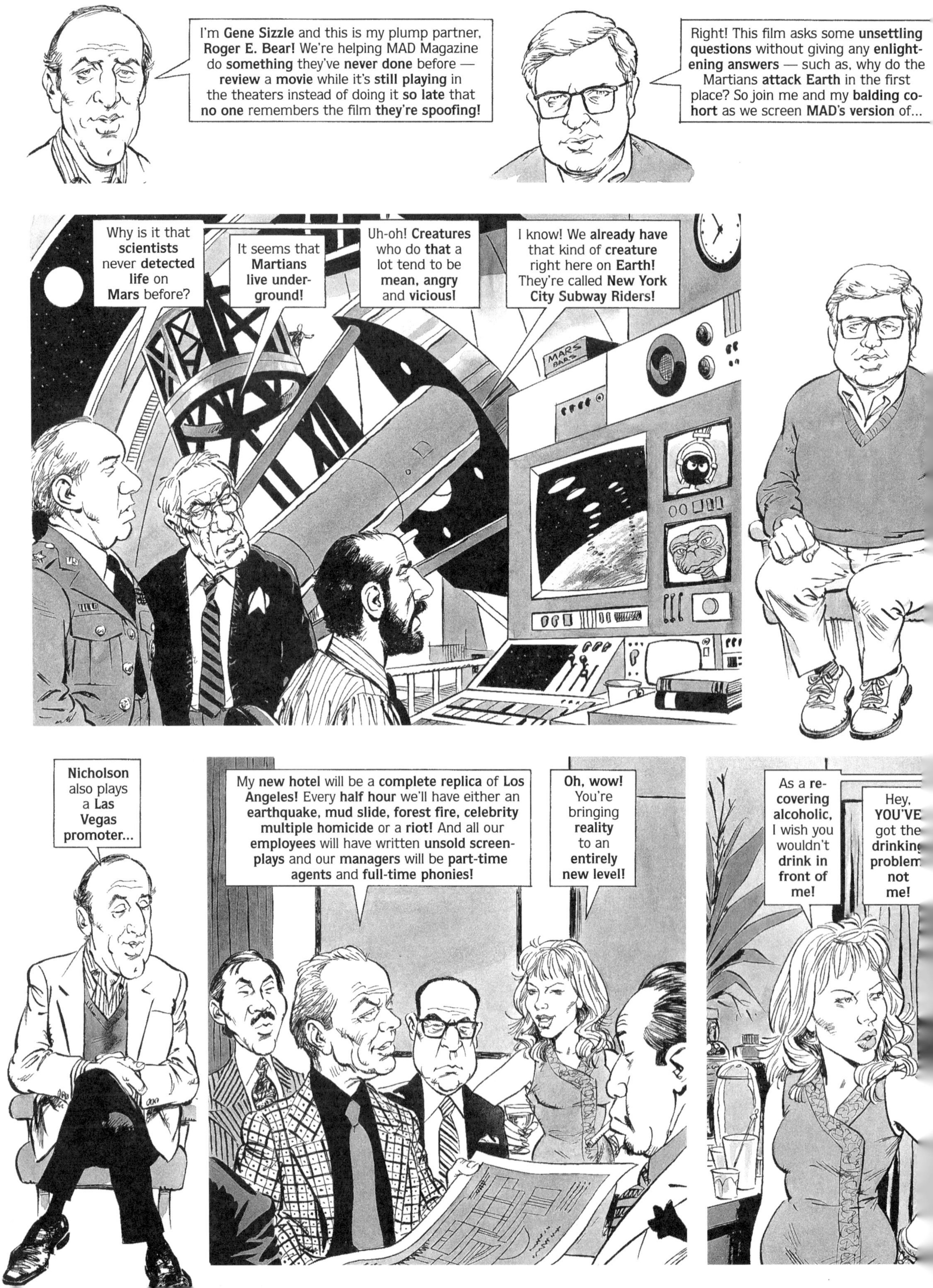
I'm Gene Sizzle and this is my plump partner, Roger E. Bear! We're helping MAD Magazine do something they've never done before — review a movie while it's still playing in the theaters instead of doing it so late that no one remembers the film they're spoofing!
Right! This film asks some unsettling questions without giving any enlightening answers — such as, why do the Martians attack Earth in the first place? So join me and my balding cohort as we screen MAD's version of...
Why is it that scientists never detected life on Mars before?
It seems that Martians live underground!
Uh-oh! Creatures who do that a lot tend to be mean, angry and vicious!
I know! We already have that kind of creature right here on Earth! They're called New York City Subway Riders!
MARS BARS
Nicholson also plays a Las Vegas promoter...
My new hotel will be a complete replica of Los Angeles! Every half hour we'll have either an earthquake, mud slide, forest fire, celebrity multiple homicide or a riot! And all our employees will have written unsold screenplays and our managers will be part-time agents and full-time phonies!
Oh, wow! You're bringing reality to an entirely new level!
As a recovering alcoholic, I wish you wouldn't drink in front of me!
Hey, YOU'VE got the drinking problem not me!

# MARRED ATTACK!

ARTIST: ANGELO TORRES WRITER: STAN HART

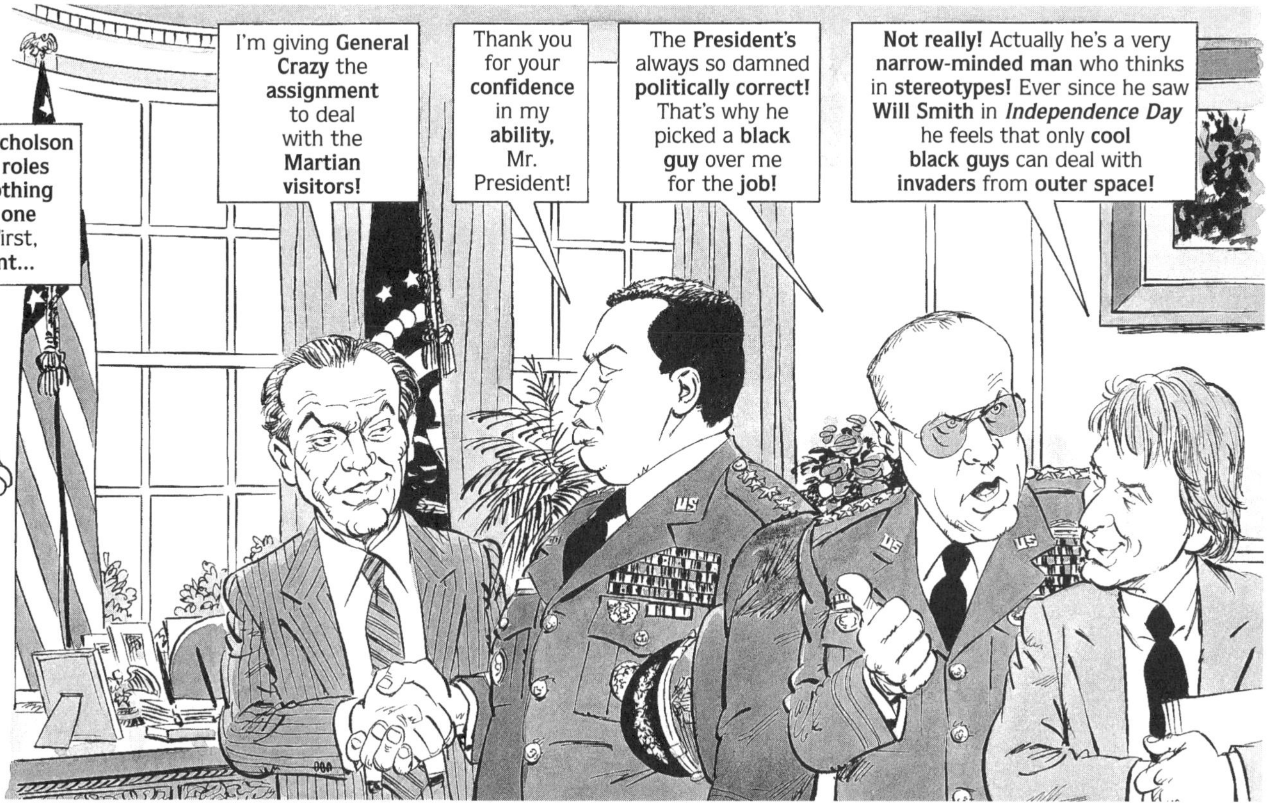
Why is **Jack Nicholson** playing **two roles** that have **nothing** to do with **one another?** First, as **President...**
I'm giving **General Crazy** the **assignment** to deal with the **Martian visitors!**
Thank you for your **confidence** in my **ability,** Mr. President!
The **President's** always so damned **politically correct!** That's why he picked a **black guy** over me for the **job!**
**Not really!** Actually he's a very **narrow-minded man** who thinks in **stereotypes!** Ever since he saw **Will Smith** in ***Independence Day*** he feels that only **cool black guys** can deal with **invaders** from **outer space!**

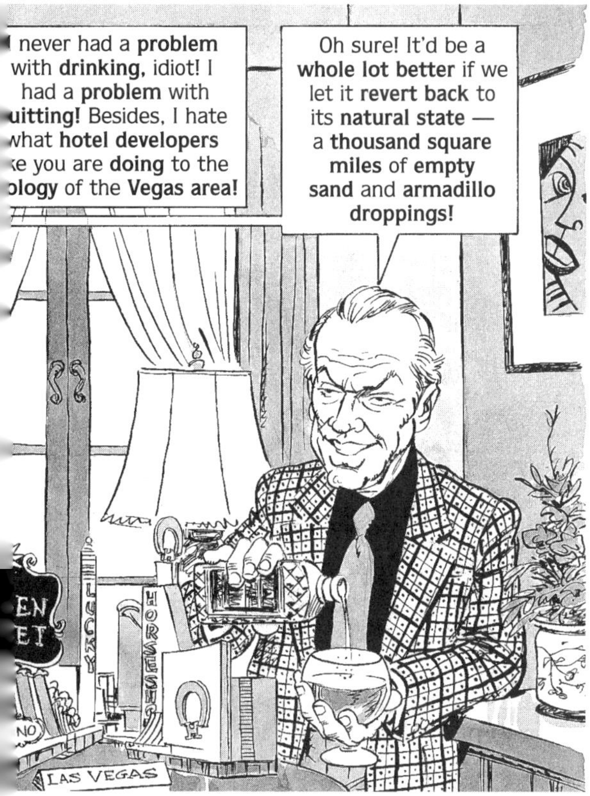
never had a **problem** with **drinking,** idiot! I had a **problem** with **uitting!** Besides, I hate what **hotel developers** e you are **doing** to the **ology** of the **Vegas area!**
Oh sure! It'd be a **whole lot better** if we let it **revert back** to its **natural state** — a **thousand square miles** of **empty sand** and **armadillo droppings!**
LUCKY
HORSESHOE
LAS VEGAS

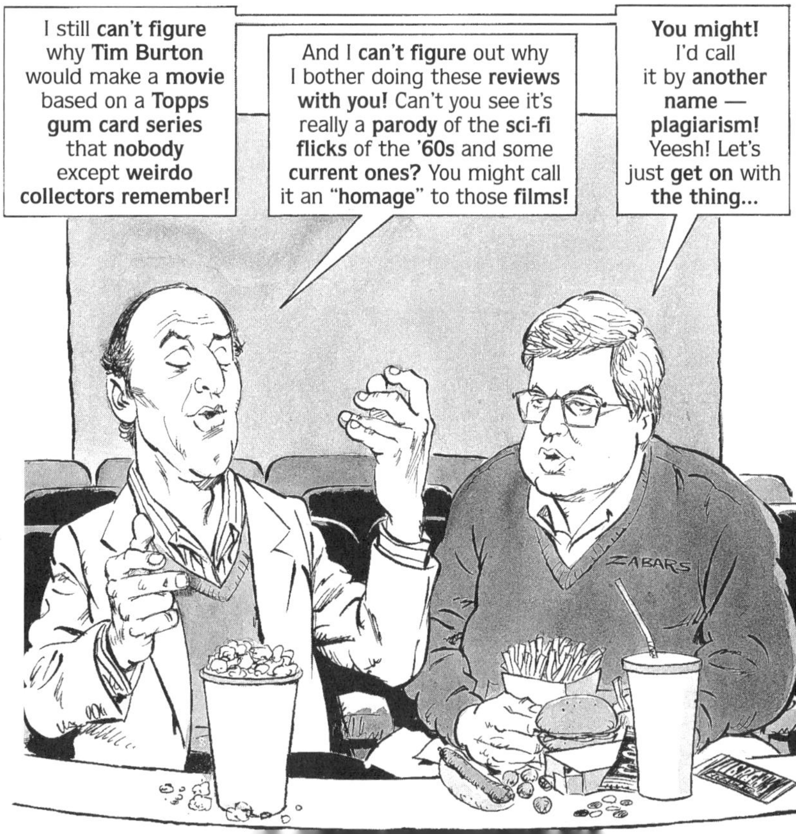
I still **can't figure** why **Tim Burton** would make a **movie** based on a **Topps gum card series** that **nobody** except **weirdo collectors remember!**
And I **can't figure** out why I bother doing these **reviews with you!** Can't you see it's really a **parody** of the **sci-fi flicks** of the **'60s** and some **current ones?** You might call it an **"homage"** to those **films!**
**You might!** I'd call it by **another name** — **plagiarism!** Yeesh! Let's just **get on** with **the thing...**
ZABARS

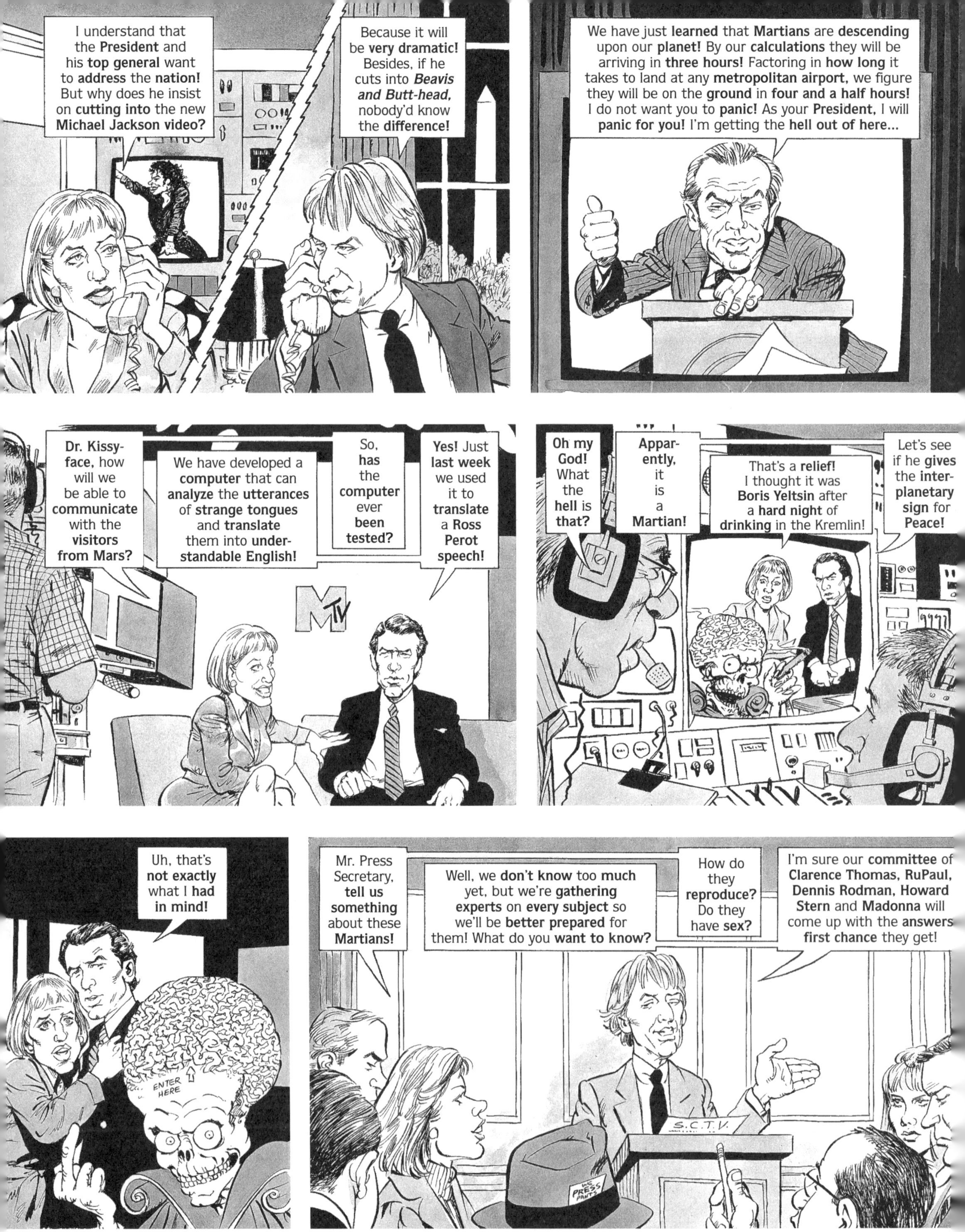
I understand that the President and his top general want to address the nation! But why does he insist on cutting into the new Michael Jackson video?
Because it will be very dramatic! Besides, if he cuts into Beavis and Butt-head, nobody'd know the difference!
We have just learned that Martians are descending upon our planet! By our calculations they will be arriving in three hours! Factoring in how long it takes to land at any metropolitan airport, we figure they will be on the ground in four and a half hours! I do not want you to panic! As your President, I will panic for you! I'm getting the hell out of here...
Dr. Kissy-face, how will we be able to communicate with the visitors from Mars?
We have developed a computer that can analyze the utterances of strange tongues and translate them into understandable English!
So, has the computer ever been tested?
Yes! Just last week we used it to translate a Ross Perot speech!
Oh my God! What the hell is that?
Apparently, it is a Martian!
That's a relief! I thought it was Boris Yeltsin after a hard night of drinking in the Kremlin!
Let's see if he gives the interplanetary sign for Peace!
Uh, that's not exactly what I had in mind!
ENTER HERE
Mr. Press Secretary, tell us something about these Martians!
Well, we don't know too much yet, but we're gathering experts on every subject so we'll be better prepared for them! What do you want to know?
How do they reproduce? Do they have sex?
I'm sure our committee of Clarence Thomas, RuPaul, Dennis Rodman, Howard Stern and Madonna will come up with the answers first chance they get!
S.C.T.V.

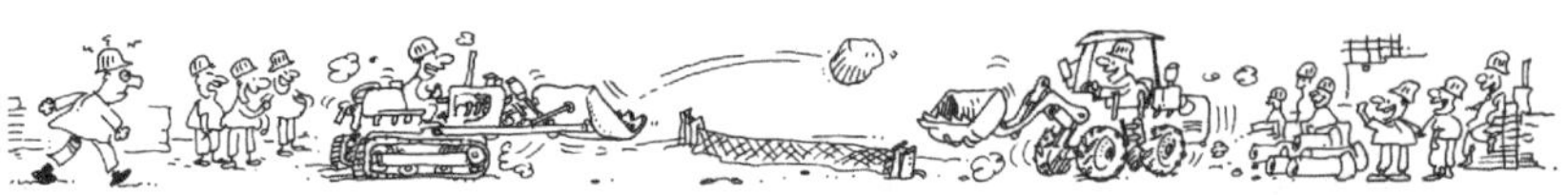

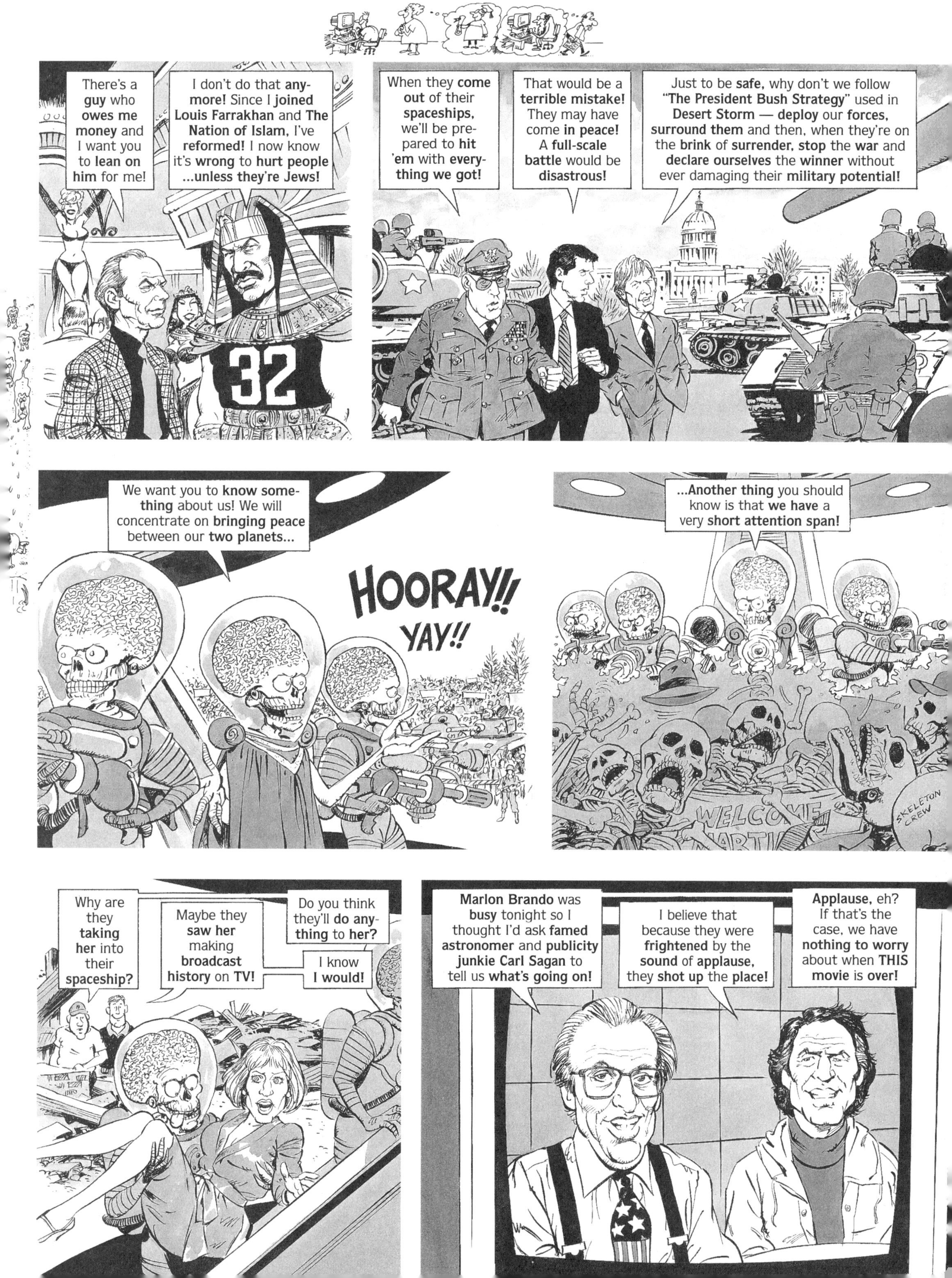
There's a guy who owes me money and I want you to lean on him for me!
I don't do that any-more! Since I joined Louis Farrakhan and The Nation of Islam, I've reformed! I now know it's wrong to hurt people ...unless they're Jews!
32
When they come out of their spaceships, we'll be pre-pared to hit 'em with every-thing we got!
That would be a terrible mistake! They may have come in peace! A full-scale battle would be disastrous!
Just to be safe, why don't we follow "The President Bush Strategy" used in Desert Storm — deploy our forces, surround them and then, when they're on the brink of surrender, stop the war and declare ourselves the winner without ever damaging their military potential!
We want you to know some-thing about us! We will concentrate on bringing peace between our two planets...
HOORAY!!
YAY!!
...Another thing you should know is that we have a very short attention span!
SKELETON CREW
Why are they taking her into their spaceship?
Maybe they saw her making broadcast history on TV!
Do you think they'll do any-thing to her?
I know I would!
Marlon Brando was busy tonight so I thought I'd ask famed astronomer and publicity junkie Carl Sagan to tell us what's going on!
I believe that because they were frightened by the sound of applause, they shot up the place!
Applause, eh? If that's the case, we have nothing to worry about when THIS movie is over!

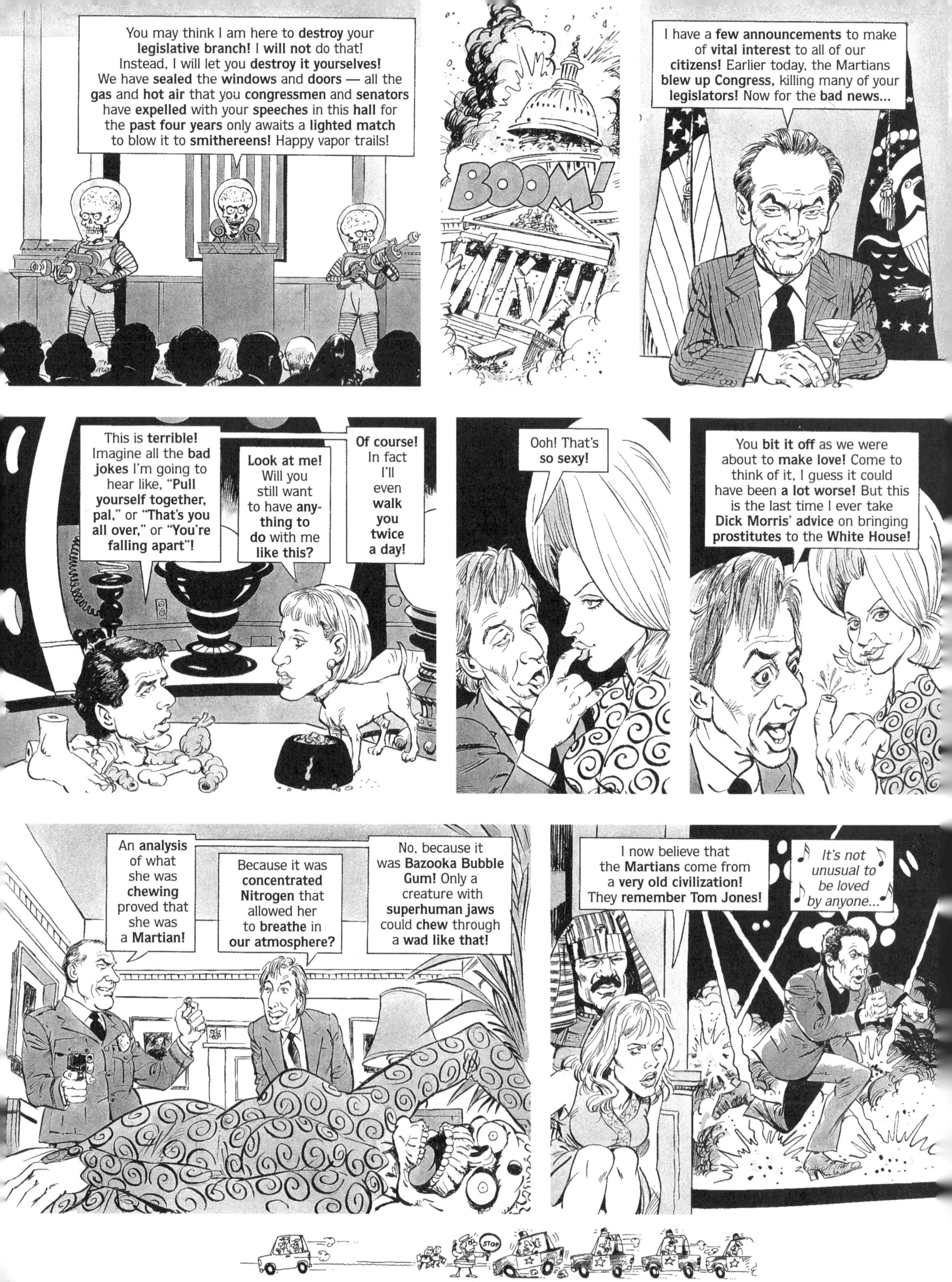
You may think I am here to destroy your legislative branch! I will not do that! Instead, I will let you destroy it yourselves! We have sealed the windows and doors — all the gas and hot air that you congressmen and senators have expelled with your speeches in this hall for the past four years only awaits a lighted match to blow it to smithereens! Happy vapor trails!
BOOM!
I have a few announcements to make of vital interest to all of our citizens! Earlier today, the Martians blew up Congress, killing many of your legislators! Now for the bad news...
This is terrible! Imagine all the bad jokes I'm going to hear like, "Pull yourself together, pal," or "That's you all over," or "You're falling apart"!
Look at me! Will you still want to have anything to do with me like this?
Of course! In fact I'll even walk you twice a day!
Ooh! That's so sexy!
You bit it off as we were about to make love! Come to think of it, I guess it could have been a lot worse! But this is the last time I ever take Dick Morris' advice on bringing prostitutes to the White House!
An analysis of what she was chewing proved that she was a Martian!
Because it was concentrated Nitrogen that allowed her to breathe in our atmosphere?
No, because it was Bazooka Bubble Gum! Only a creature with superhuman jaws could chew through a wad like that!
I now believe that the Martians come from a very old civilization! They remember Tom Jones!
It's not unusual to be loved by anyone...
STOP

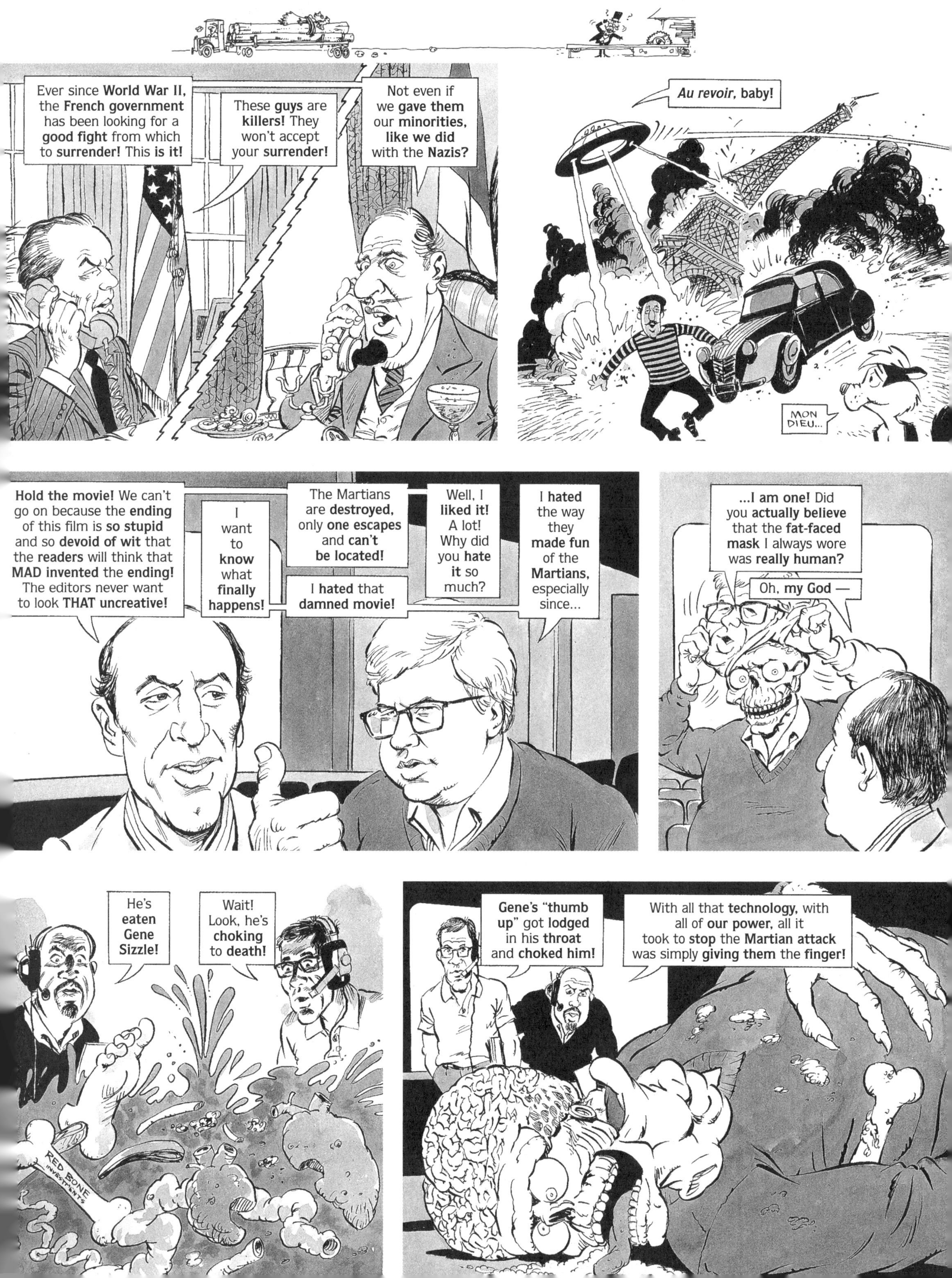
Ever since World War II, the French government has been looking for a good fight from which to surrender! This is it!
These guys are killers! They won't accept your surrender!
Not even if we gave them our minorities, like we did with the Nazis?
Au revoir, baby!
MON DIEU...
Hold the movie! We can't go on because the ending of this film is so stupid and so devoid of wit that the readers will think that MAD invented the ending! The editors never want to look THAT uncreative!
I want to know what finally happens!
The Martians are destroyed, only one escapes and can't be located!
I hated that damned movie!
Well, I liked it! A lot! Why did you hate it so much?
I hated the way they made fun of the Martians, especially since...
...I am one! Did you actually believe that the fat-faced mask I always wore was really human?
Oh, my God —
He's eaten Gene Sizzle!
Wait! Look, he's choking to death!
RED BONE INVESTMENTS
Gene's "thumb up" got lodged in his throat and choked him!
With all that technology, with all of our power, all it took to stop the Martian attack was simply giving them the finger!

**SETI AS SHE GOES DEPT.**

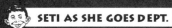

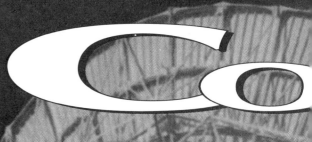

**When we recently saw the trailer for a certain Jodie Foster/Matthew McConaughey film we were psyched: it looked to be the best outer space flick in a long time! But alas there were no gory aliens, no cool light saber battles, no thrilling jumps to hyperspace, no high-speed intergalactic chases and no teeth-rattling laser blasts! It was just a bunch of preachy, pseudo-intellectual, faux-religious Carl Sagan redux tripe! They could have made a bad-assed action flick, but instead they took the...**

# Co

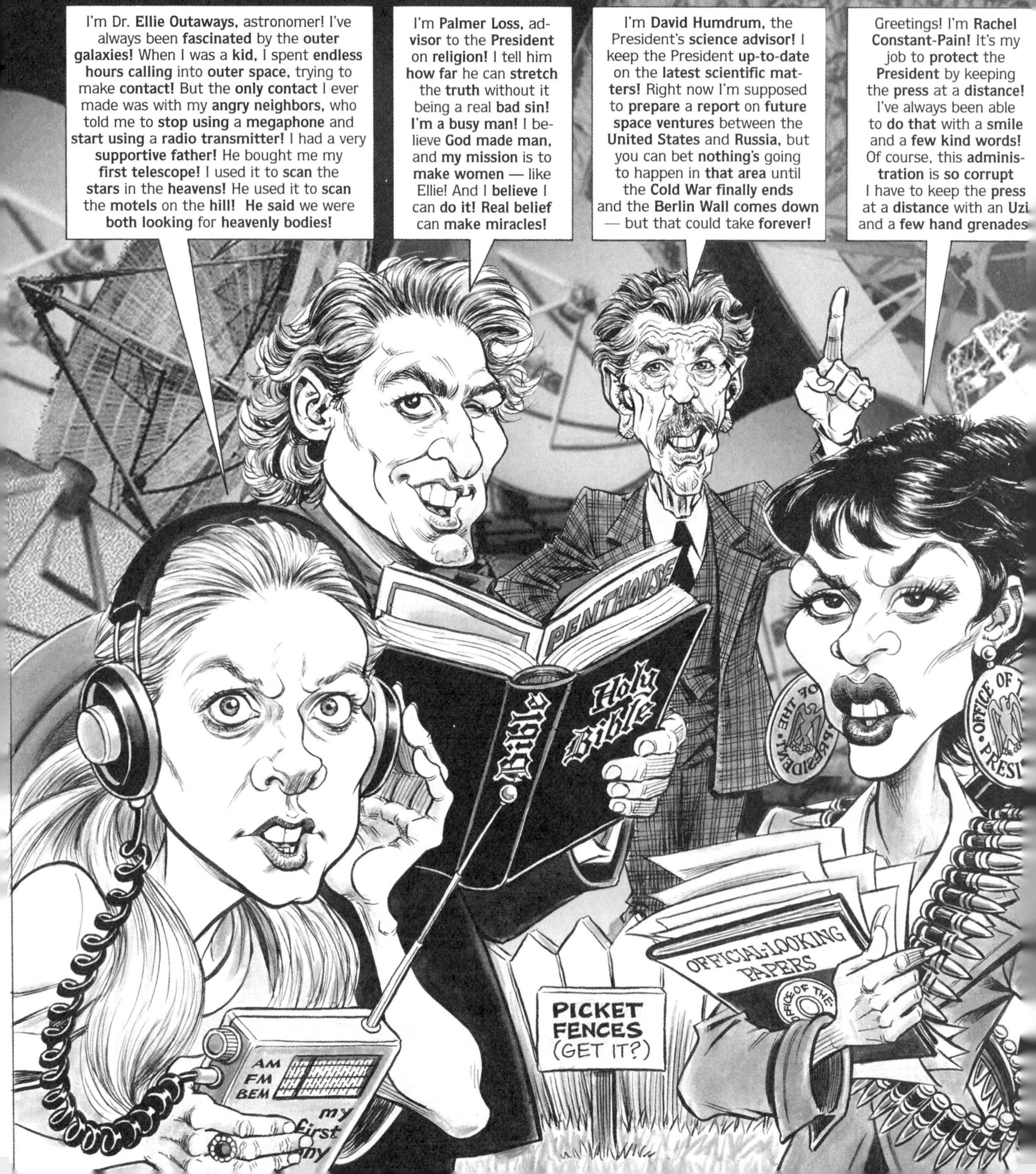

I'm Dr. Ellie Outaways, astronomer! I've always been fascinated by the outer galaxies! When I was a kid, I spent endless hours calling into outer space, trying to make contact! But the only contact I ever made was with my angry neighbors, who told me to stop using a megaphone and start using a radio transmitter! I had a very supportive father! He bought me my first telescope! I used it to scan the stars in the heavens! He used it to scan the motels on the hill! He said we were both looking for heavenly bodies!
I'm Palmer Loss, advisor to the President on religion! I tell him how far he can stretch the truth without it being a real bad sin! I'm a busy man! I believe God made man, and my mission is to make women — like Ellie! And I believe I can do it! Real belief can make miracles!
I'm David Humdrum, the President's science advisor! I keep the President up-to-date on the latest scientific matters! Right now I'm supposed to prepare a report on future space ventures between the United States and Russia, but you can bet nothing's going to happen in that area until the Cold War finally ends and the Berlin Wall comes down — but that could take forever!
Greetings! I'm Rachel Constant-Pain! It's my job to protect the President by keeping the press at a distance! I've always been able to do that with a smile and a few kind words! Of course, this administration is so corrupt I have to keep the press at a distance with an Uzi and a few hand grenades
PENTHOUSE
Holy Bible
Bible
OFFICE OF THE PRESIDENT
OFFICIAL-LOOKING PAPERS
PICKET FENCES (GET IT?)
AM
FM
BEM
my first

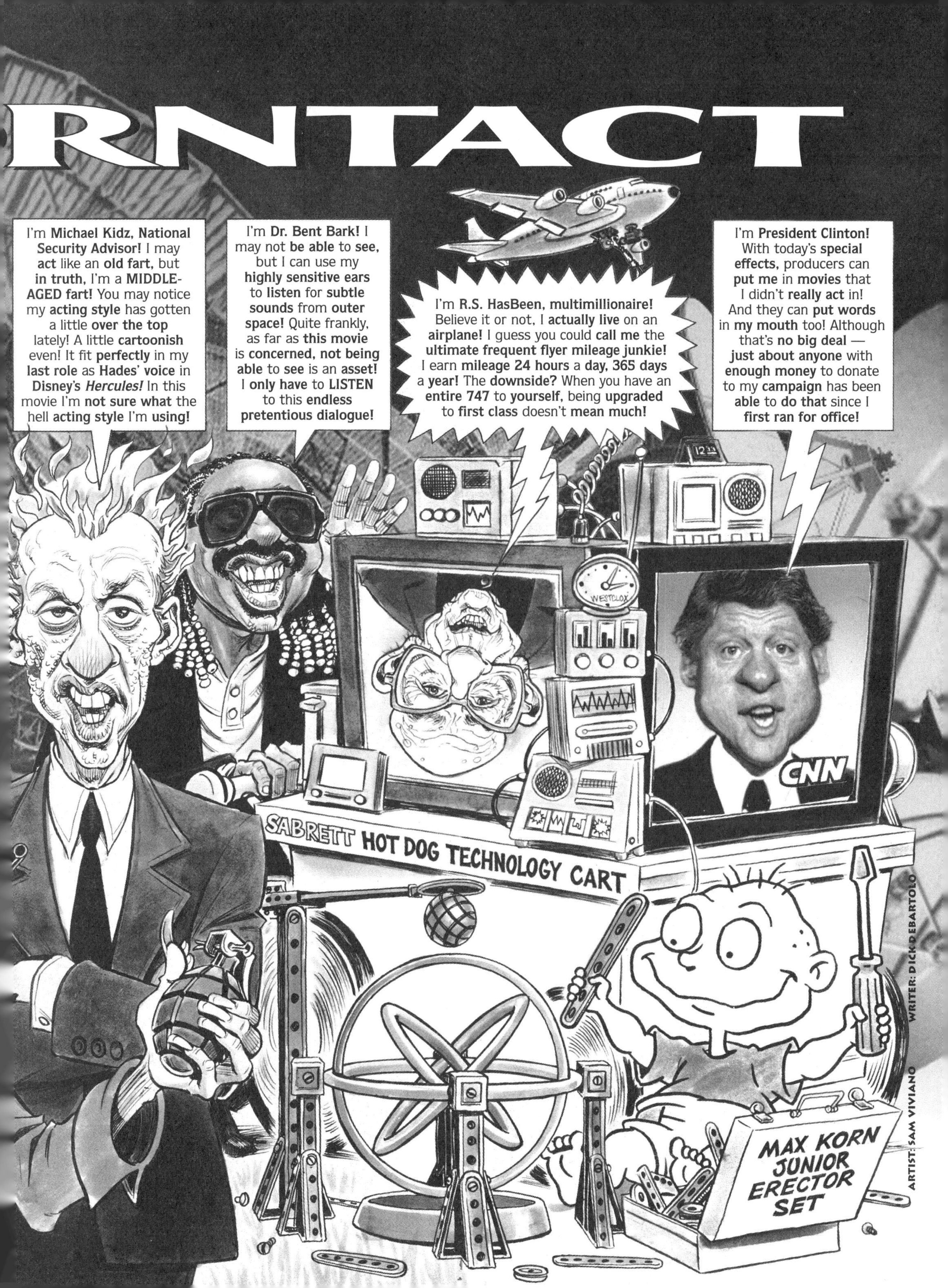
RNTACT
I'm Michael Kidz, National Security Advisor! I may act like an old fart, but in truth, I'm a MIDDLE-AGED fart! You may notice my acting style has gotten a little over the top lately! A little cartoonish even! It fit perfectly in my last role as Hades' voice in Disney's Hercules! In this movie I'm not sure what the hell acting style I'm using!
I'm Dr. Bent Bark! I may not be able to see, but I can use my highly sensitive ears to listen for subtle sounds from outer space! Quite frankly, as far as this movie is concerned, not being able to see is an asset! I only have to LISTEN to this endless pretentious dialogue!
I'm R.S. HasBeen, multimillionaire! Believe it or not, I actually live on an airplane! I guess you could call me the ultimate frequent flyer mileage junkie! I earn mileage 24 hours a day, 365 days a year! The downside? When you have an entire 747 to yourself, being upgraded to first class doesn't mean much!
I'm President Clinton! With today's special effects, producers can put me in movies that I didn't really act in! And they can put words in my mouth too! Although that's no big deal — just about anyone with enough money to donate to my campaign has been able to do that since I first ran for office!
WESTCLOX
CNN
SABRETT HOT DOG TECHNOLOGY CART
MAX KORN JUNIOR ERECTOR SET
WRITER: DICK DEBARTOLO
ARTIST: SAM VIVIANO

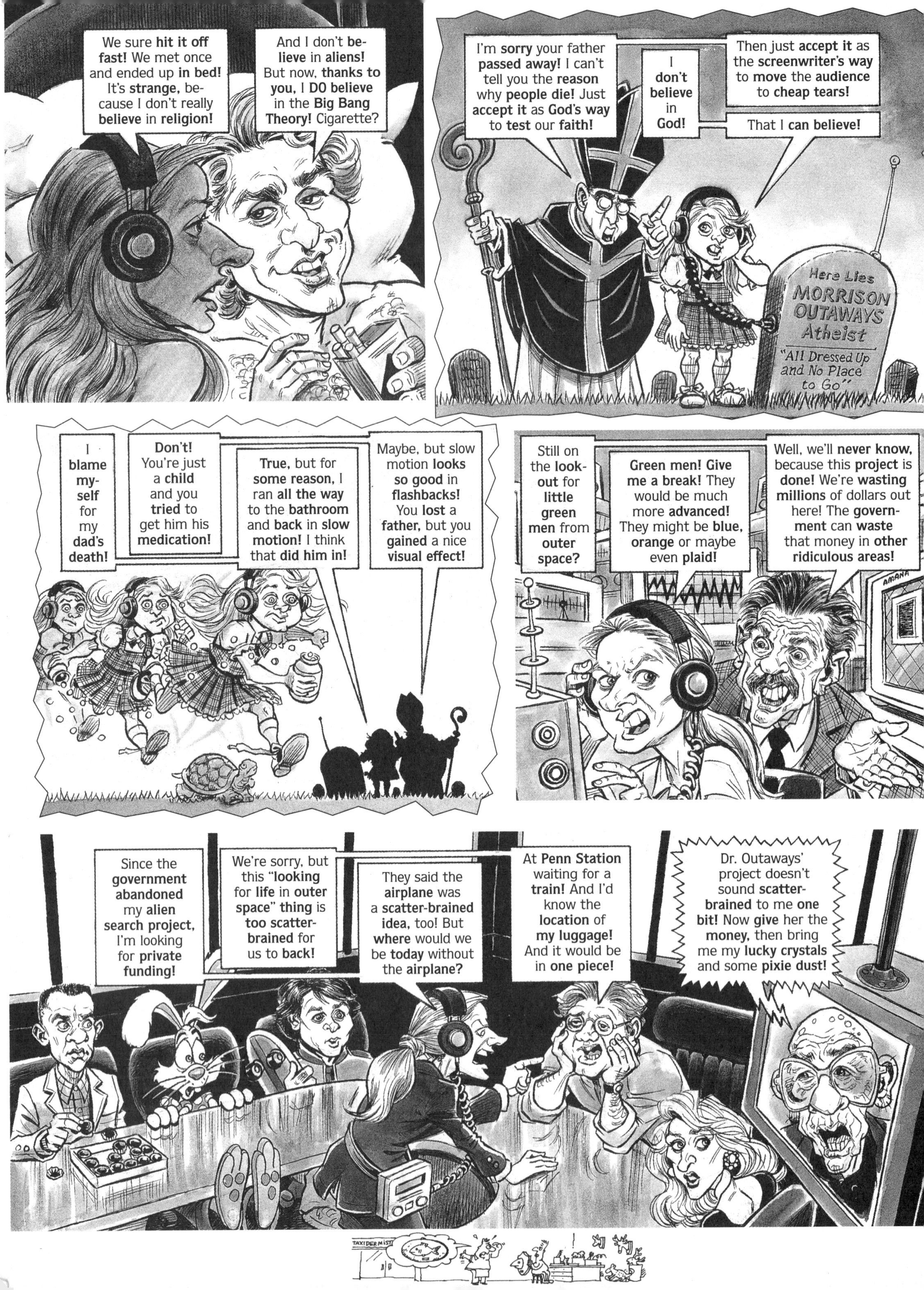
We sure hit it off fast! We met once and ended up in bed! It's strange, because I don't really believe in religion!
And I don't believe in aliens! But now, thanks to you, I DO believe in the Big Bang Theory! Cigarette?
I'm sorry your father passed away! I can't tell you the reason why people die! Just accept it as God's way to test our faith!
I don't believe in God!
Then just accept it as the screenwriter's way to move the audience to cheap tears!
That I can believe!
Here Lies MORRISON OUTAWAYS Atheist "All Dressed Up and No Place to Go"
I blame myself for my dad's death!
Don't! You're just a child and you tried to get him his medication!
True, but for some reason, I ran all the way to the bathroom and back in slow motion! I think that did him in!
Maybe, but slow motion looks so good in flashbacks! You lost a father, but you gained a nice visual effect!
Still on the lookout for little green men from outer space?
Green men! Give me a break! They would be much more advanced! They might be blue, orange or maybe even plaid!
Well, we'll never know, because this project is done! We're wasting millions of dollars out here! The government can waste that money in other ridiculous areas!
AMANA
Since the government abandoned my alien search project, I'm looking for private funding!
We're sorry, but this "looking for life in outer space" thing is too scatter-brained for us to back!
They said the airplane was a scatter-brained idea, too! But where would we be today without the airplane?
At Penn Station waiting for a train! And I'd know the location of my luggage! And it would be in one piece!
Dr. Outaways' project doesn't sound scatter-brained to me one bit! Now give her the money, then bring me my lucky crystals and some pixie dust!
TAXIDERMIST

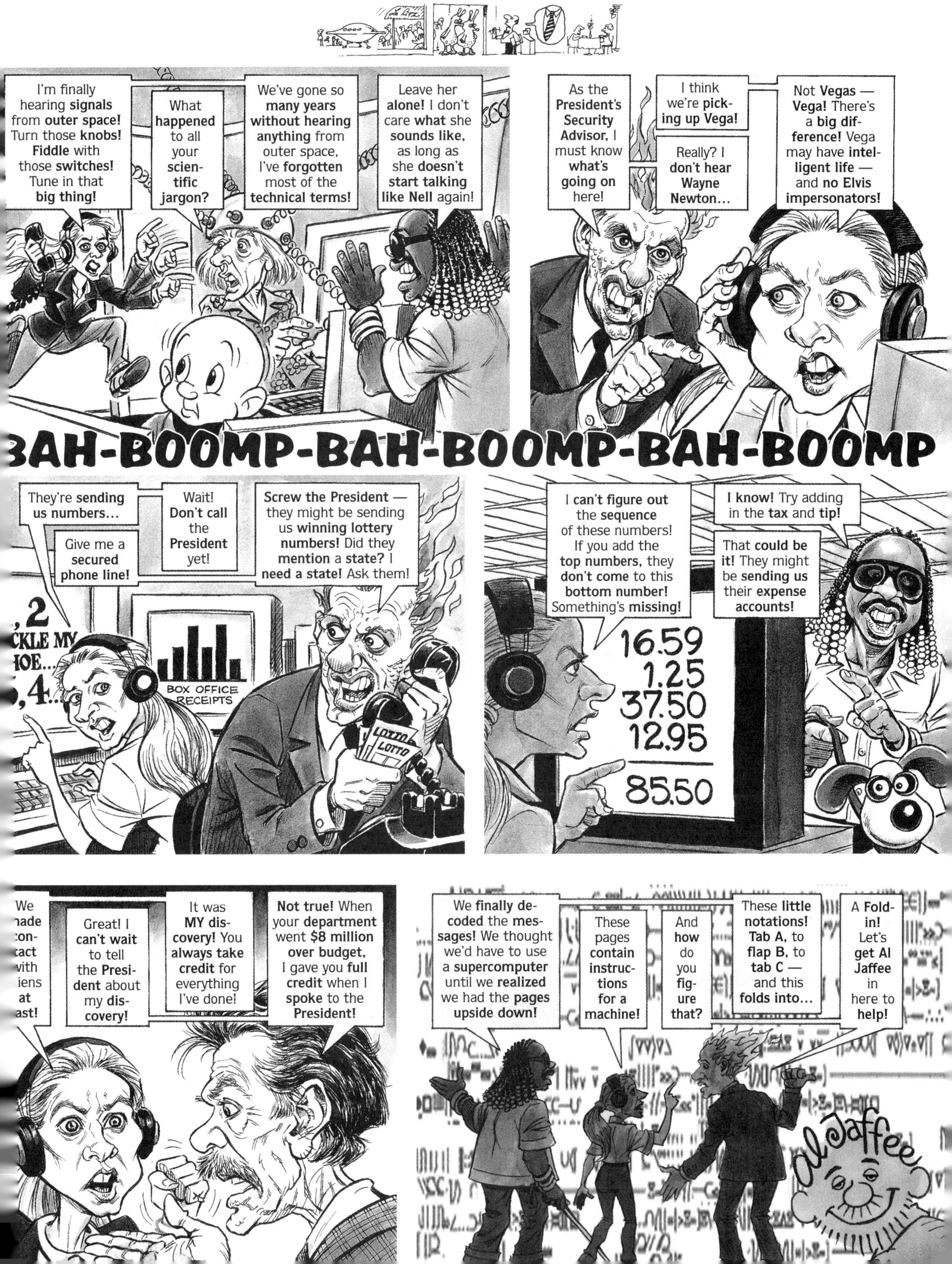

I'm finally hearing signals from outer space! Turn those knobs! Fiddle with those switches! Tune in that big thing!
What happened to all your scien-tific jargon?
We've gone so many years without hearing anything from outer space, I've forgotten most of the technical terms!
Leave her alone! I don't care what she sounds like, as long as she doesn't start talking like Nell again!
As the President's Security Advisor, I must know what's going on here!
I think we're pick-ing up Vega!
Really? I don't hear Wayne Newton…
Not Vegas — Vega! There's a big dif-ference! Vega may have intel-ligent life — and no Elvis impersonators!
BAH-BOOMP-BAH-BOOMP-BAH-BOOMP
They're sending us numbers…
Give me a secured phone line!
Wait! Don't call the President yet!
Screw the President — they might be sending us winning lottery numbers! Did they mention a state? I need a state! Ask them!
,2
CKLE MY
HOE…
,4…
BOX OFFICE RECEIPTS
LOTTO
LOTTO
I can't figure out the sequence of these numbers! If you add the top numbers, they don't come to this bottom number! Something's missing!
16.59
1.25
37.50
12.95
85.50
I know! Try adding in the tax and tip!
That could be it! They might be sending us their expense accounts!
We nade con-act vith iens at ast!
Great! I can't wait to tell the Presi-dent about my dis-covery!
It was MY dis-covery! You always take credit for everything I've done!
Not true! When your department went $8 million over budget, I gave you full credit when I spoke to the President!
We finally de-coded the mes-sages! We thought we'd have to use a supercomputer until we realized we had the pages upside down!
These pages contain instruc-tions for a machine!
And how do you fig-ure that?
These little notations! Tab A, to flap B, to tab C — and this folds into…
A Fold-in! Let's get Al Jaffee in here to help!
Al Jaffee

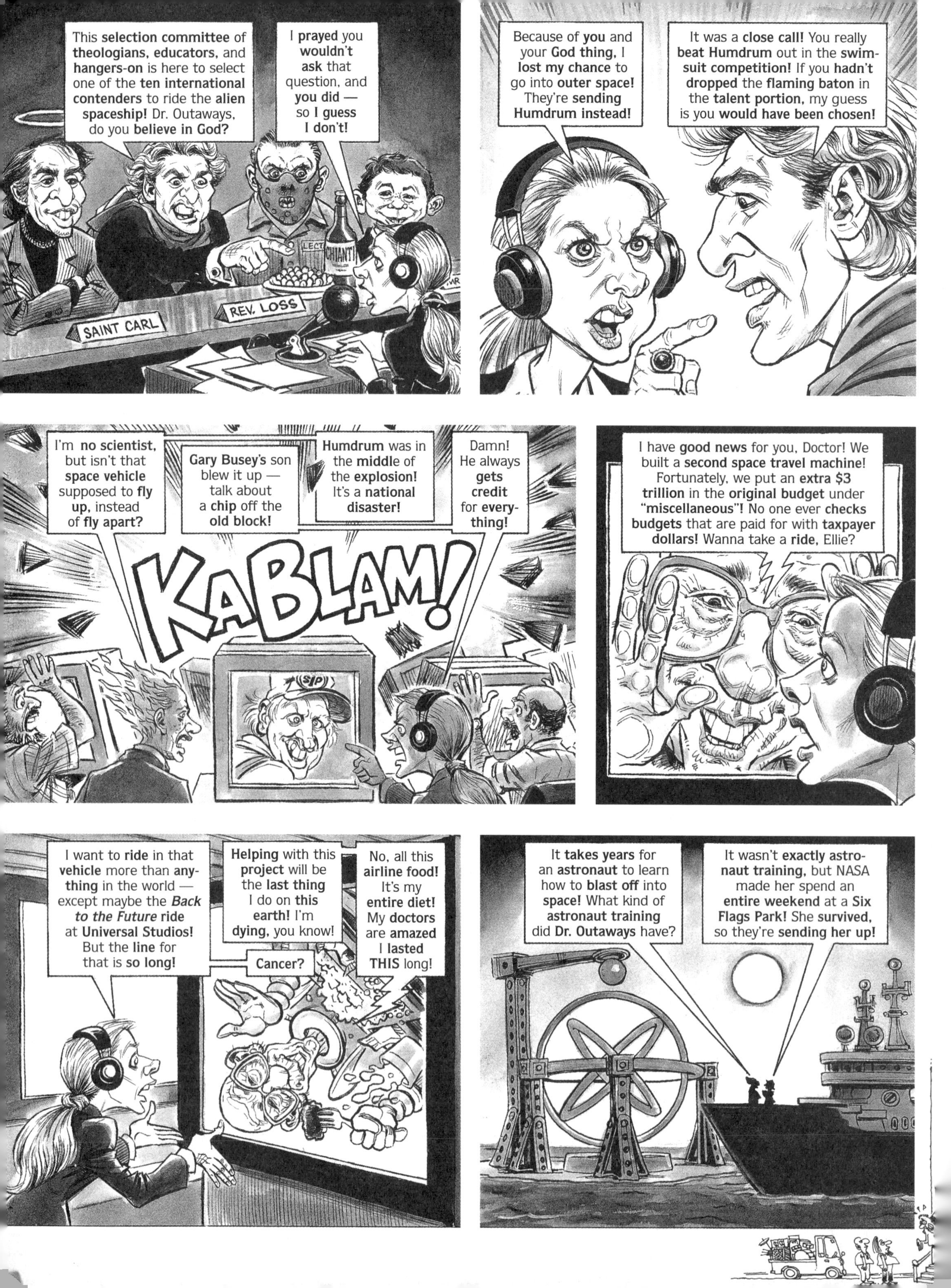

This selection committee of theologians, educators, and hangers-on is here to select one of the ten international contenders to ride the alien spaceship! Dr. Outaways, do you believe in God?
I prayed you wouldn't ask that question, and you did — so I guess I don't!
SAINT CARL
REV. LOSS
CHIANTI
Because of you and your God thing, I lost my chance to go into outer space! They're sending Humdrum instead!
It was a close call! You really beat Humdrum out in the swim-suit competition! If you hadn't dropped the flaming baton in the talent portion, my guess is you would have been chosen!
I'm no scientist, but isn't that space vehicle supposed to fly up, instead of fly apart?
Gary Busey's son blew it up — talk about a chip off the old block!
Humdrum was in the middle of the explosion! It's a national disaster!
Damn! He always gets credit for every-thing!
KABLAM!
SIP
I have good news for you, Doctor! We built a second space travel machine! Fortunately, we put an extra $3 trillion in the original budget under "miscellaneous"! No one ever checks budgets that are paid for with taxpayer dollars! Wanna take a ride, Ellie?
I want to ride in that vehicle more than any-thing in the world — except maybe the Back to the Future ride at Universal Studios! But the line for that is so long!
Helping with this project will be the last thing I do on this earth! I'm dying, you know!
Cancer?
No, all this airline food! It's my entire diet! My doctors are amazed I lasted THIS long!
It takes years for an astronaut to learn how to blast off into space! What kind of astronaut training did Dr. Outaways have?
It wasn't exactly astro-naut training, but NASA made her spend an entire weekend at a Six Flags Park! She survived, so they're sending her up!

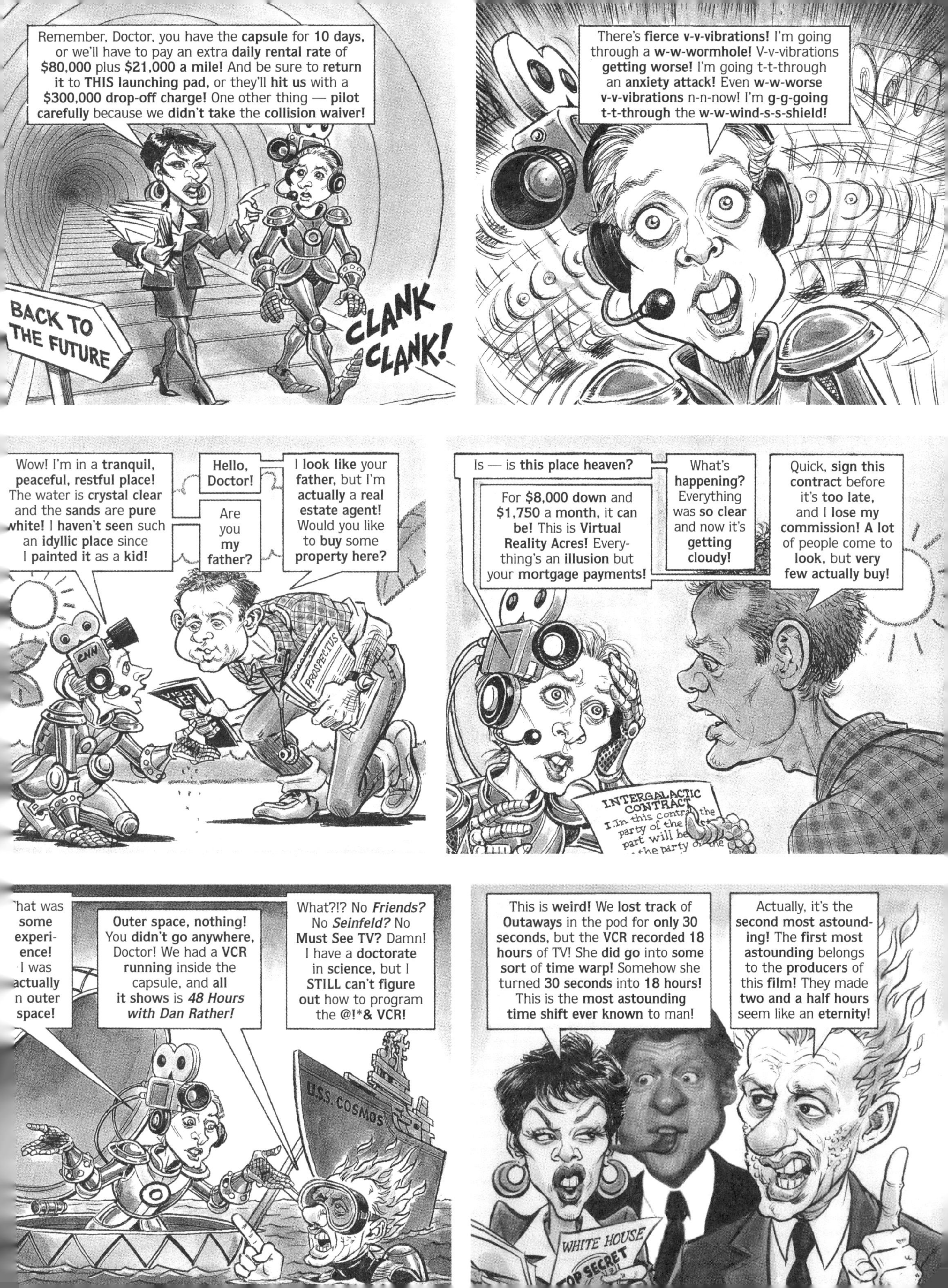
Remember, Doctor, you have the capsule for 10 days, or we'll have to pay an extra daily rental rate of $80,000 plus $21,000 a mile! And be sure to return it to THIS launching pad, or they'll hit us with a $300,000 drop-off charge! One other thing — pilot carefully because we didn't take the collision waiver!
BACK TO THE FUTURE
CLANK CLANK!
There's fierce v-v-vibrations! I'm going through a w-w-wormhole! V-v-vibrations getting worse! I'm going t-t-through an anxiety attack! Even w-w-worse v-v-vibrations n-n-now! I'm g-g-going t-t-through the w-w-wind-s-s-shield!
Wow! I'm in a tranquil, peaceful, restful place! The water is crystal clear and the sands are pure white! I haven't seen such an idyllic place since I painted it as a kid!
Hello, Doctor!
Are you my father?
I look like your father, but I'm actually a real estate agent! Would you like to buy some property here?
CNN
PROSPECTUS
Is — is this place heaven?
For $8,000 down and $1,750 a month, it can be! This is Virtual Reality Acres! Everything's an illusion but your mortgage payments!
What's happening? Everything was so clear and now it's getting cloudy!
Quick, sign this contract before it's too late, and I lose my commission! A lot of people come to look, but very few actually buy!
INTERGALACTIC CONTRACT
hat was some experience! I was actually n outer space!
Outer space, nothing! You didn't go anywhere, Doctor! We had a VCR running inside the capsule, and all it shows is 48 Hours with Dan Rather!
What?!? No Friends? No Seinfeld? No Must See TV? Damn! I have a doctorate in science, but I STILL can't figure out how to program the @!*& VCR!
U.S.S. COSMOS
This is weird! We lost track of Outaways in the pod for only 30 seconds, but the VCR recorded 18 hours of TV! She did go into some sort of time warp! Somehow she turned 30 seconds into 18 hours! This is the most astounding time shift ever known to man!
Actually, it's the second most astounding! The first most astounding belongs to the producers of this film! They made two and a half hours seem like an eternity!
WHITE HOUSE
TOP SECRET

TRITE & TRUE DEPT.

# MAD'S "LATE SHOW" CLICHÉ MOVIE SCRIPT OF THE ISSUE

ARTIST: BRUCE STARK WRITER: HARRY PURVIS

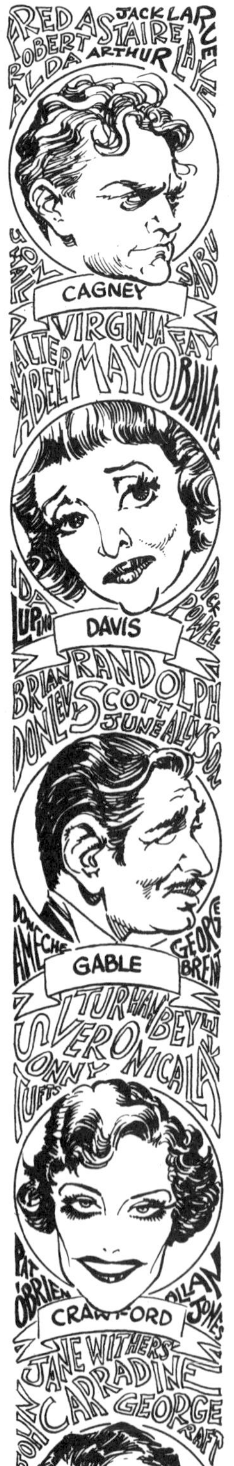
CAGNEY
DAVIS
GABLE
CRAWFORD

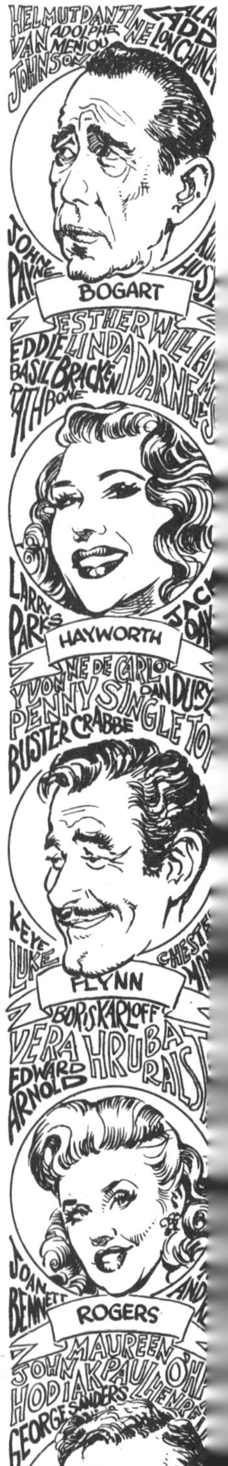
BOGART
HAYWORTH
FLYNN
ROGERS

## THE "SOCIETY" MOVIE

"I don't know what's gotten into Pamela lately. The girl seems to have lost all sense of propriety. Yesterday, I caught her dancing with the Chauffeur. Imagine that, Laureen! The Chauffeur!"

* * * * * *

"If you must know, Mother, I'm fed up with this life you seem to think is so wonderful. I'm especially fed up with all these useless, empty people who think happiness can be bought with a bank account."

* * * * * *

"Pamela, your mother and I have decided. We're shipping you off to Europe tomorrow. When you've had a few weeks in the sun at Monte Carlo, you'll come to your senses and forget all about this 'taxi-cab' person."

* * * * * *

"Perhaps we've handled this thing all wrong, Laureen. I think it's a good idea to invite this young man to the ball. When she sees how out of place he is among all this, perhaps Pamela will forget that insane idea of hers about moving to Brooklyn."

* * * * * *

". . . and did you see those dreadful people he brought with him? I understand they're his parents! I can't imagine why George and Laureen would permit such a thing!"

* * * * * *

"You needn't worry, Mrs. Smythe-Wellborne, I'll not contaminate your home with my bourgeois presence any longer. As for the check, my feelings for Pamela have no price tag. You couldn't buy them with ALL your millions! Well, how about it, Funny-Face? Are you coming with me?"

* * * * * *

"I don't know, Joe. I need some time . . . to think . . ."

* * * * * *

"Now, now, my little girl. Trust your wise old father just this once. I've lived many more years than you and I know. Someday, you'll be grateful that you made this decision. And as a special surprise for you, I've invited Freddy Van Cleef down for the week-end."

* * * * * *

"There are more important things in life than polo, Freddy. But I don't expect you to understand that. Now, if you'll excuse me, I have an important phone call to make--to a HUMAN BEING--with feelings and emotions. I only hope that he'll talk to me after all the hurt I've caused him."

* * * * * *

"I was praying you'd say that, Pam. It may be rough going at first. You won't have furs and diamonds and servants. But I can promise you one thing: you'll always have my love. Think you can live on that, Honey?"

* * * * * *

"Just try me, Darling!"

* * * * * *

"You know, Laureen, now that I've gotten to know the lad, I find that I like him. He's got some of that old spark--that 'take it with your bare hands' attitude I once had. Maybe we can all learn a thing or two from him. Anyway, that's why I've decided that he's the man to take over my entire organization!"

THE END

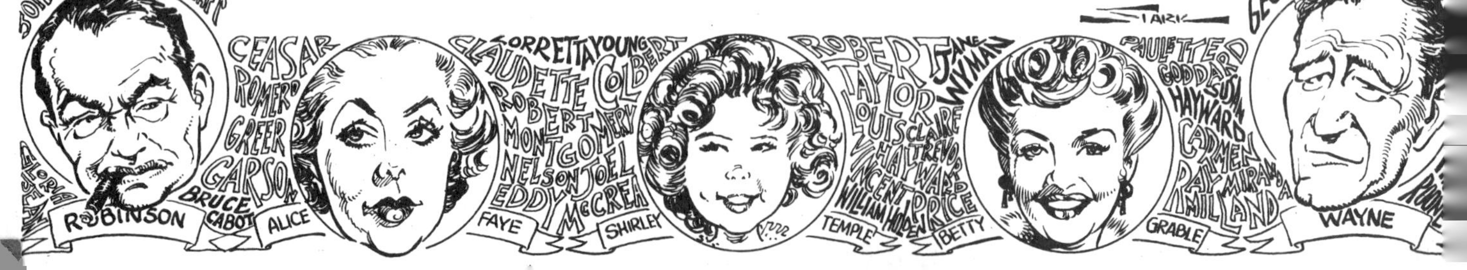
STARK
ROBINSON
ALICE
FAYE
SHIRLEY
TEMPLE
BETTY
GRABLE
WAYNE

**FRANK ON A ROLL DEPT.**

**The Caped Crusader is back on the screen, and this time they've signed yet another actor for the title role. He's George Clooney, out to scale new heights! How did this come about? Read on as we rhyme you to death with . . .**

# CLOONEY AS THE BAT

(with apologies – again – to Ernest Lawrence Thayer)

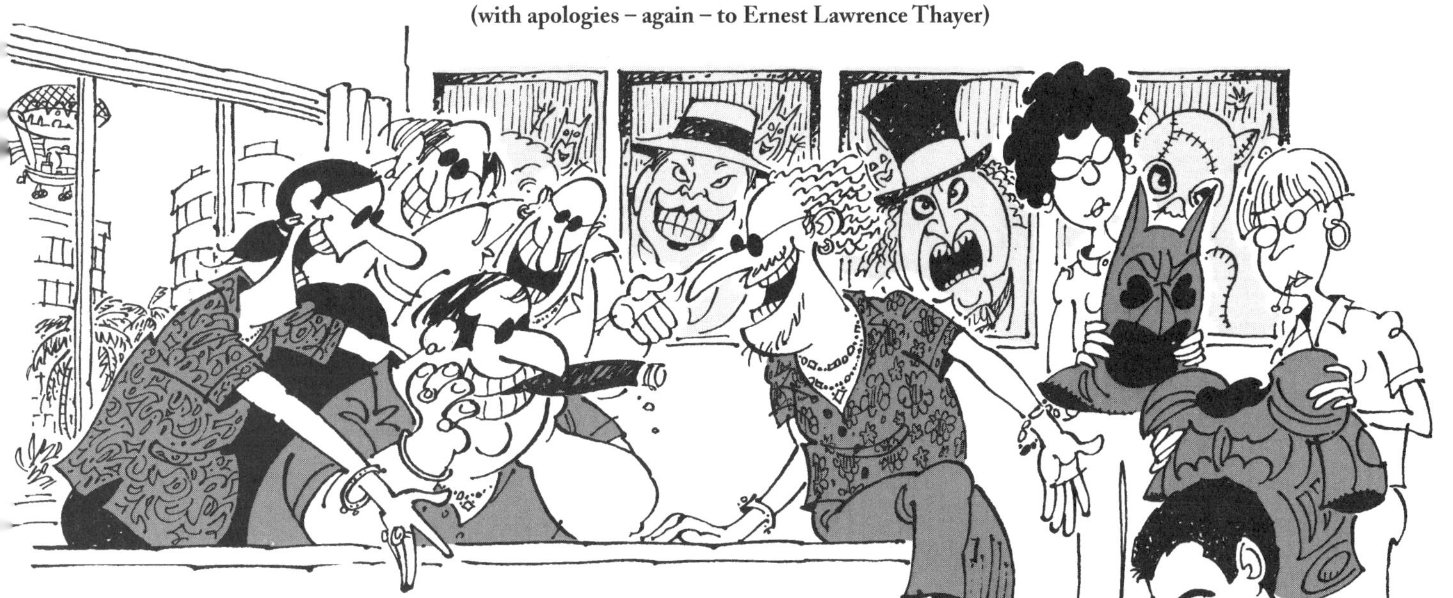

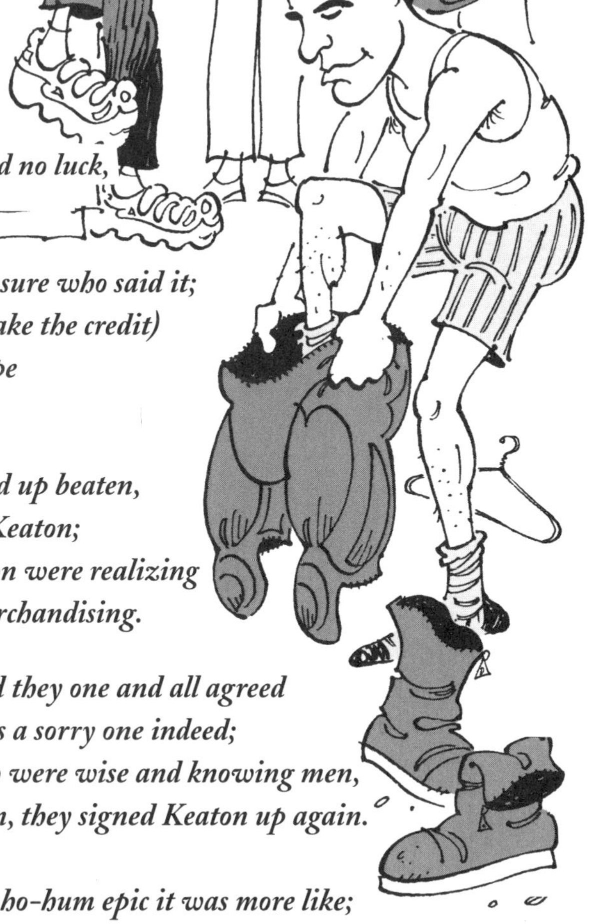

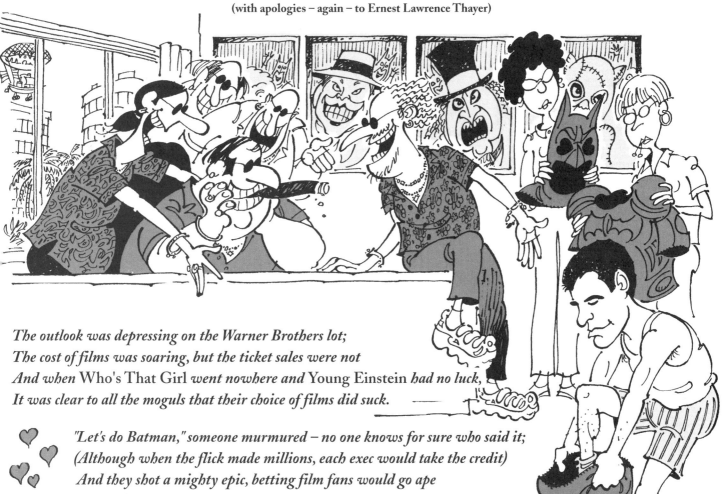

*The outlook was depressing on the Warner Brothers lot;*
*The cost of films was soaring, but the ticket sales were not*
*And when* Who's That Girl *went nowhere and* Young Einstein *had no luck,*
*It was clear to all the moguls that their choice of films did suck.*

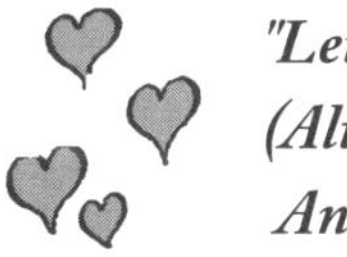

*"Let's do Batman," someone murmured – no one knows for sure who said it;*
*(Although when the flick made millions, each exec would take the credit)*
*And they shot a mighty epic, betting film fans would go ape*
*At the sight of Michael Keaton clad in latex and a cape.*

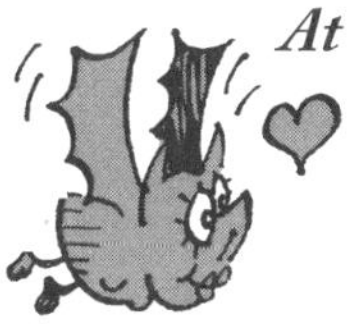

*The Joker was the villain and although he wound up beaten,*
*The performance of Jack Nicholson annihilated Keaton;*
*"Hey, that's showbiz," said the mogul, for they soon were realizing*
*That The Joker was the hero when it came to merchandising.*

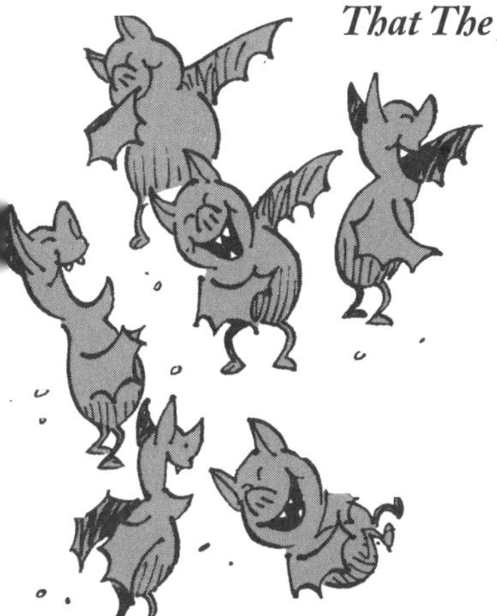

*"Strike One!" the critics thundered, and they one and all agreed*
*That the choice of Michael Keaton was a sorry one indeed;*
*"How true," concurred the moguls, who were wise and knowing men,*
*And to show they'd learned their lesson, they signed Keaton up again.*

*The sequel stumbled forth, a ho-hum epic it was more like;*
*Twice as drearisome was Keaton – many said he was Al Gore-like.*
*While The Penguin reeked with evil and Catwoman flashed her whip,*
*It was clear the Caped Crusader once again had lost his grip.*

ARTIST: PAUL COKER   WRITER: FRANK JACOBS

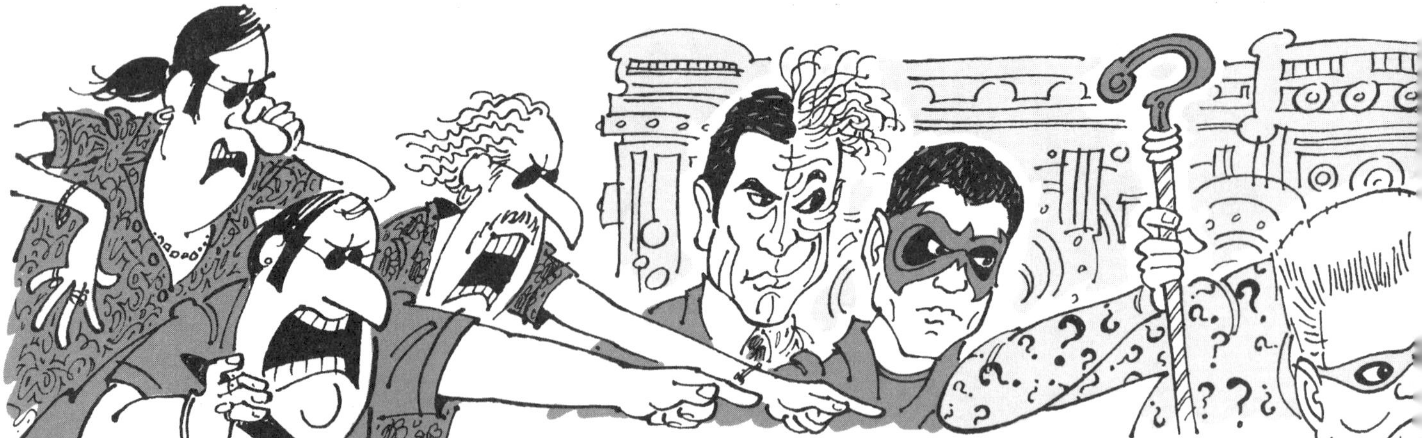

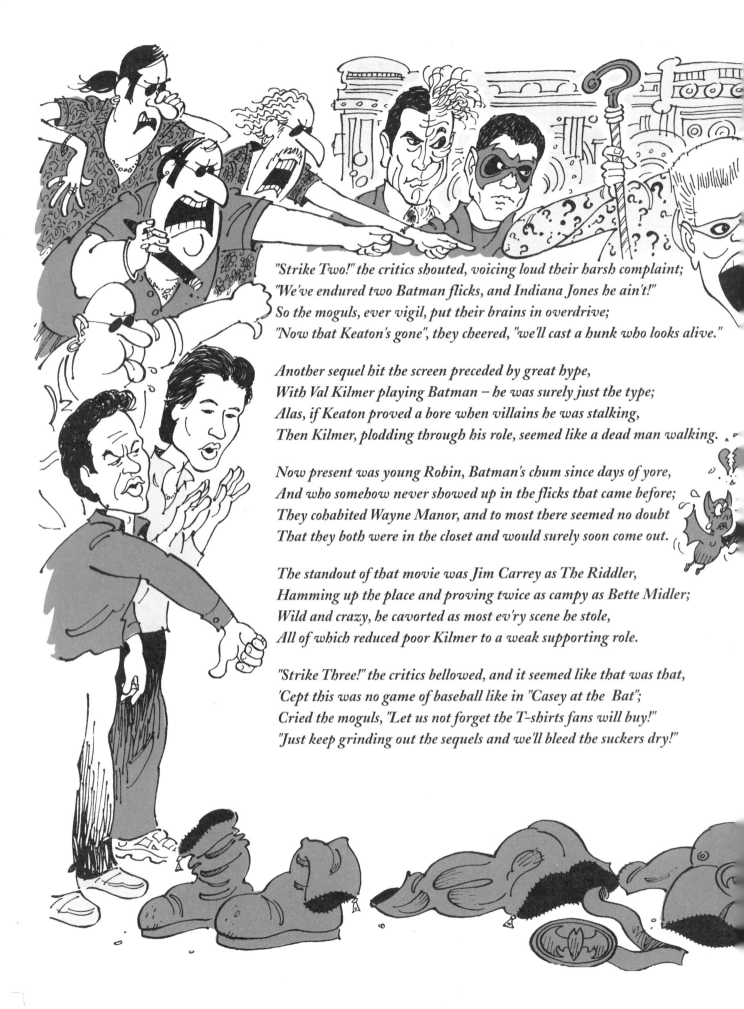

"Strike Two!" the critics shouted, voicing loud their harsh complaint;
"We've endured two Batman flicks, and Indiana Jones he ain't!"
So the moguls, ever vigil, put their brains in overdrive;
"Now that Keaton's gone", they cheered, "we'll cast a hunk who looks alive."

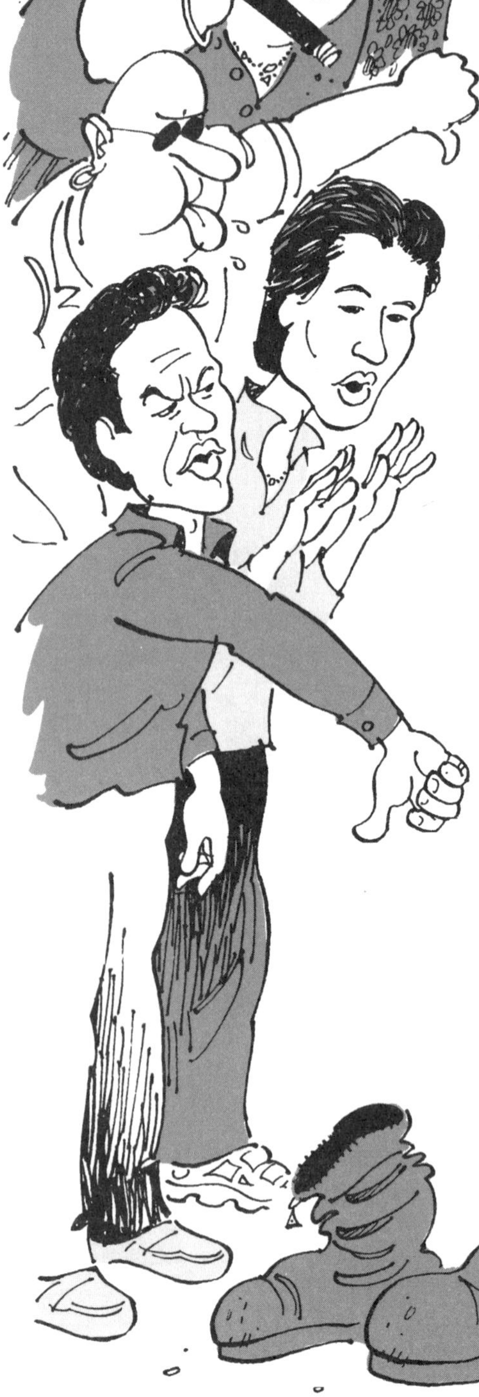

Another sequel hit the screen preceded by great hype,
With Val Kilmer playing Batman – he was surely just the type;
Alas, if Keaton proved a bore when villains he was stalking,
Then Kilmer, plodding through his role, seemed like a dead man walking.

Now present was young Robin, Batman's chum since days of yore,
And who somehow never showed up in the flicks that came before;
They cohabited Wayne Manor, and to most there seemed no doubt
That they both were in the closet and would surely soon come out.

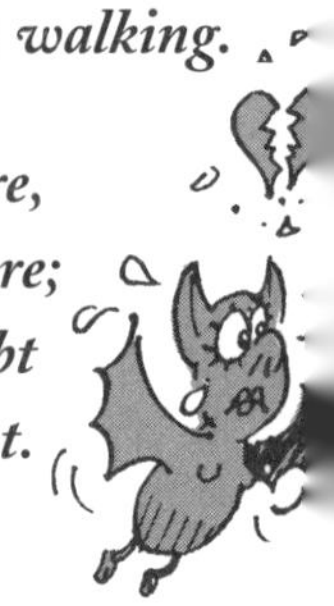

The standout of that movie was Jim Carrey as The Riddler,
Hamming up the place and proving twice as campy as Bette Midler;
Wild and crazy, he cavorted as most ev'ry scene he stole,
All of which reduced poor Kilmer to a weak supporting role.

"Strike Three!" the critics bellowed, and it seemed like that was that,
'Cept this was no game of baseball like in "Casey at the Bat";
Cried the moguls, "Let us not forget the T-shirts fans will buy!"
"Just keep grinding out the sequels and we'll bleed the suckers dry!"

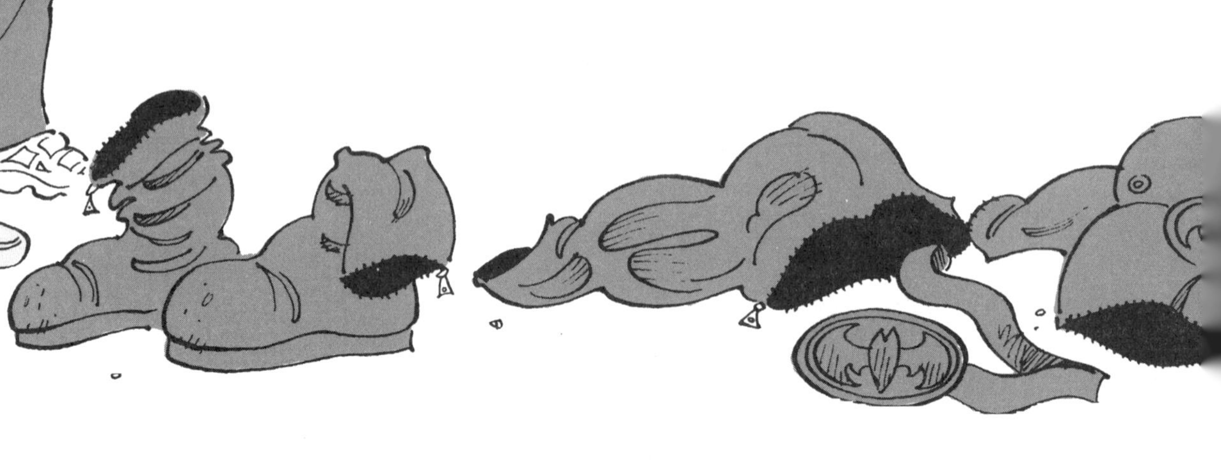

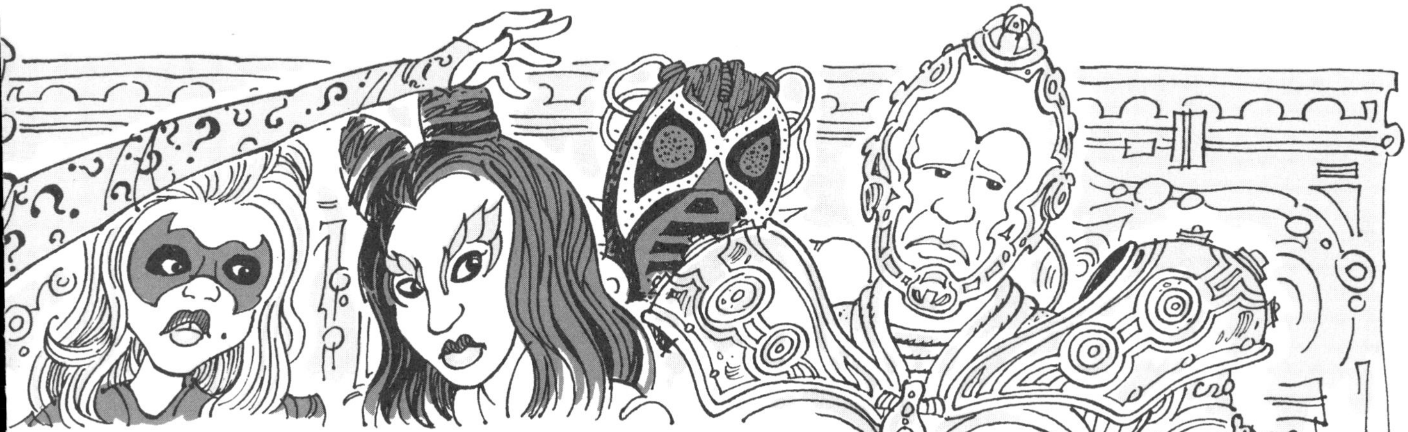

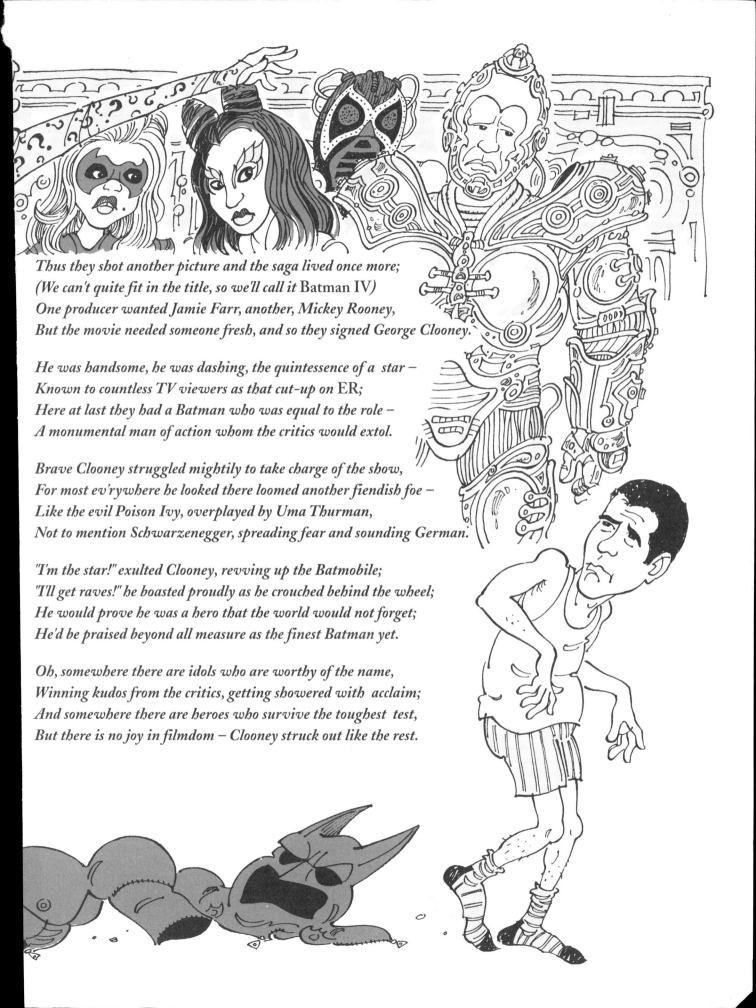

*Thus they shot another picture and the saga lived once more;*
*(We can't quite fit in the title, so we'll call it* Batman IV*)*
*One producer wanted Jamie Farr, another, Mickey Rooney,*
*But the movie needed someone fresh, and so they signed George Clooney.*

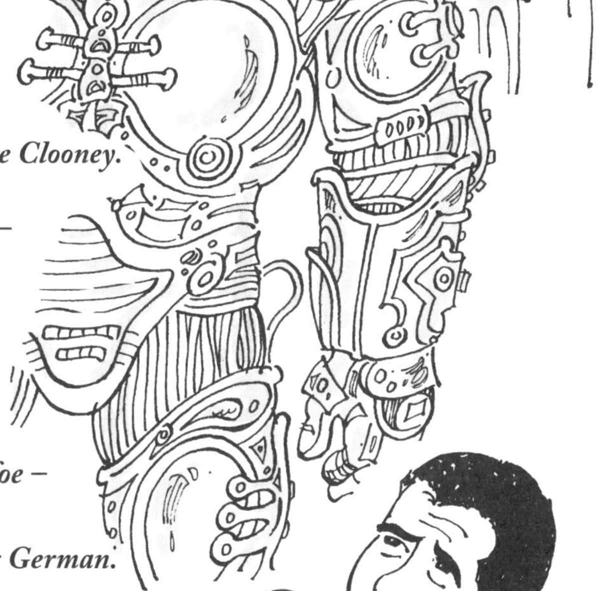

*He was handsome, he was dashing, the quintessence of a star –*
*Known to countless TV viewers as that cut-up on* ER*;*
*Here at last they had a Batman who was equal to the role –*
*A monumental man of action whom the critics would extol.*

*Brave Clooney struggled mightily to take charge of the show,*
*For most ev'rywhere he looked there loomed another fiendish foe –*
*Like the evil Poison Ivy, overplayed by Uma Thurman,*
*Not to mention Schwarzenegger, spreading fear and sounding German.*

*"I'm the star!" exulted Clooney, revving up the Batmobile;*
*"I'll get raves!" he boasted proudly as he crouched behind the wheel;*
*He would prove he was a hero that the world would not forget;*
*He'd be praised beyond all measure as the finest Batman yet.*

*Oh, somewhere there are idols who are worthy of the name,*
*Winning kudos from the critics, getting showered with acclaim;*
*And somewhere there are heroes who survive the toughest test,*
*But there is no joy in filmdom – Clooney struck out like the rest.*

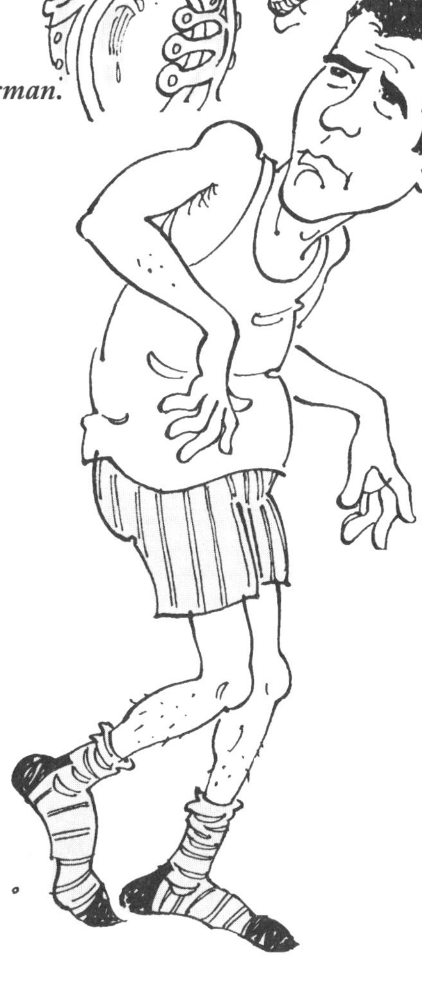

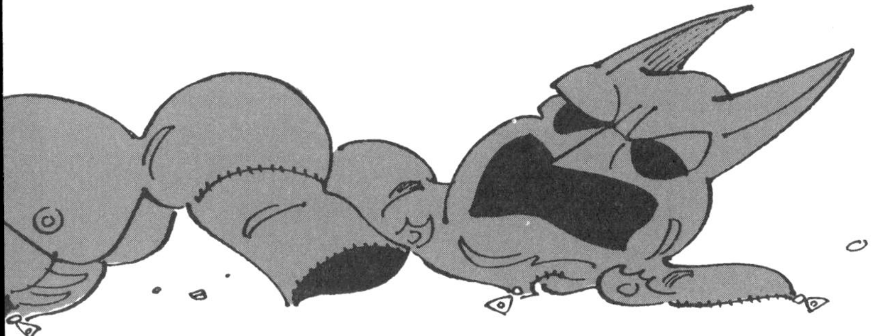

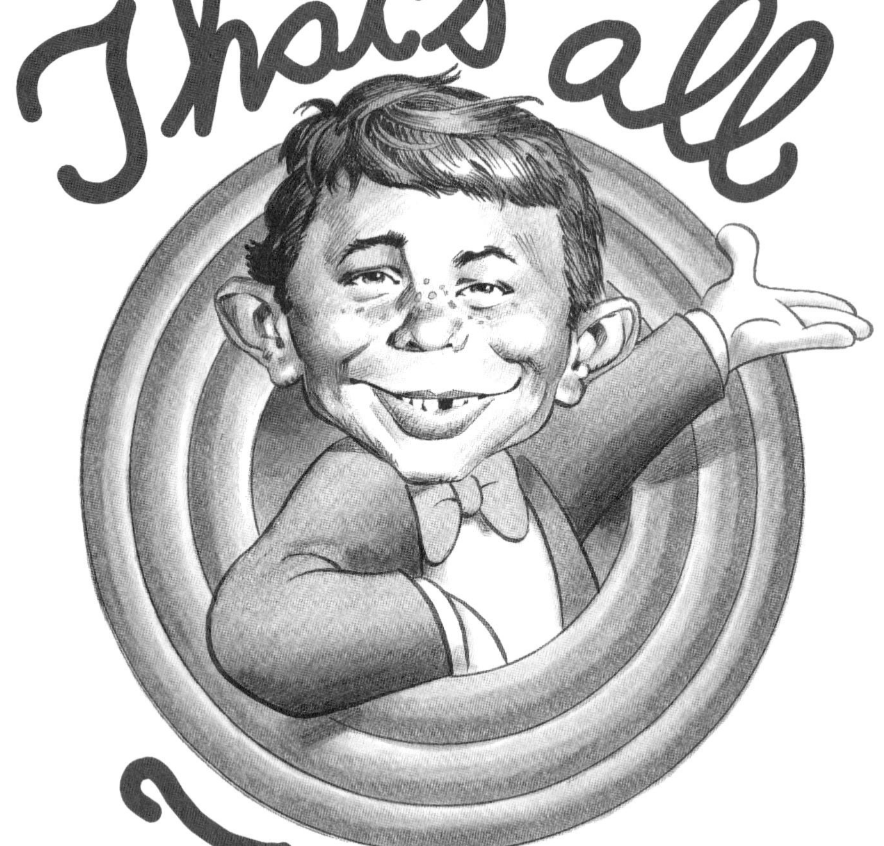

That's all
Folks